CW00722288

TAX HANDBOOK

2003-04

A. Foreman and G. Mowles

PEARSON EDUCATION LIMITED

Head Office:
Edinburgh Gate
Harlow CM20 2JE
Tel: +44 (0)1279 623623
Fax: +44 (0)1279 431059
Website: www.pearsoned.co.uk

This edition first published in Great Britain in 2003 by Pearson Education

ISBN 0 273 67529 X

British Library Cataloguing in Publication Data
A CIP catalogue record for this book can be obtained from the British Library

Typeset by Land & Unwin (Data Sciences) Ltd, Northampton
Printed and bound in Great Britain by
Biddles Ltd, Guildford and King's Lynn

The Publishers' policy is to use paper manufactured from sustainable forests.

CONTENTS

ABBREVIATIONS

AGM	annual general meeting
AIM	Alternative Investment Market
AMAP	authorised mileage allowance payments
AMT	Alternative Minimum Tax
BES	Business Expansion Scheme
CGT	capital gains tax
CIS	Construction Industry Scheme
COP	code of practice
CO_2	carbon dioxide
CPO	compulsory purchase order
CTO	Capital Taxes Office
CY	current year
DCMS	Department of Culture, Media and Sport
DETR	Department of the Environment, Transport and the Regions
DPTC	Disabled Persons' Tax Credits
ECJ	European Court of Justice
EIS	Enterprise Investment Scheme
ELS	Electronic Lodgement Service
EMI	Enterprise Management Incentive
ESC	extra-statutory concession
EU	European Union
FA	Finance Act
FICO	Financial Intermediaries and Claims Office (now called Centre for Non-Residents)
FID	Foreign Income Dividend
FIF	Foreign Investment Fund
FIFO	first in first out
FOTRA	Free of tax to residents abroad
FPCS	Fixed Profit Car Scheme
FRS	Financial Reporting Standard
FRSSE	Financial Reporting Standard for Smaller Entities
FURBS	Funded Unapproved Retirement Benefit Scheme
g/km	grammes per kilometre
GAAR	General Anti-Avoidance Rule
GWR	gifts with reservation
GP	general practitioner
HP	hire purchase
IHT	inheritance tax
IHTA	Inheritance Tax Act

IO	Integrated Office
IR(C)	Inland Revenue (Charities)
ISA	individual savings account
IT (E&P) A	Income Tax (Earnings & Pensions) Act
LEL	lower earnings limit
LIFO	last in first out
LLA	long-life asset
LLP	limited liability partnership
MAPA	Members' Agents Pooling Arrangement
NICO	National Insurance Contributions Office
NICs	national insurance contributions
NSB	National Savings Bank
OEIC	Open-ended investment company
pa	per annum
PAYE	Pay As You Earn
PEP	personal equity plan
PET	potentially exempt trust
PILON	payment in lieu of notice
pm	per month
PPS	personal pension scheme
PRP	profit-related pay
PSA	PAYE Settlement Agreement
pw	per week
QCB	qualifying corporate bond
RAC	retirement annuity contract
R&D	research and development
RPI	Retail Prices Index
SA	self-assessment
SAYE	save as you earn
SDRT	stamp duty reserve tax
SERPS	State earnings related pension scheme
SME	small or medium-sized enterprise
SMP	statutory maternity pay
SP	statements of practice
SPSS	Savings, Pension Share Schemes Office
SSAP	Statement of Standard Accounting Practice
SSP	statutory sick pay
TA	Income and Corporation Taxes Act
TCGA	Taxation of Chargeable Gains Act
TDO	Tax District Office
TESSA	Tax-Exempt Special Savings Account
TMA	Taxes Management Act
TSO	Taxpayer Service Office
UEL	upper earnings limit
UN	United Nations
VAT	value added tax
VATA	Value Added Tax Act
VCT	Venture Capital Trust
WFTC	Working Families' Tax Credits

GLOSSARY

Actual basis of assessment Where a person carrying on a trade or profession is assessed according to the profits that he has actually earned during the tax year concerned. See 5.3.

Accounting reference date The date to which accounts are made up for a company. In practice, when a company is formed the accounting reference date is normally the last day of the month in which the anniversary of its incorporation falls.

Accruals basis A system of bookkeeping which brings into account income when earned and expenditure when incurred.

Additional voluntary contribution (AVC) A contribution by an employee to secure additional benefits under his employer's approved pension scheme. See 12.10.

Ad valorem duties Duties charged as a percentage of the value of the asset concerned, particularly **stamp duty**. See Chapter 29.

Agricultural buildings allowances A form of **capital allowance** given in respect of expenditure on buildings used for agricultural purposes. See 5.5.17.

Agricultural property relief A relief given for **IHT** purposes. The relief is either 50% or 100% of the value of agricultural land. To qualify, the land must be situated in the UK, Channel Islands or Isle of Man. See 19.9.

All-employee share scheme An approved scheme for employees to receive shares tax free. See 4.12.

Alternative Investment Market The Stock Exchange launched the AIM in June 1995 to enable investors to deal in shares in unquoted companies. AIM replaced the Unlisted Securities Market, an earlier market for unquoted companies.

Annual exemption Individuals are entitled to an annual exemption for CGT purposes of £7,900 for 2003-04. See 13.1.1. There are two types of annual exemption for **IHT**. An individual may give away up to £250 to any number of people in a tax year (generally called the 'small gifts exemption'). Separately from this, he is allowed to make chargeable transfers of up to £3,000 pa which are treated as exempt. See 19.5.

Approved profit-sharing schemes Schemes under which employees of companies may be given shares without an income tax charge provided the shares are retained for a minimum period of three years. See 4.11.

Approved share option schemes There are two types: SAYE-linked schemes, which are democratic in nature and must be made available to all employees; and executive share option schemes, which can be restricted to directors and senior executives. See 4.14.2-4.14.4; see also **Enterprise Management Incentives**.

Associated companies Companies controlled by the same person or groups of people.

Basis period The period on which (usually Schedule D) profits for the tax year are based.

Bed and breakfasting A widely used way of establishing CGT losses by selling shares and repurchasing the next day. Anti-avoidance rules took effect from 17 March 1998 to prevent this. See 22.7.

Benefits-in-kind Perks received by a director or employee that are taxed as employment income and are generally subject to **NICs** from 6 April 2000. See 4.4.

Beneficial loans Loans to an employee at less than a commercial rate of interest (see **Official rate** and 4.7).

Business property relief A deduction of either 50% or 100% from the value of business property when it is assessed for **IHT** purposes. See 19.8.

Capital allowances Allowances given in respect of plant and machinery, industrial buildings and commercial property in enterprise zones. In general terms, capital allowances represent a form of relief that corresponds to depreciation. See 5.5.

Capital expenditure A 'once and for all' expense to achieve an enduring benefit for a trade. It is not a cost that may be deducted in arriving at profits for tax purposes, although **capital allowances** may be available. See 5.4.5.

Cash accounting A method of accounting to Customs & Excise for VAT as and when payment is received rather than according to when VAT invoices are issued. See 28.6.4.

Chargeable transfer A gift or other transfer of value made by an individual which is not covered by any of the various exemptions and is therefore a transfer for **IHT** purposes. See 19.2-19.5.

Charitable trust A trust where all income must be used for charitable purposes. In England and Wales, most charities have to be registered with the Charity Commissioners.

Class 1A NICs Special **NICs** charged on an employer in respect of cars made available to employees for private use. The contributions are levied on the 'scale' benefits used to arrive at the employees' taxable benefit. See Chapter 25.

Class 1B NICs Class 1B contributions were introduced from 6 April 1998 and apply where an employer settles tax in respect of employees' benefits under a **PSA**. See Chapter 25.

Close company A company where the directors control more than half of the voting shares or where such control may be exercised by five or fewer people and their associates.

Corporate venturing A relief for companies that invest in small trading companies by subscribing for ordinary shares on or after 1 April 2000. See 26.14.

Corporation tax A tax levied on companies' profits. The full rate is 30%, but many companies will qualify for the **small companies rate**.

Covenant Payments under a deed of covenant were a widely used way of transferring income to a charity. The legislation on **Gift Aid** has now superseded this.

Current year basis The Schedule D basis of assessment whereby an individual is assessed on his profits for the firm's year which ends in the tax year. It came into effect from 1997-98 onwards. See 5.3.1.

CY basis Current year basis.

Deeds of variation A special term for **IHT** purposes. Where the provisions of a person's will are varied by the beneficiaries' mutual consent, and the necessary deed of variation is executed within two years of the relevant death, IHT may be computed as if the deceased's will had contained the revised provisions from the outset. A similar treatment may apply where a person has died without making a valid will, and the individuals who would benefit under the intestacy rules mutually agree to vary the position. See 19.4.6.

Deregistration This occurs when a trader who has been registered for VAT purposes is permitted to deregister. Once deregistered, he must not charge VAT on any supplies subsequently made by him in the course of his business. See Chapter 28.

Discretionary trust A type of trust where the trustees can vary the way they use the trust monies and can choose how they pay out (or 'distribute') income to members of a class of potential beneficiaries. This is different to other types of trust where the trustees are bound to pay over the income to a particular beneficiary.

Dispensations An employer is required to make annual returns of payments and benefits provided to employees (**form P11D**). A dispensation may be negotiated with the Revenue whereby certain expenses and other payments need not be reported on the form.

Distribution A distribution of a company's assets to its members (ie shareholders), for example, a payment of a dividend. Distributions may also be made by a liquidator. Where assets are distributed to members of the company during the course of a liquidation, there is said to be a distribution in specie.

Dividends A cash amount paid to a member of a company according to the number of shares held by him. Dividends may only be declared out of distributable profits.

Domicile A legal concept that can be very important where a person has overseas income or gains or transfers property situated outside the UK. Income tax and CGT on foreign assets may be charged only on the **remittance basis**.

A person generally has a foreign domicile if he does not regard the UK as his real home and he retains strong links with another country.

The concept of domicile is not exactly the same as that of nationality, although if you are a foreign national this will be very helpful in establishing that you are not UK-domiciled. Your domicile of origin is normally that of your father when you reached age 16 (or that of your mother if she was unmarried or your father died while you were still a minor). The relevant age is 14 for individuals domiciled in Scotland.

Your domicile of origin continues to remain in force until such time as you acquire a new domicile of choice by making a permanent home elsewhere. See 24.1.

Earnings basis Accounts should be prepared so as to reflect a trader's earnings for a year, rather than just cash received. Thus, accounts should include debtors, ie bills which have been issued but which have not been paid by the year end. See 5.4.

Earnings cap An employee's earnings in excess of the cap are generally disregarded for the purpose of arriving at his benefits under an approved pension scheme. A similar rule applies for determining maximum contributions under a **personal pension scheme**. See 12.8.

Election to waive exemption A VAT term used in commercial land and property transactions. Otherwise known as the 'option to tax'. A landowner has the option to make what would otherwise be an **exempt supply** into a taxable supply. Formal notification to Customs is required. See 28.3.5.

Enhancement expenditure A term used in the context of CGT. In computing a person's capital gain, it is possible to deduct the costs incurred in acquiring the asset and any enhancement expenditure on improvements, etc reflected in the state of the asset at the date of disposal. See 14.2.4.

Emoluments Normal remuneration, bonuses and other employment income received by a director or employee. See 4.2.1 and 21.1.2.

Employment income The new term for Schedule E income introduced by the Income Tax (Earnings & Pensions) Act 2003.

Enterprise Investment Scheme A scheme under which individuals may receive income tax and CGT relief when investing in qualifying unquoted trading companies. See 11.6.

Enterprise Management Incentives A new **approved share option scheme** that allows up to 15 key employees to receive options over shares worth up to £100,000 in a small trading company. See 4.15.

Enterprise zones A Government-designated area, normally lasting for a ten-year period, during which a person carrying on a business within the zone is exempt from business rates. There is also considerable freedom from planning controls.

Expenditure on commercial buildings situated in an enterprise zone qualifies for **capital allowances**. Acquisition of an unused commercial building, or a building that has been let only during the preceding two years, attracts a 100% allowance. See 5.5.16.

Equity partner A term used to distinguish between a salaried partner taxed under Schedule E and proprietors of the business or 'full partners' taxed under Schedule D.

ESOP Employee Share Ownership Plan.

ESOT Employee Share Ownership Trust.

EU The European Union comprises Austria, Belgium, Denmark, Finland, France, Germany, Greece, Ireland, Italy, Luxembourg, the Netherlands, Portugal, Spain, Sweden and the UK.

Exempt supplies Supplies not liable to VAT. A person who makes only exempt supplies cannot recover **input VAT** suffered by him.

Exempt transfers The following transfers are exempt from **IHT**: gifts to spouse; normal expenditure out of income; £250 small gifts exemption; annual £3,000 exemption; exemption for marriage gifts; gifts to charities; gifts for national purposes; gifts for public benefit; gifts to political parties; certain transfers to employee trusts. See 19.5.

Ex gratia A person makes an *ex gratia* payment when he does so without admitting liability, for example, a payment by an employer on terminating an employment.

Filing date An individual or trustee must file his **self-assessment** return on or before 31 January following the end of the tax year concerned. See 3.1.

Financial Reporting Standards Issued by the Accounting Standards Board, and mandatory for companies.

Form CT61 A quarterly return required for a company in respect of annual payments made under deduction of tax. See 26.5.9.

Form P11D An annual return made by employers of expenses payments and **benefits-in-kind** provided for an employee.

Full-time working officers and managers A concept that applies for the purposes of CGT **retirement relief**. A person selling shares in a company qualifies for retirement relief only if he is an officer or manager, ie someone who is required to spend the greater part of his time working for the company in a managerial capacity. See 17.10.

FURBS Funded Unapproved Retirement Benefit Scheme. See 12.11.2.

Gift Aid A tax efficient system for donations to charities which was greatly enhanced by FA 2000 and also encompasses donations made under a deed of covenant. See 9.8 and 31.1.

Gross income Income from which no tax has been deducted at source. It may still be taxable income.

Group registration for VAT purposes Companies under common control may register for VAT purposes as a single unit or VAT group. Where this happens, all supplies between those companies are disregarded for VAT purposes. VAT is charged only on supplies outside the group. See 28.4.1.

Groups of companies There are various different rules under which companies may be regarded as part of a group. A parent company may have subsidiaries, ie other companies in which the parent has a majority shareholding. The companies constitute a group for company law purposes.

The conditions that need to be satisfied for companies to form a group for tax purposes vary, but in general the parent must have a 75% interest in its subsidiaries. See 26.11.

Hold-over relief Relief given to a donor or other transferor of business assets or where the gift, etc constitutes a chargeable transfer for **IHT** purposes. Where an individual, etc is entitled to hold-over relief, his gain is not charged but is deducted from the asset's market value in determining the transferee's acquisition value for CGT purposes. See 13.8 and 17.5.

IHT Inheritance tax.

Income from savings Income taxed at only 20% unless you are a higher rate taxpayer. Income from savings includes interest, dividends and purchased life annuities.

Income received gross Income received without any tax having been deducted. See **Gross income.**

Indexation An adjustment made for CGT purposes to allow for inflation up to April 1998. The adjustment is computed by reference to the increase in the retail price index between the month of acquisition (or March 1982 if later) and the month of disposal (or April 1998 if earlier). Replaced by taper relief for individuals and trustees in relation to periods after April 1998. See 14.7.

Individual savings account (ISA) A savings scheme that came into operation on 6 April 1999. All income and capital gains are free of tax. See 11.1.

Industrial buildings Buildings occupied for qualifying trade purposes may qualify as industrial buildings. The significance of this is that a person who incurs expenditure on an industrial building may claim industrial buildings allowances. Normally, allowances are given at the rate of 4% pa over a 25-year period. See 5.5.18.

Inheritance tax (IHT) A combination of a gift tax and death duties. Tax is payable on chargeable transfers made by an individual during his lifetime and on his estate at the time of his death. See Chapter 19.

Input VAT The VAT paid to suppliers of goods and services. Where a person has paid for such goods and services and is himself VAT registered, he may recover input VAT by offsetting the tax paid by him against tax charged on his own supplies. See 28.4.3.

Interest in possession trust Where the beneficiary is entitled to income arising from the trust capital and is legally entitled to demand that the trustees pay that income to him or her. An interest in possession can also exist where the trust owns a property and the beneficiary is entitled to live there rent free.

Investment companies A company that exists wholly or mainly for carrying on the business of managing investments.

IR 35 A generally used way of referring to provisions introduced in FA 2000 to combat the use of 'one man companies' to enable contractors to receive income without tax and **NICs** being withheld at source under **PAYE**.

Know-how Certain expenditure by a person carrying on a trade to acquire information required to carry out certain industrial or manufacturing processes may qualify for a form of **capital allowances**.

Market value rule Where an asset is transferred to a person by way of a gift or some other disposal which is not an arm's length transaction, CGT may be charged as if the person making the disposal had in fact received market value.

MIRAS Mortgage interest relief at source, abolished from 6 April 2000.

National insurance contributions Social Security Contributions: **Class 1 NICs** are payable by an employer and employees; Class 2 and Class 4 NICs are payable by the self-employed. The national insurance system is administered by the Department of Social Security.

NICs National insurance contributions.

Official rate A rate of interest set by Parliament which is supposed to be a commercial rate. Loans from an employer are generally treated as a benefit-in-kind if interest is paid at less than the official rate. See 4.7.

Opening years' rules There are special rules for the opening years under the Schedule D **CY basis**. See 5.3.1.

Options A legally binding contract under which one party is bound to buy or sell an asset to the other. A call option is an option under which the grantor agrees to sell an asset to the other party if he exercises his option. A put option is where a person has the right to require the other party to buy an asset from him.

Output tax VAT chargeable on goods or services supplied in the UK. The trader must account for VAT charged on such supplies by completing a VAT return, normally on a quarterly basis. See 28.4.2.

Outworkers Some industries have outworkers who work on their own premises. However, depending on the circumstances, they may be regarded as employees, and not as self-employed. This means payments made by the person using outworkers' services may be subject to **PAYE** and employers NICs. See 5.2.

Overlap relief Under the Schedule D **CY basis** of assessment, there are special provisions to cover the way profits are assessed during the opening years. The general principle is that total amount of profits assessed over the life of the business should precisely equal the actual profits earned by the business. Overlap relief covers situations where a particular year's profits are assessed more than once (usually under the **opening years' rules**) and is effectively an adjustment to ensure that this does not result in excessive amounts being assessed overall.

Overlap relief is given by way of a deduction from an individual's profits when he ceases to carry on his business or profession, or when the firm's accounting date is changed to a date that falls later in the tax year. See 5.3.3.

Partially exempt trader Under VAT, a person who makes a mixture of standard- or zero-rated supplies and supplies that are exempt for VAT purposes. A partially exempt trader may not be able to claim full credit for his input tax. See 28.4.5.

Pay As You Earn A compulsory system for deduction of tax at source from cash payments to employees.

PAYE Pay As You Earn.

PAYE Settlement Agreements Formerly known as Annual Voluntary Settlements (AVSs), these provide employers with the mechanism to meet tax liabilities arising on a wide range of staff costs that would otherwise be assessed to tax on the employees concerned as **benefits-in-kind**.

Payment in lieu of notice (PILON) The Revenue may argue that payments to an employee are taxable where the employment contract refers to the possibility of the employer making a PILON. See 4.22.8.

Personal equity plan A Government-approved way of investing in stocks and shares, replaced by ISAs from 6 April 1999.

Personal trading company A term used in the context of CGT **retirement relief**. A company is an individual's personal trading company only if he can exercise at least 5% of the voting rights. See 17.10.

Personal pension scheme Approved pension schemes run by insurance companies, banks, building societies or unit trust groups. An individual who is self-employed or in non-pensionable employment may make contributions to such scheme. See 12.8.

Plant and machinery Plant and machinery attracts **capital allowances** if used by a person in the course of a business carried on by him. There is no statutory definition of 'plant and machinery', although certain rules have evolved through decided cases. See 5.5.

Potentially exempt transfers (PETs) An outright gift made by one individual to another or to an interest in possession or accumulation and maintenance trust. The gift will be exempt from **IHT** provided the donor survives seven years. If the donor does not survive that period, the PET becomes an actually exempt transfer and becomes chargeable to IHT. See 19.6.

Premium A lump sum payment to a landlord to obtain a lease is regarded as a premium for tax purposes. Where the lease is for a period of less than 50 years, part of the premium is normally treated as income for the landlord. See 6.3.

Prescribed accounting periods Periods covered by VAT returns. Normally periods are of three-month duration ending on the dates notified in the certificate of VAT registration.

Pre-trading expenditure Certain expenditure incurred in connection with a trade that is about to be carried on may qualify for tax relief once the trade is commenced. See 5.6.

Probate value The value included for an asset in a IHT return on an individual's death. This will often be the CGT acquisition value for the person who inherits (see 14.4).

PSA PAYE Settlement Agreement.

Purchase of own shares A company may purchase its own shares. A public company is normally permitted to do so only in so far as it has distributable profits or such purchase is being funded by the proceeds from an issue of new shares. A private company may purchase its own shares out of capital. In all situations, there is a set procedure that must be followed to comply with company law.

A special tax treatment may apply where a private trading company purchases its own shares. See 7.9.7-7.9.8.

Qualifying corporate bonds (QCBs) A loan stock issued by a company may be an exempt asset for CGT purposes (ie it qualifies for exemption). However, any loss realised on a disposal of a QCB is not normally allowable for CGT purposes. See 13.4.2 and 17.1.2.

Qualifying loans An individual who is a partner is entitled to relief for interest paid on qualifying loans, ie loans used to acquire an interest in the firm or which have been taken to enable him to make a loan to his firm for use in the ordinary course of the firm's business. See 9.4.

Shareholders in a close company may also be able to raise qualifying loans to acquire shares or make loan capital available to the company. See 9.5.

Readily convertible assets A term used for **PAYE** and **NICs** purposes and replaced the former term 'tradeable assets' from 17 March 1998. PAYE and NICs have to be paid if an employee receives readily convertible assets as part of his remuneration. See 4.2.1 and 21.1.2.

Rebasing A technical term for CGT purposes whereby an individual who held an asset at 31 March 1982 may have his capital gain computed as if his cost were the market value of the asset at that date. See 14.3.

Relevant earnings Schedule D profits and earnings from a non-pensionable employment. An individual may make contributions into a **personal pension scheme** based on a percentage of his relevant earnings for a tax year. See 12.8.

Relief for reinvestment in unquoted shares CGT relief was available up to 5 April 1998 where an individual or trust invested in a qualifying unquoted trading company within three years of the date of a disposal that gave rise to a capital gain. See 17.4. Now replaced by EIS CGT deferral relief: see 11.6.

Remittance basis The rule under which foreign domiciled individuals pay tax on overseas income and gains only if they are remitted to the UK. See 24.10.

'Rent-a-room' relief A special relief for individuals who let rooms in their home. See 6.4.

Relevant discounted security A loan stock issued at a discount of more than 0.5% for each year of its life (or more than 15% if the stock has a life of more than 30 years). A gain on the sale of a relevant discounted security is taxed as income. See 7.7.

Reservation of benefit An **IHT** term. Where a person makes a gift but reserves a benefit, the transaction is not regarded as a **potentially exempt transfer**. The asset remains part of his estate for as long as he continues to reserve a benefit. If he has not relinquished his reserved benefit by the time of his death, the asset's market value will be brought into account for **IHT** purposes just as if he still owned the asset. See 19.7.

Restrictive covenant An undertaking not to do something in the future. Where an employee receives a cash sum in return for entering into such a covenant, the cash is taxed as employment income. See 4.20.

Retirement annuity contracts (RACs) These are similar to **personal pension schemes**. In effect, they are approved contracts under which a person who was self-employed or in non-pensionable employment could provide for their retirement prior to the introduction of personal pension schemes in July 1988. Many RACs make provision for premiums to be paid in subsequent years and, while no new RACs are now issued, contributions under existing policies thus continue to attract relief for some years to come. See 12.8.

Retirement benefits scheme A technical term for a pension scheme. See Chapter 12.

Retirement relief A special relief for CGT purposes which applies where an individual aged 50+ disposes of his business or an interest in a business (eg an interest in a firm). See 17.8.

Revenue expenditure Expenditure that is deductible in arriving at a company's profits. Cf **capital expenditure**.

Reverse charge A VAT charging mechanism that obliges the customer to account to Customs for VAT on the price charged for goods or services. The VAT charged is recoverable as **input VAT**, subject to the normal rules. See 28.5.3.

Roll-over relief A CGT relief that applies where an individual disposes of a business or an asset used in a business and spends the proceeds on acquiring replacement assets during a qualifying period (normally up to one year before and up to three years after the date of disposal of the original asset). See 17.4.

Roll-up fund A colloquial term for an offshore collective fund where the managers do not pay out income but accumulate it within the fund. See 8.2.

Salaried partner An individual who is subject to the supervision and direction of equity partners and who is therefore no more than a very senior employee. Salaried partners are assessable under Schedule E rather than Schedule D.

Schedule D A self-employed person's profits are assessed under Schedule D. See Chapter 5.

Schedule E Directors and employees weree assessed under Schedule E for 2002-03 and earlier years. The normal basis of assessment for Schedule E /employment income is the receipts basis, ie an individual is assessed according to remuneration received by him during the year. See Chapter 4.

Scientific research allowances Certain expenditure incurred by traders on scientific research may attract allowances. **Revenue expenditure** is allowed in full. **Capital expenditure** may attract 100% **capital allowances**. See 5.5.21.

Self-administered pension scheme A pension scheme with no more than 12 members where either the company that established the scheme or one or more of the members are trustees. See 12.9.

Self-assessment A new system for assessing tax and payment of tax liabilities which came into force in 1996-97 for individuals and trustees. See 3.1. Companies moved onto a self-assessment system for accounting periods ending on or after 1 July 1999.

Settlement Another name for a trust.

Shares Valuation Division A specialist section of the Capital Taxes Office which negotiates valuations of unquoted shares where such a valuation is required for tax purposes.

Small companies rate Corporation tax is charged at only 19% unless the company concerned has profits in excess of the lower limit (presently £300,000, provided there are no associated companies). If there are associated companies, the lower limit is divided by the number of associated companies. See 26.4.3.

Sole traders An individual is a sole trader if he carries on business on his own account rather than in partnership or through a company. Similarly, an individual carrying on a profession on his own account is termed a 'sole practitioner'.

Stakeholder pensions These replaced **personal pension schemes** with effect from 6 April 2001. See 12.8.

Stamp duty Duty payable at 0.5% on transfers of shares and at 1-4% on transfers of property. See Chapter 29.

Surcharge A penalty based on the amount of tax payable which is imposed automatically if an individual has not paid the tax due on his self-assessment return by one month after the filing date. A further surcharge is normally imposed if tax remains unpaid after a further six months have elapsed.

Taper relief Capital gains may be reduced by taper relief, depending on the number of complete years of ownership after 5 April 1998, and depending on whether the asset disposed of is a business asset. See 14.5.

There is also a taper relief for **IHT** where an individual dies within seven years of making a **potentially exempt transfer**. See 19.6.

Tax Bulletin A newsletter issued by the Revenue for practitioners. See 2.2.4.

Tax invoice An invoice issued by a supplier which must show specific information. It is the document on which VAT accounting and control procedures are based. See Chapter 28.

Tax point The time at which a transaction is regarded as taking place for VAT purposes, and when VAT becomes payable or recoverable. See **Cash accounting**.

TESSA Tax-Exempt Special Savings Account – available for new investors up to 5 April 1999. The interest is tax free if it is not drawn for a period of five years. See 11.4.

Time apportionment basis Where an asset was owned at 6 April 1965, and no universal **rebasing** election has been made, it is sometimes possible for a capital gain to be computed on the apportionment basis. This means that only a proportion of the gain achieved over the total period of ownership is brought into charge. See 14.3.

Trust Property is held in trust where trustees hold it for the benefit of clearly identified beneficiaries. The trustees must use the capital and income as directed by the trust deed and in accordance with trust law. See Chapter 20.

Unincorporated businesses A company is an incorporated business. Businesses carried on by a **sole trader** or partnership are unincorporated businesses.

Universal rebasing election An irrevocable election that may be made under which the 31 March 1982 value of assets held by that person is treated as if it were the original cost. See 14.3.

Venture Capital Loss Relief Where an individual has subscribed for shares in an unquoted trading company, any losses may be set against his income for the year in which the loss is realised. See 17.2.

Venture Capital Trust A type of investment trust established under FA 1995 provisions. VCTs must invest in unquoted trading companies with net assets of no more than £15m. See 11.7.

Wasting assets Assets with an expected useful life of less than 50 years. See 17.3.4-17.3.5.

Zero-rating A sale on which no VAT is charged. A person making zero-rated supplies may nevertheless still be able to recover **input VAT**. See 28.3.2.

KEY CHANGES INTRODUCED BY THE FINANCE ACT 2003 AND RECENT COURT DECISIONS ETC.

Chapter 2 The UK Tax System

- Schedule E abolished from 6 April 2004: see 2.1.
- Introduction of the Income Tax (Earnings & Pensions) Act 2003 from 6 April 2003: see 2.1.

Chapter 3 Coping with Self-Assessment

- High Court finds against the Revenue on discovery assessment: see 3.2.4.

Chapter 4 Employment Income

- New allowance of £2 per day for homeworkers: see 4.4.4.
- Increased tax on company cars: see 4.5.
- No tax charge where employer pays congestion charge on company car: see 4.5.6.
- Tax free allowance for Christmas parties increased to £150: see 4.9.
- Important changes to taxation of employee share schemes: see 4.14-4.16.
- New tax charge on employee options over gilts: see 4.17.
- Taxpayer secures exemption for cost of MBA course reimbursed by new employer: see 4.19.

Chapter 5 Tax and Self-employment

- 100% capital allowances for information and communication technology extended for another year.
- 100% capital allowances for water efficient technology.

Chapter 7 Income from Savings

- Loss relief abolished on Relevant Discounted Securities: see 7.7.6.

Chapter 10 Allowances and Tax Credits

- New Tax Credit system introduced from 6 April 2003: see 10.11.

Chapter 12 Life Assurance and Pensions

- Loopholes in the taxation of non-qualifying insurance policies are blocked.
- Credit for basic rate on profits from non-qualifying policies reduced from 22% to 20%.
- Earnings cap for pension contributions increased to £99,000: see 12.9.5.
- Radical changes proposed to the pension regime.

Chapter 14 The Calculation of Capital Gains

- *Mansworth v Jelley* reveals anomalies but is overruled from 9 April 2003: see 14.4.3.
- Business taper to be extended from 6 April 2004: see 14.6.11.
- New CGT treatment for earn-outs: see 14.8.1.

Chapter 15 More Complex Calculations for Certain Types of Asset

- Changes to CGT treatment of second-hand insurance policies: see 15.7.

Chapter 17 Capital Gains Tax and Business Transactions

- Hold-over relief for shares no longer available where the company has substantial investment activities: see 17.5.2.

Chapter 19 Inheritance Tax and Individuals

- Nil rate band extended to £255,000 from 6 April 2003.
- UK unit trusts and OEICs no longer subject to IHT if held by foreign domiciliaries: see 19.1.
- *Eversden* case clarifies GWR rules but is overruled from 20 June 2003: see 19.7.5.

Chapter 21 Deducting Tax at Source – and Paying it Over to the Inland Revenue

- PAYE can apply to exercise of options over shares in subsidiary companies: see 21.1.4.

Chapter 22 Anti-Avoidance Legislation

- New anti-avoidance legislation for offshore trusts: see 22.14.

Chapter 24 The Income and Capital Gains of Foreign Domiciliaries

- Government publishes Green Paper on the tax treatment of foreign domiciliaries: see 24.1.

Chapter 25 National Insurance Contributions and Social Security Benefits

- NIC charge on profits from exercise of approved options where the profit is subject to income tax: see 25.1.4.

Chapter 26 Tax and Companies

- New rules to apply to Employee Benefit Trusts.
- Revenue publishes guidance on exemption for companies' capital gains from sales of substantial shareholdings in qualifying companies: see 26.7.3.
- Relief for employee options: see 26.3.2.

Chapter 28 Outline of VAT

- Relaxation in rules of duty deferment scheme for importers to take effect from 1 December 2003: see 28.3.3.
- VAT threshold increased to £56,000: see 28.4.1.
- Limit for flat rate scheme increased to £150,000 from 1 April 2003: see 28.6.1.

Chapter 29 Stamp Duty, Stamp Duty Reserve Tax and Stamp Duty Land Tax

- New stamp duty regime to apply from 1 December 2003: see 29.5.

Chapter 31 Charities and Not for Profit Organisations

- Charities must register for Gift Aid donations of tax rebates: see 31.1.13.

USEFUL E-MAIL ADDRESSES AND WEB PAGES

The authors

Tony Foreman	tony.foreman@uk.pkf.com
Gerald Mowles	g.mowles@amicorp.com

Contributors

Chapter 5	gordon.hopkins@uk.pkf.com
Chapter 9	peter.juntai@uk.co.uk
Chapter 11	colin.walker@uk.pkf.com
Chapter 19	hilary.sharpe@uk.pkf.com
Chapter 20	mark.francis@uk.pkf.com
Chapter 23	m.price@amicorp.com
Chapter 24	mike.wilkes@uk.pkf.com
Chapter 26	peter.harrup@uk.pkf.com
Chapter 28	tim.buss@uk.pkf.com
Chapter 29	david.gubbay@dechert.com
Chapter 31	niall.ogara@uk.pkf.com

Government

Inland Revenue	www.inlandrevenue.gov.uk/
Treasury	www.hm-treasury.gov.uk/

Professional bodies

Chartered Institute of Taxation	www.tax.org.uk/
Institute of Chartered Accountants of England and Wales	www.icaew.co.uk/
The Institute of Chartered Accountants of Scotland	www.icas.org.uk/
The Institute of Chartered Accountants of Ireland	www.icai.ie/
The Law Society	www.lawsoc.org.uk/
Gray's Inn Tax Barristers	taxbar.com

General

The publishers	www.pearsoned.co.uk
PKF	www.pkf.co.uk
Zurich	www.zurichadvice.co.uk

PREFACE

This book covers a wide field and is aimed at both the professional and non-professional reader. Our main aim is always to make this Handbook a 'user friendly' but comprehensive summary of the tax legislation for a non-professional reader who is seeking guidance on his own situation. We reproduce the relevant pages of Revenue forms, cross-referenced to this book, and explain ways in which such readers may obtain further details from Government publications. We also try to go into sufficient further detail for professionals whose daily work brings them face to face with our complex tax system – accountants, solicitors and company secretaries.

We also draw attention to areas of uncertainty, potential pitfalls and tax planning points. However, it really goes without saying that this Handbook deals only with general principles and is no substitute for expert advice which takes full account of the specific facts and circumstances of your case. Readers should normally seek professional advice where substantial amounts are involved.

This book is a team effort. Our PKF colleagues – Graham Baker, Roger Bleasby, Dale Butcher, Tim Buss, Sharna Edwards, Mark Francis, Niall O'Gara, Peter Harrup, Gordon Hopkins, Peter Jun Tai, Hilary Sharpe, Colin Walker and Mike Wilkes have all updated chapters and provided a considerable amount of new material. Sue Parr has compiled the tables. Special thanks are due to our outside contributors. Vince Jerrard, Keith Williams and Stuart Reynolds of Zurich have updated their chapter on life assurance and pensions. Mike Price of Amicorp has updated the chapter on Residence. Dan Foster and Steve Dunn at DMS have added a section on Australians living in the UK. David Gubbay of Dechert (solicitors) has updated his chapter on stamp duty.

Readers can e-mail us with queries and suggestions (see p. xxx).

Note that to save needless repetition of 'he or she' we have mainly used the male gender indiscriminately to denote both genders.

Lastly, but certainly not least, our thanks to Amelia Lakin and the editorial team at Pearson Education, who have gone over the entire text with a fine-tooth comb and managed to see us through extremely tight deadlines.

Tony Foreman and Gerald Mowles

ZURICH

Other titles in the Zurich Handbook series

ESTATE PLANNING & TAXATION OF CAPITAL HANDBOOK (4th Edition)

This is an invaluable guide to estate planning, whether you are an individual wishing to control who benefits from your estate, or a professional adviser. It enables you to grasp the implications of capital taxation on personal business and family wealth and how, by careful planning, its impact can be legally mitigated.

ZURICH BUSINESS TAX AND LAW HANDBOOK (4th Edition)

The ultimate business tax reference, this handbook details the tax obligations and legal considerations facing businesses and their advisers. For business proprietors, financial advisers, company secretaries, directors and executives, this book will become the first point of reference for addressing legal questions and limiting tax obligations.

ZURICH EXPATRIATE TAX & INVESTMENT HANDBOOK (8th Edition)

For British citizens living abroad this book offers essential guidance on how to manage their financial affairs to their greatest possible advantage. It provides comprehensive coverage of every aspect of expatriate tax and investment from the effect of the single currency to advice on working abroad.

AVAILABLE SOON

PENSIONS HANDBOOK (9th Edition)

This is the complete guide to pension planning, whether you are a business owner, company director, self-employed or a professional pension planner. It examines the different pension choices available and how they work, explains the Inland Revenue requirements that must be followed and shows how individual pensions operate.

RETIREMENT PLANNING HANDBOOK (9th Edition)

The Retirement Planning Handbook focuses on the financial mechanics of planning a stress-free retirement with no financial worries. It enables you to implement a retirement plan successfully and ensures that you are fully aware of the long- and short-term investment opportunities.

ZURICH INVESTMENT & SAVINGS HANDBOOK 2003/2004

The *Investment & Savings Handbook 2002/2003* guides you through the complexities surrounding the abundance of financial products available so that you can make informed choices for your investment strategy. Completely up to date with the latest legislation, it highlights the significant changes in the law and how they will impact on your investments and savings.

For further information, contact your local bookseller, telephone Pearson Education Ltd on 02379 623333, or visit our website www.pearsoned.co.uk/

1

MANAGING YOUR TAX AFFAIRS – AND SAVING TAX

"No man in this country is under the smallest obligation, moral or other, so to arrange his legal relations to his business or to his property as to enable the Inland Revenue to put the largest possible shovel into his stores." Lord Clyde

Managing your tax affairs and planning ahead are inextricably connected with one another: you cannot plan in an effective way unless you are on top of your responsibility to file returns and you are aware of key deadlines.

In this chapter we cover:

General strategy

(1) Key points to bear in mind.

Some specific situations where you need to plan ahead

(2) If you are employed.
(3) If you are thinking of becoming self-employed.
(4) If you are already in business.
(5) Managing your investments.
(6) Tax deductible investments.
(7) Your family affairs and personal financial planning.

Managing your tax affairs

(8) Ensure that all important deadlines are kept.

1.1 KEY POINTS TO BEAR IN MIND

There is no simple solution to the question of how to pay less tax – if only there were! And there are plenty of ways of going wrong and increasing your tax problems. However, you will almost certainly do well to adopt the following basic principles of effective tax management and planning.

Carry out some background research

Your tax affairs need to be taken seriously. It is important to fill out your tax return in a meticulous way. You should carefully read the notes issued with the tax return and, if there are areas on which you are not quite sure, you should seek advice, either from the Revenue itself or from a practising accountant.

Deal with your self-assessment return issued in April 2003

Under self-assessment (SA), you need to submit your tax return, and settle your outstanding tax, by 31 January following the tax year. If you fail to do this, you automatically become liable for interest and penalties.

Do not get involved in evasion

Before you take any action, ask yourself whether you would be happy for all the documentation to be put before the Inspector of Taxes. If a scheme relies on non-disclosure, you may be getting involved in evasion. If you are found out you become liable for interest and penalties and you might be subject to prosecution.

The Government seems increasingly to put tax avoidance in the same category as tax evasion. However, taxpayers are under no obligation to arrange their tax affairs in such a way that they maximise their tax liability. The courts have drawn a distinction between acceptable tax planning and unacceptably artificial avoidance and evasion.

Plan ahead

Part of practical tax planning is to anticipate what could change in the future. For example, it may be that you are likely to sell your present home in two or three years' time when you reach retirement. If you have let a property in the past, you need to look into the position now to see whether there could be a CGT charge when you sell it and, if there is a potential problem, what steps you might take to avoid it. If you are going to sell your business when you retire in a few years' time, you need to find out what tax may be payable and what you can do to reduce this.

Do take all taxes into account

It is important to be aware that steps you might take to avoid income tax may have CGT consequences, or vice versa. For example, you may be able to get a tax deduction if you set aside part of your home for work. However, if a couple of rooms are set aside exclusively for business purposes, this may affect your main residence exemption and could result in a CGT charge when you sell the property. There may well be ways in which you could both have your cake and eat it, but you need to look into the fine detail of the rules concerning the main residence exemption.

There are also many situations where you should find out the VAT and stamp duty consequences before taking steps that will reduce the tax on your business profits: one example of this is transferring an investment property to a company.

Be flexible

It makes no sense to invest in a savings plan because the return is free of tax if the plan is not suited to your personal requirements and the capital is tied up for, say, ten years. You should bear in mind that circumstances may change. It may therefore be unwise to put all your spare investments into a trust for the benefit of your children if your own situation might change. In recent years, many individuals have suffered unexpected demands on their capital and some people are now regretting that they gave away capital that is no longer surplus to their requirements.

Do not forget the rules may change

Tax legislation is subject to a review at least once a year in the Chancellor's Budget. At one time, it was possible to obtain income tax relief for all interest payments. When the law was changed, individuals were given relief for a transitional period on existing borrowings. Nevertheless, the withdrawal of interest relief came as a serious blow to those who had come to depend on it. Another example is where the rules on non-resident trusts were changed in 1998 and individuals who had created such trusts found that they could be made to pay tax on the trustees' capital gains even though these gains might not be paid out to them. So before you carry out any tax planning that will affect your situation in future years, put down on paper how much the various tax reliefs are worth to you and the extent to which you could rearrange your affairs if the law were changed and the reliefs curtailed or abolished.

Finally, bear in mind that court decisions constantly result in changed interpretations or sometimes the Inland Revenue simply decide to interpret the legislation in a different way. It could be unwise to rely too heavily on tax breaks afforded by the present rules. A topical example is the Revenue's current attack on situations where husband and wife take out profits from a company in the form of dividends and the spouse who contributes most to the business takes an unrealistically low salary (see 22.5.3). The Inland Revenue have suddenly picked up on this and are seeking extra tax for past years which the people concerned had thought to be settled.

Do not be fooled by G&T tax advice

All professional advisers complain that clients invariably know someone who assures them that, quite legitimately, he is paying virtually no tax at all. Be wary of advice given over a gin and tonic: very often, the individual himself does not understand all the ramifications of his own affairs. Worse still, some of the schemes put forward often turn out to involve evasion (which is illegal) rather than avoidance. Even where there is some substance to what is being said, your friend's or colleague's situation may be quite different from yours. For example, someone who advises you that he pays no tax on his earnings from work carried out outside this country may have a foreign domicile (see Chap. 24) and so be entitled to reliefs that are not available to you as a UK domiciliary.

Do not wag the dog

Investment first, tax second: tax breaks may be a consideration when considering an investment, but normal investment criteria should be the deciding factor. For example, you may be able to defer gains by investing in EIS companies, but what is the benefit if the EIS company's business plan is poorly thought out?

Take professional advice

Unless your affairs are extremely straightforward, you could probably do with a financial 'health check' from time to time, ie a discussion with an accountant or tax adviser to go over your affairs to look at how you might improve your situation and pay less tax. A good accountant should be able to more than cover the fees that he charges by pointing out ways in which you can reduce personal taxes or avoid penalties.

If your affairs are more complex, you probably need to take professional advice on a regular basis. It also makes sense for a tax accountant or adviser to take over the detailed work of preparing your tax return, agreeing payments and making sure that deadlines are not missed.

Bear in mind the anti-avoidance provisions

The tax legislation contains extensive anti-avoidance provisions intended to make sure that you cannot save tax by carrying out transactions in a roundabout way. In particular, much legislation is aimed at preventing a person from converting interest income into capital gain. There are also provisions aimed against the use (or, to be more specific, the abuse) of settlements. In the main, you will be assessed on income arising to trustees of a settlement if you created that settlement and there is any way in which you, or your spouse, may benefit under the settlement.

If you are considering taking steps for tax planning that you hope will help you to escape tax, but that are contrary to the spirit of the legislation, you need to take a particularly close look at the anti-avoidance provisions. This is a situation where it is normally necessary to take professional advice. Tax evasion is illegal, but tax avoidance, maybe to the annoyance of the Treasury, is not. On the other hand, the Revenue will challenge tax avoidance arrangements, especially where they involve artificial transactions or are affected by specific anti-avoidance provisions in the legislation. Taking on the Revenue could involve expensive professional costs and, if the matter went to court, and you lost, you would be liable for the Revenue's legal costs as well as your own. An experienced tax adviser should make an informed judgement about whether a particular arrangement is likely to be regarded as acceptable tax planning or unacceptable tax avoidance.

Check on back years

Mistakes do happen, and in the past you may have failed to claim all the allowances to which you were entitled. You should therefore carry out a periodic check or 'audit' to ensure that you (and family members, eg your minor children or elderly dependent relatives) have claimed all the tax allowances and reliefs to which you are entitled. If you find that mistakes have occurred in relation to 1997-98, you need to file a repayment claim by 31 January 2004. If you do not, the overpaid tax will be lost to you for ever.

An example of this in the 2002-03 tax year was the sudden deadline imposed by the court ruling in *Mansworth v Jelley* (see 14.4.3) which necessitated a review of all open years' tax.

1.2 IF YOU ARE EMPLOYED

Whether you are a company director, a senior executive, a manager or an ordinary employee, there are all manner of ways you may be able to reduce your tax liabilities.

1.2.1 Claim expenses

It is important to claim all allowable expenses (see 4.3). There are fixed deductions for workers in certain industries (eg uniformed police officers can claim £55 pa and pharmacists £45 pa without having to produce any receipts). If you have to belong to a professional institute, the subscription is normally an allowable expense. If you are required to provide certain equipment yourself (eg a fax machine at home), make sure you put in a claim for the expenses associated with it, and claim capital allowances.

1.2.2 Keep records

If you are required to travel extensively, especially overseas, keep a note of your itinerary and the main types of expense you incur. By doing this, you will be well placed to answer any queries from the Inspector and you should be able to demonstrate that there is no benefit-in-kind if all the expenses were business related.

If you need to use your own car in the course of your employment, find out whether your employer pays the authorised mileage rates (see 4.4.9). If it does not, or if the mileage payments exceed the authorised rates, you need to keep a detailed note of your business and private mileage so that any benefit-in-kind can be calculated. Under SA, keeping good records is no longer simply a matter of 'good housekeeping' but a necessity (see 3.1.6).

1.2.3 Reduce car scale benefits and consider cash alternatives

The company car rules changed in 2002-03, if you have a company car you should consider how you are now taxed on this benefit and work out the value of having a company car versus using your own car and claiming approved mileage allowance (see 4.4.9).

1.2.4 Go for benefits that do not attract NICs

The cost of traditional benefits packages are becoming more onerous for employers because of the imposition of the Class 1A NICs charge at 12.8% (see 25.1.8). Why not suggest a package of benefits that is not subject to Class 1A, such as computers for home use, mobile 'phones and approved share schemes?

1.2.5 Other tax efficient benefits

If you have any influence over the way your remuneration package is made up, take account of the fact that some benefits are more tax efficient than others. For example, it is well worth having an interest-free loan of £5,000 since no benefit-in-kind is assessed whatsoever. The benefit of having the right to occupy a company flat is often taxed on a favourable basis, especially where it originally cost your company £75,000 or less (see 4.8).

1.2.6 Pension schemes

Pension benefits are particularly attractive as they are not normally taxable. If you do not need all your salary to cover your living costs, it may well be attractive if you can reach a 'deal' with your employer so that he makes contributions towards your pension instead of giving you a larger annual pay rise. If your employer has gone to the trouble of setting up a pension scheme for you, make sure that you get the most benefit out of it. Recent changes in legislation also mean that anyone who employs more than five employees may be required by the employees to offer a pension scheme.

Quite separately from this, do carefully consider the merits of making additional voluntary contributions. If you are not in a company pension scheme, you are most strongly advised to start a personal pension scheme or review your retirement planning strategy. See generally Chap.12.

1.2.7 Share incentives

Company directors and senior executives are often offered an opportunity to acquire shares in their company. However, there are various pitfalls that can apply if you acquire shares through an unapproved scheme (see 4.13), so you need to seek professional advice. Also plan ahead: if you have been given approved share options in the past (see 4.14), consider how you will reap the benefit. Do not forget that CGT may be payable when you exercise your share options if you go on to sell the shares that you have acquired.

The approved schemes offer significant advantages (see 4.12 and 4.15). The all-employee share scheme provides total exemption from tax after five years; the Enterprise Management Incentive Options are designed to provide larger equity profits that may be taxed at just 10%.

1.3 IF YOU ARE THINKING OF BECOMING SELF-EMPLOYED

1.3.1 Will the Revenue accept that you are self-employed?

The first question to address is whether the Revenue is likely to accept that you are self-employed. If the main thing that you have to sell is your time, and you are subject to supervision in the way in which you carry out your work, the Revenue may well regard you as an employee. It cuts no ice that your contract may state that you are self-employed.

One reason why the Revenue will look into this so closely is that, if you are self-employed, you will be able to claim certain expenses that are not allowable deductions for employees. So you should take all possible steps to ensure that your claim for self-employed status can stand up to scrutiny by the Revenue (see 5.2).

In theory, the risk of the Revenue's reclassifying a self-employed person as an employee lies with the employer. If the Revenue's view is eventually upheld, the employer is liable to pay Class 1 NICs and the Revenue may well require him to pay over the tax that he ought to have withheld under PAYE. Where this happens, the consequences can be disastrous. In law, an employer is precluded from collecting arrears of Class 1 NICs by deducting them from subsequent payments to the individual concerned. In other words, if the employer does not get it right first time round, he cannot correct his mistake later on. Similarly, the primary responsibility for deducting tax under PAYE and paying it over to the Revenue lies with the employer. The Collector of Taxes is normally reluctant to get into time-consuming disputes with the employee and will simply demand the tax from the employer, leaving him to make any adjustment by agreement with the employee. Nevertheless, most self-employed individuals also have a vested interest in the Revenue's accepting that they are genuinely self-employed. If a dispute arises with someone to whom you provide services, he is unlikely to want to deal with you again in the future, certainly not on a self-employed basis.

1.3.2 Keep the Revenue informed

Once you start to be self-employed, your best interests are safeguarded by keeping the Revenue advised about what you are doing. You are legally obliged to make your existence known to your local tax district by completing form CWF3 and advise them of when they may expect to receive accounts. New businesses have three months to register with the Revenue for Class 2 NICs or face a £100 penalty. An Inspector of Taxes is like anyone else: he is likely to be more reasonable if he is handled properly rather than irritated by the fact that he constantly has to chase you for information.

There are various other practical matters. You should make enquiries of your local VAT Office to see if you need to be registered for VAT (see 28.4.1). You should also advise the National Insurance Contributions Office (NICO) at the DSS that you are self-employed and start to pay Class 2 NICs as a self-employed person.

The Revenue issues a starter pack for new businesses, which can be obtained by either visiting www.inlandrevenue.gov.uk/employers/newbus.htm or calling 08457 646 646.

1.3.3 Should you employ your spouse?

Depending on the type of business you carry on, it may be appropriate for you to employ your spouse, or even to have your spouse as a partner (see 1.4.4). This may be a particularly good idea if your spouse would otherwise have little or no taxable income. However, if you employ your spouse, do not pay an unrealistic salary. The Revenue is almost bound to challenge a situation where the salary is disproportionate. The Revenue's argument is that you will be due a deduction only for a reasonable rate of remuneration paid to your spouse in return for services and expertise provided.

Do be careful on this; in principle you could suffer double taxation if you get it wrong since your spouse will still be taxed on his or her full salary, even if only part of that salary is allowed as a deduction in arriving at your business profits for tax purposes. Problems could also arise if you are deemed to pay your spouse too little; you should obtain advice on the implications of the minimum wage legislation (see 1.4.4).

1.3.4 Provide for tax

Finally, when you commence self-employment, do think ahead and make provision for the tax payments that you will need to make over the next 18 months to two years. Get into the habit of setting aside part of your earnings each month so that you will have something in hand to pay the Revenue when the assessments are eventually issued. Under self-assessment, the first tax payment can often be crippling as it represents a payment of tax for your first year plus a 50% payment on account.

Example

A becomes self-employed during the tax year to 5 April 2003 and draws up his accounts on a fiscal year basis. He was formerly an employee who paid all his tax under PAYE and is therefore not required to make payments on account. On 31 January 2004, *A* will have to pay all of the tax due for the year to 5 April 2003 plus a payment on account in respect of the year to 5 April 2004 equal to 50% of the 2002-03 tax.

1.3.5 Take advice on IR35

If you are setting up a limited company to supply your services, bear in mind that provisions in FA 2000 may mean that the company may have to pay over PAYE tax on notional salary that you have not actually taken out. The legislation is aimed at individuals who provide their services via intermediary companies (or partnerships) and who would otherwise be regarded as employees of the end customer. The effect of the new rules is that your company is required to account for tax on its income from 'relevant engagements' as if that income was your Schedule E earnings subject to PAYE. See 21.3 on this.

1.3.6 VAT

Research the VAT implications relating to your business. Check regularly to make sure you comply with registration requirements (see 28.4.1). The onus is on you to notify Customs & Excise if you exceed the VAT registration threshold. Make sure that you charge VAT where appropriate and allow for VAT in costings. VAT is a transaction tax, not a tax on profit, so getting VAT can be costly and putting mistakes right can often wipe-out any profit.

1.4 IF YOU ARE ALREADY IN BUSINESS

1.4.1 Keep good records

Much of the above applies to the same extent if you have already been in business for a number of years. In many businesses, some figures have to be estimated (eg the extent to which a trader's 'phone bill relates to business, as opposed to private, calls). There is nothing wrong with estimates, but do try to keep some sort of record so that the estimate can be supported if the Revenue challenges it.

You must indicate estimated entries on your SA return. The Revenue may enquire into this and the Inspector may well want to go back to previous years if he later looks into the position and decides the estimate is unreasonable. The main defence against this would be where the Inspector was already on notice about the way the estimates were arrived at.

Keep your records: the Revenue may call for them up to five years and ten months after the end of the tax year. Remember that this applies to all your tax affairs, not just the records relating to your business.

If you are a partner, keep tabs on the partnership's tax affairs. One of the partners (the 'representative partner') is responsible for filing a partnership return and you will not be able to complete your personal return without reference to this.

1.4.2 Do not cut corners on PAYE

Beware of situations where you should withhold tax, especially where you are paying casual or freelance workers whom the Revenue may regard as employees. The Revenue has teams of investigators who carry out regular reviews of PAYE compliance.

1.4.3 Take VAT seriously

VAT is a constant source of problems. Whenever you carry out a major transaction you should ask a VAT specialist for advice. Also, bear in mind that Customs & Excise make regular control visits to examine accounting records. Penalties can be levied if mistakes are uncovered during visits, so it is well worth having a review carried out in good time for errors to be corrected prior to a visit.

If you are VAT-registered, you are an unpaid tax collector. Make certain that VAT works for you by taking account of opportunities to improve cash flow, for example try to make your large value sales at the start of a VAT return period. Ideally you should organise matters so that suppliers send you invoices before the end of the return period. Ensure that you take full advantage of recovering input VAT. Consider whether special accounting schemes or flat rate schemes may be best for you (see 28.6).

1.4.4 Remunerating your spouse

Think carefully about the salary you pay to your spouse. If it is less than you have to pay to an ordinary employee, increase the amount (if only to that required under the minimum wage legislation). Consider setting up a pension scheme for your spouse, as your contributions will be tax deductible.

Think also about bringing your spouse into partnership. This is a complex matter on which it is best to seek professional advice that will take account of the nature of your business, and the time, expertise or capital brought to the business by your spouse.

1.4.5 Financing a partnership

There are some interesting possibilities for accelerating tax relief by you and your partners raising personal loans to put money into the firm to enable it to clear borrowings. Suppose your firm makes up accounts to 30 April 2004: interest on the firm's borrowings will be an expense in arriving at 2004-05 taxable profits, whereas interest paid in 2003-04 by the partners on personal loans will be a deduction from their taxable income for 2003-04 – so you get your tax relief one year earlier. (See 9.4.)

1.4.6 Relief for losses

If your business has not been going well and you suffered losses, look into the best way you can get relief. In some cases, you may be able to carry back the losses and set them against your other income (see 5.9). In other situations, the choice open to you is to set your losses against your income for the year of the loss, or against the following or preceding year's income, or carry forward the losses to be set against trading income received in later years. Obviously, it will make a great difference if you take relief in a year in which you will otherwise be subject to 40% tax rather than in a year in which your other income is relatively low and tax relief will be obtained at only 20% or 22%.

1.4.7 Stakeholder pension schemes (see Chap. 12)

It is particularly important for self-employed individuals to provide for their retirement since they qualify only for the basic State pension and not for SERPS. The Government has played its part in recent years in improving matters and the maximum contributions that may be paid to a stakeholder pension scheme are fairly generous unless you are caught because your profits exceed the 'earnings cap' (£99,000 for 2003-04).

Contributions to a stakeholder scheme are tax deductible. Furthermore, the scheme is not subject to tax of any kind and so the fund is likely to grow at a far faster rate than personal investments that are subject to tax.

It is possible to take the benefits at any time after you reach age 50. Up to 25% of the fund may be taken as a tax-free lump sum. The balance must eventually be used to purchase an annuity, although this can be postponed until age 75 if you opt for income withdrawals (see 12.8.6).

In recent years pension planning has come to mean more than simply paying into a traditional pension scheme. As a consequence of low annuity rates, individuals nowadays need to consider other investments. The tax implications of some of these alternatives are discussed at Chap 11.

The Government is also in the process of simplifying the numerous types of pension schemes that have sprouted from past legislation and it may be worth talking with your financial adviser to ensure that you are aware of these proposals and how they may affect you.

1.4.8 If you are a partner in a large professional firm

You must liaise with your firm's 'nominated partner' to obtain the information required for your SA return (see 5.10.7). If you incur any expenses, or buy plant and machinery used for the firm's business (eg a fax machine), you must arrange for the appropriate relief to be claimed in the partnership return (see 5.10.7). Your firm may convert into a Limited Liability Partnership (LLP) (see 5.11) though remember there may be other consideration when trading as a company or LLP, for example a landlord may be happy to take a guarantee from a normal partnership as he knows that each partner is jointly and severally liable, where he may not be inclined to accept a guarantee from a partner in an LLP, where each partner has a liability limited by contribution.

1.4.9 Should you transfer your business to a company?

If your business is going very well, you should consider incorporating your business, ie transfer your business to a company. Some general principles are set out in Chap. 27, but once again this is a matter where you would probably be best advised to consult an accountant or tax adviser. You will also have to consider the new rules in respect of service companies, discussed at 21.3. Another alternative is to set up an LLP (see 5.11).

1.4.10 If you already have a private company

A key issues is whether it makes sense to take a smaller salary and take the rest of your income in the form of dividends (which do not incur NICs). Another issue concerns the ownership of shares. If shares are held by your wife, she may pay a lower rate of tax on dividends. However, bear in mind that the Revenue is looking at these situations much more closely (see 22.5.3).

1.4.11 Plan for retirement and handing the business on

Finally, do plan ahead, both for retirement and for passing on your business in due course to your family. There are key questions to be addressed in relation to CGT planning: make sure that you take full advantage of taper relief available on business assets (see 14.6). Will IHT be payable on your death, or can matters be arranged so that either 100% or 50% business or agricultural property relief will be due? See 19.8-19.9 on this.

1.5 MANAGING YOUR INVESTMENTS

It is important to keep tax planning in perspective. In general, investment considerations should dictate your investment policy. Naturally, these vary according to an individual's perspective (ie his age, need for short- and medium-term liquidity, income requirements, the degree of risk acceptable, expectations for future inflation levels, perception of the economic climate, etc). Tax planning must be fitted in around these investment considerations. However, there are some quite simple steps that should be considered and that may help you to reduce the tax payable on your investment income and gains.

1.5.1 Invest in your employer?

There are valuable CGT breaks if you make gains from shares in a company for which you work (see 14.6.3). On the other hand, bear in mind the risks attached to having all your eggs in one basket.

1.5.2 Use all your family's allowances

There is generally scope for planning both in relation to income tax and capital gains tax.

Deposit interest

Spouses each have their own personal allowances and each spouse's income is taxed completely separately. If your spouse has little or no income, or is liable only at 20% or 22% whereas you have to pay 40% tax, there may be advantages in transferring incomc to him or her. A fairly straightforward way of doing this is to hold bank deposit accounts and other investments in your joint names. The basic rule is that where investments are held in this way, half of the resulting income is taxed on each spouse.

If you open a bank account in your minor child's name, the interest is treated as your income for tax purposes only if the total income arising from such potential gifts exceeds £100 pa per child (see 22.5.4), so there may be some limited opportunity for achieving tax-free savings.

Where you have adult children, it may make sense for you to lend cash to your children so that they can make tax efficient investments in ISAs (see 11.1).

Capital gains tax

Your spouse will have his or her own £7,900 CGT annual exemption and you should look for ways of using this each year, possibly by transferring investments (transfers between spouses are deemed to take place on a no gain/no loss basis) in order to put your spouse in a position to realise a gain on a sale to a third party. This is often appropriate where a gain has built up on quoted securities. A judicious transfer to your spouse of stocks and shares that show a paper gain can save significant amounts of tax even if the transfer takes place shortly before the securities are sold. But take care: the Revenue often looks very closely at the paperwork on such inter-spouse transfers and you must show that beneficial ownership of the securities actually passed to your spouse before a firm of stockbrokers was instructed to sell the shares. All other things being equal (which they seldom are), it is generally best to allow a few days to elapse between the transfer of the shares to your spouse and the sale by him or her.

There may sometimes be scope for using your children's annual CGT exemption as the £100 limit for income tax purposes does not apply for capital gains. Bear in mind that this is more difficult since a gift of shares, etc to anyone other than your spouse is normally treated as a disposal that is deemed to take place for CGT purposes at market value. However, if you hold shares in unquoted trading companies, and you can see an opportunity coming up whereby you could realise those shares at a large gain, it may be worth transferring part of your shareholding to your children. Because the shares are in unquoted trading companies, it may be possible to 'hold over' any capital gain so that your child (or other relation or friend) takes over the shares at your original acquisition value (see 18.5). This means that you will have no capital gain. The recipient will have a gain on disposal of the difference between your acquisition value (as adjusted for inflation) and the sale proceeds. However, if you plan carefully you can probably ensure that the child, etc realises a gain that is just within his £7,900 annual exemption – so no one pays tax on the capital gains.

When there is a new share listing, consideration should also be given to subscribing in your child's name as well as your own.

For CGT planning generally, see Chap. 18.

Long-term planning

You might even take out a stakeholder pension plan for a minor child and contribute up to £2,808 (£3,600 gross) pa – but bear in mind that this is a much more long-term savings plan. See 1.6.1 and 12.8 on the subject of stakeholder pensions.

1.5.3 Can you get tax relief for losses on your investments?

So many of us are nursing losses on investments in shares and unit trusts. It may make sense to cash in these investments if you have gains on other investments, for example on the sale of a property that you have been letting. Perhaps you hope that the investments will in time recover much of their value and you do not want to dispose of them altogether. There may be a way of having your loss relief without losing out on such a recovery. There are special rules aimed at 'bed and breakfast' transactions but it may be possible to side-step these if you sell and your spouse or partner buys back (see 18.2).

If you are the main beneficiary under the will of someone who dies in the last few months, it may be possible to reduce the IHT on your inheritance. If the executors sell quoted securities within 12 months of the death, and the proceeds are less than their value at the date of death ('probate value'), it may be possible to have IHT recalculated so that it is charged only on the lower value (see 19.11.3).

1.5.4 Take full advantage of tax efficient investments

Investments in an ISA are totally free from tax (see 11.1), so if possible you should open ISAs for yourself and your partner. National Savings Certificates also offer a safe and tax-free return, albeit at a relatively low interest rate.

For longer-term investments, qualifying life insurance policies are often attractive. Once a policy has been in force for ten years, there is normally no tax charge whatsoever on the policy being cashed in.

Also consider taking out a stakeholder pension plan for a non-working spouse or partner.

1.5.5 Planning for some special situations

Your circumstances may be special because of your residence status, or your plans for the future.

For example, it may be that you plan to work overseas for a few years and therefore cease to be UK-resident. In such a case, it makes sense to defer taxable income until after you have ceased to be resident as this means no tax will arise. A possible way of doing this is to invest in offshore roll-up funds, rather than bank deposit accounts, with a view to cashing in the roll-up investments after you have ceased to be a resident.

If you are about to return to the UK, having been resident abroad, then you should take advice on any investment bonds and insurance policies issued by foreign insurance companies (see 12.2). If you have been non-resident for five tax years there may be merit in realising capital gains before you resume UK residence (see 23.5.4).

Your circumstances may be special in another way: if you have suffered losses in the past on 'one-off' transactions that are dealt with under Schedule D Case VI, look out for ways of realising Case VI gains. The point is that Case VI profits may generally be set against Case VI losses brought forward from previous years, and the profits do not have to arise from the same source.

It might be, for example, that you suffered losses on a property that you let out as furnished accommodation before 1994-95 when such activities were taxed under Case VI. Perhaps you have sold the property or ceased to let it and you assumed that your losses would go to waste. However, you may be able to 'access' these Case VI losses by selling gilts shortly before they go ex-div. The point is that the sale of gilts cum-interest will normally give rise to a Case VI charge on notional income by virtue of the accrued income scheme (see 7.6). An alternative way of generating Case VI profits is to invest in offshore roll-up funds. In many cases, such investments are very similar to having money on a bank deposit overseas. Thus no income is deemed to arise until the investor realises the investment. When this happens, the profit is charged under Case VI.

1.5.6 Property investments

Investments in real estate tend to be longer-term investments. For that reason, the tax planning considerations also tend to be long term in nature.

One planning point is relevant at the time you acquire an investment property. Interest on a qualifying loan may be set against any rental income that is taxable under Schedule A, ie any income from properties in the UK that are let out for rent. However, it is not normally possible for a person who already owns a property to take a qualifying loan later on. The planning point is therefore very simple: you should normally borrow at the outset unless you are quite sure that you will not need to borrow money to finance your property investments later on. Even if you do have sufficient capital, it may be best to borrow to make property investments and use your spare capital for other purposes. For example, it would not be good tax planning to use your capital to purchase an investment property and at the same time take a long-term non-qualifying loan to finance school fees.

Do not plan for one tax in isolation. If you let part of your home, or if you let your home for a period while you are living elsewhere, check on the CGT implications (see 16.4.3). There are a number of reliefs and ESCs, but you must be very careful not to put your extremely valuable main residence exemption into jeopardy.

If you do let part of your home, bear in mind the special rent-a-room relief (see 6.4) that may mean that rental income of up to £4,250 is totally exempt from tax.

It might make sense to form a company to hold property investments. If this is your only company, and its profits do not exceed £10,000, you may have no corporation tax to pay (see 26.4).

The VAT implications of property investment are complex (see 28.3.5). It is worth obtaining professional advice as there are special rules (eg election to tax and capital goods scheme) that are not at all straightforward. There are opportunities to save VAT, but also pitfalls.

1.5.7 Qualifying loans for company directors

If you work full time for a close company or hold more than 5% of the shares, and you wish to purchase further shares, you may be able to raise a qualifying loan (see 9.5). The interest attracts tax relief at your top rate and there is no £30,000 limit as formerly applied under MIRAS.

1.5.8 Plan ahead when buying a private company

If you purchase the whole of the share capital of a private trading company, and things do not go to plan, you are not normally due income tax relief for any loss. You may be able to get a loss allowed for CGT purposes, but capital losses may be set only against capital gains, not against income, and therefore it may be some years before you get effective relief.

There may be a way around this if you follow certain steps when you acquire the company. You should speak with your accountant, but basically what will be involved is for you to form a new company, subscribe cash for new shares in that company and have the company acquire the shares in the private trading company. At the end of the day, your position will be almost exactly the same, except that you will hold shares in a company with a wholly owned subsidiary rather than hold shares in the subsidiary itself. What is important is that by dealing with matters in this way, you will be entitled to s 574 relief on any capital loss (see 17.2), ie you will be able to set the loss against your income for the year of loss or the preceding tax year.

If you need to raise equity from outside investors, see if you can structure your company in a way that qualifies under the Enterprise Investment Scheme (EIS: see 11.6). Also consider Venture Capital Trusts (VCTs) as a potential source of equity investment (see 11.7).

1.6 TAX DEDUCTIBLE INVESTMENTS

Basically, there are four types of investment that attract income tax relief when you make the investment: pension contributions; investment in enterprise zone properties; investments under the EIS; and investments in VCTs.

1.6.1 Pension contributions

We return to pension contributions because the tax situation is so attractive. There is no other type of investment where you can gain tax relief when you pay money in, enjoy the benefits of a fund that pays no tax on its income and gains, and take part of the fund as a tax-free lump sum. The last aspect is one of the most important; contributions to pension schemes allow a person effectively to convert taxable income into a tax-free capital sum.

It is precisely because the tax treatment is so beneficial that restrictions have been introduced in recent years. For example, there is the 'cap' on pensionable earnings (presently £99,000), which means you cannot make stakeholder contributions based on earnings that exceed this amount. But the percentage limits that vary according to your age have been improved, so it is now possible to make larger contributions on the first £99,000 of your annual earnings.

It is worth noting that if you make payments into a retirement annuity policy (ie a policy similar to a stakeholder pension taken out before 1 July 1988), the earnings cap does not apply. So if your earnings for 2003-04 are £200,000, you can gain income tax relief for retirement annuity premiums based on £200,000 and not on £99,000. But be careful: the tax situation is quite complicated where an individual pays a mixture of retirement annuity and stakeholder contributions, so seek advice from a specialist.

Stakeholder pensions

FA 2000 introduced legislation which allows an individual to make a payment of up to £3,600 pa even though he does not work and so has no relevant earnings. The pension payments are made net of basic rate tax even if the individual has no taxable income. If you are in pensionable employment but earn less than £30,000, you may also be able to put in £3,600 pa – you actually pay £2,808; the pensions company reclaims the difference on your behalf and credits this to your stakeholder plan. Even if you have been retired for some years, you may be able to make further pension contributions based on earnings for one of the last five tax years – so you can make stakeholder pension contributions based on earnings for as far back as 1998-99.

1.6.2 Investment in enterprise zone properties

A 100% allowance is available where a person invests in a commercial building located in an enterprise zone. Basically, the building must be unused or you must make your investment within two years of it having first been let.

Enterprise zones were designated for a period of ten years and this period has now run out for many of them. Nevertheless, a number of enterprise zone property investments remain available.

Many people prefer to invest via a syndicate or fund, often called 'enterprise zone property trusts'. A person who invests in such a trust is entitled to relief for the corresponding proportion of the trust's investments in enterprise zone properties.

1.6.3 Investments under the Enterprise Investment Scheme

Wealthy individuals should consider making selective investments under the EIS. It is now possible to invest up to £150,000 pa under the EIS. Investors are entitled to 20% income tax relief and may also be able to claim

CGT deferral relief (see 11.6). The income tax and CGT reliefs may add up to 60% of your investment. Any capital gain on a disposal of the EIS shares after three years is totally tax free.

The Government has also made the EIS more attractive in other ways. Many of the restrictions and anti-avoidance rules have been abolished. It is now possible for an investor to become a paid director and take a full part in the management of the company. If you have gains in excess of £150,000, or you have made gains in the last few years that you would like to 'roll over', you may be able to obtain CGT deferral relief by investing further amounts under the EIS. Also, one of the requirements for EIS investors to qualify for the 20% income tax relief is that they must not have more than 30% of the equity. This rule does not apply if you are investing in an EIS company only in order to secure CGT deferral relief (see 11.6).

1.6.4 Venture Capital Trusts

An individual is allowed to invest up to £100,000 pa in VCTs – although note that these may be relatively high-risk investments. There are significant tax advantages in that if you subscribe for new VCT shares you are entitled to 20% income tax relief and CGT deferral relief. In addition, the dividends you receive from your investment and any capital gain when you eventually dispose of it can be tax free (see 11.7).

1.7 YOUR FAMILY AFFAIRS AND PERSONAL FINANCIAL PLANNING

There are important personal financial planning issues to be addressed (eg making sure you claim all that is due to you under the Child Tax Credits, mortgages, tax implications of marriage (and separation and divorce), life assurance, funding school fees, providing help to elderly dependent relatives, assisting your children in buying their first home, etc). Looking further ahead, there are longer-term matters that need to be kept in mind, for example the way in which your (and possibly your spouse's) will should be drawn up. IHT planning also needs to be considered.

1.7.1 Child Tax Credits

The full credit is worth £545 pa and is payable if your family income does not exceed £50,000 (see 10.8). You can be entitled to some credit if your family income exceeds £50,000 but is less than £58,000 (£66,000 where the child is aged less than 12 months). But you have to claim your entitlement, and you should bear in mind that claims cannot be backdated by more than three months.

1.7.2 House purchase

When you purchase your home, there are several types of mortgage available. Take advice about whether an ordinary repayment, endowment or pension mortgage is the most appropriate for you.

Another alternative is to open an ISA and use this type of tax privileged savings to build up capital so that you can clear the mortgage in due course.

1.7.3 Life assurance

Income tax relief is not given for life assurance premiums on policies taken out after 13 March 1984.

If you are self-employed, it is possible to obtain income tax relief at your top rate for life assurance premiums paid under a stakeholder pension plan – consult your adviser about the possibility of securing life assurance via a stakeholder pension policy (see 12.8.3). Bear in mind that if you use up part of your relief for pension contributions in this way, it may limit the amount that you can pay to secure pension benefits.

1.7.4 Marriage

Many tax planning issues that arise in connection with marriage concern CGT or IHT.

Capital gains tax

Bear in mind that if you transfer shares or other chargeable assets to your fiancé, you are deemed to have made a disposal at market value and a capital gain may therefore arise. From this point of view, it may be better to delay matters until after you marry as no capital gain arises on transfers between spouses who are living together. However, if you are thinking of transferring an asset on which a capital *loss* would arise, it may be best to crystallise this loss by making the transfer before you marry.

Something else to bear in mind is the position if each of you already owns your own home. Basically, you have three years' grace to resolve the position, but at the end of that time only one property can qualify as your main residence (see 16.2.5). The property concerned may be a new home or one of you may move into the other's existing home.

Inheritance tax

No IHT arises on transfers of assets by one spouse to another unless the transferor is UK-domiciled and the transferee is not (see 19.5.1).

1.7.5 If you and your partner are not married

In the main, the tax legislation does not recognise common law marriages and same-sex relationships. CGT and IHT are likely to be much more of an issue here and you need advice if significant capital assets are involved.

1.7.6 Separation and divorce

Relief for maintenance payments under pre-14 March 1988 court orders was abolished with effect from 6 April 2000. Furthermore, now that the married man's allowance has been phased out, there is no relief for maintenance payments whatsoever.

So far as CGT is concerned, you could find yourself in a Catch 22 situation. The legislation provides that a man and his wife are connected persons for CGT purposes until the marriage comes to an end. The marriage comes to an end when there is a decree absolute, not a decree nisi. However, the exemption for transfers between spouses applies only if you are living together. You may therefore find yourself in a situation where a CGT charge may arise because you are required to transfer assets to your spouse as part of your divorce settlement.

It is possible to get round this problem if you plan ahead. The basic rule that transfers between spouses are not subject to CGT applies to transfers made during a tax year in which you have been living together at some time. Thus, if you and your wife separate on, say, 10 April 2003, a transfer of assets between you will not give rise to a CGT charge provided the transfer is made before 6 April 2004.

1.7.7 Funding school fees

If grandparents or other relatives are able to help, advantage could be taken of your children's tax allowances. One way is for your relatives to set up trusts and for the trustees to distribute income to your children. This money could then be used to pay school fees.

Bear in mind that this will not work if you make a trust for your own children, as any income that is paid out before they attain age 18 will be treated as if it were your income.

Where grandparents, etc cannot assist, matters are more difficult but not necessarily impossible. You should start saving as early as possible and take full advantage of privileged investments such as ISAs and qualifying insurance policies. Take advice from a specialist.

1.7.8 Providing for elderly dependants

Many readers will be making a contribution towards the support of elderly parents or other relatives. Unfortunately, recent Chancellors have significantly reduced the scope for obtaining assistance towards these costs through tax relief. In particular, it is no longer possible to transfer income via a deed of covenant and the income tax allowance for dependent relatives has been abolished altogether.

One possibility for securing tax relief is where it is necessary to purchase a property that is used by the relative as his home. There is no tax relief for a mortgage taken out for this purpose, but it may be possible to secure CGT exemption in due course if you follow a fairly involved route.

The CGT exemption is not available if you own the property yourself (unless you owned it prior to 5 April 1988). However, if you form a trust and put money into it to enable the trustees to buy the dependant's home, the trustees may be entitled to an exemption as and when they eventually sell the property. Furthermore, this exemption is not affected by your being a beneficiary under the trust yourself. So the answer may be to set up a trust under which your elderly parent is entitled to occupy the property during his lifetime, with the trust coming to an end on his death and the property passing to you as a beneficiary of your own trust.

There are other aspects to be considered, not least the IHT position if the property has a value in excess of £255,000. Talk this through with a specialist tax adviser to see if this solution would work in your particular circumstances.

1.7.9 Assisting your children in making tax privileged investments

If you can afford it, it may make sense for you to lend your adult children the money so that they can use their quota of tax exempt and tax privileged investments such as ISAs or even stakeholder pensions.

1.7.10 Inheritance tax

This is a highly specialised area (see further Chap. 19), but in general a person should:

(1) make use of the annual exemptions;
(2) preserve and maximise business property and agricultural reliefs;
(3) make a valid will;
(4) consider making exempt transfers by a deed of variation;
(5) make potentially exempt transfers that escape IHT after the donor has survived seven years; and
(6) fund insurance policies so as to provide cash to meet IHT payable on death.

1.7.11 Special reliefs for foreign nationals

There are significant planning possibilities if you have foreign domicile (see Chap. 24). The Government has once gain opened the debate on this subject and now may be the time to do a little crystal ball gazing with your tax advisor to ensure that as far as possible your tax position and wealth are insulated from any proposed changes.

1.8 ENSURE THAT ALL IMPORTANT DEADLINES ARE KEPT

It is pointless trying to arrange your affairs tax efficiently unless you get the basics right and keep your affairs tidy. This means watching deadlines for action (eg paying tax) and making elections.

The most important tax planning deadlines are listed below. Note that this section should be read subject to three cautions:

(1) Most of the deadlines are dates by which a return, claim or election must be received by the Inspector of Taxes, or a payment received by the Collector. A document or payment must be posted at least one working day before the deadline and, because of the danger of postal delays, ideally at least a week.

(2) To keep this checklist to a manageable size, only those deadlines likely to apply to the majority of people have been included; the checklist is not fully comprehensive.

(3) Many deadlines cannot be included because they are fixed by reference to the facts of the individual case. For example, most corporation tax deadlines are fixed by reference to the end of the company's accounting period.

1.8.1 Tax year ended 5 April 2003

19 April 2003 PAYE/NICs payments due at the Accounts Office by today. Interest chargeable after this date.

19 May 2003 Employers who do not file end-of-year returns (on Forms P14, P35 and P38/P38A, CIS36) by today may be fined (subject to grace period).

26 May 2003 End of grace period – automatic penalties.

31 May 2003 Last date for giving a 2002-03 form P60 to each relevant employee.

6 July 2003	Substantial fines may be imposed on any employer who does not submit Form P9D/P11D (Returns of benefits, etc provided for employees) by today (see 4.4.1). Details of benefits shown on P9D or P11D forms must be supplied to each employee.
19 July 2003	Due date for payment for 2002-03 Class 1A NICs (company cars and fuel: see 25.1.8).PAYE quarterly payment date for small employers.
31 July 2003	Second interim tax payment for 2002-03 due.
5 October 2003	To avoid the danger of incurring penalties, individuals with new sources of income in 2002-03 should have notified the Revenue by 4 pm today if no tax return has been received.
19 October 2003	Amounts agreed under PSAs due for payment – interest starts to run.
31 December 2003	Closing date for claiming, on grounds of low income, repayment of Class 2 NICs paid in 2002-03 (see 25.2.3).
31 January 2004	The Self-Assessment Tax Return for 2002-03 needs to be filed by this date.

1.8.2 Tax year ended 5 April 2002

31 January 2004

Personal tax

(1) Claiming a set-off for industrial buildings allowances on enterprise zone investments made in 2001-02 (see 11.8 and 6.6.5-6.6.6).

(2) Electing to split rents received from a furnished letting in 2001-02 between Schedule A and Case VI assessments.

(3) Claiming relief against income tax for 2001-02 for a loss on the disposal of shares in a qualifying trading company (see 17.2).

Capital gains tax

(1) Electing to compute all gains and losses on assets acquired before 31 March 1982 by reference to values on that day (possible only where the first relevant disposal which took place after 5 April 1988 occurred during 2001-02: see 14.3.2).

(2) Claiming that an asset became of negligible value during 2001-02 (see 13.4.9).

(3) Claiming relief in respect of a rolled-over or held-over gain that crystallised in 2001-02 (see 14.3.5).

(4) Claiming a set-off against capital gains assessed for 2001-02 in respect of a loss incurred on a qualifying loan to a trader (see 17.1).

(5) Electing under TCGA 1992, s 138A where an earn-out is to be satisfied by the issue of securities (see 14.8).

Business tax

(1) Claiming that a trading loss incurred in 2001-02 should be set against other 2001-02 income (see 5.9.2).

(2) Claiming that a trading loss incurred in 2001-02 should be set against a capital gain realised in 2001-02 (see 5.9.6).

(3) Claiming that a trading loss incurred in 2001-02 be carried back, where permitted under the 'new business' rules (see 5.9.5).

(4) Claiming CGT retirement relief in respect of a disposal made in 2000-01, where that claim is based on ill health (see 17.8.3).

(5) Electing to treat plant or machinery purchased in 2000–01 as a short-life asset for capital allowance purposes (see 5.5.7).

(6) Electing for post-cessation receipts received in 2001–02 to be taxed for the year the trade was discontinued (see 5.7).

1.8.3 Tax year ended 5 April 1998

31 January 2004

Personal tax

(1) Claiming personal allowances (see Chap. 10).

(2) Claiming relief for interest paid in 1997-98.

(3) Claiming relief for pension contributions paid in 1997-98.

(4) Claiming 'top-slicing' relief in respect of life assurance policy gains arising in 1997-98 (see 12.3.4).

(5) Claiming relief to correct an error or mistake made by the taxpayer that resulted in an excessive assessment being made in the year to 1997-98.

Capital gains tax

Claiming roll-over and hold-over relief in respect of disposals that took place in 1997-98 (see 17.3 and 17.5).

2

THE UK TAX SYSTEM

This chapter takes a step back from UK tax law as encountered during the course of any tax year to explain the basic structure and processes of the UK tax system. In this chapter, we look at the following:

(1) Basic principles of UK taxation.
(2) The Inland Revenue.
(3) Understanding your responsibilities and rights.
(4) Complaints and compensation.

2.1 BASIC PRINCIPLES OF UK TAXATION

Despite the introduction of SA, many of the basic principles of the UK tax system go back to the 19th century.

2.1.1 Income charged under different schedules

When Lord Addington reintroduced income tax in 1803, ironically to fund the ongoing costs of the Napoleonic wars, it was not thought to be proper or appropriate for a civil servant to be supplied with full details of an individual's total income. Consequently, income tax was made payable under several schedules, each with its own system of assessment. This made it possible for a taxpayer to report the income taxable under each schedule to a separate Inspector and so avoid the full extent of his income being known by any one official. This legacy remains with us today. Over the past two centuries, a great number of different rules have grown up so that the way in which income is assessed under each schedule varies.

Two of the schedules have been abolished since 1988. Schedule B applied to the taxation of woodlands managed on a commercial basis with a view to making a profit: it was abolished with effect from 6 April 1988. Schedule C covered paying agents (eg bankers) responsible for handling income from UK gilt-edged securities and any public revenue organisations based overseas: it was abolished by FA 1996, but this was no more than a change in name as the requirements for paying agents to withhold tax was simply transferred to Schedule D.

Income tax is now charged under four separate heads, as follows.

Schedule A

Schedule A applies to income from property (ie land and buildings) and includes rent and certain lease premiums. Income from furnished lettings is also taxed under Schedule A.

Schedule D

This schedule is itself subdivided into six cases, as follows:

- Cases I and II: profits or gains arising from trades (Case I) or professions or vocations (Case II), ie income from self-employment;
- Case III: primarily, interest and annual payments, but a whole range of related items has been included over the years;
- Cases IV and V: overseas income of UK-resident individuals. Case IV is concerned with interest on overseas securities (unless already covered by Schedule C); Case V covers income from overseas possessions;
- Case VI: miscellaneous profits that do not fall into other Schedule D cases and are not taxed through any of the other schedules.

Schedule E

Schedule E covered the taxation of all wages, salaries, benefits etc resulting from employments (including directorships). It was divided into three cases, as follows:

- Case I: earnings received by UK-resident and ordinarily resident individuals;
- Case II: earnings received by individuals resident but not ordinarily resident in the UK;
- Case III: work carried out abroad.

Schedule E was abolished with effect from 6 April 2003 but all that actually happened was that the Schedule E legislation was put into a separate Act, the Income Tax (Earnings and Pensions) Act 2003.

Schedule F

This schedule covers dividends and other distributions by companies.

2.1.2 Income tax: an annual tax

Income tax is an annual tax in that it arises on an individual's income for a tax year that ends on 5 April. Capital gains tax (CGT) is also an annual tax in this sense. In contrast, inheritance tax (IHT) may be levied by reference to a person's chargeable transfers during a seven-year period.

Furthermore, income tax is an obligation imposed by each year's Finance Act (unlike CGT, which is imposed by the Taxation of Chargeable Gains Act 1992). This can have some surprising consequences. For example, where an individual is made bankrupt after the Finance Act for the current year has received royal assent, his liability for that year comes to an end and is recoverable only out of the assets held by the individual's trustee in bankruptcy. At the end of the tax year concerned, the individual loses this exemption from income tax since a fresh liability for the following year is imposed by that year's Finance Act.

2.1.3 The Budget and Finance Bill

Each year, the Chancellor of the Exchequer introduces his Budget. Shortly after the Budget (usually during the same week) he introduces the Finance Bill and it is said to have a 'first reading'. However, this is somewhat misleading since the Bill is not actually printed for a further three weeks.

It is then read in Committee, at which time points of detail are considered and amendments made.

Next, it is brought back for a 'third reading' – in this case a formal vote of approval by the House of Commons. It is then approved by the House of Lords (their Lordships cannot amend it because it is a 'Money Bill', and since 1911 the House of Lords has been debarred from making changes to such Bills). It then receives royal assent and becomes an Act. This last stage must happen by 5 August as otherwise the Provisional Collection of Income Tax Act would cease to apply and there would no longer be a legal requirement to deduct tax at source (eg under PAYE).

The whole period during which the Chancellor's proposals move from being a Finance Bill to becoming an Act is less than 100 working days for Parliament. The draft legislation is often complex (several recent Finance Acts have been so long that they have had to be printed in two volumes) and it is not surprising when it subsequently emerges that the legislation is ambiguous or uncertain – hence the need for statements of practice and extra-statutory concessions (see 2.3.1).

How the money is raised

Figure 2.1 is taken from the Treasury's figures released following the 2003 Budget statement.

2.2 THE INLAND REVENUE

No book on UK taxation would be complete without an overview of the Revenue and how it operates. The following is therefore an overview of the Revenue and how it deals with its 'clients', the taxpayers.

Figure 2.1

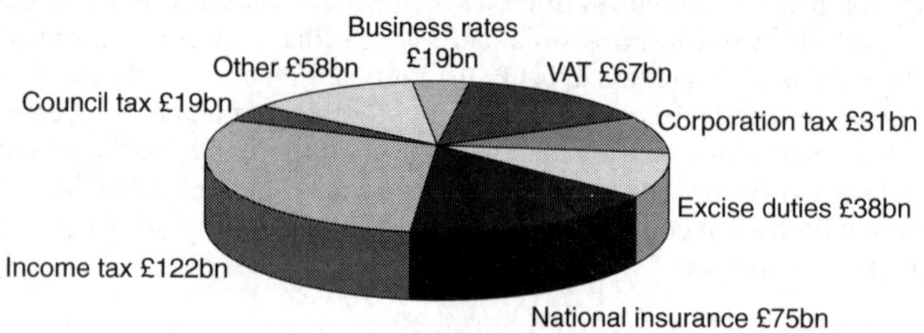

2.2.1 Inland Revenue organisation and structure

The Inland Revenue is the government department responsible for assessing and collecting direct taxes (income tax, corporation tax, CGT, petroleum revenue tax, IHT and stamp duty) and national insurance contributions (NICs). It also has responsibility for enforcing the national minimum wage, paying the Working Families' and Disabled Persons' Tax Credits and collecting student loans. In dealing with Revenue officials, taxpayers should bear in mind that there are three main divisions of responsibilities:

(1) Inspectors of taxes.
(2) Certain specialist offices including the following 'business streams':
   - **IR Charities**, dealing with work on charities previously done in both the Financial Intermediaries and Claims Office (FICO) in Bootle and Edinburgh and the Capital and Savings Division;
   - **IR Capital Taxes**, which deals with all the work previously done in the Capital and Savings Division and the Capital Taxes Office on IHT and CGT, including shares valuation;
   - **IR Stamp Taxes**, which handles work on stamp duty and stamp duty reserve tax previously dealt with in both the Stamp Office and the Capital and Savings Division;
   - **IR Savings, Pensions, Share Schemes**, which is responsible for work on pensions, including personal pensions, savings products, employee share schemes and equity remuneration, and any continuing MIRAS issues. This includes all the work previously done on these topics in the Capital and Savings Division, FICO and the Pension Schemes Office;
   - **IR Trusts**, which manages the operational work on trusts and administration periods previously dealt with in the five Trust Offices and FICO (Scotland), as well as the advisory and policy work previously carried out by FICO and the Capital and Savings Division; and

- **Centre for Non-Residents**, a new division that is part of Inland Revenue International rather than the Capital and Savings Division. This team is responsible for dealing with all the non-resident work formerly handled in FICO.

(3) Collectors of taxes – responsible for collecting tax and NICs. There are various collection offices around the country. Staff at the Collector's office do not get involved at all in assessing the tax payable; this is the job of the Inspector of Taxes.

Each individual taxpayer dealt with by the Revenue has a single tax district or tax office, which deals with all aspects of his income tax and CGT liabilities. A director or employee's tax district is determined by his employer's address. Where a taxpayer is self-employed, the main tax district is decided by the address from which the business is carried on. Individuals who have only investment income are normally dealt with by the tax district that deals with the area in which they live.

The Revenue has three main types of tax office that are supported by the tax enquiry centres and various specialist offices.

Taxpayer Service Office (TSO)

TSOs combine assessment with preliminary collection work to improve customer service. They deal specifically with personal tax matters, such as:

- PAYE coding;
- Assessments and personal reliefs;
- Employer-based (including PAYE-related) compliance work;
- Checks and telephone calls to taxpayers on certain local collection action cases (although in London, this involves all local collection action, including enforcement);
- Income tax accounts processing.

Tax District Office (TDO)

TDOs are locally based to handle investigation and compliance work, including the following:

- All corporation tax;
- In-depth accounts examination and income tax compliance, including Schedule D;
- Local recovery action, including enforcement.

Integrated Office (IO)

These are single offices set up in some areas to cover all TSO and TDO functions.

Tax enquiry centre

Tax enquiry centres perform the following services:

- Answering enquiries and providing assistance by telephone or in person;
- Providing leaflets and forms;
- Arranging for staff from the three main offices (above) to provide specialist help;
- Accepting payments where a taxpayer wishes or needs to pay tax locally.

2.2.2 The Revenue's Code

The Revenue publishes codes of practice (COPs), some of which are examined in this chapter, explaining their approach and procedures in certain areas of work, which set out the legal rights of taxpayers (and the Revenue) and explain what the taxpayer can expect to happen. The COPs (which can be found at www.inlandrevenue.gov.uk/leaflets/ include the following:

- COP1 Putting things right when we make mistakes;
- COP3 Review of employers' and contractors' records;
- COP4 Inspection of schemes offered by financial intermediaries;
- COP6 Collection of tax;
- COP7 Collection of tax due from employers and contractors in the construction industry;
- COP8 Special Compliance Office investigations. Cases of other than suspected serious fraud;
- COP9 Special Compliance Office investigations. Cases of suspected serious fraud;
- COP10 Information and advice;
- COP11 Enquiries into tax returns by local offices;
- COP14 Enquiries into Company Tax Returns;
- COP17 Enquiries into applications for Working Families' Tax Credit or Disabled Persons' Tax Credit;
- COP19 National Minimum Wage. Information for Employers;
- COP20 National Minimum Wage. Information for Workers;
- COP22 Orders for the delivery of documents;
- Consultation Code of Practice on Consultation;
- COP-AT Anti-Terrorism, Crime and Security Act 2001: Code of Practice on the Disclosure of Information.

2.2.3 The Revenue's open government policy

In April 1994, the Government introduced the *Code of Practice on Access to Government Information*, and in May 1995 the Revenue published leaflet IR141, *Inland Revenue: Open Government*. This leaflet explains how the Revenue is complying with the promise of increased openness and accountability so as to improve the democratic process and public's understanding of the way the Government works. The Revenue is committed to make information about policies and decisions more extensively available.

The Revenue makes certain information generally available through press releases, leaflets, booklets and other publications including their internal guidance manuals, which were published at the end of 1995. This information covers:

(1) details of major policy proposals and decisions that the Government considers to be relevant and important;
(2) explanatory material on the Revenue's dealings with the public; and
(3) information about standards of service, complaints procedures and other aspects of the way the Revenue runs its services.

Except where there is an established convention or legal authority not to do so, the Revenue will provide reasons for administrative decisions affecting individual taxpayers. It will also respond to questions about the general working of the tax system where taxpayers need the information, say, to complete their tax returns, to understand how their tax is worked out or to appeal.

In addition, the Revenue will generally meet requests for information about Government policy on taxes, their actions and decisions, and interpretation of legislation where it has a settled view. Information will not be given if it is in the public interest for it to remain confidential. Such examples are where it would prejudice the assessment or collection of tax, or assist tax avoidance or evasion.

The Revenue charges for providing some information. The charge is based on the nature of the request and the time needed to deal with it, and calculated at a rate of £15-£20 per hour, unless it is of a specialist nature. A flat-rate charge of £15 applies for dealing with straightforward requests where the estimated cost is less than £50. There is no charge for Revenue leaflets (which explain different aspects of the tax system), copies of the Taxpayer's Charter, COPs or other similar types information that set out the services provided by the Revenue and the standards it aims to achieve. Explanations of the reasons for decisions, answers to questions about the general working of the tax system and information about the right of appeal or how to complain are also free.

The Revenue's COP on open government sets a response date target of 20 working days from receipt of a straightforward request and outlines the complaints procedure.

2.2.4 Revenue information and advice

COP10 outlines Revenue practice in giving post-transactional rulings, statutory clearances and approvals, together with interpretations of tax law (in certain circumstances), and provides details of the other information published. Post-transactional rulings are rulings given by the Revenue on the application of tax law to a specific transaction after it has taken place. Such rulings bind the Revenue unless material information was withheld. The scheme requires the following information to be submitted before a ruling can be obtained:

- The taxpayer's name and tax reference;
- Full particulars of the transaction or event;
- A statement of the issue(s) to be considered;
- Copies of all relevant documents, with the relevant passages identified;
- A statement that, to the best of the taxpayer's knowledge and belief, the facts as stated are correct and all relevant facts have been disclosed;
- A statement of the specific point(s) of difficulty giving rise to the ruling request;
- A statement of the ruling requested or suggested as appropriate by the applicant;
- Particulars of sections of the Taxes Acts considered to be relevant;
- Particulars of any case-law, statements of practice, extra-statutory concessions, etc considered to be relevant;
- Particulars of any previous discussions or correspondence about the tax treatment of the transaction, or of any similar transaction between the taxpayer and any Revenue office; also, when the taxpayer or his advisers are aware of correspondence on the transaction between any other person and any Revenue office, particulars of that correspondence;
- A statement of the applicant's opinion of the transaction's tax consequence, along with reasons to the extent that they are capable of being supplied.

The following information is available from the Revenue:

- Explanatory leaflets, booklets and helpsheets, designed to explain different aspects of the tax system and provide assistance with tax return completion;
- Statements of practice (SPs), which explain the Revenue's interpretation of legislation and the application of the law in practice;
- Extra-statutory concessions (ESCs), which are relaxations providing a reduction in tax liability that would not be available under the strict letter of the law;
- Press Releases, which announce a proposed change in the law, in Revenue practice or other change;
- The *Tax Bulletin*, which provides insight into the thinking of technical Revenue specialists on technical issues and interpretation of tax law (published every two months);
- Internal Guidance Manuals, which cover the Revenue's interpretation of tax law and the operation of the tax system.

With the exception of the last item, most of the above information is available on the Revenue's website www.inlandrevenue.gov.uk. Any Revenue Enquiry Centre, Tax Office or the Revenue Information Centre should be able to provide leaflets, booklets, SPs and ESCs and certain items can be obtained through the Self-Assessment Orderline.

The website is a significant and valuable source of information, not only in the large amount of information it makes available, but also in the speed in which it is updated. As well as providing the aforementioned information, return forms (eg SA and employers forms) can be downloaded and there are a number of specialist featured areas such as:

- Construction Industry Scheme;
- E-business and e-commerce;
- IR35 regulations;
- Employee Share Schemes;
- Working Families' Tax Credit.

Over the last few years, access to the Revenue's Internal Manuals has increased and at present over 50 different manuals are in the public domain, covering a wide range of subjects. The manuals are available for reference in Revenue Enquiry Centres or can be purchased from independent publishers. A selection of these manuals is also available at www.inlandrevenue.gov.uk/manuals/index.htm.

It must not be forgotten that the Revenue's information sources do not have the force of law, but are merely interpretations of the legally binding statute and case-law. Therefore, potentially they could be open to challenge through the courts.

2.3 UNDERSTANDING YOUR RESPONSIBILITIES AND RIGHTS

The Revenue is now increasingly run more like a business. At the same time, the Government requires it to operate quality management and to assess its efficiency in terms of 'satisfied customers'.

It is the Revenue's policy to help taxpayers understand their rights and obligations, get their tax affairs right and pay their tax on time. Their standards in dealing with the public are explained in *Our Service Commitment to You*. The work must be done thoroughly, timely and cost-efficiently and its staff must get it right first time. Targets are set each year and measured regularly to see if they are being achieved. The Revenue has also issued a joint charter with Customs & Excise, a Charter for Inland Revenue taxpayers (IR167) and a charter for national insurance contributors (CA4).

What this means in practice

In practice, this means that a taxpayer should attend promptly to correspondence from the Revenue and complete tax returns within a reasonable period. If you find there are some aspects of your tax return that are complex and prevent you from completing the entire form, you should contact the Inspector and explain the reason for the difficulty.

2.3.1 Statements of practice and extra-statutory concessions

It is extremely important that the Revenue operates a uniform interpretation of the tax legislation. This is all part of the Taxpayer's Charter, which requires the Revenue to deal with two taxpayers in the same way if their circumstances are identical.

In cases where the legislation is obscure, or its precise implication is uncertain, the Revenue publishes statements of practice (SPs). These operate as a shield for the taxpayer rather than a sword for the Revenue. You can rely on the Revenue applying these SPs but they do not affect your statutory rights and, if you believe that the Revenue interpretation is wrong, it is still open to you to appeal to the Commissioners.

The Revenue also publishes extra-statutory concessions (ESCs). These apply in cases where the legislation is quite clear but the letter of the law produces an unreasonable result. In effect, the Revenue recognises that Parliament could never have intended to impose certain tax liabilities, and ESCs are commonsense rules that the Revenue applies so as to avoid an unreasonable result. Once again, the Revenue publishes these ESCs because it recognises the need to treat all taxpayers alike. In general, and unless your circumstances are special, or you are seeking to apply an ESC so as to avoid tax, you can rely on the Inspector of Taxes applying a published ESC if it covers your particular circumstances.

2.3.2 If you and the Revenue cannot reach agreement

There will be cases where an Inspector and a taxpayer (or his professional adviser) form different conclusions about whether, or how, tax should apply to a particular transaction. In such cases where there is an honest difference of opinion, or even in cases where there is an argument about the actual facts, the Revenue does not have the last word. The procedure for resolving such disputes is to require an appeal to be heard by the Commissioners.

There are two types of Commissioners: General Commissioners and Special Commissioners. The difference lies mainly in the type of disputes that each type of Commissioner is best equipped to deal with. Questions of fact, requiring local knowledge, are best heard by General Commissioners. Special Commissioners are generally lawyers and are normally regarded as more competent to deal with technical issues arising from the interpretation of the legislation.

The Commissioners are an independent body and are not connected with the Inspector of Taxes or the Revenue. Their findings on matters of fact are normally final, but if a taxpayer (or the Revenue) is dissatisfied with his (or its) decision on a point of law, an appeal may be made to the courts. Normally, the appeal is heard by the High Court (Court of Session in Scotland). It is even possible to appeal against decisions by the courts and ultimately the matter may go right up to the House of Lords for a decision.

2.4 COMPLAINTS AND COMPENSATION

If a taxpayer is not happy with the way he has been treated by the Revenue, he is entitled to complain. In this first instance, it is recommended that the complaint be raised with the Officer in Charge of the local district before approaching the Director or Controller with overall responsibility for that office. Further details are provided in leaflet IR120. If this still proves unsatisfactory, the complaint should be raised with the Adjudicator (see leaflet AO1); failing that, the case could be referred through the taxpayer's local MP to the independent Parliamentary Commissioner for Administration (the Ombudsman).

If the Revenue makes a mistake or causes unreasonable delay, the taxpayer is entitled to an apology, an explanation of what went wrong and, if appropriate, details of the steps taken to ensure the mistake does not reoccur. If reasonable and possible, the Revenue will also have the mistake corrected.

The Revenue has a 28-day target for replying to all letters and enquiries; if there is a delay in excess of six months, without good reason, it will give up interest on unpaid tax and pay repayment interest on overpaid tax arising because of the delay. Furthermore, any reasonable costs incurred as a direct result of the delay will also be paid. The Revenue's policy on remitting tax where there has been a delay in using information provided to it is explained at 3.2.8.

If the mistake or delay is serious, it may be possible to claim additional costs arising from the mistake. According to the Revenue's internal Redress Manual, a serious error is something that no responsible person, acting in good faith and with proper care, could reasonably have done; this would indicate that a non-serious error was a pardonable error, or even an innocent misunderstanding. Although the interpretation of 'serious' is dependent on the facts of each situation, the Revenue considers the following to fall within the definition:

(1) taking a wholly unreasonable view of, as opposed to having a genuine difference of opinion about, the law;
(2) starting or pursuing enquiries into matters that were obviously trivial on the basis of the facts available at the time;
(3) making what would normally be a simple or trivial mistake, but the particular circumstances required more care because the Revenue should have known that such a mistake could have serious consequences.

Even if the mistakes are not serious, reasonable costs may be paid for persistent errors (eg where the Revenue makes the same type of mistake or continues in the mistake even after it has been revealed, unless there is a genuine difference of opinion). If a number of unconnected mistakes were made in any 12-month period, for the same tax year or for the same period of assessment, this may also be regarded as persistent (eg if an assessment keeps being amended because of new facts, but each time the Revenue gets the amendment wrong).

The reasonable costs that may be paid extend to professional fees, incidental personal expenses, or wages or fees that would have been earned but were lost through having to sort things out. They could also include such items as postage and telephone charges.

In exceptional cases, where a serious error has resulted directly in a significant and unwarranted intrusion into the taxpayer's personal life, the Revenue will consider making a payment as consolation for any worry and distress suffered as a direct result of that error. Significant and unwarranted intrusions may comprise confidentiality breaches, inappropriate use of information, poorly handled investigations, and misleading advice or mistakes affecting vulnerable taxpayers (such as those suffering medical or physical illness, emotional trauma (eg bereavement) or the elderly). If the unreasonable delay exceeds more than two years, a consolatory payment may also be made. In handling the complaint itself, if there has been significant delay for no good reason or where it has been seriously mishandled, consolatory payments may be made. Unsurprisingly each case will be considered on its own merits and payments are likely to be in the region of £50-£250, could be higher in more extreme cases, but are unlikely to ever exceed £2,000.

2.4.1 Revenue Adjudicator

If you find that you are dissatisfied with the treatment you receive from the Revenue (or Customs & Excise) you can ask an independent body to investigate your complaint. The matter should be referred to

Revenue Adjudicator's Office
3rd Floor
Haymarket House
28 Haymarket
London SW1Y 4SP
Tel: 020 7930 2292

The Revenue Adjudicator has issued a leaflet, *How to Complain about the Inland Revenue*.

3

COPING WITH SELF-ASSESSMENT

This chapter looks at the following:

(1) Self-assessment (SA).
(2) Revenue enquiries into tax returns.
(3) Internet filing of SA tax returns.
(4) Ten golden rules for dealing with your 2003 tax return.
(5) Common errors.
(6) Finding your way around the SA form.

3.1 SELF-ASSESSMENT (SA)

The chances are that if you are going to receive a 2003 SA tax return, you will have received it just after the start of the new tax year in April. If you do not receive a form and you had a new source of income or capital gains in the year just ended, you should report this to the Revenue by 5 October 2003. If you have received the form, this must be filed no later than 31 January 2004.

If you want the Revenue to work out your tax for you or have underpayments collected under PAYE in the following tax year, you need to file your return by 30 September 2003.

3.1.1 An overview of the SA system

Do not be put off by the fact that the form seems complicated: the Revenue has produced a number of helpsheets and your tax office will be only too pleased to clarify anything that is not covered by the notes. There are still teething problems, but the system is proving to be a great improvement on what went before: a system designed afresh rather than a set of procedures that evolved gradually in a piecemeal fashion over the previous 200 years. For example, you only need to deal with one tax office. Also, you or the Revenue work out the tax that you owe (or are owed) as a global figure, whereas in the past many taxpayers had to contend with several different tax districts making assessments on particular types of income, sometimes from opposite ends of the country.

The Revenue form contains a 'core' section that applies to all taxpayers. Beyond that, there are a number of special schedules that you need to complete only if you have a specific type of income, etc.

The basic principle is that by completing the form you should work out your own tax liability and settle what you owe by 31 January each year. However, provided an SA return is filed not later than 30 September following the end of the tax year, the Revenue will calculate the amount of tax payable for you. Where a person does not submit the forms by 30 September he has until the following 31 January to complete the form (ie the SA return for 2002-03 will need to be filed by 31 January 2004). See Figure 3.1 for the deadlines.

Figure 3.1 – Deadlines

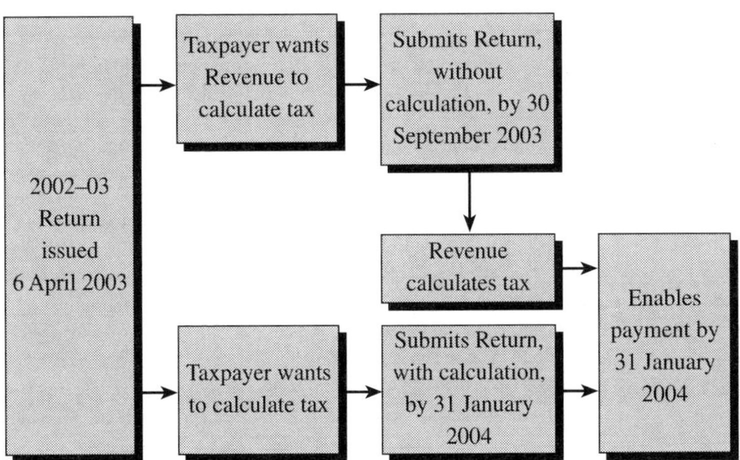

The legislation contains a number of 'incentives' to ensure that people comply with their obligations. If a person does not file his or her SA return by the 31 January deadline, he or she becomes liable for a fixed penalty of £100. If the return has still not been sent in by six months later, there is a further £100 fixed penalty. If the individual continues to be dilatory, the Revenue may apply to the Commissioners for further penalties to be imposed of up to £60 per day that the return remains outstanding.

The penalties for late submission of the return forms are in addition to surcharges that may be imposed on outstanding tax (see below).

3.1.2 Payment of tax

Having submitted his SA return, the taxpayer must settle his tax liability for the year concerned. Of course, some income will have borne tax during the course of the year, either under PAYE or because a self-employed person has made payments on account of his tax liability. If tax is still outstanding after the 31 January payment date, interest is charged and the following surcharges are imposed:

Table 3.1 – Diary under self-assessment

Date	*Who is affected*	*What happens*
6 April 2003	Everybody who gets a tax return	Self-assessment tax return for 2002-03 sent out
31 May 2003	Employees	Employer should have given employee P60 for 2002-03 by this date
6 July 2003	Employees who receive expenses and benefits-in-kind (not covered by a dispensation)	Employer should have given employee details of expenses and benefits for 2002-03 by this date
31 July 2003	Some people: the Revenue will notify in advance where it applies	Second interim payment on account of 2002-03 tax
30 September 2003	People who want the Revenue to calculate their 2002-03 tax	Send in tax return by now
30 September 2003	People who pay tax under PAYE and want the Revenue to collect any tax due (up to £2,000) through their PAYE code during 2004-05	Send in tax return by now
5 October 2003	People with new sources of income or capital gains arising in 2002-03, who have not received a return	Report to Revenue by now or risk penalty
31 January 2004	Everybody who receives a return	This is the deadline for sending in the return and paying the tax due (£100 penalty for those failing to comply)
31 January 2004	Everybody who had an income tax liability for 2002-03 of more than £500 and less than 80% of liability not accounted for by tax deducted at source	First interim payment on account in respect of 2003-04 tax
28 February 2004	Everybody who has not paid tax due on 31 January 2004	Automatic surcharge will arise
6 April 2004	Everybody who gets a tax return	Tax return for 2003-04 will be sent out

(1) a 5% surcharge on any tax that is unpaid by 28 February after the end of the tax year (a month after the tax fell due);
(2) a further 5% surcharge on any tax still outstanding by 31 July (ie six months after the date that the tax fell due for payment on 31 January).

3.1.3 Payments on account

When a person files an SA return, he may be required to make payments on account of his tax liability for the current year. Basically, the person should take the total tax liability for the previous year (ie the year covered by the SA return) and deduct CGT and tax withheld at source. If the balance is £500 or more, the taxpayer must make equal payments on account on 31 January and 31 July, which add up to this amount.

Example

A files an SA return for 2002-03 in January 2004. There is tax to pay of £10,000, but £4,500 of this is CGT. A must pay £2,750 on 31 January 2004 as a payment on account for 2003-04 and he must make a similar payment on account on 31 July 2004.

There is also no need to make payments on account if 80% of your liability (ignoring any CGT) is covered by tax deducted at source. You can apply for a reduction in your 2003-04 payments on account if you have reason to believe that your tax liability will be lower than that for 2002-03, but if you turn out to be mistaken you will be charged interest.

3.1.4 Process now, check later

The Revenue has designed the SA return with its own data processing in mind. Returns are normally read by an OCR (optical character recognition) machine. Some returns may be submitted electronically – the Revenue would much prefer that their 'customers' use the ELS (Electronic Lodgement Service) method of filing.

Past experience has shown that many returns need correcting because of arithmetical errors, figures being transposed, amounts being entered in the wrong column, etc. When the Revenue officer identifies such mistakes he issues a notice to the taxpayer advising him of the correction (or 'repair') needed. The taxpayer can object, but if the Revenue does not hear further within three months, the correction is deemed to form part of the return.

Routine checking and making corrections must not be confused with Revenue officers carrying out an enquiry. The Revenue must issue a formal notice within a period of 12 months of the filing date (31 January) unless the return is submitted after that date. The Revenue need not give any reason for wanting to check a return and, indeed, between 5,000 and 10,000 taxpayers will be selected each year on a totally random basis. The Revenue has said that it expects to carry out around 40,000 enquiries each year.

3.1.5 Protection against unnecessary enquiries

The Revenue has issued a number of Codes of Practice (see 2.2.2) and has stressed to its staff that enquiries should be brought to an end as soon as possible. Furthermore, the Revenue cannot open fresh enquiries into a return once the original enquiry has been brought to a conclusion.

3.1.6 Keeping proper records

Because the Revenue operates on a 'process now, check later' basis, you need to keep records in order to be able to back up your entries on your SA return. The length of time that you need to retain your records depends on whether you have a business or are letting property. If you do, the required period is five years and ten months after the end of the tax year. If you do not have either of these sources of income, the minimum period for retaining your records is normally one year and ten months after the end of the tax year concerned. You may find it helpful to read Revenue leaflet SA/BK4, *Self Assessment: a general guide to keeping records.*

3.2 REVENUE ENQUIRIES INTO TAX RETURNS

The Revenue has a period of 12 months from the 31 January filing date to issue a notice that it is carrying out an enquiry into a tax return. Once that enquiry is completed, the position becomes final and the Revenue cannot reopen enquiries into that year unless it can show 'discovery', ie that the taxpayer acted negligently or fraudulently so that key information was withheld from the Revenue. Enquiries can be made into partnership returns under the same rules as apply to individual returns, but any amendments to partnership profits then need to be taken through to the individual partners' tax returns.

3.2.1 Provisional figures, estimates and valuations

The maximum time permitted for completion and submission of a return is ten months (ie for 2002-03, 6 April 2003 to 31 January 2004). Final figures may not always be available by the submission deadline and therefore it may be necessary to estimate these amounts. The Revenue recognises this and has said that this is acceptable in certain circumstances. Initially, the Revenue's attitude to provisional figures was somewhat relaxed and it did not normally regard a return containing them as incomplete, provided the taxpayer took all reasonable steps to obtain the final figures and the estimate was corrected as soon as they were available.

However, in *Tax Bulletin* September 1998, the Revenue announced that it would regard provisional returns as incomplete in circumstances where the taxpayer had made little or no effort to obtain the final figures. It stated that general pressure of work or complexities of tax affairs did not validate provisional figures and in the case of accounts information it must genuinely be impossible for final figures to be submitted. A single figure of estimated business profit would only, in all likelihood, be acceptable for a newly commenced business where the first accounting period does not end until close to or after the submission date. A change of accounting date may also give rise to provisional standard accounts information, and this should fulfil the requirements as being a complete return. Despite all this, the Revenue confirmed that it would not reject such returns, but would process them as received and flag them for enquiry review if the ultimate figures were not supplied by the expected date.

The Revenue's leniency narrowed further in December 1999, when it stated returns would be rejected if an 'acceptable explanation for the delay' were not included in the return along with a date by which final figures were expected.

In January 2002, the Revenue retracted this, saying that it will now accept a return (assuming there are no other problems) where the taxpayer has used a provisional or estimated figure and it will no longer send back a return that does not have an adequate explanation for why such figures are needed or does not give a date for the supply of final figures. The Revenue goes on to say that the omission of that information will be a factor to be taken into account in order to decide whether to open an enquiry into the return. The Revenue also made two further points:

- 'Past Revenue practice ... was based on our legal advice ... and any resulting late filing penalties charged before 23 October 2001 were correctly charged.'
- It is possible for the use of provisional or estimated figures to result in an incorrect return for which a penalty may be charged. This can be because the customer did not take reasonable care when calculating the figures or because final figures could have been obtained before the Return was sent to the Revenue.

There will be situations where an estimated figure is submitted that will not be amended in the future (eg where there is inadequate information to reach a precise figure). If the estimate is considered to be sufficiently reliable to make a complete return (eg where it is based on detailed records for a sample representative period in the case of private proportion expenses (eg motoring expenses)), it is not necessary to refer specifically to the estimate. However, if the figure is not so reliable (eg because the records may have been lost or destroyed), the Revenue requires identification of the amounts and an explanation of its calculation.

The Revenue also draws a distinction between estimates and judgemental figures. A valuation at 31 March 1982 for CGT is a good example of a judgemental figure. That is, there is no right or wrong answer, and the figure to be included is basically the taxpayer's best judgement as to the figures, which could be agreed with the Revenue. Again, the Revenue requires identification of, and details about, the valuation. The Revenue has agreed that where no enquiry is made into a valuation within the 12-month enquiry period, and the valuation falls within the range of bona fide valuations that could arise in negotiations between valuers who were fully instructed on the facts, it will not try to reopen the position.

3.2.2 Return amendments by the taxpayer and the Revenue

The taxpayer may within 12 months of the filing date (in most cases, 31 January) give a notice to the Revenue amending his SA return.

The Revenue may repair an SA return within nine months of receiving it to correct obvious errors of principle, transpositions of figures and arithmetical errors. The Revenue is required to issue a notice in this connection and the taxpayer can then accept the repair or file an objection.

3.2.3 Selection of returns for Revenue enquiries

The Revenue has a statutory power to enquire into any tax return without giving a reason. However, because of its limited resources, it has to be selective. It is more likely to target cases where a larger amount of tax is perceived to be at risk; enquiries are also likely to arise in cases where the Revenue's internal procedures require a mandatory review. A number of returns not suspected of being incorrect will also be selected at random each year (see 3.1.4).

An examination of the Revenue's Internal Enquiry Handbook indicates that Revenue staff are required to review certain returns such as:

- Returns filed late;
- Returns that include provisional figures;
- Cases that involve large capital gains;
- Situations where there has been a change in accounting year; and
- Returns for Lloyd's Names.

Revenue procedure for enquiries

The Revenue must give written notice that an enquiry is to be made into an SA return. This notice must be served within a strict time limit:

- 12 months after the 31 January filing date; or
- where it is delivered after the normal 31 January filing date, the quarter date following 12 months after delivery.

For these purposes, the quarter dates are 31 January, 30 April, 31 July and 31 October. Thus, if an SA return is not delivered until 31 March, the

Revenue can give notice that it is starting an enquiry up to 30 April of the following year.

The Revenue will not give any reason for having opened an enquiry. However, it should soon become apparent whether it is initially an enquiry into one particular aspect of the return or a full enquiry under which the Revenue requires access to all the taxpayer's records. An aspect enquiry can extend into a full enquiry as the Revenue receives information, so the distinction is not completely clear cut.

The opening of an enquiry is not meant to imply that the Revenue believes that anything is untoward, merely that it is carrying out checks to test the return's accuracy and reliability.

The Enquiry Handbook states repeatedly that Revenue officers should adopt a non-confrontational approach and keep an open mind. The Revenue intends that the opening of enquiries should be less contentious, and that its aim is to develop a more neutral and less confrontational approach in this area. It is acknowledged that the information initially available in the return and elsewhere is unlikely to be sufficient to establish whether the return is incorrect, and even where it appears incorrect it could be that the information is incomplete, misleading or capable of explanation. The Handbook advises officers that unless they are reasonably certain that there have been omissions (and often it will not be possible for them to be certain), they should ask the taxpayer in a neutral way whether there is anything further that he has to say, taking account of what has already been said. They should make it clear that no allegations are being made at this point. When the Revenue opens an enquiry, it will issue details of its COP, which will be either the full code or a short version in straightforward cases.

Information required

The Revenue is instructed to request informally any information needed, rather than using its formal powers to require the production of the information. A formal notice would, however, be issued for documents in the taxpayer's power or possession, if he had refused to co-operate with the informal request or had failed to comply within the specified timescale. Such a notice must allow the taxpayer at least 30 days to comply. Moreover, the taxpayer may appeal to the Commissioners if he thinks that the notice is invalid. If the Commissioners decide that the notice is valid, the documents must then be produced within 30 days of their decision.

The Revenue should only request information and documents that are relevant and reasonably required to determine whether the self-assessment is correct. Its approach varies according to whether the taxpayer is a business taxpayer (ie a taxpayer who is self-employment or in receipt of income from property). In the case of a full enquiry into the business taxpayer's affairs, the Revenue considers that the following items can be reasonably requested without providing an explanation:

- Business records generally;
- Cash book, petty cash book, sales and purchase invoices and bank account statements;
- Details of how any adjustments by the accountant had been calculated;
- An analysis of drawings;
- Details of any balancing figures or estimates used in the accounts.

Private bank statements are not normally required at the initial stage of an enquiry.

Where there is a full enquiry into a non-business taxpayer, which is a complex case, officers should seek to verify in the first place the income and gains declared by reference to any third-party information held (eg a form P11D). The information requested directly might then comprise:

- Dividend vouchers;
- Certificates of loan interest paid;
- Form PPCC (a certificate confirming payment under a personal pension scheme);
- A detailed CGT computation;
- A copy of a property valuation;
- An account of the precise use made of a company asset, such as a private plane.

As for business taxpayers, the advice to officers is that they should not ask to see private bank statements at this early stage unless it can be demonstrated that the statements are relevant to the return and can be reasonably required for checking the return's accuracy.

In aspect cases, the information requested should, unsurprisingly, concentrate on information relevant to the particular point under review.

Meetings with the Revenue

The Enquiry COP states that taxpayers are not obliged to attend any meeting requested by the Revenue, but are expected to provide promptly any information considered essential to the enquiry. The Revenue believes meetings allow taxpayers to clarify and explain any points that may have been misunderstood, and to ask questions of the Revenue. The taxpayer will be told if the Revenue considers correspondence is an inadequate substitute for a meeting. However, an officer cannot insist that a taxpayer attends any meeting, and his only alternative in terms of asking questions of the taxpayer face-to-face is to take an appeal to a personal hearing before the Commissioners and put his questions to the taxpayer during cross-examination (assuming the taxpayer is put forward as a witness).

The Revenue has confirmed that the taxpayer should be sent an agenda in advance of such a meeting. The March 2002 edition of the Revenue newsletter *Working Together* states:

> Enquiry staff should provide an agenda covering the main areas for discussion … It should be case specific but not a detailed list of questions and should not be seen by either party to be exhaustive or restrictive. We would not expect a completely new major agenda item to be introduced at the meeting unless something unexpected is revealed during the course of the meeting

There is no reason in principle why enquiries should not be conducted entirely through correspondence. COP11 commits the Inspector to being mindful of the taxpayer's compliance costs and it may be possible to agree with the officer that matters should proceed by way of correspondence without this being viewed as lack of co-operation on the taxpayer's part. It should be borne in mind, however, that a refusal to attend a meeting may, in certain circumstances, be seen as a lack of co-operation when it comes to assessing penalties in the event that the enquiry reveals an under-declaration of tax.

A request for a meeting can often be taken as an indication that the officer, having considered the information initially supplied, has concluded that there are grounds for doubting the return's accuracy or that there are matters that require further detailed enquiry. Officers are instructed that where irregularities are suspected they would need to consider how to give the taxpayer the opportunity to disclose them and to co-operate actively in quantifying them. Whether the taxpayer does take this opportunity could have a bearing on the level of penalty that could be levied on him or her. Officers are instructed to seek early meetings.

Closure of the enquiry

The legislation does not specify any time limit in which the Revenue must complete its enquiries. However, if the taxpayer feels that the Revenue has had sufficient information, he may appeal to the Commissioners for them to direct the Revenue to bring the enquiry to an end.

When the Revenue officer who has conducted the enquiry has completed his investigation, he must issue a notice stating this and setting out the conclusions of the correct amount of tax that should be payable for the year in question. Once the notice has been issued, the Revenue is debarred from starting new enquiries in relation to that return.

Faster Working enquiries

The Revenue is keen to reduce the time taken to deal with enquiries into business returns and therefore introduced 'Faster Working'. Since April 1998, business taxpayers whose returns are selected for enquiry have had the opportunity to elect for Faster Working. This is voluntary for taxpayers, and either side can pull out of the agreement if, for example, the enquiry proves to be unexpectedly complex. It involves setting an agreed but flexible timetable for the enquiry; the total time will vary according to circumstances. The Revenue's aim is for enquiries under Faster Working to be completed within about six months. Leaflet IR162, *A better approach to local office enquiry work under self-assessment,* and *Tax Bulletin Supplement to Special Edition 2*, provide more information. Despite the Revenue's intentions, there is little evidence that Faster Working has been embraced by local districts, which are rumoured to be reluctant to agree to it, even if it is specifically requested.

3.2.4 Protection from discovery assessments

Even though an assessment has been accepted, the time limit for starting an enquiry has expired and all enquiries have been completed, the Revenue may still revisit the past if fresh information comes to light or if it turns out that the taxpayer had negligently or fraudulently withheld that information. An assessment to collect underpaid tax in these circumstances is called a 'discovery assessment'.

No discovery assessment may be made where the Revenue could reasonably have been expected to identify the point at issue from information provided in an SA return. Moreover, information provided in SA returns for the two previous years is also to be taken into account in this connection. It follows that taxpayers should provide the Revenue with too much information rather than too little to avoid discovery assessments. The provision of business accounts is particularly useful in this context, although the Revenue guidance notes for taxpayers state that it is not necessary to send them.

The recent case of *Langham v Veltema* (2002) STC 1557 sheds interesting light on all this. The taxpayer had bought a property from his company and it did not occur to the Inspector that the valuation needed to be agreed. It was held that no discovery assessment could be made.

An additional form of protection may be secured by obtaining post-transaction rulings (see 2.2.4).

3.2.5 What happens if the SA return is found to be incorrect?

If the Revenue's enquiry shows that the taxpayer has self-assessed and paid too much tax, he is refunded the difference, together with interest (normally from the date of payment). If the enquiry reveals material errors in the taxpayer's favour, he is likely to be charged interest from the 31 January filing date plus a surcharge for the tax unpaid at 28 February and 31 July following that filing date. If the errors revealed in the enquiry were duplicated in previous tax years, the Revenue is likely to raise discovery assessments for those years and to seek interest and surcharges. Penalties may also be imposed where the enquiry reveals under-declarations, which amount to negligence or fraud.

3.2.6 What penalties can the Revenue impose?

Deliberate deception

Anyone who has deliberately understated his taxable income or chargeable gains may be prosecuted for fraud, false accounting, theft or the beautifully old-fashioned, but still rather serious, offence of 'cheating our Sovereign Lady the Queen'. If business profits have been understated, there has been failure to declare all investments or the taxpayer has claimed allowances to which he is not entitled, he is in serious trouble and at risk of imprisonment. A taxpayer in this position should immediately seek the advice of a solicitor or accountant experienced in settling 'back duty' cases, even if the Revenue has not yet shown signs of suspecting the deception. Although it is very difficult for the Revenue to amass enough evidence to mount a successful criminal prosecution, an unrepresented taxpayer may find himself out of depth at a Revenue enquiry.

Failure to submit a return

If a taxpayer fails to submit his SA return by the required filing date, usually 31 January following the end of the tax year, there is an automatic flat-rate penalty of £100. For continuing failure, the Commissioners may impose an additional penalty of up to £60 per day. If there has been no application for an additional daily penalty and the return has not been submitted within six months of the filing date, a further automatic £100 penalty arises. If the return is still outstanding within 12 months of the filing date, a penalty not exceeding the tax that would have been payable under the return is charged – in other words, there can be a double assessment. However, according to the Revenue's SA/BK6, these late return fixed penalties cannot exceed the tax liability for the year payable at the filing date, which is after taking into account payments made on account or otherwise. For example:

		£	£
2002-03 SA shows total liability			50,000
Less: payments on account	31 Jan 2003	23,000	
	31 July 2003	23,000	
Additional payment on account	20 Jan 2004	2,000	
Tax deduction under PAYE for 2002-03		1,925	49,925
Balance payable at filing date	31 Jan 2004		75

Any penalties for late submission in respect of 2002-03 would be reduced to £75. If, however, the additional payment of £2,000 had been made after the filing date (say 20 February 2004 rather than 20 January 2004), the automatic penalties would not be reduced. It is possible to appeal against the penalties if the taxpayer can satisfy the Commissioners that he had a reasonable excuse throughout the period of default.

The same fixed penalties apply for failures to submit partnership returns, although there is no tax-geared penalty or provision for reducing the penalties as for individuals. Each partner is liable to a £100 penalty if the partnership return is submitted late.

Failure to notify Revenue of taxable income or gains

A taxpayer who has not received a return form is still obliged to inform the Inspector of any taxable income or gains (other than income taxed under the PAYE scheme, income taxed by deduction at source, and income and gains already assessed) within six months of the end of the year of assessment. If the taxpayer fails to do so, he becomes liable to a penalty equal to the tax unpaid at the filing date.

Submission of an incorrect return

If a taxpayer submits an incorrect return, he is liable to a penalty equal to the difference between the tax charged on the income or gain returned and the true income or gain. Strictly, such a penalty is chargeable only if the taxpayer has been fraudulent or negligent, but the Revenue's approach has always been that the mere fact that the return is wrong proves that the taxpayer must have been guilty at least of negligence. Moreover, the taxpayer is not allowed to blame a third party (eg an accountant) for the error, although he may be able to insist that the accountant reimburses any penalty suffered.

Similar provisions apply for partnership returns; penalties for incorrect partnership returns may be levied on each partner.

Mitigation of penalties for incorrect return

The penalty for an error in a return (including a set of business accounts submitted with a return) is, therefore, a potential doubling of the tax chargeable on the income or gains under-declared. This could be levied in addition to any interest charge. However, the Revenue's practice is to reduce or mitigate the potential penalty by reference to three factors. Taking the maximum penalty as a surcharge of 100%, the possible reductions are as follows:

(1) For disclosure, a maximum of 30% if the taxpayer goes to the Inspector admitting that a mistake has been made and a maximum of 20% if the taxpayer makes a complete disclosure as soon as he is challenged by the Inspector.

(2) For co-operation, a maximum of 40%. 'Co-operation' means, for example, answering the Inspector's questions and providing any back-up documentation within a reasonable time span.

(3) For reduced culpability, a maximum of 40%. For example, nothing will be allowed under this heading if it is clear, even though the Inspector cannot prove it, that the taxpayer set out deliberately to cheat the Revenue. A reduction of perhaps 15-25% will be allowed if the taxpayer has been guilty of gross carelessness and between 30% and 40% where he has simply misunderstood information supplied by a third party (eg where he has entered the net instead of the gross interest received on a building society account).

The usual procedure is for the Inspector to suggest an overall settlement figure to include underpaid tax, interest and any penalty. However, he will also provide a computation showing how the overall figure was calculated and it is open to the taxpayer to argue for a bigger reduction of the penalty element. If the Inspector does not agree, he must submit the case to his Head Office, which is sometimes willing to accept a lower settlement than originally proposed by the Inspector.

Payment by instalments is possible where the taxpayer does not have readily realisable capital, but this will increase the interest (though not the penalty) payable.

3.2.7 Certificates of tax deposit

A taxpayer can make deposits with Collectors of Taxes to cover tax liabilities. A certificate is issued and the deposit held for the general benefit of the individual until such time as he surrenders all or part of the certificate to cover tax liabilities.

Where a deposit is used to cover a tax liability, interest on overdue tax cannot run from the date that the deposit was made. Deposits are therefore commonly used to cover a tax liability that cannot easily be quantified, for example a capital gain on a sale of unquoted shares where a value at 31 March 1982 needs to be negotiated with the Shares Valuation Division.

Interest is credited from the date the deposit is made to the date it is used (or cashed) for a maximum of six years. The rate of interest is fixed by reference to money market rates and is taxable. Interest is paid at a lower rate where deposits are encashed rather than used to settle tax liabilities.

Deposits are not transferable except to personal representatives of a deceased person. They cannot even be transferred to a spouse, although the Collector of Taxes will accept a certificate on the basis that it is treated as encashed with the resultant proceeds being applied to cover a spouse's tax liability. The problem with this procedure is that it does not protect the spouse from a liability to interest on underpaid tax. The Revenue has confirmed that a certificate of tax deposit held in the name of a partnership may be used to discharge personal tax liabilities of any of the partners.

3.2.8 Remission of tax by the Revenue

The Revenue's policy, detailed in ESC A19, is to give up arrears of tax that have arisen because of failure by the Revenue to make proper and timely use of information supplied. Remission of tax in this way is normally available where the taxpayer could have reasonably believed that his tax affairs were in order and was notified of the arrears more than 12 months after the end of the tax year in which the Revenue was informed. Alternatively, in the case of an over-repayment, it is available if the taxpayer was notified after the end of the tax year following the year in which the repayment was made.

3.2.9 Error or mistake relief

Sometimes errors are made against the taxpayer and relief can be claimed against any over-assessment to income tax or CGT owing to an error or mistake in a return. However, relief does not extend to an error or mistake in a claim included in the return. Relief will not be available on the ground of an alleged error in the basis of computation of liability if the return was made on the basis of, or in accordance with, the practice generally prevailing at the time when the return was made. According to the Revenue's internal manuals at IM3751A, the term 'error or mistake' includes errors of omission such as the non-deduction of an admissible expense, errors of commission (eg computational or arithmetical errors), errors arising from a misunderstanding of the law and erroneous statements of fact.

The relief is also available for an error or mistake in a partnership statement where the partners claim that their self-assessments were excessive. If the claim results in an amendment to the partnership statement, any necessary amendments to the partners' individual self-assessments are made by notice by the Board of the Revenue.

Relief may be claimed within five years of 31 January following the tax year to which the return relates. For years prior to SA, a six-year time limit applied.

3.3 INTERNET FILING OF SA TAX RETURNS

The Inland Revenue is keen that we embrace new technology as it essentially cuts down on filing space requirements. To register for Internet filing of your SA tax return, go to inland.revenue.gov.uk. You will need to have the following items to hand:

- Your UTR – unique taxpayer reference;
- Your national insurance number;
- Your postal code.

The site asks also for an e-mail address and the optional provision of a password. Once you have succesfully registered, an ID number will be generated on screen and an activation PIN number sent out via the postal system. A note of all of the above should be kept in at least one safe place.

If you have given an e-mail address when registering you will receive the following notification:

> *'Thank you for enrolling for the Internet Service for Self Assessment service through the Government Gateway.*
>
> *Within 7 days we will send you an Activation PIN through the post, however, for some services a PIN is not required and the services will be activated immediately.*
>
> *If you have registered on behalf of an organisation, the letter containing the Activation PIN will be sent to the contact name and address held by the government department providing this service for your organisation. In this letter, the contact will be asked to give the Activation PIN to you, authorising you to act on behalf of your organisation for this service.*
>
> *Once you have received the Activation PIN you will be able to activate the service, and be able to submit forms over the Internet.*
>
> *If you have not received a letter from us within 7 days, please contact the Internet Service for Self Assessment Helpdesk on 0845 60 55 999.'*

When you receive the activation PIN and user ID log into the government site at www.gateway.gov.uk to activate your Inland Revenue account. Once activated you can file your tax return over the Internet. Remember that the same deadlines apply as under paper filing.

3.4 TEN GOLDEN RULES FOR DEALING WITH YOUR 2003 TAX RETURN

The SA system requires that you carry out certain tasks by fixed deadlines. If you fail to deal with your tax affairs in a business-like way, you will be charged interest and surcharges (and possibly worse).

The SA tax return may still be unfamiliar but is not as difficult as it seems at first glance. A review carried out by the Revenue showed that 30% of returns contained clerical errors that needed correction (eg arithmetical mistakes, figures entered in the wrong columns, etc), but 90% of the mistakes could be readily identified to enable the return to be 'processed' and the taxpayer's details entered on the Revenue computer. The standard eight-page return may need to be supplemented by additional schedules so this is probably your first task: to see if you have been sent all the extra schedules that you will need. The tax legislation can be very complicated but the Revenue has gone to considerable expense to provide detailed notes and 'helpsheets' that accompany the extra schedules and these should enable you to cope with most straightforward situations.

The next thing to take on board is that the Revenue has powers enabling it to check up on taxpayers. Tax officials will be using these powers and will not find it amusing if you are audited and found wanting, even where the shortcomings amount only to carelessness. The Inland Revenue Enquiry Manual makes it quite plain that SA will not be allowed to degenerate into 'pay what you like'. Furthermore, even though there is a set time limit for the Revenue to announce that a return will be audited ('selected for enquiry'), it will be able to reopen back years if the taxpayer has omitted key information (this is called 'discovery': see 3.2.4).

Therefore, you are advised to do the following:

(1) Get organised; start to collect together the information you will need (see Table 3.2).

(2) Do not throw anything away for the time being. In fact, you should keep your 2002-03 records until 31 January 2005 (2009 if you run a business or receive rental income). Remember that the Revenue's policy is 'process now, check later'. The Revenue will be able to open an enquiry into your 2002-03 return by serving a notice before 1 February 2005 – and it will not have to give any justification for doing so.

(3) Do not leave everything until the last minute. There will be an automatic £100 penalty if you are late in filing your return and, while 31 January 2004 is a long way off, it will be easier to tackle the return while things are still fresh in your mind. If there are any gaps in your records (you have been under a legal obligation to keep adequate records since 6 April 1996), you may be able to reconstruct them by getting down to the task before the trail goes completely cold.

(4) Do not try sending in an incomplete return, as it will be rejected. If you had benefits-in-kind, such as a company car or a mobile 'phone, you will need to put down a figure for your taxable benefit: just reporting 'per form P11D' or 'as PAYE' is not acceptable.

(5) Start to put cash aside now so that you can settle your 2002-03 tax and make a payment on account for 2003-04 next 31 January. If you are short of funds after Christmas you may find yourself exposed to interest (APR currently at 6.5%). Worse still, if you are unable to clear your 2002-03 tax by 28 February, you will be liable for an automatic 5% surcharge (equal to an APR of over 60%).

(6) Consider filing by 30 September. Somerset House has given repeated assurances that filing early will not increase the likelihood of your return being selected for enquiry. On a positive note, the Revenue will collect underpayments of up to £2,000 via the PAYE system if you submit your return by the end of September. This may be much more convenient than having to make a lump sum payment.

(7) Work on the basis that your return will be selected for enquiry. The Revenue will be selecting around 10,000 returns each year on a random basis; this means there is less than a 1% chance of being selected, but you are considerably more likely to be selected for random enquiry than to win the National Lottery. Tax offices are also expected to check another 30,000 returns with the selection being made on a more scientific assessment of risk of undeclared tax.

(8) Remember to tick the box if your return contains any estimated or provisional figures. It will probably be in your own best interests to give an explanation of how you have arrived at the figures concerned as this may pre-empt queries from the Revenue. It may also afford a degree of protection against the Revenue coming back after 31 January 2005 and reopening 2002-03 by making a 'discovery assessment'.

(9) Think twice about not drawing attention to any assumptions you have made in completing your return that could be challenged by the Revenue. You do not have to follow the Revenue's line on everything, especially if you receive advice that the Revenue's interpretation of the legislation is open to doubt, but you should not be coy about this. From time to time the Revenue is shown to be wrong, but the Revenue wins more often than it loses and you could be liable for penalties if the courts uphold the Revenue's interpretation and it emerges that you had not put all your cards face up on the table.

(10) Finally, get professional advice if your affairs are complicated. DIY tax returns may be a false economy if your situation is non-standard, however hard the Revenue has tried to explain the rules in its helpsheets.

Table 3.2 – Information you will need

If you are employed:	
Form P60, ie the annual certificate of pay and tax deducted at source. Taxable figures for any benefits-in-kind (company car, mobile 'phone, cheap loans in excess of £5,000) from your employer. Details of amounts paid to you under the Fixed Profit Car Scheme for using your own car for company business.	Your employer should have provided this automatically by 5 July 2003.
If you changed jobs during the year ended 5 April 2003, details of benefits provided by your previous employer.	You may have to ask for this.
Advice from your employer as to what to report if you received free shares or exercised (or were given) a share option in 2002-03.	Speak to your Personnel Department.

If you were self-employed:	
You will need to prepare accounts or have an accountant do this for you. The Revenue requires your details in a set format so that it can use its computer to assist it in identifying cases which should be taken up for enquiry.	See 5.4.1 and 5.4.5.
If you have rental income:	
You should keep an analysis of rents receivable for 2002-03 and a note of any bad debts, details of expenditure such as fees paid to managing agents, repair bills and redecoration, replacement of electrical goods and furniture. If you have borrowed to fund your property 'business', the interest should be an allowable expense.	Rent charged for 2002-03 will normally be taxable even if you did not receive it until after the end of the year.
If you have income from savings:	
Keep a copy of your bank deposit account statements, your building society passbook and dividend vouchers.	
If you had trust income:	
You need form R185 which sets out the amount of income paid to you and the tax deducted at source.	
If you have made capital gains:	
You will need the stockbroker's contract notes for sales of shares and copies of the sale contract and completion statement if you made real estate sales. If you gave assets to your children you may be liable for CGT as if you had sold at market value so seek advice in such situations.	The gains are exempt if they totalled less than £7,500.

3.5 COMMON ERRORS

The Revenue's Press Office has kindly provided us with a note of the more common errors on the SA form:

- No signature;
- Not ticking all the mandatory boxes;
- Not ticking the repayment box;
- Not nominating who the repayment is to go to;
- Not nominating where the repayment is to go;
- Not completing the relevant supplementary pages;
- Not attaching the relevant supplementary pages;
- Including the capital on your bank/building society account in the interest box as interest;
- Entering weekly/monthly pension in the annual box.

... and finally – using the space for additional information

At the end of the SA form, the Revenue has left you a number of blank pages for additional information. You may take the view that this is the Revenue's way of giving you enough rope to hang yourself, but in fact it should be grasped as a lifeline. There may be aspects of the form where you or your tax adviser has relied on a certain interpretation of the tax law. The Revenue may not agree with your interpretation but will be unaware of the basis on which you have completed the form unless you draw its attention to this. If this emerges later on, the Revenue may seek to re-open your self-assessment and possibly charge interest and penalties. One way of covering yourself is to make appropriate entries in the additional information box. If you make your assumptions and interpretations explicit, you will protect yourself against the Revenue using its discovery powers (see 3.2.4).

3.6 FINDING YOUR WAY AROUND THE SA FORM

When you examine your return, you will see the following questions that we have cross-referred to this book (see following pages).

INCOME AND CAPITAL GAINS *for the year ended 5 April 2003*

Step 1 Answer Questions 1 to 9 below to check if you need supplementary Pages to give details of particular income or capital gains. Pages 6 and 7 of your Tax Return Guide will help. (Ask the Orderline for a Guide if I haven't sent you one with your Tax Return, and you want one.) If you answer 'Yes' ask the Orderline for the appropriate supplementary Pages and Notes. Ring the Orderline on 0845 9000 404, or fax on 0845 9000 604 for any you need (closed Christmas Day, Boxing Day and New Year's Day).

If you do need supplementary Pages, tick the boxes below when you've got them.

Q1 Were you an employee, or office holder, or director, or agency worker or did you receive payments or benefits from a former employer (excluding a pension) in the year ended 5 April 2003? If you were a non-resident director of a UK company but received no remuneration, see the notes to the Employment Pages, page EN3, box 1.6. YES ☐ EMPLOYMENT ☐ — See Chap. 4

Q2 Did you have any taxable income from share options, shares or share related benefits in the year? (This does not include
- dividends, or
- dividend shares ceasing to be subject to an Inland Revenue approved share incentive plan within three years of acquisition

they go in Question 10.) YES ☐ SHARE SCHEMES ☐ — See 4.10-4.16

Q3 Were you self-employed (but not in partnership)? (You should also tick 'Yes' if you were a Name at Lloyd's.) YES ☐ SELF-EMPLOYMENT ☐ — See Chap. 5

Q4 Were you in partnership? YES ☐ PARTNERSHIP ☐ — See 5.10

Q5 Did you receive any rent or other income from land and property in the UK? YES ☐ LAND & PROPERTY ☐ — See Chap. 6

Q6 Did you have any taxable income from overseas pensions or benefits, or from foreign companies or savings institutions, offshore funds or trusts abroad, or from land and property abroad or gains on foreign insurance policies? YES ☐ — See 8.2, 8.3-8.8 and 12.4

Have you or could you have received, or enjoyed directly or indirectly, or benefited in any way from, income of a foreign entity as a result of a transfer of assets made in this or earlier years? YES ☐ — See 22.4

Do you want to claim foreign tax credit relief for foreign tax paid on foreign income or gains? YES ☐ FOREIGN ☐

Q7 Did you receive, or are you deemed to have, income from a trust, settlement or the residue of a deceased person's estate? YES ☐ TRUSTS ETC ☐ — See 8.11.2 and Chap. 20

Q8 Capital gains - read the guidance on page 7 of the Tax Return Guide.
- If you have disposed of your only or main residence do you need the Capital Gains Pages? YES ☐ — See Chap. 16
- Did you dispose of other chargeable assets worth more than £15,400 in total? YES ☐
- Were your total chargeable gains more than £7,700 or do you want to make a claim or election for the year? YES ☐ CAPITAL GAINS ☐ — See Chaps. 13-15

Q9 Are you claiming that you were not resident, or not ordinarily resident, or not domiciled, in the UK, or dual resident in the UK and another country, for all or part of the year? YES ☐ NON RESIDENCE ETC ☐ — See Chaps. 2 and 24

Step 2 **Fill in any supplementary Pages BEFORE going to Step 3.**
Please use blue or black ink to fill in your Tax Return and please do not include pence. Round down your income and gains. Round up your tax credits and tax deductions. Round to the nearest pound.
When you have filled in all the supplementary Pages you need, tick this box. ☐

Step 3 Fill in Questions 10 to 24. If you answer 'Yes', fill in the relevant boxes. If not applicable, go to the next question.

BS 12/2002net TAX RETURN: PAGE 2

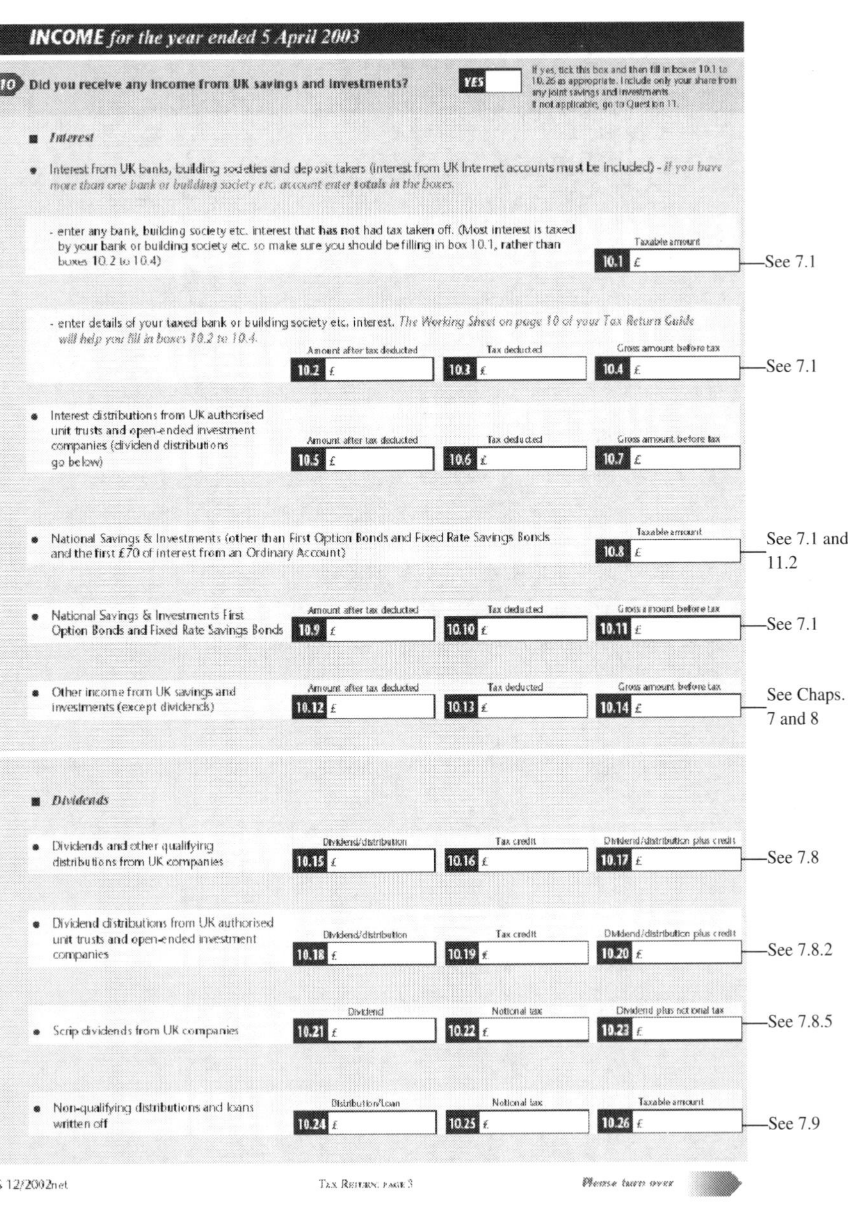

INCOME *for the year ended 5 April 2003*

Q10 Did you receive any income from UK savings and investments? YES

If yes, tick this box and then fill in boxes 10.1 to 10.26 as appropriate. Include only your share from any joint savings and investments. If not applicable, go to Question 11.

■ *Interest*

- Interest from UK banks, building societies and deposit takers (interest from UK Internet accounts must be included) - *If you have more than one bank or building society etc. account enter totals in the boxes.*

- enter any bank, building society etc. interest that **has not** had tax taken off. (Most interest is taxed by your bank or building society etc. so make sure you should be filling in box 10.1, rather than boxes 10.2 to 10.4) — Taxable amount **10.1** £ — See 7.1

- enter details of your taxed bank or building society etc. interest. *The Working Sheet on page 10 of your Tax Return Guide will help you fill in boxes 10.2 to 10.4.*

	Amount after tax deducted	Tax deducted	Gross amount before tax	
taxed bank or building society etc. interest	**10.2** £	**10.3** £	**10.4** £	See 7.1
• Interest distributions from UK authorised unit trusts and open-ended investment companies (dividend distributions go below)	**10.5** £	**10.6** £	**10.7** £	

- National Savings & Investments (other than First Option Bonds and Fixed Rate Savings Bonds and the first £70 of interest from an Ordinary Account) — Taxable amount **10.8** £ — See 7.1 and 11.2

	Amount after tax deducted	Tax deducted	Gross amount before tax	
• National Savings & Investments First Option Bonds and Fixed Rate Savings Bonds	**10.9** £	**10.10** £	**10.11** £	See 7.1
• Other income from UK savings and investments (except dividends)	**10.12** £	**10.13** £	**10.14** £	See Chaps. 7 and 8

■ *Dividends*

	Dividend/distribution	Tax credit	Dividend/distribution plus credit	
• Dividends and other qualifying distributions from UK companies	**10.15** £	**10.16** £	**10.17** £	See 7.8
• Dividend distributions from UK authorised unit trusts and open-ended investment companies	**10.18** £	**10.19** £	**10.20** £	See 7.8.2

	Dividend	Notional tax	Dividend plus notional tax	
• Scrip dividends from UK companies	**10.21** £	**10.22** £	**10.23** £	See 7.8.5

	Distribution/Loan	Notional tax	Taxable amount	
• Non-qualifying distributions and loans written off	**10.24** £	**10.25** £	**10.26** £	See 7.9

BS 12/2002net TAX RETURN: PAGE 3 *Please turn over*

INCOME *for the year ended 5 April 2003, continued*

Q11 Did you receive a taxable UK pension, retirement annuity or Social Security benefit?
Read the notes on pages 13 to 15 of the Tax Return Guide.

YES [ ] If yes, tick this box and then fill in boxes 11.1 to 11.14 as appropriate. If not applicable, go to Question 12.

■ ***State pensions and benefits***

	Taxable amount for 2002-03
• State Retirement Pension - *enter the total of your entitlements for the year*	11.1 £
• Widow's Pension or Bereavement Allowance	11.2 £
• Widowed Mother's Allowance or Widowed Parent's Allowance	11.3 £
• Industrial Death Benefit Pension	11.4 £
• Jobseeker's Allowance	11.5 £
• Invalid Care Allowance	11.6 £
• Statutory Sick Pay, Statutory Maternity Pay and Statutory Paternity Pay paid by the Inland Revenue	11.7 £

—See Chap.

	Tax deducted	Gross amount before tax
• Taxable Incapacity Benefit	11.8 £	11.9 £

■ ***Other pensions and retirement annuities***

	Amount after tax deducted	Tax deducted	Gross amount before tax
• Pensions (other than State pensions) and retirement annuities - *If you have more than one pension or annuity, please add together and complete boxes 11.10 to 11.12. Provide details of each one in box 11.14*	11.10 £	11.11 £	11.12 £

	Amount of deduction	
• Deduction - *see the note for box 11.13 on page 15 of your Tax Return Guide*	11.13 £	11.14

—See 8.8

Q12 Did you make any gains on UK life insurance policies, life annuities or capital redemption policies or receive refunds of surplus funds from additional voluntary contributions?

YES [ ] If yes, tick this box and then fill in boxes 12.1 to 12.12 as appropriate. If not applicable, go to Question 13. —See 12.1

	Number of years	Tax treated as paid / Tax deducted	Amount of gain(s)
• Gains on UK annuities and friendly societies' life insurance policies where no tax is treated as paid	12.1		12.2 £ —See 11.3
• Gains on UK life insurance policies etc. on which tax is treated as paid - *read pages 15 to 18 of your Tax Return Guide*	12.3	Tax treated as paid 12.4 £	12.5 £ —See 12.3
• Gains on life insurance policies in ISAs that have been made void	12.6	Tax deducted 12.7 £	12.8 £ —See 11.

	Amount
• Corresponding deficiency relief	12.9 £

	Amount received	Notional tax	Amount plus notional tax
• Refunds of surplus funds from additional voluntary contributions	12.10 £	12.11 £	12.12 £

—See 12.

Q13 Did you receive any other taxable income which you have not already entered elsewhere in your Tax Return?
Fill in any supplementary Pages before answering Question 13. (Supplementary Pages follow page 10, or are available from the Orderline.)

YES [ ] If yes, tick this box and then fill in boxes 13.1 to 13.6 as appropriate. If not applicable, go to Question 14.

	Amount after tax deducted	Tax deducted	Amount before tax
• Other taxable income – also provide details in box 23.5 - *read the notes on pages 18 to 20 of your Tax Return Guide*	13.1 £	13.2 £	13.3 £

		Losses brought forward	Earlier years' losses used in 2002-03
• Tick box 13.1A if box 13.1 includes enhanced capital allowances for environmentally friendly expenditure	13.1A	13.4 £	13.5 £

2002-03 losses carried forward: 13.6 £

BS 12/2002net TAX RETURN: PAGE 4

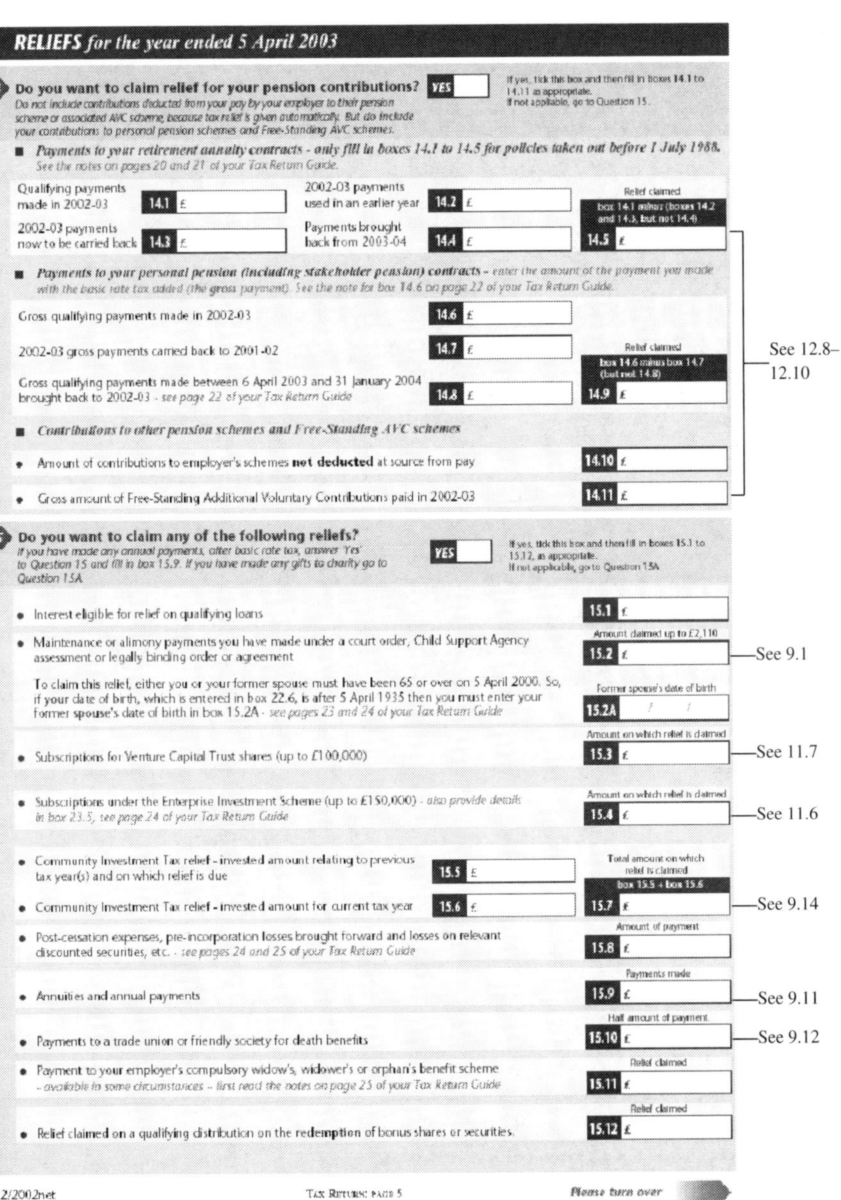

RELIEFS *for the year ended 5 April 2003*

Q14 Do you want to claim relief for your pension contributions? YES [ ] If yes, tick this box and then fill in boxes 14.1 to 14.11 as appropriate. If not applicable, go to Question 15.

Do not include contributions deducted from your pay by your employer to their pension scheme or associated AVC scheme, because tax relief is given automatically. But do include your contributions to personal pension schemes and Free-Standing AVC schemes.

■ ***Payments to your retirement annuity contracts - only fill in boxes 14.1 to 14.5 for policies taken out before 1 July 1988.*** *See the notes on pages 20 and 21 of your Tax Return Guide.*

Qualifying payments made in 2002-03	14.1 £	2002-03 payments used in an earlier year	14.2 £	Relief claimed box 14.1 minus (boxes 14.2 and 14.3, but not 14.4)
2002-03 payments now to be carried back	14.3 £	Payments brought back from 2003-04	14.4 £	14.5 £

■ ***Payments to your personal pension (including stakeholder pension) contracts*** *- enter the amount of the payment you made with the basic rate tax added (the gross payment). See the note for box 14.6 on page 22 of your Tax Return Guide.*

Gross qualifying payments made in 2002-03	14.6 £	
2002-03 gross payments carried back to 2001-02	14.7 £	Relief claimed box 14.6 minus box 14.7 (but not 14.8)
Gross qualifying payments made between 6 April 2003 and 31 January 2004 brought back to 2002-03 - *see page 22 of your Tax Return Guide*	14.8 £	14.9 £

■ ***Contributions to other pension schemes and Free-Standing AVC schemes***

- Amount of contributions to employer's schemes **not deducted** at source from pay — 14.10 £
- Gross amount of Free-Standing Additional Voluntary Contributions paid in 2002-03 — 14.11 £

See 12.8–12.10

Q15 Do you want to claim any of the following reliefs? YES [ ] If yes, tick this box and then fill in boxes 15.1 to 15.12, as appropriate. If not applicable, go to Question 15A

If you have made any annual payments, after basic rate tax, answer 'Yes' to Question 15 and fill in box 15.9. If you have made any gifts to charity go to Question 15A

- Interest eligible for relief on qualifying loans — 15.1 £
- Maintenance or alimony payments you have made under a court order, Child Support Agency assessment or legally binding order or agreement — Amount claimed up to £2,110 — 15.2 £ — See 9.1

  To claim this relief, either you or your former spouse must have been 65 or over on 5 April 2000. So, if your date of birth, which is entered in box 22.6, is after 5 April 1935 then you must enter your former spouse's date of birth in box 15.2A - *see pages 23 and 24 of your Tax Return Guide* — Former spouse's date of birth — 15.2A / /
- Subscriptions for Venture Capital Trust shares (up to £100,000) — Amount on which relief is claimed — 15.3 £ — See 11.7
- Subscriptions under the Enterprise Investment Scheme (up to £150,000) - *also provide details in box 23.5, see page 24 of your Tax Return Guide* — Amount on which relief is claimed — 15.4 £ — See 11.6
- Community Investment Tax relief - invested amount relating to previous tax year(s) and on which relief is due — 15.5 £
- Community Investment Tax relief - invested amount for current tax year — 15.6 £ — Total amount on which relief is claimed box 15.5 + box 15.6 — 15.7 £ — See 9.14
- Post-cessation expenses, pre-incorporation losses brought forward and losses on relevant discounted securities, etc. - *see pages 24 and 25 of your Tax Return Guide* — Amount of payment — 15.8 £
- Annuities and annual payments — Payments made — 15.9 £ — See 9.11
- Payments to a trade union or friendly society for death benefits — Half amount of payment — 15.10 £ — See 9.12
- Payment to your employer's compulsory widow's, widower's or orphan's benefit scheme *- available in some circumstances - first read the notes on page 25 of your Tax Return Guide* — Relief claimed — 15.11 £
- Relief claimed on a qualifying distribution on the **redemption** of bonus shares or securities. — Relief claimed — 15.12 £

SA100 2/2002net — TAX RETURN: PAGE 5 — *Please turn over*

ALLOWANCES *for the year ended 5 April 2003*

Q15A Do you want to claim relief on gifts to charity? YES

If you have made any Gift Aid payments answer 'Yes' to Question 15A. You should include Gift Aid payments to Community Amateur Sports Clubs here. You can elect to include in this Return Gift Aid payments made between 6 April 2003 and the date you send in this Return. See page 26 in the Tax Return Guide and the leaflet enclosed on Gift Aid.

If yes, tick this box and then read page 26 of your Tax Return Guide. Fill in boxes 15A.1 to 15A.5 as appropriate. If not applicable, go to Question 16.

- Gift Aid and payments under charitable covenants made between 6 April 2002 and 5 April 2003 — **15A.1** £
- Enter in box 15A.2 the total of any 'one off' payments included in box 15A.1 — **15A.2** £
- Enter in box 15A.3 the amount of Gift Aid payments made after 5 April 2003 but treated as if made in the tax year 2002-03 — **15A.3** £
- Gifts of qualifying investments to charities – shares and securities — **15A.4** £
- Gifts of qualifying investments to charities – real property — **15A.5** £

Q16 Do you want to claim blind person's allowance, married couple's allowance or the Children's Tax Credit? YES

You get your personal allowance of £4,615 automatically. ***If you were born before 6 April 1938, enter your date of birth in box 22.6*** *- you may get a higher age-related personal allowance.*

If yes, tick this box and then read pages 26 to 31 of your Tax Return Guide. Fill in boxes 16.1 to 16.33 as appropriate. If not applicable, go to Question 17.

- ***Blind person's allowance*** — Date of registration (if first year of claim) **16.1** / / — Local authority (or other register) **16.2** — See 10.6

- ***Married couple's allowance*** *- In 2002-03 married couple's allowance can only be claimed if either you, or your husband or wife, were born before 6 April 1935. So you can only claim the allowance in 2002-03 if either of you had reached 65 years of age before 6 April 2000. Further guidance is given beginning on page 27 of your Tax Return Guide.*

If both you and your husband or wife were born after 5 April 1935 you cannot claim; do not complete boxes 16.3 to 16.13.

If you can claim fill in boxes 16.3 and 16.4 if you are a married man or if you are a married woman and you are claiming half or all of the married couple's allowance.

- Enter your date of birth (if born before 6 April 1935) — **16.3** / /
- Enter your spouse's date of birth (if born before 6 April 1935 and if older than you) — **16.4** / /

Then, if you are a married man fill in boxes 16.5 to 16.9. If you are a married woman fill in boxes 16.10 to 16.13.

- Wife's full name — **16.5**
- Date of marriage (if after 5 April 2002) — **16.6** / /
- Tick box 16.7, or box 16.8, if you or your wife have allocated half, or all, of the minimum amount of the allowance to her — Half **16.7** All **16.8**
- Enter in box 16.9 the date of birth of any previous wife with whom you lived at any time during 2002-03. *Read 'Special rules if you are a man who married in the year ended 5 April 2003' on page 28 before completing box 16.9.* — **16.9** / /
- Tick box 16.10, or box 16.11, if you or your husband have allocated half, or all, of the minimum amount of the allowance to you — Half **16.10** All **16.11**
- Husband's full name — **16.12**
- Date of marriage (if after 5 April 2002) — **16.13** / /

See 10.3

- ***Children's Tax Credit*** *– even if you have already completed a separate Children's Tax Credit (CTC) claim form and received the relief in your tax code, you should still fill in boxes 16.14 to 16.26, as directed. Any reference to 'partner' in this question means the person you lived with during the year to 5 April 2003 – your husband or wife, or someone you lived with as husband or wife.*

Guidance for claiming CTC is on pages 28 to 31 of your Tax Return Guide. Please read the notes before completing your claim, particularly if either you, or your partner, were liable to tax above the basic rate in the year to 5 April 2003.

- Enter in box 16.14 the date of birth of a child living with you who was born on or after 6 April 1986. *If you have a child living with you who was born on or after 6 April 2002 make sure you enter their date of birth in this box in preference to claiming for an older child.* — **16.14** / /
- Tick box 16.15 if the child was your own child or one you looked after at your own expense. If not, you cannot claim CTC – go to box 16.27, if appropriate, or Question 17. — **16.15**
- Tick box 16.16 if the child lived with you throughout the year to 5 April 2003. — **16.16**
  If you ticked box 16.16 and
  - you were a lone or single claimant, you have finished this question; go to Question 17.
  - you have a partner, go to box 16.18.
- If the child lived with you for only part of the year you may only be entitled to a proportion of the CTC. Enter in box 16.17 your share in £s that you have agreed with any other claimants that you may claim for this child. But leave boxes 16.17 to 16.25 blank if you separated from, or started living with, your partner during the year to 5 April 2003. Special rules apply to work out your entitlement; ask the Orderline for *Help Sheet IR343: Claiming Children's Tax Credit when your circumstances change* which explains how to complete box 16.26. — **16.17** £

See 10.8 10.11

BS 12/2002net TAX RETURN: PAGE 6

ALLOWANCES *for the year ended 5 April 2003, continued*

■ ***Children's Tax Credit**, continued*

If you lived with your partner (for CTC this means your husband or wife, or someone you lived with as husband and wife) for the whole of the year to 5 April 2003, fill in boxes 16.18 to 16.25 as appropriate.

- Enter in box 16.18 your partner's surname — **16.18**
- Enter in box 16.19 your partner's National Insurance number — **16.19**
- Tick
  - box 16.20 if you had the higher income in the year to 5 April 2003, — **16.20**

  or

  - box 16.21 if your partner had the higher income in that year — **16.21**
- Tick box 16.22 if either of you were chargeable to tax above the basic rate limit in the year to 5 April 2003. — **16.22**

*If you ticked boxes 16.20 and 16.22 your entitlement will be reduced – see page 30 of your Tax Return Guide; **your partner cannot claim** CTC - go to box 16.28, or Question 17 as appropriate.*

*If you ticked boxes 16.21 and 16.22 your partner's entitlement will be reduced; **you cannot claim** CTC - go to box 16.27, or Question 17, as appropriate.*

*If **neither** of you were chargeable above the basic rate and **you** had the lower income **and***

- *you don't want to claim half of the entitlement to CTC, and*
- *you didn't make an election for CTC to go to the partner with the lower income*

you have finished this part of your Return - go to boxes 16.27 or 16.28, or Question 17, as appropriate (your partner should claim CTC if they have not already done so).

Otherwise, tick one of boxes 16.23 to 16.25.

- I had the higher income and I am claiming all of our entitlement to CTC — **16.23**
- We are both making separate claims for half of our entitlement to CTC — **16.24**
- We elected before 6 April 2002, or because of our special circumstances, during the year to 5 April 2003 (see page 31 of your Tax Return Guide), for the partner with the lower income to claim all of our entitlement to CTC — **16.25**
- If you separated from, or starting living with, your partner in the year to 5 April 2003, enter in box 16.26 the amount of CTC you are claiming *(following the guidance in Help Sheet IR343: Claiming Children's Tax Credit when your circumstances change)* — **16.26** £

See 10.8–10.11

■ ***Transfer of surplus allowances** - see page 31 of your Tax Return Guide before you fill in boxes 16.27 to 16.33.*

- Tick box 16.27 if you want your spouse to have your unused allowances — **16.27**
- Tick box 16.28 if you want to have your spouse's unused allowances — **16.28**
- Tick box 16.29 if you want to have your partner's unused CTC — **16.29**
- Tick box 16.30 if your surplus CTC should be transferred to your partner — **16.30**

Please give details in the 'Additional information' box, box 23.5, on page 9 - *see page 31 of your Tax Return Guide for what is needed.*

If you want to calculate your tax, enter the amount of the surplus allowance you can have.

- Blind person's surplus allowance — **16.31** £
- Married couple's surplus allowance — **16.32** £
- Surplus CTC — **16.33** £

OTHER INFORMATION *for the year ended 5 April 2003*

17 **Are you liable to make Student Loan Repayments for 2002-03 on an Income Contingent Student Loan?** *You must read the note on page 31 of your Tax Return Guide before ticking the 'Yes' box.* — **YES**

If yes, tick this box.
If not applicable, go to Question 18.

If yes, and you are calculating your tax enter in Question 18, box 18.2A the amount you work out is repayable in 2002-03

12/2002net TAX RETURN: PAGE 7 *Please turn over*

4

EMPLOYMENT INCOME

GRAHAM BAKER

This chapter deals with the following matters:

(1) Basis of assessment.
(2) How tax is collected.
(3) Allowable expenses.
(4) Benefits-in-kind in general.
(5) Company cars.
(6) Free use of assets.
(7) Beneficial loans.
(8) Living accommodation.
(9) Miscellaneous benefits.
(10) Gifts of shares.
(11) Profit-sharing schemes.
(12) All-employee share schemes.
(13) Non-approved share options.
(14) Approved share option schemes
(15) Enterprise Management Incentives (EMI)
(16) Restricted shares and shares in subsidiary companies
(17) Options to acquire gilts
(18) Options to acquire other company assets
(19) Golden hellos
(20) Restrictive covenants
(21) Redundancy payments
(22) Golden handshakes and other termination payments.
(23) Special rules for working outside the UK
(24) Designing a 'tax efficient' remuneration package.

4.1 BASIS OF ASSESSMENT

4.1.1 Introduction

An individual who holds an office or employment is now taxed under the Income Tax (Earnings and Pensions) Act 2003 which came into force on 6 April 2003. This Act has replaced Schedule E TA 1988 but has made no substantive changes. The Act retains (under another name) the three cases under Schedule E regarding the individual's residence, ordinary residence and domicile, and where the employment duties are carried out:

Table 4.1 – Different treatment according to residence/domicile of employee

Case I	Individual resident and ordinarily resident in the UK: tax is due on total remuneration received. The legislation is now s 15 IT(E&P)A 2003.
Case II	Individual resident but not ordinarily resident in the UK: tax is due on total remuneration received (subject to special treatment of foreign emoluments (see 24.2) and remuneration taxed under Case III (see below)). Individual not resident in the UK: tax is due on total remuneration received for duties performed in the UK. The relevant legislation is now s 25 IT(E&P)A 2003.
Case III	Individual resident but not ordinarily resident in the UK where the duties are performed outside the UK. Case III may also apply to foreign domiciled individuals' earnings from duties performed outside the UK (see 24.2). In both situations, tax is due on earnings brought into the UK. The relevant legislation is now s 26 and s 22 IT(E&P)A 2003.

The remainder of this chapter concentrates on employees who are taxed under Schedule E Case I. See Chaps. 23 and 24 for the taxation of non-ordinarily resident and foreign domiciled individuals under Schedule E Case III.

4.1.2 Receipts basis

(IT(E&P)A 2003, s 10)

The amount that is assessable for a tax year is the amount of earnings received in that year.

4.1.3 Date remuneration is deemed to be received

(IT(E&P)A 2003, s 18)

Special provisions define the date that an individual is deemed to receive remuneration as the earlier of:

(1) the date when payment is actually made; and
(2) the time when the employee becomes entitled to payment.

In the case of directors, the date can be earlier than above, in that payment is deemed to take place on the earliest of (1) and (2); and

(3) the date that income is credited to the director in the company's accounts or records;

(4) the date when the amount of income for a period is determined; or
(5) the end of a period if the director's remuneration for a period is determined before the period has expired.

The employer is required to operate PAYE when payment is deemed to take place (see 21.1).

4.1.4 Amounts deducted in arriving at pay

(IT(E&P)A 2003, s 713)

Contributions made by an employee to an approved retirement benefit scheme and contributions to a payroll giving scheme ('give as you earn') are deducted from an individual's salary in arriving at taxable pay for both PAYE and for assessment purposes. Note that NICs are based on pay before such amounts are deducted (see 25.1).

4.1.5 Amounts added in arriving at pay

Since 6 April 2000, an employer has been required to pay Working Families' and Disabled Persons' Tax Credits (see 25.6).

4.2 HOW TAX IS COLLECTED

4.2.1 Tax deductions under PAYE

All payments of 'emoluments' by a UK-resident employer to directors and employees are subject to Pay As You Earn (PAYE). Emoluments are cash payments (salary, wages, bonus, etc) other than expense payments.

PAYE code numbers

The Revenue issues code numbers that determine the amount of PAYE deductions. Such code numbers are based on the latest information available to the Revenue and are intended to ensure that the amounts withheld under PAYE approximate closely to the individual's actual liability. Nevertheless, deduction of tax under PAYE is provisional in that if the actual liability exceeds the amount withheld under PAYE, the Revenue may collect the balance either by increased PAYE deductions in subsequent years or by raising an assessment.

Although the top rate of tax is 40%, the Revenue may issue K codes under which increased deductions may be taken of up to 50% of an individual's pay. The principle behind K codes is that notional pay is added to an employee's actual pay, and PAYE is operated accordingly. This is intended to cover the situation where the benefits-in-kind that are taxable exceed a person's allowances.

What the letters in your code mean

A Basic personal allowance plus one half of the Children's Tax Credit, and the Revenue estimates that you are liable at the basic rate of tax.

H Basic personal allowance plus the full Children's Tax Credit, and the Revenue estimates that you are liable at the basic rate of tax

L Basic personal allowance.

P Full personal allowance for those aged 65-74.

V Full personal allowance for those aged 65-74, *plus* the full married couple's allowance for those born before 6 April 1938 and aged under 75 and the Revenue estimates that you are liable at the basic rate of tax.

Y Full personal allowance for those aged 75+.

T Any other items the Revenue needs to review in your tax code or if you ask the Revenue not to use any of the other tax code letters listed.

K 'K' followed by a number means that the *total allowances* in your code are less than the *total deductions* to be taken away from your allowances.

BR Tax deducted at the basic rate, currently 22%.

D0 Tax deducted at a flat rate of 40%.

0T No allowances, salary charged at progressive rates.

NT No Tax, usually used for non-residents being paid from the UK.

The Revenue publishes a leaflet (P3), which is available from your local tax office or from the Revenue's website containing its example of how a K coding works.

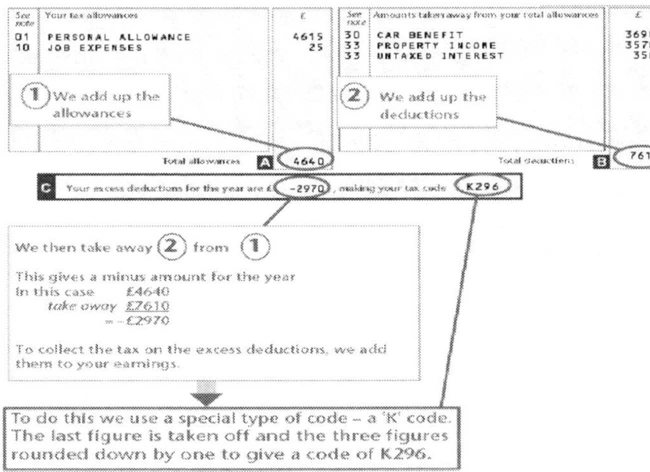

How tax is worked out using this tax code for 2003-04

Pay from employment		£ 18,720
Plus the excess deductions for the year		£ 2,970
Pay on which tax will be paid		£ 21,690
On £ 21,690, the tax payable is		
Starting rate 10% on £1,960	= £ 196.00	
Basic rate 22% on £ 19,730	= £ 4,340.60	
Tax payable for the year	= £ 4,536.60	

To work out the weekly amounts of pay and tax, divide the pay and the tax payable for the year by 52.

4.2.2 Foreign employers that are unable to operate PAYE

Where a person is employed by a foreign employer that has no place of business in the UK, PAYE is not normally operated. Tax is payable by the employee as if he were self-employed, ie two payments on account based on the previous year's tax bill plus a balancing payment on 31 January following the end of the tax year.

4.2.3 Self-assessment

An employee has until 31 January following the year of assessment to file a return and pay any additional tax due (ie for 2002-03, by 31 January 2004). If the employee wants the tax underpaid (of up to £2,000) to be collected by way of an adjustment in the code operated against his salary, he is requested to file the return by 30 September following the year of assessment (ie for 2002-03, by 30 September 2003).

Where the taxpayer fails to notify the Revenue and pay any tax due by 31 January, interest penalties and surcharges may arise (see Chap. 3).

A practical point when completing the SA form is to have copies of your PAYE Codings (P2) to hand. For 2002-03, question 18.1 on the main form asks for 'unpaid tax included in your tax code for 2002-03', and question 18.2 asks for 'tax due for 2002-03 included in your tax code for a later year'. The former should be taken from the last P2 notice of coding received for 2002-03 and the latter from your current 2003-04 coding. If in doubt, contact your PAYE district office or the Inspector of Taxes at the number shown on the front of the tax return.

4.3 ALLOWABLE EXPENSES

4.3.1 Schedule E expenses

(IT(E&P)A 2003, s 327)

The rules governing the amounts that may be deducted for tax purposes from remuneration subject to Schedule E tax are extremely strict. The legislation provides for a deduction to be made only in respect of expenses that are wholly, exclusively and necessarily incurred in the performance of the duties of the employment or office.

Wholly, exclusively ...

The courts have held that the following expenses are not deductible for Schedule E purposes because they are not deemed to have been incurred wholly and exclusively in the performance of the employment duties:

(1) meal expenses paid out of meal allowances;

(2) the rent of a telephone installed for business reasons but not used wholly and exclusively in the performance of duties;
(3) the cost of domestic assistance where the taxpayer's wife is employed;
(4) the cost of looking after a widower's children; and
(5) the cost of ordinary clothing.

... and necessarily ...

The situation often arises that the employer has reimbursed the expense because it is regarded as essential. This is helpful, but not conclusive. The Revenue will assess the amount paid to a director or P11D employee (see 4.4.1) but may then seek to disallow the individual's expenditure claim on the grounds that it is not necessary. Two of the leading cases involved reimbursed expenditure by journalists on newspapers and other periodicals. The point at issue was whether reading such newspapers was part, or inherent in the performance, of the journalists' duties. The key point here is that it is not the employer's decision that determines the case. The employer may be fully prepared to reimburse the expenditure but the Revenue may still argue that it fails to meet the very strict guidelines on what constitutes 'necessary'.

... in the performance of the duties

Other expenses were rejected on the grounds that they were not incurred in the performance of the duties of the relevant employment:

(1) employment agency fees (although entertainers specifically are now entitled to claim a deduction for such expenses up to 17.5% of their earnings);
(2) a headmaster's course to improve background knowledge;
(3) an articled clerk's examination fees;
(4) travelling costs from home to the place where the employment duties were performed;
(5) living expenses paid out of living allowances paid to an employee when working away from home; and
(6) expenditure by a rugby league player on diet supplements in order to improve and maintain his fitness (*Ansell v Brown* 2001 STC 1166);
(7) Expenses incurred by a supply teacher in keeping a room at her home for preparation of lessons, marking, etc (*Warner v Prior* 2003 SpC 353);
(8) Expenses incurred by a Civil Servant who was allowed to work from home in Norfolk but was required to travel to the Department's offices in Leeds on a weekly basis (*Kirkwood v Evans* 2002 STC 231).

Cases where the taxpayer has succeeded

There have been cases where travelling expenses have been allowed because the courts were satisfied that a person's duties started as soon as he left home. For example, in *Gilbert v Hemsley* [1981] STC 703 a plant-hire company director's duties involved his using his home as a base and travelling to various sites. The court held that once he left home he was travelling in the course of his duties. Similarly, in *Pook v Owen* (1969) 45 TC 571 a doctor was 'on call' and his duties started once he was telephoned by the hospital to ask him to attend.

4.3.2 Expenses that are allowable

(IT(E&P)A 2003, ss 333-360)

Certain expenses are specifically allowable, such as the cost of professional subscriptions to an approved body that is relevant to the individual's employment (eg the annual subscription to the Institute of Chartered Accountants or The Law Society). Also, flat rate expenses are given to employees in certain industries to cover expenditure on tools, overalls, special clothing, etc.

Despite the very restrictive rules outlined in 4.3.1, you may be able to secure a deduction if you pay interest on a loan used to purchase equipment used by you in the course of your employment (eg a computer or a fax machine at your home that you use for business purposes).

In addition to claiming a deduction for loan interest, relief may be due for expenses such as running costs and (in the case of a fax machine) the line rental. Capital allowances may also be due, subject to a restriction if the equipment is used for private purposes as well as for your employment.

At one time, directors or employees could not obtain tax relief for expenditure on items such as directors' and officers' liability insurance, or professional indemnity insurance. FA 1995 introduced relief for such premiums where they are paid by employees. Moreover, tax relief is also available where an employee has to meet his own uninsured liability.

The relief for insurance or payment of uninsured liabilities is also available to former employees who incur such expenses within a six-year period after the year in which the employment ceased.

4.3.3 Capital allowances for cars

2001-02 was the last tax year for which you could claim capital allowance on a car or motorbike used for work-related purposes, see the *Zurich Tax Handbook 2002/2003* at 4.3.3 regarding this.

4.4 BENEFITS-IN-KIND IN GENERAL

4.4.1 Directors and 'higher paid employees'

(IT(E&P)A 2003, s 201)

The legislation distinguishes P11D employees (ie directors and employees earning £8,500+ pa) from other employees. An employer is required to submit form P11D in respect of each P11D employee, who may then be assessed on the cost to the employer of benefits-in-kind received by them. Other employees are normally taxed on benefits only if they are convertible into cash.

An employee will fall within the P11D category where remuneration, together with benefits and reimbursed expenses, is £8,500+ pa. Such employees formerly were called 'higher paid' employees. The £8,500 threshold was set in 1979 and, in accordance with the Government's intentions that all employees should pay income tax on the whole of their earnings whether received in cash or in kind, this limit has not been increased. By 1989 the term 'higher paid' had become inappropriate and consequently, while there was no change made in the level of the threshold, references to 'higher paid employees' were deleted from the legislation.

Employees are treated as earning £8,500+ if they are remunerated at the rate of £8,500+ pa. For example, a person whose employment began on 1 January 2003 and who had received a salary of £2,000 and reimbursed expenses of £200 by 5 April 2003 would be within the P11D category as the total amount of £2,200 would give an annual rate greater than £8,500.

All reimbursed expenses and other benefits have to be reported on form P11D and count towards the £8,500 limit, even though they may be justified as being for business purposes and ultimately no taxable benefit-in-kind arises, unless a dispensation has been agreed by the Revenue (see 4.4.2).

Directors are normally within the P11D regime, regardless of whether their remuneration reaches or exceeds the £8,500 limit (subject to one exception: see below). Furthermore, individuals who control a company's affairs and take management decisions may be treated as directors, even if they do not hold a formal position with the company and may have another title or job description within the company.

A person remunerated at a rate below £8,500 by a particular company is still within the P11D category if a directorship is held with another company in the same group, or if the total remuneration from group companies amounts to £8,500 pa whether or not any directorships are held. Certain directors are exempt from these rules by virtue of s 168 and therefore are excluded from the definition. To qualify for this favourable treatment, certain conditions need to be satisfied. The director:

(1) must not hold more than 5% of the company's ordinary share capital (holdings by his 'associates' may need to be included as if he held the shares); and

(2) must be employed on a full-time basis (or the company must be a non-profit making organisation); and
(3) must be receiving remuneration and benefits which in aggregate are less than £8,500 pa.

An employer must provide employees with details of the taxable amounts for benefits shown on his form P11D. This must be done before 5 July following the tax year unless the employee had left the firm before the end of the tax year (in which case the employer must provide the information within 30 days of the former employee requesting him to do so). The P11D must include the cost of benefits provided by third parties where they were arranged by the employer.

4.4.2 Dispensations

The Revenue may grant a dispensation so that certain reimbursed expenses need not be reported on form P11D. This clearly is useful in reducing administration and accounting work and, wherever possible, employers should apply for a dispensation. The Revenue will set out expenses covered by it; any expenses not covered must still be reported. Any changes in the method of reimbursing expenses or scales of allowances must be notified to the Revenue.

4.4.3 Benefits-in-kind provided by third parties

(IT(E&P)A 2003, s 265)

It is not uncommon for wholesalers and distributors to offer benefits-in-kind to employees of retailers with whom they do business. Subject to certain *de minimis* rules, such benefits are taxable just as if they had been provided by the retailer himself.

However, non-monetary gifts costing no more than £250 (£150 up to 2002-03) received by an employee or his family from someone other than his employer is generally exempt from income tax. Likewise, no income tax liability usually arises on entertainment that an employee receives from a third party. These exemptions apply only where the gift or entertainment is not provided directly or indirectly by the employer and, furthermore, where it is not provided as a reward for, or in recognition of, specific services done or to be done by the employee.

Where the third party benefits have not been arranged by the employer, the provider must give the employee details of any taxable benefits by 5 July following the tax year.

4.4.4 Benefits for director's family

(IT(E&P)A 2003, s 201(2))

A fundamental point is that an assessment may arise even though the director or employee has not personally received a benefit-in-kind. A tax liability may arise if the benefit was made available to a member of the director's or employee's household by reason of his employment. The Revenue may argue that substantial benefits-in-kind enjoyed by a director's family are provided by reason of that person's employment even though the recipient may also be a company employee. The Revenue is especially likely to argue this where a director's spouse is employed by the company and receives abnormally large benefits-in-kind for employees of that category.

The legislation defines an individual's family or household as his spouse, children, parents, servants, dependants and guests. Note that this definition does not include grandparents, brothers, sisters and grandchildren, although there can be situations where such relatives count as dependants.

4.4.5 Scholarships

(IT(E&P)A 2003, s 213)

There is a general exemption for scholarships, but a scholarship provided to a child by reason of his parent's employment is normally treated as a benefit-in-kind of the parent. The benefit is taxable unless it can be shown that the scholarship was not awarded by reason of the employment and 75% of the scholarships awarded by the fund are awarded to children whose parents are not employed by the company.

4.4.6 Benefits that may result in a tax charge for non-P11D employees

The general rule is that employees not within the P11D category are assessable only on benefits capable of being converted into cash or on any benefits provided through an employer meeting an employee's own personal liability. This principle has been modified to some extent so that, for example, credit vouchers are an assessable benefit even if the employee is not within the P11D category. However, the principle continues to hold good with regard to benefits such as the provision of a company car, free use of assets, beneficial loans, etc.

Table 4.2 sets out the position.

4.4.7 Tax treatment of specific benefits where received by a non-P11D employee

Benefits capable of being converted into cash

Where the benefit is convertible into cash, the measure of assessable benefit is the amount of cash that could be realised. For example, an employee provided with a new suit by the employer would be taxable on its second-hand value.

Table 4.2 – Treatment of benefits received by non-P11D employees

	Taxable	*Non-taxable*
Benefits capable of being turned to pecuniary account, ie convertible to cash	✓	
Luncheon vouchers in excess of 15p per working day	✓	
Credit tokens and vouchers	✓	
Transport vouchers (ie any ticket, pass or other document or token intended to enable a person to obtain passenger transport services)	✓	
Living accommodation	✓	
Payment of employees' personal liabilities	✓	
Company cars		✓
Free use of assets		✓
Beneficial loans		✓
Medical insurance		✓

Credit tokens and vouchers

(IT(E&P)A 2003, s 90)

The taxable amount in respect of credit tokens and vouchers is the cost to the employer of providing them. Vouchers other than cheque vouchers are deemed to be taxable emoluments as and when they are allocated to a particular employee, not when they are used by that employee.

Transport vouchers

(IT(E&P)A 2003, s 82)

Specific legislation was introduced some years ago to ensure that season tickets provided by employers should be taxable. Once again, the measure of the assessable benefit is the cost to the employer of providing the voucher.

Living accommodation

(IT(E&P)A 2003, s 97)

The assessable amount is the greater of the property's gross rateable value or the rent payable by the employer, less any amount made good by the employee. Following the abolition of domestic rates, estimated values are used for new or substantially altered properties. No assessable benefit arises where the employee occupies representative accommodation (see 4.4.8).

Payment of employee's personal liabilities

A liability arises where the employer pays a personal liability of the employee. This would include such items as home heating, lighting bills and water rates, but special rules apply where the employee is in representative accommodation (see 4.4.8).

4.4.8 Benefits not taxable for any category of employees

There are certain benefits that are not usually taxable even when the employee is within the P11D category. The most widely used tax-free benefits are as set out below.

Retirement benefits

Payments by an employer to an approved occupational pension scheme to secure retirement benefits for an employee do not give rise to an income tax liability for that employee. Payments into a non-approved scheme are taxable as additional remuneration for the year that the employer makes the relevant contribution. To secure approval, a pension scheme must be established for the sole purpose of providing 'relevant benefits' (ie pensions, death-in-service payments and widows' and dependants' pensions). In addition, an employee's contributions must not exceed 15% of his remuneration. The pension benefits payable by an approved scheme must not exceed certain limits. Pension schemes are covered in more detail in Chap. 12.

Luncheon vouchers

Non-transferable luncheon vouchers (ie vouchers that are not capable of being exchanged for cash) are exempt from income tax up to a limit of 15p per working day. Vouchers for larger amounts are partly exempt, with the excess over 15p being taxable in full, whether or not the employee is within the P11D category.

Staff canteen and dining facilities

No taxable benefit-in-kind arises where the canteen, etc is used by all staff. Furthermore, the use of a separate room by directors and more senior staff does not prejudice this exemption, unless the meals provided are superior. The Revenue also accepts that facilities provided by a hotel or restaurant for staff to 'eat in' may come within the definition of a 'canteen', provided that the meals are taken at a time or place when they are not being served to the public or where part of the restaurant or dining room is designated specifically as being for staff use only.

Sports facilities

(IT(E&P)A 2003, s 261)

No taxable benefit arises in respect of the use or availability of sports facilities owned by the employer. At one time, no assessment was normally made where an employer took out corporate membership of an outside sports club so that all the employees were able to use its facilities. However, the Revenue's current literature states that the exemption is not available for sports facilities that are available to the general public.

Workplace nurseries and crèches

Employees are exempt from income tax on the benefit derived from the use of a workplace nursery provided by the employer. The exemption applies only to nurseries run by employers alone or jointly with other employers or bodies, either at the workplace or elsewhere. The provision by an employer of cash allowances to employees for childcare, or the direct meeting of an employee's childcare bills by an employer, are taxable benefits.

Pool cars

(IT(E&P)A 2003, s 167)

No tax charge arises by reason of the use of a pooled car. A car qualifies as a pooled car only if all the following conditions are satisfied:

(1) It is available for, and used by, more than one employee and is not used ordinarily by any one of them to the exclusion of the others.
(2) Any private use of the car by an employee is merely incidental to its business use.
(3) It is not normally kept overnight at or near the residence of any of the employees unless it is kept on the employer's premises.

These requirements are interpreted strictly. Note that a car only qualifies as a pooled car for a tax year. There is a danger, therefore, in a car being taken out of pooled use and allotted to a specific employee towards the end of a tax year. As the car now no longer qualifies as a pooled car, any employee who has had the car available for private use during the same tax year may be assessed. So, if the car is ordinarily parked overnight near the home of one of the users, it does not qualify as a pooled car and creates a tax problem for any other employees who use it.

Disabled employees' travel costs

Assistance with travelling costs between home and work is not taxable where it is given to disabled persons. This includes contributions towards the cost of travel by public transport. A car provided for travel between home and work is not taxed where:

(1) the employee is severely and permanently disabled; and
(2) the car has been specially adapted; and
(3) no private use is made other than travel between home and work occupied by the employer.

'Green commuting' facilities

There is no taxable benefit in respect of:

- works buses with a seating capacity of 9 or more (12 or more until 5 April 2002);
- subsidies to public bus services, provided the employee pays the same fare as other members of the public;
- bicycles and cycle safety equipment made available for employees to get to and from work; and
- workplace parking for bicycles and motorcycles.

For employees who may need to shower and change clothes after arriving at the office because, for example, they cycle or run to work, tax is not chargeable on the free use by employees of changing and shower room facilities at an employer's premises, provided they are generally available to all employees. The employer can also provide breakfast on designated 'cycle to work days' without this constituting a taxable benefit (for 2002-03 the exemption was limited to six breakfasts pa).

Late travel

There is an exemption for the cost to an employer of providing transport to get an employee home (after 9 pm) where public transport is not available or it is not reasonable for the employer to expect the employee to use it. The exemption does not apply if the employee has to work late on a regular or frequent basis.

The exemption has been extended to cover extra travel costs where car-sharing arrangements temporarily break down. This can include situations where the employee travels home at his normal time (eg where the employee whose car he shares is unexpectedly kept late).

Employees' rail strike costs

(IT(E&P)A 2003, s 245)

There is now a statutory exemption which covers extra costs incurred by employees in getting to work because of a rail strike. The exemption (which may also cover the cost of hotel accommodation near the place of work) means that no Schedule E tax is payable where the employer meets these expenses.

Homeworking allowance

The Finance Act 2003 has introduced an exemption for payments of up to £2 per week to cover extra expenses where the employee is required to work from home.

Relocation expenses
(IT(E&P)A 2003, s 271)

There is an exemption from tax on certain removal expenses borne by an employer when an employee has to change his residence to take up a new job within the same organisation, or to take up completely new employment. It is not necessary for the employee to sell his former home, but the exemption is available only where it would be unreasonable to expect him to work at the new location without moving closer to it. Abortive costs where a particular purchase falls through can be covered by the exemption provided the employee does eventually move house. The exemption is subject to a ceiling of £8,000 for any one move.

Payments made to compensate employees for losses on the sale of their former houses are regarded as taxable.

The Revenue has published a guide for employees on relocation packages and their tax treatment (IR134, obtainable from tax offices and tax enquiry centres). Sometimes employers provide guaranteed selling prices for the employee's former home, either directly or through a relocation agency. The Revenue published its views on the tax consequences of such arrangements in *Tax Bulletin* May 1994, available from the Revenue Press Office.

Gifts by third parties

The exemption for non-monetary gifts by third parties covered at 4.4.3 applies to all categories of employees.

Long service awards
(IT(E&P)A 2003, s 323)

Awards to directors and employees to mark long service are exempt provided the period of service is at least 20 years and no similar award has been given to the employee within the previous ten years. The gift must not consist of cash and the cost should not exceed £50 per year of service (£20 pa up to 2002-03). The exemption also applies to gifts of shares in the company that employs the individual or in another group company.

Awards under suggestion schemes
(IT(E&P)A 2003, ss 321-322)

Provided the employee is not engaged in research work, he may receive a tax-free payment under a firm's suggestion scheme. Making suggestions should not, however, be regarded as part of the employee's job. The size of the award should be within certain limits, ie £25 or less where the suggestion, although not implemented, has intrinsic value. Where the suggestion is implemented, the amount should be related to the expected net financial benefit to the employer. In any event, any excess over £5,000 is taxable.

Use of company computers

Since 6 April 1999, employees have been able to take up the loan of a computer without being faced with a tax charge. This concession applies to computer equipment with a value of up to £2,500. The normal benefit-in-kind rules (20% × market value), see 4.6, apply to any excess over £2,500. The exemption is not given if the equipment is confined to directors and senior staff.

Representative accommodation

(IT(E&P)A 2003, s 99)

Living accommodation qualifies as representative accommodation if any one of the following conditions is satisfied:

(1) it is necessary for the performance of the employee's duties that he should reside in the accommodation;
(2) the accommodation is provided for the better performance of the employee's duties and it is customary to provide accommodation for such employees; or
(3) the employee has to live in the accommodation because of a special threat to his security.

The exemption under the first two conditions is usually available only to directors who (together with their associates) hold 5% or less of the company's ordinary share capital and are full-time working directors. Where the employer pays for heating, lighting, repairs, maintenance, etc, the representative occupiers cannot be assessed in respect of such benefits on more than 10% of their emoluments of the employment.

The main occupations that satisfy the conditions for exemption are:

(1) agricultural workers living on farms or agricultural estates;
(2) lock-gate and level-crossing gatekeepers;
(3) caretakers who live on the premises for which they are responsible;
(4) stewards and greenkeepers who live on the premises they look after;
(5) managers of public houses who live on the premises;
(6) wardens of sheltered housing who live on the premises;
(7) police officers and Ministry of Defence police;
(8) prison governors, officers and chaplains;
(9) clergymen and ministers of religion, unless engaged on administrative duties only;
(10) members of the armed forces;
(11) members of the Diplomatic Service;
(12) managers of newspaper shops that have paper rounds;
(13) managers of traditional off-licences (ie those with opening hours that are the same as for public houses);

(14) head teachers and teachers at boarding schools who have pastoral responsibility, if the accommodation is at or near the school;
(15) veterinary surgeons who live near their practice so that they can respond regularly to emergency calls; and
(16) managers of camping and caravan sites living on or near the premises.

Retraining

(IT(E&P)A 2003, ss 311-312)

Where an employer pays the cost of a course undertaken by an employee (or former employee) to provide him with skills for future employment elsewhere, that cost can be a deductible expense of the employer, and may not be a taxable benefit of the employee. The employee must have been full time and have completed at least two years' service.

The exemption is normally dependent on the employee leaving his job no later than two years after completing the course.

Sandwich courses

(SP4/86)

Where an employer releases an employee to take a full-time educational course at a university, technical college or similar educational institution that is open to the public at large, payments for periods of attendance may be treated as exempt from income tax. There are various conditions that attach to this exemption:

(1) the course must last for at least one academic year with an average of at least 20 weeks of full-time attendance; and
(2) the rate of payment must not exceed the greater of £7,000 and the rate of payment that an individual would have received had he been granted a public grant.

Where the rate of payment exceeds the above limits, the full amount is taxable; where the amount of payment is increased during a course, only subsequent payments are taxable.

Education and training

(IT(E&P)A 2003, ss 255-260)

No tax charge arises on payments made to a provider in respect of the costs of providing 'qualifying education or training' for a fundable employee. Similar relief is available for payment or reimbursement of any incidental costs incurred wholly and exclusively as a result of the employee undertaking the course. The exemption is available only where participation is available on similar terms to all employees.

'Qualifying education or training' is education or training which qualifies for grants under the Learning and Skills Act 2000 and its Scottish equivalent. A fundable employee is one who holds an account qualifying under the Learning and Skills Act, s 104 or who is a party to arrangements under s 105 or s 106 of that Act.

4.4.9 Expenses relating to directors and P11D employees

This section deals with problem areas that arise regularly in practice where expenses are paid on behalf of directors and senior employees or where the employer reimburses them.

Travelling expenses

(IT(E&P)A 2003, ss 336-340)

Travel between home and the ordinary place of work does not rank as business travel. Where an individual is 'on call' and assumes the responsibilities of the employment upon leaving home, it may be possible to argue that home to work travel is business, not private, travel, but usually this applies only in exceptional cases. Other travelling expenses are not normally treated as a benefit-in-kind so long as the individual has a 'normal place of work' that he attends the majority of the time. Where an employee performs incidental duties of the employment at another location and travels there directly to or from his home, the allowable expense is the lesser of the travel and subsistence expenses actually incurred, and the expenses that would have been incurred if the journey had started and finished at the normal place of work.

In order to secure tax relief on reimbursed travelling expenses, the employee must keep adequate records so as to distinguish business from non-business travel. Ideally, expenses claims to the employer should show the actual cost of such travel and, if the employer is to obtain a dispensation, the Revenue will need to be satisfied that such internal controls exist.

Approved Mileage Allowance Payments (AMAP)

There is a statutory scheme of flat-rate allowances for business mileage which has applied since 6 April 2002. The fixed rates are the same for the tax years 2002-03 and 2003-04:

	Per mile
Cars and vans:	
First 10,000 miles in tax year	40p
Each additional mile	25p
Motorcycles	24p
Bicycles	20p

The employee cannot claim tax relief for interest on a loan used to buy his car (this was permitted up to 2001-02).

Where an individual is required to use his own car for business, and he is reimbursed at less than the authorised rates, he can claim a deduction equal to the shortfall.

In addition to the mileage allowance payment, an employer can also pay up to 5p per passenger per mile free of tax and NICs for fellow employees carried in the employer's or employee's car or van where the journey constitutes business travel for both driver and passengers. The employee cannot claim any relief if the employer does not pay the passenger rate.

A non-statutory scheme of Fixed Profit Car Scheme rates applied up to 2001-02 (see *Zurich Tax Handbook 2002/2003* at 4.4.9).

Mileage allowances for business travel in a company car

Where an employer reimburses fuel costs which relate to business mileage, the following mileage rates may be paid tax free.

Petrol			*Diesel*	
1400cc or less 10p	1401cc to 2000cc 12p	Over 2000cc 14p	Up to 2000cc 9p	Over 2000cc 12p

It may be possible to negotiate higher rates in particular circumstances (Revenue internet statement 28 January 2002).

Using your bicycle for business

Employees can claim capital allowances on bicycles used for business travel. A tax-free cycling allowance of 20p per business mile can be paid. Where the employer pays less than this rate, the employee can claim a tax deduction for the difference.

Subsistence

The Revenue's view is that it is strictly only the extra costs of living away from home that are allowable. If there are continuing financial commitments at home, the whole cost of living away from home is normally allowed. This concession is not available if the employee has no permanent residence, for example an unmarried person who normally lives in a hotel or club and who gives up that accommodation when away on a business trip. There is a specific exemption where an employee performs his duties wholly overseas and needs board and lodging abroad to do so.

Miscellaneous personal expenses

There is a statutory exemption for employees' miscellaneous personal expenses when they are required to stay away from home overnight on business. This exemption allows employers to meet expenses of up to £5 a night (£10 if overseas). Under the previous rules, incidental personal expenses such as newspapers, laundry and 'phone calls home were often met by employers but, because relief is only available for expenses necessarily incurred in the performance of the duties, these were liable to tax. Payments up to these limits are exempt, which should reduce employers' compliance costs and simplify their administrative procedures. But if the limits are exceeded, the whole of the expense payment is taxable, not just the excess.

Employees' travel and subsistence

There are special rules covering 'triangular travel'.

Triangular travel

Triangular travel occurs where an employee with a normal place of work travels not between home and normal place of work, but between home and another place at which he is required to perform his employment duties.

Example of triangular travel

An employee usually commutes by car from home in Oxford to a normal place of work in London. This is a daily round trip of 114 miles. On a particular day, the employee drives instead to a temporary place of work in Brighton, a round trip of 120 miles.

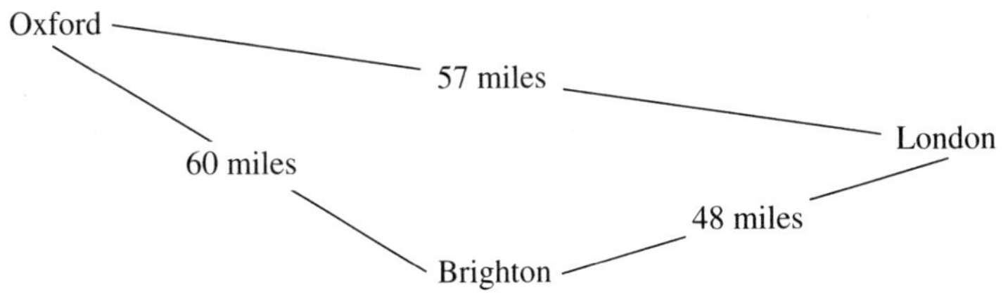

The new rules allow a claim for the full mileage cost of 120 miles. It is not necessary to restrict the claim for the normal commuting costs that would have been incurred if the employee had travelled to London.

Of course, nothing in tax is ever as straightforward as this; for example, the Revenue would not allow the cost of the employee travelling to Brighton if he worked there so regularly that it became a normal place of employment. The Revenue's criterion here is that a place of work becomes a normal place of employment if the employee spends 40% of his time there.

The Revenue has issued a comprehensive guide, *Tax relief for business travel*, to employers.

These rules affect employees in employment that involves travel where tax relief is available for travel between home and various places visited.

The Revenue will review whether the travelling is 'on the job', as opposed to 'to the job'. Such employees are expected to visit a number of places each day and have no base to which they report regularly. Thus, the definition of 'permanent workplace' may create difficulties where an employee reports regularly to a head office or regional base, say, every Tuesday.

Employees who are based at home may also be affected by these rules. The key issue is often whether the home base is an objective requirement of their duties, rather than a personal choice.

Area-based employees whose duties are defined by reference to a specific area (ie a county) have their tax relief restricted if they live outside that area. Tax relief is due only on necessary business journeys within the designated area or to a temporary workplace outside the area.

There are specific anti-avoidance measures (including a 'necessary attendance rule') that require attendance to be an objective requirement of the duties, and not from personal choice or to claim tax relief. It is also a requirement that any changes to a workplace must be significant in the effect on the journey. The Revenue has suggested adopting a ten-mile 'common sense' rule.

Employers should review their travel and subsistence expenses reimbursement policies in the light of the new legislation and determine if changes need to be made.

Site-based employees

A deduction is allowed for the costs of travel to or from any place where attendance at that place is in the performance of the duties of a person's employment. The subsistence costs of site-based employees are also an allowable expense.

Temporary absence from normal place of work

Where an employee is required to work temporarily at a place other than his normal workplace, the deductions for travel expenses described above are available.

Temporary relocation to another office, etc

The Revenue has clarified the circumstances in which employees who are temporarily absent from their normal place of work can claim a deduction for travelling and subsistence expenses. Normally an employee is regarded as temporarily absent from his normal place of work if:

(1) the absence is not for more than 24 months; and
(2) the employee returns to the normal place of work at the end of the period.

If these conditions are satisfied, the employer can pay a subsistence allowance free of tax.

The Revenue takes the view that an individual may also qualify if these conditions are expected to be satisfied at the outset but circumstances subsequently change. Relief is available for the period up to the time when it becomes clear that either condition will be breached.

There are special rules for subsistence allowances given to employees of overseas companies who are seconded to work in the UK for periods of up to two years. While it is not a statutory requirement that the employee is not UK-domiciled, in practice most employees who are temporarily seconded to the UK fall into this category. These rules are dealt with in 24.4.

Overseas travelling expenses

(IT(E&P)A 2003, s 370)

Where some or all of the employment duties are performed abroad, travelling expenses to and from the UK to carry out these duties are specifically regarded as having been necessarily incurred in the performance of the overseas employment. It follows that if those expenses are reimbursed by the employer, no benefit-in-kind arises. Legislative changes have relaxed the rules further so that, while the employee is serving abroad, the employer may pay for an unlimited number of journeys made by the employee to and from the UK without any tax charge arising. However, these journeys must be made wholly and exclusively for the purpose of performing the employment duties.

Moreover, where an employee travels between places where different jobs are performed, and one or more of these jobs are performed wholly or partly overseas, the expenses incurred in travelling overseas are also deemed to be necessarily incurred in performing the duties carried out overseas, so that once again no benefit-in-kind arises. In many cases, there is dual purpose in travelling and a taxable benefit-in-kind arises on the private element. Consequently, where travel expenses relate partly to a foreign holiday taken at the end of the business trip, there would be a taxable benefit-in-kind.

Similarly, a benefit-in-kind may be assessed on some or all of the expense where a spouse accompanies a director or employee and where this is not necessary for business purposes.

The maximum allowance to cover an employee's miscellaneous personal expenses is £10 per night when he is abroad.

A director or employee who travels overseas should be able to substantiate a claim that expenses were necessarily incurred for business purposes by producing details of the expenses and the time spent away from home. A brief itinerary should be available where travel is undertaken within the overseas country or countries. Inspectors of Taxes normally expect that an employer will properly control expenditure, but in certain cases they may wish to see receipted bills or other vouchers.

Spouse's travelling and subsistence expenses

Where a spouse or other member of the family accompanies the director or employee abroad on a business trip, it will be helpful in satisfying the Revenue that no benefit-in-kind arises if the board of directors minutes its decision that the director should be so accompanied. However, this is not generally sufficient in itself and it must be shown that the spouse, etc was able to perform certain tasks that could not be performed by the director.

It may be possible to show this if the spouse has some practical qualification, for example an ability to speak the foreign language concerned. A relative's expenses might also be allowable where the director or employee is in poor health and to travel alone would be impracticable or unreasonable. Where the individual's presence is for the purpose of accompanying his or her spouse at business entertainment functions, the expenses of the trip may be disallowed in calculating the employer's tax liability under the entertainment legislation, even though the expenses may be allowable in determining the employee's tax liability.

Employees working overseas: family visits

(IT(E&P)A 2003, s 371)

Where an employee is abroad for a continuous period of 60 days or more, there is an exemption for amounts borne by the employer in respect of the travelling expenses for visits by the employee's spouse and minor children. The exemption is available for only two journeys by the same person in each direction in a tax year. There is no relief if ultimately the employee bears the expense personally.

Entertaining expenses and round-sum allowances

It is not uncommon for directors or employees to have a round-sum allowance to cover such things as travelling, subsistence and entertaining. In the case of travelling and subsistence, the allowance counts as the director's or employee's taxable income, but a tax deduction may be claimed in respect of any part of the allowance that can be shown to have been spent for business purposes. It is very important to have a record-keeping system that enables such claims to be substantiated. In some situations, it may be better for the employer to dispense with round-sum allowances and reimburse the director or employee for properly substantiated expenditure, since no benefit-in-kind should then arise.

The situation is rather more complex in the case of entertaining expenditure. If an employer reimburses a director's or employee's entertaining expenditure or pays a round-sum allowance that is specifically intended for entertaining, the expense to the employer is disallowed for tax purposes. The reimbursement or allowance is entered on the director's or employee's P11D, but a deduction may be claimed for all the expenditure which is for genuine business purposes. If, on the other hand, the director or employee is given a round-sum allowance not specifically designated as being for entertaining, there is no question of the allowance being disallowed in the employer's tax computation. However, the director or employee would only escape liability on any part of the allowance that could be shown to have been used for business expenditure other than entertainment.

4.5 COMPANY CARS

(IT(E&P)A 2003, s 114)

4.5.1 Car benefits for 2002-03 and future years

With effect from 6 April 2002, a more environmentally friendly regime for calculating the cash equivalent of the benefit where an employer provides a car to an employee or member of his family or household has been introduced. This is based on the published carbon dioxide (CO_2) emissions figure (in grams per kilometre) for a given car. From 1 March 2001 that figure appears in the car log book. For cars registered between 1 January 1998 and 1 March 2001, the emissions figure can be obtained from a booklet published by:

The Vehicle Certification Agency
1 The Eastgate Office Centre
Eastgate Road
Bristol BS5 6XX
Web page: www.vca.gov.uk

The emissions figure is rounded down to the nearest whole 5gm below and is then converted to a percentage using the Revenue table (see Table 4.3). The maximum percentage to be applied to the list price of the car is 35%. The list price is still subject to an overall limit of £80,000.

Diesel cars have a low CO_2 figure but produce other emissions. To maintain an environmental balance with petrol vehicles, the percentage is increased by 3% (up to the maximum 35%), for example if diesel emissions in 2002-03 are 255 grams per kilometre, the percentage is 33% + 2%.

Electric cars are taxed on 9% of list price.

Cars registered before 1 January 1998 do not have a CO_2 emissions figure and the percentage for these vehicles will continue to be based on engine size, but with no discounts for age or business use, as follows:

Engine size (cc)	*Percentage of car's price taxed*
0-1400	15%
1401-2000	22%
2001 and over	32%

A limited number of cars produced on or after that date will also not have a CO_2 figure and the percentage to be used then is:

Engine size (cc)	*Percentage of car's price taxed*
0-1400	15%*
1401-2000	25%*
2001 and over	35%

*Plus 3% supplement for diesel cars

Table 4.3 – CO2 emissions: cars registered from 1 January 1998

CO_2 emissions in grams per kilometre			*Percentage of car's price taxed*
2002-03	*2003-04*	*2004-05*	
165	155	145	15
170	160	150	16
175	165	155	17
180	170	160	18
185	175	165	19
190	180	170	20
195	185	175	21
200	190	180	22
205	195	185	23
210	200	190	24
215	205	195	25
220	210	200	26
225	215	205	27
230	220	210	28
235	225	215	29
240	230	220	30
245	235	225	31
250	240	230	32
255	245	235	33
260	250	240	34
265	255	245	35

Automatic cars

These have higher CO_2 emissions. However, where an employee is disabled (ie holds an 'orange badge'), and can only drive an automatic, the emission figure is taken as that of the 'equivalent manual car', ie the closest non-automatic variant of the car concerned.

Second cars

Second cars are charged at the same rate as first cars.

Reductions in the scale benefit

The scale figures are reduced where an employee was provided with a company car part way through the tax year, or where he ceased to have a company car. However, there is no reduction where the car was not available for use because of repairs, unless it was incapable of being used for at least 30 consecutive days.

Contributions made by an employee towards the cost of the car can be deducted from the list price, up to a maximum of £5,000.

4.5.2 Car benefits for 2001-02 and earlier years

A different system applied up to 2001-02 (see *Zurich Tax Handbook 2002/2003* at 4.5.2).

4.5.3 Private petrol

(IT(E&P)A 2003, s 149)

An additional scale benefit applies where an employer provides private petrol for use in a car to which a scale benefit charge arises. The scale charge for 2002-03 depended entirely on engine size (for cars with a recognised cylinder capacity) as follows:

	Petrol	*Diesel*
Up to 1,400 cc	2,240	2,850
1,401 to 2,000 cc	2,850	2,850
Over 2,000 cc	4,200	4,200

For cars without a cylinder capacity, the scale charge was £4,200 for 2002-03.

For 2003-04 and future years, the charge is calculated by taking the vehicle's CO_2 emissions percentage figure shown in Table 4.3 and multiplying it by £14,400.

The scale figures apply regardless of the amount of private fuel provided. If any is provided, the fuel scale charge is always applied unless the employee reimburses the employer for the full cost. In some cases it may be cost effective for employee to do this and the position should therefore be reviewed before the start of each new tax year.

The charge is reduced if the car is not available for part of the tax year (see 4.5.1) or where fuel is not provided for part of a tax year or the employee makes good the cost during part of the tax year.

4.5.4 Car parking spaces

(IT(E&P)A 2003, s 266(1))

The provision of a car parking space at or near the employee's place of work has not been treated as a taxable benefit since 1988-89. Where an employee pays for car parking himself, he cannot claim a deduction for those charges.

4.5.5 Private use of company vans

(IT(E&P)A 2003, s 154)

FA 1993 introduced a scale charge for employees who have private use of company vans. An employee may be assessed on a standard amount of £500 pa in respect of private use of a van. The amount is reduced to £350 for vans that are four or more years old at the end of the tax year. Any vehicles in excess of 3.5 tons are exempt from tax altogether (unless the vehicle is used wholly or mainly for the employee's private purposes). Where an employee has two or more vans made available for private use at the same time, tax is charged on the scale figure for each van. The standard amount is reduced pro rata where the van is only available part of the year. As for company cars, a £1-for-£1 reduction is made for any contributions made by the employee towards the private use. Where a van is shared among several employees, the standard amount is apportioned among the employees.

It is possible for employees to elect to pay tax on a flat benefit of £5 for every day that the van was made available to them for private use.

4.5.6 Congestion charge

No Schedule E charge arises where an employer pays the congestion charge on a company car or van. It does apply where the congestion charge relates to a vehicle which is not owned by the employer unless the travel into London was an expense incurred wholly and necessarily in the performance of the employee's duties.

4.6 FREE USE OF ASSETS

(IT(E&P)A 2003, s 203)

A taxable benefit arises where an employer makes an asset available for use by a director or P11D employee. The annual amount is 20% of the asset's market value when it was first made available for use by the employee. Assets that may be involved include yachts, furniture, television sets, stereo equipment, company vans, etc – virtually any asset apart from living accommodation and company cars. If the employer rents or hires the asset for a sum in excess of 20% of its original market value, the higher rental charge is substituted as the assessable benefit. A deduction is allowed for any contribution or rental payable by the employee.

A further charge may arise if the ownership of assets is eventually transferred to the employee. The amount may be determined by either the asset's market value at the time of transfer of ownership or, where a higher figure results, its original cost at the time it was first made available as a benefit for any person, less any amounts already charged as benefits in connection with its availability.

The second alternative does not apply to cars.

Example – Transfer of assets

A company provides an employee with the use of a yacht that costs £40,000, with the employee paying a rental of £2,000 pa. After two years the yacht is sold to the employee for its second-hand market value of £20,000. The assessable benefit would be:

		Benefit
		£
Year 1:	£40,000 × 20%	8,000
	Less: rental paid	(2,000)
		6,000
Year 2:	£40,000 × 20%	8,000
	Less: rental paid	(2,000)
		6,000
Year 3:	Cost of yacht	40,000
	Less: benefits assessed in Years 1 and 2	(12,000)
	Amounts paid by employee	(24,000)
		4,000

Where an asset previously made available to an individual is transferred to him (or to another employee) at a time when its market value is still high, it is possible that the total amount charged as a benefit for tax purposes exceeds the original cost. In other cases, the rules may operate to impose a high benefit charge on the transfer of an asset despite its value having depreciated rapidly during the period of use.

Such rules must therefore be considered carefully when planning the provision of an asset for use by an employee or arranging for its transfer to him. It may be that where a tax-efficient remuneration package is desired, transfer of ownership should be avoided where assets have a relatively short useful life.

Example – Ownership of assets

A company provides employees with the use of suits that remain the property of the company. The suits cost £200 and have a useful life of two years, after which they are scrapped. An employee could therefore have an effective benefit of £200, but would be charged tax on only £40 for each of the two tax years.

4.7 BENEFICIAL LOANS

(IT(E&P)A 2003, s 184)

4.7.1 Type of loans that are caught

A charge generally arises for directors and P11D employees on the annual value of beneficial loan arrangements. A loan's 'annual value' is taken as interest at the 'official rate' less the amount of interest (if any) paid by the employee. The official rate is now set annually in advance and is 5% for 2003-04 (also 5% for 2002-03). An additional taxable benefit arises if the loan is subsequently written off or forgiven. The beneficial loan provisions can also apply if a loan is made to a member of an employee's family.

Moreover, the Revenue can assess benefits where credit has been involved, even though there may be no formal loan. In particular, a director who overdraws his current account with the company is regarded as having obtained a loan.

Almost all loans by employers (and persons connected with them) are caught as the legislation deems such loans to have been given by reason of the employment. Originally there was only a single exception in that this rule did not apply where the employee was related to the employer and it could be shown that the loan was given for family reasons. Loans made by an employer whose business includes lending money to the general public do not give rise to a charge on the employees provided the loans are made on similar terms to the public.

4.7.2 Beneficial loans used for qualifying purpose

No charge arises in respect of a cheap loan where the money borrowed has been applied for a qualifying purpose, for example to purchase shares in a close company in which the individual has a material interest or where he is employed full time in the conduct and management of the company's business.

4.7.3 *De minimis* exemption

All cheap or interest-free loans made to an individual employee that do not exceed £5,000 are exempt. This figure excludes loans used to buy shares in employee-controlled companies (see 9.6).

4.7.4 Employee loans written off

If the loan is written off, the amount forgiven is treated as assessable income for that year even if the company no longer employs the person concerned. The only exception here is if the loan is forgiven on the employee's death.

Some care must be taken if it is decided to clear a loan by making an *ex gratia* or compensation payment to an employee on termination of employment. An income tax liability will arise if the loan is formally written off. However, no liability normally arises if the employee receives a cheque as an *ex gratia* or compensation payment and uses that sum to clear his outstanding loan. It is recommended that professional advice be taken in such circumstances.

4.7.5 Further information

The Revenue issued leaflet IR145, which explains how loans provided by employers to employees are taxed.

4.8 LIVING ACCOMMODATION

(IT(E&P)A 2003, ss 105-106)

4.8.1 Introduction

The income tax charge that generally applies where an employee is provided with accommodation (unless it is representative accommodation: see 4.4.8) depends on whether the property is owned or rented by the employer. In the past, where the employer owned the property, the assessable amount was usually the gross annual value for rating purposes. Despite the abolition of domestic rates, this treatment continued to apply for properties on existing rating lists (see 4.4.7). For new properties and those where there have been major improvements, the Revenue makes an estimate of what the gross annual value would have been had rates continued.

Where the property is rented by the employer, the assessable amount is the greater of the rent paid and the annual value as above. In addition, a charge may arise on the annual value of any furniture and fixtures, and on any occupier's expenses borne by the company such as water rates, decorations, gardener's wages, etc.

An additional charge may arise where the employer paid more than £75,000 to acquire the property. The amount assessable is a percentage of the excess of the property's cost over £75,000. The percentage to be applied is the official rate of interest used for beneficial loans (see 4.7) as at the beginning of the tax year.

Example – Charge on living accommodation in excess of £75,000

A company director occupies a property owned by the company that has a gross annual value of £2,000. The cost of the property in 1998 was £95,000. The director will be assessed on the following amount for 2003-04:

	£	£
Gross annual value		2,000
Additional charge:		
Cost in 1998	95,000	
Less:	(75,000)	
Total	20,000	
Assessment on £20,000 at official rate of 5%		1,000
Total		3,000

4.8.2 Properties owned for more than six years

Where the company has owned the property for at least six years, the figure taken into account in computing the additional charge is the market value at the time it was made available, rather than the cost. The actual cost (including improvements) to the employer is still used to determine whether the provisions apply. Consequently, properties the actual cost of which was less than £75,000 (including the cost of any improvements) are not within the scope of this additional charge even if their market value exceeds £75,000. Where the actual cost exceeded £75,000, the additional charge is based on the market value.

Example – Charge on living accommodation purchased over six years ago

In the example in 4.8.1, assume the company has owned the property for more than six years and that in May 1998, when the director first occupies it, the market value is £191,000. As the original cost of the property exceeded £75,000, the director will be assessed on the following amount for 2003-04:

	£	£
Gross annual value		2,000
Additional charge:		
Market value in 1998	191,000	
Less:	(75,000)	
Total	116,000	
Assessment on £116,000 at official rate of 5%		5,800
Total		7,800

4.8.3 Possible reduction in taxable amount

It may be possible to reduce the taxable amount where the employee is required to occupy a property that is larger than would normally be needed for his own purposes. In *Westcott v Bryan* (1969) 45 TC 476 a director was required to live in a large house so that he could entertain customers. He was allowed a reduction in the taxable amount to cover the relevant proportion of the annual value and the running expenses.

Some care is needed if it is intended to claim relief in this way. This claim succeeded because the house was larger than needed for the director and his family. It would not have succeeded had the property merely been more expensive than he would have chosen. It was also helpful that the company directors had approved board minutes setting out their requirement and the business reason for it.

Where part of the property is used exclusively for work, the taxable amount may be reduced on a pro rata basis. Revenue Helpsheet IR202 contains working sheets that enable you to compute your taxable benefits in this situation.

4.8.4 Possible increase in taxable benefit

It is sometimes the case that an employer offers a choice: salary of £x or salary of £y plus a house. In this situation, the difference between £x and £y may be taxed if this exceeds the normal benefit-in-kind calculated along the lines set out in 4.8.1-4.8.2.

4.8.5 Holiday accommodation and foreign properties

Some employers buy holiday flats, cottages, etc for use by staff. In practice, generally the Revenue apportions the assessable amount for the year among those employees who have occupied the property. The assessment can be reduced by letting the accommodation to third parties when directors and employees do not require it.

A practical problem arises with overseas properties. Because there is no rateable value, the benefit is the annual rent that the property would normally command on the open market. However, where this applies, there is normally no additional charge based on the excess of the property's cost over £75,000 (see 4.8.1). An ESC avoiding such a double charge was published on 28 November 1995.

4.9 MISCELLANEOUS BENEFITS

Council tax

Where an employer pays the council tax on behalf of an employee, this is normally chargeable as part of the employee's remuneration package, resulting in a charge to both income tax and NICs. The one exception to this is where the employee is a representative occupier (see 4.4.8).

Mobile 'phones

(FA 1991, s 30)

Tax was charged on a standard amount of £200 pa per 'phone where it was used privately. 'Private use' meant making personal calls or accepting reverse charge calls; it did not include receiving normal personal calls. The charge was abolished from 6 April 1999.

Telephone rental

The Revenue treats the full amount of the rental paid by the employer as a taxable benefit-in-kind even though the 'phone may be partly (or mainly) used for business calls. The decision in *Lucas v Cattell* (1972) 48 TC 353 was that the expenditure on rental had a dual purpose (ie that a 'phone is intended to be used for both business and personal use) and therefore no part of it was allowable.

Liability insurance and payment of uninsured liabilities

FA 1995 provides that employees are not subject to tax on a benefit-in-kind where their employer pays premiums on items such as directors' and officers' liability insurance or a professional indemnity insurance policy. Furthermore, the Act also provides that payment of an employee's uninsured liabilities does not give rise to a benefit-in-kind provided they arise from the employee's work. This is subject to the overriding requirement that the liabilities could have been insured against and this means that those arising from, for example criminal convictions, cannot attract relief.

Medical insurance

The cost of medical insurance is normally assessable on P11D employees. Where the employer has a group scheme, a proportion of the total premiums is related to individual employees. There is an exception in that the premiums are exempt to the extent that they provide cover for an employee working outside the UK.

Club subscriptions

A benefit-in-kind is deemed to arise where an employer pays or reimburses an employee's subscription to a club, even though the employee may only belong to the club to entertain the employer's customers.

In-house tax and financial advice

This is a type of expenditure that the Revenue has ignored in the past, but certain Inspectors of Taxes are now treating this as a benefit-in-kind where the cost can clearly be allocated to particular employees. Similarly, the Revenue will seek to assess directors on a benefit-in-kind where work on their personal taxation affairs has been carried out by the company's auditors, the cost being recovered in whole or in part from the company.

Christmas parties and other functions

The Revenue does not assess a benefit in respect of 'modest' expenditure on a Christmas party for staff, provided the party is open to all staff. The limit regarded as modest in this context is currently £150 per head (£75 up to 2002-03). If the cost (including VAT) amounts to £151 or more, the whole amount is taxable, not just the excess. Although this rule is generally attributed to Christmas parties, it may apply to a function at another time of year. The £150 annual 'allowance' can be used to cover the cost of more than one function.

Legal fees

There may be expenditure incurred for the benefit of the company's business but nevertheless is deemed to give rise to a benefit-in-kind. A leading case in this connection concerned a company director who was accused of dangerous driving. It was necessary for the company's business that he should not be imprisoned and the company paid his legal expenses. Although the lawyers engaged by the company were more expensive than the director would have used himself, the expenditure by the company was treated as a benefit-in-kind.

Outplacement counselling

(IT(E&P)A 2003, s 310)

The value of outplacement services provided to employees made redundant is exempt from income tax. Such services may include assistance with CVs, job searches, office equipment provisions and advice on interview skills.

Goods and services provided at a discount to the normal price ('in-house benefits')

Where employees are allowed to purchase goods or services from their employer, no tax charge arises provided they pay an amount equal to the employer's cost. The House of Lords eventually decided that 'cost' meant marginal, and not average, cost (*Pepper v Hart* [1992] STC 898). This will normally produce a significantly lower benefit.

Following this case, the Revenue published an SP with regard to teachers, employees within the transport industry and other employees who receive goods or services from their employer. It stated that the *Pepper v Hart* decision means that:

(1) rail or bus travel by employees on terms that do not displace fare-paying passengers involves no or negligible additional costs;
(2) goods sold at a discount that leave employees paying at least the wholesale price involve no or negligible net benefit;
(3) where teachers pay 15% or more of a school's normal fees, there is no taxable benefit;
(4) professional services that do not require additional employees or partners (eg legal and financial services) have no or negligible cost to the employer (provided the employee meets the cost of any disbursements).

Funded Unapproved Retirement Benefit Schemes (FURBS)

(IT(E&P)A, s 386)

Some employers make contributions to a FURBS. The creation of a FURBS must be reported to the company's Inspector of Taxes within three months.

The employer's contributions must also be reported on Form P11D and the employee is treated as if he had received a benefit the cost of which is equal to the amount paid into the FURBS. See 12.11 for further details.

Making good benefits-in-kind for previous years

The cash equivalent of any benefit chargeable to tax under s 203 IT(E&P)A 2003 is the cost of the benefit 'less so much (if any) of it as is made good by the employee to those providing the benefit'. The Revenue accepts that there is no time limit for making good and, provided the relevant year's assessment has not been determined, there could be some merit in the person concerned taking further remuneration now and using the net cash left to him after PAYE to make good benefits provided for earlier years. This could be a particularly good idea where a director of a family company is faced with a Schedule E assessment plus penalties and interest in respect of prior year incorrect returns because benefits have not been reported properly in the past.

For beneficial loans, however, the Revenue's view is that the cash equivalent can be reduced by a payment in a later year only if the interest is paid under an obligation that existed at the time of the loan.

4.10 GIFTS OF SHARES

A gift of shares to an employee is normally a taxable benefit, the charge being based on the shares' market value. Much the same applies where an employee buys shares for less than their real market value. If the shares are given to the employee by a shareholder, he is normally treated as if he had made a disposal of the shares at their market value, and therefore may be liable for CGT.

The tax position where an employee is allowed to subscribe for new shares at an undervalue is broadly the same. The employee is taxed on the difference between the amount he pays to subscribe for the shares and their market value. However, dealing with matters in this way usually avoids any CGT problems for the shareholders (since there is no disposal by the existing shareholders or the company, merely an issue of new shares).

A company must report the acquisition of shares by an employee within 92 days of the end of the relevant tax year to:

Inland Revenue
Employee Share Schemes Unit
Savings and Investment Division
First Floor, South West Wing
Bush House, Strand
London WC2B 4RD

PAYE must be accounted for if either the shares are marketable securities or trading arrangements are in place.

4.11 PROFIT-SHARING SCHEMES

(TA 1988, ss 186-187)

These schemes were effectively phased-out in 2002-03.

They operated by means of a trust, with the trustees receiving payments from the company's profits to enable them to buy shares on the employees' behalf. The amount that could be appropriated to an employee under the scheme could not exceed £3,000 or, if greater, 10% of the employee's remuneration for PAYE purposes, with an overall limit of £8,000.

The trustees must retain the shares for a period of two years; if the trustees then retain the shares for a further year, there is no income tax charge on him. If the employee sells them within three years of appropriation, an income tax charge arises based on the 'locked-in value', ie the lower of the shares' market value when they were appropriated by the trust fund or the sale proceeds. This charge is reduced by 50% where the individual is no longer an employee because of his leaving through injury, disability, redundancy or reaching pensionable age.

Provided the shares are held in trust for three years, normally the only liability arising to the employee is CGT when he disposes of the shares appropriated to him. The capital gains liability arises on the difference between the disposal proceeds of these shares less their open market value on the day on which they were appropriated to him. The growth in value from the date of acquisition by the trust to the date of appropriation is tax free.

The employee is entitled to dividends paid on the shares during the period of retention by the trustees. Such dividends are taxable in the normal way.

Following the introduction of all employee share ownership schemes (see 4.12), approved profit-sharing schemes have been phased out. No application for approval could be granted if received by the Revenue after 5 April 2001, and no appropriation of shares under such a plan can be made after 31 December 2002.

For further details, see Revenue leaflet IR95.

4.12 ALL-EMPLOYEE SHARE SCHEMES

(IT(E&P)A 2003, ss 488-515)

FA 2000 established a new type of share scheme which enjoys a much more generous range of tax reliefs than any previous all-employee share scheme. The new scheme may involve one or more of the following elements:

- Free shares
- Partnership shares
- Matching shares.

The basic principle behind this scheme is that all employees should participate on similar terms. However, if an employer awards free shares, the award may be partly or wholly by reference to performance targets. Under the scheme, trustees acquire shares in the employing or holding company of a group. No Schedule E tax or NICs are payable on the award of shares. All income and capital growth that arises while the trustees hold shares will normally be tax free. The shares must be fully paid-up ordinary shares in a company that is not controlled by another company or shares in a quoted subsidiary of a company that is not a close company (see 26.13).

4.12.1 Free shares

An employee may be awarded free shares with a value of up to £3,000 pa. The shares may be awarded partly by reference to criteria based on salary, length of service, etc. In such a case, other employees may be awarded shares by reference to performance provided the highest performance-linked award does not exceed four times the highest award by reference to non-performance linked criteria. In other cases (eg where all awards are by reference to performance), the employer must demonstrate to the Revenue's satisfaction that the performance targets are broadly comparable.

Wherever awards are to be made by reference to performance, the targets and other criteria must be communicated to employees in advance. Performance criteria may be linked to individual, team, divisional or corporate performance.

Free shares must be held by the trustees for a period of between three and five years. Shares can, at the employer's discretion, be awarded so that they will be forfeited if the employee leaves within three years.

4.12.2 Partnership shares

Employees may relinquish up to £1,500 of their pay in return for 'partnership' shares being acquired by the trustees on their behalf. No Schedule E tax or NICs arise on salary foregone in this way, but the employing company receives a deduction in arriving at its taxable profits equal to the amount relinquished. The partnership shares cannot be subject to forfeiture, but the scheme rules can require the trustees to pay out on the employee leaving.

Where an employee withdraws from the scheme within three years, income tax and NICs are payable on the shares' market value at the date of withdrawal. Where he withdraws after three but before five years have elapsed, the employee is charged on the lower of the shares' initial value or their market value at the time that he withdraws.

Where an employment comes to an end because of disability or redundancy, the shares may be withdrawn tax free even if this occurs within the three-year period.

4.12.3 Matching shares

If an employer so wishes, matching shares can be awarded to employees on a basis of up to 2:1 (ie shares worth £3,000 for an employee who relinquished salary of £1,500 in order to 'buy' partnership shares worth £1,500). An award of matching shares may be made on the basis that they are forfeited if the employee leaves within three years or withdraws his partnership shares during that period.

4.12.4 Dividends

The legislation gives employers a choice of whether to offer dividend reinvestment. If dividends are paid out they are taxable income for the employees. However, dividends may be reinvested tax free up to £1,500 pa.

4.13 NON-APPROVED SHARE OPTIONS

(IT(E&P)A 2003, s 471)

4.13.1 Introduction

A Schedule E income tax charge may arise on the exercise of a share option that was granted by reason of the individual's office or employment. The legislation was introduced on a piecemeal basis and it is often difficult to discern any clear or logical structure or principles that underlie it.

4.13.2 Non-approved share options

(IT(E&P)A 2003, s 471)

A tax charge may arise on either the grant or the exercise of the option.

Grant of the option

A charge may arise only if the option has a potential life of more than ten years (seven years for options granted before 17 March 1998). Even if the option is capable of being exercised more than ten years later, the Revenue is unlikely to assess a value greater than the difference between the shares' value at the time the option is granted, and the aggregate of the amount (if any) paid for the grant of option and the amount payable under the option.

Exercise of the option

A person who is subject to tax under Schedule E Case I (see 4.1.1) may be subject to an income tax charge when he exercises a non-approved share option that has been granted to him by reason of his office or employment. The charge is not dependent on his selling the shares but arises on any profit or gain that he is deemed to have made by exercising the option. Normally the profit is simply the difference between the shares' market value at the time he exercises his option and the price payable under the option.

Example – Exercise of share options

A was granted an option to acquire 1,000 shares in XYZ Ltd at a price of £2 per share. After five years have elapsed, he exercises the option and pays £2,000 to acquire the 1,000 shares. By this time the shares have grown in value to £5 per share. *A* will be assessed for the year in which he exercises the option. His profit will be assessed as £3,000, ie:

	£
Market value of 1,000 shares	5,000
Less: amount paid	(2,000)
	3,000

If the employee agrees to pay his employer's NICs on the profit from exercising the option, the NICs are deducted in arriving at the taxable amount.

4.13.3 Employee's residence status

No charge arises under these provisions if the employee was not resident and ordinarily resident in the UK at the date the option was granted. This is because the individual must be UK-resident and ordinarily resident if he is to be chargeable to tax under Schedule E Case I. However, the charge still arises where an individual who was resident and ordinarily resident when the option was granted ceases to be UK-resident before it is exercised. In some cases, the Schedule E charge may be reduced because of relief due under a double taxation agreement. There is a helpful article on the way the Revenue applies the Schedule E rules to internationally mobile employees in *Tax Bulletin* October 2001.

4.13.4 Other employee share options

(IT(E&P)A 2003, ss 193-197)

Where an individual exercises an option that was granted to him as an employee, but at a time when he was not chargeable to tax under Schedule E Case I, and he retains the shares, an income tax charge may arise on their eventual disposal. The legislation on beneficial loans contains deeming provisions that treat the difference between the shares' market value at the time the option is exercised and the amount payable to exercise the option as if it were a loan. On a subsequent sale or disposal of the shares, the loan is deemed to be written off and a Schedule E charge arises if the individual is UK-resident at that time. If you think you may be in this situation, you should seek professional advice.

4.13.5 Reporting requirements

Ask your accountant to obtain a copy of *Tax Bulletin* February 1994 for your reference. The grant or exercise of options must be notified within 92 days of the end of the tax year.

PAYE must be accounted for on profits from options that are both granted and exercised after 25 November 1996 and where the shares are marketable securities or trading arrangements are in place. A further charge can arise unless the employee reimburses his employer within a defined period (see Q6 at 21.1.4).

4.13.6 Capital gains tax

See 14.4.3 on the CGT consequences of disposing of shares acquired under an unapproved share option.

4.14 APPROVED SHARE OPTION SCHEMES

(IT(E&P)A 2003, ss 517-526)

4.14.1 Introduction

There are three main types of approved share option schemes for employees: save as you earn (SAYE)-linked share option schemes, executive share option schemes and the EMI scheme (see 4.15).

Approved SAYE-linked schemes were introduced in 1980. Their main features are that there is a limit on the value of the shares that may be allocated to an employee, and participation in the scheme must be open to all full-time employees who have completed five years' service.

In 1984 the Government introduced a further category of approved share options intended to cover special arrangements for senior executives. The maximum amounts involved are much more generous and there is no requirement that the option be granted to all employees.

It is possible for an employer to establish both types of scheme and, indeed, to grant non-approved share options as well.

4.14.2 Approved SAYE-linked share option schemes

These schemes entail the grant of an option for employees to purchase company shares at a price that must not be 'manifestly less' than 80% of their market value at the time the options are granted. The employee is required to take out an SAYE-linked savings scheme (maximum £250 pm) and may use the proceeds to exercise the share option three, five or seven years later, depending on the rules of the particular scheme. No income tax liability arises on the grant or exercise of the options. CGT is charged on an eventual disposal of the shares.

For further details obtain a copy of Revenue leaflet IR97.

4.14.3 Executive share option schemes

The general principle is that an income tax charge may arise on the exercise of a share option, but certain approved share option schemes may be established that avoid such an income tax liability. CGT may still apply, but only on a subsequent disposal of the shares concerned.

4.14.4 Conditions for approval

In order to receive Revenue approval, the following conditions must be satisfied:

(1) Participation in the scheme must be open only to full-time directors or employees or to part-time employees working at least 20 hours pw. Part-time directors may not participate in this scheme: the Revenue has indicated that it regards a director who works 25 hours pw as full-time. The employer may choose which of the employees are to be permitted to participate in the scheme.

(2) Where the employer is a close company, no participant must own (or be entitled to acquire as a result of the grant of the option) more than 10% of the company's shares. Furthermore, no individual who has owned more than 10% of the company's shares within the previous 12 months can participate.

(3) The price at which the option is to be exercised must not be 'manifestly less' than the shares' value at the time the option is granted.

(4) There is a limit on the number of shares over which a particular employee may be granted options. The scheme must limit the employee's options to shares with a market value at the time the options are granted that does not exceed £30,000.

(5) The shares issued under the scheme must be fully paid ordinary shares of the company or its parent company. They must be shares either quoted on a recognised stock exchange, or in a non-close company controlled by a quoted company, or in a company not under the control of another company.

(6) Options must not be transferable.

(7) The exemption from income tax applies only to options exercised between three and ten years after they are granted.

(8) There has been an income tax charge on individuals who exercise options under the scheme more than once every three years. This three-

year time limit was waived if a director or employee died and the option was exercised by the personal representatives within one year of death. The charge has been removed altogether by FA 2003 in relation to options exercised after 8 April 2003.

You may find it helpful to obtain a copy of Revenue leaflet IR101.

4.14.5 Options granted before 17 July 1995

Different rules applied up to 17 July 1995. Basically, an executive could be granted approved options over shares with a market value of up to four times his remuneration. Furthermore, in certain circumstances, options could be granted at a discount of up to 15% on the market value.

Profits realised from the exercise of such options are still exempt from income tax (provided the other conditions in 4.15.4 are satisfied).

4.15 ENTERPRISE MANAGEMENT INCENTIVES (EMI)

(IT(E&P)A 2003, ss 527-541)

Key aspects of the EMI option scheme are as follows:

(1) Share options can be issued to employees (until FA 2001 received royal assent, there was a limit of 15 employees).
(2) The shares over which options are granted can have a value of up to £100,000 per employee. This refers to the value at the time the options are granted. The total value of shares over which options can be granted is £3m (£1.5m before FA 2001).
(3) The price at which options may be exercised may be more or less than market value at the time the options are granted.
(4) The only income tax charge is on exercise of the options and is equal to the difference between the shares' market value at the time of grant less the exercise price. If the options are granted at the market value, no tax is payable.
(5) If the shares are readily convertible assets at the time the option is exercised, NICs are charged on the same basis as the income tax charge described above. If the options were issued at market value, there is no charge. There are also significant CGT benefits for the employees.
(6) The shares acquired by the employees qualify for the business asset rate of taper relief. Taper relief provides relief for CGT for individuals based on the length of ownership. Under the EMI rules, the period of ownership is deemed to start from when the share options are granted (the rules for other share option schemes are that the period starts when the shares are acquired). Overall this means that, provided the shares are sold two years after the options are granted (calculated by income tax year), the CGT rate will be 10%.

Only certain companies can operate the scheme, and certain employees may be ineligible. A summary of the rules is as follows:

(a) the company must be independent and not under the control of another company;
(b) it must be carrying on a qualifying trade defined as for EIS purposes (see 11.6.4) – this trade must be carried on mainly in the UK;
(c) its gross assets cannot exceed £30m at the time the options are granted (£15m up to 31 December 2001);
(d) the employee must be employed for at least 25 hours pw or, if less, 75% of his working time;
(e) the option ceases to qualify once the employee no longer meets the 25 hour per week requirement (this rule has been relaxed for reservists who were required to serve in the Iraq war);
(f) the employee must not own more than 30% of the shares in the company; and
(g) he can only participate in one Revenue-approved share option scheme.

4.16 RESTRICTED SHARES AND SHARES IN SUBSIDIARY COMPANIES

(IT(E&P)A 2003, ss 417-470)

4.16.1 General

FA 1988 contained provisions that may apply in relation to shares acquired by reason of an individual's employment charged under Schedule E Case I (see 4.1.1). The legislation may apply to any shares acquired in this way whether by exercise of an option, subscription for new shares or purchase of existing shares. Liability to tax under Schedule E may arise:

(1) when any restrictions affecting the employee's shares are removed; or
(2) when the employee shareholder receives any special benefit by virtue of ownership; or
(3) where the shares are in a 'dependent subsidiary' (this charge was removed with effect from 16 April 2003).

Tax charged in this way can be especially onerous as the individual may not have realised any cash.

4.16.2 Removal of restrictions

Tax may be charged on the increase in value that accrues from the removal of restrictions. There are, however, certain circumstances in which restrictions can be removed without a tax charge (see Figure 4.1).

Figure 4.1 – Does removal of restrictions mean there is an income tax charge under Schedule E?

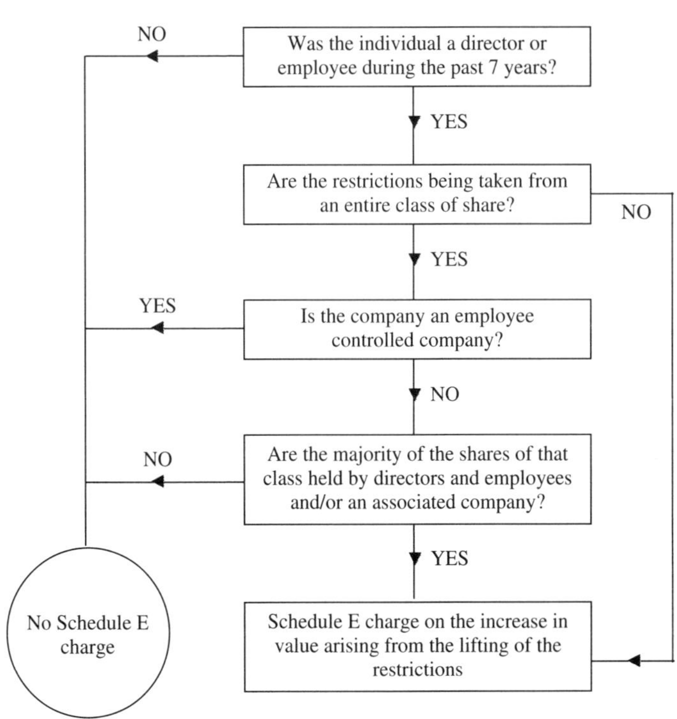

Example of tax charge on removal of restrictions

X acquires 1,000 shares in the company for which he works. The shares do not have any rights to dividend. Two years later, the restrictions are removed so that the shares have normal dividend rights. Suppose the figures work out like this:

Value of shares with full dividend rights	£3 per share
Value of shares with no dividend rights	£1 per share
Increase in value from removal of restrictions	£2 per share

X will therefore be taxed on £2,000 (1,000 × £2 per share)

4.16.3 Shares in a dependent subsidiary

This legislation ceased to apply with effect from 16 April 2003. However, the following may still be relevant in relation to 2002-03 and for the period 6-15 April 2003.

A company was regarded as a dependent subsidiary if there is any significant amount of trading with the parent company or another member of the group. A company that was a subsidiary was deemed to be a dependent subsidiary unless the directors certified each year that it is not and the auditors confirmed their agreement to this. There was a two-year deadline for the directors to issue their certificate; if they failed to do so the subsidiary is automatically regarded as a dependent subsidiary. Attempts to persuade the Revenue to extend this period have consistently been rebuffed.

Where an employee held shares in a dependent subsidiary, a tax charge could arise on the growth in the value that takes place at the earliest of the following times:

(1) the time when he actually disposes of the shares;
(2) the date the company ceases to be a dependent subsidiary;
(3) the expiry of seven years from the date of acquisition.

A charge could arise even though the company was not a dependent subsidiary when the person acquired his shares if it subsequently becomes a dependent subsidiary.

The SA return pack contains some very useful helpsheets that should enable you to compute any taxable benefit for 2002-03.

The FA 2003 abolished the legislation on shares in dependent subsidiaries because it introduced a new charge which catches profits arising from the artificial manipulation of share rights.

4.16.4 Long-term incentive plans

FA 1998 introduced two new provisions which apply in relation to shares acquired during the period 17 March 1998-16 April 2003.

Shares subject to forfeiture

An award of shares to employees can be subject to certain targets being met, or sometimes the shares are given at the outset on condition that they will be forfeited if a target is not met. The risk of forfeiture is lifted when a target is met and the employee then becomes the unconditional owner of the shares.

FA 1998 clarified the tax position. There is a charge to tax when shares are first awarded if there is a risk of forfeiture more than five years after they are first awarded. Otherwise there is no charge to income tax until the risk of forfeiture is lifted or, if sooner, when the shares are sold.

These provisions apply to shares awarded on or after 17 March 1998. Advice on practical aspects and what counts as restrictions, etc are contained in *Tax Bulletin* April 2000.

As regards the treatment of shares awarded prior to 17 March 1998, see *Tax Bulletin* June 1998.

Convertible shares

An income tax charge arises on the value of any new class of shares, less an allowance for any income tax already paid, when a share conversion takes place. This is designed to cover schemes where an employee receives shares with a low value that are later converted to shares with a much higher value.

These provisions apply to shares awarded on or after 17 March 1998, but will not normally apply if the majority of the shares of the class converting are held by people who are not employees or directors.

PAYE must also be operated where any shares or conversions are readily convertible assets.

4.16.5 New legislation on restricted shares and convertible shares

The Inland Revenue has found that the legislation on Long Term Incentive Plans allows scope for avoidance.

The FA 2003 contains new provisions which are intended to impose an income tax charge on the full amount of the economic benefit obtained by the employee. The new rules do not apply to securities acquired before 16 April 2003 nor to disposals of shares acquired after that date if the disposal occurs before an 'Appointed Day' in August 2003.

In the past, an employee could acquire shares which were subject to forfeiture. The Schedule E charge by reference to acquisition would normally have been trivial. Before the forfeiture period came to an end, the company might pay a substantial dividend. When the forfeiture period expired, the market value of the shares was substantially reduced by the payment of that dividend and the amount charged under Schedule E would have been limited to this. The overall effect was that the employee received his profit as a dividend which was subject to income tax at a more favourable rate. The intention behind the new rules is that the amount charged under Schedule E should be the market value before reduction by reason of the dividend.

On the other hand, the FA 1998 legislation has worked against some employees in that the full increase in value has been subject to income tax at the time that restrictions ceased to apply. The new rules will impose income tax only on the increase in value that arises from the removal of restrictions.

Example of difference between the old and new rules

Mr T is given shares on 1 January 2004 that have an open market value of £1,000. However, Mr T has to forfeit them if he leaves his employer before 1 January 2010. The effect of this restriction is to depress the value on acquisition to £650 (ie a 35% discount). When the forfeiture provisions cease to apply on 1 January 2010, the shares are worth £5,000.

The old rules would have produced a tax charge on £650 for 2003-04 and on £4,350 for 2010-11.

The new rules impose the same charge for 2003–04 but limit the charge in 2010-11 to £1,750, ie 35% of £5,000.

4.17 OPTIONS TO ACQUIRE GILTS

The treatment of non-approved employee share options was regarded as disadvantageous, but this was because of specific legislation on **share** options; the rules governing options involving other assets has been quite different. However, the FA 2003 introduced new rules that apply to options over other securities such as British Government securities ('gilts') which are granted after 15 April 2003.

Under the old rules, an income tax charge could arise at the time an option is granted if the option has a market value. However, if the exercise of the option was conditional on the employee achieving demanding performance targets it is arguable that the option had little or no value at the time it is granted. Furthermore, no Schedule E income tax charge would normally arise on the exercise of the option.

The FA 2003 provisions mean that a profit on the exercise of such an option granted after 15 April 2003 will generally be subject to income tax under Schedule E.

4.18 OPTIONS TO ACQUIRE OTHER COMPANY ASSETS

The treatment of options involving other assets is quite different. An income tax charge may arise at the time an option is granted if the option has a market value. However, if the price at which the option may be exercised is higher than the asset's present market value, it is arguable that the option has little or no value at the time it is granted.

No Schedule E income tax charge would normally arise on the exercise of the option. Furthermore, on a subsequent disposal of the asset there would normally be liability only for CGT on the profit over the amount paid. Although special care needs to be taken where the director or employee is connected (perhaps as a shareholder) with the company that grants the option, this type of option can provide substantial benefits.

Example – Option to acquire assets

A company director, who is not a shareholder, is granted the option to purchase surplus development land owned by the company for £150,000 at any time during a period of ten years. The land has a market value of only £125,000 at the time the option is granted and the option, therefore, has only a small value at that time. When the option is exercised the land has a market value of £250,000 and the director has in effect acquired a capital asset at a discount of £100,000 on its current market value. This discount would not normally be subject to income tax.

4.19 GOLDEN HELLOS

These are payments made to induce a prospective employee to take up employment with the company and are occasionally not taxable. In *Pritchard v Arundale* (1971) 47 TC 680, which involved a firm of chartered accountants, a senior partner was approached by a client to leave his practice and become a director of the client's company. In order to induce him to do this, he was given shares in the company that were held to be not a reward for services to be rendered in the future, but an inducement to leave his practice and take up the employment. It was therefore not taxable.

In *Vaughan-Neil v IRC* [1979] STC 644 a barrister received £40,000 to induce him to give up his practice and join a company as its 'in-house adviser'. Once again it was held that the payment was not taxable. By contrast, in *Glantre Engineering Ltd v Goodhand* [1983] STC 1 a payment by an engineering company to induce an employee of a firm of accountants to join them was held to be taxable.

The principles that emerge from these three cases are as follows:

(1) it must be clear from the facts that the payment is an inducement and not a reward for future services;
(2) the payment must not be returnable if the person does not take up the employment; and
(3) it is probably more likely that the payment will be accepted as non-taxable if the recipient has previously been in practice or self-employed rather than an employee of another company.

Shilton v Wilmshurst [1991] STC 88 extended these principles by deciding that a payment made by a football club to a footballer about to transfer as an inducement to him to join his new club was taxable. The House of Lords held that an emolument from an employment meant an emolument for being or becoming an employee and therefore would include a sum paid by a third party as an inducement to enter into a contract of employment to perform services in the future. It was not necessary for the payer to have any interest in the performance of those services.

In *Silva v Charnock* 2202 SpC 332, the taxpayer had taken a career break in order to study for a MBA. Her tuition fees cost her £18,000. After getting her MBA, she took a new job and received a signing-on bonus of £18,000. It was held that this was not taxable as it fell within the exemption contained in TA 1988, s200B.

4.20 RESTRICTIVE COVENANTS

(IT(E&P)A 2003, s 155)

Where the present, past or future holder of an office or employment gives an undertaking that restricts his conduct or activities, any sum paid in respect of that restrictive covenant is treated as remuneration from the office or employment for the year in which the payment is received. This rule applies even where the covenant is not legally valid. In some cases, valuable consideration other than money is given for the restrictive covenant and in such a situation a sum equal to the value of that consideration is treated as having been paid. The payment may not necessarily come from the employer and so a payment to an employee that was made by a major shareholder in a family company might well be caught under these provisions.

4.21 REDUNDANCY PAYMENTS

(IT(E&P)A 2003, s 309)

A statutory redundancy payment made under the Employment Protection (Consolidation) Act 1978 is exempt from tax, although it may need to be taken into account in computing the tax payable on a termination payment (see 4.22). The Revenue generally treats payment to an employee under a non-statutory redundancy scheme as exempt under SP1/94 where the following conditions are satisfied:

(1) payments are made only on accounts of redundancy as defined in s 81 of the 1978 Act;
(2) the individual has at least two years' continuous service;
(3) payments are made to all relevant employees and not merely to a selected group of employees; and
(4) the payments are not excessively large in relation to earnings and length of service.

In *Mairs v Haughey* [1993] STC 569 the Revenue sought to tax a payment made to an employee for giving up contingent redundancy rights. The Revenue argued that the payment constituted an emolument of the employment, but it was held that a redundancy payment is not an emolument and a lump sum paid in lieu of a right to receive such payment is equally not an emolument. This case has also cast doubt on the view generally held within the Revenue that a termination payment is always taxable where the employee is contractually entitled to it.

4.22 GOLDEN HANDSHAKES AND OTHER TERMINATION PAYMENTS

(IT(E&P)A 2003, s 401)

4.22.1 Introduction

Where a director's or employee's contract of service is terminated, it may be possible for a compensation or *ex gratia* payment to be made that is either wholly or partly tax free provided the employee is not entitled to the compensation under a contract of service and the payment is not deemed to be a benefit under a retirement benefit scheme. Where the individual receives compensation under a term of his employment contract, the Revenue's view is that it is taxable under Schedule E in the usual way. A payment made to a director as compensation for accepting a reduced salary or any other variation of his service contract is not regarded as a termination payment, and the amount received is normally taxable in full.

4.22.2 Exemptions from the charge under s 401

There are various types of termination payment that are exempt:

(1) Payments made because of termination of employment through death, injury or disability. Disability covers not only a condition arising from a sudden affliction, but also a continuing incapacity to perform the duties of an office or employment because of the culmination of a process of deterioration of physical or mental health caused by chronic illness (see SP10/81).
(2) Terminal grants and gratuities to members of HM forces.
(3) Lump sum payments from Commonwealth government superannuation schemes or compensation for loss of career owing to constitutional changes in Commonwealth countries.
(4) A special contribution by an employer into an approved retirement benefit scheme.
(5) A lump sum payment where the employment has constituted foreign service that exceeds the following limits:
    (a) three-quarters of the whole period of service;
    (b) the last ten years;
    (c) one-half of the period of service provided this amounted to at least 20 years and subject to at least ten of the last 20 years of service being foreign service.

'Foreign' service is defined as meaning a period of service during which the earnings were not assessable under Schedule E Case I because either the individual was not resident in the UK or the 100% deduction was available because the period spent working overseas exceeded 365 days (see 4.23).

4.22.3 Basic £30,000 exemption
(IT(E&P)A 2003, s 404)

Where a termination payment is not wholly exempt, the first £30,000 is normally tax free and only the balance is chargeable. Where an individual receives both statutory redundancy payments and a termination payment, the amount of the statutory redundancy payments uses up part of the £30,000 exemption and only the balance is available to cover part of the termination payment.

4.22.4 Employment includes a period of foreign service

The £30,000 exemption may be increased where the employment has included 'foreign service' (see 4.22.2).

Example – Increased exemption owing to foreign service

B was non-resident in the UK from 1980 to 1988. He then qualified for the 100% deduction from 1988 to 1990, so that he was not subject to UK tax on his salary even though he was resident. He retired in December 2001 and received compensation of £80,000. The exemption is found by using the fraction:

$$\frac{\text{Foreign service}}{\text{Total period of employment}}, \quad \text{ie in this case} \quad \frac{10 \text{ years}}{21 \text{ years}}$$

This fraction is applied to the amount of the golden handshake after deduction of the £30,000 exemption. The taxable amount would be arrived at as follows:

	£
Compensation	80,000
Less: 'normal exemption'	(30,000)
	50,000
$^{10}/_{21}$ thereof	(23,809)
Taxable amount	26,191

4.22.5 Year for which a termination payment may be taxed

Until recently, the time when a termination payment was made did not affect the tax liability as it was always treated as taxable income for the year in which the employment was terminated. However, from 1998-99 onwards, it is the year of receipt that counts and termination payments are taxed as income of the year in which they are received.

4.22.6 Taxation of continuing payments and benefits

Redundancy and other termination settlements often include provisions for payments to be made or benefits to continue after termination. The legislation that applied up to 5 April 1998 was regarded as unfair and to some extent unworkable, as what was taxed was the value of the promise to provide the ongoing benefits rather than the benefits themselves. Valuing the entitlement of a future benefit could be difficult and normally involved a significant up-front tax charge at a time when the former employee could least afford it. The assessment, once finalised, could not later be adjusted to reflect the level of benefit actually enjoyed or received.

Where cash was paid after termination of the employment, it was also assessed in the year of termination, but in practice a charge could not arise before the payment was made. A former employee's tax liability for the year of termination might therefore have to be revised on several occasions if he continued to receive payments in later years. This caused problems under self-assessment, which is designed to provide certainty for the taxpayer. It required the taxpayer to self-assess by estimating the value of the right to receive continuing benefits.

An optional alternative approach was applied for 1996-97 and 1997-98 allowing the ex-employee to elect for ongoing benefits to be taxed only to the extent that they are received. However, the tax charge still arose in respect of the year of termination, not the year of receipt.

The rules are now simpler and involve less administrative costs for employers. Benefits are taxable only as they arise: both benefits and payments will be taxable in the year when received or enjoyed (not in the year of termination).

Example – Benefits-in-kind following redundancy

M is made redundant on 6 October 2002 and receives a lump sum of £20,000 plus a further £20,000 on 6 April 2003. She also continues in the company medical insurance scheme for 18 months at an ongoing cost to the employer of £350 in 2002-03 and £650 in 2003-04.

In 2002-03 *M* receives a combined redundancy package of £20,350 that is covered by the £30,000 exemption. The £9,650 exemption balance is carried forward to the following year. In 2003-04 she receives the balance of the package of £20,650, of which £9,650 is exempt. The medical benefit of £650 is covered by the balance of the exemption as is £9,000 of the cash payment, leaving £11,000 to be taxed at the basic rate under PAYE.

4.22.7 *Ex gratia* payments

There has been concern that *ex gratia* payments may be subject to tax under Schedule E as unapproved retirement benefits taxable under IT(E&P)A 2003, s 393. If this charge arises, the £30,000 exemption is not available. The Revenue issued SP13/91 in October 1991 and subsequently has clarified the position. An *ex gratia* payment is normally regarded as a retirement benefit taxable under s 393 only where it is paid in connection with an individual's retirement. The Revenue has also given the following guidelines on hypothetical situations:

(1) A person who has worked for a company for 20 years leaves at age 54 to take a senior executive position in another company – 'golden handshake'.

(2) A long-service employee leaves to take a senior executive position in another company at age 60 – borderline, probably retirement.

(3) A division of a company is sold and the 55-year-old manager responsible for running it leaves to take a job with the purchaser – 'golden handshake'.

(4) A person in his 50s has a heart attack and is advised by his doctor to leave and seek a less stressful position – 'golden handshake'.

(5) An employee aged 35 is involved in an accident and suffers disabilities that make him unable to continue with his job – 'golden handshake'.
(6) An employee aged 50 leaves to take a job nearer home to nurse her aged parents – borderline, 'golden handshake': if the employee did not take a new job, or was nearer normal retirement age, this situation would be treated as retirement.

4.22.8 Payments in lieu of notice (PILONs)

PILONs have featured increasingly in employment contracts in recent years as employees have tried to formalise their rights and employers have wanted to be able to enforce restrictive covenants and prevent ex-employees using confidential information that they have acquired in the course of their employment. The Revenue set out its opinion in a lengthy article in *Tax Bulletin* August 1996. In large measure, the Revenue's interpretations have been upheld by the courts (see *EMI Electronics Group Ltd v Coldicott*).

The term 'PILON' is sometimes used loosely to include payments to employees on 'garden leave'. This is not correct, as an employee who is on garden leave is still an employee: he cannot take another job until the end of the notice period. All that has changed is that he is not required to carry out any duties. Payments to such an employee are taxable in the normal way and the employer should deduct tax under PAYE.

There are also situations where the employee's service contract actually provides for a PILON, usually at the employer's option. The Revenue's view is that where an employer decides to make a PILON, the payment is made under the contract rather than as compensation for the contract having been broken. As such, it remains taxable in full and PAYE deductions should be made.

Rather more controversially, the Revenue argues that there may be an implied term to an employment contract where an employer customarily makes PILONs. This is common in certain industries (IT, stockbroking, asset management) where the last thing an employer wants is for an employee who is serving out a notice period to have continued access to confidential information or to clients. You should take professional advice if you are an employer who has a history of regularly making PILONs.

Virtually the only circumstances in which you can be completely confident that a PILON will be treated as a golden handshake (see 4.22.1) is where the payment is a 'one-off' exception to your normal rule, and there is no reference to the possibility of such a payment in the service contract or related documents such as the staff handbook. In this situation, the first £30,000 is normally exempt from tax.

4.23 SPECIAL RULES FOR WORKING OUTSIDE THE UK (MAINLY ABOLISHED 17 MARCH 1998)

(IT(E&P)A 2003, s 328)

4.23.1 Introduction

Where a person was resident and ordinarily resident in the UK but worked overseas for a continuous period of at least 365 qualifying days, a 100% deduction was available up to 17 March 1998. This meant that no UK tax was payable on the earnings concerned.

4.23.2 Abolition of 100% deduction

With effect from 17 March 1998 the 100% deduction ceased to be available except to seafarers. The Revenue has confirmed that where a qualifying 365-day period straddled 17 March 1998, the relevant proportion of the individual's earnings for 1997-98 qualified for relief.

Because of the loose definition of 'seafarer', it was possible for employees who worked on particular types of oilrigs to qualify. However, following a decision by the Court of Appeal, with effect from 17 March 1998, employees who work on jack-up rigs or similar structures in the offshore oil and gas industry can no longer be regarded as seafarers and are therefore not entitled to the 100% deduction. Employees who worked on jack-up rigs before March 1998 may be entitled to the deduction provided they satisfy all the conditions and are eligible to make the claim (see *Tax Bulletin* February 2002).

4.24 DESIGNING A 'TAX EFFICIENT' REMUNERATION PACKAGE

Where an individual has a real degree of influence over the way his total remuneration package of salary and benefits is made up, the following should be borne in mind.

(1) Pension schemes are very tax efficient.
(2) Approved share options are treated more favourably than non-approved options.
(3) The legislation on benefits-in-kind still leaves some scope for manoeuvre.
(4) Golden handshakes are not always taxable.

4.24.1 Advantages of pension funds in general

There can be no better medium- to long-term investment than a pension scheme. The fact that pension schemes are not subject to tax internally because of the funds' exemption from UK income tax and CGT, combined with the facility to take a tax-free lump sum at retirement, means that the overall return will almost certainly beat any comparable investment.

4.24.2 Pension schemes not subject to the earnings cap

Some individuals may be in a company pension scheme that they had joined prior to 17 March 1987. If there is any element of choice, and the individual can afford to do so, it may well be better to forgo salary in return for an increased level of funding for the company pension. The fact that there is no ceiling on the tax-free lump sum of 1.5 times final remuneration is obviously extremely attractive.

In practice, even if the company operates a first-class pension scheme, there is likely to be some scope for augmenting the individual's pension entitlement. For example, many company schemes do not define final remuneration so as to include the maximum amount that the Revenue would permit. In these cases, it may be possible for an individual to have his pension entitlement increased to take account of 'fluctuating emoluments' such as benefits-in-kind, etc.

4.24.3 Stakeholder pension schemes

The maximum allowable premiums for Stakeholder pensions is the greater of £3,600 or the maximum allowable premium computed as under the normal limits for personal pension contributions (PPCs). Therefore, the new provisions allow a taxpayer with no earnings to contribute £3,600 pa to a PPC and obtain basic rate tax relief by retaining it out of the premium (higher rate relief also being given if investment income is high enough). The net relevant earnings can be the highest of such earnings for the current year and any of the preceding five years. If the earnings cease, then contributions can continue to be paid for the tax year of cessation and the five following years, based on the highest net relevant earnings of the year of cessation and the previous five years. Any excess PPCs paid must be refunded.

4.24.4 Schemes where individual subject to earnings cap

Where an individual is subject to the earnings cap (see 12.9.4) because he has taken up employment after 31 May 1989, or has become a member of a company pension scheme only after that date, there may still be considerable scope for increasing the level of benefits. If the individual can afford it, he should pay the maximum additional voluntary contributions and arrange matters so that his employer funds the scheme to the maximum extent permitted. In most cases, the individual will not receive the full pension if he accrues benefits at the standard rate of 1/60 final remuneration for each year of service, whereas the Revenue will permit a scheme to be funded so that the full pension is due after 20 years' service (see 12.9.5).

In the case of a family company, where both spouses are active in the business, it may well be possible for each to have the maximum permitted pension benefits.

4.24.5 Approved share option schemes

The tax treatment of an individual who exercises an approved share option or receives shares via an approved profit-sharing scheme is significantly better off than someone who benefits via an unapproved arrangement. Basically, no tax charge arises on the exercise of an approved share option provided that the necessary conditions have been observed (see 4.14).

The conclusion must be that wherever an individual has a choice, he should normally participate via an approved rather than a non-approved scheme.

The new approved schemes introduced in FA 2000 must also be borne in mind, especially the EMI scheme (see 4.15).

4.24.6 Tax efficient benefits-in-kind

Despite the Government's long-term intention to remove any discrimination between the tax treatment of benefits-in-kind and cash remuneration, there are still certain benefits-in-kind that are treated favourably for tax purposes. If a person is a company director, or someone else who has a degree of say in the way his remuneration package is made up, significant tax benefits can be secured by a judicious choice of benefits-in-kind.

Company cars or cash allowance?

You need to check that you will be better off with a company car as opposed to receiving a cash allowance with which you can buy your own car and then charge for business mileage at the flat-rate mileage allowances (see 4.4.9).

It may pay to buy your company car

Because of the high rate of depreciation in the first year, it may be advantageous for a director to arrange for his company to purchase a car with a view to its being sold to him after it has been used for a period. Provided he pays the full market value for the car in its second-hand condition, there will be no Schedule E charge on the difference between the cost of the car to the company and the amount at which the director purchases it. Admittedly, there is a scale benefit for the period the company owns the car, but this is often significantly less than the vehicle's depreciation during the period concerned.

Car fuel

Where an employee or director has a company car, it is clearly beneficial that he should have as much free petrol as possible as the scale benefit does not vary according to how much private petrol is provided.

Use of company computers

Since 6 April 1999, subject to certain restrictions, employees have been able to take up the loan of a computer with a value of up to £2,500 without being faced with a tax charge.

Employee shares

With taper relief at 10% on business assets after two years, an employee share scheme can form part of a very attractive benefits package. This is of course providing your company shares go up in value – see above regarding share schemes.

Interest-free loans

There is a *de minimis* limit so that, if an individual has a beneficial loan from his company, no Schedule E charge arises unless the loan exceeds £5,000.

Company accommodation

It may be possible to secure a reduction in the taxable benefit that arises where a director or employee occupies a company property. This is a complex area where you should take professional advice.

4.24.7 Golden handshakes are not always taxable

Despite the rules being tightened up, a termination payment can still be treated favourably, either because of the £30,000 exemption or because it qualifies for total exemption (see 4.22).

5

TAX AND SELF-EMPLOYMENT

GORDON HOPKINS

If you are self-employed, either in business on your own or in a partnership, you will be taxed under Schedule D Case I (if you carry on a trade) or Case II (if your business is regarded as a profession). In practice, the rules for determining taxable profits are virtually the same and therefore all references in this chapter to a person carrying on a trade apply equally to a person who is engaged in a profession.

The following key aspects of taxation of the self-employed are covered in this chapter:

(1) How self-employed individuals pay tax.
(2) Are you really self-employed?
(3) Basis of assessment.
(4) How taxable profits are computed.
(5) Capital allowances.
(6) Pre-trading expenditure.
(7) Post-cessation receipts.
(8) Post-cessation expenses.
(9) Relief for trading losses.
(10) Partnerships.
(11) Limited liability partnerships.
(12) Partnerships controlled outside the UK.

5.1 HOW SELF-EMPLOYED INDIVIDUALS PAY TAX

5.1.1 Payment of tax

Unlike employees who suffer deduction of tax from their earnings under PAYE, self-employed individuals pay tax directly to the Revenue. Tax payable by them for 2003-04 needs to be paid in two instalments on 31 January 2004 and 31 July 2004. The amount payable for each instalment is normally half the liability for 2002-03.

If you started self-employment fairly recently, and previously almost all your tax was collected under PAYE, you may find that you do not have to make instalment payments for 2003-04. However, the system will catch up with you on 31 January 2005 as you will then have to settle the whole of your 2003-04 tax and make the first payment on account for 2004-05.

5.1.2 Completing your tax return

You will need to complete a special schedule as part of your SA tax return; this asks for details of the type of business you are carrying on. It also asks whether your sales exceed £15,000 pa.

Very small businesses

If your sales are less than £15,000 pa you can simply file your tax return on the basis of three entries: sales, expenses and profit. There is no obligation to prepare accounts, although it may be advisable to do so for other reasons.

5.1.3 Ascertaining taxable profits based on accounts

If your sales (or 'turnover') exceed £14,999 you will need to complete further forms; to do this, you need accounts for your business. It is advisable to send in accounts with the SA return, whether or not the Revenue wants them, as this limits the scope for the Revenue to reopen back years by making 'discovery assessments'.

Very often, accounts are drawn up for other reasons as well (eg for production to banks and other lenders) and it is important to bear in mind that there may need to be some specific adjustments for tax purposes. There are also specific rules that govern the amount of 'capital allowances' that a trader may claim – in broad terms, capital allowances are an adjustment for depreciation or wear and tear on equipment, etc used in the business. This is dealt with in greater detail at 5.4.

5.2 ARE YOU REALLY SELF-EMPLOYED?

5.2.1 Introduction

It is not possible to elect to be self-employed; whether you are self-employed is a matter of fact. However, since the Taxes Acts do not define 'self-employment', the rules have evolved through decisions handed down by the courts.

The real distinction between being self-employed and an employee is that there is no 'master-servant' relationship. Yet in practice it is often difficult to discern the dividing line and the Revenue may take a different view from the parties concerned. For example, freelance workers may not necessarily be recognised as being self-employed and salaried partners may be classified as employees. Before 6 April 1999, the position could be complicated further in that the Contributions Agency was responsible for assessing liability for NICs and occasionally reached a different conclusion from the Revenue. These grey areas can sometimes result in companies treating freelance workers as if they were employees and deducting tax and NICs under PAYE accordingly. This reflects the Revenue's practice of seeking unpaid tax from employers in cases where a company has not operated PAYE. As a result, it is very difficult, for example, for workers in the computer field to secure payment on a self-employed basis. Similar problems are often experienced by workers in the TV industry, journalists, actors and artistes and many other industries where freelance workers are required to work 'on-site'.

The Revenue has addressed this issue by the introduction of new legislation with effect from 6 April 2000, known colloquially as IR35. These rules are covered in more detail at 21.3 as they deal primarily with individuals who offer their services through a service company. During the consultation period leading up to the introduction of the new legislation, the Revenue consolidated its statements on the dividing line between being employed and self-employed: see *Tax Bulletin* 45, available at www.inlandrevenue.gov.uk/bulletins/tb45.htm, and leaflet IR175, *Supplying Services*.

5.2.2 The Revenue's criteria

Guidelines issued by the Revenue in conjunction with the DSS to clarify employment status (leaflet IR56, *Employed or self-employed?*) included the following points:

(1) An employee generally does the work in person (and does not hire someone else to do it), working at times and places and in the way specified by the firm for whom the work is done and normally paid at hourly, weekly or monthly rates, possibly including overtime.
(2) A self-employed person may hire and pay others to do the work, or do it personally, in either case specifying the time and the way it is done, providing major items of equipment, being responsible for losses as well as profits and correcting unsatisfactory work in his own time and at his own expense.

These criteria are only for guidance, and in some cases the Commissioners and the courts have held that a person who did not fulfil the requirements in (2) above was nevertheless self-employed. Thus, a journalist who worked as a freelance sub-editor at various national newspapers was held by the Commissioners to be self-employed even though she carried out all the work at the newspapers' offices. Similarly, a test case sponsored by Equity resulted in the Special Commissioners finding that actors engaged in London West End theatre work are not employees.

Commissioners' decisions, unlike court decisions, do not set binding legal precedents. It was therefore even more important that the Court of Appeal held in *Hall v Lorimer* [1994] STC 23 that a TV vision mixer was self-employed even though he failed to satisfy virtually all of the above tests. The taxpayer used extremely expensive equipment provided by the TV companies concerned and his work was controlled rigorously.

The moral is to take professional advice if you are a borderline case rather than simply accept a 'ruling' from the Revenue. The borders are shifting constantly; for example FA 2000 contains provisions that can treat certain partnership income as if it were employment income subject to PAYE.

5.3 BASIS OF ASSESSMENT

The same rules apply for Schedule D Cases I and II. A self-employed person may draw up accounts to any date he chooses; there is no requirement that accounts be made up to 5 April to fit in with the fiscal year, although the Revenue will encourage him to adopt that basis. All self-employed individuals are now taxed on the 'current year' (CY) basis.

5.3.1 Current year basis

A business's assessable profits are dealt with on the CY basis. This means that the assessment is determined by the profits for the accounting year that ends in the year of assessment. Thus a business with a 31 May year end will be assessed for 2003-04 on its profits for the year ended 31 May 2003. Taxable profits for these purposes are after deducting capital allowances (see 5.5).

Special rules govern the first tax year since there are normally no accounts that end in that tax year (see below).

Opening years

Special rules apply for the first two tax years:

(1) The first tax year's assessment is made by reference to profits actually earned during that year.
(2) The second tax year's assessment is normally determined by the profits of the first 12 months.
(3) The third tax year's assessment is on the CY basis.

Example of opening years rules under the CY basis

A started in business on 6 October 2002. His accounts for the year to 5 October 2003 show profits of £48,000. Profits for the year ending 5 October 2004 are £72,000. *A* will be assessed as follows:

	£
2002-03 'actual' basis (6/12 × £48,000)	24,000
2003-04 first 12 months' profits	48,000
2004-05 CY basis	72,000

Example of position where first accounts not drawn up for 12-month period

The precise way in which the opening year rules work is slightly more complicated where there are no accounts for a period of 12 months ending in the second tax year. This is covered by the following examples:

(1) *B* started in business on 1 January 2002. The first set of accounts was made up to 30 April 2002, then to 30 April 2003. *B* will be assessed on profits computed as follows:

2001-02	Profits of period 1 January to 5 April 2002.
2002-03	Profits of first 12 months, ie 4/4 profits of period 1 January to 30 April 2002 *plus* 8/12 of profits for year ended 30 April 2003.

(2) *C* started up on 1 March 2002 and the first set of accounts was made up to 30 April 2003, ie there are no accounts ending in the second year. *C*'s assessable profits are:

2001-02	1/14 × profits for 14 months ended 30 April 2003.
2002-03	Profits of first 12 months, ie 12/14 profits for 14 months ended 30 April 2003.
2003-04	12/14 × profits for 14 months ended 30 April 2003.

5.3.2 Final year of trading

Where an individual ceases to carry on a business, he is taxed under the CY basis on his profits for a notional period that starts immediately after the basis period for the previous tax year and ends on the date that he ceases. This can be illustrated by a case where a person makes up accounts to 30 April. Assume his profits for the year ended 30 April 2003 are £80,000. He ceases business on 30 November 2003 and his profits for the final six months amount to £50,000. The assessable income for 2003-04 is his share of profits for the period 1 May 2002 to 30 November 2003, ie £80,000 plus £50,000 (but subject to either overlap or transitional relief: see below).

5.3.3 Overlap relief

Because of the way a new business is assessed under the CY basis for the first two tax years, some profits may be taxed more than once. To compensate for this, and to ensure that over the life of the business tax is paid only on the actual amount of profits, overlap relief is given when the business is discontinued or, in the case of partners, when they leave the firm.

If the overlap relief exceeds the taxable profits for the final year, the balance may be treated as an allowable loss and either set against the individual's other income for that year or the preceding year, or carried back against Schedule D Case I profits of the last three years as terminal loss relief (see 5.9.7).

Example of overlap relief

In the first example at 5.3.1, in which *A*'s first accounts end on 5 October 2003, 6/12 of the first 12 months' profits are assessed twice. Accordingly, a figure of £24,000 is carried forward and is deducted from *A*'s profits for the final year of trading. Thus, if *A* retires on 5 October 2005 and his final year's profits are £60,000, the assessment for 2005-06 will be as follows:

	£
CY basis	60,000
Less: overlap relief	24,000
Taxable profits	36,000

Change of accounting dates

Unless a business from the date of commencement draws up annual accounts ending in the period 31 March to 5 April, there will be overlap relief.

Example – Change of accounting dates (1)

G started trading on 1 October 2002. The profit for the first year of trading was £45,000. The basis of assessment for the opening years would be:

2002-03	1 Oct 2002 to 5 Apr 2003
2003-04	12 months to 30 Sept 2003
2004-05	12 months to 30 Sept 2004

The overlap period is the 187 days to 5 April 2003 that will be assessed both in 2002-03 and 2003-04. The overlap profit is £23,055.

If during the business's lifetime the accounting date is extended to bring it nearer to 5 April, the overlap relief is utilised. The intention of the legislation is to give relief in full when accounts are drawn up on a fiscal year basis, ie for the year to 5 April. If the accounting period is shortened, additional overlap relief is created.

Example – Change of accounting dates (2)

G changes his accounting date to 30 April 2006. The profit in the year to 30 September 2005 is £90,000.

2005-06	12 months to 30 September 2005
2006-07	12 months to 30 April 2006

The period of overlap is 1 May 2005 to 30 September 2005. The overlap profit is therefore £37,726 over 153 days, which is combined with the earlier overlap profit to give an overlap profit of £60,781 over 340 days.

If *G* extends his basis period towards 5 April, the overlap relief is used: logically, if *G* were to extend the accounting date to 5 April, all of the relief would be utilised.

Commercial consideration should be given to the value of overlap relief over the life of a business as the value of the relief will diminish in real terms with time. Professional advice should be taken in respect of using this relief during the course of the business by advancing the accounting date towards the following 5 April.

5.3.4 Transitional relief

The basis of assessment for a pre-6 April 1994 business changed to the CY basis (see 5.3.1) in 1997-98. This meant that a businessman with a year end of 5 May was assessed for 1997-98 on the whole of his profits for the year ended 5 May 1997 even though he had already been assessed for 1996-97 on a full year's profits, albeit profits which were computed in a different way. It was argued that this amounted to double taxation, and the legislation therefore allows transitional relief that works like overlap relief (see 5.3.3). The relief represents the amount assessed under the CY basis for 1997-98 but earned before 6 April 1997. Thus, if a business made up accounts to 5 May, the 1997-98 assessment was based on profits for the year ended 5 May 1997 and the transitional relief is 11/12 of those profits. Incidentally, the Revenue is content to split years in these situations by either months or days providing there is consistency. Transitional relief will be enjoyed when the accounting date is moved to a point later in the tax year, or the individual ceases to carry on business.

Example

J makes up his accounts to 5 June and has been in business for many years prior to 1994. His 1996-97 assessment was made on 50% of the profits for the two years ended 5 June 1996. Assume that this computation produced an assessment for 1996-97 of £100,000.

For 1997-98, *J* was assessed on the CY basis, ie his assessment was made on the profits for the year ending in 1997-98. Thus, if *J*'s profits for the year ended 5 June 1997 amounted to £180,000, that was his assessable income for 1997-98.

If *J* ceases to carry on the business in 2002-03, he is entitled to transitional relief equal to 10/12 of £180,000, ie £150,000. This amount will be allowed as a deduction in arriving at his assessable profits for 2002-03.

5.4 HOW TAXABLE PROFITS ARE COMPUTED

5.4.1 Self-assessment tax return

At the centre of SA for the self-employed is the schedule that contains a series of boxes designed to adjust account figures for tax purposes (see p. 131).

Example

Z's profit and loss account for the year ended 31 December 2002 shows the following:

	£	£
Income		97,500
Expenses		
Wages	27,500	
Rent	6,000	
Insurance	1,650	
Utilities	1,060	
Repairs	2,100	
Telephone	980	
Accountancy	500	
VAT surcharge	400	
Depreciation	1,400	
Entertaining	1,200	
Miscellaneous	250	
		(43,040)
Net profit		£54,460

Notes:

(1) Goods taken out for personal use and not reimbursed at full cost: £600.
(2) Telephone costs not relating to business: £200.
(3) Non-staff entertaining: £565.

5.4.2 What type of accounts are required?

The nature and complexity of accounts should be governed by the business. An individual in business as a window-cleaner can keep his accounts as simple as possible. Moreover, the Revenue allows certain 'short-cuts'; for example if you use your car for business you generally can use the approved mileage allowance rates designed for employees (see 4.4.9) and merely claim, say, 4,000 miles at the appropriate rate rather than keep all your motoring bills and claim capital allowances. Larger businesses require more complex accounting. The following covers the rules that govern the tax treatment of income and expenses and deals with adjustments to accounts that are required for tax purposes. For example, a set of accounts prepared

Income and expenses - annual turnover £15,000 or more

You must fill in this Page if your annual turnover is £15,000 or more - read the Notes, page SEN2

If you were registered for VAT, do the figures in boxes 3.29 to 3.64, include VAT? **3.27** [ ] or exclude VAT? **3.28** ✓

Sales/business income (turnover) **3.29** £ 97,500

	Disallowable expenses included in boxes 3.46 to 3.63	Total expenses	
• Cost of sales	3.30 £	3.46 £	
• Construction industry subcontractor costs	3.31 £	3.47 £	
• Other direct costs	3.32 £	3.48 £	
		Gross profit/(loss)	box 3.29 *minus* (boxes 3.46 + 3.47 + 3.48) 3.49 £ 97,500
		Other income/profits	3.50 £
• Employee costs	3.33 £	3.51 £ 27,500	
• Premises costs	3.34 £	3.52 £ 7,650	
• Repairs	3.35 £	3.53 £ 2,100	
• General administrative expenses	3.36 £ 200	3.54 £ 2,040	
• Motor expenses	3.37 £	3.55 £	
• Travel and subsistence	3.38 £	3.56 £	
• Advertising, promotion and entertainment	3.39 £ 565	3.57 £ 1,200	
• Legal and professional costs	3.40 £	3.58 £ 500	
• Bad debts	3.41 £	3.59 £	
• Interest	3.42 £	3.60 £	
• Other finance charges	3.43 £ 1,400	3.61 £ 1,400	
• Depreciation and loss/(profit) on sale	3.44 £	3.62 £ 650	
• Other expenses	3.45 £	3.63 £	
	Put the total of boxes 3.30 to 3.45 in **box 3.66 below**	Total expenses	total of boxes 3.51 to 3.63 3.64 £ 43,040
		Net profit/(loss)	boxes 3.49 + 3.50 *minus* 3.64 3.65 £ 54,460

Tax adjustments to net profit or loss

• Disallowable expenses	boxes 3.30 to 3.45 3.66 £ 2,165	
• Adjustments (apart from disallowable expenses) that increase profits. Examples are goods taken for personal use and amounts brought forward from an earlier year because of a claim under ESC B11 about compulsory slaughter of farm animals	3.67 £ 600	
• Balancing charges (from box 3.23)	3.68 £	
Total additions to net profit (deduct from net loss)		boxes 3.66 + 3.67 + 3.68 3.69 £ 2,765
• Capital allowances (from box 3.22)	3.70 £	
• Deductions from net profit (add to net loss)	3.71 £	boxes 3.70 + 3.71 3.72 £ 57,225
Net business profit for tax purposes (put figure in brackets if a loss)		boxes 3.65 + 3.69 *minus* 3.72 3.73 £

for commercial reasons may include a provision for wear and tear to a building. Such a provision needs to be 'added back' (as no relief is available for depreciation as such, relief is due only via the capital allowances system).

5.4.3 Accounts should be on the 'earnings basis'

The Revenue's view is that accounts should normally be prepared to reflect a trader's earnings for a year rather than just the cash received. For example, the accounts should include debtors, ie bills that have been issued but not paid by the year end. Similarly, the accounts should include work in progress.

5.4.4 Sound commercial accountancy principles

The Master of the Rolls stated in *Gallagher v Jones* [1993] STC 537, CA:

> Subject to any express or implied statutory rule … the ordinary way to ascertain the profits or losses of a business is to apply accepted principles of commercial accountancy. That is the very purpose for which such principles are formulated. As has often been pointed out, such principles are not static: they may be modified, refined and elaborated over time as circumstances change and accounting insights sharpen. But so long as such principles remain current and generally accepted they provide the surest answer.

Accountancy principles are constantly being refined and are published by the Accounting Standards Board as Financial Reporting Standards. In particular, FRS18 brought together and updated a number of earlier statements on accounting policies. Some FRSs are mandatory only for businesses of a certain size; others apply more generally. Smaller businesses that do not require an audit are governed by the regularly updated FRSSE.

Key concepts for accountants include the 'going concern' concept, the need for consistency, and the accruals principle whereby income and expenses related to earning it are matched. Until recently, the concept of prudence was also regarded as a fundamental principle, ie that income and profits should not be anticipated, but accountants now place increasing weight on accounts showing a 'realistic' position rather than an approach that might be regarded as excessively prudent.

5.4.5 Expenditure that is specifically disallowed
(TA 1988, ss 74 and 577)

As mentioned above, certain types of expenditure are disallowed, although it may be sound accounting practice to deduct such costs in a trader's accounts. See Table 5.1 for a summary contained in the Revenue guide. The rest of this section looks more closely at specific types of business expenses.

Table 5.1 – Inland Revenue summary of allowable and non-allowable business expenses

	Allowable	*Not allowable*
Basic costs	Light, heat and power; telephone; insurance; stationery and postage; business rates and rent; advertising; protective clothing; repairs; replacement loose tools (unless capital allowances claimed instead); transport of goods to customers or materials from suppliers; subcontractors (see Leaflet IR14/15)	Private and personal expenses; non-business part of running costs of premises used only partly for business; own insurance; ordinary, everyday clothing even if bought specially for business use; parking and other fines; buying, altering or improving fixed assets; depreciation or losses on sale of fixed assets
Employee costs	Employees' wages and salaries; employers' NICs; redundancy payments; pension contributions on employees' behalf; employees' expenses and benefits	Own wages or salary and drawings from the business; own pension payments and other benefits; own NICs
Finance costs	Interest on loans and overdrafts used solely for business purposes; costs of arranging such finance	Repayment of loan or overdraft (as opposed to the interest)
Professional	Accountancy fees; preparation of ordinary business costs agreement; debt recovery (if debt is for a taxable receipt); renewing leases of less than 50 years (where no premium is paid); defending business rights; appeals against business rates	Costs of settling tax disputes; legal costs of buying fixed assets (treated as part of the cost of fixed asset); costs and fines or penalties for breaking the law
Travel	Travel on business to meet customers, suppliers, etc; travel between business premises; accommodation and reasonable cost of meals on overnight business trips; vehicle running expenses (less proportion of private use)	Travel between home and place of business (unless agreed with the Tax Office that your home is your base); costs of buying vehicles (but capital allowances can be claimed); meals (except on overnight business trips)
Bad debts	Irrecoverable debts written off, if taxed when they arose; recovery costs; provisions against specific doubtful debts; debts recovered later should be shown in box 3.16 or 3.37 of the self-assessment return	General bad debts reserve; debts not taxed when they arose, eg because they relate to sale of a fixed asset
Subscriptions	Payments to certain professional bodies (Tax Office can tell you which)	Payments to political parties; most payments to clubs, charities or churches
Entertaining	Costs of entertaining staff; gifts (not food or drink) up to £10 per person per year which advertise your business	All other entertaining and hospitality
VAT	Any VAT which is not recoverable is an allowable expense. This does not include any input VAT paid on capital items. However, this can be included in their cost if a claim can be made to capital allowances for them. Where allowable expenses net of recoverable input VAT are shown then the turnover should be shown on the same basis, that is net of output VAT charged. Alternatively, you may prefer to show receipts and allowable expenses gross of VAT and the net payment to Customs & Excise as an expense or the net repayment as a taxable receipt.	

Capital expenditure

(TA 1988, s 74)

The acquisition of a capital asset is not a cost that may be deducted in arriving at profits for tax purposes. This may seem obvious where an asset such as a building is acquired, but the definition of capital expenditure goes a long way beyond the acquisition of tangible assets. The generally accepted definition was given by Lord Cave in *British Insulated and Heisby Cables Ltd v Atherton* (1925) 10 TC 155; he stated:

> when an expenditure is made … with a view to bringing into existence an asset or an advantage for the enduring benefit of a trade there is very good reason (in the absence of special circumstances leading to the opposite conclusion) for treating such expenditure as properly attributable not to revenue but to capital.

The acquisition of, for example goodwill, is capital expenditure. Less obviously, a lump sum payment to secure release from an onerous liability (eg a lease at a high rent or a fixed rate loan) is also regarded as capital expenditure.

Entertaining

(TA 1988, s 577)

Any expenses relating to entertaining customers or suppliers that are included in a set of accounts normally need to be added back. There is a modest exemption that may apply where the entertaining is provided by an hotelier, restaurateur or someone else who provides entertainment in the ordinary course of his trade. Staff entertainment is also an allowable expense, but the individual employee may be assessed on a benefit-in-kind.

Gifts to customers, etc

(TA 1988, s 577)

The cost of gifts to customers and to potential customers and introducers is also disallowed unless the gift carries a conspicuous advertisement and is neither food, drink, tobacco or a voucher exchangeable for such goods, nor an item that costs more than £50 per recipient per year (£10 for 2000-01 and earlier years).

Illegal payments

A specific provision disallowing illegal payments such as bribes came into force on 11 June 1993 (the date the relevant clause was introduced in the committee stage of the Finance Bill 1993). Prior to 11 June 1993, it was open to a business to claim a deduction for such payments where they were incurred wholly and exclusively for the purposes of the trade – although this was often difficult to prove in practice.

The disallowance was extended by FA 1994 to cover payments made on or after 30 November 1993 in response to threats, menaces, blackmail and other forms of extortion. The disallowance in respect of bribes was further extended for expenditure incurred after 31 March 2002 to cover any payment that would constitute a criminal offence if made in the UK, effectively amending the law to cover bribes made outside the UK.

Lease rentals on expensive cars

(CAA 1990, s 35)

Where a trader uses a leased car or provides a car to an employee and the original cost was £12,000+ (£8,000+ prior to 10 March 1992), part of the lease rentals must be added back as a disallowable expense. The amount disallowed is the following proportion of the lease rental:

$$\tfrac{1}{2} \times \frac{(\text{Cost of car} - £12{,}000)}{\text{Cost of car}}$$

Thus, if a car costing £16,000 is leased for a rental of £2,400 pa, the amount disallowed is:

$$\tfrac{1}{2} \times \frac{(£16{,}000 - £12{,}000)}{£16{,}000} \times £2{,}400, \text{ ie } £300.$$

This treatment does not apply to maintenance costs included in the lease rentals provided they are identified separately under the terms of the leasing agreement. Amounts paid under an HP agreement are dealt with differently (see 5.4.6).

Provisions for bad debts

(TA 1988, s 74(j))

A general provision against bad debts is not allowable, but provisions against specific debts are a proper deduction for tax purposes provided it can be shown the amount is a reasonable provision (see further 5.4.8).

Remuneration not paid within nine months of year end

(FA 1989, s 43)

Bonus payments to employees may be made after the end of a year. If they clearly relate to a period of account, it would be normal for the trader's accounts to include a provision. However, this provision is allowable only if the remuneration is paid within nine months of the year end.

Pension contributions for employees
(FA 1993, s 112)

A deduction is due only if the contribution is paid during the course of the trader's year, whether to an approved or unapproved scheme.

Pension contributions for the trader himself are not an allowable deduction in computing profits, although relief is available as a deduction from taxable profits (see 12.8 for details of the method of dealing with personal pension contributions).

Expenditure not wholly for trade purposes
(TA 1988, s 74(a))

The legislation requires the expenditure to be incurred 'wholly and exclusively' for the purposes of the trade. Consequently, expenses incurred partly for trade purposes and partly for personal reasons are not allowable. For example, the cost of black dresses worn in court by a female barrister was disallowed on the grounds that the expenditure had a dual purpose (warmth and decency as well as the need to dress in a particular way when appearing in court), as was the cost of meals incurred by a self-employed carpenter when he was working away from home.

Where an expense is incurred for mixed purposes the whole amount is disallowed; this rules out relief where an individual travels abroad mainly to have a holiday but carries out some work while there. However, where it can be shown that an additional cost was incurred wholly for business reasons, a deduction may be due for this. Consequently, if a person uses part of his home for business, the extra heat and light bills are an allowable expense for tax purposes. In practice, quite a number of expenses are apportioned between private (not allowable) and business (allowable) use. 'Phone bills and car expenses are two particular examples that arise often.

In *McKnight v Sheppard* HL 1999 STC 669 a stockbroker incurred legal expenses in defending charges brought by The Stock Exchange. He was found guilty of gross misconduct and suspended from trading. Because a suspension would have resulted in the destruction of his business, he appealed and his suspension was reduced to a fine. He was allowed tax relief for his legal expenses because these had been incurred wholly and exclusively for the purposes of the trade, but the fines imposed were disallowed.

Payments of reverse premiums

FA 1999 provides that no relief is due to a trader who pays a reverse premium to induce a tenant to take a lease.

Sums recoverable from insurance policy, etc
(TA 1988, s 74(c))

Where a trader can get back from an insurance company the money that he has paid out, there is no deduction due for the expenditure. The same treatment applies where a trader has been indemnified against a particular cost.

Annual payments

(TA 1988, s 74(p) and (q))

Certain annual payments (eg patent royalties) generally need to be paid net of basic rate tax. The payments are not deductible in arriving at profits assessable under Schedule D Case I or II, although they are allowed as a deduction for higher rate purposes.

5.4.6 Other expenditure where adjustments may be required

Interest

Relief for interest payments on qualifying loans taken by partners are given against the partner's general income (see 9.4). Interest paid by a sole trader or partnership may be deducted in arriving at the business's taxable profits provided it passes the 'wholly and exclusively' test (see above).

Problems may arise where overdraft interest is charged in a set of accounts and the proprietor's capital account is overdrawn. The Revenue is likely to argue that the interest (or, at any rate, part of it) was incurred not for business purposes, but to finance drawings. If you find yourself in this situation you should take advice from an accountant.

Cost of raising business finance

(TA 1988, s 77)

There are often certain costs in raising long-term finance, and for many years the Revenue regarded these as capital expenditure. A statutory deduction is now available provided the costs:

(1) were incurred wholly and exclusively for the purposes of obtaining loan finance, providing security or repaying a loan; and
(2) represented expenditure on professional fees, commissions, advertising, printing or other incidental expenses in relation to raising finance.

In some cases a deduction is available even though the expenditure failed and the loan finance was not in fact obtained.

Lease rentals

The way lease rentals are treated depends on the type of lease. If it is an 'operating lease', ie a lease for a period that is less than the asset's anticipated useful life, it is normal for rentals to be deducted in arriving at the profits for the period to which the rentals refer. In practice, most leasing agreements provide for rentals to be payable in advance. Thus, if a trader pays lease rentals of £12,000 on 1 December which cover a period of six months, and he makes up accounts to the following 31 March, the amount deducted in arriving at the profits for the year ended 31 March would be:

$$\frac{4 \text{ months}}{6 \text{ months}} \times £12{,}000 = £8{,}000.$$

A different treatment is required where a trader pays rentals under a 'finance lease', ie a lease agreement under which the trader acquires almost all the benefits of outright ownership. There is a special accounting standard that governs the accounting treatment of such leases, and the Revenue's view is that the amount that should be deducted is that charged in the trader's accounts in accordance with SSAP 21 (ie the relevant Statement of Standard Accounting Practice issued by the Institute of Chartered Accountants).

Hire purchase

Where equipment is acquired under an HP contract, its cost counts as capital expenditure (in most cases capital allowances will be available). The 'interest' element is apportioned over the contract term and relief is given for the amount of interest that relates to the accounting period concerned.

Example – Adjustments for HP contracts

A trader acquires a computer under a three-year HP agreement. The cost of the computer was £12,000, but the trader pays 36 monthly HP payments of £420.

The interest payable over the three years totals £3,120. This would normally be allocated roughly as follows:

Year 1:	£1,715
Year 2:	£1,040
Year 3:	£365

This type of allocation reflects the amount of the HP 'loan' outstanding during each year.

Legal and professional expenses

Where an Inspector of Taxes examines a trader's business accounts, he normally asks for an analysis of any substantial amounts relating to legal and professional expenses. Legal costs in connection with the acquisition of capital assets are disallowable as capital expenditure, as are legal costs in connection with renewing a lease of more than 50 years. In contrast, legal costs incurred to protect a capital asset are generally allowable as a revenue expense. Professional costs incurred in connection with tax appeals are not allowable on the grounds that such costs relate to tax on profits rather than an expense incurred in earning profits. However, in practice the costs of preparing and agreeing tax computations are usually allowed.

5.4.7 Relief for premiums

(TA 1988, s 87)

A trader may be required to make a lump sum payment to a landlord to obtain a lease. Where the lease is for a period of less than 50 years, part of the lump sum may be treated as income in the landlord's hands (see 6.3) and the trader may claim a deduction for this amount as if it were rent payable over the period of his lease. The part taxed in the landlord's hands is 100% of the premium less 2% for each complete year of the lease other than the first year.

There is no relief if the lease is for more than 50 years or if the premium is paid to someone other than the landlord since such a third party (eg an outgoing tenant) is not subject to income tax under Schedule A.

Sometimes the lease will require a tenant to have certain building work carried out that will increase the value of the landlord's interest in the property. The landlord may be assessed under Schedule A on a notional premium (see 6.3.3). Where this applies, the trader can claim a deduction just as if he had been required to pay a premium in cash. However, the notional premium is generally far less than the actual cost of carrying out the work concerned.

Example – Treatment of premiums

B pays a premium for a lease of ten years of which £40,000 is treated as income of the landlord for Schedule A purposes. Of this sum, 82% (ie £32,800) is taxed in the landlord's hands as income for the year in which the premium is payable.

B can claim a deduction in his accounts for the ten years as if he had paid rent of £3,280 pa. If it were not for s 87, the expenditure would be treated as capital expenditure and would attract no relief.

5.4.8 Provision for bad or doubtful debts

The Revenue has explained its approach with regard to provisions for bad or doubtful debts. Its interpretation is that a trader may be entitled to a deduction provided the following circumstances are satisfied:

(1) the debt existed at the balance sheet date; and
(2) before the accounts were finalised, the company's trader/directors discovered that the debtor's financial position at that date was such that the debt was unlikely to be paid.

The Revenue stated that a common example of this is where a debtor at the balance sheet date goes into administration or liquidation shortly after that date and before the date on which the trader approves the financial statements. Where the administration or liquidation commences after the balance sheet date, its occurrence before the accounts were finalised normally sheds light on the debtor's financial position at the balance sheet date. If the period between the balance sheet date and approval of the accounts is short, it is unlikely that a debtor would have gone from financial good health to insolvency in that period. In these circumstances it would normally be reasonable for the trader to regard the debt as doubtful. The acceptable amount of provision would depend on the information available.

The Revenue contrasts this with a situation where a debtor is an habitually slow payer and there are no grounds to believe his financial position has changed. In such a case, the Revenue argues that the length of time a debt has been outstanding is not in itself a sufficient reason to regard it as doubtful.

5.4.9 Provisions against liability to pay sums after year end

This is an aspect of a trader's accounts to which Tax Inspectors pay particular attention. The Revenue needs to be satisfied that relief is not sought for expenditure that will be incurred only in the future. Consequently, an Inspector will almost certainly withhold relief unless he is satisfied that a trader became liable to make the payment concerned before the year end. For example, in the past it was not generally possible to secure a deduction for redundancy costs unless the necessary redundancy notices were served by the end of the trader's accounting period. Similarly, the Revenue will often argue that a provision for an amount that may be due to a client for professional negligence is not allowable unless the client's claim has been admitted by the year end.

This approach can be challenged where the accounts comply with generally accepted accountancy principles, but you should seek professional advice if sizeable amounts of tax are at issue.

The Revenue's rather restrictive approach was challenged successfully in *Johnston v Britannia Airways Ltd* [1994] STC 763. Civil Aviation Authority rules required each aeroplane to have a certificate of airworthiness. This would not be issued unless each engine was overhauled every 17,000 flying hours which, in Britannia's case, meant every three to five years. Accordingly, a provision for the overhaul costs was made in each year's accounts based on the average cost of the overhaul per hour flown and the number of hours flown in the period.

The Inspector took the view that the correct treatment was to make no provision before the cost of the major overhaul was incurred, to capitalise the overhaul cost when incurred, and then to write it off gradually over the period up to the next overhaul. The Special Commissioners found that the accruals method used by Britannia gave the most accurate picture of the airline's profits and was more effective in matching costs with revenue than the capitalise and amortise method favoured by the Revenue. Furthermore, the company's method was in accordance with ordinary principles of commercial accountancy. Accordingly, since there was nothing in statute or case-law to contradict it, the company's appeal succeeded. This decision was upheld by the High Court.

Bear in mind that accountancy principles are being refined and updated constantly and FRS12 now sets out 'best practice' on provisions for sums payable after the year end. The Revenue will resist an accounting treatment that does not comply with FRS12. The *Britannia Airways* decision has since been overtaken by changes in generally accepted accountancy principles.

There are sometimes circumstances where a payment will almost certainly be required in the future, although the precise amount has yet to be ascertained. An example contained in a Revenue publication concerns an insurance broker who may be required to refund commission to an insurance company if clients allow policies to lapse. The Revenue has accepted that a provision may be allowable in these circumstances provided it is arrived at scientifically by reference to past experience. A 'rough and ready' general provision is not allowable.

During 1999 the Revenue decided not to appeal against a High Court decision on provisions for sums that would be payable only in the future. *Herbert Smith v Honour* [1999] STC 173 concerned a firm of solicitors that had taken long leases over office premises that turned out to be surplus to requirements. The offices could only be sublet at a much lower rent and the firm's accounts made a provision for the loss that would accrue in later years. The Revenue's decision not to appeal followed from its acceptance that the accounting treatment was in accordance with generally accepted accountancy principles.

These issues also arose in the so-called *Jenners* case. The Commissioners held that a company operating a department store could make provisions for repairs that would have to be carried out in later years. Again, the Revenue decided not to appeal.

5.4.10 Valuation of stock and work in progress

A trader's accounts should include his stock in hand at his year end. Individual items of stock should be valued at the lower of cost or net realisable value. Cost should normally include a proportion of overheads.

Similarly, work in progress should be valued at the year end on the same basis. Where the accounts relate to a profession, it is not necessary to include in the cost the time value of work put in by the sole proprietor or partner, since this represents the proprietor's profit rather than a cost incurred in carrying on the profession.

The treatment of long-term work in progress can involve complex issues and should be discussed with the firm's accountant.

5.4.11 Withdrawal of 'cash basis' practice for professions

Relatively large businesses have been able to prepare accounts purely on a cash receipts basis without taking into account income from unpaid invoices nor the value of work in progress. The cash basis was widely used by barristers, solicitors, surveyors, actuaries, doctors and accountants, supported by a Revenue SP that allowed such businesses to use this basis subject to conditions that profits were computed on the earnings basis for the first three fiscal years and thereafter could be accounted on a purely cash basis. The cash basis also applied to expenses.

This has now been abolished. Businesses must use the earnings basis for accounting periods starting on or after 6 April 1999. Furthermore, there is a one-off catching-up charge based on the value of work in progress and debtors, net of creditors, at the start of the first accounting period affected.

The catching-up charge will be payable over ten years of assessment starting with the 2000-01 year of account. The amount chargeable in each year except the last will be restricted to the smaller of:

(1) one-tenth of the total charge; and
(2) 10% of the 'normal' profit.

In the tenth year, the balance of the catching-up charge will be taxed.

Example of catching-up charge

K has prepared his accounts on a cash basis for many years using a 31 October year end. He will have a catching-up charge based on the value of his work in progress and debtors less creditors as at 1 November 1999. The first of his ten instalments will be taxable for the year 2000-01 and the tax will be due on 31 January 2002.

5.4.12 Other consequences of the catching-up charge

Although the charge itself is not welcome, there are some measures of relief:

(1) As the catching-up charge will be taxed under Schedule D Case VI, it will not be liable to Class 4 NICs.
(2) There will be no charge in a loss-making year, unless this is the final year of the business.
(3) Existing losses arising from the same business can be set against the charge.
(4) Relief will be given for any initial double charge.

Example of initial double charge

L began to practise on 1 May 1990, preparing his accounts to 30 April each year. For the first three years, he used the earnings basis to compute his profits. With effect from 1 May 1991, he used a purely cash basis. Closing debtors on 30 April 1991 were £40,000. He was taxed on profits as follows:

Year of assessment		*Basis period*
1990-91	1 May 1990 to 5 April 1991	Earnings basis
1991-92	1 May 1990 to 30 April 1991	Earnings basis
1992-93	Year ended 30 April 1991	Earnings basis
1993-94	Year ended 30 April 1992	Cash basis

In addition to the normal overlapping of early profits, he will have been taxed yet again when he received payment for the £40,000 unpaid invoices, following adoption of the cash basis in 1992. (This could also work the other way around, resulting in a net saving from changing the way the accounts were prepared.)

5.4.13 Cessation of trade

Where a business ceases, the ten-year spread of the charge will continue; there will be no 10% profits cap because there are no longer any profits.

5.4.14 Barristers and advocates

Barristers (in Scotland, advocates) have always been regarded as a 'special case': few other professions experience such delay between completing an assignment and being paid. In recognition of the particular difficulties facing new barristers especially, they are allowed to remain on the cash basis until the seventh anniversary of the start of their practice. They then have to change to the earnings basis and meet the catching-up charge at that time.

It is possible for a barrister to change to preparing accounts within the seven-year period, but this decision will depend on a number of factors, including his marginal rate of income tax and the reliability of future profit projections (see 30.2 *re* barristers generally).

5.4.15 Use of 'true and fair view' approach

The 'true and fair view' approach to computing taxable profits and losses is intended merely to ensure that profits are calculated in accordance with appropriate accounting standards and that time is not wasted on immaterial amounts. The Revenue confirmed that sole traders and partnerships do not need to have an audit even though their taxable profits must now be based on accounts that would comply with the true and fair view recognised for audited accounts.

Guidance on the application of accounting principles for traders who were formerly on the cash basis is contained in *Tax Bulletin* December 1998. See also the ICAEW technical release Tax 30/98.

5.4.16 Miscellaneous matters

Enterprise allowance should not be included
(TA 1988, s 127)

Where a trader has received an enterprise allowance, this should not be included in the computation of profits assessable for Schedule D Case I purposes. The allowance is taxable, but is charged to tax under Schedule D Case VI rather than Case I.

Class 4 NICs

No deduction is due for the trader's liability for Class 4 NICs (see 25.4) in arriving at the trader's taxable profits.

Gifts in kind to charities

FA 1999 gives relief for traders who donate computers or other equipment to charities. Relief is also due for the employer costs of staff seconded to educational establishments.

5.5 CAPITAL ALLOWANCES

5.5.1 Introduction

A trader is entitled to capital allowances on plant and machinery used in the trade. Capital allowances are also available on commercial buildings located in an enterprise zone, agricultural buildings, industrial buildings and hotels.

Allowances may also be claimed for expenditure on know-how and scientific research expenditure. All these are dealt with differently, and various rates of initial and annual allowances are given.

Capital allowances are treated like any other business expense. The allowances are computed on the CY basis, but once again with special rules for the first tax year.

Successive Finance Acts have overlaid one another during the last 50 years and this makes it difficult to see the wood for the trees. The key issues are addressed in this section (5.5.2–5.5.21).

5.5.2 What is plant and machinery?

Despite the introduction of specific legislation in 1994, the definition of 'plant and machinery' is unclear. The statutory definition focuses mainly on what is *not* plant as it forms part of a building, and the Revenue's practice and interpretation are still based largely on decisions handed down by the courts. The earliest judicial definition was provided in *Yarmouth v France* (1887) 19 QBD 647, in which Lindley LJ stated:

> in its ordinary sense, it includes whatever apparatus is used by a businessman for carrying on his business – not his stock-in-trade, which he buys or makes for sale, but all goods or chattels, fixed or movable, live or dead, which he keeps for permanent employment in his business …

Some items are clearly within this definition (eg typewriters, dictating machines, telephone equipment, computers, manufacturing equipment, vans and other motor vehicles). What is less obvious is that a building may contain items that are P&M. In some cases the plant will have become part of the building (eg a lift). Also, there may be structures that are items of plant (eg a dry dock or a grain silo, or a mezzanine floor put into a factory to create storage space). Capital allowances are also due on building work needed to enable plant and machinery to be installed (ie if a floor had to be strengthened to install a computer).

You should take professional advice if you acquire a building or adapt premises to meet the requirements of your trade in order to ensure that you obtain the Inspector of Taxes' agreement on the full amount eligible for capital allowances.

5.5.3 Allowances for plant and machinery

(CAA 2001, ss 11-15)

Plant and machinery qualifies for a 25% writing-down allowance, computed on the balance of the 'pool' at the year end. The pool's opening balance represents the cost of plant brought forward from previous years, less capital allowances already received. A trader receives writing-down allowances based on the opening balance plus the cost of additional plant acquired during the year, less any disposal proceeds.

Example – Writing-down allowances

S and *T* are in partnership. In their year to 31 March 2001 they had acquired plant and machinery at a cost of £30,000 and received capital allowances of £7,500. During their year ended 31 March 2002, they sell some of this plant for £2,000 and buy new plant for £20,000. Their pool would be as follows:

	£
Written-down value brought forward at 1 April 2001	22,500
Additions during year ended 31 March 2002	20,000
	42,500
Less: disposal proceeds	(2,000)
	40,500
Writing-down allowances (25%)	(10,125)
Written-down value carried forward	30,375

5.5.4 Expenditure treated as incurred in a period

(CAA 2001, s 67)

Expenditure is deemed to be incurred in a period if a trader enters into an unconditional contract; it is not necessary that the trader should actually have paid for it or brought it into use by his year end. There is an exception for plant and machinery acquired under an HP contract where entitlement to allowances arises only when the plant is actually brought into use.

5.5.5 Assets brought into use part way through year

(CAA 2001, ss 55 and 67)

An asset acquired towards the end of a trader's accounting period still attracts the full 25% allowance unless the trade has not been going for 12 months. In such a case, the 25% allowance may be scaled down.

Example – Assets bought in year in which trade is commenced

U commenced trading on 5 October 2000. On 5 April 2001 he acquired plant and machinery for £60,000. The capital allowances due to him for 2000-01 are:

$\frac{6}{12} \times 25\% \times$ £60,000, ie	£7,500

5.5.6 Assets kept separate from the pool

(CAA 2001, s 74)

Cars that cost £12,000+ need to be kept separate. The maximum writing-down allowance for such a car is £3,000, but a balancing allowance (or charge) arises on disposal.

Example – Writing-down allowances for cars

V operates an advertising business. She makes up her accounts to 30 April. On 1 May 2001 she acquired a car that costs £30,000 and this was used by an employee. After two years, the car is sold for £10,000.

The car is deemed to be in a separate pool and the position is as follows:

		£
Year 1:	Cost	30,000
	Writing-down allowances for 2001-02	3,000
		27,000
Year 2:	Writing-down allowances for 2002-03	3,000
		24,000
Year 3:	Disposal proceeds	10,000
Balancing allowance for 2003-04		14,000

Cars that cost less than £12,000 were kept in a separate pool until the start of the accounting period that includes 6 April 2000. Any balance in this pool was transferred to the general pool either on 6 April 2000 or 6 April 2001 at the taxpayer's option.

Other assets kept separate

(CAA 2001, s 206)

Certain other assets are kept separate from the pool. One particular category is assets used partly for the purposes of the trade and partly for other purposes. For example, a van used by a sole trader for 40% business and 60% private motoring is deemed to form a separate pool. The trader is entitled to 'scaled down' allowances, ie he would receive 40% of the full writing-down allowance and 40% of any balancing allowance. 'Short-life' assets are also kept separate.

5.5.7 'Short-life' assets

(CAA 2001, ss 83-84)

Where expenditure is added to the pool, the trader receives writing-down allowances that are likely to get smaller and smaller. For example, a trader invests expenditure of £100,000 on plant in Year 1. He does not acquire any other plant and machinery for five years. His writing-down allowance in Year 1 will be £25,000 (ie 25% of £100,000), £13,750 in Year 2 (ie 25% of the residual £75,000) and so on. By the end of Year 5, the written-down value will be just under £24,000, but the equipment itself may be worn out and have a scrap value of only £2,000. To cover this type of situation, the legislation allows for a trader to designate certain assets as short-life assets. The cost of these assets is kept in a separate pool and a balancing allowance (or charge) arises on a sale within five years, or on the assets being scrapped by then. If an asset is not sold within that period, the asset's written-down value is transferred to the general pool.

(1) In the above example, if the plant were actually scrapped at the start of Year 5 and the trader received no scrap value at all, he would receive a balancing allowance of £31,640.
(2) Again using the same basic facts, if the plant and machinery were still in use at the end of Year 5, the written-down value of £23,730 would be transferred to the trader's pool of other plant.

The following cannot be short-life assets:

(1) Cars.
(2) Assets used partly for non-trade purposes.
(3) Assets originally acquired for non-trade purposes (eg assets acquired prior to the trade being commenced).

(4) Ships.
(5) Certain assets leased out in the course of a trade.

An election needs to be made for an asset to be treated as a short-life asset. This needs to be submitted to the Inspector of Taxes within two years of the accounting period in which the asset is acquired. The Inspector will require sufficient information to be able to identify the assets at a later stage (see SP1/86).

5.5.8 First-year allowances for small and medium-sized businesses

(CAA 2001, SS 47-49)

The first Labour Budget in July 1997 introduced a first-year capital allowance of 50% for a 12-month period for investment in plant and machinery. The allowance was available to unincorporated businesses and to companies provided they qualified as SMEs (small or medium-sized businesses). The 25% writing-down allowance applies for the second and subsequent years.

Expenditure on plant incurred during the 12 months from 2 July 1997 to 1 July 1998 qualified for a first-year allowance of 50%. The rate of first-year allowance was then reduced to 40%. At first, the first-year allowance was renewed on a year-by-year basis, but FA 2000 put the relief on a permanent basis. In order to establish whether a business is regarded as 'small' or 'medium-sized', the tax legislation relies on the Companies Act definitions. Three conditions arise from the legislation:

(1) turnover of not more than £11.2m;
(2) assets of not more than £5.6m; and
(3) no more than 250 employees.

(These limits are currently under review by the EU and the turnover figure is expected to be increased to £20m later this year.)

Provided two of the above three conditions are satisfied for the current or previous year, the business is regarded as an SME. Specifically in the case of companies, the company must be an SME for the year in which the expenditure is incurred. If the company is a member of a group, the group as a whole must satisfy two of the three conditions.

First-year allowances apply to businesses carried on by individuals and partnerships made up of individuals, provided the business would qualify if it were carried on by a company. There are two specific exclusions:

(1) expenditure on plant and machinery for leasing, cars, sea-going ships and railway assets;
(2) expenditure on long-life assets (LLAs – plant with an expected useful

life of at least 25 years) but the £100,000 pa limit (see 5.5.13) should exclude the majority of SMEs.

Northern Ireland
(CAA 2001, s 40)

Expenditure incurred by SMEs on plant and machinery for use in Northern Ireland during the period 12 May 1998 to 11 May 2002 may qualify for 100% first-year allowances. Such allowances are not available for expenditure on plant used for leasing or for cars, LLAs, sea-going ships, aircraft and railway assets.

5.5.9 100% allowances for IT equipment
(CAA 2001, s 45)

Small businesses that invest in information and communications equipment (ie computers, software and Internet-enabled mobile 'phones) during the period 1 April 2000 to 31 March 2004 are entitled to 100% allowances. The definition of 'small business' for this purpose is that it must satisfy two of the following requirements:

(1) a turnover of not more than £2.8m;
(2) a balance sheet total of not more than £1.4m; and
(3) not more than 50 employees.

The Revenue confirmed that costs of designing a website may qualify for the 100% allowance.

5.5.10 100% allowance for energy-saving equipment
(CAA 2001, ss 45A-45C)

Expenditure after 31 March 2001 on designated energy-saving technologies and products qualifies for 100% first-year allowances. The qualifying items are set out in a list issued by the DETR: see www.eca.gov.uk.

5.5.11 Expenditure on water technologies

All businesses can claim 100% first-year allowances for expenditure on or after 1 April 2003 on designated plant and machinery to reduce water use and improve water quality. The designated technology classes are:

- Meters and monitoring equipment;
- Flow controllers;
- Leakage detection;
- Efficient toilets;
- Efficient taps.

Qualifying technologies and products can be found at www.eca.gov.uk.

5.5.12 100% capital allowances for refurbishing flats over shops

(CAA 2001, ss 393A-393W)

Qualifying expenditure on flats over shops has attracted 100% allowances since 11 May 2001. There are various conditions:

(1) the expenditure must be incurred on the renovation or conversion of vacant or underused space above shops and other commercial premises;
(2) the property must have been built before 1980, have no more than five floors and all upper floors must have originally been constructed primarily for residential use;
(3) the upper floors must have been either unoccupied or used only for storage for at least one year before the conversion work was put in hand;
(4) the properties must be in traditional shopping areas and the whole or greater part of the ground floor must be 'authorised for business use', ie designated as such for business rates imposed by the local authority;
(5) the conversion must not be part of any scheme to extend the building;
(6) there must not be more than four rooms in each flat;
(7) each flat must have separate external access (ie not through the shop); and
(8) the flats must not have a notional weekly rent exceeding the following limits

Number of rooms	*Flats in Greater London*	*Elsewhere*
1-2	£350	£150
3	£425	£225
4	£480	£300

No balancing charge will arise if the flats are retained for seven years and are either let or made available for letting throughout that period.

5.5.13 Long-life assets (LLAs)

(CAA 2001, ss 90-104)

FA 1997 introduced the concept of LLAs. An LLA has an expected working life of 25+ years. Where a trader incurs expenditure of more than £100,000 on an LLA, capital allowances are restricted to 6%.

This rule affects assets purchased on or after 26 November 1996, but not those purchased before 1 January 2001 where the contract was entered into prior to 26 November 1996. A number of categories of expenditure are specifically excluded from the general definition. Thus LLAs do not include any machinery or plant that is a fixture in, or is used in, a dwelling-house, retail shop, showroom, hotel or office or for ancillary purposes. Also there are specific exclusions for motor or hire cars. There is a transitional exception for expenditure contracted for before 2 November 1996 and incurred by 31 December 2000 and to which the long-life rules do not apply.

Expenditure on LLAs is segregated into a separate pool that qualifies for writing-down allowances at 6% instead of 25%. This categorisation of an asset as long life is irrevocable and it cannot later be reclassified as non-long life. The LLA rules do not apply where second-hand plant is purchased from a person who qualified for 25% writing-down allowances.

5.5.14 Expenditure on landlord's fixtures

(CAA 2001, s 172)

The *Stokes v Costain Property Investments Ltd* [1984] STC 204 decision established that capital allowances were not due on expenditure on plant by a tenant where the plant became part of a building and therefore became a landlord's fixture. This is because the items of plant did not 'belong' to the tenant. This was clearly unsatisfactory as tenants are often required to install plant within a building such as lifts, air conditioning, etc. Accordingly, the legislation was amended and now specifically provides that a tenant who incurs expenditure on such plant can receive allowances, but a balancing charge may be made on the expiry or surrender of the lease, according to the plant's market value at that time. There are complex provisions dealing with situations where more than one person incurs expenditure on the same fixture or where expenditure is incurred by an equipment lessor.

5.5.15 Acquisition of second-hand buildings

(CAA 2001, ss 172-204)

There are anti-avoidance provisions that:

(1) prevent allowances being given on fixtures as plant and machinery and under some other category (eg enterprise zones or scientific research);
(2) limit allowances given on fixtures as plant in total to the fixtures' original cost (or, where capital allowances were claimed on the fixtures for periods before 24 July 1996, the cost price to the most recent claimant). This applies only where the disposal by the previous claimant took place on or after 24 July 1996;
(3) treat a fixture as sold at its tax written-down value if it is sold for less than that value to accelerate allowances (other than where the disposal is for good commercial reasons and is not part of a tax avoidance scheme).

5.5.16 Buildings located in an enterprise zone

(CAA 2001, ss 298-299)

Qualifying expenditure on a commercial building located in an enterprise zone can qualify for a 100% initial allowance. 'Commercial building' is defined as a building or structure, other than an industrial building or hotel, used for the purposes of a trade, profession or vocation or as an office. The definition specifically excludes a building wholly or partly used as a dwelling-house. Certain conditions must be fulfilled, in that the building must:

(1) have been constructed under an unconditional contract entered into before the enterprise zone came to the end of its designated life; and
(2) be acquired unused or within two years of its having been let for the first time.

The part of the purchase price relating to the cost of the land does not qualify for capital allowances. Plant and machinery contained in the building that have become an integral part of it may also qualify for the 100% allowance. The initial allowance can be disclaimed, in whole or in part, and the remaining amount of qualifying expenditure is then available at 25%. The 25% writing-down allowances are given on a straight-line basis over four years rather than on the reducing basis that applies for plant.

Example – Capital allowances on buildings in an enterprise zone

An enterprise zone building is acquired for £200,000. The land cost is £20,000, so £180,000 qualifies for capital allowances. The purchaser disclaims the whole of the initial allowance. He receives annual allowances as follows:

	£
Year of expenditure	45,000
Year 2	45,000
Year 3	45,000
Year 4	45,000

If the purchaser had disclaimed only £80,000, the position would have been:

	£
Year of expenditure	
Initial allowance	100,000
Annual allowance	45,000
	145,000
Year 2 annual allowance	35,000
Year 3 annual allowance	Nil
Year 4 annual allowance	Nil

The point to note is that the annual allowances are based on the total qualifying costs, not on the balance left over after deducting the initial allowance.

Example – Disposal of a building in an enterprise zone

A disposal of an enterprise zone building within 25 years of acquisition gives rise to a balancing charge.

Y acquires an enterprise zone building in Year 1 and takes the full 100% initial allowance on the qualifying expenditure of £95,000. In Year 4 he disposes of the building. If he receives disposal proceeds of £75,000, there will be a balancing charge of £75,000. If he receives £120,000 (ie more than the trader's qualifying expenditure), the balancing charge is limited to £95,000.

5.5.17 Agricultural buildings allowances
(CAA 2001, ss 361 and 372)

Expenditure on agricultural buildings qualifies for a 4% annual allowance given on a straight-line basis. A balancing allowance or charge may arise on a disposal that takes place within a 25-year period.

The term 'agricultural buildings allowances' is misleading in that the expenditure does not need to be on a building. The allowances are given in respect of expenditure on farmhouses, farm or forestry buildings, cottages, fences, ditches, and drainage and sewerage works. The land must be used for agricultural purposes.

Expenditure incurred during the year ended 31 October 1993 qualified for an initial allowance of 20%.

5.5.18 Industrial buildings
(CAA 2001, s 271)

Expenditure on an industrial building brought into use for a trade by the year end qualifies for a 4% annual allowance, again given on the straight-line basis. An 'industrial building' is a building or structure used for the purpose of a trade consisting of:

(1) manufacturing or processing goods or materials; or
(2) maintaining or repairing goods or materials for customers; or
(3) maintaining or repairing goods or materials owned by the trader himself provided the relevant trade consists of manufacturing or processing goods or materials; or
(4) storaging:
    (a) raw materials for manufacture;
    (b) goods to be processed;
    (c) goods manufactured or processed, but not yet delivered to any purchaser;
    (d) goods on arrival by sea or air into the UK; or
(5) working mines, oil wells, etc or foreign plantations.

In addition, a sports pavilion provided for the welfare of workers employed in any trade qualifies for industrial buildings allowances. Qualifying expenditure again excludes the land element in the purchase price. A balancing charge or allowance may arise on a disposal within 25 years.

Example – Disposal of industrial buildings

An industrial building was acquired for a cost of £250,000. The land element was £20,000. If the purchaser brought the building into use immediately, allowances would be due as follows:

		£
	Qualifying cost	230,000
Year 1:	Annual allowance	(9,200)
	Residue	220,800
Year 2:	Annual allowance	(9,200)
	Residue	211,600

If the building is sold in Year 3, a balancing allowance or charge will arise according to whether the proceeds exceed £211,600. If the proceeds were £225,000 there would be a balancing charge of £13,400. If the proceeds were £150,000 there would be a balancing allowance of £61,600. The maximum balancing charge would be £18,400, ie the allowance received in Years 1 and 2.

5.5.19 Hotels

(CAA 2001, s 279)

A qualifying hotel attracts industrial buildings allowances (see 5.5.18). A qualifying hotel must fulfil the following conditions:

(1) Accommodation must be provided in a building of a permanent nature.
(2) The hotel must be open for at least four months during April to October.
(3) There must be at least ten bedrooms available for letting to the public in general that must not normally be in the same occupation for more than a month.
(4) The services provided must normally include the provision of breakfast and evening meals, making beds and cleaning rooms.

5.5.20 Expenditure on know-how

(CAA 2001, s 452)

Expenditure on acquiring know-how for use in a trade attracts capital allowances. 'Know-how' means any industrial information and techniques of assistance in manufacturing or processing goods or materials, or working or searching for mineral deposits, or that may be relevant to agricultural, forestry or fishing operations. Allowances are given on 'qualifying expenditure', which is the aggregate of any capital expenditure on know-how during the basis period, together with any unused balance of expenditure brought forward from the previous basis period and less any disposal value for know-how that has been sold.

Writing-down allowances are given at the rate of 25%.

5.5.21 Expenditure on scientific research

(CAA 2001, s 437)

Any capital expenditure incurred by a trader on scientific research related to a trade attracts a 100% allowance. 'Scientific research' was traditionally defined as activities in the fields of natural or applied science for the extension of knowledge. It has been redefined in FA 2000 to make it clear that it includes scientific research:

(1) that may lead to or facilitate an extension of trade; or
(2) of a medical nature that has a special relation to the welfare of workers employed in particular industries.

5.6 PRE-TRADING EXPENDITURE

(TA 1988, s 401, as amended by FA 1989, s 114 and FA 1993, s 109; CAA 2001, s 12)

A person may incur expenditure before he starts to trade such as:

- Rent for business premises;
- Rates, insurance, heating and lighting;
- Advertising wages or other payments to employees;
- Bank charges and interest;
- Lease rentals on plant and machinery and office equipment;
- Accountancy fees.

Expenditure qualifies for relief only if it is incurred within seven years of the date trade is commenced. The expense is treated as an ordinary trading expense incurred on the day the trader starts business.

Pre-trading capital expenditure that qualifies for capital allowances is also treated as having been incurred at the date trade is commenced.

5.7 POST-CESSATION RECEIPTS

(TA 1988, ss 103-104)

Where a person has been assessed on the cash basis (see 5.4.11), special rules apply if the trade or profession is discontinued. Subsequent receipts are normally taxed under Schedule D Case VI as income for the year in which they come in, although an election may be made for the post-cessation receipts to be treated as arising in the year of discontinuance.

Expenses may be deducted in so far as they were incurred wholly and exclusively for business and are not otherwise allowable. For example, a solicitor who had post-cessation receipts could deduct premiums paid on a professional indemnity policy where the cover related to the period after the solicitor had ceased to carry on his profession.

A similar charge may arise where a change occurs in the treatment of a trader's profits so that the cash basis ceases to apply and his profits are assessed on the earnings basis. Amounts received from customers after the change that relates to invoices issued when the business was dealt with on the cash basis are treated as post-cessation receipts.

5.8 POST-CESSATION EXPENSES

(TA 1988, s 109A)

Until 1995, no tax relief was available for expenditure incurred after a trade or profession had ceased (except to the extent to which the expense could be set against post-cessation receipts). This gave rise to serious problems for professional people such as architects who need to retain professional indemnity insurance after they have retired, in case a defect should subsequently come to light. The Revenue proved most intractable on this and stated that even if an insurance premium was paid prior to cessation, the part of the premium relating to the post-cessation period was not considered to be an allowable expense.

FA 1995 corrected this anomaly and expenditure may now be allowable if it is incurred within seven years of a business ceasing. The following types of expenditure may qualify for this relief:

(1) the costs of remedying defective work done, goods supplied, or services rendered while the trade or profession was continuing and damages paid by the taxpayer in respect of such defective work, goods or services whether awarded by a court or agreed during negotiations on a claim;
(2) insurance premiums paid to insure against the above costs;
(3) legal and other professional expenses incurred in connection with the above costs;
(4) debts owed to the business that have been taken into account in computing the profits or gains of the trade or profession before discontinuance but that have subsequently become bad;
(5) the costs of collecting debts that have been taken into account in computing the profits of the trade before discontinuance.

The amount of the relief will be reduced by any expense allowed as a deduction in the final accounting period that remains unpaid at the end of the year of assessment in which the new relief is given.

Expenditure that qualifies for the relief will be set against income and capital gains of the year of assessment in which the expense is paid. Where there is insufficient income or capital gains to cover the expenditure, the unrelieved expenditure of that year cannot be carried forward under the relief arrangements against future income or capital gains. However, the unrelieved expenditure will still be available to be carried forward under the existing rules and set against subsequent post-cessation receipts from the trade or profession.

The legislation requires a formal claim to be made within 22 months of the end of the year of assessment in which the expense is paid.

5.9 RELIEF FOR TRADING LOSSES

Relief may be available for a loss incurred by an individual in a trade or profession. Relief may also be due for pre-trading expenditure treated as a loss incurred when the trade was commenced (see 5.6). The provisions that govern the relief for trading losses are complex and there are several ways in which you may claim that losses be utilised.

Table 5.2 – Losses under self-assessment for 2002-03

Reference	*Description*	*Deadline*
TA 1988, s 380 FA 1991, s 72	Deduction from income or gains for 2002-03	31 Jan 2005
TA 1988, s 380	Deduction from income or gains for 2001-02	31 Jan 2005
TA 1988, s 381	Loss in first four years of trade carried back	31 Jan 2005
TA 1988, s 385	Carry forward against future profits	31 Jan 2009
TA 1988, s 388	Terminal loss relief	31 Jan 2009

5.9.1 Carry forward relief against subsequent assessments (TA 1988, s 385)

A loss incurred by a sole trader or a partner's share of his firm's trading loss may be carried forward and deducted in assessments for later years in respect of the same trade or profession. With the introduction of the CY basis of assessment (see 5.3.1), capital allowances are treated as trading expenses and can therefore increase or create a loss. Where losses are carried forward in this way, they must be used against the assessable profits for the first subsequent year in which profits arise. The loss carried forward in this way may also be relieved against certain income connected with the trade even though it is assessed under a different schedule (eg interest earned on temporary investment of trade receipts and dividends from trade investments). There is no limit on the number of years for which a loss may be carried forward provided the same trade is carried on. For 1996-97 onwards the loss must be claimed within five years of the filing date (ie for a loss arising in 2002-03, by 31 January 2009).

5.9.2 Relief against general income
(TA 1988, s 380)

Where a sole trader or partner incurs a loss and the trade was carried on with a view to profit, the loss may be relieved against his general income for the year of assessment in which it was incurred (ie his total income for the year). Relief may also be claimed against his general income for the preceding tax year. The claim for a loss to be set against his general income for the preceding tax year is an alternative to the claim for the loss to be relieved against income of the year of loss. In other words, either the loss may be set against income of the current year (with any balance being set against income of the following year) or the individual may forgo the chance to set the loss against his income for the current year and set the full amount against income of the preceding year.

Where an individual takes relief for trading losses against his general income, he must use up the losses to the extent to which he has taxable income. It is not possible for a claim to be made to restrict the amount of losses so as to enable sufficient income to be left to make use of his personal allowances. On the other hand, the legislation permits him to deduct certain items before arriving at his general income against which trading losses can be offset. These items include relief for allowable expenses for Schedule E purposes, retirement annuity and personal pension contributions, interest relief and relief for donations to charities by deed of covenant or Gift Aid.

Relief for losses against other income must be claimed within 22 months of the end of the tax year in which the loss arises (ie one year after the filing date for the return relating to that year of assessment) so that a 2002-03 loss must be claimed by 31 January 2005.

5.9.3 Relief by aggregation

Where the profits of different accounting periods are time apportioned (eg on commencement of a business), a loss may be relieved by aggregation with a profit. This situation could arise if a first period of trading were less than 12 months.

Example – Loss relief by aggregation

W started business on 1 January 2001. She made a loss of £6,000 for the period ended 30 September 2001 and a profit of £24,000 for the year ended 30 September 2002. Relief by aggregation would produce the following result:

Profits assessable 2000-01	Nil
Profits assessable 2001-02	Nil
Profits assessable 2002-03	£24,000

This is because the first 12 months' trading would be deemed to produce a net loss computed as follows:

	£
Loss for period 1 Jan to 30 Sept 2001	(6,000)
$\frac{3}{12}$ of profit for year ended 30 Sept 2002	6,000
	Nil

If a loss is set against other income, it cannot also be relieved by aggregation. Thus, if *W* had claimed relief for the £3,000 loss that she had incurred in 2000-01, only the balance of the loss for the period ended 30 September 2001 which relates to the period 6 April to 30 September 2001 could be taken into account in arriving at the profits of the first 12 months' trading. The 2001-02 assessment would then be £3,000.

Example – Loss set against other income

Y commenced trading on 1 August 2001. He has a loss during the nine months ended 30 April 2002 of £36,000. He has profits for the year ended 30 April 2003 of £60,000.

If the 2001-02 and 2002-03 losses are used by being set against *Y*'s other income, the Schedule D assessments will be as follows:

		£
2001-02		Nil
2002-03	Profits of first 12 months:	
	9 months ended 30 April 2002	Nil
	$\frac{3}{12}$ × profits for year ended 30 April 2003	15,000
		15,000
	CY basis profits for year ended 30 April 2003	60,000

Contrast this with the situation where relief for the loss is obtained by aggregation:

2001-02		Nil
2002-03	Loss for 9 months to 30 April 2002	(36,000)
	Profits for year ended 30 April 2003	15,000
	Loss carried forward	(21,000)
2003-04	Profits assessed on CY basis	60,000
	Less: loss brought forward	(21,000)
		39,000

5.9.4 Losses arising from a business taxed under CY basis

Under the CY basis (see 5.3.1), losses are attributed to a tax year in the same way as profits are assessed. This means that once the business has got past the opening years, a loss will be treated as arising in the tax year in which the trader's accounting period ends. Losses for the opening years are computed on exactly the same basis as profits.

5.9.5 Losses in early years of a trade

(TA 1988, s 381)

In certain circumstances, relief may be claimed against an individual's general income for the three years of assessment preceding the year in which the loss is incurred. Relief is given against income for the earliest year first. There are certain preconditions for a loss to be claimed in this way:

(1) The loss must arise during the first four tax years in which the business is carried on.
(2) Where a trade is acquired from a spouse, the four years run from the date the spouse first commenced trading (unless the trade is taken over on the spouse's death).
(3) The trade must be carried on, on a commercial basis and with a reasonable expectation of profits.

A claim for a 2002-03 loss to be relieved in this way must be made by 31 January 2005.

5.9.6 Relief for trading losses against capital gains

(FA 1991, s 72)

An individual who has incurred a trading loss may have it set against any capital gains that arise in the same or preceding year. It is not possible to claim relief for losses in this way without first having made a claim for relief under s 380 for the loss to be set against the individual's general income for the year (see 5.9.2 for the time limit for making such a claim).

5.9.7 Terminal loss relief

(TA 1988, s 388)

Where a trade, profession or vocation is permanently discontinued, a loss incurred during the last 12 months can be deducted from the profits charged to tax in the three tax years before the final year. The relief can include a claim for the loss arising in the tax year in which the cessation takes place, and a proportion of the loss for the previous tax year.

Capital allowances for the final tax year may also be claimed, as can an appropriate proportion of the preceding year's capital allowances, representing the allowances due for the period beginning 12 months prior to the cessation.

The terminal loss may be carried back against profits from the same trade for the three tax years preceding the year of cessation. The relief is given against the latest year's profits first.

If interest and dividends would have been included as trading profits (except that they were subject to deduction of tax at source), the terminal loss may be set against such income.

5.9.8 Anti-avoidance provisions

Losses from limited partnerships

(FA 1988, s 117)

Limited partnerships were widely used in tax avoidance arrangements. The House of Lords decided in *Reed v Young* [1986] STC 285 that a limited partner could be entitled to loss relief for an amount that exceeded his actual liability under the Limited Partnership Act. This led to specific legislation to limit the amount of loss relief to the capital that is 'at risk'. Any losses incurred beyond this amount must be carried forward to be set against any future share of profits received by the limited partner from the firm. The s 117 provisions apply to individuals who are limited partners or members of a joint venture arrangement under which their liability is limited to a contract, agreement, guarantee, etc.

5.9.9 Loss relief where business transferred to a company

(TA 1988, s 386)

Where a business has been carried on by an individual (either as a sole trader or in partnership) and is transferred to a company, it is possible for any unused trading losses to be relieved against his income from the company in subsequent years. This relief is available only if the business is transferred to a company wholly or mainly in return for an allotment of shares and then only if the individual has retained ownership of those shares throughout the tax year concerned. In practice, the Revenue does not withhold relief provided he has retained at least 80% of the shares.

5.9.10 Schedule D Case V losses

(TA 1988, s 391)

Profits from a trade managed or controlled abroad are taxed under Schedule D Case V. Loss relief is calculated in the same way as for a loss incurred in a trade, profession or vocation taxed under Schedule D Case I or II. Relief for such losses is given in the same way as relief is given for UK trading losses, except that where a loss is to be set against other income, a Case V loss can be deducted only from:

(1) profits from other foreign trades assessable under Case V;
(2) foreign pensions and annuities where a 10% deduction is available;
(3) foreign emoluments assessable under Schedule E.

5.10 PARTNERSHIPS

A partnership's profits are computed in the same way as a sole trader's (see 5.4-5.5). However, there are a number of additional complications.

5.10.1 Salaried partners

A salaried partner is engaged under a contract of employment. He is normally taxed under Schedule E rather than under Schedule D. His remuneration is treated as a normal employee cost in arriving at the firm's profits. Sometimes partners have a fixed share of profits. It is not always easy to determine whether they are Schedule D or salaried partners. The key indicators that a partner is assessable under Schedule D are that the individual has capital at risk and that he is not subject to the control and direction of the Schedule D partners.

5.10.2 How partnership profits are taxed

There was a difference between firms that were carrying on business on or after 6 April 1994 and those carrying on business before that date. The difference in treatment disappeared in 1997-98 with the introduction of the CY basis for all unincorporated businesses.

Partners in a firm that started business on or after 6 April 1994, or who are deemed to have started a new business because the old firm had a cessation, have always been taxed separately. Assessments are raised on individual partners rather than on the firm as a whole. There is no principle of partners being jointly and severally liable for the firm's tax.

For pre 1994-95 businesses, assessments were made on the firm rather than on individual partners. The partnership's assessable profits for a year were assessed in one amount payable by the firm as a whole with each partner jointly and severally liable. The assessment reflected the way in which income was divided among the partners, their allowances, etc. This came to an end in 1996-97 and partners are now always assessed separately.

5.10.3 Treatment of partners under CY basis

Partners assessed individually

Assessments under the CY basis have always been made on individual partners rather than on the firm itself. Each partner is responsible for settling his own tax liabilities and is not jointly and severally liable for the total amount of tax payable by the partners. There may be a minor exception to this where there are non-resident partners in the firm.

Application of CY basis to partners

Basically, each partner is treated separately and the rules described at 5.3.1-5.3.3 are applied.

Example of how partners' taxable income is computed

> *K* and *L* start a new firm on 6 October 1999. They share profits equally. On 6 January 2001, *M* joins them and takes a one-third entitlement to profits. Accounts to 5 October 2000 show a profit of £132,000. The accounts for the years to 5 October 2001 and 5 October 2002 show a profit of £240,000 and £300,000 respectively. The position is as follows:
>
> *1999-00* *K* and *L* are each assessed on the actual basis, ie the firm's profits of £66,000 for 1999-2000 ($\frac{6}{12}$ × £132,000 profits for the year ended 5 October 2000) are divided equally between them, so *K* and *L* are each assessed on £33,000.
>
> *2000-01* *K* and *L* are assessed on their share of the firm's profits for the first 12 months, ie profits of £132,000 are divided equally and each is assessed on £66,000. *M* is assessed on the actual basis, because 2000-01 is her first tax year as a partner in this firm, so she is assessed on £20,000 ($\frac{3}{12}$ × her one-third share of the profits for the year ended 5 October 2001).
>
> *2001-02* *K* and *L* are assessed on the CY basis on their share of the firm's profits for the year ended 5 October 2001, ie £80,000 each. *M* is assessed on the profits for her first 12 months (ie $\frac{9}{12}$ × £80,000 plus $\frac{3}{12}$ × £100,000).
>
> *2002-03* All three partners are assessed on the CY basis, ie their one-third share of the firm's profits for the year ended 5 October 2002 of £300,000.

Similarly, the provisions on overlap relief are applied separately in relation to each partner. Thus, in the above example, if *K* retired on 5 October 2002, he will be entitled to overlap relief in arriving at his taxable profits for 2002-03. The other ongoing partners would get their overlap relief only when they retire or the firm changes its accounting date (see below). Their overlap relief is as follows:

	£
K	33,000
L	33,000
M	45,000 ($\frac{3}{12}$ × £80,000 + $\frac{3}{12}$ × £100,000).

5.10.4 Partnership interest and other investment income

A partner may be entitled to a share of interest earned by the firm on surplus cash – or indeed any other investment income.

Each partner is assessed on his share of such income, but it is assessed on the CY basis. Thus, if a firm makes up accounts to 31 May, the partners will be assessed for 2002-03 on their share of investment income in the firm's accounts for the year ended 31 May 2002 – even though the relevant income may actually have been received during the tax year 2001-02. The exception to this is investment income taxed at source which is assessable on a tax year basis, i.e. bank interest received net.

5.10.5 Catching-up charge: partnerships formerly on cash basis

The catching-up charge for businesses taxed on the cash basis up to 1998-99 is described at 5.4.11. The total catching-up charge for partnerships is based on the first accounting period starting on or after 6 April 1999 as for individuals. The part of the charge allocated to the first year is then allocated to the persons who were members of the partnership:

(1) during the 12 months ending on the date that the catching-up charge is calculated; and
(2) using the profit-sharing arrangements for that 12-month period.

The same method is used for the parts of the charge being levied in future years, using the profit-sharing arrangements for the 12 months ending on the anniversary of the catching-up charge that falls into the tax year. This applies irrespective of a future change in accounting date.

5.10.6 Limits and changes in partners

The one-tenth and 10% limits operate at partnership level for the first nine years as they do for individuals. A partner remains liable for his share of the catching-up charge only for the period up to the date he leaves the partnership. Similarly, anyone joining the partnership during the ten-year spreading period becomes liable for his share of the charge in the future.

5.10.7 Partnership tax returns

As well as requiring returns from individual partners, the Revenue issues a partnership tax return to the 'nominated partner'. The return requires full details of the firm's profits and capital gains and the way profits (and losses) are divided between the partners. A partner needs to refer to the self-assessment reference under which the partnership return has been filed. The legislation means that all business expenses must be claimed on the partnership return, even where the expenditure is borne by an individual partner (eg his car expenses or the purchase of a fax machine for business use at home). However, the Revenue states in Helpsheet IR231 that:

> the only legal basis for giving relief for expenditure that qualifies for capital allowances is as a deduction in the calculation of the profits of the partnership business (unless there is a formal leasing agreement between the partner and the partnership, when the allowances will be due against the leasing income).
>
> However, this does not mean that any legitimate expenditure incurred by a partner – that is any expense that would be allowable if met from partnership funds – can only be relieved if it is formally included in the partnership accounts. Nor does it mean that capital allowances can only be claimed on vehicles, or other assets, that feature in the partnership accounts.
>
> Providing that:
>
> - any expenditure, or claim to capital allowances, is correctly calculated for tax purposes, and
> - records relevant to those calculations are made and kept as if the expenditure, or assets, were part of the partnership accounts
>
> the Revenue will accept entries in the relevant sections of the Partnership Tax Return that, though based on the partnership accounts, include adjustments for such expenditure, or allowances. But once the adjustments have been made the expenditure will be treated, for all practical purposes, as if it had been included in the partnership's accounts.

5.10.8 Interest paid by partners on personal loans

Where a partner has taken a personal loan to finance his buying into the firm or to provide part of its working capital, he can claim relief for the interest paid by him on such borrowings. However, this relief is given by way of a deduction from his total taxable income rather than as an expense in computing his Schedule D profits (see 9.4).

5.11 LIMITED LIABILITY PARTNERSHIPS

5.11.1 Background

The legislation on limited liability partnerships (LLPs) came into effect on 6 April 2001. In essence, an LLP is a hybrid. Legally it takes the form of a body corporate (a company), with its own legal personality, but for tax purposes it may be treated as transparent. Provided the LLP is carrying on a lawful business with a view to profit, its members are taxed as if they were partners in a partnership.

Members are assessed on their share of the LLP's profits and capital gains. Unlike a conventional partnership, there is no joint and several liability between the members. Their liability, in most cases, is limited to the capital contributed to the LLP, together with any further capital they may have agreed to contribute in the event of winding up the LLP. Undrawn profits do not automatically become part of a member's capital contributed (unless otherwise agreed). The member ranks equally with other unsecured creditors for repayment of his current account balance. This contrasts with conventional partnerships where the partner is jointly and severally liable to the full extent of his personal assets. An LLP may therefore have attractions as compared with conventional partnerships, but there can also be drawbacks. For example, the LLP is technically a company and has to file accounts and disclose certain financial information, broadly in line with similar sized companies.

5.11.2 Restriction of loss relief

If a loss arises, there may be a restriction on the member's ability to set the loss against his other income. The limit is the amount of capital contributed by the member.

This restriction does not apply where the LLP carries on a profession.

Guidance notes on LLP can be obtained from Companies House. www.companieshouse.gov.uk

5.12 PARTNERSHIPS CONTROLLED OUTSIDE THE UK

(TA 1988, s 112)

A UK resident may be a partner in a partnership controlled outside the UK. His earnings from such a partnership are normally assessable under Schedule D Case V (rather than under Case I or II – but note that profits earned by a UK branch are taxed under Case I or II).

5.12.1 Current year basis

A partner in a foreign partnership is assessable on the CY basis (see 5.3.1).

5.12.2 Classification of overseas entities

In practice, it is often not clear whether an overseas legal entity will be treated as a partnership or a company for UK tax purposes. This is so especially where an entity combines some of the characteristics of UK partnerships and companies. The Revenue set out its opinion of the correct tax treatment of various US and European entities in *Tax Bulletin*, December 2000.

6

INCOME FROM UK PROPERTY

This chapter deals with rental income from land or property in the UK. All such income is now taxed under Schedule A. Rents received from letting an overseas property are taxed under Schedule D Case V and the tax treatment of such income is covered in 8.4.

The following matters are covered in this chapter:

(1) Basis of assessment and administration.
(2) How to calculate your taxable profit.
(3) Lump sums deemed to be rent (premiums).
(4) 'Rent-a-room' relief.
(5) Furnished holiday accommodation.
(6) Capital allowances on investment properties.
(7) Mineral royalties.
(8) Woodlands.

Do not overlook VAT: it is possible to register many rental businesses for VAT purposes and this can mean that you will recover input tax. However, you will have to charge VAT on the rent. See further 28.3.5.

6.1 BASIS OF ASSESSMENT AND ADMINISTRATION

6.1.1 All rental activities treated as single business

All rental income received by an individual from UK properties is now assessed under Schedule A, whether the property is let unfurnished or furnished. All income and expenses are brought together in a single business of letting UK property. The income is brought in on normal commercial accountancy principles. Expenses are allowed if they satisfy the test that the expense is incurred wholly and exclusively for business purposes and this rule applies to interest (including overdraft interest) just as for any other expense.

6.1.2 Exceptional types of rental income

Rental income for Schedule A purposes includes ground rents. It also includes 'other receipts from an estate' in land such as charges levied by a landlord in return for maintaining a block of flats and payments made to a landowner for sporting rights. It does not include admission charges made by hotels, boarding houses, theatres, etc since the profits of such businesses are chargeable to tax under Schedule D Case I.

Income from taking in lodgers is generally treated as trading income rather than rental income assessable under Schedule A. However, see 6.4 on 'rent-a-room' relief.

6.1.3 Schedule A assessed on fiscal year basis

An individual must report his income on a tax year basis, ie he must draw up accounts to 5 April.

6.1.4 Partnership income dealt with separately

Rental income received by a partnership is treated as a separate source. If the partnership does not have any trading income, the rental income is assessed on a fiscal year basis, irrespective of the date to which the partnership draws up accounts. In contrast, if the partnership also has some trading income taxed under Schedule D Case I or II, its Schedule A income is assessed on the same basis. Thus, if a trading partnership has a 30 April year end, the partners will be assessed for 2002-03 on their share of the partnership's Schedule A income for the year ended 30 April 2002.

6.1.5 Schedule A income is investment income

Although all rental income is treated as arising from a single business of letting property, the income is still treated as investment income. Any losses can only be carried forward for offset against Schedule A income and cannot be set against the individual's other income for the year (there is an exception to this for deficits arising from letting agricultural properties where the deficit may be set against other income: see below).

Schedule A income is not 'income from savings'.

6.1.6 Deficiency on agricultural property

(TA 1988, s 33)

Where an estate consists of or includes agricultural land, a deficiency may be set against any Schedule A income. Any balance that cannot be relieved in this way may be set against the individual's other income for the year, or the following tax year.

'Agricultural land' is defined as land, houses or other buildings in the UK occupied wholly or mainly for husbandry purposes. 'Estate' means any land and buildings managed as one estate. Where only part of the estate is used for husbandry, only a proportion of any deficiency can be relieved in this way.

6.2 HOW TO CALCULATE YOUR TAXABLE PROFIT

The legislation requires that landlords should calculate their income and expenses in accordance with normal accountancy principles but subject to the same specific rules that apply for Schedule D Case I purposes.

You may find it helpful to obtain Revenue booklet IR150, *Taxation of Rents*. You should also study the notes and helpsheets issued by the Revenue to enable landlords to complete their SA tax returns. The Revenue's guide to the SA return sets out the normal treatment of certain common expenses.

6.2.1 Rent receivable

The Revenue confirms in its booklet that you do not bring rent into a year's tax computation merely because you receive it in, or it is due to be paid to you in, the year. Equally, you do not exclude rent merely because you receive it outside, or it is due outside, the tax year. You bring in the proportion of rent earned in the year from the tenants' use of the property in the year. You exclude the proportion earned from the tenant's right to use the property outside the year. So, you may need to make an adjustment where rent is receivable on, say, a quarterly basis, either in advance or in arrears.

Incidentally, the Revenue's notes to the SA return point out that rental income includes receipts in kind as well as in cash.

6.2.2 Bad debts

A landlord can claim a deduction for rent that is due to him but has not been paid where the debt is clearly irrecoverable. A deduction can also be claimed for doubtful debts. Such a deduction is available only where the landlord has taken all reasonable steps to recover the debt. Furthermore, if the outstanding rent is collected in a later tax year, he should bring the recovery into his accounts as a receipt for his rental income for that year.

No deduction is available for a general bad debt reserve (ie a landlord cannot deduct 5% of the outstanding rents due to him at the year end just to be on the safe side). Tax relief is available for provisions for doubtful debts only if the provisions relate to specific debts and the facts relating to each debtor have been taken into account. Furthermore, as the Revenue literature makes clear, you cannot deduct a bad or doubtful debt merely because the tenant is always a slow payer. There has to be good reason for thinking the debt is likely to be bad.

A landlord who waived rent due from farmers, etc because of foot and mouth is not taxed on the amount waived: see *Tax Bulletin* May 2001.

6.2.3 Rent-free periods

The Revenue approach follows the accounting principles set out in SSAP21. If the landlord, for example grants a lease for a five-year period with no rent being payable in Year 1 and rent of £10,000 being payable in Years 2-5, the landlord should spread the total amount of rent receivable over the five years (ie £40,000) and bring into his accounts one-fifth of that total income for each year of the lease. In other words, the treatment reflects the substance of the transaction; in essence there is not really a rent-free year at all since the £40,000 payable over the first five years is rent for the whole of that period.

6.2.4 Expenses

Expenses should also be brought into account on normal accountancy principles. This means that a landlord should deduct any allowable expenses that relate to work done, or goods or services supplied to him, for a particular year. There is no requirement that the supplier should have been paid during the tax year. Thus if you have raised a loan for the purchase or improvement of repairs of properties that are let out, you can claim relief for interest that has accrued up to 5 April even though the bank or building society may debit interest on a different basis (eg at 30 June and 31 December).

Expenses are deductible only if they meet the 'wholly and exclusively' rule (ie expenditure that is part business/part private is not allowable). For example, the cost of travelling to Wales to supervise repairs to a holiday cottage is not an allowable deduction for tax purposes if the landlord also took a holiday while there (ie the visit had a dual purpose). But where a definite part or proportion of an expense is wholly incurred for business purposes, that part may be deducted. This might well arise where a landlord lives in part of the property that is rented out: here, a proportion of the insurance premium relating to the property as a whole may be deducted in the landlord's Schedule A computation. Remember that where expenditure is partly for business and partly for personal use, you have to complete a specific box on the SA return.

6.2.5 Repairs, maintenance and renewals

Examples of common repairs normally deductible in computing income for tax purposes are:

- Exterior and interior painting and decorating;
- Stone cleaning;
- Damp and rot treatment;
- Mending broken windows, doors, furniture and machines such as cookers or lifts;
- Re-pointing;
- Replacing roof slates, flashing and gutters.

The Revenue has confirmed that the cost of replacing worn out single-glazed windows with double glazing may be an allowable expense in computing Schedule A profits (see *Tax Bulletin* 59).

Substantial repairs carried out shortly after a landlord has occupied a property to put it into a fit state are generally disallowed as constituting capital expenditure.

The *Jenners* case (see 5.4.9) means that a specific and scientifically calculated provision for the cost of repair work to be carried out in the future might be allowable. You need to take specialist advice on whether making such a provision accords with the generally accepted accountancy principles set out in FRS12.

Expenditure on improvements that obviated the need for repairs used to be allowed by concession, but is no longer allowed in relation to expenditure incurred after 5 April 2001.

6.2.6 Renewals

The landlord can claim the cost of replacing furniture, furnishings and machinery. However, expenditure on renewals is not available where the landlord claims a standard 10% wear and tear allowance (see 6.2.9).

Where expenditure on renewals is claimed, the landlord should bring into account of his income any amounts he receives for items that have been scrapped or sold. Also, expenditure on renewals should not normally include the cost of items that represent a significant improvement or addition to the furniture and furnishings, etc previously made available to the tenant.

6.2.7 Legal and professional costs

The Revenue view is as follows:

Non-allowable expenses

(1) Expenses in connection with the first letting or subletting of a property for more than one year (including eg legal expenses (such as the cost of drawing up a lease), agents' and surveyors' fees and commission).
(2) Any proportion of the legal, etc costs that relate to the payment of a premium on the renewal of a lease.
(3) Fees incurred in obtaining planning permission or on the registration of title when buying a property.

Allowable expenses

(1) Expenses for granting a lease of a year or less.
(2) The normal legal and professional fees incurred on the renewal of a lease, provided it is for less than 50 years (the Revenue confirmed in its *Tax Bulletin* that the costs of granting a lease to a new tenant are normally allowable provided the replacement lease follows closely on the previous one and is broadly similar in terms).

(3) Professional fees incurred
   (a) in evicting an unsatisfactory tenant, with a view to re-letting;
   (b) on an appeal against a compulsory purchase order; and
   (c) in drawing up accounts.

6.2.8 Costs of services provided, including wages

A landlord who provides any service to a tenant (eg gardening, the provision of a porter, cleaning, etc) can claim the cost of these services, provided they are incurred wholly and exclusively for the purposes of the letting.

6.2.9 10% wear and tear allowance

A landlord who lets a dwelling-house as furnished accommodation can claim (as an alternative to claims on a renewals basis) an allowance amounting to 10% of the rent received after deducting charges or services that would normally be borne by the tenant but are, in fact, borne by the landlord (eg council tax). This allowance, known as 'wear and tear allowance', is accepted by the Revenue as broadly covering the cost of normal renewals of furniture.

A landlord who lets non-residential property (eg offices) can normally claim capital allowances for any items provided (eg furniture).

Table 6.1 – Computing your Schedule A income (straightforward situation)

For each property, bring in the rental income that relates to the tax year (ie if rent is receivable on 25 March 2003 for the quarter ending 24 June 2003, include a proportion for the period 25 March to 5 April 2003).

Deduct

- Charges made by an agent for rent collection and management;
- Any rent you have to pay on the property (eg ground rent);
- Any service charges you have to pay (particularly likely to apply if you are letting out a flat);
- Insurance premiums paid for the period covered by the tax year: if you pay insurance for a calendar year, include $\frac{3}{12}$ of the premium for 2003 + $\frac{9}{12}$ of the premium for 2002;
- Repairs and similar expenses (eg gardening) incurred in the tax year. Note that the expense need not actually have been incurred in the tax year so long as it is clear that it relates to the tax year;
- Interest on borrowings used to finance the original purchase of a property, improvements or repairs.

Aggregate all the income and expenses for your different properties except for properties not let on a commercial basis (any deficit on such properties will almost certainly not be allowable). Add in any lump sums taxable as premiums (see 6.3).

6.3 LUMP SUMS DEEMED TO BE RENT (PREMIUMS)

(TA 1988, ss 34-39)

6.3.1 Introduction

A landlord faced with the choice of letting a property for five years at £10,000 pa, or taking a lump sum in return for granting a lease for five years at an annual rent of £100, would regard the two transactions as very similar in their overall consequences. The purpose behind the tax legislation that deals with lump sums (or 'premiums') is to ensure that the tax treatment of both transaction types is similar in nature. The principle is that a proportion of a premium received by a landlord for granting a lease of less than 50 years should be taxed as if it were rent.

The following sections apply only where the person who receives the premium is the landlord, ie a person who continues to hold a superior interest in the property. An outgoing tenant who assigns the whole of his interest in the property is not regarded as receiving a premium for Schedule A purposes.

6.3.2 How premiums are apportioned between income and capital

(TA 1988, s 34)

The rule is that the full amount of the premium is treated as rent except for 2% for every complete year of the lease after the first year. For example, if a ten-year lease is granted for a premium of £25,000, the amount subject to tax under Schedule A is 82% of £25,000, ie £20,500. See Table 6.2.

Table 6.2 – Extract from Inland Revenue helpsheet

Working sheet for chargeable premiums – leases up to 50 years

Premium	**A**	£
Number of **complete periods of 12 months** in lease *(ignore the first 12 months of the lease)*	**B**	£
A multiplied by B	**C**	£
C divided by 50	**D**	£
A less D	**E**	£

Copy figure in box E to box 5.22.

6.3.3 Payments in kind
(TA 1988, s 34(2))

It is provided that if a tenant is required to carry out work as a term of his lease, the whole of the benefit accruing to the landlord is deemed to be a premium receivable at the commencement of the lease.

6.3.4 Deemed premiums
(TA 1988, s 34(5))

Any lump sum paid by a tenant to vary the lease can be treated as a premium receivable at the time the contract for the variation is entered into.

Example – Deemed premium

A is the landlord of a property used as offices and let on a 15-year lease. It is a term of the lease that the tenant should not use the premises for any other purpose.

The tenant secures planning consent to use the property for light industrial use. He makes a payment to *A* of £12,000 in Year 4 to induce him to vary the lease so that the property can be used for industrial purposes. *A* is deemed to receive a premium in Year 4. The taxable amount is:

	£
	12,000
Less: (10 × 2%)	(2,400)
	9,600

Similarly, if *A* had received a lump sum to induce him to waive the relevant term in the lease, the lump sum would be treated as a premium.

6.3.5 Sale with right to repurchase the property
(TA 1988, s 36)

Where the freehold or leasehold of a property is sold subject to a condition that at a future date the purchaser may be required to sell it back to the vendor at a lower price, the vendor is liable to tax under Schedule D Case VI on the excess of the sale price over the repurchase price. The difference is treated as a premium so that the amount charged is reduced by 2% for each complete year between the date of sale and the date of resale less one year. A similar rule applies where a vendor sells a property but retains an option to repurchase it.

6.3.6 Which year?

The SA return pack and the Revenue's internal guidance indicate that the taxable amount of any premiums should be taxed as income for the year in which the landlord becomes entitled to them. This could be challenged on the grounds that the income for granting, say, a five-year lease should be spread evenly over the period, with part of the premium being taxed for each of the years to which it relates. Seek professional advice if substantial amounts are involved.

6.4 'RENT-A-ROOM' RELIEF

(F(No 2)A 1992, s 59 and Sched 10)

Special relief is available to an individual who receives payment for letting furnished accommodation in a qualifying residence. The relief provides total exemption from income of £4,250 unless sums accrue to another person in respect of lettings of furnished accommodation in the same property, in which case the exemption is reduced to £2,125, regardless of the number of other people (ie if three people qualified in respect of the same property, the limit for all three would be £2,125 each).

A qualifying residence is a residence that is the individual's only or main residence at some time in the basis period for the year of assessment in relation to the lettings. 'Residence' means a building (or part of a building) occupied or intended to be occupied as a separate residence.

Rent-a-room relief is available automatically unless the taxpayer elects otherwise or the gross sums received exceed the £4,250 limit.

Where the gross sums received exceed the £4,250 limit for the year of assessment (or the £2,125 limit where some other person receives income from furnished lettings within the same property), the taxpayer may elect for his profits or gains for the basis period to be treated as equal to the excess. For example, if a taxpayer has gross rent of £5,000, he may compute his taxable income as £750 or he can compute it in the normal way by reference to the expenses he actually incurred.

Need for caution

The Revenue has commented on the suggestion that rent-a-room relief might be available where part of an individual's residence is let to a company for use as an office (or for some other trade or business purpose). The Revenue's view is that the relief is available only where the person paying rent uses the premises for residential purposes.

6.4.1 Revenue leaflets

For further information on rent-a-room relief, obtain leaflets IR87, *Rooms to let*, and IR223, *Rent-a-Room for Traders*.

6.5 FURNISHED HOLIDAY ACCOMMODATION
(TA 1988, ss 503-504)

6.5.1 Definition

Where a person lets furnished holiday accommodation (including caravans), it may be treated as a trade provided the following conditions are satisfied:

(1) The property must be situated in the UK.
(2) It must be let on a commercial basis.
(3) It must be let as furnished accommodation.
(4) It must be available for commercial letting to the public as holiday accommodation for at least 140 days in a 12-month period.
(5) It must be let for at least 70 such days.
(6) It must not normally be occupied by the same person for more than 31 consecutive days at any time during a seven-month period within the 12-month period.

Where a person lets more than one such property, the 70-day test may be satisfied by averaging any or all of the accommodation let by that person. A claim for averaging must be made within 22 months of the end of the tax year (ie for 2001-02, by 31 January 2004).

Some extra latitude is allowed for 2000-01 and 2001-02 for accommodation in foot and mouth-affected rural areas: see *Tax Bulletin* May 2001.

6.5.2 Lettings classified as furnished holiday lettings

The following consequences will follow if a property is treated as being let as furnished holiday accommodation.

Relief for interest

Interest on loans used to purchase the property and to finance the lettings should qualify as an expense incurred in the trade. In some cases, the inclusion of such interest will give rise to a loss for tax purposes.

Capital allowances for plant and machinery

Equipment, furniture and furnishings may attract capital allowances: see 5.5.

Relief for pre-trading expenditure

Expenditure incurred before the business of letting such properties actually commences may be allowed as a loss incurred at the point in time when the lettings commence as pre-trading expenditure (see 5.6).

Relief for losses

Because the activity of letting such property is regarded as a trade for Schedule D purposes, relief can be obtained for losses against the individual's other income (see 5.9). This applies whether the loss arises from interest, capital allowances or pre-trading expenditure or for other reasons provided it can be shown that the activity was carried on on a commercial basis.

Profits classified as earned income

The legislation provides that profits arising from letting such property should be treated as earned income. This is not dependent on the owner taking any active involvement in the lettings: the whole activity can be dealt with by an agent where desired. Because the profits are regarded as earned income, they rank as 'relevant earnings' for personal pension contribution and retirement annuity premium purposes (see 12.8).

Capital gains tax

Roll-over and retirement reliefs may be available: see 17.4 and 17.8.

The property is regarded as a business asset for taper relief (see 14.6).

6.6 CAPITAL ALLOWANCES ON INVESTMENT PROPERTIES

6.6.1 Introduction

Capital allowances are usually given when the Revenue assesses the profits of a trade. It is also possible to qualify for capital allowances in respect of expenditure on investment properties, for example where a landlord installs a lift, air-conditioning, electrical equipment, etc, or incurs capital expenditure on a flat over a shop (see 5.5.12). The allowances must first be set against the income of a defined class (see below), but any surplus of allowances may be set against the individual's other income for that year or the following tax year.

6.6.2 Expenditure that may attract allowances

The following are often installed by landlords and generally qualify as plant:

- Electrical, cold water, gas and sewerage systems designed to meet the particular requirements of a trader to whom the building is let;
- Water-heating systems;
- Powered systems of ventilation, air cooling or air purification;

- Lifts, hoists and moving walkways;
- Sprinkler systems and fire alarms;
- Burglar alarm systems.

6.6.3 Purchase of second-hand buildings

A landlord who acquires a building can often claim capital allowances for the plant contained in it (see 5.5.15).

6.6.4 Agricultural buildings allowances
(CAA 1990, ss 132(3) and 141)

Agricultural buildings allowances (see 5.5.17) are available for relief by 'discharge or repayment of tax' if the landlord does not carry on a farming trade. The allowances must first be set against agricultural or forestry rental income.

It is necessary to make a claim under CAA 1990, s 141 within two years of the end of the year of assessment in order that agricultural buildings allowances may be set against other income rather than carried forward. If the individual wishes, the surplus allowances may be set against income of the following tax year.

6.6.5 Industrial buildings allowances
(CAA 1990, ss 9 and 141)

An individual who owns the relevant interest in an industrial building may qualify for industrial buildings allowances (see 5.5.18) because the property is occupied and used for a qualifying trade. Similarly, an individual who owns a property in an enterprise zone generally qualifies for allowances where the building is occupied for commercial purposes.

The allowances on such buildings must first be set against rental income from the buildings and then against any balancing charge that arises on the disposal of an interest in an industrial building. Any surplus of allowances may then be set against the individual's income for the year, or the following tax year. Again, a formal claim is required under s 141.

6.6.6 Enterprise zone trust

It is possible to invest in properties in enterprise zones through a syndicate or 'enterprise zone property trust'. An individual who invests in the trust is treated as if he had incurred a proportion of the trust's expenditure on enterprise zone properties and the allowances may be set against his other income in the same way as described at 6.6.5. In some cases, there may be a delay in that an individual invests in a trust at the end of one tax year and becomes entitled to allowances only for the following year (because that is the year in which the trust acquires the relevant properties).

6.7 MINERAL ROYALTIES

(TA 1988, s 122 and Sched 6)

Mineral royalties are normally received net of tax at the basic rate. However, only part of the royalties is taxable as income.

Where the recipient is resident or ordinarily resident in the UK, one-half of the mineral royalties is treated as capital gains rather than income. Similarly, only 50% of any management expenses or other sums deductible for Schedule A purposes may be set against the part of the mineral royalties treated as income.

When the mineral lease comes to an end, the person may claim a capital loss as if he had disposed of the land at its market value at that time. The loss may be set against capital gains for the year in which the mineral lease expires or against capital gains taxed on mineral royalties during the preceding 15 years.

'Mineral royalties' is defined as including rents, tolls, royalties and other periodic payments relating to the winning and working of minerals (other than water, peat and topsoil) under a lease, licence or other agreement.

6.8 WOODLANDS

(FA 1988, s 65 and Sched 6)

At one time, profits arising from the occupation of woodlands in the UK were taxed under Schedule B. This charge was abolished with effect from 6 April 1988. Profits or gains arising from the occupation of woodlands are now exempt and woodlands are not chargeable under Schedule A.

7

INCOME FROM SAVINGS

This chapter deals with the types of income that need to be reported on page 3 of the SA tax return (reproduced on p. 61). Such income does not fit neatly into the traditional categories or 'Schedules'. The chapter encompasses:

Income taxed under Schedule D Case III

(1) Bank and building society interest.
(2) Other interest income.
(3) Loans to individuals and other private loans.
(4) Gilts and loan stocks.

Interest received net of tax

(5) Rate of tax deducted at source.

Income taxed under Schedule D Case VI

(6) Accrued income scheme.

Other interest-type income

(7) Relevant discounted securities.

Dividends from UK companies

(8) Dividends.
(9) Sundry receipts treated as dividends.

Certain interest and dividends received from foreign companies are taxed as income from savings: this is dealt with in Chap. 8 as they need to be reported on another part of the SA tax return. Income from savings is always taxed at 20% unless the taxpayer is liable for higher rate tax.

INCOME TAXED UNDER SCHEDULE D CASE III

7.1 BANK AND BUILDING SOCIETY INTEREST

7.1.1 Interest receivable without tax deducted at source

The National Savings Bank (NSB) always pays interest without deduction of tax. The first £70 interest paid on an ordinary NSB account is exempt, but interest on an NSB investment account or from deposit bonds, income bonds or capital bonds is taxable in full.

Interest payments by UK banks or building societies on deposit accounts are normally subject to deduction of tax at source unless the depositor completes form R85. This form requires the depositor's full name, address, date of birth and national insurance number and contains a declaration that the depositor is unlikely to be liable for income tax.

Banks are permitted to pay interest without deduction on non-transferable fixed deposits for amounts of £50,000+ and where the deposit is for a fixed period not exceeding five years.

Interest payments may be made without deduction of tax on certificates of deposit provided the deposit is for at least £50,000 and the bank or building society takes the deposit for a fixed period (which must not exceed five years). Interest may also be paid without deduction of tax on deposits where no certificate of deposit has been issued, but the depositor would be entitled to a certificate if he called for one to be issued.

Interest may also be received without tax being deducted at source from loans to individuals, deposits held by a solicitor and on certificates of tax deposit (see 7.2).

7.1.2 How taxable amount is arrived at

The assessable income is the actual income that arises during the tax year, ie the CY basis. This means that for 2002-03 the assessable income is the income receivable for the year ended 5 April 2003.

7.1.3 Date of receipt

Interest is regarded as received when it is credited to the account. Occasionally, cases arise where an individual is required to make a deposit with a bank as a condition of the bank advancing money to a company. In some situations, he is precluded from making withdrawals from the deposit account as long as the company's borrowings are outstanding.

The courts have held that an individual who has a deposit account subject to such a block may nevertheless be taxed on interest credited to that account. Furthermore, there is no relief if he never receives the interest because the company goes into liquidation and the bank appropriates the money outstanding to his credit on the deposit account.

7.1.4 Minor children's accounts

A parent who gifts the capital to his unmarried minor child's account is generally charged tax on interest credited to it, unless the total income from that gift does not exceed £100 (see 22.5.4 on aggregation of minor children's income in general).

7.1.5 Rate of tax on income from savings

All interest income assessed under Schedule D Case III counts as income from savings. Tax is charged at 20% unless the recipient is liable for the 40% higher rate.

Example

B received untaxed interest of £15,000 in the year ended 5 April 2003. She is single and has other income of £12,000, so she is not subject to higher rate tax. She will pay tax on the interest as follows:

	£
Non-savings	12,000
Savings	15,000
	27,000
Less: allowance	(4,615)
	22,385
Non-savings income	
Covered by personal allowance £4,615	Nil
Starting rate £1,920 @ 10%	192.00
Basic rate £5,465 @ 22%	1,202.30
Savings income	
Lower rate £15,000 @ 20%	3,000.00
Tax due	4,394.30

7.1.6 Holocaust victims' bank accounts: compensation

Compensation paid by banks on dormant accounts opened by Holocaust victims and frozen during World War II is exempt from tax. See the Revenue Press Release dated 8 May 2000.

7.2 OTHER INTEREST INCOME

7.2.1 Interest payable by a solicitor

Interest may be received without deduction of tax from client's accounts held by a firm of solicitors or accountants. Such income is taxable under Schedule D Case III.

7.2.2 Interest receivable on compulsory purchase monies

Where a property is the subject of a compulsory purchase order that goes to appeal, and the amount payable is increased, interest is generally payable on the increase. This is regarded as income for the year in which the entitlement arises, ie when the CPO appeal is settled by agreement or on appeal and the interest is received. This principle is not affected by the fact that the interest may have accrued over several years and may be calculated using six-monthly rests.

7.2.3 Certificates of tax deposit

Interest is credited to an individual where he has invested in certificates of tax deposit that are either applied to cover tax payable by assessments or are encashed. The interest is taxable and is income for the year of receipt.

7.2.4 Exempt interest

Interest paid by the Revenue or Customs & Excise on over-payments of tax (called 'repayment supplement') is not subject to tax. However, interest paid by Customs in respect of official error is taxable.

7.2.5 Interest awarded by the courts

This may be exempt. The treatment turns on whether the court order or arbitration award provides for payment of interest as such (taxable) or is merely an element taken into account in arriving at the amount to be awarded (which is capital and not income taxable under Schedule D Case III).

7.3 LOANS TO INDIVIDUALS AND OTHER PRIVATE LOANS

Interest on a private loan to an individual or trust is generally received without deduction of tax. Interest paid by cheque is received when the sum is credited to the recipient's account, not when the cheque is received.

Interest is not assessable where an individual waives the interest before it falls due for payment, provided he receives no consideration for the waiver.

7.4 GILTS AND LOAN STOCKS

Interest payments on British Government Securities ('gilts') can be received gross from 1998-99 onwards, although this must be requested where interest was previously received net. There are two exceptions:

(1) Interest on 3½% War Loan is always paid without deduction.

(2) Where interest is paid on gilts held on the NSB register, interest is also automatically paid without deduction.

Interest payments on loan stocks issued by companies are normally subject to deduction of tax at source.

Again, interest from gilts and loan stocks is regarded as income from savings and so qualifies for the 20% rate from 1996-97 (see 7.1.5).

INTEREST RECEIVED NET OF TAX

7.5 RATE OF TAX DEDUCTED AT SOURCE

(TA 1988, ss 480A-482)

Interest payments made by UK banks and building societies are normally subject to deduction of tax at source (for exceptions see 7.1.1).

Interest paid on gilts may also be paid net of tax except in the case of 3½% War Loan and stocks held on the NSB register. Interest paid on local authority loan stocks and company loan stocks and debentures is subject to deduction of tax, as indeed is all interest paid by UK companies to persons other than group companies.

Because such income is income from savings, tax is deducted at 20%.

Certain unit trusts that invest only in bank deposits or gilts are treated as 'transparent' so that distributions of income are treated as interest rather than dividends. Once again, 20% tax is withheld at source.

INCOME TAXED UNDER SCHEDULE D CASE VI

7.6 ACCRUED INCOME SCHEME

(TA 1988, ss 710-728)

7.6.1 Introduction

An individual who sells a gilt or fixed-interest loan stock may sell either cum- or ex-interest. In the former case, the buyer receives the next interest payment; in the latter, the seller receives the next interest payment even though it is paid after he has sold the gilt or loan stock. In practice, gilts, etc are quoted on an ex-interest basis from six weeks or so before interest is due for payment.

The price at which a gilt or loan stock is sold generally reflects an adjustment for accrued interest. For example, if a gilt pays interest every six months, a person who sells at the end of Month 4 will receive a price that reflects four months' accrued interest. Conversely, a person who sells at the end of Month 5 would normally sell on an ex-interest basis and the purchaser would take a deduction for one month's interest (as the seller would receive this).

7.6.2 Accrued income taxable

The accrued income scheme may apply where the nominal value of gilts or loan stocks held at any point in the year exceeds £5,000. It brings into charge the interest credited to sellers of gilts and loan stocks. The interest deemed to accrue on a daily basis is treated for tax purposes as if it had been received by the seller. The amount of any adjustments in the other direction (interest received but not earned over the period of ownership) is deducted and the net amount charged to tax under Schedule D Case VI on the CY basis.

Example

C subscribes £30,000 for a new Government Stock, 5% Treasury Stock 2050 issued on 1 August 2002. He holds the stock for 86 days and then sells it to *D*, who holds the stock at 1 February 2003 when the first six months' interest is payable. *C* will be assessable for income tax purposes on £353, ie $^{86}/_{183}$ × £750 (the half-yearly interest payable on stock). *D* will be entitled to a deduction of the same amount in computing his taxable income. His position will therefore be as follows:

	£
D receives six months' interest of	750
He deducts 'rebate interest'	353
Taxable income	397

7.6.3 Types of securities within accrued income scheme
(TA 1988, s 710)

The scheme applies to acquisitions and disposals of virtually all types of fixed interest securities by UK-resident individuals. The securities must be loan stock and not shares, but the scheme may apply to foreign securities as well as to UK loan stocks.

Savings certificates, certificates of deposit and zero coupon bonds are excluded. Bills of exchange and Treasury bills are not regarded as securities because they are within the definition of certificates of deposit (see 7.2.3), which are also excluded.

7.6.4 Types of disposal that may be caught
(TA 1988, s 710)

The scheme applies to transfers. This term is widely defined in TA 1988 and includes:

(1) a sale (s 710(5));
(2) an exchange (s 710(5)) or a conversion of securities (s 710(13));
(3) a gift (s 710(5));

(4) any transfer other than under (1)-(3) above (s 710(5));
(5) death (s 721(1));
(6) a change in the true ownership where a person entitled to securities becomes a trustee in relation to them (s 720(4)).

7.6.5 Year of assessment
(TA 1988, s 714)

The assessment is under Schedule D Case VI. It is made for the tax year in which the interest period ends, ie if a loan stock pays interest on 30 April, a disposal of the stock on a cum-interest basis on 5 April 2003 produces taxable income for 2003-04.

7.6.6 Income from savings

Amounts of accrued income taxed under Schedule D Case VI have counted as income from savings (see 7.1.5) since 1998-99.

7.6.7 Calculation of accrued amount and rebate amount
(TA 1988, ss 710, 713 and 714)

Where transactions go through The Stock Exchange, the accrued and rebate amounts are calculated by the broker and appear on the contract note. Where the transaction does not go through the market, the calculation is made in the same way.

If there is more than one transaction in 'securities of the same kind', the accrued and rebate amounts can be netted off. This term is interpreted strictly: £5,000 9% Treasury Stock 2020 is 'of the same kind' as £10,000 9% Treasury Stock 2020, but is not 'of the same kind' as some other issue of Treasury stock.

Separate calculation of all accrued and rebate amounts is necessary. Relief is given for a rebate amount against the next interest received on that security or, if a transfer intervenes, against the accrued amount. Thus it is possible for a rebate amount in one tax year to be set against interest received in the next.

OTHER INTEREST-TYPE INCOME

7.7 RELEVANT DISCOUNTED SECURITIES
(FA 1996, Sched 13)

7.7.1 Introduction

Schedule D Case III may also bring sums deemed to be interest income into charge.

A loan stock may be issued at a discount, or be redeemable at a premium. In either case, the borrower undertakes that when the loan is repaid the borrower will receive more than the amount originally paid on the issue of the stock. A typical situation is where a loan stock is issued at £80 for every £100 nominal and when the loan stock is redeemed the investor is entitled to receive £100. There are no provisions for the payer to deduct tax from discount.

The discount or premium is charged to tax under Schedule D Case III where the loan stock is within the definition of a relevant discounted security and the company that issues the bond is a UK company. If the issuer is an overseas company, the discount is charged under Case V.

7.7.2 Definition of 'relevant discounted security'

(TA 1988, Sched 4, para 1)

A loan stock is not a relevant discounted security just because it is issued at a discount; it must be issued at a deep discount. A discount is regarded as a deep discount only where it exceeds 0.5% for every year of the loan stock's intended life, or where the discount exceeds 15% in total.

The following types of loan stock cannot be a relevant discounted security:

(1) indexed-linked gilts.
(2) gilts issued prior to 14 March 1989;
(3) a loan stock that is convertible into shares; and
(4) certain corporate loan stocks the redemption price of which is linked to shares or other assets.

Examples – Relevant discounted security

(1) A five-year loan stock is issued at £95 for every £100 nominal. This is a relevant discounted security because the discount exceeds 0.5% pa.
(2) A 35-year loan stock is issued at £80 for every £100 nominal. This is a relevant discounted security, even though the discount is less than 0.5% pa, because it exceeds 15% in total.

7.7.3 Events that give rise to a tax charge

(TA 1988, Sched 4, para 4)

A disposal of a relevant discounted security can give rise to a charge under Schedule D Case III. The whole of the profit is taxable as if it were interest.

Example – Disposal of deep discount security

A bond is issued at £82, redeemable at £100 after two years. This reflects a compound interest rate of approximately 10% since $82 \times (^{110}/_{100})^2 = 100$. If the holder sells for £93 after 12 months, he will be assessed on the difference between £82 and £93, ie £11. If the purchaser holds the bond until it is redeemed in Year 2 he will be chargeable under Schedule D Case III on the redemption profit of £18 as income for that year.

7.7.4 Stripped gilts

There is one exception to the general rule that individuals and trustees are taxed on discounted securities only when a disposal takes place. Where a stripped gilt is held, it is necessary to revalue it at the end of each tax year and the owner must pay tax on any increase in value as if it were income. These rules were changed with effect from 27 March 2003 so that they now also apply to strips of non-UK government securities.

7.7.5 Income from savings

Discounts taxed under Schedule D Case III count as income from savings (see 7.1.5).

7.7.6 Losses

An individual who realised a loss on the disposal of a relevant discounted security was allowed to deduct this from his taxable income for the year. However, the loss could not be carried back or forward to a future year.

This loss relief has been withdrawn by FA 2003 in relation to most losses realised on disposals made on or after 27 March 2003. Loss relief can still be available for quoted securities acquired before that date.

DIVIDENDS FROM UK COMPANIES

7.8 DIVIDENDS

7.8.1 Taxable for year in which they fall due for payment
(TA 1988, s 834(3))

The dividends that need to be reported on a tax return, and that are income for a tax year, are the dividends that were due for payment in the year. If you have shares in a company that declared a dividend that was payable on 5 April 2003, you must report the dividend as 2002-03 income. This is not affected by the fact that you may not have received the dividend cheque until early in the next tax year.

The period for which the dividend is paid is not relevant. A final dividend for a company's year that ended on 31 December 2002 would be income for 2003-04 if it was paid in (eg) June 2003.

A dividend from a UK company carries a tax credit (see 7.8.3).

7.8.2 Dividends paid by unit trusts

Dividends from unit trusts are treated in exactly the same way as dividends from companies except in regard to 'equalisation'. This is an amount paid to holders of units who have acquired them since the last dividend was paid. The equalisation payment is not taxable as income but is instead treated as a return of capital.

7.8.3 Rate of tax on dividends received from UK companies

A shareholder is entitled to a tax credit of one-ninth of the dividend. This credit is non-refundable.

An individual whose income is within the basic rate band does not have to pay any additional tax on a UK dividend, the tax credit is treated as covering his liability. Higher rate taxpayers pay a special 32.5% rate on dividends and are able to set the tax credit against this. In practice, this means that the effective rate of higher rate tax is one-quarter of the actual dividend receipt.

A different treatment applied up to 1998-99, for details see the *Zurich Tax Handbook 2002/2003* at 7.8.4.

7.8.4 Stock dividends

(TA 1988, s 249)

A company may make a 'scrip' or bonus issue so that shareholders receive new shares in proportion to their existing shareholdings. This is not taxable income since in reality all that has happened is that the company has subdivided its share capital by issuing new shares.

In contrast to this, a company may offer shareholders the choice between a cash dividend or additional shares to a similar value. This is called a 'stock dividend' and is taxable income.

'Enhanced scrip dividends' are a special type of stock dividend where the company offers a premium to shareholders who take stock rather than cash and makes prior arrangements to enable the shareholders to dispose of the shares that they have acquired by taking the stock alternative.

7.8.5 How stock dividends are assessed

(SP A8)

A shareholder who accepts extra shares in lieu of a cash dividend is normally treated as if he had received a dividend equal to the cash that he could have taken. Tax is deemed to have been paid at the lower rate.

A slightly different treatment applies where the value of the shares taken as the stock dividend differs from the cash dividend by 15% or more. In such a case, the shareholder is deemed to have received a dividend equal to the shares' value at the date of issue. The shareholder may therefore be required to pay higher rate tax on the 'grossed up' value of the dividend or the shares.

Example – Taxation of dividends

E was entitled to a dividend of £2,100 or extra shares in X plc. He took the shares. If the shares were worth £1,900, he will nevertheless be charged higher rate tax on £2,100 plus an amount equal to the tax credit; the amount charged to higher rate tax for 2002-03 is £2,333 (£2,100 grossed up for the 10% tax credit).

If the shares were worth £2,600 when they were issued, he would be charged higher rate tax on £2,600 'grossed up', ie £2,888.

7.8.6 Consequences for CGT of taking a stock dividend

In the example in 7.8.5, the shareholder's acquisition value for CGT purposes of the shares that he acquires through the stock dividend is the amount on which he is assessed for higher rate purposes less basic rate tax.

7.8.7 Dividends that form part of a demerger

(TA 1988, s 213)

A dividend may take the form of an issue of shares formerly held by the company in a subsidiary. Where the necessary Revenue clearances have been obtained, such a dividend is treated as capital and not as taxable income. The documentation issued by the company normally states that clearance has been obtained from the Revenue and that the demerger is an exempt distribution.

7.8.8 Other dividend income

See 7.9 on sundry receipts from UK companies that are treated as distributions. See also 8.10.2 on dividends paid by foreign companies that are treated as income from savings.

7.9 SUNDRY RECEIPTS TREATED AS DIVIDENDS

7.9.1 Deemed dividends

(TA 1988, s 209)

There are various transactions that can count as a distribution, particularly where a person holds shares in a close company (see 26.13). From the recipient's point of view, a distribution is for all practical purposes the same as a dividend.

7.9.2 Interest at more than commercial rate

(TA 1988, s 209)

Interest paid to a shareholder may constitute a distribution in so far as it exceeds a normal commercial rate.

7.9.3 Issue of redeemable shares

(TA 1988, s 209(2)(c))

An issue to shareholders of redeemable preference shares (or other redeemable shares) counts as a distribution. The redeemable shares' value at the date they are issued is treated as if it were a dividend paid in cash at that time. This rule does not apply where the redeemable shares are issued for new consideration.

7.9.4 Bonus issue following repayment of share capital

(TA 1988, s 210)

Where a company has repaid share capital in the past, a subsequent bonus issue is treated as a dividend paid to the shareholders who receive the bonus shares. These shareholders may not be the same people whose shares were previously bought back by the company, but this does not make any difference to the way in which the current shareholders are taxed on receipt of a bonus issue of shares in these circumstances.

7.9.5 Benefits-in-kind provided to shareholders

(TA 1988, s 418)

Where shareholders in a close company (see 26.13) are provided with benefits-in-kind, they may be assessed under Schedule E. If they are not employed by the company, it is not possible for the Revenue to assess benefits-in-kind under Schedule E. In these circumstances, the company may be deemed to have made a distribution equal to the value of the benefits-in-kind concerned.

7.9.6 Assets transferred by or to close company

(TA 1988, s 209(4))

A deemed distribution may arise where assets are transferred from the members of a company to the company at a price that exceeds their market value, or company assets are transferred to shareholders at a price that is less than market value.

7.9.7 Purchase by company of its own shares

(TA 1988, s 209)

The general rule is that where a company buys back its shares, the amount paid by the company is treated as a distribution in so far as it exceeds the shares' original issue price.

The amount treated as a distribution is not affected by the shares' value at the time they were acquired by an individual. Consequently, where a person has acquired shares by inheritance or bought them from an existing shareholder, his acquisition value may exceed the original issue price (ie the amount paid to the company in return for the shares being issued). In the event of a purchase of own shares by a company, it is the issue price that is important.

Example – Purchase by company of own shares

> *F* acquires 1,000 shares in Y Ltd for £10,000. The shares were originally issued at their par value of £1 per share. It subsequently transpires that *F* cannot get on with the company's directors. If her shares are bought back by the company at £9 per share, *F* is deemed to have received a distribution of £8,000, even though she had actually made a capital loss.

7.9.8 Relief under TA 1988, s 219

In certain circumstances it may be possible for a company to purchase its own shares without the transaction being treated as giving rise to a distribution. Clearance must be obtained from the Revenue that the purchase of own shares is for the benefit of the company's trade. The conditions that must be satisfied are:

(1) the company must be unquoted;
(2) it must be a trading company or the holding company of a trading group;
(3) the seller must be resident and ordinarily resident in the UK;
(4) the seller must have owned the shares for at least five years;
(5) the seller's interest in the company must be 'substantially reduced'; and
(6) the purchase must be undertaken to benefit the company's trade.

Alternatively, s 219 may apply where shares are being bought back within two years of the shareholder's death and the reason for this is that the personal representatives would not otherwise be able to pay the IHT due on the estate.

8

OTHER INCOME

This chapter deals with income received both without deduction of tax and net of tax.

Income from which no tax is deducted at source

Investment income taxed under Schedule D Case VI

(1) Sale of certificates of deposit.
(2) Gains from roll-up, and other offshore, funds.

Schedule D Cases IV and V: untaxed income from abroad

(3) Foreign interest and dividends.
(4) Foreign real estate income.
(5) Alimony and maintenance payments.
(6) Investment in overseas partnerships.
(7) Double tax relief.
(8) Pensions taxable under Schedule D Case V.

Other income taxed under Schedule D Case VI

(9) Sundry income assessed under Case VI.

Income received net of tax

(10) Foreign interest and dividends received via UK paying agents.
(11) Other income received net of tax.

INCOME FROM WHICH NO TAX IS DEDUCTED AT SOURCE

INVESTMENT INCOME TAXED UNDER SCHEDULE D CASE VI

8.1 SALE OF CERTIFICATES OF DEPOSIT

(TA 1988, s 56)

A certificate of deposit is a document that entitles the holder to receive the amount held on deposit. An owner of such a deposit can assign it to someone else. Where this is done for valuable consideration, the profit is taxable under Schedule D Case VI.

At one time it was possible to avoid having taxable income by assigning ownership of a deposit without there being a certificate of deposit. Profits on such transactions are now also caught as income taxable under Schedule D Case VI. They are not treated as income from savings.

8.2 GAINS FROM ROLL-UP, AND OTHER OFFSHORE, FUNDS

(TA 1988, ss 757-763)

A Schedule D Case VI charge may arise on gains from disposals of certain offshore funds. The types of funds concerned are generally collective investment schemes similar to unit trusts. In many cases the fund earns bank interest that is accumulated within the fund rather than distributed as dividend. When the shareholder disposes of his investment he receives the benefit of this accumulated interest in the price that he obtains for his shares.

8.2.1 No charge on distributor funds

(TA 1988, s 760 and Sched 27)

Gains from distributor funds are generally exempt from the charge under s 757. Offshore funds qualify for distributor status where at least 85% of investment income received by the fund is distributed as dividend. In the case of commodity funds, the 85% distribution requirement is reduced to 42.5%.

Where a fund does not qualify as a distributor fund, a Case VI charge arises on a disposal. This includes certain disposals not taken into account for CGT purposes, for example a share exchange on a takeover of a fund. It also includes a deemed disposal on the shareholder's death.

The charge arises on the gain as it would be computed for CGT purposes, but with no allowance for indexation.

Example – Tax on offshore funds

A has held shares in an offshore fund since June 1993. The shares cost £14,000 and are worth £17,000 when sold in August 2002. If the offshore fund does not have distributor status, the gain of £3,000 is Case VI income for 2002-03.

If the offshore fund had distributor status, the gain would have been charged to CGT rather than as income. The amount charged would have been less than £3,000 because of indexation allowance and the gain may have been covered by *A*'s annual exemption for CGT purposes (see 13.1.1).

It is necessary for the fund to have had distributor status for the whole period of an individual's ownership if the gain is to be taxed as capital gain rather than Case VI income, ie it is an 'all or nothing' test.

8.2.2 Equalisation arrangements

(TA 1988, s 758)

Where an overseas fund has distributor status, and there are equalisation arrangements, any sum paid to a shareholder on the sale of his shares or units and treated as equalisation is income for Schedule D Case VI purposes. There is no income tax charge on the balance of the disposal proceeds.

8.2.3 Gains realised by foreign domiciliaries

(TA 1988, s 762)

A gain from a disposal of an offshore fund by a person of foreign domicile is taxed under Schedule D Case V, not Case VI, and the remittance basis applies (see 24.10).

8.2.4 Gains not income from savings

Gains realised from the disposal of offshore funds are taxed under Schedule D Case VI, not Case III, and do not count as income from savings (see 7.1.5).

8.2.5 Changes in the future?

The Government has been reviewing the tax treatment of non-distributor funds as the UK treatment is at variance from that in most EU countries. Changes were expected to be announced in the 2003 Budget but the subject was not mentioned.

SCHEDULE D CASES IV AND V: UNTAXED INCOME FROM ABROAD

If you have untaxed income from abroad, a special schedule of your SA tax return must be completed.

8.3 FOREIGN INTEREST AND DIVIDENDS

Debenture and Government bond interest and dividends paid by overseas companies are taxed under Case IV or V only if they fall outside the paying agent procedures described in 8.10. Interest on overseas bank deposits and private loans are always taxable under Case V. Such income is normally treated as being from savings.

8.3.1 How the taxable amount is computed

The CY basis has applied since 1997-98. A point to watch with all foreign investments is that income tax is charged on the interest credited or dividends received, without reference to any exchange gain or loss on the money deposited or invested.

Example – Foreign currency deposit account

In June 2001, *F* deposited £10,000 with a foreign bank. At the then exchange rate of £1 = 20 units of foreign currency, that sum was credited as 200,000 units. In June 2002, when the exchange rate was £1 = 25 units, interest of 30,000 units was credited to the account. In June 2003, *F* closed the account, receiving back his original capital, the interest credited in June 2002 and a further 20,000 foreign currency units as interest to close. By then the exchange rate was £1 = 30 units, so the sterling equivalent of the 250,000 units was only £8,333.

In commercial terms, *F* has suffered a loss of £1,667, but for tax purposes he received interest of £1,200 in June 2002 (30,000 units at £1 = 25) and £667 in June 2003 (20,000 units at £1 = 30) and income tax must be paid on that interest. He has also made a capital loss of £3,534, calculated as follows:

			£	£
Proceeds of	250,000	units		8,333
	200,000	units cost (June 2001)	10,000	
	30,000	units cost (June 2002)	1,200	
	20,000	units cost (June 2003)	667	
				11,867
Capital loss				(3,534)

Unfortunately, that capital loss may only be used by set-off against capital gains on the disposal of other assets. If *F* has no such gains, he cannot utilise the loss and so has paid tax on a profit of £1,867 when he has in fact made a loss of £1,667.

8.3.2 Income from savings

Foreign dividends and interest taxed under Schedule D Case IV or V count as income from savings unless the income is taxed under the remittance basis (see 24.10).

8.4 FOREIGN REAL ESTATE INCOME

It is not unusual for a UK resident to have bought – or inherited – a villa or flat abroad. It is less usual to own commercial premises, but the tax rules are the same. And the same rules also apply to properties bought under 'time-share' arrangements.

The CY basis of assessment has applied since 1997-98.

8.4.1 How income is computed

In calculating the assessable rent, the landlord may deduct expenses paid, for example repairs, redecoration, insurance, maid service, gardening, management fees and advertising. If the landlord sometimes uses the property himself, then an apportionment of these expenses must be made in the same way as for a UK property (see 6.2).

There are three important differences between the tax treatment of rent from real property in the UK and rent from property abroad:

(1) The 'rent-a-room' scheme (see 6.4) applies only to properties in the UK; this exemption cannot be claimed against rents from an overseas property.
(2) Similarly, the special rules allowing the provision of furnished holiday accommodation to be treated as a trade (see 6.5) apply only where the relevant property is situated in the UK.
(3) If the rental income statement for an overseas property shows a deficit for a year (ie if expenses excluding interest paid exceed rent received), that deficit may be carried forward and deducted from the rent received in respect of the same property in the next year (and the deduction may be rolled forward indefinitely until there is rental income against which it can be set). However, no other form of loss relief is available. In particular, the deficit may not be set against rents received from other properties, whether in the UK or abroad.

Interest payments can be deducted even if the interest is paid overseas.

8.4.2 Accounts

In the past, rental income statements should have been drawn up to 5 April, but in practice the Revenue often accepted statements drawn up to any convenient date. For example, the rental statement for the calendar year will often have been taken as the measure of the income for the tax year. This is no longer acceptable and it is necessary to report the income that has actually arisen in the tax year.

One possible complication is that income may be received, and expenses incurred, in either UK or local currency. In practice, the Revenue accepts any reasonable basis of currency conversion. For example, if a local agent collects the rents, disburses local expenses and remits a net sum to the landlord, that net amount may be converted at the spot rate for the day it was remitted. However, the Revenue expects the same basis of conversion to be retained from one year to the next.

8.5 ALIMONY AND MAINTENANCE PAYMENTS
(TA 1988, s 347A(4))

A UK resident may receive maintenance or alimony payments from a spouse, former spouse or parent resident abroad. This income is almost always exempt from tax.

It used to be that the tax treatment was dependent on whether the maintenance or alimony payments counted as an 'existing obligation'. Broadly, an existing obligation was one created by a court order or agreement made before 15 March 1988 either in the UK or abroad. Even payments under existing obligations were taken out of charge from 6 April 2000.

8.6 INVESTMENT IN OVERSEAS PARTNERSHIPS
(TA 1988, s 391)

A UK resident may be a sleeping partner in a business carried on abroad. For example, a man might provide the finance for his son to set up in business abroad in return for a share of the profits. It may be difficult to tell whether the father has become a sleeping partner in the son's business or has made a loan at interest to the son. If the father is entitled to a stated proportion of profits (say, one-quarter), then he is certainly a sleeping partner; if he is entitled to a fixed annual sum, he may be a sleeping partner or may simply have made a loan. In practice this is not important, as both interest and a sleeping partner's profit share are taxed according to the usual Case IV or V rules.

The important question is whether the UK resident is a sleeping or an active partner. If he is an active partner, the partnership business is likely to be carried on at least partly within the UK, in which case complex questions arise that are outside the scope of this book; specialist advice therefore should be sought.

If the sleeping partner is entitled to a fixed sum, at annual or other intervals, and that sum is stated in a foreign currency, then each instalment must, for tax purposes, be converted into sterling at the spot rate for the date it falls due. If he is entitled to a stated proportion of profits, and the business accounts are prepared in a foreign currency, the appropriate profit figure must be converted into sterling at the spot rate for the last day of the accounting period. If the sleeping partner is obliged to bear a share of a trading loss, that loss may be relieved against overseas trading and pension income, but not against overseas investment income or any UK income. In most cases, therefore, it is relieved by deducting the loss amount from the partnership profit share assessable for a later year.

8.7 DOUBLE TAX RELIEF
(TA 1988, s 790)

Basically put, foreign tax paid can be deducted from the UK tax charged on the same income.

Example – Double tax relief

D, a basic rate taxpayer, receives an interest payment of £1,000 from abroad, on which the foreign tax is £150. The UK tax position is:

	£
Gross interest	1,000
Foreign tax deducted or paid	(150)
Net receipt	850
UK tax at 20% of £1,000	200
Less: foreign tax paid	(150)
UK tax to be paid	50
After-tax income	800

If *D* were liable for tax at only 10%, the foreign tax would bring his UK tax liability down to nil, but he would not be entitled to reclaim the difference of £50.

8.7.1 An important practical point

Relief for overseas tax is not given unless the individual can prove that he has indeed paid the tax. It is not sufficient simply to demonstrate that tax is payable under foreign law: the claimant must be able to show that he has indeed paid that tax by producing an official receipt or tax deduction certificate.

8.7.2 Foreign tax adjustments

The Revenue must be notified if an amount of foreign tax paid is later adjusted and this means that too much credit has been allowed as double taxation relief. Failure to notify the Revenue within one year of an adjustment results in a taxpayer becoming liable to a penalty (not exceeding the tax underpaid) because of the claim that has proved to be excessive.

If a foreign tax adjustment means that you have not claimed enough you are under no statutory duty to report this, but it is clearly in your own interests to do so.

8.8 PENSIONS TAXABLE UNDER SCHEDULE D CASE V
(TA 1988, s 58)

Certain pensions are taxable under Case V rather than Schedule E:

(1) Pensions paid by a person outside the UK.
(2) Pensions paid on behalf of a person outside the UK.
(3) Voluntary pensions paid by a person outside the UK.

Pensions charged to tax under Case V are assessed on pensioners who are:

(a) resident, ordinarily resident and domiciled in the UK – 90% of the pension is charged to tax;
(b) resident but not ordinarily resident in the UK – the pension is assessed on the remittance basis by reference to sums brought into the UK;
(c) resident and ordinarily resident, but not domiciled, in the UK – the pension is assessed on the remittance basis.

Pensions assessed under Case V have been taxed on the CY basis since 1997-98.

Nazi compensation pensions
(TA 1988, s 330)

Annuities and premiums paid under German or Austrian law to victims of Nazi persecution are exempt from income tax. These are pensions paid because of serious damage to the individual's health; they are also exempt from tax in Germany and Austria.

OTHER INCOME TAXED UNDER SCHEDULE D CASE VI

8.9 SUNDRY INCOME ASSESSED UNDER CASE VI
(TA 1988, s 15)

Tax may be charged under Case VI in respect of any annual profits or gains that do not fall under any other Schedule D case and are not charged by virtue of any other schedule.

Post-cessation receipts (see 5.7) and enterprise allowances are charged under Case VI. In addition, Case VI applies to gains from roll-up funds, profits under the accrued income scheme and gains on foreign life policies. Furthermore, where tax is charged under various anti-avoidance provisions (see Chap. 22) the charge is normally made under Case VI.

In addition, profits from certain 'one-off' or isolated business activities in the nature of a trade have been charged under Case VI. Thus, the following have been held by the courts to be Case VI income:

(1) commission for guaranteeing overdrafts;
(2) underwriting commission on share issues;
(3) insurance commission;
(4) receipts for the use of copyright material;
(5) payments made to the wife of a train robber for their life story;

(6) profits realised by an 'angel', ie a person who sponsored a play and was entitled to a share of the profits.

Case VI income may be earned income or investment income.

8.9.1 Schedule D Case VI losses

(TA 1988, s 392)

Case VI losses may be set against any profits assessable under Case VI, whether or not the profits arise from the same activity. However, they may not be set against income taxed under any other schedule.

Where an individual has suffered losses from an isolated transaction in the past, it may be sensible to arrange matters so that income arises that is taxable under Case VI. For example, an investment in an offshore roll-up fund (see 8.2) could be made with a view to producing a predictable level of Case VI profits that will be tax free because of the relief for Case VI losses.

INCOME RECEIVED NET OF TAX

8.10 FOREIGN INTEREST AND DIVIDENDS RECEIVED VIA UK PAYING AGENTS

(TA 1988, ss 17, 44 and 123, and Sched 3; F(No 2)A 1992, Sched 11)

8.10.1 Foreign interest income

Interest on bonds issued by overseas governments or companies may be received via a 'paying agent'.

The paying or collecting agent receives, from the overseas government or company, a remittance representing the interest due less the foreign tax payable on that interest. The rate at which foreign tax is deducted depends partly on the laws of the country concerned and partly on the terms of any double tax treaty between the UK and that country. At worst, tax is deducted at the full rate payable by residents of the overseas country. At best, no foreign tax at all is deducted. More usually, tax is deducted at a 'treaty' or 'withholding' rate of, typically, 10% for interest and 15% for dividends.

Before paying the interest over to the individual bondholders, the paying agent must deduct UK tax so that the total tax paid (foreign and UK) equals tax at 20%. The interest is treated as income from savings.

Example – Tax deducted by paying agent

G has a holding of foreign government bonds on which the interest, payable annually through a British bank, is 500 dinars, equivalent to £100 sterling. Foreign withholding tax is charged at 10%. The bank will send *G* a cheque for £80 (or will credit her account with that amount) and provide a voucher showing:

	£
Gross income	100
Less: foreign withholding tax	(10)
	90
Less: UK income tax	(10)
Net payment	80

The bank will pay the £10 UK income tax over to the Revenue.

If *G* is a basic rate taxpayer, that is the end of the story: the deduction made by the paying agent clears her basic rate liability and gives her relief for overseas tax paid. If she is a higher rate taxpayer, she is in the same position as if she had received income on a British Government security: her total liability is £40 (40% of £100) of which she has paid £20 by deduction. She must therefore pay a further £20, probably on her annual tax assessment.

If *G* is not a taxpayer at all, the Revenue will repay only the £10 UK income tax deducted by the British bank – it will not repay the £10 foreign tax deducted by the foreign government. In certain circumstances it may, theoretically, be possible to reclaim this money direct from the foreign authorities, but it is certain to be a difficult and time-consuming process, especially if correspondence in a foreign language is necessary. In almost all cases, it simply will not be worth the effort.

Care is needed with regard to foreign dividends as in some cases the tax shown as 'deducted' on the dividend certificate is really tax suffered by the foreign company on its profits rather than foreign tax withheld from the dividend, and such tax is not eligible for double tax relief. This is often the case where the company is based in Australia or the Channel Islands.

8.10.2 Foreign dividends

A UK paying agent deducts UK tax so as to bring the total of foreign and UK tax up to 10%. Foreign dividends are taxed at only 10% unless the recipient is a higher rate taxpayer, when the rate is 32.5%.

If the shareholder is liable to higher rate tax, the rate on foreign dividends is 32.5%.

8.10.3 High overseas tax rate

In some instances, overseas tax may be deducted at a rate higher than the 10% UK rate on dividends. In such a case, the UK paying agent simply passes on whatever net payment is received from overseas.

Example – High overseas tax rate

H has a shareholding in a foreign company, on which a dividend equivalent to £100 is declared during 2002-03. However, the foreign authorities withhold tax at 30%. The net remittance received by *H* will be £70.

If he is a basic rate taxpayer, no UK tax will be payable on the foreign dividend, because the UK tax is reduced to nil by relief for the £30 foreign tax paid. However, the excess foreign tax paid cannot be set against *H*'s UK tax liability on other sources of income – it is simply lost. If *H* is a higher rate taxpayer, his UK liability of £32.50 (32.5% of £100) will be reduced to £2.50 by deducting the £30 foreign tax paid.

There are thus two basic rules. First, the Revenue never refunds tax paid to a foreign government; secondly, foreign tax paid in respect of a particular source of income may only be set against UK tax charged on that same source.

8.10.4 Which year of assessment?

(TA 1988, s 835(6) and Sched 3, para 8; F(No 2)A 1992, Sched 11)

Interest and dividends within the 'paying or collecting agent' scheme count as income of the year in which they are paid to the investor by the UK paying or collecting agent. Accordingly, the operative date is the date the agent issues a cheque or authorises a credit transfer. This cannot be before, but may be a few days after, funds become available in the UK. Therefore, it is possible that a dividend or interest payment due, say, at the end of March 2003 will be assessable either as income of the 2002-03 or 2003-04 tax year. The payment date will be clearly shown on the paying or collecting agent's voucher, so no particular difficulty should arise.

8.10.5 Stock dividends and other peculiarities

(TA 1988, s 249)

As explained in 7.8, an investor who opts to take a stock dividend (ie additional shares in lieu of a cash dividend) from a UK company is taxed as if he had received an equivalent amount in cash. This rule does not apply where a non-UK resident company pays the stock dividend.

A higher rate taxpayer offered the choice between a stock and a cash dividend is therefore usually better off taking the stock dividend. However, this assumes that the additional shares offered are worth at least as much as the cash option and that they are readily saleable. As always, the 'tax-saving' tail must not be allowed to wag the 'sensible investment policy' dog. Moreover, in one court case it was suggested that, if stock dividends are taken year after year, and the shares so obtained are sold to provide the shareholder with an income, then income tax may be charged on that income. The Revenue is unlikely to take this point unless a substantial amount of money is at stake.

In a number of other cases also, payments by an overseas company may escape tax where an equivalent payment by a UK company would be taxable as a dividend. Most often this occurs where a payment that under UK law would count as a distribution of profits counts, under the relevant foreign law, as a partial return of the shareholders' original investment. The overseas company or the UK paying agent usually advise on the correct position.

8.10.6 Reporting the income

Interest and dividends from foreign companies collected by paying agents should be included on page F1 of the SA return.

8.11 OTHER INCOME RECEIVED NET OF TAX

8.11.1 Annuities

(TA 1988, ss 349 and 656-658)

Annuities paid by an insurance company are dealt with at 12.5. Where an annuity is payable by an individual or a private company, the payer must deduct tax at basic rate. Note that such income is not treated as savings income and therefore tax is still deducted at basic rate and not at 20% where payment is made.

Example – Annuity income received net of basic rate tax

M sells his business to *N* for a cash sum plus an annuity of £10,000 a year payable by *N* out of the business profits. In 2002-03, *N* paid *M* only £7,800 (£10,000 less tax at 22%).

(1) *M* may set any available personal allowances against the annuity, so that if he is aged 67, is single and has no other income, the position for 2002-03 will be:

	£	£
Annuity (gross amount)		10,000.00
Personal allowance (over-65 rate)		(6,100.00)
		3,900.00
Tax payable		
£1,920 charged at 10%	192.00	
£1,980 charged at 22%	435.60	
Total tax due	627.60	
Less: tax paid by deduction	(2,200.00)	
Revenue will repay	1,572.40	

(2) If *M*'s other income is sufficient to utilise both his personal allowances and the lower rate band, there will be no repayment. If he is a higher rate taxpayer, he will have to pay additional tax on the annuity, as follows:

	£	£
Higher rate tax on annuity (40% of £10,000)		4,000
Less: Already paid by deduction		(2,200)
Additional tax payable by assessment		1,800

(3) The buyer, *N*, can obtain relief for the annuity paid to *M* not as a trading expense, but as a deduction in computing total taxable income.

(a) If he is only a basic rate taxpayer, he obtains the relief to which he is entitled by keeping for himself the £2,200 difference between the gross amount of the annuity and the £7,800 actually paid to *M*.

(b) If he is a higher rate taxpayer, additional relief is given by not charging higher rate tax on an amount equal to the gross annuity paid – a process usually referred to as 'extending the basic rate band'.

(4) Suppose *N*'s profits are £50,000, he has no other income and is entitled only to the basic personal allowance of £4,615. If he did not have to pay the annuity, his tax position would be:

		£
Income		50,000
Personal allowance		(4,615)
Tax payable on		45,385
£1,920	charged at 10%	192.00
£27,980	charged at 22%	6,155.60
£15,485	charged at 40%	6,194.00
£45,385		12,541.60

(5) As he does have to pay the annuity, the basic rate band is extended by the gross amount of that annuity (£10,000), so the position becomes:

		£
£1,920	charged at 10%	192.00
£37,980	charged at 22%	8,355.60
£5,485	charged at 40%	2,194.00
£45,385		10,741.60

This is a reduction of £1,800 and so overall the position is:

	£
Gross annuity	10,000
Net payment to *M*	(7,800)
Basic rate tax relief	2,200
Reduction in tax payable by assessment	1,800
Total tax relief (40% of £10,000)	4,000

8.11.2 Income from trusts

Income paid to a beneficiary of a fixed interest trust is normally taxed at source at 20%. However, tax will sometimes have been charged on the trustees at basic rate on income received by them that is not income from savings. For example, rental income falls into this category. In such a situation, the beneficiary will have a credit for basic rate tax on that element of his income from the trust that represents income that is not income from savings.

Income payments to discretionary beneficiaries carry a credit of 34%.

8.11.3 Estates of deceased persons

(TA 1988, ss 695-702)

When someone dies, it takes time for his executors or personal representatives to identify all his assets, pay all his debts, settle any IHT liability and work out the best way of dividing the estate between those entitled (eg one beneficiary may want to take specific investments, another may prefer cash). During this time, known as 'the administration period', it is quite likely that income will be received by the executors or personal representatives, both on the deceased's existing investments and, for example, as interest on a bank account into which the executors have paid money collected on behalf of the estate.

The executors or personal representatives must pay tax on all income received. Items such as share dividends and bond interest are received net of tax and this tax will cover the executors' liability. Income from savings is taxed at 20%. Other income is subject to tax at the basic rate and, where no tax has been withheld at source (eg rental income), the executors will need to go through the self-assessment procedures.

The executors or personal representatives must therefore pool income on which tax has been paid. That pool must be divided between the beneficiaries in accordance with the terms of the deceased's will, or of the laws of intestacy if he left no will.

Example – Tax treatment of estate income

The gross income from an estate is £200, on which the executors have paid tax of £44. The deceased's son is, under the will, entitled to half that income. He will receive a cheque for £78 plus a certificate, signed by the executors, confirming that tax of £22 has been paid to the Revenue. The son's income for tax purposes is £100, but he is treated as having already paid basic rate tax on that £100. If he has personal allowances or other reliefs available, he can obtain (from the Revenue) a repayment of some or all of the £22 tax paid; if he is a higher rate taxpayer, he will have to pay over to the Revenue the difference between basic and higher rate tax.

In some cases, the executors will have suffered tax at only 20%, rather than at basic rate, and the certificate issued by them to the beneficiary must make this clear.

8.11.4 Allocation of estate income to particular tax years

The tax treatment of beneficiaries of deceased persons' estates was simplified by FA 1995, with a view to facilitating the introduction of self-assessment. Payments made to beneficiaries out of the income of the residue of an estate are taxable as income for the year of payment.

9

DEDUCTIONS IN ARRIVING AT TAXABLE INCOME

PETER JUN TAI

In this chapter, we look at the various deductions you may claim on page 5 of the SA tax return.

(1) Alimony and maintenance.
(2) Loans used to purchase an annuity from an insurance company.
(3) Loans to purchase investment property.
(4) Loans to invest in partnerships.
(5) Loans to invest in close companies.
(6) Loans to invest in employee-controlled companies.
(7) Loans to purchase plant and machinery.
(8) Gift Aid.
(9) Gift of listed shares and securities.
(10) Gift of land and buildings.
(11) Annuities, etc.
(12) Trade union and friendly society subscriptions.
(13) Life assurance premiums.
(14) Community investment tax relief.

9.1 ALIMONY AND MAINTENANCE

No relief is normally given whatsoever for payments made after 5 April 2000.

If the payer or recipient was born before 6 April 1935, an allowance of up to £2,110 can be claimed for 2002-03 (relief given at only 10%).

9.2 LOANS USED TO PURCHASE ANNUITY FROM AN INSURANCE COMPANY

MIRAS relief, abolished from 6 April 2000, was given for interest loans secured on the borrower's main residence if he was aged 65+ and at least 90% of the loan on which the interest was payable was used to buy an annuity for the remainder of his life. Interest payable on these types of loan continues to attract relief at 23% despite the general abolition of MIRAS and the reduction in the basic rate to 22%.

9.3 LOANS TO PURCHASE INVESTMENT PROPERTIES

Interest on loans used to acquire a property that is let out may be allowed in computing the rental income assessable under Schedule A (see Chap. 6 on this). Relief has not been due for interest on such loans under any other provisions since 1994-95.

9.4 LOANS TO INVEST IN PARTNERSHIPS

(TA 1988, s 362)

Tax relief may be obtained on loan interest where the money is used to invest in a partnership which is not an investment LLP.

9.4.1 Conditions for relief

It does not matter that such loans may be secured by way of a mortgage against the partner's main residence; the availability of relief depends on the purpose for which the loan is raised, not the way in which the lender secures its position. Relief is basically available where the loan is applied:

(1) in purchasing a share in a partnership; or
(2) in contributing capital to a partnership or advancing money to a partnership where the money advanced is used wholly for the purposes of the partnership's trade, profession or vocation; or
(3) in paying off another loan the interest on which would have been eligible for tax relief.

However, there are further conditions that must be satisfied. The borrower must be a member of the partnership throughout the period in which the interest accrues (and not just as a limited partner). Also, he must not have recovered any capital from the partnership since raising the qualifying loan.

9.4.2 Recovery of capital

(TA 1988, s 363)

If, at any time after the application of the proceeds of the loan, a partner recovers capital from the partnership, he is deemed to have used the money he has withdrawn to repay the qualifying loan on which he is claiming interest relief. This applies whether or not he actually uses the proceeds in this manner. It is therefore advisable to segregate the partners' capital and current accounts in the partnership's books so that any withdrawal can be clearly identified.

9.4.3 Property occupied rent free by partnership

Where a partner takes out a loan to purchase property occupied by the partnership for business purposes and the interest is paid by the partnership, technically no deduction is due to the partnership as the interest is not its liability but the partner's. However, SP4/85, issued in February 1985, regards the interest paid as rent so that it then becomes allowable as a deduction. In the partner's hands, the rent is taxable but the interest paid is allowed as a deduction in arriving at the amount taxable under Schedule A.

9.4.4 Incorporation of partnership

(ESC A43)

Where a partnership business is transferred to a limited company in return for shares, any qualifying loan in existence at the time continues to attract tax relief provided the conditions for relief in 9.5 below would be met if a new loan was taken out.

9.4.5 Tax planning: withdrawing partnership monies and replacing working capital by raising qualifying loans

Where a partner has a surplus balance on either his current or capital account with a partnership and he does not already have a qualifying loan, he may withdraw the balance due to him (with his partners' consent), use the money to pay off non-qualifying borrowings and then borrow further funds to introduce capital into the partnership with tax relief.

Example – Replacement capital

B is a partner in the XYZ partnership. He has a credit balance of £100,000 in his capital account. Outside the partnership, he has bought a yacht for his private use with the help of a £40,000 loan from his bank and he has a house mortgage of £20,000. *B* would withdraw £60,000 from his capital account in the partnership and use the money to make the following repayments:

	£
Yacht bank loan	40,000
Building society	20,000
	60,000

Once these transactions have been completed, *B* would borrow £60,000 as a loan (not overdraft) and use the funds to reintroduce capital into the partnership with full tax relief on the interest payable. Professional advice should be sought well in advance before setting up this sort of loan.

9.4.6 Another planning point: raising qualifying loans to replace partnership borrowings

Another situation where it may be appropriate to restructure existing borrowings is where the partnership has taken a loan, typically in order to purchase another business or the property from which the business is carried on. In this situation, each partner is normally required to borrow privately his share of the partnership loan and introduce the monies raised into the partnership. The partner can then personally claim tax relief on the interest paid as a charge on his income.

The partnership collects the monies raised by each partner's loan and uses the funds to redeem the partnership loan. As a result, each partner's share of profits becomes correspondingly higher because no interest is now payable by the partnership. However, the situation redresses itself because the higher profits must be used to finance the private borrowing.

Rearranging matters in this way can provide significant cash-flow benefits since relief is available for interest up to one year earlier than where the borrowings remain within the partnership. For example, if the partnership makes up its accounts to 30 April, interest paid on partnership borrowings in the year to 31 March 2004 will normally attract tax relief in 2004-05 (ie as an expense in arriving at the partnership profits for its year falling in 2004-05), whereas replacing these borrowings with qualifying loans raised by the partners will mean that the interest attracts tax relief against their income for the tax year 2003-04.

9.5 LOANS TO INVEST IN CLOSE COMPANIES

(TA 1988, s 360)

Where interest is paid on a loan used to purchase shares in a close company, or in lending money to such a company that is used for the company's business purposes, the interest may be eligible for tax relief. For the definition of a close company, see 26.13.1.

Relief is due provided the borrower meets one of two conditions and the company is a qualifying company:

(1) The borrower either alone or together with certain associates owns a material interest in the close company (defined broadly as more than 5% of the ordinary share capital).
(2) The borrower holds less than 5% of the ordinary share capital, but works for the greater part of his time in the actual management or conduct of the company or an associated company (a works manager, a production manager or a company secretary would normally satisfy this condition).

The company must exist wholly or mainly for one of the following purposes:

(a) To carry on a trade or trades on a commercial basis.
(b) To make investments in land or property let commercially to unconnected parties.
(c) To hold shares or securities or make loans to 'qualifying companies' or an intermediate company, all of which are under its control. A qualify-

ing company is one that is under the close company's control and satisfies the conditions at (a) and (b) above.

(d) To co-ordinate the administration of two or more qualifying companies.

If the company holds property, the individual must not reside in it unless he has worked for the greater part of his time in the actual management or conduct of the company.

Once again, relief is dependent on the way the loan is used, not on the way it is secured; the borrower may therefore have a qualifying loan that is secured by way of a mortgage on his home.

9.5.1 Close EIS and BES companies

(TA 1988, s 360(3A); FA 1989, s 47)

Loan interest relief is not available in respect of shares issued under the Enterprise Investment Scheme. Similar rules apply where an individual has used a loan to acquire shares on which relief was due under the Business Expansion Scheme.

9.5.2 Company ceases to be close after loan taken out

Relief can continue to be due for interest paid on a loan even though the company has ceased to be a close company.

9.5.3 Close company taken over on share-for-share basis

Where an individual has borrowed in order to invest in a close company and that company is taken over by another close company on a share-for-share basis, his loan can continue to be a qualifying loan.

9.6 LOANS TO INVEST IN EMPLOYEE-CONTROLLED COMPANIES

(TA 1988, s 361)

It is also possible for an individual to establish a qualifying loan where he uses it to acquire shares in an employee-controlled company, even if it is not a close company. The conditions that need to be satisfied for a loan to qualify under this provision are:

(1) during the year of assessment in which the interest is paid, the company must either become employee-controlled for the first time or be employee-controlled for at least nine months;

(2) the individual or his spouse must be a full-time employee throughout the period commencing with the application of the loan and ending with the date on which the interest is paid. He can also continue to obtain

relief for interest paid within 12 months of his having ceased to be an employee;

(3) the shares must be acquired before, or not later than 12 months after, the date on which the company first becomes an employee-controlled company; and

(4) the individual must not have recovered any capital from the company during the period from applying the loan proceeds to pay interest.

The legislation requires that the company be unquoted and resident only in the UK and either a trading company or the holding company of a trading group. A company is 'employee-controlled' if more than 50% of its ordinary share capital and voting power is owned by full-time employees or their spouses. If a full-time employee owns more than 10%, the excess is disregarded. For this purpose, a spouse's holding is attributed to the employee unless the spouse is also a full-time employee.

9.7 LOANS TO PURCHASE PLANT AND MACHINERY (P&M)

(TA 1988, s 359)

Where a partner incurs capital expenditure in the purchase of plant and machinery used for the partnership's business purposes and eligible for capital allowances, he can claim tax relief on interest paid if the plant is financed by a loan. The relief is available only in the tax year in which the loan is taken out and the following three tax years.

Example – Use of loans to purchase plant and machinery

A partner borrowed £10,000 at 10% pa on 6 October 2001 to buy a van that is used for the partnership's business. His private use is agreed at 25%.

Interest relief is available on £375 in 2001-02 and on £750 for the ensuing three tax years.

Similar relief is available for employees who are required to purchase plant for use in carrying out their duties but the relief is not available for loans used to buy a car, van or motor cycle.

9.8 GIFT AID

(FA 1990, s 25; F(No2)A 1992, s 26)

9.8.1 Introduction

Gift Aid, introduced in 1990, is a way in which the Government seeks to encourage taxpayers to support charities. The scheme originally gave income tax relief only for substantial cash donations to charity. Prior to 6 April 2000 there was a minimum limit for gifts to qualify under this scheme of £250. This limit was abolished from 6 April 2000.

Example – Gift Aid donation

In 2002-03, *A* gave £780 to a recognised charity. Under the Gift Aid scheme, that will be treated as a donation of £1,000, from which basic rate tax of £220 has been deducted. The charity can claim that tax from the Revenue, so it will receive a total of £1,000.

If *A* is a basic rate taxpayer, that is the end of the story: he has paid over £780 that the Revenue has 'topped up' to £1,000. If *A* is a higher rate taxpayer, he may claim higher rate relief on the gift, calculated as follows:

	£
Gross donation made	1,000
Tax relief at 40%	400
Less: deducted when gift made	(220)
Reduction in *A*'s own tax liability	180

If *A* is not a taxpayer at all, the Revenue will require him to make good the £220 it has paid to the charity, but if he has paid sufficient tax at the lower rates to cover the £220 this is sufficient.

Relief can also be obtained against tax on an individual's capital gains.

9.8.2 Carry back of relief

It is possible to carry back Gift Aid donations made after 5 April 2003. The amount that may be carried back will the amount of donations made by 31 January following the tax year.

This relief may apply when filing the 2002-03 tax return.

An individual will need to make a formal carry back election. The deadline for making this election is the date that he files his tax return or (if earlier) 31 January following the year to which the donations are being carried back.

9.8.3 Giving a tax refund to charity

The 2004 Tax Form will allow individuals to nominate any tax repayment to charity. This will be under Gift Aid and, subject to any restriction imposed after this book has gone to press, be available to set against an individual's tax liability as a carry back in the 2003-04 tax form.

9.8.4 Qualifying donations

Several conditions must be satisfied before a donation can qualify under the Gift Aid scheme:

(1) The recipient must be a recognised charity established in the UK (ie the charity must be administered in the UK: it may carry out its charitable

work anywhere in the world) or, from 6 April 2002, a community amateur sports club (see 31.2).

Many appeal funds and societies established for the public benefit are not technically charities. In case of doubt, intending donors should ask for evidence of charitable status or should consult:

The Charity Commission
57-60 Haymarket
London SW1Y 4QX

By way of exception, four bodies that technically are not charities *are* deemed to be charities for Gift Aid purposes: the British Museum, the National History Museum, the National Heritage Memorial Fund, and the Historic Buildings and Monuments Commission for England.

(2) The gift must be of money: it is not possible to claim Gift Aid relief for donated works of art, or even for goods (eg clothing or blankets) to be used to assist distressed people. Also, it is not possible to give money on condition that it be used to buy something from the donor, a member of his family or a company in which he has an interest.

(3) The gift may be made in cash, by cheque or bank transfer, or by credit card. However, the Revenue does not accept that writing-off an existing loan to the charity is equivalent to a gift of money.

(4) There is no minimum or maximum donation.

(5) Any reciprocal benefit received from the charity (by the donor or a member of his family) must fall within prescribed limits (see 9.8.6-9.8.8).

(6) Until 6 April 2000, the donor had to be a UK resident.

9.8.5 Payments under deeds of covenant

Where an individual makes payments under a deed of covenant in favour of a charity that was entered into before 6 April 2000, the payments are now treated as Gift Aid donations.

9.8.6 Permissible benefits for Gift Aid donors

A charity may wish to give a token of its appreciation to donors by way of thanks for their donations. Modest benefits received in consequence of making a donation will not stop the donation from qualifying as a Gift Aid donation, provided their value does not exceed certain limits. If a charity wishes to provide benefits to donors (eg as part of a membership scheme) it should consider whether the proposed benefits fall within the limits in the donor benefit rules. If they exceed the limits, the membership subscriptions cannot qualify as Gift Aid donations.

The following need to be determined to decide whether a donation can qualify as a Gift Aid donation:

(1) whether the donor, or a person connected with him, receives any benefits in consequence of making the donation; and
(2) if so, whether their value exceeds the limits in the donor benefit rules.

9.8.7 The donor benefit rules

The rules contain two limits for the value of benefits that a donor, or a person connected with him, may receive in consequence of making a donation. If such value:

- exceeds the limits in 9.8.8 (the relevant value test); or
- plus the value of any benefits received in consequence of any Gift Aid donations made by the same donor to the same charity earlier in the same tax year exceeds £250 (the aggregate value test);

the donation will not qualify as a Gift Aid donation.

9.8.8 The relevant value test

The limits for the relevant value test are:

Amount of donation	*Value of benefits*
£0-100	25% of the donation
£101-1,000	£25
£1,001-£10,000	2.5% of the donation
£10,001+	£250

9.8.9 The aggregate value test

In addition to satisfying the relevant value test, the value of benefits received in consequence of a donation must also satisfy the aggregate value test if the donation is to qualify as a Gift Aid donation. In other words:

(1) the value of benefits received in consequence of making the donation;
(2) plus the value of any benefits received in consequence of any Gift Aid donations by the same donor to the same charity earlier in the same tax year;
(3) must not exceed £250.

9.9 GIFT OF LISTED SHARES AND SECURITIES

From 6 April 2000, both individuals and companies who make gifts to charity of listed shares and securities have been able to claim relief in calculating their taxable income. The relief applies where listed shares or securities are given or sold at undervalue to a charity. The shares must be listed on a recognised stock exchange in the UK or overseas. A gift of AIM shares can qualify.

The deduction is equal to the shares' or securities' market value on the date of disposal (inclusive of the incidental cost of disposal) less any consideration received for or in consequence of their disposal.

Example

C gives listed shares with a market value of £10,000 to a charity. The shares show an unrealised gain of £9,000. *C* obtains income tax relief of £10,000 and CGT relief of £9,000. For a 40% taxpayer this amounts to tax relief of £7,600.

No CGT arises on a gift of shares to charity, so the donor's 40% income tax relief may be in addition to a significant saving of CGT that would apply if he were to sell the shares. The deduction is given only against income, not against capital gains.

An important planning point to bear in mind is that in the same way that no capital gain is recognised on the gift, no loss is allowed. Therefore, if you are making a gift of shares ensure first that there would be a chargeable gain if you actually disposed of the shares. If not, then a better alternative would be to actually sell the shares and make a cash donation to the charity, especially if you had other chargeable gains arising during the tax year.

9.10 GIFT OF LAND AND BUILDINGS

FA 2002 introduced a new tax relief for gifts made on or after 6 April 2002. The relief allows the donor to deduct the value of land or buildings in arriving at his taxable income. The relief is basically the same as that for gifts of listed shares; therefore, the same considerations apply.

9.11 ANNUITIES etc

(TA 1988, ss 347A, 663 and 683; FA 1988, s 36)

9.11.1 Introduction

Most annuities are payments under deed of covenant, ie a written promise to pay another person a certain sum of money each year (or each week, month, quarter, etc), either for a fixed number of years or for a period determined by events (eg until the payer's or the payee's death).

At one time, all deeds of covenant operated so as to transfer taxable income from the payer to the payee, so that the payer's taxable income was reduced by the amount of the covenanted payment and the payee's similarly increased. This could save a great deal of money where (as would usually be the case) the payee was subject to a lower rate of tax than the payer. As a result, deeds of covenant were often used to redistribute income around a family. Inevitably this has led to anti-avoidance legislation that has gradually become all-embracing.

Payments under deed of covenant are now deductible only where the covenant represents

(1) part of the purchase price of a business; or
(2) a payment made by a partnership to a retired partner, or to a former partner's widow or other dependant.

9.11.2 Business purchase and partnership annuities

Business purchase and partnership annuities attract higher rate relief as well as basic rate. The payer can deduct basic rate only at source, and must claim the higher rate relief from the Revenue. For details of such annuities, see 8.11.1.

9.12 TRADE UNION AND FRIENDLY SOCIETY SUBSCRIPTIONS

(TA 1988, s 266(6) and (7))

Some trade unions provide pensions and/or death benefits (often called 'funeral benefits') for their members. Each member is entitled to tax relief on half of that part of his subscription that relates to the provision of such benefits. However, this relief is sometimes given by the Revenue making a block payment to the union and the union then charging reduced subscriptions to its members.

The members of some friendly societies also pay a subscription that covers both a death benefit and a sickness benefit (ie a 'mixed policy'). Half of the amount referable to the death benefit qualifies for tax relief.

There is a distinction between relief under the special arrangements for trade union subscriptions and mixed friendly society policies and the general relief for life assurance premiums (see 9.13). Relief under the special arrangements is available only in the exact circumstances described – and not, for example, for a premium paid under a simple life assurance policy issued by a friendly society. Relief under the special arrangements is, however, available irrespective of the date the insurance came into force, whereas the general relief for life assurance premiums is available only for policies entered into force before 14 March 1984.

9.13 LIFE ASSURANCE PREMIUMS

(TA 1988, s 266)

Most life assurance polices that came into force before 14 March 1984 qualify for a form of tax relief. (The operative date is the day the policyholder's proposal was accepted by the insurance company, not the day the policy was issued.) The Revenue makes a block payment to the insurance company, equal to half the basic rate of tax on the premiums payable on qualifying policies, and the insurance company correspondingly reduces the amount actually paid by the policyholder. For example, if the standard premium was £100, the Revenue would pay £12.50 and the policyholder only £87.50. That £12.50 is the sum total of the relief available: no additional relief may be claimed if the policyholder is a higher rate taxpayer. Relief is lost completely if any material change is made to the policy – for example if a term policy is converted into an endowment or if the insurance company makes a loan to the policyholder without charging a commercial interest rate.

No tax relief is available for the premiums on life assurance policies that came into force on or after 14 March 1984. However, an alternative route to tax relief is to arrange your life cover through a personal pension plan, as explained in Chap. 12.

9.14 COMMUNITY INVESTMENT TAX CREDIT

The Community Investment Tax Credit (CITC) scheme was announced in July 2001 and the legislation included within Finance Act 2002. The scheme came into effect on 23 January 2003 and applies to investments in accredited Community Development Finance Institutions (CDFIs) made on or after 17 April 2002. The relief is intended to stimulate private investment in disadvantaged communities by providing a tax incentive to individuals and companies investing in not-for-profit and profit-seeking enterprises in or for those communities.

The tax relief is worth up to 25% of the value of the investment in the CDFI and is spread over five years, starting with the year in which the investment is made: for example for 2002-03 the tax relief given on a qualifying investment of £100 will be the lower of £5 or that which reduces the tax liability to nil.

The relief for a year should normally be claimed on the tax return for that year, see boxes 15.5 to 15.7 of the 2003 SA form. However individual investors having received a tax relief certificate may also request a change to their PAYE code number, or claim a reduction their self-assessment payments on account.

10

ALLOWANCES AND TAX CREDITS

DALE BUTCHER

This chapter looks at allowances and tax credits that may be claimed by taxpayers. The following topics are covered:

(1) Personal allowances.
(2) The basic personal allowance.
(3) Married couple's allowance.
(4) Pensioner couples.
(5) Allowances recently abolished.
(6) Blind persons.
(7) Time limits.
(8) Children's tax credits.
(9) Working Families' Tax Credit.
(10) Disabled Person's Tax Credit.
(11) Tax credits from 6 April 2003.

10.1 PERSONAL ALLOWANCES

(TA 1988, ss 256-278)

Income tax is not charged on the whole of a person's taxable income. In calculating the amount on which tax must be paid, he may claim a personal allowance that depends on his individual circumstances (eg age).

Personal allowances may be claimed by anyone resident in the UK. There is no minimum age requirement so that eg a newborn baby is entitled to a personal allowance. Sometimes it is possible, through the use of trusts or settlements, to redirect part of a family's income to a child, so that it may (being covered by his personal allowance) be enjoyed tax free (although the scope for transferring taxable income in this way has been whittled down by a succession of complex anti-avoidance provisions: see 22.5.4).

British subjects and certain other categories of people not resident in the UK may also claim personal allowances.

10.2 THE BASIC PERSONAL ALLOWANCE

(TA 1988, s 257)

Every individual resident in the UK is entitled to the basic personal allowance – often called the 'single person's allowance', a throwback to the days when there was also a 'married man's allowance'. The allowance for the current year is £4,615. If the individual is born or dies halfway through a year of assessment, the allowance is not scaled down.

Example – Death during tax year

Suppose *D* died at the end of September 2003, by which time he had earned only half his annual salary. His tax bill for 2003-04 would be:

		£
Salary		10,000
Professional subscription paid		(135)
		9,865
Personal allowance		(4,615)
Tax payable on		5,250
£1,960	charged at 10%	196.00
£3,290	charged at 22%	723.8
£5,250		£919.80

Because the PAYE scheme assumes that personal allowances will be used in equal monthly (or weekly) instalments over the year, about £1,574 will have been deducted from *D*'s salary while he was alive. On request, the Revenue will therefore repay his executors the excess tax deducted (£654.20).

10.2.1 Higher allowances for the over-65s

Higher allowances are given to those who have attained age 65 and are of limited means. The allowance is currently £6610 for those between ages 65 and 74 and £6,720 for those aged 75+. If an individual attains age 65 or 75 during a year of assessment, he is entitled to the appropriate allowance for the whole of that year. For example, a man born on 1 June 1938 attained age 65 on 1 June 2003 and is entitled to the higher allowance of £6,610 for the 2003-04 tax year.

The higher allowance is also given where the individual was alive on the first day of the tax year and would have achieved age 65 or 75 within the tax year had he not died.

The allowance is designed to assist only those of limited means. The allowance is reduced by £1 for every £2 by which the individual's 'total income' exceeds £18,300, until it falls back to the standard allowance for the under-65s.

Within this band, every £2 of income can cost 66p in tax (44p on the £2 itself, plus 22p on the £1 of allowances withdrawn). This is an effective percentage rate of 33%. For 2002-03, the £1-for-£2 reduction operated between 'total incomes' of £17,900 and £20,870 for those between the ages of 65 and 74 and between £17,900 and £21,410 for those aged 75+.

Example – Reduced higher allowances

In 2002-03, *E* was aged 70. He received a State pension of £5,500 pa, an occupational pension of £13,500 and rental income of £1,000. His 'total income' was £20,000; his overall income tax liability for 2002-03 is therefore:

	£	£	£
Total income			20,000
Higher personal allowance		6,100	
Total income	20,000		
Income limit	17,900		
Excess	2,100		
Half of excess		1,050	
Reduced higher personal allowance[1]			5,050
Tax payable on			14,950

[1]This cannot be reduced below the standard personal allowance of £4,615

£1,920	charged at 10%	192.00
£13,030	charged at 22%	2,866.60
£14,950		£3,058.60

The definition of 'total income' is, accordingly, very important, especially as in certain circumstances it is possible for an individual to rearrange his investments so that his 'total income', as defined by the Taxes Acts, is less than his real income. This is explained in 10.2.2.

10.2.2 Calculating 'total income'

(TA 1988, s 835)

A person's 'total income', as defined by the Taxes Acts, differs from his real income, first because not all receipts count towards total income and secondly because certain deductions can be made from real income in calculating total income.

The first step in calculating total income is to add together all the income that is assessable to tax. Income not assessable to tax is excluded. Examples include letting income exempt under the 'rent-a-room' scheme (see 6.4), the interest credited to an ISA or an existing TESSA (see 11.4), the dividends earned by a PEP (see 11.5) or a venture capital trust (see 11.7), the growth in value of National Savings certificates (see 11.2.1) and amounts withdrawn from insurance bonds up to the 5% limit (see 12.3.3). A person whose income falls within the marginal age relief band would, therefore, clearly do well to consider placing his money in tax-exempt investments.

The second step is to deduct, from the sum of assessable income, the following outgoings:

(1) Interest paid, insofar as it qualifies for tax relief under the usual rules other than under MIRAS (see 9.2).
(2) All of the 'other outgoings' listed in Chap. 9, insofar as each qualifies for tax relief under the normal rules. (The 'other outgoings' that may qualify are Gift Aid donations.)
(3) Contributions paid to an occupational or personal pension scheme.
(4) Any surplus capital allowances arising from investment in enterprise zone property (see 11.8).

Example – Total income

Suppose that *E* in the example above received a windfall of £5,000. He invests £1,800 in an enterprise zone property trust and the balance in National Savings Certificates. To celebrate his good fortune, he makes a Gift Aid donation of £200 (gross) in favour of his local church. His tax liability for the year 2002-03 will in fact fall to £2,167.60, as follows:

	£	£	£
Pension and interest received			19,000
Enterprise zone property investment		1,800	
Gift Aid payment (gross)		200	
			(2,000)
'Total income'			17,000
Higher personal allowance			
Total income	17,000		
Income limit	17,900		
Excess	Nil		
			(6,100)
Tax payable on			£10,900
£1,920 charged at 10%			192.00
£8,980 charged at 22%			1,975.60
£10,900			£2,167.60

10.3 MARRIED COUPLE'S ALLOWANCE

(TA 1988, s 257A)

This relief was abolished with effect from 6 April 2000, though it still exists for married couples where either spouse was born before 6 April 1935. See *Tax Handbook 2000-01* at 7.5.

10.4 PENSIONER COUPLES

(TA 1988, s 257A)

A higher married couple's allowance is still available if either spouse was born before 6 April 1935. The allowance for 2003-04 is £5,565 if the elder spouse is aged between 65 and 74, and £5,635 if he or she is aged 75+. Relief is restricted to 10%. The allowance is subject to claw-back if the individual's income exceeds £18,300 (see 10.2.1).

10.4.1 Pensioner couples: transfer of excess allowances

(TA 1988, s 257B; F(No 2)A 1992, s 20 and Sched 5)

The whole of a higher, age-related married couple's allowance may be transferred to the wife if the husband has insufficient income to use it himself. An election to do this must be lodged with the Revenue within five years and ten months from the end of the tax year.

10.5 ALLOWANCES RECENTLY ABOLISHED

The widow's bereavement allowance under TA 1988, s 262 was abolished completely from 2001-02. The additional personal allowance under TA 1988, ss 259-261A was abolished with effect from 6 April 2000.

10.6 BLIND PERSONS

(TA 1988, s 265)

A person who is blind may claim a special, additional personal allowance of £1,510 for 2003-04 (£1,480 for 2002-03). A person counts as 'blind' if:

(1) he lives in England or Wales and his name appears on the local authority's register of blind persons; or
(2) he lives in Scotland or Northern Ireland and is so blind that he cannot perform any work for which eyesight is essential.

This definition means that a person resident abroad can never, for tax purposes, count as blind – an odd rule strictly enforced by the Revenue.

A person who becomes blind during a year of assessment may claim the full blind person's allowance for that year.

10.6.1 Married couples

If husband and wife are both blind, each may claim a separate blind person's allowance.

A blind husband with insufficient income to use all his personal allowances may be able to transfer the whole or part of his blind person's allowance to his wife (whether or not she also is blind). However, the transfer of the married couple's allowance took priority, so a transfer of blind person's allowance was only possible where the husband's income was insufficient to use his basic personal allowance and the blind person's allowance itself. Similarly, a wife may transfer her unused blind person's allowance to her husband (whether or not he also is blind).

A claim to transfer a blind person's allowance to a spouse must be made, on Revenue Form 575, within five years of the 31 January following the end of the relevant year of assessment.

Example – Blind married couple

G, who is sighted, earns £10,000 a year. His wife, *H*, who is blind, has a pension of £5,000. The position for 2002-03 is:

H	£	£
Pension		5,000
Basic personal allowance	4,615	
Blind person's allowance	1,480	
		(6,095)
Excess, transferable to husband		1,095
G		
Salary		10,000
Basic personal allowance	4,615	
Transferred excess from wife	1,095	
		(5,710)
Tax payable on		£4,290
£1,920 charged at 10%		192.00
£2,370 charged at 22%		521.40
£4,030		713.40

10.7 TIME LIMITS

As noted at 10.2, every individual resident in the UK is automatically entitled to the basic personal allowance.

Other allowances must be claimed within five years and ten months of the year to which they relate, for example a claim in respect of blind persons allowance relating to the year ended 5 April 1998 must be made by 31 January 2004.

In general, most claims for allowances are made annually in the tax return. However, where a claim is overlooked or a formal return is not issued, a claim can be made to the taxpayer's tax office, normally in writing, though in certain circumstances 'phone claims will be accepted.

10.8 CHILDREN'S TAX CREDITS UP TO APRIL 2003

This scheme came into effect on 6 April 2001. A reduction in an individual's tax liability is given as a tax credit for each qualifying child. A qualifying child is one aged under 16 who lives with the individual during the tax year. The individual who claims the credit must be a parent or someone maintaining the child.

The basic credit for 2001-02 is £5,200 per child, with the credit being given at the rate of 10%. However, the credit is reduced by £2 for every £3 of the claimant's income charged to higher rate tax.

Where the child lives with husband and wife, or with a couple living together as man and wife, the reduction in the tax credit is generally by reference to the spouse with the higher income.

Relief for child tax credits are given under PAYE for claimants who are employed. A self-employed individual claims a credit when making his SA return.

From 2002-03, an extra tax credit of £5,200 is given for the tax year in which the child is born.

10.8.1 Claiming the credit

To claim, you must have at least one child who is:

- Your own child, a stepchild, an adopted child or a child you look after at your own expense,
- Under age 16 at the start of the tax year, and
- Living with you for at least part of the tax year.

If someone else can also claim for the same child, you may have to share the tax credit with him or her.

If the child reaches age 16 during the tax year, you are still entitled to the tax credit for the whole year as long as the child is living with you during the period before his or her 16th birthday.

The Children's Tax Credit is an income tax relief. It is not a payment to you, but a way of reducing the tax you pay on your income. Unlike the personal tax allowance, the tax credit is not an amount of income you can receive without paying tax. Instead, it reduces your tax bill by up to a set amount and this is reflected in your tax code. In 2001-02 it is worth up to £442 off the tax you have to pay.

There is only one credit for each family. If you are living with a partner, you or your partner can have only one credit between you, even if you have more than one child living with you.

If the person claiming it is a higher rate taxpayer, the credit of £520 is reduced at the rate of £1 for every £15 of income taxed at the higher rate. It is unlikely that you will receive any credit if your income is above £41,735. The credit is expressed as an allowance of £5,200 given at the rate of 10%. If you are a higher rate taxpayer, you may see the reduction of the credit expressed as £2 of the allowance withdrawn for every £3 of income in the higher rate band.

Example

J and *K* have two children under age 16. *K* earns £36,010 and *J* earns £25,000 pa. *K* has to claim the Children's Tax Credit as she is the higher rate taxpayer. She is taxed as follows in 2001-02:

0% on the first £4,535 of her income (personal allowance)
10% on the next £1,880
22% on the next £27,520
40% on the remaining £2,075

The credit is reduced by £1,383 to £3,817. Therefore the credit is worth £520 – £382 off the tax *K* has to pay.

If neither partner in the couple pays tax at the higher rate in the tax year, then either of them can have the whole credit, or they can decide to share the credit equally between them. Both partners have to agree if the partner with the lower income is to have all the credit allocated to him or her. If the partner who receives the credit does not pay enough tax to use all the credit, he or she can transfer the unused credit to the other partner after the end of the tax year. If either, or both, partners pay higher rate tax, the partner with the larger income must claim the credit. You cannot share the credit or transfer it to the partner with the lower income. This is to ensure that the reduction in the credit is based on the income of the higher earning person.

Example of credit in a split year

L and *M* have been living together and sharing the credit equally. Both are basic rate taxpayers. They separate on 21 August 2002 and the children go and live with *M*. The year is then split into two parts.

For the first part of the tax year, from 6 April to 20 August 2002 (137 days), the couple live together. The credit is worth £520 for a full year. So for this period it is worth up to £520 × 137) ÷ 365 = £195, which means for this part of the year it is worth up to £97 each for *L* and for *M*.

For the second part of the tax year, from 21 August 2002 to 5 April 2003 (228 days), the children live with *M*. For this period the credit is worth up to (£520 × 228) ÷ 365 = £325 for *M* only. Therefore, over the whole year it is worth up to £97 for *L* and £422 for *M* (£97 + £325).

10.8.2 Children's tax credit and the SA form

Even if you have claimed the Children's Tax Credit on the CTC claim form and received the relief via the tax code operated against your earnings in the tax year to 5 April 2003, the 2002 SA form must be completed and Question 16 of the form ticked 'YES'. If there has been a change in your circumstances during the course of the tax year then the Revenue provides helpsheet IR343. Specifically, this helpsheet deals with the position where during the course of the tax year you and your partner separate or start living together. If following a separation you cannot agree on how the credit should be split, the Revenue guidance is that you make an estimate of the credit and make a note in the space provided on the form as to how you arrived at your estimate. If there is no subsequent agreement on how the credit should be divided, the matter will be decided before the General Commissioners.

10.9 WORKING FAMILIES' TAX CREDIT UP TO APRIL 2003

The Working Families' Tax Credits (WFTC) scheme topped up the earnings of individuals with children. For both WFTC and Disabled Persons' Tax Credits (see below), a childcare tax credit could be available to assist with the childcare costs incurred by a working parent.

WTFC could be claimed by couples or lone parents who were UK-resident, had at least one child, worked at least 16 hours pw and did not have savings of more than £8,000. The tax credit was based on four elements:

(1) a basic tax credit (£60 for 2002-03);
(2) a supplement of £11.65 for a person who worked more than 30 hours pw;
(3) a tax credit for each child dependent on age (£26.45 from birth to age 16 and £27.20 from September following the 16th birthday up to the day before their 19th birthday); and
(4) a childcare credit of up to 70% of eligible costs up to a maximum of £135 pw for one child and £200 pw for two or more children.

The total award was calculated by adding all the credits together. See also 25.6.

The amount of WFTC that a person was entitled to was calculated as follows:

(1) Add together all income of the claimant and that of their partner in respect of net income from employment, self-employment income after deducting expenses, tax and NICs, most social security benefits (except those that are tax-free), Statutory Sick Pay, occupational or personal pension and any 'assumed income from capital'. Assumed income from capital is calculated as £1 per £250 of savings over and above £3,000 up

to the maximum permitted savings of £8,000 to qualify for entitlement to WFTC.

(2) If the total income was less than £94.60 pw, the claimant was awarded the maximum WFTC that they are entitled to. If their income was more than this amount, then maximum WFTC was reduced by 55p for each £1 of income above £94.60.

Example

A lone parent with one child aged 12 had take-home pay of £140 pw for work of less than 30 hours and child benefit. She paid £30 pw in childcare costs. The WFTC entitlement was computed as follows:

WFTC maximum amount:	£
Basic	60.00
Child tax credit	26.45
Childcare tax credit (70% of £30)	21.00
	107.45
Less 55% of income in excess of £94.60	
(£140 – £94.60 = £45.40)	24.97
WFTC payable	82.48

Applications for WFTC were made by post on form WFTC1 and evidence of earnings was required.

Self-employed and non-earning applicants could be paid by either automated credit transfer direct into the claimant's bank or building society account or by cashing weekly orders at the Post Office. Employees normally received their WFTC with their wages or salary.

10.10 DISABLED PERSON'S TAX CREDIT (DPTC) UP TO APRIL 2003

A person could apply for DPTC if he worked 16+ hours pw and had a physical/mental disability that put him at a disadvantage in getting a job, either as an employee or as a self-employed person. It was calculated in the same way as WFTC except the basic credit and thresholds for savings are different.

The basic credit was £62.10 for a single person or £92.80 for couples and lone parents. The supplements for working over 30 hours pw and for children and childcare were identical to those of the WFTC.

The savings threshold above which no DPTC is available was £16,000, with savings of less than £3,000 being disregarded in calculating 'assumed income from capital'.

Applications for DPTC were made by post on form DPTC1 and evidence of earnings was required. The payment method was the same as for WFTC. See also 25.6.

10.11 TAX CREDITS FROM 6 APRIL 2003

From 6 April 2003, the above tax credits were replaced by two new tax credits, the child tax credit and the working tax credit.

Child tax credit

As its name suggests, the child tax credit is meant to support families with children and can be claimed if you have responsibility for a child.

The credit, which can be claimed in addition to any child benefit or working tax credit, is available for the support of:

- A child until 1 September following their 16th birthday
- A person aged 16-18 who
  - is in full time education, up to and inclusive of A levels or their equivalent (NVQ3/Scottish Highers); or
  - if not in education has no job/training place and has registered with the Careers or Connexions Service

The 'child' must not be claiming income support or tax credits and must not be serving a custodial sentence of more than four months.

The following table is a guide to how much child credit can be claimed in the current tax year (2003-04) by an individual who is not claiming working tax credit.

Child Tax Credit (£)

Gross	*One Child*		*Two Children*		*Three Children*	
Annual Joint Income (£)	*Annual*	*Weekly*	*Annual*	*Weekly*	*Annual*	*Weekly*
5,000	1,990	38.00	3,435	65.70	4,880	93.30
10,000	1,990	38.00	3,345	65.70	4,880	93.30
15,000	1,335	25.50	2,780	53.20	4,225	80.80
20,000	545	10.40	930	17.80	2,375	45.40
25,000	545	10.40	545	10.40	545	10.40
30,000	545	10.40	545	10.40	545	10.40
40,000	545	10.40	545	10.40	545	10.40
50,000	545	10.40	545	10.40	545	10.40
60,000	0	0	0	0	0	0

Working tax credit

The new working tax credits is available as a top up for individuals in low paid jobs, with additional payments being available for working households in which an individual has a severe disability.

In general a qualifying individual is:

- aged 16 or over, works 16 hours a week and is responsible for a child; or
- aged 25 or over and work at least 30 hours a week; or
- aged 16 and over, has a disability that puts him at a disadvantage in getting a job and work at least 16 hours a week; or
- the individual or their partner is aged over 50 and is returning to work for at least 16 hours a week after time spent on qualifying benefits.

The following tables offer a guide as to the amounts that could be receivable in 2003-04.

Working Tax Credit (£)
if you are responsible for at least one child or young person

Gross Annual Joint Income (£)	*Couple or lone parent working between 16 and 30 hours a week*		*Couple or lone parent working between 16 and 30 hours a week*	
	Annual	*Weekly*	*Annual*	*Weekly*
5,000	3,000	58.00	3,645	69.70
7,500	2,000	40.50	2,745	52.50
10,000	1,150	22.70	1,820	34.80
12,500	250	4.90	895	17.10
15,000	0	0.00	0	0.00

Working Tax Credit (£)
if you are *not* responsible for at least one child or young person

Gross Annual Joint Income (£)	*Single person aged 25 or over working 30 hours or more a week*		*Couple (working adult aged 25 or over) working 30 hours or more a week*	
	Annual	*Weekly*	*Annual*	*Weekly*
5,000	2,145	41.00	3,645	69.70
7,500	1,245	23.80	2,745	52.50
10,000	320	6.10	1,820	34.80
12,500	0	0.00	895	17.10
15,000	0	0.00	0	0.00

The general rule is that to qualify for tax credits you must be aged 16 or over and usually live in the United Kingdom. You may also qualify if you do not live in the UK but you are:

- A citizen of another country in the European Economic Area (EEA) and you work in the United Kingdom, or
- A Crown Servant posted overseas, or

- A citizen of a country in the European Economic Area (including the UK) living abroad and you receive a UK state pension or contributions-based Jobseeker's Allowance.

If you are in the above situation and feel that that you meet the other requirements for tax credits then you should phone the Inland Revenue helpline 0800 500 222. Further details on tax credits and an assessment of whether you qualify can be found at www.taxcredits.inlandrevenue.gov.uk/home.aspx.

11

TAX EFFICIENT INVESTMENT

COLIN WALKER

There is a range of investments where the interest and any gains are exempt from tax. This chapter covers the following:

Investments providing tax exempt return

(1) Individual savings accounts (ISAs).
(2) National Savings investments.
(3) Friendly society investments.
(4) TESSAs.
(5) Personal equity plans (PEPs).

Investments qualifying for tax deduction

(6) Enterprise investment scheme.
(7) Venture capital trusts (VCTs).
(8) Enterprise zone trusts.
(9) Investment in British films.

INVESTMENTS PROVIDING TAX EXEMPT RETURN

11.1 INDIVIDUAL SAVINGS ACCOUNTS (ISAs)

11.1.1 Basic outline of scheme

ISAs are designed to encourage new saving. They are offered by financial institutions, or 'providers' (eg banks, building societies and insurance companies). All UK-resident and ordinarily resident individuals aged 16+ can take out an ISA. The annual limit is £7,000, of which up to £3,000 can be kept on deposit and up to £1,000 in life assurance policies. The balance must be invested in stocks and shares, and unit trusts.

Investors in ISAs are exempt from income tax and CGT on their investments and the ISA manager can reclaim the 10% tax credit on UK dividends until 5 April 2004. This applies to shares held both directly within the ISA and by an insurance company in a special fund for policies issued as part of an ISA.

Normally, contributions to an ISA are made in cash (but see below on shares acquired under approved schemes).

11.1.2 Transfers of shares into an ISA

It is possible to transfer into an ISA shares received from an approved profit-sharing scheme (see 4.11) or from an approved savings-related share option scheme (see 4.14.2). The market value of shares transferred into the ISA counts towards the £7,000 annual limit, but no CGT is payable on the transfer. The transfer must take place within three years of the shares being appropriated in the case of a profit-sharing scheme and within 90 days of acquisition under a savings-related share option scheme.

It is not possible to transfer other shares into an ISA, for example shares acquired under a public offer or on a building society demutualisation (as was permitted with PEPs).

11.1.3 Withdrawals

It is possible to make withdrawals from an ISA at any time without loss of tax relief, but it is not possible to return sums to an ISA unless the amounts fall within the annual 'allowance'.

11.1.4 Practical aspects

The regulations permit an individual to take out a 'maxi' ISA or up to three 'mini' ISAs in a tax year. An individual is not allowed to take out a maxi and a mini ISA in the same year.

A maxi ISA can be invested wholly in quoted (but not AIM) shares, unit trusts, investment trusts and OEICs, gilts, and corporate bonds with a life of at least five years. This is sometimes called the 'equity' component, although the range of investments is wider than equities. Alternatively, the maxi may be split into three separate components with cash deposits of up to £3,000 and life assurance of £1,000. With a maxi, you can 'top-up' the stocks and shares component so that if, for example, only £1,000 were put into the cash component and £750 in life assurance, £5,250 could be put into the stocks and shares component. Once you have set up a maxi ISA with two or more components, you are stuck with it, as the rules do not permit internal transfers from one component to another.

Alternatively, it is possible for an individual to take out three mini ISAs, possibly with different managers, for each separate component. In this case it is not possible to top-up the stocks and shares component, so if you take out a £1,000 mini cash ISA and a £750 mini insurance ISA, you can still put in only £3,000 into a stocks and shares ISA.

11.1.5 CAT standards

The Government introduced a system of voluntary 'CAT' (Charges Access Terms) standards. These vary according to the different types of ISA. For example, the CAT for mini cash ISAs requires seven-day access and interest of no less than base minus 2%; for mini insurance ISAs, annual charges should not exceed 3% and the surrender value after three years must be at least equal to the premiums paid. The standards are voluntary, but providers must inform potential investors whether their products meet or exceed the standards.

11.1.6 Consequences if rules are broken

With an ISA invested in stocks and shares, if the rules are broken (eg because the individual has taken out both a maxi and a mini ISA in the same year), the individual must report any capital gains.

With a cash ISA, the provider must withhold 20% tax and the individual must include the interest on his SA return and pay any higher rate tax due. In the case of an insurance ISA, the policy will be cancelled and the insurance company must deduct tax at basic rate. If the investor has made a profit, he is liable for higher rate tax. An individual who has knowingly broken the rules may also be liable for a penalty.

11.2 NATIONAL SAVINGS INVESTMENTS

11.2.1 National Savings certificates

(TA 1988, s 46)

These are certificates that pay an accumulating rate of interest over a five-year period. All returns are tax free. Index-linked certificates accumulate at a rate related to the RPI. If held for the full five years a bonus is payable.

11.2.2 NSB ordinary account interest

(TA 1988, s 325)

The first £70 of interest paid on a National Savings Bank (NSB) ordinary account is exempt from tax (see 7.1.1).

11.3 FRIENDLY SOCIETY INVESTMENTS

Friendly societies issue qualifying insurance policies and there is no tax charge for investors when such policies mature. In this respect the position is no different from policies issued by insurance companies. The difference lies in the way friendly societies are treated favourably for tax purposes in that they are not normally subject to tax on life assurance business; this has generally enabled them to produce attractive returns.

Friendly society policies are essentially a long-term investment. For many years they were prevented within the first ten years from paying a surrender value that exceeded the amount of premiums paid, but FA 1995 removed this limitation. This is often academic since the surrender value can be very low where plans are cancelled or surrendered before the ten-year term has expired, because penalties tend to be heavy and frequently the charges on friendly society plans are high.

The maximum premiums are still very low: the maximum permitted is £270 pa. Some societies do permit a lump sum investment to be made to cover the full ten-year plan. Most of the larger friendly societies are governed by the same investment regulations as life assurance companies. All investment income and capital gains within the fund are free of all UK tax, which enhances the rate of return.

11.4 TESSAs

(TA 1988, ss 326A-326C)

An individual was permitted to open a Tax-Exempt Special Savings Account in 1998-99 and earlier years. This is basically a five-year plan under which an individual aged 18+ could save up to £9,000. The sum must be held on deposit by a bank, building society or other institution authorised under the Banking Act 1987, but the regulations permit an investor to switch from one group to another. The resulting interest is not taxable provided the individual makes no withdrawals during the five-year period, or any such withdrawals do not exceed the amount of interest credited to the account less tax at basic rate.

Up to £1,800 pa may be invested in a TESSA opened before 6 April 1999 provided the total sums invested do not exceed £9,000.

Where a TESSA ceases to qualify, the interest credited to it becomes taxable income that is deemed to arise at that point in time.

Replacement by ISAs

No new TESSAs can be opened after 5 April 1999, although it is still possible to pay into a TESSA opened before 1999-2000. When existing accounts mature the capital can be transferred into the cash component of an ISA (see 11.1). Neither the annual subscriptions to TESSAs nor any maturing capital are treated as included in the annual subscription limit for the ISA.

11.5 PERSONAL EQUITY PLANS (PEPs)

(TA 1988, s 333)

An individual aged 18+ who is resident and ordinarily resident in the UK was permitted to invest up to £6,000 in a PEP in 1998-99, the final year of the scheme. In addition, a further £3,000 could be invested in a single company PEP (see below). The investments are held by a PEP manager and it is possible for a plan to be transferred to another authorised manager.

PEPs were intended to be a way of encouraging investment in shares. Up to £6,000 pa could be invested in shares in companies quoted on the Stock Exchange, shares quoted on the unlisted securities market (USM), or authorised unit trusts or investment trusts which in turn invest at least 50% of their funds in UK equities or shares quoted on EU Stock Exchanges. A PEP manager was (and can continue to do so on existing PEP funds) also allowed to invest in qualifying corporate bonds and convertible stocks. As an alternative, up to £1,500 could be invested in any other authorised unit trust or investment trust. The balance of any investments over the £1,500 limit then had to be invested in qualifying equities, or in unit trusts or investment trusts that met the 50% requirement.

An individual could also invest up to £3,000 pa in a single company PEP where the investment was restricted to shares in one particular company.

All income and capital gains arising within the PEP are exempt from tax.

All PEPs held at 6 April 1999 can continue to be retained and attract the same tax advantages as ISAs.

INVESTMENTS QUALIFYING FOR TAX DEDUCTION

11.6 ENTERPRISE INVESTMENT SCHEME

(FA 1994, s 135 and Sched 14)

The scheme is intended to provide a 'targeted incentive' for new equity investment in unquoted trading companies and to encourage outside investors to introduce finance and expertise to a company. The reliefs allow minority investors to secure 20% income tax relief in addition to CGT deferral relief, which could be worth up to another 40% of the amount invested.

FA 1998 extended the EIS to enable some investors to secure EIS CGT deferral relief even though they do not qualify for the income tax relief (eg because they take a controlling stake in the company). This effectively replaced CGT reinvestment relief and subsumed this into a 'unified' scheme under which companies in which investors take up shares have to conform to a common set of rules.

11.6.1 Summary of main aspects

Tax relief is due only if an individual subscribes for new shares in a qualifying company. Income tax relief may be given at 20% on the amount invested; this relief is forfeited if there is a disposal within three years (five years for shares issued before 6 April 2000). CGT deferral relief may also be obtained so that in some situations total tax relief of 60% can be secured.

Income tax relief is not available if the individual acquires a shareholding that exceeds 30%, but CGT deferral relief can still be available.

There is a ceiling for investment by individuals who qualify for income tax relief under the EIS of £150,000 per tax year. The ceiling does not apply for CGT deferral relief.

Up to one-half of the amount invested by an individual between 6 April and 5 October in any year can be carried back to the previous tax year if he did not invest the full amount during that year (subject to a maximum of £25,000).

Income tax relief is not available to an individual if he was previously connected with the company. This does not prevent a connected investor from qualifying for the CGT deferral relief.

EIS relief is available only where the company has gross assets of less than £15m before and no more than £16m after the EIS share issue. Where EIS shares are sold at a loss, relief is available either against capital gains or against the individual's income by virtue of TA 1988, s 574 (see 17.2).

Shares that attract the 20% income tax relief are exempt from CGT, except to the extent that EIS relief has been withdrawn.

The Revenue publishes a most informative booklet, IR137, *The Enterprise Investment Scheme*.

11.6.2 Conditions to be satisfied for relief to be available

Subscription for new shares in a qualifying company

Both EIS income tax relief and EIS CGT deferral relief are available only if an individual subscribes for shares. The shares must be ordinary shares that are not preferred in any way. EIS income tax relief is available only if he invests at least £500. The company must be a qualifying company.

Certificate EIS 3

An investor should normally obtain certificate EIS 3 from the company before claiming either type of EIS relief.

11.6.3 Qualifying companies

A qualifying company can be a UK-resident or non-resident company, but it must be an unquoted company that either:

(1) exists wholly for the purpose of carrying on one or more qualifying trades (see 11.6.4) or 'so exists apart from purposes capable of having no significant effect (other than in relation to incidental matters) on the extent of the company's activities'; or
(2) has a business that consists wholly of:
   (a) holding shares or securities of, or making loans to, one or more qualifying subsidiaries of the company; or
   (b) both holding such shares or securities, or making such loans, and carrying on one or more qualifying trades.

Company must be unquoted

A company does not qualify if any of its shares or securities are dealt in on The Stock Exchange or USM. The fact that a company's shares are dealt in on the AIM does not disqualify it, but the £15m gross asset test will rule out many AIM companies.

Other conditions

There are certain other conditions that need to be satisfied if it is to be a qualifying company:

(1) it must not control another company apart from a qualifying subsidiary, either on its own or together with a connected person, and there must not be any arrangements in place under which the issuing company can acquire such control;
(2) it must not be under the control of another company, or of another company and persons connected with it, and again there must be no arrangements in place whereby such a company may acquire control of the issuing company; and
(3) there must be no arrangements for the company to become quoted.

11.6.4 Meaning of qualifying trade

There are certain trades that are excluded under s 297. The company's business must not consist to any substantial extent of any of the following:

(1) dealing in land, commodities or futures, or shares, securities or other financial instruments;
(2) dealing in goods otherwise than in the course of any ordinary trade of wholesale or retail distribution;
(3) banking, insurance (but not insurance broking), money-lending, debt-factoring, HP financing or other financial activities;
(4) oil extraction activities;
(5) leasing (except for certain short-term charters of ships) or receiving royalties or licence fees;

(6) providing legal or accountancy services;
(7) providing services or facilities for any trade carried on by another person (other than a parent company) that consists to any substantial extent of activities within any of (1)-(6) above and in which a controlling interest is held by a person who also has a controlling interest in the trade carried on by the company;
(8) any of the following property-backed activities where the shares were issued on or after 17 March 1998:
    (a) farming and market gardening;
    (b) forestry and timber production;
    (c) property development;
    (d) operating or managing hotels or guest houses; and
    (e) operating or managing nursing or residential care homes.

Wholesale and retail distribution trades

Wholesale and retail distribution trades qualify only if they are 'ordinary' trades. Section 297(3) states that a trade does not qualify as an ordinary trade of wholesale or retail distribution if:

(1) it consists to a substantial extent of dealing in goods of a kind that are collected or held as an investment; and
(2) a substantial proportion of those goods are held by the company for a period that is significantly longer than the period for which a vendor would reasonably be expected to hold them while endeavouring to dispose of them at their market value.

The following are taken as indications that a company's trade is a qualifying trade:

(a) The trader buys the goods in quantities larger than those in which he sells them.
(b) The trader buys and sells the goods in different markets.
(c) The company incurs expenses in the trade in addition to the costs of the goods, and employs staff who are not connected with it.

The following are 'indications' that the trade is not a qualifying trade:

(i) There are purchases or sales from or to persons who are connected with the trader.
(ii) Purchases are matched with forward sales or vice versa.
(iii) The trader holds the goods for longer than is normal for such goods.
(iv) The trade is carried on otherwise than at a place or places commonly used for the type of trade.
(v) The trader does not take physical possession of the goods.

The above are only indications and are not conclusive that a company's trade is or is not a qualifying trade, but it will be difficult to persuade the

Revenue that a trade qualifies if there are a number of indications to the contrary.

11.6.5 Definition of 'qualifying subsidiary'

(TA 1988, s 308(2))

A qualifying subsidiary is one in which the issuing company or one of its subsidiaries holds at least 75% of the share capital. In addition, the company must meet one of the following tests:

(1) it must be carrying on a qualifying trade; or
(2) it must exist to hold and manage a property used by the parent company, or by a fellow 75% subsidiary, for qualifying trade purposes; or
(3) it must be dormant.

It was originally necessary for the activities of each member of a group of companies to be a qualifying activity. This was relaxed with effect from 27 November 1996 so that a group's activities are considered as a whole, rather than on an individual company basis. The Revenue stated that relief will no longer be withdrawn where the non-qualifying activities do not form a substantial part of the group's activities as a whole, but no indication has been given of what percentage is considered to be 'substantial'.

11.6.6 Reliefs available to an EIS investor

There are two types of relief: income tax and CGT deferral relief (see 11.6.1). They are separate, and either can be claimed without the other. An individual who invests, say, £100,000 can claim both reliefs by reference to the same £100,000 invested. Trustees can only claim the CGT relief.

11.6.7 Income tax relief

An investor is entitled to the lower of the income tax payable by him and relief at the lower rate (20%) on the amount invested up to a limit of £150,000 (£100,000 for 1997-98 and earlier years). For this purpose, his tax liability is calculated without regard to any reliefs given as a reduction expressed in terms of tax.

His tax liability is also computed without regard to double taxation credits and basic rate tax deducted at source on annual payments.

11.6.8 Further conditions for income tax relief

Individual must not be connected with the company

The legislation provides that an individual may be treated as connected with the issuing company, and therefore not entitled to EIS income tax relief, if he directly or indirectly possesses or is entitled to acquire more than 30% of the:

(1) issued ordinary share capital of the company, or any of its subsidiaries;
(2) loan capital and issued share capital of the company or any subsidiary; or
(3) voting power in the company or any subsidiary.

A connected individual can still be eligible for CGT deferral relief.

An individual is also regarded as being connected with the issuing company if he directly or indirectly possesses, or is entitled to acquire such rights as would, in the event of the winding-up of the company (or any of its subsidiaries), mean he is entitled to receive, more than 30% of the assets available for distribution to the company's equity holders.

Rights of 'associates' need to be taken into account. For these purposes, an 'associate' means partner, spouse, parent, grandparent, great-grandparent, child, grandchild, great-grandchild and certain family trusts. The necessity to take account of partners' interests was confirmed by the decision in *Cook v Billings & others*.

An individual is also regarded as connected with the company if he possesses any loan capital in a subsidiary of the company.

Individual must not be previously connected with the company

An individual is deemed to be connected with the company if he is:

(1) a paid director of the issuing company or any of its subsidiaries; or
(2) an employee of the issuing company or any of its subsidiaries; or
(3) a partner of the issuing company or any subsidiary; or
(4) an associate of someone who is a director, employee or partner of the issuing company, or any of its subsidiaries.

An individual is disqualified if he falls into any of the above categories during the two years prior to the date the EIS shares are issued. Furthermore, he will not qualify for EIS relief if he is connected with the issuing company at the time the shares are issued, unless he is a business angel who qualified for EIS relief on his original investment and is now acquiring additional shares and he is connected only because he is a paid director (see Figure 11.1).

11.6.9 CGT deferral relief

(FA 1995, s 65 and Sched 13)

This relief involves a concept of deferred gain. Basically, an individual who has realised a gain may secure deferral relief if he invests in the EIS during the period beginning one year before and ending three years after the disposal giving rise to the chargeable gain. However, the deferred gain is separately identified and will come back into charge if certain events happen (see 11.6.16).

Figure 11.1 – Is an investment by a 'business angel' eligible for EIS relief?

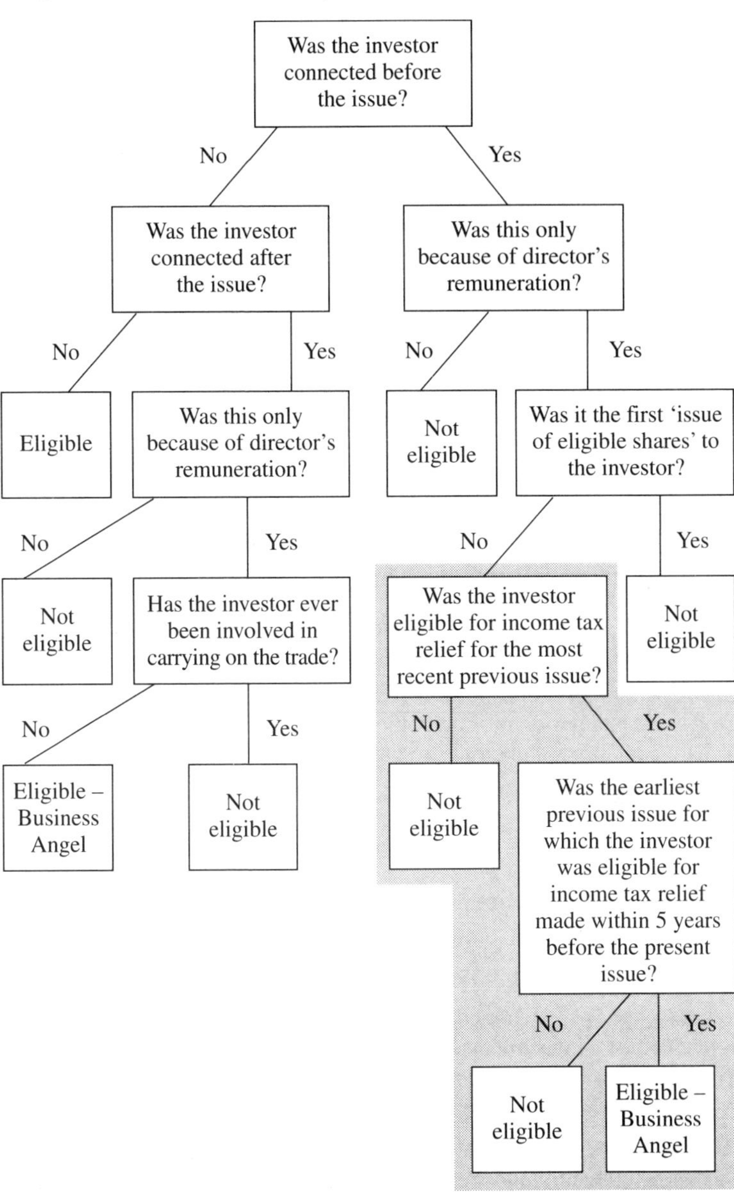

NB. The shaded area deals only with cases where there was only one issue of eligible shares to the investor before he or she became connected with the company because of director's remuneration.

Example of EIS CGT deferral relief

N sold quoted shares for £20,000 in December 2000. The shares were originally purchased in January 1985 for £5,000. In June 2002, *N* had invested £10,000 in ordinary shares in an EIS company. The CGT position for 2000-01 would then be as follows:

		£	£
Proceeds			20,000
Less:	Cost	5,000	
	Indexation relief, say	3,000	
			(8,000)
Net gain			12,000
Less:	EIS CGT deferral relief		(10,000)
Net chargeable gain for 2000-01			2,000

Note: If *N* were a higher rate taxpayer, the combined income and CGT relief could amount to 60% (20% income tax relief and 40% deferral of CGT).

The CGT deferral relief can be claimed even where the investor is 'connected' with the company (see 11.6.8).

11.6.10 Withdrawal of relief where company redeems share capital

All EIS investors lose a proportion of their relief if at any time during the investor's relevant period the company repays, redeems or repurchases any of its share capital which belongs to any member other than:

(1) the qualifying individual in question; or
(2) another EIS investor who thereby loses relief under the disposal of shares rule; or

the total relief withdrawn from EIS investors is the greater of:

(a) the amount receivable by the non-EIS investor; or
(b) the nominal value of the share capital in question.

The relief so lost is apportioned between the EIS investors in proportion to the amounts of the investments that have qualified for relief.

11.6.11 Withdrawal of relief where value is received from the company

Relief is withdrawn to the extent that an investor receives value from the company within three years of making his investment. An investor is regarded as having received value where the company:

(1) repays, redeems or repurchases any part of his holding of its share capital or securities, or makes any payment to him for the cancellation of rights;
(2) repays any debt to him (other than a debt incurred by the company on or after the date on which he subscribed for the shares that are the subject of EIS relief);
(3) pays him for the cancellation of any debt owed to him other than an ordinary trade debt, ie a debt incurred for a supply of goods or services on normal trade credit terms. The legislation specifically provides that normal trade credit does not allow for payment to be left outstanding for a period that exceeds six months; or
(4) releases or waives any liability of his to the company (the liability is deemed to have been waived if the liability is outstanding for more than 12 months) or discharges or undertakes to discharge any liability of his to a third person.

Further, he is regarded as having received value where the company:

(a) makes a loan or advance to him if this includes the situation where the individual becomes indebted to the company other than by an ordinary trade debt;
(b) provides a benefit or facility for him;
(c) transfers an asset to him for no consideration or for consideration less than market value;
(d) acquires an asset from him for consideration exceeding market value; or
(e) makes any other payment to him except:
    (i) one that represents payment or reimbursement of allowable expenditure;
    (ii) interest at a commercial rate on a loan from the individual;
    (iii) dividends representing a normal return on investment;
    (iv) payment for supply of goods by the individual to the company (provided the price does not exceed the goods' market value);
    (v) reasonable and necessary remuneration for services rendered to the company where the individual is chargeable under Schedule D Case I or II (this does not cover remuneration for secretarial or managerial services).

In addition, he may receive value from a company if it is wound up and he receives a payment or asset in the course of the liquidation.

11.6.12 Withdrawal of relief where company ceases to be a qualifying company

EIS relief is withdrawn completely where any of the following events occurs during the three-year relevant period:

(1) the company issues shares that are not fully paid up;

(2) the company ceases to exist wholly for a qualifying trade purpose;
(3) the company comes under the control of another company, or of another company and persons connected with it;
(4) arrangements come into being whereby another company could acquire control.

Prior to 7 March 2001, relief was also clawed back if the company became a quoted company during the three-year relevant period.

11.6.13 Clawback of income tax relief where investor becomes connected with the company

EIS income tax relief (but not CGT deferral relief) is withdrawn completely where an investor becomes connected with the company during his relevant period (three years from the date the shares are issued).

Definition of 'connected'

An individual is regarded as becoming connected with the company if he is:

(1) the owner (directly or indirectly) of more than 30% of the company's voting shares, its issued ordinary share capital, or its loan capital and issued share capital taken together;
(2) the owner of rights entitling him to more than 30% of the company's assets available for distribution to equity holders;
(3) entitled to acquire more than 30% of the company's voting shares, its issued share capital or its share and loan capital taken together;
(4) entitled to acquire rights entitling him to more than 30% of the company's assets available for distribution to the company's equity holders;
(5) the associate of a person who owns or is entitled to acquire more than a 30% interest;
(6) the owner of any loan capital in a subsidiary of the company;
(7) an employee of the company;
(8) a partner of the company;
(9) an associate of an employee or a partner of the company; or
(10) a director of the company – unless he receives only 'normal and necessary' remuneration.

11.6.14 Withdrawal of income tax relief on disposal within three years

If a disposal takes place within three years (five years for shares issued before 6 April 2000), and the disposal is not to the investor's spouse, relief is withdrawn. If the disposal is anything other than a sale to an unconnected party at an arm's length price, EIS income tax relief is withdrawn completely. Where the disposal is on an arm's length basis, relief is withdrawn only on the sale consideration received by the investor.

The grant of an option during the relevant period may be treated as a disposal, ie where the exercise of the option would bind the grantor to purchase any EIS shares.

The receipt of a loan during the relevant period may also be treated as a disposal. This applies where the loan is made to the investor or an associate of his, if 'the loan is one which would not have been made, or would not have been made on the same terms' if the EIS investment had not been made.

11.6.15 Loss relief on arm's length disposal at less than cost

Where a loss arises on disposal or the company goes into liquidation within the three-/five-year period, further income tax/CGT relief may be due to the investor. In a case where the investor receives no payment under the liquidation, the net amount of his investment may qualify as a capital loss.

Example – EIS income tax relief

O invests £80,000 under the EIS. He receives income tax relief at 20% of £80,000, ie £16,000. If the entire investment has to be written off, he will be entitled to a capital loss of £64,000. This loss may be set against *O*'s income or relieved against capital gains.

11.6.16 Clawback of CGT deferral relief

A gain that has been deferred is brought back into charge if any of the following events happens:

(1) the investor disposes of the shares other than to his spouse (unless the conditions for exemption set out in 11.6.18 are satisfied);
(2) the investor (or, where there has been a transfer between spouses, his spouse) ceases to be UK-resident at any time within three years of the issue of the EIS shares (five years for shares issued before 6 April 2000);
(3) the company ceases to be a qualifying company for EIS purposes within three years of the issue of the shares, or within three years of the date that it starts trading if this happens later.

The rule in (2) above does not apply if an individual temporarily becomes non-resident because of his employment, and he returns to the UK within three years still owning the shares.

Example of withdrawal of CGT deferral relief

> During the year 1999-2000, *P* realised a capital gain of £60,000 and made an investment into an EIS company of £55,000 in August 2000. Her other income is sufficient to warrant full EIS relief.
>
> For 2000-01 *P* received EIS relief of £55,000 × 20% = £11,000. She could also elect to defer her 1999-2000 gains of £52,900 (£60,000 less the annual exemption £7,100). This would defer a potential CGT liability of £21,160.
>
> In July 2003 *P* decides to emigrate. This causes the deferred gain of £52,900 to be reinstated as if it were a 2003-04 capital gain.

11.6.17 Taper relief

Where a capital gain arising after 5 April 1998 has been reduced by taper relief (see 14.5) and the gain is deferred by an EIS investment, the gain clawed back on disposal is the original gain (ie there is no further taper relief). Where EIS shares are issued after 5 April 1999 and sold at a gain that is reinvested in new EIS shares, extra taper relief may eventually be due.

11.6.18 Disposal after three years of shares that qualified for EIS income tax relief

Once shares that qualify for the 20% income tax relief have been held for three years (or five years if the shares were issued before 6 April 2000: see 11.6.14), there is no clawback of relief on a disposal of shares. Furthermore, these shares are an exempt asset for CGT purposes so that no CGT will be payable on any gain. However, and in contrast to the rules that applied under the BES, a loss realised on the disposal of the shares after the three-year period may still attract either income tax or CGT relief. Again, the loss is calculated as the difference between the net of tax cost and the disposal proceeds (see 11.6.15).

CGT may still be payable on disposal to the extent that CGT deferral relief has been obtained (see 11.6.16), even though any capital gain may be exempt.

11.7 VENTURE CAPITAL TRUSTS (VCTs)

(TA 1988, s 842 and Sched 28)

11.7.1 Qualifying trusts

VCTs are companies broadly similar to investment trusts. The main conditions for approval are that, in its most recent accounting period, the VCT meets the following requirements:

(1) its ordinary share capital has been quoted on The Stock Exchange;
(2) it has not retained more than 15% of the income that it derived from shares or securities;

(3) its income must have been derived wholly or mainly from shares or securities;
(4) at least 70% by value of its investments comprise of shares or securities in qualifying holdings (see below). Securities can include medium-term loans for a period of at least five years;
(5) at least 30% by value of its qualifying holdings are made up of ordinary shares; and
(6) no holding in any one company represents more than 15% of the VCT's investments.

A VCT may be given provisional approval provided the 70% and 30% requirements are met within three years and the other conditions are met in the current or next accounting period. If the trust fails to meet the conditions within these time periods, provisional approval is withdrawn.

Qualifying holdings

'Qualifying holdings' are holdings in unquoted companies that exist wholly for the purpose of carrying on wholly or mainly in the UK one or more qualifying trades (defined as for the EIS).

VCTs may count annual investments of up to £1m in total in any one qualifying unquoted trading company as a qualifying holding. The unquoted company's gross assets must not exceed £16m immediately after the VCT's investment.

VCTs can treat certain quoted investments as qualifying holdings where the companies were unquoted at the time the VCT made its investment, and no more than five years have elapsed since the company became quoted.

Finance Act 1998 changes

The rules that govern the types of companies in which VCTs may invest were aligned with the EIS rules (see 11.6) with effect from 17 March 1998. In addition:

(1) guaranteed loans and securities cannot qualify as part of the fixed proportion of qualifying investments that a VCT must hold in order to preserve its approved status; and
(2) VCTs must ensure that at least 10% of their total investment in any company is held in ordinary, non-preferential shares.

These latter changes apply to VCTs for accounting periods ending on or after 2 July 1997, but not in respect of funds raised by the issue of shares before that date.

Finance Act 1999 changes

Some of the anti-avoidance rules were relaxed with effect from 16 June 1999.

It is now permissible for a VCT to exchange its shares in an unquoted company for shares in a new holding company where that holding company has a 100% interest in the original company and the share exchange is being carried out in order to facilitate a flotation. In broad terms, the VCT may treat its shares in the new holding company as a qualifying investment provided the VCT has the same interest in the holding company and the VCT's shares in the original company were a qualifying investment.

Similarly, where a VCT holds convertible loan stock or preference shares, and it exercises its conversion rights, the resulting shareholding can be a qualifying investment.

Finance Act 2002 changes

The legislation was amended by FA 2002 to enable VCTs to retain their approved status where they merged with another VCT. The rules were also relaxed to enable VCTs to maintain their approved status during a winding-up. Prior to this, either of these events would have resulted in the investors losing their tax reliefs.

11.7.2 Income tax reliefs

There are two kinds of income tax relief available for investments in VCTs:

(1) Individuals aged 18+ are exempt from income tax on dividends from ordinary shares in VCTs to the extent that the shares acquired each year do not exceed £100,000 in value (relief on distributions). As from 9 March 1999, this relief can be withheld if the Revenue can show that the VCT shares were acquired in order to avoid tax (eg where they were acquired shortly before the VCT paid a dividend and sold shortly afterwards).

(2) Individuals aged 18+ who subscribe for new ordinary shares in VCTs are, in addition, entitled to claim income tax relief at 20%, subject to the amount subscribed in any one year not exceeding £100,000. This relief on investment will be withdrawn unless the shares are held for at least three years (five years for shares issued before 6 April 2000).

11.7.3 CGT reliefs

There are two kinds of CGT relief available for investors as follows:

(1) Individuals aged 18+ are exempt from CGT on disposals of ordinary shares in VCTs in respect of which they qualify for relief on investments (relief on disposals).

(2) Individuals aged 18+ who have subscribed for new ordinary shares in VCTs for which they have been given income tax relief on investment may also be able to defer tax on a chargeable gain arising from the dis-

posal of any asset provided the VCT shares for which the individual subscribes are issued in a period beginning 12 months before and ending 12 months after the disposal (deferred relief on reinvestment). The deferred gain is reinstated if and when any of the following events happens:

(a) the investor disposes of the shares other than to his spouse;
(b) the investor (or where there has been a transfer between spouses, his spouse) ceases to be UK-resident at any period within three/five years of the issue of the VCT shares;
(c) the company ceases to be a qualifying VCT within three years of the issue of the shares, or within three years of the date that it starts trading if this happens later;
(d) the investor ceases to qualify for the 20% income tax relief, or some event occurs as a result of which the income tax relief is withdrawn or reduced.

11.8 ENTERPRISE ZONE TRUSTS

It is possible to invest in properties in enterprise zones through a syndicate or 'enterprise zone property trust'. An individual who invests in the trust is treated as if he had incurred a proportion of the trust's expenditure on enterprise zone properties. Similarly, rents (and sometimes interest) received by the trust are apportioned among the investors, ie the Revenue looks through the trust and treats the individual as if he had acquired an interest in the underlying properties.

Where an individual is treated as having acquired such an interest in an enterprise zone property, the allowances may be set against his other income (see 6.6.6). However, an individual who invests in such a trust is entitled to capital allowances only for the year in which the trust invests in enterprise zone properties. In some cases, there may be a delay in that he invests in a trust at the end of one tax year and becomes entitled to allowances only for the following year (because that is the year in which the trust acquires the relevant properties).

11.9 INVESTMENT IN BRITISH FILMS

A number of schemes have evolved from tax relief introduced in 1997.

The legislation allows for a 100% write-off for tax purposes, on completion, of the production and acquisition costs of 'British qualifying' films the budgets of which do not exceed £15m. Films are certified as British qualifying by the Department for Culture, Media and Sport if they meet certain criteria, such as 70% of the film's cost being spent on film activity in the UK.

The relief was intended originally to run for five years, so that it would apply to expenditure incurred between 2 July 1997 and 1 July 2002 inclusive. FA 2001 extended the end date by a further three years so that it will now apply to expenditure incurred between 2 July 1997 and 1 July 2005 inclusive.

This is a very specialised form of investment and, because of the amount of capital involved in making films, many of the schemes that have evolved are partnerships. Under such schemes an individual can benefit from the opening year rules for new businesses (see 5.3.1) and losses may also be utilised under TA 1988, s 380 (see 5.9.2). Investments and investors are subject to close scrutiny by the Inspector of Taxes. If you are considering this type of investment, you are strongly advised to take professional advice.

For more information visit the Department of Culture's website at www.culture.gov.uk or telephone the DCMS on 020 7211 6200.

The Government recently announced that it would enter a period of consultation with the film industry with a view of refocusing the relief in line with the original intent of the legislation to stimulate the production of British films.

12

LIFE ASSURANCE AND PENSIONS

VINCE JERRARD, KEITH WILLIAMS AND STUART REYNOLDS

This chapter covers the tax treatment of life assurance and pensions plans and looks at the treatment of the contributions paid in the funds while they are invested, and the benefits paid out. It covers the following topics:

Life assurance

(1) Introduction.
(2) Qualifying and non-qualifying policies.
(3) Taxation of life policy proceeds.
(4) Offshore life policies.
(5) Annuities.
(6) Permanent health insurance.
(7) Life policies effected by companies.

Pensions

(8) Personal pensions (including stakeholder plans).
(9) Occupational schemes.
(10) Free-standing AVC (FSAVC) schemes.
(11) Unapproved schemes.
(12) State pension benefits.
(13) Contracting out.

Miscellaneous

(14) Taxation of commission, cashbacks and discount.

LIFE ASSURANCE

12.1 INTRODUCTION

A life assurance policy is simply the evidence of a contract between the individual policyholder and the life assurance company. The general principle is that the company is the collecting house for pooled investments and mortality risks, offering benefits directly to policyholders based on personal contracts.

Life assurance policies can be classified in a number of different ways, but the most common practical classification reflects the nature of the benefits provided under the policy and the periods for which they are provided. Types of policy are:

(1) whole of life policies, where the sum assured is payable on the death of the life assured, whenever that occurs;
(2) term policies, where the sum assured is payable on death during the policy term only; and
(3) endowment policies, where the sum assured is payable on death during the policy term, or on survival to the end of the term.

Each type of policy has its own characteristics in terms of the blend of life assurance protection and potential investment return. Term policies for a relatively short period are most likely to offer the highest sum assured for each pound of premium while, towards the other end of the spectrum, an endowment policy will have a greater investment element.

An important characteristic of life assurance policies is that they do not produce income as such, but are essentially medium- or long-term accumulators. While a policy is held intact, the income and gains arising from the underlying investments held by the life company are taxed in the hands of the life company itself. In general, the policyholder's prospective tax liability arises only when he receives payment under the policy.

This chapter deals with the tax consequences on the policyholder paying premiums or receiving benefits under a life assurance policy issued by a UK company or a foreign insurer operating through a branch in the UK (for 'foreign' life policies see 12.4).

Over the years many changes have been made to this complex and technical area. Unless the contrary is clearly the case, this chapter deals with the current life policy tax regime, which took effect from its 'appointed day' of 1 April 1976, and assumes enactment of FA 2003.

12.1.1 The company's tax position

Taxation of life companies is extremely (and increasingly) complex. Broadly speaking, in respect of their life assurance business, companies are generally taxed on the excess of their investment income and realised capital gains over management expenses (the 'I-E' basis). For proprietary companies there is a formula to determine the proportions of the company's income and gains that should be allocated to policyholders and shareholders, respectively. With effect from 2000-01, tax was charged on the policyholder's share of income and gains at the rate of 22% (20% on some items, eg the income from directly held equities and, since 1996-97, for the policyholders' shares of the investment returns corresponding to savings income). However, with effect from 1 April 2003 the rate charged on the policyholder share of all life fund income drops to 20%. The company's profits attributable to shareholders are, on the other hand, chargeable to corporation tax at the usual rates.

To enable UK life companies to compete more equally for the business of residents of other EU states, companies are able to write such business in an 'overseas' life fund, broadly on a gross roll-up basis with no UK tax on the income and gains, but with no relief for expenses.

Registered friendly societies are in a somewhat different position, being exempt from corporation tax in respect of tax-exempt life or endowment business. This is life and endowment business where total premiums under contracts do not exceed £270 pa with effect from 6 April 1995. Policies that can be written on the tax-exempt basis are generally qualifying policies provided they satisfy a minimum sum assured test. Such policies can give tax-free proceeds even to higher rate taxpayers, but non-qualifying friendly society policies are taxable at basic and higher rates. The remainder of this chapter does not deal specifically with friendly society business.

12.1.2 Review of life assurance taxation

In recent years the Revenue has conducted a number of reviews of life assurance taxation covering both taxation of life companies and of life policy proceeds. The current I-E regime collects an aggregated tax in respect of both the company's trading profit and the bulk of the income and gains accruing to the individual's policy, but an alternative would be a gross roll-up regime (similar to those found in most EU countries). Under such a regime, life companies would be taxed on their profits with the remaining tax charge being levied directly on the individual policyholder when his policy comes to an end.

It was intended that decisions should be reached during 1995, but the timescales slipped drastically, although the first results of the review (correction of some technical anomalies and the removal of what the Revenue saw as avoidance through the use of some reassurance arrangements) appeared in FA 1995. Implementation of any far-reaching changes still appears to be some years away.

Whatever the outcome of the life company tax review, it did seem likely that there would be changes to the life assurance qualifying rules. The Revenue interpreted the EC 3rd Life Directive as requiring the removal of pre-certification of life policies (see 12.2.1), and the 1994 Budget announced consultations with a view to removing pre-certification and amending the policy tax regime for 6 May 1996. In fact, the Revenue's proposals were not published until after the 1996 Budget and consultation continued until the end of April 1997.

The proposals would have introduced an 'exit testing' regime under which the tax consequences of a policy coming to an end, or paying out benefits, would have been determined by looking at how the policy had been maintained previously. This contrasts with the current 'qualifying rules' approach under which the tax treatment of the policy proceeds is determined, to a significant extent, by reference to the policy design at outset.

The tests to be applied on 'exit' would have been similar to those used in the qualifying rules, and under the new regime favoured policies would still have been able to pay tax-free proceeds, even to higher rate taxpayers.

However, the proposals had a number of significant drawbacks that the industry and other interested parties drew to the Revenue's attention. Among these were the following:

(1) *Complexity* The aim was to produce a simpler regime, but the 93 draft clauses published were far from simple.
(2) *Cost* It was not the Revenue's aim to increase the tax-take from life policies. Against this background it was difficult to see the cost/benefit justification for the change, given that early industry estimates put the cost of implementing the new regime in the order of £1bn.
(3) *Legitimate expectations of existing policyholders* As life policies are medium- to long-term contracts, policyholders must be able to have confidence that subsequent tax changes, even if not actually retrospective, recognise and safeguard their reasonable expectations regarding the benefits their policies will produce. The proposals provided for all policies to move on to the new regime, with little in the way of protection for existing policyholders – something the industry would have found difficult to accept.
(4) *Specific proposals* As proposed, the new regime would have been disadvantageous to policies held in trust (both new and existing policies in existing trusts).

Later in 1997 it was announced that the wide-ranging reforms canvassed would not be introduced. FA 1998 contained clauses dealing with certain specific matters, namely 'dead settlor' trusts, the appointment of fiscal representatives by offshore life companies selling to UK residents, and changing the taxation of 'personal portfolio bonds' (see 12.3.12). Pre-certification has been retained.

The 2002 Budget Day Press Releases promised further consultation on the modernisation of corporation tax. The Sandler Report, also in 2002, proposed changes to life assurance taxation (specifically the removal of qualifying policy status and of the '5% withdrawals' – see 12.2.1 and 12.3.3 respectively) and the introduction of new simpler and cheaper products.

Although implementation of the Sandler proposals on life policy taxation was a distinct possibility for the 2003 Budget it did not happen. Instead, the Chancellor appears to have listened to the industry's lobbying and an amendment was made to the effect that the recommendations would be considered within a wider framework taking account of regulatory change and corporation tax reform. It is clear that yet further change is likely in the near future.

FA 2003 does contain a number of measures relating to life company and policy taxation. For life policies, the majority of these are in the nature of clarification or (as with group life policies and premiums charged for exceptional risk of a critical illness) restoration of the positions always intended, if not properly reflected, in existing legislation.

12.1.3 Individual savings accounts (ISAs)

This new form of tax-favoured savings was introduced in April 1999. In outline, the scheme as it affects life insurance is as follows.

Life assurance policies are permitted ISA investments, but only to the extent of £1,000 of premium in any year, out of a personal subscription limit of £5,000 pa (originally to be £7,000 in the first two years of the scheme, but now continuing at this higher level until April 2006). ISA policies may not require payment of regular premiums, but it is anticipated that 'regular single premium' policies will be allowed to offer greater investment benefits, reflecting the duration of the policy and repeated investment in them. The proceeds of such policies will be free of tax and the funds to which the policies are linked will grow tax free, with the benefit of a 10% credit in respect of UK dividend income for the first five years of the scheme.

12.2 QUALIFYING AND NON-QUALIFYING POLICIES

For tax purposes, the key classification of policies is between qualifying and non-qualifying policies.

The distinction is only relevant to the *individual*. There is no differentiation between qualifying and non-qualifying policies in respect of taxation of the income and gains from the underlying assets in the life company's hands.

Each of the three types of policy already identified (whole life, endowment and term assurances) is capable of being a qualifying or non-qualifying policy depending on its initial design and the way in which it is dealt with once in force.

12.2.1 Qualifying policies
(TA 1988, s 267 and Sched 15)

These are policies that satisfy the conditions set out in TA 1988, Sched 15, and do not fall foul of the various anti-avoidance provisions. The main features of the qualifying rules are as follows.

Premiums

(1) must be payable for a period of ten years or more (though term assurances may be written for shorter periods) and must be payable annually or more frequently; and

(2) must be fairly evenly spread so that premiums payable in any one period of 12 months are neither more than twice the amount of premiums paid in any other 12-month period, nor more than ⅛ of the total amount of premiums payable over the first ten years (in the case of whole life policies) or over the term of the policy (in the case of an endowment).

Premiums payable for an exceptional risk of death have always been left out of account for these purposes. FA 2003 also provides that this is the case for premiums payable for exceptional risk of a critical illness (see 12.3.8).

The sum assured

(1) for an endowment policy must not be less than 75% of the total premiums payable during the term of the policy. This percentage is reduced by 2% for each year by which the life assured's age exceeds 55 years at the issue of the policy;

(2) for a whole of life policy must not be less than 75% of the total premiums payable if death were to occur at age 75;

(3) for a term policy that has no surrender value and ends before the life assured's 75th birthday need not satisfy any minimum requirement.

Benefits

(1) may include the right to participate in profits, the right to benefits arising because of disability or the right to a return of premiums on death under a certain specified age (not exceeding 16 years); but

(2) may not include any other benefits of a capital nature.

The rules for certain special types of policy may vary from those referred to above, for example, mortgage protection policies, family income policies and industrial assurances.

Life assurers usually submit standard policy wordings to the Revenue so that they can be certified as satisfying the qualifying rules (pre-certification). Policies in those standard forms can then be marketed as qualifying.

Where a policy contains options by which the policyholder may, for example, increase the sum assured or the premium, or extend the policy term, these options are tested at the outset to ensure that, however any options are exercised, the policy will still satisfy the qualifying rules.

12.2.2 Non-qualifying policies

Non-qualifying policies are all other life policies not satisfying the qualifying rules, and those that, although they may have satisfied the qualifying rules at the outset, have subsequently been changed in some way such that they no longer satisfy those rules.

The most significant category of policies that are non-qualifying is single premium investment contracts (usually referred to as 'bonds'). These are written as whole of life contracts and provide for only a small amount of life cover, being primarily investment vehicles.

A High Court decision in 1994 cast doubt on the status of some policies such as life assurance contracts where no (or possibly insubstantial) life cover is provided. In 1996, the Court of Appeal restored the previous industry understanding.

12.2.3 Taxation of premiums

(TA 1988, ss 266 *et seq* and Sched 14)

No specific tax relief is available to an individual in respect of premiums paid under a non-qualifying life assurance policy. Similarly, there is no specific relief for premiums paid under qualifying policies issued in respect of contracts made after 13 March 1984.

However, for qualifying policies issued before that date, Life Assurance Premium Relief (LAPR) is still available where the policy was issued on the life of the payer of the premium (or the payer's spouse) and where the payer is UK-resident at the time premiums are paid.

Relief is given currently at the rate of 12.5% on premiums up to the greater of £1,500 or one-sixth of total income, and is usually obtained by deducting the tax relief from the premiums payable to the life company. Relief is lost if the policy becomes non-qualifying or if the benefits secured by the policy are increased, or its term extended, after 13 March 1984.

Where an individual receives the benefit of LAPR but, in effect, recoups himself for his outlay in premiums by withdrawing money from the policy, there is a process by which some or all of the LAPR is 'clawed back' by deduction from the amount withdrawn by him.

12.3 TAXATION OF LIFE POLICY PROCEEDS

(TA 1988, ss 539-554)

In view of life policies' position as income accumulators, where liability for gains and income in respect of the underlying assets is dealt with by taxing the life company, the usual income tax principles are inappropriate to life policy taxation. Accordingly, the tax regime that applies to the individual policyholder has been specifically constructed for the purpose. It caters separately for qualifying and non-qualifying policies and for mortality and investment profits realised from policies.

It is first necessary to determine whether any particular action constitutes a chargeable event in respect of the policy. If it does not, no income tax consequence arises under the life policy regime from that action. If it does, it is then necessary to calculate the 'gain', to determine the rate of tax applicable to the gain, and to determine who is liable to pay the resulting tax.

Despite references to 'chargeable events' and 'gains', it is the income tax regime that applies to life policies (for the CGT position, see 12.3.10).

For the tax treatment of life policies that qualify as an ISA investment, see 12.1.3. For the taxation of personal portfolio bonds, see 12.3.12.

12.3.1 Chargeable events

Non-qualifying policy

(TA 1988, s 540)

For a non-qualifying policy, the five chargeable events are:

(1) the death of the life assured;
(2) the maturity of the policy;
(3) the total surrender of the policy;
(4) the assignment of the policy for money or money's worth; and
(5) excesses arising on partial surrenders or partial assignments in any policy year commencing after 13 March 1975 (see 12.3.3).

No chargeable event occurs where an assignment takes place by way of security for a debt (or on the discharge of the security). Similarly, an assignment between spouses living together is not a chargeable event.

Qualifying policy

For a qualifying policy, the chargeable events are the same but subject to the following amendments:

(a) death or maturity are only chargeable events if the policy has previously been made paid-up (ie premiums have ceased but the policy has remained in force) within the first ten years (or three-quarters of the term of an endowment policy, if shorter);
(b) surrender, assignment for money or money's worth or an excess will only be a chargeable event if it occurs before the expiry of ten years (or three-quarters of the term of an endowment policy, if shorter) or if the policy was made paid-up within that period.

Three key consequences of the chargeable event rules are that:

(i) the gift (ie assignment of the whole policy with no consideration) of qualifying or non-qualifying policies is not a chargeable event and so triggers no income tax consequence;
(ii) there is no chargeable event on death of the life assured under, or on the maturity of, a qualifying policy where all due premiums were paid prior to the event in question;
(iii) there is no chargeable event on the assignment for value or surrender (in whole or part) of a qualifying policy where premiums have been paid for the first ten years (or three-quarters of the term for an endowment policy).

Where there is no chargeable event in respect of a life policy, there is no income tax charge under the specific life policy tax regime, irrespective of the tax position of the individual policyholder. In particular, points (ii) and (iii) above illustrate the key current advantage of qualifying policies – ie their ability to provide tax-free proceeds, even for higher rate taxpayers.

12.3.2 Calculating life policy gains

(TA 1988, s 541)

Broadly speaking, where the chargeable event is either a maturity, total surrender or an assignment for consideration, the chargeable gain is the investment profit made under the policy. This is calculated by reference to the value of the benefits being received as a result of the chargeable event, plus the amount of any 'relevant capital payments' previously received under the policy (ie any sum or other benefit of a capital nature, other than one paid as a result of an individual's disability), less the amount paid by way of premiums and any taxable gains as a result of previous partial surrenders.

This principle of charging tax only on investment gains also applies where the chargeable event is the death of the life assured. The exclusion of mortality profit from the taxable gain is achieved by using the policy's surrender value immediately before death instead of the value of the benefits being received under the policy.

A policy capable of paying benefits on more than one death could have the considerable disadvantage that, on a death, lump sums paid on previous deaths were taken into account when calculating the 'investment gain' under the policy. This result was not intended and FA 2003 confirms this to be the case (both for the future and the past), subject to certain conditions.

12.3.3 Partial surrenders

(TA 1988, s 546)

The chargeable event listed in 12.3.1(5) creates a potential income tax liability on the policyholder surrendering part of his policy (often referred to as making 'withdrawals' from the policy). Partial surrenders include the surrender of a right to a bonus and loans to the policyholder made by (or by arrangement with) the insurance company (unless the policyholder's policy is qualifying and the loan bears a commercial rate of interest or is lent to a full-time employee of the insurer for the purposes of house purchase or improvement).

At the end of each policy year, the policy attracts a 'notional allowance' of 5% of the total premium then paid under the policy. This allowance is then set against the value of any partial surrenders made up to that date. If the value of those partial surrenders exceeds the current cumulative allowance, a chargeable event occurs; if the cumulative allowance is equal to or exceeds cumulative withdrawals, no chargeable event occurs. Allowances are given up to 100% of the total premiums paid so that, for a single premium investment bond, the allowances are given at the rate of 5% for 20 years.

Once an 'excess' (ie an occasion on which the cumulative partial surrenders exceed the cumulative allowances) has occurred, the cumulative withdrawals and allowances up to that date are considered to have been used and the process of accumulating allowances and withdrawals starts afresh (subject to the '100% of premiums' limit that applies to the allowances).

Example – Cumulation of allowances and withdrawals

X invests £10,000 in a single premium investment bond; £1,200 is withdrawn after four policy years, a further £4,500 after six policy years and £1,000 after eight policy years.

Policy Years	*A* *Cumulative allowances chargeable events* £	*B* *Partial surrender (C – A)* £	*C* *Cumulative surrender between* £	*D* *Taxable gain* £
1	500 (1 × 500)	0	0	0
2	1,000 (2 × 500)	0	0	0
3	1,500 (3 × 500)	0	0	0
4	2,000 (4 × 500)	1,200	1,200	0
5	2,500 (5 × 500)	0	1,200	0
6	3,000 (6 × 500)	4,500	5,700	2,700
7	500 (1 × 500)	0	0	0
8	1,000 (2 × 500)	1,000	1,000	0
9	1,500 (3 × 500)	0	1,000	0
10	2,000 (4 × 500)	0	1,000	0

Note: (1) A chargeable event occurs only when C exceeds A.
(2) The value of the policy is irrelevant to these calculations so that it is possible to have a taxable gain under a policy at a time when the policy itself is worth less than the premiums paid.

When the final chargeable event occurs under the policy (ie death, maturity, final surrender or assignment for value), the total profit on the policy is brought into account. The profit is the final proceeds (excluding any mortality profit where the event is death), plus previous partial surrenders, less premiums paid and any taxable gains from previous partial withdrawals.

Example – Total surrender after partial surrenders

> Using the example immediately above, if the policy were totally surrendered at the end of the tenth policy year for £10,400, the taxable gain on that final encashment would be as follows:
>
> £10,400 + £1,200 + £4,500 + £1,000 – (£10,000 + £2,700) = £4,400
>
> *Note:* If, on final termination, the 'gain' calculated in this way is a negative figure, it may be deducted from taxable income for the purposes of higher rate tax only (see 12.3.4).

Partial assignments of policies

FA 2001 clarified the position on partial assignments of policies (eg where a husband and wife jointly own a policy and want to transfer it to one of them only, such as on divorce). will clarify the position so that:

(1) partial assignments for no consideration will not be chargeable events (but note that the Revenue believes that assignment on divorce will almost invariably be for consideration); and
(2) any tax liability will fall on the person whose interest in the policy is reducing.

12.3.4 Taxing gains on chargeable events
(TA 1988, ss 547 and 550)

In the majority of cases where the policyholder owns the policy for his own absolute benefit, the gain is treated as the top slice of his income and is taxed appropriately.

However, because the income and gains attributable to the policy's underlying assets have already been taxed in the hands of the life company, life policy gains are not chargeable to income tax at the basic rate. This applies to both qualifying and non-qualifying policies. Despite the fact that, in effect, the gain is treated as having already suffered basic rate tax, there is no grossing up of the gain for higher rate tax purposes.

Accordingly, for an individual paying tax at the higher rate, the maximum rate of tax payable on life policy gains at present (tax year 2002-03) will be 18% (40% less 22%). An individual whose income (including the gain) is taxable at the basic rate only will have no further income tax liability on the policy gain. Non-taxpayers or those paying tax at the lower rate of 20% will not be able to make any reclaim in respect of tax notionally paid by the life company.

If the individual realises a loss under the policy, that loss is only available as a deduction from taxable income for the purposes of higher rate tax.

To reflect the reduction, with effect from 1 April 2003, of the tax rate on the policyholder share of life fund income and gains from 22% to 20%, the 'credit' given on chargeable event gains will fall from 22% to 20% with effect from 6 April 2004.

Top-slicing

In view of the fact that the gain will have arisen over a period of years, the legislation recognises that it would be harsh to treat the total gain as part of the taxpayer's income in the year of receipt. A measure of relief is afforded by a process known as 'top-slicing'.

Top-slicing first requires calculation of the 'appropriate fraction' of the gain, more usually referred to as the 'slice'. Where the chargeable event in question is death, maturity, total encashment or assignment for value, the slice is calculated by dividing the gain by the number of complete policy years for which the policy has been in force. Where the chargeable event is caused by a partial surrender, the gain is divided by the number of complete policy years since the last excess caused by a partial surrender (or by the number of years for which the policy has been in force where the chargeable event is the first excess).

The slice (and not the whole of the gain) is treated as the top part of the policyholder's income, and the average rate of tax applicable to the slice (less the basic rate) is calculated. That tax rate will then apply to the whole of the gain to determine the total income tax liability on the gain. The result is that relief is given to individuals whose other income would mean that they pay the tax at no more than the basic rate, but who would be taken into the higher rates of tax if the whole of the gain were added to their income.

Example – No tax on the gain

A invests £20,000 in a single premium investment bond in May 1998 and cashes it in after five years for £27,500. The gain is therefore £1,500 and the 'slice' is £1,500 (£7,500 divided by five).

	£
Taxable income (excluding policy gain)	15,000
'Slice'	1,500
Taxable income	16,500

The tax rate applicable to the 'slice' is therefore 22% less 22% = 0%.

Example – Slice falling into basic and higher rate bands

B invests £12,000 in a single premium investment bond in May 1998. After five years he cashes it in for £17,000. The gain is £5,000 and the slice is £1,000 (£5,000 divided by five). In that year his other taxable income after reliefs is £30,000.

	£
Tax calculation on gain:	
Taxable income + 'slice'	31,000
Tax applicable to slice	
On £500 (ie £30,000 to £30,500) at 0% (22% – 22%)	Nil
On £500 (ie £30,500 to £31,000) at 18% (40% – 22%)	90
Total tax on slice	90

Average rate on slice

$$\frac{90}{1{,}000} \times 100 \qquad 9\%$$

The tax payable is £5,000 × 9% = £450.

To illustrate the effect of top-slicing, if it had not been available the calculations would have been:

	£
Tax applicable to the gain	
On £500 at 0% (22%)	Nil
On £4,500 at 18% (40% – 22%)	810
Tax payable	810

Notes:

(1) The whole gain (without top-slicing) is counted as income in determining whether any age allowance or entitlement to children's tax credit should be reduced.

(2) There is no top-slicing where the taxpayer is a company.

(3) Any business expansion scheme relief is left out of account when calculating top-slicing relief.

(4) For top-slicing purposes, total income is computed without reference to amounts chargeable in respect of loss of office or lease premiums chargeable as rent.

(5) The examples given in this chapter assume no reliefs or amounts as mentioned in (3) and (4).

Age allowance for over 65s

If an individual is entitled to the higher personal allowance, the gain on a life policy can reduce (or eliminate) that additional allowance. Top-slicing relief does not apply in respect of this reduction of the additional allowance. See 10.2.1 for an example of how higher allowances can be reduced.

Children's tax credit

The gain on a life policy can affect entitlement to children's tax credit. As for age allowance, top-slicing relief does not apply.

12.3.5 Two policy gains in one tax year

(TA 1988, s 550)

Where an individual has two policies with chargeable gains in a tax year, tax is calculated as if the gains arose under only one policy, with a slice equal to the sum of the individual slices. Thus, if two policies are surrendered in the same tax year, one with a gain of £10,000 (having been in force for five years) and one with a gain of £24,000 (having been in force for eight years), tax on the gains is calculated as if one policy had been surrendered, yielding a gain of £34,000 and with a slice of £5,000.

This approach can have the effect of increasing or decreasing the total tax payable (compared to disposing of the policies in separate tax years) depending on the individual's tax position and the performance of the relevant policies.

12.3.6 Persons liable for the charge

(TA 1988, ss 547 and 551)

Where a policy is held by an individual for his own benefit, the tax charge falls on him. The same applies to an individual where the policy is held as security for a debt owed by him.

If the policy is held in trust, the charge falls on the settlor, who can recover the tax paid from the trustees. If a policy is held by a trust created by a settlor who has since died, it is possible that gains realised by trustees in these circumstances may escape tax altogether in view of the impossibility of taxing somebody who has not been alive in the appropriate year of assessment. Although somewhat anomalous, this has been very useful if an individual owned a policy that would not come to an end on his death (eg a joint life policy paying out on the second death). By declaring a suitable trust of the policy in his Will, he may have been able to put future gains realised under the policy outside the income tax net.

FA 1998 included provisions to counter this by enabling the trustees, or perhaps even the trust's beneficiaries, to be taxed where the settlor is dead (or not UK-resident at the time of the chargeable event). The rules do not apply where the settlor had died before 17 March 1998 and the policy is not 'enhanced' after that date.

Where the policy is held by a company, or on a trust created by or as security for a debt owed by a company, the charge falls on the company (with the right for the company to recover the tax paid from the trustees where the policy is held on trust).

If a policy is assigned by way of gift, chargeable excesses arising during that policy year, but prior to the assignment, are taxed on the assignor. Future gains are taxed on the new beneficial owner.

12.3.7 Timing of the taxation of gains

Where the chargeable event is death, maturity, total surrender or assignment for value, the gain is treated as arising at the time of the appropriate event.

Excesses arising from partial surrenders, on the other hand, are generally only regarded as arising at the end of the policy year in which the excess occurs. Accordingly, if the policy was taken out in June 1993 and an excess occurs as a result of a partial surrender in February 2002, the gain resulting from that partial surrender is treated as arising in June 2002 and so is taxable in 2002-03.

12.3.8 Critical illness policies

A development in the UK life assurance market in recent years has been the ability to include critical illness or 'dread disease' benefits in a variety of policies. In general, this benefit pays a capital sum if the life assured is diagnosed as suffering from any of the specified 'dread diseases or events'. The diseases or events specified vary from company to company, but usually include heart attack, stroke, cancer and heart by-pass surgery.

It is understood that the Revenue accepts that the payment of a benefit on the happening of a dread disease is not a chargeable event, so that this benefit is paid free of tax under the life policy tax regime.

12.3.9 Chargeable event certificates
(TA 1988, s 552)

When a chargeable event occurs, the life assurance company is required to provide the Revenue with a chargeable event certificate that gives the policyholder's name and address, the nature and date of the chargeable event and information required for computing the gain.

FA 2001 introduced some changes to these rules. Life companies now have to supply policyholders with chargeable event certificates to help them include the gains in their SA returns. The certificates also have to include more information about the chargeable event and the gain produced.

Chargeable event certificates only have to be sent to the Revenue where the gain exceeds a threshold (set at half the basic rate tax band).

12.3.10 Capital gains tax and life policies
(TCGA 1992, s 210)

Until FA 2003 a policyholder had no personal liability to CGT on a disposal of the policy if he was its original beneficial owner, or if he was an assignee and acquired the policy other than for money or money's worth.

If a policy is in the hands of an individual who is not the original beneficial owner and who did acquire it for money or money's worth, the policy is an asset potentially liable to CGT. However, where the policy is issued in respect of an insurance made after 25 June 1982, the policy also remains subject to the income tax regime that applies to life assurance policies. This may also affect some policies issued before that date. The potential for double taxation (income tax and CGT) is resolved by TCGA 1992, s 37, which provides, broadly, that money or money's worth charged to income tax will be taken into account and excluded from the CGT calculations. FA 2003 has widened this so that now, if the policy is disposed of by a person who is not the original beneficial owner, and the policy *at any time* prior to that disposal changed hands for money or money's worth, the policy will be an asset potentially liable to CGT.

Where a life policy is subject to the CGT regime, the occasion of the payment of the sum(s) assured and the surrender of the policy are treated as disposals.

12.3.11 Guaranteed income bonds

In 1996, the Revenue raised questions concerning the taxation of some policies that could provide regular payments to the policyholder. Most common among these policies were guaranteed income bonds. The Revenue view was that such payments were interest or annual payments, rather than policy part surrenders. FA 1997 reinstated, with retrospective effect, the industry's understanding of the position, confirming such payments as part surrenders to be dealt with under the life policy tax rules.

12.3.12 Personal portfolio bonds

These are policies usually, but not exclusively, written offshore where the benefits due under the policy are – or may be – closely linked with the value of a portfolio of assets personal to the policyholder.

FA 1998 included the introduction of a new charge on such policies, which deems a gain of 15% of the total premiums paid to the end of each policy year and deemed gains from previous policy years chargeable under the new legislation. This is an additional charge but is not imposed in respect of any policy year ending before 6 April 1999. This charge does not apply to 'managed portfolio bonds', ie those that do not allow 'personalisation' by restricting the policy investment to pooled assets generally available to investors.

12.4 OFFSHORE LIFE POLICIES

(TA 1988, s 553 and Sched 15, paras 23-27; FA 1995, s 56)

In general, policies issued in respect of contracts made after 17 November 1983 cannot be qualifying unless they are issued by a UK insurance company or the UK branch of a foreign insurer. Before that date, foreign policies could be qualifying if they satisfied the normal qualifying rules.

Other amendments to the life policy tax regime, as it applies to such foreign policies, are as follows:

(1) The gain calculated on a chargeable event is reduced by reference to the amount of time, during the life of the policy, the policyholder was not UK-resident.
(2) In calculating the 'appropriate fraction' for top-slicing purposes, any complete years during which the policyholder was not UK-resident are excluded.
(3) Taxable gains arising under such policies are charged to basic rate as well as higher rate tax, as appropriate. An exception to this applies where the insurer is taxed on the investment income and gains accruing for the policyholder's benefit at a rate of not less than 20%. In such cases, the policy gains will not be liable to basic rate UK income tax. This exception will apply only to policies issued by EU or EEA insurers.

FA 1998 included a framework requiring certain categories of offshore life companies to appoint a fiscal representative in the UK to be responsible for reporting, to the Revenue, gains on life policies in accordance with TA 1988, s 552 (see 12.3.9). Discussions between the Revenue and the offshore insurers have resulted in regulations that enable insurers to comply with local secrecy laws while giving the insurers time to develop systems to comply with the reporting requirements.

12.5 ANNUITIES

(TA 1988, ss 656 and 685)

An annuity is an arrangement under which one person agrees to pay another a sum of money for a known period, or a period to be determined by some specified contingency.

Annuities may be immediate (ie the payment will start straightaway) or deferred (where payments will start at some predetermined point in the future). Many annuities are established to continue for the lifetime of the annuitant, but temporary annuities cease at the end of a fixed period or on the annuitant's death, whichever comes earlier. Annuities may be effected on the lives of two or more individuals and, for example, continue until the death of the last survivor. Annuities may be paid monthly, quarterly or annually, and may be of a fixed amount or subject to some sort of index-linking. Annuities may also be written with a guaranteed minimum period so as to reduce the loss that might otherwise be suffered by an individual who dies shortly after purchasing an annuity.

There are four main types of annuity:

(1) Purchased life annuities, where an individual pays a lump sum to an insurance company in return for the annuity.

(2) Annuities received as a gift (eg at one time it was common for testators to direct that annuities be paid out of their estates).
(3) Annuities paid as part of the purchase price of a business or by continuing members of a partnership to a former partner who has retired.
(4) Compulsory purchase annuities, for example, those purchased out of pension funds.

Significant changes were made in FA 1991 to the taxation of life companies in respect of general annuity business, with effect for accounting periods commencing after 31 December 1991. The changes apply to existing business, subject to transitional relief.

These changes brought the taxation of life company general annuity funds broadly into line with the regime that applies to ordinary life business. Previously, a general annuity fund was not taxed on its income and gains if annuities paid by the company during the tax year equalled or exceeded the fund's investment income and realised gains.

For the annuitant, a purchased life annuity attracts a special relief in that amounts received by him are treated in part as a return of the money paid for by the annuity (the capital element) and in part as interest on that purchase price. The capital element of each payment is calculated by reference to actuarial tables and is not taxable. This tax exemption applies even where the annuitant lives long enough for the capital element of annuity payments he receives to exceed the original purchase price of the annuity.

Other types of annuity do not receive this favourable treatment in respect of the capital element of annuity payments.

Purchased life annuities are also subject to an income tax regime similar to that previously described as applying to life policies (see 12.3.4).

Chargeable events for life annuities are total surrender, assignment for money or money's worth and 'excesses' (calculated in much the same way as in respect of life policy partial surrenders).

Where a gain arises on a chargeable event, the gain is not charged to basic rate tax where the company offering the annuity has been taxed under the new life company tax regime described above because of the 'credit' that is, in effect, given in respect of tax paid by the life company on the income and gains of its general annuity fund.

For CGT purposes, deferred annuities are also treated in a similar way to life policies, with the effect that no chargeable gain accrues on the disposal of such a contract except where the person making the disposal is not the original beneficial owner and acquired the rights for consideration in money or money's worth or, following FA 2003, the person making the disposal is not the original beneficial owner and the annuity at any time changed hands for money or money's worth.

12.6 PERMANENT HEALTH INSURANCE

12.6.1 Introduction

Permanent health insurance (PHI) policies provide a replacement income for an individual who is unable to work through illness or disability. Contracts are usually available to those aged between 16 and 60 but terminate on the insured reaching his normal retirement date.

Once the disability or illness arises, benefits commence on expiry of a deferred period, typically between one and twelve months, selected by the policyholder. The longer the deferred period, the fewer claims the insurer will expect to pay and so the lower the premium will be per £ of benefit.

PHI contracts can be written as life assurance policies – typically as non-qualifying policies to avoid provision of substantial sums assured payable on death. If structured as a life policy, payment of disability benefits is not treated as a surrender of rights for the purposes of life policy taxation.

12.6.2 Tax consequences

If an individual effects a PHI contract for himself, premiums are not deductible for tax purposes. If an employer effects a policy on an employee to enable him to continue to pay the employee's salary during a period of disability or illness, or if the policy covers a revenue loss during such a period, the employer might be able to claim the premiums as a business expense.

For 1995-96, benefits received from an individual's own PHI policy were taxable under Schedule D Case III but received the benefit of ESC A26, which gave him a 'tax holiday'.

The tax holiday was a period of 12 months (before April 1996 the holiday ran for a complete tax year and so could have been up to 23 months). An individual's tax holiday commenced when he became entitled to claim appropriate benefits, so that if he had two PHI policies with different deferred periods, the tax holiday on the one with the longer deferral would be less than 12 months.

No tax holiday was available if the benefit did not compensate for loss of income from employment or self-employment.

Insurers had to deduct basic rate tax from payments to individuals where entitlement to those benefits arose on or after 6 April 1994 (even if the policy was effected before that date). Before April 1994, the industry practice was to pay benefits gross, even after the end of the tax holiday.

With effect from 1996-97, benefits from most individually owned PHI policies are tax free.

If the contract is effected by an employer to maintain the employee's salary during the period of illness or disability, the income is taxable in the individual's hands, in the same way as salary would have been.

12.7 LIFE POLICIES EFFECTED BY COMPANIES
(TA 1988, s 540)

There are a number of circumstances in which a company can effect a life policy. For example, it may do so on the life of a director or other key executive to provide the company with compensation for the death of that individual. Similarly, policies may be effected to provide funds to repay loans.

In general, if a company effects a term assurance for a short period (usually not more than five years), which does not acquire a surrender value and is effected solely to provide protection against the loss of profits resulting from the death of a key person, the premiums are tax deductible and the proceeds taxable in the hands of the company.

If, on the other hand, the policy is for a longer term, may acquire a surrender value, is effected for a capital purpose, or where the life assured has a material shareholding in the company, the premiums are not tax-deductible but the proceeds are unlikely to be charged to corporation tax in the company's hands, other than by virtue of the life assurance chargeable event rules.

Prior to FA 1989, policies owned by companies could be qualifying policies (provided they satisfied the qualifying rules) and so could provide tax-free proceeds to the company in the same way as for individuals. Gains from non-qualifying policies were also tax-free in the hands of the company, except where the company was a close company.

The rules changed for policies effected after 13 March 1989 (or those effected before that date but subsequently varied to increase the benefits or the policy term). Such policies cannot be qualifying policies (irrespective of their compliance with the qualifying rules) if, immediately prior to the chargeable event, the policy was owned by a company or was held on trusts created, or as security for a debt owed, by the company. Gains from such policies are treated as the company's income and are chargeable under Schedule D Case VI.

There is an exception to this denial of qualifying status where policies are used to secure company debts incurred in purchasing land to be occupied by the company for the purposes of its trade (or in constructing, extending or improving buildings occupied in that way). Broadly speaking, provided the policy has been used for this purpose since its inception, the chargeable gain will only be the amount by which the policy proceeds exceed the lowest amount of the loan that has been secured by the policy.

PENSIONS

12.8 PERSONAL PENSIONS (INCLUDING STAKEHOLDER PLANS)

A personal pension scheme (PPS) is a money purchase arrangement, which means that the level of benefit provided will depend on both the amount and timing of contributions to it, and the rate of investment growth.

12.8.1 Development

The personal pension concept was introduced originally by FA 1956 with the launch of retirement annuity contracts (RACs, also known variously as section 226 plans, self-employed retirement annuities, etc). RACs were intended to enable both self-employed and employed people, for whom membership of an occupational pension scheme was not available, to pension their earnings.

The concept was extended enormously in July 1988 when RACs were replaced by PPSs, which are capable of both receiving employer contributions and contracting out of the State Earnings Related Pension Scheme (SERPS: see 12.12.2).

Most recently, with effect from 6 April 2001, the concept has been refined and yet further extended by the application of the 'stakeholder' framework to PPSs. Now, membership of a PPS or a stakeholder pension (SHP) is potentially open to all UK residents (whether employed or not, and including children).

12.8.2 Personal pension providers

Retirement annuity contracts, as their name suggests, were issued by life insurance companies. PPSs could be provided by life insurance companies, in addition to banks, building societies and authorised unit trust schemes. The stakeholder changes to personal pensions included the expansion of permitted providers to include managers of open-ended investment companies and, most significantly, employers. It is also possible to adopt a self-administered approach with investment in a range of permitted assets.

12.8.3 Eligibility and contribution limits

(1) Any individual under age 75, who is UK-resident and ordinarily resident, and who is not a member of an employer's occupational pension scheme (but see (9), (10) and (11) below), is eligible to join a PPS or SHP and to contribute up to £3,600 in each tax year. This limit may be amended in subsequent years by Treasury Order.

(2) An individual under age 75 may become a member of a PPS or SHP solely in order that the scheme may receive:

(a) a transfer payment from another approved or acceptable pension scheme;
(b) *minimum contributions* where the member has contracted out of SERPS. Minimum contributions are not included in the overall limits for contributions by members and employers (see (1) above and (4) below)

(3) An ex-spouse may join a PPS or SHP in order to invest pension credit rights derived from a pension sharing order.

(4) A contribution greater than £3,600 may be paid in the tax year if the PPS member has relevant earnings, which are defined as income:

- taxable under Schedule D, derived from a trade, profession or vocation, either as an individual or a partner;
- taxable as 'employment income' under the Income Tax (Earnings and Pensions) Act 2003;
- from any property related to an office or employment;
- from patent rights treated as earned income.

Where an individual has relevant earnings, it is not necessary that he should be ordinarily resident in the UK.

(5) Relevant earnings for the tax year ending 5 April 2004 are capped at £99,000 for the purpose of paying contributions to a PPS or SHP.

(6) The maximum percentage of capped relevant earnings, which may be paid by and on behalf of PPS or SHP members within specified age bands, is as follows:

Age at Beginning of tax year	*Percentage of net relevant earnings 1987-88 1988-89*	*1989-90 onwards*	*Maximum contribution 2003-04*
below 36	17.5	17.5	£17,325
36-45	17.5	20.0	£19,800
46-50	17.5	25.0	£24,750
51-55	20.0	30.0	£29,700
56-60	22.5	35.0	£34,650
61-74	27.5	40.0	£39,600

(7) Contributions to RACs are not subject to capped limits, and it is possible to pension total net relevant earnings. The maximum percentage, however, will be that for the relevant age band shown in the second column above. Aggregate contributions to both RACs, PPSs SHPs and in any single tax year are restricted to the percentage of capped earnings shown in the third column above.

(8) If a controlling director receives income from either an investment company or an employer's occupational pension scheme, contributions to a PPS or SHP are restricted to the maximum universal contribution in the relevant year (£3,600 in 2003-04).

(9) Membership of an employer's occupational pension scheme, which provides benefits only if the member dies in the employer's service, does not preclude an employee from pensioning all his or her income from that employment through a PPS or SHP.

(10) Where there are two sources of earnings, one of which is pensioned by an employer's occupational pension scheme, it is possible to contribute to a PPS or SHP in respect of the other earnings, subject to certain limits.

(11) Concurrent membership of both an employer's occupational pension scheme and a PPS or SHP is permitted, provided that:

- the member is not a controlling director, and

- the member's pay in the relevant year does not exceed £30,000 (excluding P11D benefits).

If these conditions are satisfied, the member and his or her employer may, in aggregate, contribute up to £3,600 in the relevant tax year to the PPS or SHP.

(12) Members of unapproved retirement benefits schemes (FURBS and UURBS) are eligible to join a PPS or SHP.

(13) Of contributions to a PPS or SHP within the overall limits set out above, 10% may be allocated to provide a lump sum death benefit by means of life assurance payable at the discretion of the scheme manager (or trustee, if applicable) after taking into account any nomination made by the member. It is possible to assign the death benefit, for example, to trustees of a discretionary trust, or to a lender.

(14) Arrangements made before 6 April 2001 to provide a lump sum death benefit by means of life assurance under PPSs and RACs, whereby a contribution of up to 5% of net relevant earnings was permitted, may continue.

(15) There is no requirement in law for an employer to pay contributions to a PPS or SHP. Contributions made by an employer to a PPS or SHP must be within the overall limits shown above. Employers' contributions are not treated as income for the purpose of assessing the employee's liability for income tax and NICs.

12.8.4 Tax relief on contributions

(1) Contributions to a PPS or SHP attract full income tax relief in the year of payment, even where the member did not have any tax liability for the year in question. Members pay contributions net of basic rate tax (22% in 2003-04). Any higher rate tax relief is obtained either by application to the tax inspector using form PP120, or by completing the relevant section of the SA return. The 10% tax band is not affected by the deduction of basic rate tax from the contribution.

(2) The basis on which tax relief on contributions to RACs is given has not changed. Contract holders should continue to apply for relief through their tax return after initial submission of a form SEPC. The self-employed can continue to set off contributions against their Schedule D income.

12.8.5 Year for which tax relief granted and 'carry back'

(1) Relief for contributions to a PPS or SHP is normally only given against net relevant earnings of the tax year in which contributions are paid. It is possible, however, to elect to have any contribution treated for tax purposes as if it had been paid during the preceding tax year.

(2) The amount of any claim for higher rate relief is calculated by reference to the tax payable for the year of payment (or where carry back is being used, for the year in which the contribution is treated as being paid). The maximum amount on which tax relief is available in any year is the

appropriate percentage of the net relevant earnings for that year (or, where carry back is being used, for the year in which the contribution is treated as being paid).

(3) An election for carry back does not alter the rate of tax deducted, which remains the basic rate for the year in which the contribution is actually paid.

(4) Employer contributions cannot be carried back. They are always treated as contributions for the tax year in which they are actually paid.

(5) Claims to relief for carry back are made by an amendment to the SA return. Claims can only be made by inclusion in the tax return, or by a separate stand-alone claim using form PP43 once the SA return has been completed. Relief is not given by adjustment to the assessment for the earlier year but by a repayment of tax already paid or a set off against outstanding liabilities. Carry back claims do not affect payments on account.

(6) With effect from 31 January 2002, it ceased to be possible to combine carry back with the facility to carry forward unused relief from previous years.

Note that the facility to offset contributions to PPSs against unused relief carried forward from previous years was abolished with effect from 6 April 2001 (with the exception of the January 2001 provision above).

(7) The facility to carry back contributions to the previous two years and to carry forward unused relief from the previous six years in respect of contributions to RACs remains undisturbed.

12.8.6 Benefits payable and age at which they may be taken

(1) The PPS established by the pension provider can allow the individual to take benefits in stages.

(2) The pension may start being paid at any age between 50 and 75. Normally this pension has to take the form of an annuity (but see (9) below). It is not necessary actually to retire before the annuity may commence. In certain occupations, the Revenue allows an annuity to start earlier than age 50 (eg jockeys, motor racing drivers, cricketers, etc). The pension can also start to be paid before age 50 on retirement because of ill health. Under no circumstances may the annuity start later than at age 75.

(3) The annuity payable can take one of several forms: sterling or unit-linked, guaranteed or non-guaranteed, etc. In most contracts there is a provision that on death before the beginning of the annuity, an annuity is payable to any widow(er) or dependants nominated by the individual or, alternatively, a lump sum could be paid, not exceeding the amount of the contributions plus a reasonable amount of interest or bonuses (this includes capital growth and income attributable to the contributions paid under a unit-linked plan).

(4) The PPS or SHP can also incorporate a sum assured, so that on death an additional lump sum would be paid. This can be arranged to be free of IHT by writing it in trust where the PPS itself is not set up under trust.

(5) Any annuity payable to a widow, widower or dependant would be free of IHT (IHTA 1984, s 152).

(6) The whole of any annuity payable either to the individual, any spouse or dependants is currently treated and taxed as pensions income under the Income Tax (Earnings and Pensions) Act 2003 (and not, as is the case with purchased life annuities, partly as income and partly as a return of capital). The PAYE system is applied to these payments.

Prior to 6 April 1995 all personal pension annuities were taxed under Schedule D and basic rate income tax was deducted at source when the pension was paid.

(7) A lump sum may be taken from the PPS or SHP, between ages 50 and 75, up to a maximum of 25% of the fund excluding any part of the fund built up from contributions paid by the DSS. For PPSs effected prior to 27 July 1989, the value of the DSS contributions could be taken into account in calculating the cash lump sum available, but any fund used to provide benefits for a widow(er) or dependants had to be excluded.

(8) Instead of taking the annuity from the life company that issued the original pension contract, it is possible to use the fund built up to buy an annuity from any other company, thus obtaining the best terms then available ('open market option'). If the PPS or SHP is provided by an organisation that is not a life assurance company, the pension (and life assurance) must be provided by a life company.

(9) With effect from 1 May 1995, it is possible for PPSs or SHPs to allow members to defer the purchase of the annuity up to age 75. Before the annuity is purchased, it is possible to take income withdrawals. These withdrawals are taxable under the PAYE system in the same way as annuity payments. The maximum amount of income withdrawal is set by reference to the amount of a level, single life annuity, using rates laid down by the Government, and must be reviewed every three years.

(10) Where the option is exercised to defer the purchase of the annuity, no further contributions or transfers, other than transfers from other personal pension arrangements, from which income withdrawals are being taken, can be paid to the personal pension arrangement. The fund will continue to grow free of income and capital taxes. If the member dies during the deferral period, withdrawals can continue to be paid to any surviving spouse or dependant up to the date when the member would have reached age 75. Alternatively, the fund can be used to purchase an annuity or taken as a lump sum. Where the fund is taken as a lump sum there is a special charge to tax of 35% of the fund.

(11) The benefits available under RACs have been unaffected by the changes to PPSs and SHPs. The key differences between RACs and PPSs include the following:

(a) employers are not allowed to pay direct contributions into an employee's RAC;
(b) the Pensions Relief at Source system does not apply to RACs;

(c) RACs cannot be used to contract out of SERPS;
(d) the earliest age at which benefits could be taken was age 60 (except for those specific occupations where the Revenue permitted an earlier retirement age or in the case of ill health);
(e) annuities from RACs remain taxable under Schedule D and did not become subject to the PAYE system when the new rules on the taxation of personal pension annuities were introduced in the 1995-96 tax year; and
(f) the rules allowing the purchase of an annuity to be deferred do not apply to RACs.

In addition, there are different rules for determining the maximum lump sum cash that can be taken from an RAC. Instead of being restricted to 25% of the fund, the lump sum can equal three times the annual annuity payable after the cash has been taken (but contracts entered into on or after 17 March 1987 are subject to a maximum cash lump sum of £150,000 per contract).

12.9 OCCUPATIONAL SCHEMES

(TA 1988, ss 590 *et seq* and Sched 23; FA 1989, Sched 6)

12.9.1 Types of plan

(1) Occupational pension schemes may be either money purchase schemes or 'final salary' schemes, where the benefits are determined as a fraction of the employee's salary at retirement. Final salary schemes are sometimes called 'defined benefit' schemes.

(2) All occupational pension schemes require the involvement of an employer who will make some contribution to the scheme.

(3) Occupational pension schemes may be insured, where all benefits are provided in the form of insurance policies either on a group or individual basis, or self-administered with investment in a range of permitted assets. There are special rules for small self-administered schemes with 12 or fewer members.

12.9.2 Eligibility

(1) All employees, whether part time or full time, are eligible for membership of an occupational pension scheme if their employer participates in such a scheme. There are special rules for employees of overseas employers and for employees who are temporarily seconded outside the UK.

(2) Persons assessable under Schedule D (eg agents and consultants) are not eligible.

(3) Directors are also eligible for membership of an occupational pension scheme, but controlling directors of investment companies normally are not able to benefit from schemes approved under the Revenue's discretionary powers (see 12.9.3).

(4) It is not possible for an employer to make membership of an occu-

pational scheme (other than one providing death benefits only) compulsory. In general, leaving a good occupational scheme is unlikely to be wise except where its benefits are poor; expert advice should be sought if this is contemplated.

12.9.3 Approval of schemes

(1) Approval of occupational pension schemes is given by the Savings, Pension Share Schemes Office (SPSS), which is a branch of the Inland Revenue. 'Approval' will prevent contributions paid by the employer being taxed in the employees' hands as a benefit-in-kind.

(2) In addition, 'exempt approval' will give the additional benefits of the gross roll-up in the fund and tax relief for the employee in respect of regular contributions he makes to the scheme. Exempt approval will also mean that the employer's contributions will be deductible business expenses without relying on the normal rules for deductibility applying to Schedule D income. In order to be exempt approved, the scheme must be set up under irrevocable trusts.

(3) In most cases approval is given under the SPSS's discretionary powers, which are extremely wide-ranging. The main conditions for approval include the following:

(a) The sole purpose of the scheme must be to provide 'relevant benefits' in respect of service as an employee. Relevant benefits, broadly speaking, include most types of financial benefit given in connection with the termination of an employee's service with a particular employer.
(b) The scheme must be recognised by employer and employee and the employee must be given written particulars of its essential features.
(c) The employer must contribute to the scheme, although the employee may indirectly provide the necessary funds by agreeing to a reduction in salary, known as a 'salary sacrifice'.
(d) Pension benefits must be payable on retirement at any age between 50 and 75 and must not exceed a maximum permitted benefit calculated by reference to the employee's final remuneration and the length of service with that employer (see 12.9.5). Benefits may be available in respect of early retirement at any earlier age where retirement is because of ill health. There is also a maximum limit on the permitted pension that can be provided for widow(er)s and dependants.
(e) No pension may be surrendered, commuted or assigned, save for commutation on retirement up to a maximum lump sum (see 12.9.5(7)).
(f) A scheme may also provide for a lump sum payment of up to four times the employee's final remuneration on death in service and for a return of the employee's contributions in certain cases.

12.9.4 Tax relief on contributions and limits

(1) Contributions by the employer to an exempt approved scheme are deductible business expenses, although relief in respect of non-regular contributions may be deferred by being spread over a maximum of five years.

(2) The employee may make personal contributions of up to 15% of his remuneration subject to the £99,000 salary cap (see 12.9.5(6)). Personal contributions attract tax relief at the highest rate paid by the individual.

(3) Unlike PPSs, there are no specific limits on the amount of contributions that may be made to an occupational scheme other than those applicable to personal contributions. Instead, the controls operate on the level of benefits that is allowed. If a scheme becomes 'over-funded' (ie where the scheme has more capital than is necessary to meet its prospective liabilities), payment of further contributions may be restricted or capital may have to be returned to the employer after deduction of tax of 40%.

(4) Where a surplus arises from an employee's voluntary contributions, any refund to the employee will have tax deducted at 32% (33% for refunds made before 6 April 2000, and 34% for refunds made for the period before 6 April 1997). The amount received by the employee is treated as being paid net of tax at the basic rate. An employee who is a higher rate taxpayer will be subject to a further charge on the equivalent gross amount of the payment received, taking the total effective rate to approximately 47.8%.

12.9.5 Benefits

(1) The maximum pension benefits under an occupational pension scheme are expressed as a fraction of the member's final salary for each year of service with the employer. For example, many schemes provide a pension of one-sixtieth of final salary for each year of service so that the maximum pension of two-thirds of final salary is reached after 40 years' service.

(2) The maximum rate at which pension benefits can accrue is one-thirtieth of final salary for each year of service. In order to obtain a maximum pension of two-thirds of final salary, it is necessary to complete 20 years' service.

(3) Final salary or 'final remuneration' must be calculated in a way which is approved by the PSO. The two permitted definitions are:

(a) the remuneration in any of the five years preceding retirement, leaving service or death (as applicable), together with the average of any fluctuating emoluments (bonuses, commissions, etc), averaged over at least three consecutive years ending with the year in question; or

(b) the highest average of the total emoluments from the employer over any period of three consecutive years ending within ten years before retirement, leaving service or death (as applicable).

Company directors who are treated as controlling directors may only calculate final salary using the second permitted definition.

(4) Final salary excludes any income and gains from shares and options acquired through share option, share incentive and profit-sharing schemes. In addition, payments on the termination of employment (eg golden handshakes) cannot be used as part of the calculation of final salary.

(5) It is possible to increase final salary for previous years in line with the increase in the RPI up to the date when benefits are paid. This increase is known as 'dynamisation'.

(6) There is a maximum amount of final salary that may be taken into account for pension purposes. For 2003-04, this amount is £99,000. The 'salary cap' is subject to the same rules relating to annual increases in line with the RPI as the limit on contributions to PPSs (see 12.8.3(6)).

(7) Instead of taking all benefits in pension form, the member may commute part of his pension for a tax-free cash lump sum. The maximum lump sum is three-eightieths of final salary for each year of service up to a maximum of 40 years' service or 2.25 times the pension available before commutation, if greater. The maximum lump sum is, therefore, one and a half times final salary.

(8) A lump sum of up to four times final salary, together with a refund of the employee's personal contributions, can also be paid on the death of the employee in service. It is also possible to provide a pension for a spouse or dependant up to two-thirds of the maximum pension to which the deceased would have been entitled at his normal retirement date. A pension of a similar amount can also be provided for a spouse or dependant on death after retirement.

(9) Pensions payable are treated as earned income and taxed under Schedule E. The payments are subject to the deduction of income tax under the PAYE system.

12.9.6 Cessation of approval

Where an approved occupational scheme ceases to be approved after 2 November 1994, there is a special tax charge of 40% of the accumulated fund valued immediately before the scheme ceases to be approved. This tax charge was introduced primarily to prevent avoidance of tax by the appointment of offshore trustees to small self-administered schemes, but the tax charge applies whenever a scheme ceases to be approved. From 17 March 1998, the tax charge was extended to apply where a scheme ceases to be approved and has received a transfer value from another approved scheme in respect of a controlling director of a company (or a person whose earnings were chargeable to tax under Schedule D). The tax charge is payable by the scheme administrator or, in the event of non-payment, by the employer or, from 17 March 1998, by the scheme members who were controlling directors (or whose earnings were chargeable to tax under Schedule D).

12.9.7 'Grandfathering'

The maximum limits on contributions to and benefits from occupational pension schemes have been restricted over the years. The most notable changes were in 1987 and 1989 when restrictions, including the introduction of the salary cap in 1989, were announced in the Budget. Members who joined schemes prior to the Budget Days in those years may continue to benefit from the old rules, which have been preserved or 'grandfathered' for those members eligible. Minor changes have also been made to the Revenue's discretionary practice at other times. Further details can be found in the *Zurich Pensions Handbook.*

12.10 FREE-STANDING AVC (FSAVC) SCHEMES

12.10.1 Types of plan

FSAVC schemes are money purchase schemes that provide benefits in addition to the benefits provided by an employer's occupational pension scheme. They are similar to PPSs in that they may be offered by life assurance companies, banks, building societies and authorised unit trust schemes. FSAVC schemes are occupational pension schemes for Revenue purposes and must be set up under irrevocable trusts for the sole purpose of providing relevant benefits of the type provided by occupational pension schemes.

12.10.2 Eligibility

An employee will only be eligible to contribute to an FSAVC scheme if he is a member of an occupational pension scheme to which his employer is currently contributing or of a statutory scheme such as the Civil Service scheme. Contributions may only be paid to one FSAVC scheme in any tax year, although if there are earnings from more than one employment, separate contributions may be made to an FSAVC scheme in respect of each employment.

Directors who are treated as controlling directors are not eligible for membership of an FSAVC scheme.

12.10.3 Contributions

The maximum contribution is 15% of the employee's remuneration in any one tax year. In order to calculate the maximum contribution, the contribution to the FSAVC scheme must be aggregated with the employee's contributions to his employer's scheme. The salary cap of £99,000 will apply if it applies to the benefits provided by the employer's scheme, so that the maximum contribution will be £14,850 in 2003-04 for an employee who is subject to the salary cap.

Where contributions to the FSAVC scheme exceed £2,400 pa, the scheme's administrator must calculate the maximum contribution that is not likely to produce benefits in excess of the Revenue limits. To do this, information is provided by the administrators of the employer's scheme (or the member himself) about the benefits provided by that scheme. If necessary, contributions to the FSAVC scheme must be restricted. Contributions to an FSAVC scheme must be paid net of basic rate tax under the PRAS system. Higher rate tax relief is obtained by either an adjustment to the employee's PAYE coding or to his end-of-year tax assessment.

12.10.4 Benefits

The benefits provided by an FSAVC scheme must be aggregated with the benefits provided by the employer's scheme to ensure that the limits on benefits provided by occupational schemes are not exceeded.

An FSAVC scheme may not provide a tax-free cash lump sum on retirement, although the pension provided may be used as part of the '2.25 times pension before commutation' calculation in order to enhance the tax-free lump sum provided by the employer's scheme where the rules of the employer's scheme allow this.

Where the funds accumulated in the FSAVC scheme are such that the maximum limits on benefits are exceeded, the excess must be returned to the employee after deduction of tax at 33% (34% for refunds made before 6 April 1997). The amount received by the employee is treated as being paid net of tax at the basic rate. An employee who is a higher rate taxpayer will be subject to a further charge on the equivalent gross amount of the payment received, taking the total effective rate to approximately 47.8%.

Pensions payable are treated in the same way as those from occupational schemes and are subject to the PAYE system.

12.11 UNAPPROVED SCHEMES

Unapproved occupational pension schemes were introduced to allow employers the flexibility to provide benefits for those employees who had earnings in excess of the salary cap. However, their use is not restricted to such employees and they may be used to provide benefits in excess of the normal two-thirds maximum pension benefit or to provide greater benefits for those with less than 20 years' service.

12.11.1 Eligibility

Any person in receipt of income taxed under Schedule E is eligible for an unapproved scheme. There is no requirement that the employee is also a member of an approved scheme.

12.11.2 Types of plan

Such schemes may be funded (ie contributions set aside in order to fund the promised benefits) or unfunded (ie at retirement the benefits will be paid by the company out of current income or investments). A funded scheme is often called a FURBS. There is no requirement that funded schemes are established under trust, but this is commonly the case.

12.11.3 Contributions

If the scheme is funded, the employer will obtain tax relief on the contributions as a normal business expense. There is no set limit on the contributions that may be paid, although excessive contributions may be disqualified from tax relief.

The employee is taxed on contributions paid by the employer as if they were earnings. If no benefits are received by the employee, it may be possible to reclaim some of the tax. Employee contributions are not tax deductible and are to be avoided.

In an unfunded scheme there is no charge to tax on any reserves set up to provide for future benefits. Equally, the employer will not obtain any tax relief until the benefits are actually paid.

12.11.4 Taxation of scheme investments

Unapproved schemes do not benefit from 'gross roll-up', but are not subject to the special rate of income tax of 34% payable by trusts that accumulate their income. Tax is payable at 20% or 22%, depending on the type of income.

Since 6 April 1998, the trustees of unapproved schemes pay CGT on realised gains at the rate of 34% applicable to all trusts. Prior to 6 April 1998, realised gains were taxed at the basic rate (23% for 1997-98).

Prior to 30 November 1993, extra tax benefits could be achieved by establishing a funded scheme under an offshore trust, although care had to be taken to avoid the anti-avoidance legislation that applied to such trusts. FA 1994 effectively removed the tax advantage of offshore schemes, although existing schemes can continue unchanged.

12.11.5 Benefits

The scheme must be set up to provide relevant benefits, but there are no set limits on the benefits that can be provided. Pensions from unapproved schemes, whether funded or unfunded, are subject to income tax as earned income.

Lump sums paid from funded schemes may be paid free of tax, but those from unfunded schemes are subject to income tax as earned income. Lump sums paid from funded schemes set up after 30 November 1993, or from schemes set up before then that are varied to provide a lump sum, may be taxed if they exceed the amount of the contributions on which the employee was taxed, where the scheme invests in assets that are not subject to income tax or CGT.

12.12 STATE PENSION BENEFITS

The State currently provides a number of pension benefits with a range of eligibility conditions and contribution requirements. There are also a number of additional means-tested benefits payable in retirement that are beyond the scope of this book. The main State pension benefits are as follows.

12.12.1 The basic pension

This is a contributory scheme that aims to provide a pension of approximately 20% of national average earnings. It is not related to salary, but to obtain the maximum pension an individual must have paid (or have been credited with) NICs for about 90% of his expected working life. The pension (which is taxable as earned income if attributable to an individual's own contributions) is increased each year in line with the RPI.

12.12.2 State Earnings Related Pension Scheme (SERPS)

SERPS was introduced in 1978 and is based on earnings between the lower and upper earnings limits (for 2003-04, £89 and £595 pw, respectively). The earnings between these two figures are often called 'band earnings'. The self-employed neither contribute towards, nor benefit from, SERPS.

SERPS provides a pension at state retirement age expressed as a percentage of band earnings. For those retiring in 2009-10 or later the percentage is currently 20%, with those retiring before then receiving a higher percentage up to a maximum of 25% of band earnings. Band earnings are based on an average over the whole of your working life, although individuals retiring before 6 April 1999 can use their best 20 years to calculate band earnings.

State pensions do not provide any cash lump sum at retirement or any opportunity of retiring and receiving benefits before state retirement age. Benefits can be postponed for up to five years, in which case the pension will be increased.

The main benefit from the state scheme is a lifelong pension for the individual, but SERPS can also, in certain circumstances, provide a widow's pension which will be of a reduced amount unless the widow is aged over 40 and has dependent children (or over 50 with no dependent children).

Accrual of SERPs benefits ceased from 6 April 2002, but benefits accrued prior to that date continue to be calculated in accordance with the existing rules at that date.

12.12.3 State Second Pension (S2P)

S2P was introduced on 6 April 2002. Like SERPs, which it replaces, S2P is based on NICs made by employers and employees. However, S2P provides better benefits than SERPs for low and moderate earners, broadly those earning up to £24,600 for 2002-03.

To achieve this, earnings are divided into three bands rather than the single 'band earnings' used to calculate SERPs. In addition to the lower and upper earnings limits, there is now a 'low earnings threshold' broadly equal to half of national average earnings (£11,200 for 2003-04) and a second earnings threshold (£25,600 for 2003-04).

The rate of accrual for the lowest band (ie for earnings between the lower earnings limit and the lower earnings threshold) is double that of the highest band and four times that of the middle band, as shown below:

	Earnings	*Maximum S2P*
Band 1	£4,004-11,200	40%
Band 2	£11,201-25,600	10%
Band 3	£25,601-30,940	20%

In addition to the improved benefits for low and moderate earners, S2P also provides coverage for some carers and people with long-term disabilities or illness. In these cases, it is possible to build up an entitlement to S2P for periods where individuals are unable to work.

12.13 CONTRACTING OUT

It is possible to leave SERPS and S2P provided appropriate provision is made to replace the SERPS/S2P benefits with a suitable approved alternative. To encourage this, individuals and employers who 'contract out' in this way receive benefits in the form of reduced NICs and/or a direct payment into individual PPSs.

There are currently three ways in which an employee can be contracted out. These are:

(1) membership of an appropriate personal pension plan (APPP);
(2) membership of a contracted-out money purchase pension scheme (COMPS); or
(3) membership of an occupational scheme providing guaranteed minimum pension (GMP) or from 6 April an occupational scheme that satisfies a 'Reference Scheme' test.

12.13.1 Appropriate personal pension plan (APPP)

APPPs require no employer involvement at all and are open to all employees who are not contracted-out by another scheme, even those who are also members of an occupational scheme. In order to contract out, the employee and the chosen personal pension plan provider must complete a Joint Notice (Form APPI), which is submitted to the DSS. An individual can use only one APPP to contract out at any time and must contract out for a complete tax year.

Once the Joint Notice is accepted by the DSS payments are made, normally once a year, directly by the DSS to the pension provider. These payments, called 'protected rights contributions', consist of the National Insurance Rebate but both the employee and employer continue to pay the full rate of NICs. For 1997-98 and onwards, a system of age-related rebates applies. From 2002-03, the age-related rebates range from 4.2% to a maximum of 10.5%.

The protected rights contributions must be used to provide a pension benefit at state retirement age, or a widow(er) or dependant's pension or a lump sum on death.

12.13.2 Contracted-out money purchase scheme (COMPS)

COMPSs are occupational pension plans where the employer takes the initial decision to contract out, although the employer may allow individuals the choice of whether to contract out or not.

Both the employer and employee pay a reduced rate of NICs, but this saving is balanced by the protected rights contributions that the employer must ensure are paid into the pension scheme on a monthly basis. Normally, both the employer and the employee will contribute their respective shares of the protected rights contributions. In addition to the basic flat-rate rebates, the DSS pays an additional age-related payment after the end of the tax year. From 2002-03, the total rebates from all sources range between 2.6% and 10.5%.

The protected rights contributions must be used to provide benefits in the same way as those provided by an APPS.

12.13.3 Guaranteed minimum pension

This method of contracting out involved an occupational pension scheme providing a guaranteed minimum level of pension equivalent to that provided by SERPS. Both the employer and the employee benefited from a reduced level of NICs, but the employer had to be prepared to provide the pension scheme with sufficient funds to enable it to meet the guarantee.

Since 6 April 1997, no further GMPs can accrue. Since then, occupational schemes can be contracted out either on a money purchase basis (ie a COMPS) or by satisfying the 'Reference Scheme test'. The latter involves the scheme's actuary certifying that the pension benefits from the scheme are 'broadly equivalent' to the pension benefits of a standard Reference Scheme.

The Reference Scheme is a basic scheme providing one-eightieth of earnings between the lower and upper earnings limit (for 2003-04, £89 and £595 pw, respectively) for each year of pensionable service for 90% of the scheme's membership.

Employees who contracted out using an APPP or a COMPS must consider whether the money purchase benefit is of benefit to younger people, with older persons likely to benefit more from SERPS.

MISCELLANEOUS

12.14 TAXATION OF COMMISSION, CASHBACKS AND DISCOUNTS

The Revenue published SP4/97 on the taxation of commission, cashbacks and discounts, further commenting on this subject in *Tax Bulletin* Issue 33. The Revenue has offered its assurances to the 'ordinary retail customer' that there normally will be no tax liabilities on rebated commissions or discounts. However, the position is more complex with regard to insurance products. SP4/97 states:

> **Life insurance and personal pensions**
>
> *Qualifying life insurance policies*
>
> **36** Where commission in respect of a policy holder's own qualifying life insurance policy is received, netted off or invested, that policy will not be disqualified as a result of entitlement to that commission if the contract under which commission arises is separate from the contract of insurance. In practice, the Revenue will not seek to read two contracts as one in a way that would lead to the loss of qualifying policy status.
>
> **37** Where a policy holder pays a discounted premium in respect of his or her own policy, the premium payable under the policy will be the discounted premium. It is this amount that must be used for the purposes of establishing whether the relevant qualifying rules are met.
>
> *Calculation of chargeable event gains in respect of life policies, capital redemption policies and life annuity contracts*
>
> **38** Chargeable event gains are computed by reference to the premiums or lump sum consideration paid. The amount paid will be interpreted as follows –
>
> – where a policy holder pays a gross premium and receives commission in respect of that policy, the chargeable event gain is calculated using the gross amount paid without taking the commission received into account;
> – where an amount of commission is received or due under an enforceable legal right and subsequently invested in the policy, that amount is included as a premium paid when calculating the chargeable event gain;
> – where a policy holder nets off commission from an insurer in respect of his or her own policy from the gross amount of premium payable and the

commission is not taxable as income on the policy holder, the chargeable event gain is calculated using the net amount paid to the insurer;

- where a policy holder pays a discounted premium, the chargeable event gain is calculated using the discounted amount of premium paid;
- where extra value is added to the policy by the insurer (for example by allocation of bonus units), the premium for the purpose of calculating the chargeable event is the amount paid by the policy holder without taking the extra value into account.

Tax relief in respect of personal pension contributions

39 Tax relief for contributions to personal pension schemes is due in respect of 'a contribution paid by an individual'. The amount of the contribution will be interpreted as follows where the contract under which the commission arises is separate from the personal pension scheme contract -

- where a contributor pays a gross contribution and receives commission in respect of that contribution, tax relief is given on the gross amount paid without taking the commission received into account;
- where an amount of commission is received by, or is due under an enforceable legal right to, the contributor and subsequently invested in the personal pension that gave rise to the commission, tax relief is given on that amount;
- where a contributor deducts commission in respect of his or her own pension contribution from the gross amount payable, relief is due on the net amount paid;
- where a contributor pays discounted contributions, tax relief is due on the discounted amount paid;
- where extra value is added to the policy by the insurer (for example by allocation of bonus units), relief is due on the amount paid by the contributor without taking the extra value into account.

40 If commission were to be rebated to the contributor under the same contract as the personal pension contract, this would be an unapprovable benefit (since it would involve leakage of the pension fund to the member) which would jeopardise the tax-approved status of the arrangement.

41 The consequences of paying commission on transfers between tax-approved pension schemes may be different from those outlined if such payment is effectively a benefit not authorised by the rules of the pension scheme. Alternatively, the misrepresentation as an annual premium of any premium applied to new pensions business so that a higher rate of rebated commission is generated will call into question the bona fides of the pension arrangement and jeopardise its approval from inception.

The statement also encompasses the Revenue's two previous press releases by stating that:

(1) other commission rebates to ordinary customers will not be taxed; and
(2) cashbacks offered by banks and building societies as an inducement to take out a mortgage will not be regarded as chargeable to CGT.

12.14.1 Payments arising from trade or employment

If a cashback is received in the course of either the recipient's business or employment, the cashback may be chargeable as income.

The income tax consequences of the new statement are that employees who receive commission arising from, and discounts in connection with, goods, investments or services sold to third parties are assessable regardless of whether the commission is passed on by them to the customer and whether the commission is paid by the employer or anyone else.

The Revenue takes the view that PAYE will apply in any situation where the commission, etc falls to be taxed under Schedule E.

13

CAPITAL GAINS TAX

This chapter deals with the following areas of capital gains tax (CGT):

(1) Basic outline of CGT.
(2) CGT and the self assessment form.
(3) Who is subject to CGT?
(4) What assets are chargeable assets?
(5) Which types of transaction may produce a chargeable gain?
(6) How gains may be deferred or 'rolled over'.
(7) Sales of shares to all-employee share trusts.
(8) Hold-over relief where a gift is a chargeable transfer for IHT purposes.

Unless otherwise stated, the statutory references refer to the Taxation of Chargeable Gains Act (TCGA) 1992.

13.1 BASIC OUTLINE OF CGT

Capital gains are assessed for a tax year. Under self-assessment the due date for payment of the tax is 31 January following the tax year (ie for gains arising in the year ended 5 April 2003, tax is payable by 31 January 2004). There is no requirement to make payments on account: indeed capital gains do not form part of the payment on account calculation (see 3.1.3).

The way chargeable gains are computed is quite different from the rules that determine assessable income for tax purposes. A range of exemptions and reliefs may apply, and a major distinction between CGT and income tax is that capital gains may be reduced by taper relief (and by indexation relief, an adjustment for inflation up to April 1998).

The rate of CGT is now governed by whether the individual's income and capital gains are sufficient to put him into the 40% band.

13.1.1 Annual exemption
(TCGA 1992, s 3)

You are not liable for CGT unless you make gains of more than the annual exemption, which for 2003-04 is £7,900. The exemptions for the past six years were:

	£		£
2002-03	7,700	1999-00	7,100
2001-02	7,500	1998-99	6,800
2000-01	7,200	1997-98	6,500

13.1.2 No gain/loss on spouse transactions

Provided a couple has not separated on a permanent basis, there can be no chargeable gains on any assets transferred from one spouse to the other, whether by gift or sale. The asset is treated as passing across on a no gain/no loss basis, with the recipient acquiring it at his spouse's cost plus indexation to date (see 14.7 on indexation relief and 14.5 on taper relief). There is an exception to this rule in respect of the transfer of an asset that becomes part of the trading stock used in the spouse's business.

13.1.3 Losses

Losses may arise as well as capital gains. The normal rule is that capital losses cannot be offset against an individual's income but may be carried forward against capital gains of future years. Losses arising from transactions involving connected persons may only be set against gains arising from transactions with the same person.

Brought forward losses do not need to be set against gains that are covered by the annual exemption. However, current year losses must be set against capital gains before using the annual exemption.

13.1.4 Rate of tax

(TCGA 1992, s 4)

Once the gains for the year have been computed (net of any losses), the annual exemption is deducted. The balance is then added to the individual's taxable income and the CGT is normally ascertained by working out the additional income tax that would be payable if the capital gains had been income from savings.

Example

B has 2002-03 taxable income, after personal allowances, of £25,000. Her capital gains for the year are £17,300. After deducting the £7,700 annual exemption, this means adding in an amount of £9,600. The CGT payable would be computed as:

	£
Balance of basic rate band	
£29,900 – £25,000 = £4,900 at 20% =	980
£4,700 at 40% =	1,880
Total CGT payable	£2,860

However, if *B* had no taxable income at all, the calculation is slightly different. If the gains were again £17,300, the CGT payable would be:

	£
First £7,700	Nil
£1,920 at 10%	192
£7,680 at 20%	1,536
	1,728

Any unused personal allowances for income tax purposes simply go to waste.

13.1.5 Trading losses

If relief for trading losses has been claimed against income from other sources for the year, any balance of loss may be set against capital gains for that year, or against income and capital gains of the preceding tax year.

A formal claim must be lodged with the Revenue by one year and ten months after the tax year of loss, ie a claim to utilise a 2002-03 trading loss must be made by 31 January 2005. Similar claims can be made for losses arising from letting furnished holiday accommodation, from post-cessation expenditure or from post-employment deductions (see 6.5 and 5.8).

13.2 CGT AND THE SELF-ASSESSMENT FORM

The FA 2003 set out the following circumstances under which an individual is required to complete the CGT pages of the SA form:

- If there is CGT to pay;
- Total proceeds for the tax year are more than four times the annual CGT exemption, for example for 2003-04 £31,600 (for 2002-03 this limit was twice the annual exemption, ie £15,400);
- Chargeable gains exceed the annual exemption and are reduced by losses;
- A CGT relief (other than taper) is to be claimed;
- A CGT election is being made;
- CGT losses are being claimed.

13.3 WHO IS SUBJECT TO CGT?

An individual's residence and domicile status may have a crucial bearing on his CGT liability.

13.3.1 Significance of residence status

(TCGA 1992, s 2)

An individual is subject to the CGT legislation only if he is either resident or ordinarily resident in the UK for the year in which relevant disposals take place. Residence and ordinary residence are determined in the same way as for income tax (see 23.2). There are two exceptions:

(1) Where a non-resident and non-ordinarily resident person carries on a trade or profession through a branch or agency in the UK, CGT may be charged on a disposal of assets used in that branch despite the fact that he would normally be outside the charge on capital gains.

(2) An individual who has been resident or ordinarily resident in the UK for any part of at least four of the seven tax years prior to his ceasing to be resident for a period of less than five complete tax years may be taxed on his return to the UK (see 13.3.2 and 23.5.4).

13.3.2 Individual non-resident for part of tax year

Technically, an individual is resident or non-resident for the whole of a tax year. The Revenue practice of treating certain individuals as resident for only part of a tax year for income tax purposes is really no more than an extra-statutory concession. The 'split year' treatment (see 23.5.1) is therefore subject to two exceptions.

The first concerns the year of departure. An individual who moves abroad is taxed on all capital gains for the year of departure, even if the gains are realised after the date he leaves the UK. Different rules apply to individuals who left the UK before 17 March 1998: see *Tax Handbook 1998-99* at 13.2.2.

Secondly, the Revenue can assess capital gains where the individual has returned to the UK during the year in question and was non-resident for less than five years. In such a case, capital gains realised in the tax year in which he resumes UK residence may be charged to tax even though the disposals took place prior to his return.

Example – Non-residence for part of tax year

C was classified as non-resident in the UK from 1 January 1999 when she took up a job in the Middle East. She returned to the UK on 24 July 2003. For income tax purposes she is regarded as not resident and not ordinarily resident from 1 January 1999 to 23 July 2003, but she would be subject to CGT for 1998-99 on disposals made during the period 1 January to 5 April 1999.

Gains realised in the period 6 April 1999 to 5 April 2003 are not subject to CGT for the tax year concerned as *C* is neither resident nor ordinarily resident in those years. However, the gains will be taxed as if they were realised in 2003-04, ie the year in which *C* resumes residence in the UK. *C* will also be taxed on all her gains for 2003-04, not merely those realised after her return on 24 July 2003.

In some cases the provisions of a double taxation agreement may override the five-year rule and prevent the Revenue from taxing gains realised in the year in which the individual resumes UK residence. This is an area where specialist advice is essential.

13.3.3 Foreign domicile may make an important difference
(TCGA 1992, s 12)

(See 24.1 on domicile.)

An individual who is resident (or ordinarily resident) and domiciled in the UK is subject to CGT on a worldwide basis (ie on gains realised both in the UK and abroad). By contrast, a non-UK domiciled individual is charged tax on gains from foreign assets only if the proceeds are brought into (or, as the legislation puts it, the gains are 'remitted' to) the UK. There are further details on the treatment of foreign domiciled individuals in 24.12. The rest of this chapter deals only with UK-domiciled people.

13.4 WHAT ASSETS ARE CHARGEABLE ASSETS?

13.4.1 Assets within the scope of CGT
(TCGA 1992, s 21)

Gains on virtually all types of assets are potentially subject to CGT, subject to certain stated exceptions. TCGA 1992, s 21(1) states:

> All forms of property shall be assets for the purposes of this Act, whether situated in the UK or not, including:
> (a) options, debts and incorporeal property generally, and
> (b) any currency other than sterling, and
> (c) any form of property created by the person disposing of it, or otherwise coming to be owned without being acquired.

The asset need not be transferable or capable of being assigned. The term 'any form of property' is all embracing. For example, the courts have held that CGT was due on an employer's right to compensation from an employee who wished to be released from his service agreement. In another case, the right to compensation for property expropriated by the USSR in 1940 was held to be a form of property and therefore an asset for CGT purposes. Similarly, the High Court held in *Zim Properties Ltd v Proctor* [1985] STC 90 that the right to bring an action before the courts constitutes an asset that can be turned to account by the potential litigant negotiating a compromise and receiving a lump sum.

The conclusion therefore is that virtually all forms of property that can yield a capital sum are subject to CGT unless they are specifically exempt.

13.4.2 What assets are specifically exempt?

The following are the main categories of exempt assets:

(1) Principal private residence (see 16.1) [s 222].
(2) Chattels that are wasting assets, unless used in a business (see 15.3.1) [s 44].
(3) Chattels where the sale consideration is less than £6,000. There is some alleviation of the charge when more than £6,000 is received (see 15.3.2) [s 262].
(4) Decoration for valour so long as sold by the original recipient [s 268].
(5) Foreign currency acquired for personal expenditure outside the UK. This includes money spent on the purchase or maintenance of any property situated outside the UK [s 269].
(6) Winnings from betting (eg the pools, horses, bingo and lotteries) [s 51].
(7) Compensation or damages for wrong or injury suffered in a profession or vocation [s 51]. Certain compensation from foreign governments for property lost or confiscated by concession.
(8) Debts [s 251].
(9) National savings certificates and non-marketable securities, ie those that cannot be transferred or are only transferable with a Minister of the Crown's or National Debt Commissioner's consent [s 121].
(10) Gilt-edged securities and qualifying corporate bonds (QCBs) and any options to acquire or dispose of such investments [s 115]. A QCB is a loan stock that is not convertible and is not a relevant discounted security (see 7.7).
(11) Shares held in ISAs (see 11.1) and PEPs (see 11.5) [s 151].
(12) Shares issued by way of business expansion schemes after 18 March 1986 provided the BES relief has not been withdrawn and the shares are sold, etc by the original subscriber or his spouse.
(13) Shares that qualified for income tax relief issued under an enterprise investment scheme (see 11.6) provided the EIS relief has not been withdrawn.
(14) Shares in a venture capital trust (see 11.7).
(15) Motor cars, unless not suitable for use as a private vehicle or commonly used for the carriage of passengers [s 263]. Also veteran and vintage cars.
(16) Woodlands [s 250].
(17) Gifts to charities and for national purposes to any one mentioned in the Inheritance Tax Act (IHTA) 1984, Sched 3 [s 257].
(18) Works of art where they are taken by the Revenue in lieu of death duties such as IHT (IHTA 1984, Sched 3) [s 258].
(19) Gifts to housing associations; a claim is made by both transferor and the association [s 259].
(20) Mortgage cash-backs: the Revenue conceded on 21 March 1996 that

mortgagees who receive cash inducements from banks and building societies are not liable to CGT on such receipts.

(21) Compensation for missold personal pensions taken out as a result of disadvantageous advice given between 29 April 1988 and 30 June 1994.

(22) Life assurance policies, but only where the policy is disposed of by the original owner or beneficiaries or by a person who acquired it by way of a gift from a person who had not himself acquired it by purchase [s 210]. The rules were recently tightened by FA 2003 (see 15.7.1).

Where an asset is exempt, no gain is assessable. Unfortunately, it follows that no relief is normally given for losses (losses on a disposal of shares in an EIS are an exception to this general rule).

13.5 WHICH TYPES OF TRANSACTION MAY PRODUCE A CHARGEABLE GAIN?

(TCGA 1992, s 28)

13.5.1 Introduction

The most obvious type of disposal is an outright sale with immediate settlement, but there are many other transactions that count as a disposal for CGT purposes, for example:

- Outright sale (possibly with payment by instalments);
- Conditional sale;
- Exercise of an option;
- Exchange of property;
- Compulsory acquisition of asset by local authority, etc;
- Sums payable as compensation or proceeds under an insurance policy;
- Gifts;
- Asset destroyed or becoming of negligible value.

The liability to CGT is determined by the tax year in which the date of disposal falls.

13.5.2 Outright sale

(TCGA 1992, s 28)

The date of disposal is the day on which the unconditional contract is entered into, which may be different from the date the vendor receives payment.

Sale with payment by instalments

The date of disposal is fixed by the time the parties enter into an unconditional contract. It may be possible to pay CGT arising from such transactions as the instalments come in over a period of up to eight years (provided the instalments are spaced over a period of at least 18 months: TCGA 1992, s 280).

The Revenue operates a concession where a vendor grants a mortgage to a purchaser who defaults and the vendor takes back the asset in satisfaction of the sums due to him. The disposal is effectively treated as if it has never happened (see ESC D18).

13.5.3 Conditional sale

(TCGA 1992, s 28)

A conditional sale is a contract that does not take effect until a stated condition is satisfied.

Example

> *D* agrees to purchase *E*'s shares in XYZ Ltd provided the local authority grants planning permission over land owned by XYZ by April 2003. Under this type of agreement, *E* remains the legal owner of his shares until the condition is satisfied. If the local authority does not in fact grant planning permission, *D* is under no obligation to buy *E*'s shares.
>
> The date of disposal under such contracts is the day the condition is satisfied and the contract becomes unconditional, for example in the above example, the date planning permission is granted.

13.5.4 Exercise of an option

(TCGA 1992, s 144)

A 'call' option is a legally binding agreement between the owner of an asset and a third party under which the owner agrees to sell the asset if the other party decides to exercise his option. The purchase price payable upon the exercise of the option is normally fixed at the outset; this constitutes one of the terms of the option.

A 'put' option is one where the other party agrees to buy the asset if the owner decides to exercise an option requiring him to do so.

The grant of either type of option does not constitute a disposal of the asset concerned. This happens only when the option is exercised and the day on which this happens is the date of disposal.

In some cases, payment is made for the option to be granted. This is treated as a disposal of a separate asset unless the option is subsequently exercised.

13.5.5 Exchange of property

An agreement to exchange an asset for another is a disposal of the old asset and an acquisition of the new asset. If there is any cash adjustment, this must also be brought into account. For example, if *F* exchanges his holding in ICI for *G*'s shareholding in Glaxo, *F* is treated as if he has disposed of the ICI shares for the market value of the Glaxo shares at the time of the exchange. This type of transaction commonly occurs where an individual transfers portfolio investments to a unit trust in return for units.

There is an important exception to the rule that an exchange constitutes a disposal that may apply where a shareholder takes securities offered to him on a company takeover (see 15.1.6 on such share exchanges). Provided certain conditions are satisfied, the exchange does not count as a disposal and the securities issued by the acquiring company are deemed to have been derived from the original shares, with the shareholder carrying forward his original acquisition value.

Example – Exchange of shares on company takeover

H holds 1,000 shares in XYZ plc that he acquired in 1993 for £9,000. Another company, ABC plc, makes a takeover bid and offers all XYZ shareholders a share exchange whereby they receive one ABC share (worth £30 each) for every two XYZ shares that they own. The offer document confirms that agreement has been obtained from the Revenue that TCGA 1992, s 136 applies.

If *H* accepts, he will receive 500 ABC shares worth £15,000, but he will be deemed to have acquired them in 1993 for £9,000. No disposal is deemed to have occurred on the share exchange.

13.5.6 Compulsory acquisition of asset
(TCGA 1992, s 22)

The transfer of land to, for example, a local authority exercising its compulsory purchase powers is a disposal for CGT purposes. In some cases, once the compulsory purchase order has been served, contracts are drawn up and the land is transferred under the contract. The rules in relation to outright sales and conditional sales apply.

Where the CPO is disputed, the date of disposal is normally the earlier of:

(1) the date on which compensation for the acquisition is agreed or otherwise determined, and
(2) the date on which the local authority enters the land in pursuance of its powers.

13.5.7 Sums payable as compensation or proceeds under insurance policy
(TCGA 1992, s 22)

In some cases, an asset (eg a building) may be destroyed or damaged and a capital sum received as compensation. In such cases, the asset is deemed to have been disposed of at the date the capital sum is received. Similarly, where a capital sum is received from an insurance policy following such damage, receipt of insurance monies is treated as constituting a disposal.

An ESC was issued on 19 December 1994 which covers the receipt of compensation under the Foreign Compensation Act 1950, the Ugandan Expropriated Properties Act, compensation payable by the UN Compensation Commission for property lost during the Gulf War and compensation payable under German Law. The concession may provide exemption for a person who receives compensation for property lost or confiscated, for example by the Nazis or under the East German regime.

13.5.8 Gifts

(TCGA 1992, s 17)

A gift is treated as a disposal at market value (except where it is from one spouse to the other: see 13.1.2). At one time it was possible for assets to be transferred at cost, but this general form of hold-over relief was abolished in 1989. In some specific situations the capital gains may still be held over, for example where the gift involves business property or is a lifetime chargeable transfer for IHT purposes, such as a gift to a discretionary trust (see 19.10) but not a PET (see 19.6.1). See on this 13.8.

A gift often constitutes a transaction between connected persons: see 22.9.

13.5.9 Asset destroyed or becoming of negligible value

(TCGA 1992, s 24)

The total destruction or entire loss of an asset constitutes a disposal. This could be physical destruction (eg by fire) or legal/financial destruction (eg bankruptcy or winding-up).

The legislation also permits a person to elect that he should be treated as having disposed of an asset that has become of negligible value. Normally, a capital loss will arise on such an occasion.

'Negligible value' is interpreted by the Revenue as meaning considerably less than small. For example, the Revenue will only agree that shares, loan stock and other securities are of negligible value on being satisfied that the owner is unlikely to recover anything other than a nominal amount on the liquidation of the company. The mere fact that shares have been suspended or de-listed by The Stock Exchange is not regarded as sufficient.

The legislation provides that a disposal is deemed to take place in the year during which the Inspector of Taxes agrees that the asset has become of negligible value. However, the Revenue permits a claim to take effect up to two tax years prior to the claim provided the asset was of negligible value in the prior year (see ESC D28).

In practice it is not always beneficial for an individual to claim the ESC D28 benefit, or indeed for a claim to be made, until such time as there are gains against which the loss can be set (see 13.1.3).

13.6 HOW GAINS MAY BE DEFERRED OR 'ROLLED OVER'
(TCGA 1992, ss 164A-164N)

A roll-over relief was available up to 5 April 1998 whereby an individual (or trustee) who realised a gain on the disposal of an asset of any description could roll over the gain if he reinvested it in shares in a qualifying unquoted trading company. Where gains were rolled over they were not charged to tax, but the gain was deducted from the cost of acquiring the new asset (ie the unquoted shares).

An example of this relief would be if *J* sold quoted shares and realised a gain of £150,000. Provided he reinvested at least £150,000 in qualifying unquoted shares and claimed roll-over relief, the gain was not chargeable at all. If he reinvested only £95,000, the chargeable gain was limited to £55,000.

This relief is dealt with in detail at 17.4. From 6 April 1998, a similar relief is available under the EIS (see 11.6 on EIS CGT deferral relief) and also in respect of VCTs.

13.7 SALES OF SHARES TO ALL-EMPLOYEE SHARE TRUSTS
(TCGA 1992, Sched 7C)

Where an individual transfers unquoted shares to trustees who hold them for employees under an approved all-employee share scheme (see 4.12), the individual may roll over any capital gain arising from this transfer provided he reinvests in chargeable assets within six months. The all-employee trust must acquire at least a 10% interest in the company. The chargeable assets into which the individual's gain is rolled over cannot consist of shares in the company concerned or a property that is exempt as the individual's main residence.

13.8 HOLD-OVER RELIEF WHERE A GIFT IS A CHARGEABLE TRANSFER FOR IHT PURPOSES
(TCGA 1992, s 260)

Where a gift or a sale at an undervalue is a chargeable transfer for IHT purposes, and the donee is UK-resident, the donor and donee can elect for any gain to be held over. This generally means that the asset is deemed to pass across to the donee on a no gain/no loss basis but with the donee inheriting the donor's acquisition cost.

You should obtain a copy of Helpsheet IR295 if you make such a chargeable transfer.

Section 260 relief is not available where the gift is a potentially exempt transfer for IHT purposes (see 19.6).

14

THE CALCULATION OF CAPITAL GAINS

The computation of a capital gain (or loss) is more complicated than it looks. Basically, a gain (or loss) is the difference between the disposal value and the original cost after certain expenses, allowances and deductions have been taken into account. However, there are a number of variables. This chapter deals with the following aspects:

(1) Amount to be brought in as disposal value.
(2) What costs are allowable?
(3) Assets held at 31 March 1982 and 6 April 1965.
(4) Other acquisition values.
(5) Taper relief.
(6) What is a 'business asset' for taper relief purposes?
(7) Indexation
(8) Earn-outs.

14.1 AMOUNT TO BE BROUGHT IN AS DISPOSAL VALUE

14.1.1 Market value

(TCGA 1992, s 17)

The general rule is that market value must be used unless the transaction is at arm's length. In the straightforward situation where a contract is entered into with a third party on a commercial basis, the disposal proceeds are the actual sale proceeds. An individual is not penalised because he has made a bad bargain and sold an asset for less than it is really worth. However, if the bargain is not at arm's length and the individual deliberately sells the asset for an amount less than its true value, the legislation requires market value to be substituted. If the disposal is to a connected person, for example a relative or the trustee of a family settlement or a family company, there is an automatic assumption that the bargain is not at arm's length and market value is always substituted for the actual sale proceeds if the two amounts are different. There are three exceptions:

(1) Transactions between spouses (see 13.1.2).
(2) Gifts to charities and similar bodies (see 13.4.2).
(3) Situations where a hold-over election can be made (see 17.5).

14.1.2 Contingent liabilities

(TCGA 1992, s 49)

There may be occasions where the contract may require part of the proceeds to be returned at some time in the future. This is known as a sale with 'contingent liabilities'.

Suppose a vendor receives £150,000 for the disposal of a plot of land, but is under an obligation to return £60,000 in certain circumstances. Will the capital gain be charged on sale proceeds of £150,000 or £90,000? In fact, s 49 provides that in these circumstances the capital gain must be computed in the first instance without any deduction for the contingent liability. However, if and when the vendor is required to refund part of the sale proceeds because the contingent liability has become an actual liability, the CGT assessment is adjusted accordingly.

14.1.3 Contingent consideration: quantifiable

(TCGA 1992, s 48)

In a similar way, it is possible that the contract may provide that additional sums may be payable if certain conditions are satisfied in the future. If it is possible to put a value on the further amount of consideration that is 'contingent' (ie payable only if certain conditions are satisfied), the full amount that may be received is brought into account at the date of disposal without any discount. If the conditions are not satisfied, so that the further amounts are never received, an adjustment is made later to the CGT assessment.

14.1.4 Contingent consideration: unquantifiable

The position is different where the contingent consideration cannot be ascertained at the date of disposal (this is normally the situation where the contingent consideration may vary and is not a fixed amount). Basically, the legislation requires that the market value of the right to receive the future consideration should be regarded as the disposal proceeds. The difference between this amount and the amount eventually received forms a separate CGT computation for the year in which the final amount of the actual contingent consideration is determined. The treatment of contingent consideration, especially variable contingent consideration, is fairly complex. It normally arises in relation to either land or shares in private companies. This is an area where it is essential to take professional advice. However, see 14.8 on earn-outs.

14.1.5 Deduction for amounts charged as income

(TCGA 1992, s 31)

In some cases the disposal of an asset may give rise to an income tax charge. Where this happens, the amount taken into account in arriving at taxable income is deducted from the sale proceeds and only the balance is brought into account for CGT purposes. This commonly arises where a private company buys back its own shares and the transaction is treated as a distribution (see 7.9.7).

14.2 WHAT COSTS ARE ALLOWABLE?

14.2.1 Certain specific types of expenditure

The legislation permits only a limited range of expenses to be deducted in computing capital gains and losses. TCGA 1992, s 38(1) states:

> the sums allowable as a deduction from the consideration in the computation of the gain accruing to a person on the disposal of an asset shall be restricted to:
>
> (a) the amount of value of the consideration, in money or money's worth, given by him or on his behalf wholly and exclusively for the acquisition of the asset, together with the incidental costs to him of the acquisition or, if the asset was not acquired by him, any expenditure wholly and exclusively incurred by him in providing the asset,
>
> (b) the amount of any expenditure wholly and exclusively incurred on the asset by him or on his behalf for the purpose of enhancing the value of the asset, being expenditure reflected in the state or nature of the asset at the time of the disposal, and any expenditure wholly and exclusively incurred by him in establishing, preserving or defending his title to, or to a right over, the asset,
>
> (c) the incidental costs to him of making the disposal.

14.2.2 The cost of the asset

The asset's market value at 31 March 1982 or 6 April 1965 may be substituted for actual cost if the asset was held at those dates (see 14.3.1 and 14.3.4).

14.2.3 Incidental costs of acquisition

These are limited to:

(1) fees, commission or remuneration paid to a surveyor, valuer, auctioneer, accountant, agent or legal adviser;
(2) transfer/conveyancing charges (including stamp duty); and
(3) advertising to find a seller.

14.2.4 Enhancement expenditure

The legislation permits a deduction to be claimed in respect of expenditure incurred in order to enhance the asset's value provided such expenditure is reflected in the state or nature of the asset at the time of disposal. The latter condition excludes relief for improvements that have worn out by the time the asset is disposed of. Certain grey areas are worth mentioning:

(1) Initial expenditure by way of repairs to newly acquired property that is let may be allowable if no relief has been given in computing Schedule A income.
(2) Expenditure means money or money's worth; it does not include the value of personal labour or skill.

14.2.5 Expenditure incurred in establishing, preserving or defending legal title

The case-law concerned with the allowable nature of this expenditure hinges on the interrelationship between the words 'incurred', 'establishing', etc. The High Court held in *IRC v Richards' Executors* (1971) 46 TC 626 that the cost of making an inventory and providing a valuation for a grant of probate was allowable under this head (see SP8/94).

14.2.6 Incidental costs of disposals

The following expenses may be deductible under this head:

(1) Fees, commission or remuneration for the professional services of a surveyor, valuer, auctioneer, accountant, agent or legal adviser.
(2) Transfer/conveyancing charges (including stamp duty).
(3) Advertising to find a buyer.
(4) Any other costs reasonably incurred in making any valuation or apportionment for CGT purposes, including in particular expenses reasonably incurred in ascertaining market value where this is required. Professional costs incurred in getting a valuation agreed with the Revenue are not allowable.

14.2.7 Part disposals

(TCGA 1992, s 42)

Where a person disposes of part of an asset, the cost is apportioned between the part disposed of and the part retained according to the formula [A ÷ (A + B)] where A is the consideration received or deemed to have been received and B is the market value of the part retained.

Example – Part disposals

B holds 1,000 shares in XYZ Ltd that cost him £10,000. The company is taken over and he receives cash of £5,000 and convertible loan stock issued by the acquiring company worth £15,000 (assume that in this particular case no capital gain arises in respect of the loan stock because it is issued on the occasion of a takeover and the necessary Revenue clearances have been obtained (see 13.5.5 and 15.1.3)). *B*'s acquisition value will be apportioned as follows:

$$£10{,}000 \times \frac{5{,}000}{5{,}000 + 15{,}000} = £2{,}500,$$

ie the proportion of acquisition value that relates to the part sold. £7,500 is treated as the acquisition value of the part retained, ie it will be taken into account in computing any gain or loss as and when the loan stock is sold.

Special rules may apply where shares are sold out of a shareholding that includes shares held on 31 March 1982 and shares acquired after that date (see 15.1.3).

14.2.8 Small capital receipts

(TCGA 1992, s 122)

There are occasions where the formula [A ÷ (A + B)] does not have to be used, and the amount received is simply deducted from the owner's acquisition value. The most common situation where this arises is where a shareholder sells his entitlement under a rights issue, normally on a nil paid basis. Provided the amount received is less than £3,000 or is small as compared with the asset's value, the receipt can be deducted from the owner's acquisition value. 'Small' in this context is interpreted by the Revenue to be an amount not exceeding 5% of the market value.

14.2.9 Capital sums applied in restoring assets

(TCGA 1992, s 23)

Under normal circumstances, an asset is regarded as having been disposed of for CGT purposes if it is lost or destroyed. However, where a capital sum is received from such an asset (eg insurance policy proceeds), the owner may claim that the asset is not treated as disposed of if at least 95% of the capital sum is spent in restoring the asset.

14.3 ASSETS HELD AT 31 MARCH 1982 AND 6 APRIL 1965

(TCGA 1992, s 35 and Scheds 2-3)

14.3.1 General rebasing

(TCGA 1992, s 35)

The general rule is that where assets were held at 31 March 1982, it is to be assumed that they were sold on that date and immediately reacquired at their market value at that time. This is known as 'rebasing'.

The resulting gain or loss is then compared with the gain or loss calculated by reference to the original cost, with the following consequences:

Original cost	*March '82 value*	*For CGT*
Gain	Gain	The lower gain is assessed
Loss	Loss	The lower loss is allowed
Loss	Gain	Nil assessed – no gain/loss
Gain	Loss	Nil assessed – no gain/loss

However, original cost is ignored altogether if a universal rebasing election has been made.

14.3.2 Universal rebasing election

(TCGA 1992, s 35(5))

If a person so elects, the rebasing rule is applied to all disposals made by him of assets held on 31 March 1982. In other words, original cost is ignored completely, and regard is had only for the value of the assets held at that date. In some cases, making this election will mean that losses can be claimed that would not otherwise be available (because of the no gain/no loss rule).

A universal rebasing election is precisely that. If the election is made the rebasing rule is applied to all assets held at 31 March 1982. Furthermore, once made, the election is irrevocable.

There is a time limit for making the election. The legislation requires it to be made within two years of the end of the year of assessment in which a disposal first takes place of assets that were held at both 6 April 1988 and 31 March 1982. If no election has been made and assets held at 31 March 1982 have been disposed of during the period 6 April 1988 to 5 April 1998, it is now too late to make the election.

Married persons

The election may be made by each spouse separately. Where an asset passes from one spouse to another and the spouse who received it subsequently disposes of it, the gain or loss on that particular asset is governed by whether the spouse who transferred the asset had made the universal rebasing election.

14.3.3 Time apportionment for assets held at 6 April 1965

(TCGA 1992, Sched 2, para 16)

Special rules apply to the disposal of assets that were held at 6 April 1965, and where a universal rebasing election has not been made and the assets concerned are not quoted shares or land with development value.

When CGT was first introduced in 1965, it was recognised that it would be unfair to charge tax on capital gains that had accrued before that date. For assets other than shares that were quoted at 6 April 1965 and land that (either at that time or subsequently) had development value, taxpayers were given the general right to compute gains on the basis that the appreciation had occurred at a uniform rate and to exclude the part relating to the period before 6 April 1965. This is known as the 'time apportionment' basis. The capital gain computed on this basis is arrived at by using the following formula:

$$\text{Overall gain} \times \frac{\text{Period between 6 April 1965 and date of disposal}}{\text{Total period of ownership}}$$

For example, if an asset had been acquired in, say, April 1960 and sold for an overall gain of £40,000 in April 2003, the time apportionment formula would produce the following result:

$$£40{,}000 \times \frac{\text{April 1965 to April 2003 (38 years)}}{\text{April 1960 to April 2003 (43 years)}}$$

ie a chargeable gain of £35,349. When using this formula, the fraction should be calculated by reference to months of ownership and the divisor cannot reflect a period prior to 6 April 1945.

Where land has development value at the date of disposal, it is not possible to time apportion the capital gain. One must either use the land's market value at 6 April 1965 or its value at 31 March 1982.

14.3.4 Market value at 6 April 1965

There may be circumstances where the fact that no universal rebasing election has been made means that an asset's market value at 6 April 1965 can or must be used instead of original cost.

Quoted shares

Where an election was made under TCGA 1992, Sched 2, para 4 in respect of quoted securities held on 6 April 1965, either in respect of equity investments or fixed interest investments, all the securities falling into that particular category are deemed to have been disposed of and reacquired on 6 April 1965 so that the original cost is not relevant. This election would normally have been made some years ago as the deadline was two years after the first relevant disposal that took place after 19 March 1968.

Unquoted shares and other assets

In this situation, capital gains are calculated on the time apportionment basis unless a specific election is made within two years of the disposal date, in which case the gain is computed by reference to the asset's market value at 6 April 1965.

In practice, this election is beneficial only where the asset's market value at 6 April 1965 was higher than its value at 31 March 1982.

14.3.5 Assets acquired via a gift made between 1 April 1982 and 5 April 1988

(TCGA 1992, Sched 4)

This section may be relevant where all of the following conditions are satisfied:

(1) The asset was acquired as a gift or transfer from a trust during the period 1 April 1982 to 5 April 1988.
(2) The donor held the asset at 31 March 1982.
(3) The donor claimed hold-over relief so that the recipient was deemed to have acquired the asset at the donor's original cost.

When rebasing was first introduced, it was recognised that it would be unfair not to permit some relief where an asset had been transferred prior to 6 April 1988 and the gain had been held over. The person who received such a gift cannot claim rebasing because he did not own the gifted asset at 31 March 1982. To give rough and ready compensation for this, the legislation included provisions so that when the recipient of such a gift made a disposal after 5 April 1988, half of the held-over gain could be 'forgiven' or left out of account.

Example – Transfer prior to 6 April 1988 with held-over gain

P received a gift of shares in August 1986 from his father *Q*. At the time of the gift, the shares were worth £180,000. *Q*'s acquisition value was only £40,000, and indexation (see 14.7) amounted to £10,000. This would normally have meant that *Q* would have had a chargeable gain of £130,000. However, he made a claim under the legislation prevailing at the time that permitted the capital gain to be held over. This meant that *Q* did not suffer a CGT charge, but *P* was deemed to have acquired the assets with an acquisition value as follows:

	£
Market value at date of gift	180,000
Less: held-over gain	(130,000)
Acquisition value	50,000

When *P* disposes of the asset, his acquisition value is increased by 50% of £130,000 so that his acquisition value becomes £115,000.

14.3.6 Relief not automatic

A formal claim for the relief described in 14.3.5 must be made within one year and ten months of the end of the tax year in which the recipient makes his disposal.

14.4 OTHER ACQUISITION VALUES

14.4.1 Assets acquired via inheritance or family trust (TCGA 1992, ss 62 and 71)

Where a person inherits an asset, he is generally deemed to have acquired it for its market value at the date of the testator's death (ie probate value). There is one exception to this: it is possible to claim a form of relief from IHT where quoted securities have gone down in value after the person has died (see 19.11.3). Where such relief has been claimed for IHT, a corresponding adjustment is made so that the person taking the assets concerned is deemed to have acquired them not at probate value, but at the value actually brought into account for IHT purposes after taking account of the fall in value.

Where assets have been acquired from a trust, the beneficiary's acquisition value is normally the market value at the time the asset is transferred to him. However, the acquisition value may be lower than this where the trustees have claimed hold-over relief under either the general hold-over relief provisions that prevailed up to 5 April 1989 or the more restrictive provisions that have applied subsequently (see 17.5).

14.4.2 Deemed acquisition value where income tax charged (TCGA 1992, ss 120 and 141)

Where a person is subject to a Schedule E income tax charge when he acquires an asset (eg where he exercises a non-approved share option), he is deemed to have acquired it for an amount equal to the value taken into account in computing a Schedule E charge on him. Similarly, where a person acquires shares by way of a stock dividend (ie where there is a choice between a cash dividend or further shares issued by a UK company), the shares are deemed to be acquired for a consideration equal to the amount brought into account for income tax purposes by reason of the stock dividend (see further 7.8.6).

14.4.3 Share options exercised up to 9 April 2003

A 2002 decision by the Court of Appeal in the case of *Mansworth v Jelley* [2002] STC 1013 revealed an anomaly. The Court held that where an employee acquired shares by exercising an option, his acquisition cost was market value at that date *plus* an amount equal to the sum on which he was assessed for income tax purposes. This amounts to a form of 'double-counting' and generally meant that a CGT loss would arise on the sale of those shares.

This anomaly was corrected in relation to share options exercised after 8 April 2003 but the amending legislation was not retrospective. You should take professional advice if you exercised such options.

Table 14.1 – Computing your capital gains before taper relief

Sale proceeds (consider whether the market value provisions may apply) – see 14.1).	A	
Deduct incidental costs of disposal (see 14.2).	B	
Net sale proceeds (A – B).		C
If the asset was acquired after 31 March 1982, enter cost.	D	
Amount of any enhancement expenditure.	E	
If the asset was owned at 31 March 1982 and a universal rebasing election is in force, enter value at 31 March 1982 (see 14.3).	F	
If the asset was owned at 31 March 1982, but no universal rebasing election is in force, enter cost or value at 31 March 1982, whichever is the higher.[1]	G	
Enter the amount of enhancement expenditure – if 31 March 1982 value is entered at F or G, include only post-31 March 1982 enhancement expenditure.	H	
Enter the total of figures entered in any of D to H.		I
Unindexed gain (C – I).		J
Indexation relief on figure in D, F or G (see 14.7).	K	
Indexation relief on figure in E or H.[2]	L	
Enter total of K and L.		M
Deduct M from J. The result is the indexed gain.		N

[1]Note that there will not be an allowable loss if there is an overall gain taking the original cost, but a loss taking the 31 March 1982 value.
[2]The figure of indexation relief cannot exceed the figure at J, except in relation to assets disposed of prior to 30 November 1993.

14.4.4 Working out your gains

Table 14.1 can be used as a 'pro forma' when calculating capital gains or losses.

14.5 TAPER RELIEF

14.5.1 Introduction

One of the most significant changes to the CGT legislation was the introduction in 1998 of taper relief, which replaced indexation allowance (see 14.7). The main attraction of taper relief over indexation allowance is that it reduces the amount of the gain regardless of base cost. Another attraction is that employee shares generally qualify as business assets. FA 2002 changes mean that capital gains on such shares may be subject to an effective tax rate of only 10% once the shares have been held for two years.

For gains realised on or after 6 April 1998, indexation allowance is given for periods up to April 1998, but not thereafter. Where an asset was held at 6 April 1998 and disposed of after that date, indexation allowance is computed only for the period from the date of acquisition (or the date the expenditure was incurred) to April 1998. For assets acquired on or after 5 April 1998, no indexation allowance is available to reduce the chargeable gain.

The taper reduces the amount of the chargeable gain according to how long the asset has been held for periods after 5 April 1998. The taper is more generous for business than for non-business assets.

Taper relief is given on the net gains that are chargeable after deduction of indexation allowance and any capital losses realised in the same tax year or brought forward from previous years. Where an individual has gains that attract no taper relief, losses are set against those first to produce the lowest tax charge.

14.5.2 Period of ownership

Taper relief operates as follows in respect of periods of ownership after 5 April 1998:

(1) where there has been a transfer of an asset between spouses, the taper relief on a subsequent disposal is based on the combined period of holding by both spouses;
(2) for other no gain/no loss transfers, taper relief is given by reference to the period of ownership only of the new owner;
(3) where a shareholding is increased by a bonus issue, taper relief is given by reference to the date the original shares were acquired;
(4) where shares are acquired through a rights issue or other reorganisation, they are treated as if they were acquired when the original shares were acquired;
(5) where a relief defers the gain on a disposal until a later occasion (eg the relief on reinvestment in a VCT), the taper relief on the deferred gain relates to the period during which the person owned the original asset (there is an exception to this where EIS shares issued after 5 April 1999 are sold for a gain and the gain is reinvested in new EIS shares); and
(6) where gains have been relieved under a provision that reduces the cost of a replacement asset (eg roll-over relief for business assets), the taper relief operates by reference to the period of ownership of the new asset.

14.5.3 Non-business assets

The rates of taper relief on non-business assets acquired before 17 March 1998 are:

Number of complete years of ownership	*Taper relief (%)*
Less than 3	nil
3	5
4	10
5	15
6	20
7	25
8	30
9	35
10	40

Assets acquired before 17 March 1998 qualify for an addition of one year to the period for which they are treated as held after 5 April 1998. This addition is the same for all assets, whenever they were actually acquired. So an asset purchased on 1 January 1998 and disposed of on 1 July 2000 is treated for taper relief purposes as if it had been held for three years (two complete years after 5 April 1998 plus one additional year). Therefore, a non-business asset held at 17 March 1998 did not qualify for any taper relief until 6 April 2000 and qualified for 5% taper if sold in 2000-01.

14.5.4 Taper relief on business assets up to 5 April 2000

The rate of taper relief was originally 7.5% for each complete year of ownership plus an extra year's relief where the asset was held on 17 March 1998.

14.5.5 Taper relief on business assets disposed of between 5 April 2000 and 5 April 2002

The rate of taper relief in respect of business assets altered significantly in FA 2000. For business assets disposed after 5 April 2000, taper relief was calculated according to the following table:

Complete years of ownership	*Taper relief* %	*Effective tax rate for 40% taxpayer* %
1	12.5	35
2	25	30
3	50	20

For these purposes, the period 17 March to 5 April 1998 no longer gave rise to a bonus year.

14.5.6 Taper relief on business assets disposed of after 5 April 2002

The Government has reduced the period of ownership needed for full taper relief to two years. For business assets disposed of after 6 April 2002, taper relief is now calculated according to the following table:

Complete years of ownership	*Taper relief* %	*Effective tax rate for 40% taxpayer* %
1	50	20
2	75	10

14.6 WHAT IS A 'BUSINESS ASSET' FOR TAPER RELIEF PURPOSES?

As explained at 14.5, taper relief may reduce a chargeable gain realised after 5 April 1998. The rate of taper relief depends on whether the asset sold is regarded as a business asset.

14.6.1 Basic definition of 'business assets'

A 'business asset' is defined broadly as:

(1) Shares and securities held by the individual in a qualifying company.
(2) An asset used by a qualifying company for the purposes of its trade.
(3) An asset held for the purposes of a qualifying office or employment
(4) An asset used for the purposes of a trade carried on by the individual (whether alone or in partnership).

The rules in (4) have remained fairly constant since 1998 and we deal with such assets at 14.6.9.

14.6.2 Definition of 'qualifying company' from 6 April 2000

Different rules apply according to whether the company is quoted.

All shares in unquoted trading companies qualify as business assets. AIM counts as unquoted. However, a company that is controlled by a quoted company is regarded as a quoted company for these purposes.

Furthermore, all shares in quoted trading companies are business assets if the individual is employed (full- or part-time) by the company concerned.

If an individual is employed by a non-trading company and he does not have a material interest in that company (10% or more), his shares also qualify as business assets.

Where an individual is not employed by a quoted trading company, his shares still qualify as business assets if he has at least 5% of the voting rights. This also covers trustees who hold a 5% interest.

Table 14.2 – Defining a qualifying company

Is the company a trading company or the holding company of a trading group?	*Is the company listed?*	*Is the individual an officer or employee of the company or of a connected company?*	*6 April 1998 to 5 April 2000*	*From 6 April 2000 (per Finance Act 2000)*	*From 6 April 2000 (per Finance Act 2001)*
Yes	Yes	Yes	Business asset – if the individual was a full-time working officer/employee and held 5% of the voting rights	Business asset	Business asset
Yes	Yes	No	Business asset if the individual held 25% of the voting rights Non-business asset otherwise	Business asset if the individual held 5% of the voting rights Non-business asset otherwise	Business asset if the individual held 5% of the voting rights Non-business asset otherwise
Yes	No	Yes	Business asset – if the individual was a full-time working officer/employee and held 5% of the voting rights	Business asset	Business asset
Yes	No	No	Business asset – if the individual held 25% of the voting rights Non-business asset otherwise	Business asset	Business asset
No	Yes	Yes	Non-business asset	Non-business asset	Business asset if no material interest Non-business asset otherwise
No	Yes	No	Non-business asset	Non-business asset	Non-business asset
No	No	Yes	Non-business asset	Non-business asset	Business asset if no material interest Non-business asset otherwise
No	No	No	Non-Business asset	Non-Business asset	Non-Business asset

Shares in an unquoted company that exists in order to hold shares in a joint venture company can also qualify as business assets.

Table 14.2 can be used to define a qualifying company.

14.6.3 Definition in force up to 5 April 2000

A company was a qualifying company if it was a trading company, or a holding company of a trading group, and the individual met one of the following tests:

(1) he was a full-time officer or employee of that company and his shares gave him at least 5% of the voting rights; or
(2) where he did not meet the full-time condition, his shares gave him 25% of the voting rights in the company.

14.6.4 Shares held prior to 6 April 2000 sold after that date

Where shares did not qualify under the old rules, a capital gain will be time apportioned and business taper will apply only to the post-5 April 2000 proportion of the capital gain.

Example

S works for X plc and on 6 October 2002 he realises a gain of £45,000 on selling X plc shares. These shares did not qualify as business assets until 6 April 2000 as *S* did not meet the 5% requirement.

The gain is time apportioned and the proportion found by the following formula attracts business taper relief:

$$\frac{\text{6 April 2000 – 6 October 2002}}{\text{6 April 1998 – 6 October 2002}} \quad \text{ie} \quad \frac{30}{54} \quad \text{months}$$

S therefore gets 75% taper on £25,000.

The remainder of the gain (ie £20,000) attracts non-business taper relief based on five qualifying years of ownership because of the bonus year.

14.6.5 Definition of 'trading company'

A company must exist to carry on a trade and must not exist to any substantial extent for any other purpose, for example holding investments. In practice, the Revenue accepts that a trading company can invest surplus cash while it looks for suitable opportunities to invest the money in its trade. Where longer-term investments are held, the Revenue is likely to regard them as substantial if they exceed 20% of the company's net worth. Some guidance is given in *Tax Bulletin* June 2001. This is an area where specialist advice may be required.

14.6.6 Apportionment of gain

Where shares in a company do not qualify as business assets for the whole period of ownership since 6 April 1998 (eg because the company infringed the 20% test described in 14.6.5), the gain needs to be time apportioned and business taper relief is due for the proportion relating to the period when the shares qualified.

14.6.7 Companies that hold investments in a joint venture company

The rules have changed on several occasions. Originally shares in such a company did not qualify as a business asset. From 6 April 2000, a company could be regarded as a trading company if

(1) it existed in order to hold shares in a joint venture company;
(2) at least 75% of the shares in the joint venture company were owned by five or fewer companies; and
(3) the company owned at least 30% of the joint venture company's shares.

From 17 April 2002, the requirements are that

(a) the company existed to hold shares in the joint venture company;
(b) at least 75% of the shares in the joint venture company are owned by five or fewer persons (not necessarily companies); and
(c) the company owns at least 10% of the joint venture company's shares.

The changes made from 6 April 2000 and 17 April 2002 do not apply retrospectively.

14.6.8 Shares or securities may include loan notes and debentures

Where an individual holds loan notes issued by a company, they may attract taper relief provided they are securities and are not qualifying corporate bonds (see 22.10). Furthermore, if the company is an unquoted trading company or is a quoted trading company that employs the individual, the loan notes may in certain circumstances attract taper relief at the business rate.

Bear in mind that a company that is a subsidiary of a quoted company is regarded as being a quoted company for taper relief, so the business taper relief will normally be available only if the company that has issued the loan notes is neither a quoted company nor a subsidiary of a quoted company or the individual is employed by the group. It is, however, possible that certain loan notes issued by subsidiaries of quoted companies may have qualified as business assets up to 17 April 2002.

FA 2002 changed the legislation retrospectively so that debentures and loan notes that are issued on company take-overs may be regarded as securities for taper relief purposes even though they may not meet the criteria for being regarded as securities for other CGT purposes. This retrospective change was beneficial as such debentures would otherwise not have attracted taper relief.

14.6.9 Assets used by individual's qualifying company

An extremely wide range of assets can qualify. The most common example is land and buildings used in the business. Sometimes an individual owns goodwill, but the business is carried on by his company.

The status of such an asset as a business asset is not jeopardised by the owner charging rent (eg where he lets premises to a qualifying company for use in its trade).

Up to 5 April 2000, the assets will have counted as business assets only if the individual held 5% of the voting shares and worked for the company on a full-time basis or the individual held at least 25% of the voting shares.

14.6.10 Mixed use

Where an asset has been used as a part business/part non-business asset, the gain on the its disposal is apportioned pro rata. Part of the gain qualifies for the business asset taper relief and the other part for the non-business asset taper relief. A switch to non-business asset use during the last ten years of ownership will always adversely affect the taper.

Example of taper relief in case of mixed use

T acquired a freehold office in 1996. The offices were rented out as an investment until 5 April 2001. The office were then used by his qualifying company until 30 September 2004 when they were sold, realising a chargeable gain (after indexation to April 1998) of £325,000.

For taper relief the relevant period is from 6 April 1998 to 30 September 2004, ie 6.5 years. During this period the office was a non-business asset for 3 years (April 1998 to April 2001) and a business asset for the remaining 3.5 years. Therefore 3/6.5 of the gain is charged as a non-business asset (£150,000) with the balance as a business asset. As the asset was held prior to 17 March 1998 it qualifies for the one-year addition in respect of the non-business portion.

	Non-business asset	*Business asset*	*Total*
	£	£	£
Chargeable gains	150,000	175,000	325,000
Deduct taper relief 25%/75%	37,500	131,250	168,750
Taxable gains (before annual exemption)	112,500	43,750	156,250

Note that if there were allowable losses for the year they would be set firstly against the gain attracting the lower rate of taper relief.

14.6.11 FA 2003 – Business taper to be extended from 6 April 2004

The most important point is that everything which qualifies as a business asset under the current rules will continue to qualify under the new rules. The good news is that certain situations not covered by the current rules will qualify from 6 April 2004.

These borderline situations not covered by the current rules involve assets owned by individuals, trustees and personal representatives where they are used for the purposes of a trade carried on by:

- any individual, or any partnership which has an individual as a member;
- the trustees of any settlement, or any partnership whose members include any person acting in the capacity of a trustee of a settlement;
- the personal representatives of any deceased person, or any partnership whose members include any person acting in the capacity of a personal representative;
- a partnership whose members include a company which is a 'qualifying company' by reference to the owner of the asset; or
- a partnership whose members include a company which belongs to a trading group whose holding company is a qualifying company by reference to the owner of the asset.

The term 'qualifying company' includes all unlisted trading companies and unlisted holding companies of trading groups. The new measure will not make any changes to the rules for qualifying companies.

14.7 INDEXATION

(TCGA 1992, ss 53-57)

Indexation was a relief which gives an allowance for inflation up to April 1998.

A person who makes a capital gain is allowed to deduct not only his actual acquisition value, but also a proportion that represents the increase in the RPI between the month of acquisition and the month of disposal. The formula used is [(RD – RI) ÷ RI] where:

RD = RPI in month of disposal or April 1998, whichever is the earlier;
RI = RPI for March 1982 or month in which expenditure incurred, whichever is the later.

Note that where the date of disposal is after 30 April 1998, indexation allowance is given only by reference to the April 1998 figure because of the introduction of taper relief from 1998-99 (see 14.5).

Example

> *S* acquired shares in X plc on 1 June 1991 for £20,000. She sells them in June 1999 for £30,000. She has a capital gain of £10,000 before indexation, and a gain of £5,740 after taking indexation into account. The indexation relief is computed as follows:
>
> $$\text{Cost £20,000} \times \frac{\text{RPI for April 1998} - \text{RPI for June 1991}}{\text{RPI for June 1991}}$$
>
> That is £20,000 × (162.6 – 134.1 ÷ 134.1) = £20,000 × 0.213 = £4,260. The RPI figures are set out in Table 32.8 (pp. 635-6).

14.7.1 Restriction to indexation relief
(FA 1994, s 93)

Indexation relief may only reduce or extinguish a gain; it cannot convert a gain into a loss or increase a loss.

Examples of restriction

Acquisition cost £4,000, indexation allowance £750.

	£	£	£
Sale proceeds	5,000	4,500	3,000
Less: Cost	(4,000)	(4,000)	(4,000)
Unindexed gain/(loss)	1,000	500	(1,000)
Indexation allowance	(750)	(500)	Nil
Chargeable gain/(capital loss)	250	Nil	(1,000)

A different rule applied up to the November 1993 Budget, so that indexation relief could have created or increased a loss in relation to transactions prior to 30 November 1993.

14.8 EARN-OUTS

Earn-outs can create a problem, as already touched on in 14.1.2.

An earn-out is where a person sells shares and part of the consideration is dependent on the company's subsequent performance. For example, an individual might sell his private company for £1m cash plus a further amount based on the company achieving certain profit targets for the next three years.

The right to receive further cash if the profit targets are achieved is a valuable one, but its value will not normally be the maximum sum: it depends on whether the targets will be achieved. The case-law (*Marren v Ingles*) indicates that a present (discounted) value should be ascertained and this should be included as part of the sale consideration that is taxable for the year in which the sale takes place. When the earn-out period is over, and the actual amount due under the earn-out is known, a further capital gain (or loss) occurs for the year in which the entitlement is ascertained.

This has meant that a person who is entitled to receive an earn-out could be taxed on sums that he never in fact received. Fortunately, there is a way of avoiding this. Provided the sale contract specifies that the earn-out consideration must be satisfied by the acquiring company issuing securities or debentures (eg loan notes), and provided the person entitled to the earn-out makes an election under TCGA 1992, s 138A, there is no question of anything being taxed in respect of the earn-out until the person makes a disposal of the securities that he receives in satisfaction of his rights to the earn-out.

The s 138A election must be made within 22 months of the end of the tax year in which the person enters into a contract under which he may receive an earn-out.

14.8.1 New CGT treatment for earn-outs

Twenty-three years after the House of Lords decided *Marren v Ingles* [1980] STC 500 in favour of the Revenue, the Chancellor tackled the problem in his 2003 Budget.

There is now a carry-back relief whereby a vendor who has been taxed on a higher amount than he eventually receives may carry back the difference as a loss. In other words, the end result is that he will pay CGT only on the amount that he actually collects.

This new relief will apply only to earn-out rights disposed of after 9 April 2003.

15

MORE COMPLEX CALCULATIONS FOR CERTAIN TYPES OF ASSET

The last chapter dealt with basic CGT calculations; this chapter deals with the following:

(1) How gains are computed on quoted securities.
(2) When may a chargeable gain arise on foreign currency?
(3) Special rules for disposals of chattels.
(4) Specific rules that apply to disposals of land and investment properties.
(5) How the Revenue computes gains on unquoted shares.
(6) Disposal of foreign property.
(7) Gains and losses on second-hand insurance policies.

15.1 HOW GAINS ARE COMPUTED ON QUOTED SECURITIES

'Quoted securities' means shares, loan stock, warrants, etc that are dealt in on the London Stock Exchange and other similar stock exchanges recognised by the Revenue as having similar rules and procedures to the London Exchange. This section deals with the tax treatment of transactions such as:

- Sale of part of a shareholding;
- Bonus issues and rights issues;
- Takeovers and mergers.

15.1.1 Identification rules

Specific rules apply where a person sells part of his holding in securities of the same class. Securities are treated as being of the same class if they are treated as such under Stock Exchange practice. For example, all ICI ordinary shares are securities of the same class, whereas BP ordinary shares are not and form a different class.

The identification rules for disposals after 5 April 1998 are that shares disposed of should be matched with:

(1) acquisitions made on the same day;
(2) acquisitions within the next 30 days: if more than one acquisition is made in this period they are dealt with on a FIFO basis, ie the first shares acquired are deemed to be the ones sold;

(3) acquisitions made after 5 April 1998 on a LIFO (last in first out) basis; and
(4) shares held in a 'pool' at 5 April 1998.

FA 2002 introduced an exception to the 'same day' rule. Where an employee acquires shares from more than one employee share scheme and sells some of those shares all on the same day, the employee will now be able to elect as to which shares have been sold.

15.1.2 Old identification rules may still be relevant

If you are working out the gains on sales of some of the shares that you held before 6 April 1998, you may still need to know the rules which previously applied. These are covered in 15.1.3 to 15.1.5.

15.1.3 Sale of part of shareholding up to 1997-98

(TCGA 1992, ss 104-109)

For most quoted securities, the general rule for 1997-98 and earlier years was that securities sold on a disposal of part of a shareholding were identified as follows:

(1) With securities of the same class acquired on or after 6 April 1982 deemed to form part of a 'new holding' (see below).
(2) With securities deemed to form part of a 1982 holding, ie securities held at 5 April 1982 other than those held at 6 April 1965.
(3) With other securities on a LIFO basis. This applied only where a universal rebasing election was not made (see 14.3.2).

15.1.4 Pooling

Any securities of the same class acquired on or after 6 April 1982 were 'pooled', ie treated as a single asset that grew or diminished as acquisitions and disposals were made. The technical term for this asset is a 'new holding' (to distinguish it from holdings at 31 March 1982).

Securities of the same class acquired for the first time after 5 April 1985 were pooled as a single asset in the same way.

Technically, the indexed cost of the pool had be recomputed every time there was an operative event, ie something that had the effect of either increasing or decreasing the qualifying expenditure.

Example – Securities acquired on or after 6 April 1982

A held 10,000 XYZ plc shares at 6 April 1985. They were all acquired in July 1984 at a cost of £3 per share. On 1 August 1989 she acquired a further 5,000 shares at a cost of £50,000 (£10 per share). Her new holding had an indexed cost computed as follows:

	£
10,000 shares cost July 1984	30,000
Indexation July 1984 to August 1989	9,000
	39,000
5,000 shares cost August 1989	50,000
Indexed cost of 15,000 shares at August 1989	89,000

If *A* sold 5,000 shares in November 1997 the calculation is:

	£
Indexed cost of pool at August 1989	89,000
Indexation August 1989 to November 1997	30,868
Indexed cost of 15,000 shares at November 1997	119,868

$\frac{5,000}{15,000}$ × £119,868 = Indexed cost of shares sold

$\frac{10,000}{15,000}$ × £119,868 (ie the balance) = the indexed cost of the remaining shares

Thus, the cost of the 5,000 shares sold would be taken as £39,956. *A* could not take as her cost the actual amount paid for the most recent acquisition of 5,000 shares.

1982 holdings

Similarly, an individual's shareholding at 6 April 1982 was also treated as a single asset the cost of which reduced as and when sales took place.

15.1.5 Bonus issues and rights issues before 6 April 1998

A bonus issue or rights issue was related to the shares that produced the entitlement.

Example

C had acquired 4,500 shares in XYZ plc between 1982 and 1995 and also holds 13,500 shares acquired before 5 April 1982. The company provides a scrip issue of one new share for every three shares held. *C* would therefore acquire 6,000 new shares free of charge of which a proportion would be treated as an addition to her new holding, with the balance being added to her 1982 holding, ie:

Addition to new holding	1,500 shares
Addition to 1982 holding	4,500 shares

Similarly, if *D* had a total of 40,000 shares in Y plc, which was made up of a new holding of 10,000 shares and a 1982 holding of 30,000 shares, and the company announced a rights issue in March 1997 of one new share at £2 for every existing share held, *D* might acquire 20,000 new shares at a cost of £40,000. Only the cost of the rights shares that related to his new holding of 10,000 shares could be added to the indexed cost of the new holding. The other rights shares would be treated as forming part of the 1982 holding.

Shareholders sometimes dispose of rights nil paid. Sums received for such disposals were normally deducted from the indexed pool cost unless (exceptionally) the amount received exceeded 5% of the shareholding's market value at the time of disposal (see 14.2.8).

15.1.6 Takeovers and mergers

There is a special relief that may apply where a company issues shares or securities in order to take over another company. The shareholders who accept this offer will not be treated as making a disposal provided they meet one of the following requirements:

(1) together with persons connected with them, they do not hold more than 5% of the company's share capital; or
(2) the Revenue is satisfied that the share exchange is a bona fide commercial transaction that is not entered into with a view to tax avoidance.

So far as quoted securities are concerned, the position is generally straightforward. The offer document forwarded to shareholders normally states whether clearance has been obtained from the Revenue under TCGA 1992, s 138 confirming that TCGA 1992, s 135 applies. Provided this is the case, no capital gain will arise on the exchange of shares for securities issued by the company making the takeovers.

What happens if there is a mixture of shares and cash?

Suppose a shareholder in X plc is offered a share in Y plc plus cash of £1 in exchange for every share that he holds in X plc. If he accepts this offer there will be a part disposal. The value of the new Y plc shares on the first day of trading is taken and the following computation is required:

Amount received via cash element	A
Take proportion of indexed cost of holding in X plc	
$\frac{\text{Cash received}}{\text{Cash + value of Y plc shares}} \times \text{Indexed cost}$	B
Capital gain/(loss) on cash element	C

What happens if there is a mixture of shares and loan stock?

Suppose the shareholder in X plc had instead accepted an offer of one share in Y plc plus £1.25 loan stock. Assume that when the new Y plc shares were first traded they had a price of £2 and the loan stock was traded at £80 for every £100 nominal. The cost of the two types of new securities would be determined like this:

Example – Takeover by mixture of shares and loan stock

Apportioned to Y plc shares:

$$\frac{\text{Value of Y shares}}{\text{Value of Y shares + Y loan stock}}$$

$$\text{ie} \quad \frac{£2}{£2 + £1} \times \text{Cost of X shares = deemed cost of Y shares}$$

Apportioned to Y plc loan stock:

$$\frac{\text{Value of loan stock}}{\text{Value of loan stock + shares}}$$

$$\text{ie} \quad \frac{£1}{£1 + £2} \times \text{Cost of X shares = Deemed cost of Y loan stock}$$

This division of the indexed cost of the original holding in X plc will be relevant as and when there is a disposal of either the Y plc shares or loan stock.

15.1.7 Special rules where share exchange involves qualifying corporate bonds

(TCGA 1992, s 116)

Loan stock is often a type of qualifying corporate bond (QCB), ie an exempt asset for CGT purposes (see 13.4.2). The offer document sent to shareholders on a company takeover normally draws attention to whether the loan stock falls into this category. If it does, the investor is not entitled to indexation relief for periods after the takeover. Furthermore, disposal of the loan stock creates a capital gain calculated according to values at the time of the takeover and not the loan stock's value at the time it is eventually sold or redeemed.

As a matter of fact, the deferred gain is triggered by any kind of disposal of the QCBs. For example, a gift of the loan stock causes the deferred gain to become chargeable. Indeed, a chargeable gain could even arise on a deemed disposal such as would apply if the company that had issued the loan stock went into liquidation.

15.2 WHEN MAY A CHARGEABLE GAIN ARISE ON FOREIGN CURRENCY?

There is an exemption for foreign currency provided it was acquired for an individual's personal expenditure abroad. In all other situations, foreign currency is a chargeable asset and a gain (or loss) will arise when the currency is disposed of. A disposal may take place on the foreign currency being spent, converted into another foreign currency, or converted into sterling. In each of these situations, the sterling equivalent of the foreign currency at the date of acquisition is compared with the sterling equivalent at the date of disposal.

In theory, each separate bank account denominated in foreign currency counts as a separate asset. In practice, the Revenue permits taxpayers to treat all bank accounts containing the particular foreign currency as one account (see SP10/84).

15.3 SPECIAL RULES FOR DISPOSALS OF CHATTELS

(TCGA 1992, s 262)

A chattel is defined by the legislation as a tangible, movable asset. Examples are a picture, a silver teapot and a first edition of a famous novel.

15.3.1 Chattels that are wasting assets

(TCGA 1992, s 45)

Special rules apply for chattels that fall within the definition of 'wasting assets'. These are assets with a useful life expectancy of less than 50 years. They are exempt regardless of the amount of the sale proceeds. Equally, there is no relief for any losses realised on their disposal.

This exemption is not available for an asset on which the owner was entitled to capital allowances because it had been used in a trade.

15.3.2 Other types of chattel

(TCGA 1992, s 262)

A gain arising on the disposal of a chattel not covered by the exemption in 15.3.1 is exempt only if the sale proceeds do not exceed £6,000. However, there is a form of marginal relief under which, if the sale proceeds are more than £6,000, the maximum chargeable gain cannot exceed five-thirds of the excess. For example, if a picture costing £900 is sold for £6,900, the chargeable gain cannot exceed $\frac{5}{3}$ × £900, ie £1,500.

In some cases the marginal relief will not help, for example if the sale proceeds were £6,900, but the picture had cost £5,800, the chargeable gain would be computed on normal principles.

Losses

A capital loss may arise on the disposal of a chattel. Where the sale proceeds are less than £6,000, the loss must be calculated on the basis that notional sale proceeds of £6,000 were received. For example, if an uninsured antique table costing £10,000 were destroyed by fire, the proceeds are taken to be £6,000, not nil.

Assets forming a set

Several chattels may be deemed to form a single asset, for example a set of antique chairs and a table. Where these are sold to the same person, or to persons acting in concert, they may be regarded as the disposal of a single asset. This rule may apply even though the sales take place at different times. As a consequence, gains that would otherwise be exempt because of the £6,000 limit may be brought into charge.

So, someone may own four antique chairs each worth £6,000. If they were to be sold one at a time to the same person, the total sale would be regarded as the sale of a single asset for £24,000 and the £6,000 exemption would not apply.

15.4 SPECIFIC RULES THAT APPLY TO DISPOSALS OF LAND AND INVESTMENT PROPERTIES

15.4.1 Will the gain be subject to income tax?

Speculative or short-term transactions in land may well give rise to a claim by the Inspector that the individual was dealing in land and therefore subject to tax under Schedule D Case I. Whether a trade is being carried on is a matter of fact. The Inspector may cite the following 'badges of trade' in support of an assessment under Schedule D Case I:

(1) Evidence that an asset was acquired with a view to its being resold in the short term.
(2) A large part of the purchase price being financed by borrowings, especially short-term borrowings such as an overdraft.
(3) The taxpayer has a background of similar transactions or has special expertise that assists in achieving a profit on disposal of the asset.

In *Kirkby v Hughes* [1993] STC 76, the court held that the taxpayer was carrying out a trade and the following were regarded as badges of trade:

(a) The properties were larger than would be expected for sole occupancy.
(b) The periods of occupancy were short.
(c) Another property was purchased while the taxpayer was still resident in the first without any clear intention of selling the first.

(d) There was no proof that the taxpayer had intended to acquire the first house as a personal asset.

Quite separately from the above, TA 1988, s 776 may enable the Inspector to assess a gain under Schedule D Case VI. Section 776 may apply where a capital gain is realised and UK land:

(i) was acquired with the sole or main object of realising a gain on its disposal; or
(ii) is developed with the sole or main object of realising a gain on the disposal of it when developed.

There are also circumstances where disposal of shares in a company that owns land may give rise to a Case VI assessment (see 22.2.3).

Section 776 can apply whether or not the person is UK-resident. Furthermore, the capital gain may be received by a third party and yet still give rise to an assessment under s 776 if an individual has transferred the opportunity of making a gain to the third party. Moreover, s 776 can apply to one or more transactions that form a scheme and any number of transactions may be regarded as constituting a single arrangement or scheme if a common purpose can be discerned in them, or if there is other sufficient evidence of a common purpose. For a fuller account of s 776, see 22.2.

The main disadvantage for a UK resident who is assessed to income tax on gains from land, under Schedule D Case I or VI, is that he cannot deduct either the indexation allowance or the annual exemption. Also, the fact that gains are assessed as income may mean that he cannot make use of capital losses that have been brought forward from earlier years or have arisen during the same year on other transactions. On the other hand, where an individual has borrowed to acquire the land, he may be able to deduct the interest in calculating the gain for income tax purposes, whereas no deduction is normally available for CGT purposes.

The fact that since 6 April 1988 CGT is normally charged at the same rate as income tax means that it is now less common for Inspectors to argue that gains on land transactions should be assessed as income. The main circumstances where the Revenue is likely to argue on these lines is where the individual concerned is a builder, developer or estate agent or has entered into a large number of land transactions or the amounts involved in a particular transaction are substantial.

15.4.2 Specific points on computation of gains on transactions involving land

(TCGA 1992, Sched 8)

Wasting assets

Where a person disposes of a wasting asset, his cost or acquisition value may need to be restricted. This applies where a person disposes of a leasehold interest in land and the lease has less than 50 years to run at the date of disposal. Table 15.1 shows how the cost of a lease must be adjusted.

Table 15.1 – Depreciation of leases

Years	*Percentage*	*Years*	*Percentage*	*Years*	*Percentage*
50 (or more)	100	33	90.280	16	64.116
49	99.657	32	89.354	15	61.617
48	99.289	31	88.371	14	58.971
47	98.902	30	87.330	13	56.167
46	98.490	29	86.226	12	53.191
45	98.059	28	85.053	11	50.038
44	97.595	27	83.816	10	46.695
43	97.107	26	82.496	9	43.154
42	96.593	25	81.100	8	39.399
41	96.041	24	79.622	7	35.414
40	95.457	23	78.055	6	31.195
39	94.842	22	76.399	5	26.722
38	94.189	21	74.635	4	21.983
37	93.497	20	72.770	3	16.959
36	92.761	19	70.791	2	11.629
35	91.981	18	68.697	1	5.983
34	91.156	17	66.470	0	0

The fraction of the cost of the lease which is not allowed is given by the fraction

$$\frac{P(1) - P(3)}{P(1)}$$

where

P(1) = the percentage derived from the table for the duration of the lease at acquisition

P(3) = the percentage derived from the table for the duration of the lease at the time of disposal

Example – Wasting assets

E purchases a 48-year lease in 1992 for £10,000. In 2000 she spends £2,000 on improvements that affect the value of the lease. She disposes of it with 36 years left in 2004. Her allowable expenditure is therefore as follows:

$$\text{Original cost £10,000} \times \frac{(99.289 - 92.761)}{99.289} = \text{£657}$$

$$\text{Additional £2,000} \times \frac{(95.457 - 92.761)}{95.457} = \text{£56}$$

£713

Total allowable expenditure = £12,000 – £713 = £11,287

Enhancement expenditure

It commonly happens that a person has spent money over the years on improvements. This expenditure can be taken into account provided the improvements are reflected in the state of the property when it is sold.

Where such enhancement expenditure occurred after 31 March 1982, the expenditure is added to the acquisition value and attracts indexation allowance from the time it is incurred.

Enhancement expenditure prior to 31 March 1982 may be taken into account only if the universal rebasing election (see 14.3.2) has not been made and the total of original cost and pre-31 March 1982 enhancement expenditure exceeds the market value at 31 March.

Time apportionment and enhancement expenditure

Where a universal rebasing election has not been made, it may be possible to compute the capital gain on the time apportionment basis (see 14.3.3). This can be difficult where there has also been enhancement expenditure because the overall gain has to be split between the gain on the original cost and the gain relating to the enhancement expenditure. This is an area where professional advice is essential.

15.5 HOW THE REVENUE COMPUTES GAINS ON UNQUOTED SHARES

There are some special features to the way in which gains on unquoted shares are computed. Other aspects follow the principles already covered in this chapter. For example, the identification rules where a person disposes of part of a shareholding of unquoted shares are exactly the same as for quoted securities (see 15.1.3).

There are also practical considerations that do not arise in relation to quoted securities such as the need to negotiate a valuation of the shares at 31 March 1982. Retirement relief also needs to be borne in mind (see 17.8-17.10).

In the case of gifts, the value used for CGT purposes is normally the value of the asset taken by the acquirer, not the reduction in value for the person making the disposal. From this point of view, CGT works differently from IHT (see 19.3.3).

15.5.1 Shares held at 31 March 1982

Where an individual has made a universal rebasing election (see 14.3.2), the original cost is not relevant and the capital gain is computed only by reference to the shares' value at 31 March 1982. Even where the election has not been made, it is often fairly clear that the market value at 31 March 1982 will be higher than either original cost or market value at 6 April 1965.

Inevitably, the market value at 31 March 1982 will be the subject of negotiation with the Revenue's Shares Valuation Division and professional advice should be taken. The shares' value will reflect factors such as the nature of the company, its assets and the size of the shareholding. See leaflet SVD1 *Share Valuation Division*.

The general approach adopted by the Division is to determine the value of the unquoted shares and securities by reference to a completely hypothetical market. It is assumed that any prospective purchaser will have available to him all of the information that a prudent prospective purchaser of the asset might reasonably require if he were proposing to purchase it from a willing vendor by private treaty and at arm's length. Open market value must be assumed and the yardstick is always the requirement of the willing and prudent purchaser and not the wishes, etc of the directors of the private company.

The company's underlying assets are largely irrelevant if a person has only a relatively small minority shareholding; they may be a more important consideration if he has control. Therefore, a quite different valuation might be placed on shares that form, say, a 7% shareholding from a 51% shareholding that gives the owner control. In the former case the valuers will be looking at factors such as the level of dividends paid in the past and the likelihood of such dividends being paid in the future. At the other extreme, a 51% shareholder would place great value on a 7/51 part of his shareholding as a disposal of such shares will cause him to lose voting control over the company.

On a practical aspect, it is possible to enter into negotiations with the Revenue in advance of filing your SA tax return. If you wish to reduce any uncertainty to the minimum by trying to agree 31 March 1982 values before filing your return, ask the Revenue for form CG34.

15.5.2 Shares held at 6 April 1965

Where a universal rebasing election has not been made it may be possible (and beneficial) for the capital gain to be computed on the time apportionment basis.

Example – Shares held at 6 April 1965

F acquired 1,000 shares in a family company on 1 April 1950 and they were then worth £10,000. He sold his shares on 1 April 2000 for £750,000. Assume for illustration purposes that indexation allowance amounts to £150,000. The capital gain on the time apportionment basis is:

$$\frac{\text{Period since 6 April 1965}}{\text{Overall period of ownership}} \times \text{gain of £600,000 (ie gain after indexation)}$$

The figures work out as follows:

$$\frac{\text{420 months}}{\text{600 months}} \times \text{£600,000} = \text{£420,000}$$

The £420,000 gain may then be reduced by taper relief (and in some cases by retirement relief: see 17.8-17.10).

15.5.3 Situations where time apportionment relief is not available

It is not possible to claim time apportionment relief on the disposal of unquoted shares if there was a capital reorganisation prior to 6 April 1965. A capital reorganisation would include a rights issue or a merger between two companies.

Furthermore, time apportionment relief may be severely restricted where an individual has, since 6 April 1965, transferred or sold a property to a company in which he holds shares. Once again, this is a situation where you should seek professional advice.

15.5.4 Retirement relief and taper relief

Retirement relief may be available for gains realised before 6 April 2003 (see 17.8). The conditions for business taper relief should also be borne in mind.

15.6 DISPOSAL OF FOREIGN PROPERTY

15.6.1 Gains must be computed in sterling

Just as a chargeable gain may arise on the disposal of foreign currency, there may similarly be a currency gain on the disposal of certain foreign assets, such as a house or flat in a foreign country. Where overseas assets are disposed of, it is not correct to calculate the gain or loss in terms of the foreign currency and then convert that gain or loss into sterling at the time of the disposal. Instead, the following formula should be used:

Market value of foreign currency received at sale (converted at exchange rate applying at that time)	v
Deduct sterling equivalent of cost of asset on acquisition (converted at exchange rate applying at the time of acquisition)	w
	x
Deduct indexation relief	y
Chargeable gain	z

Example – Disposal of foreign property

G acquired a property in West Germany in 1987 for DM 1m (exchange rate DM 4 = £1) and sold it in 2001 for DM 1,350,000 (exchange rate DM3 = £1). The gain would be computed as follows:

	£
Sale proceeds	450,000
Less: cost	(250,000)
	200,000
Less: indexation on £250,000 – say	(150,000)
Chargeable gain	50,000

This can produce some unexpected consequences. Suppose that *G* had borrowed the purchase price in deutschmarks. When she repaid the mortgage on selling the property, she might well be left with no cash in hand. In fact, the profit on the sale of the property in sterling terms was matched by the increase in the sterling value of her mortgage debt. However, there is no CGT relief for this increase and the gain of £50,000 would still be chargeable.

15.6.2 Relief for foreign tax
(TCGA 1992, ss 277-278)

Many overseas countries reserve the right to charge CGT on the disposal of real estate situated in that country, whether or not the owner is resident there. Where a UK resident has had to pay foreign tax in these circumstances, he may claim double tax relief. In effect, the overseas country's tax is available as a credit against the UK tax.

Example – Relief for foreign tax

H has a property in Italy that cost 160m lire (at the time of purchase this was the equivalent of £90,000). The property is sold for 220m lire and there is a chargeable gain for UK tax purposes of £50,000 (assume that Italian CGT of £7,000 is payable). If *H*'s £50,000 gain was chargeable to tax at 40%, the position would be:

	£
UK CGT	20,000
Less: double tax relief	(7,000)
UK CGT actually payable	13,000

However, there is no relief for any excess. Thus, if *H* had unrelieved losses brought forward such that his UK tax had been only £6,500, there would be no relief for the balance.

Sometimes there will be a liability for foreign tax, but no capital gains for UK tax purposes.

Example – Foreign CGT only

> *J* disposes of a property in Sierra Leone at a £40,000 loss in sterling terms. However, there was a gain in terms of local currency and the tax bill in Sierra Leone is £10,000. *J* can claim a deduction for this amount as if it were a deduction from his sale proceeds, and this would mean that his loss for UK CGT purposes would be increased from £40,000 to £50,000.

15.6.3 Foreign gains that cannot be remitted

(TCGA 1992, s 279)

Where a person realises a gain on the disposal of assets situated abroad, but is genuinely unable to transfer that gain to the UK because of restrictions imposed abroad or because the foreign currency is not convertible, the amount of the gain may be omitted from assessment for the year in which it arose. Instead, the gain will be assessed to CGT only when it becomes remittable. Claims to this relief must be made within six years of the year in which the gain was realised.

15.7 GAINS AND LOSSES ON SECOND-HAND INSURANCE POLICIES

The Finance Act 2003 has made two changes.

15.7.1 Is a second-hand insurance policy a chargeable asset for CGT purposes?

Until recently, a second-hand insurance policy has been a chargeable asset for CGT purposes only if the person making the disposal acquired it by purchase. This allowed the CGT charge to be avoided in many circumstances. For example, where the person who purchased a policy gave it to his wife, she would not be regarded as disposing of a chargeable asset because she had acquired it by gift rather than purchase.

From 9 April 2003, a second-hand policy is a chargeable asset where it is received as a gift from a person who acquired it by purchase.

The new rules will also cater for more complex situations where policies have at any stage been bought second-hand. However, these rules will allow exemption in three circumstances. Where consideration is given only on transfers between:

- husband and wife;
- former spouses under the terms of a divorce settlement;
- two companies within a group;

the policy will not constitute a chargeable asset.

15.7.2 Computation of CGT losses

Where a second-hand insurance policy is sold, the amount brought into account in computing taxable income has been excluded from the consideration used in computing a CGT gain (or loss). In practice, this has produced substantial CGT losses. From 9 April 2003, the CGT loss is restricted to the economic loss.

16

THE MAIN RESIDENCE

The largest capital gain that most people make comes from the sale of their main (or only) residence. This is not surprising as their home is likely to be their single largest investment. In the majority of circumstances, this gain is exempt from CGT provided certain conditions are satisfied.

In this chapter, we look at the following

(1) Main residence exemption.
(2) Possible restrictions on exemption.
(3) Living in job-related accommodation.
(4) Treatment where property not occupied throughout ownership period.

16.1 MAIN RESIDENCE EXEMPTION

16.1.1 Basic conditions that must be satisfied (TCGA 1992, s 222)

There is a total exemption from CGT where a gain is realised by an individual on the disposal of a property that has been his sole or main residence throughout his period of ownership. The legislation also provides exemption for land that forms part of the property (the garden or grounds) up to the 'permitted area'. The permitted area is always at least 0.5 of a hectare (approximately one acre), but may be more where the land is required for the reasonable enjoyment of the property (see 16.1.3).

A married couple living together can have the exemption in respect of only one property for a particular period. Note that the exemption can also apply to a property outside the UK.

16.1.2 Occupation test (TCGA 1992, s 223(3); SP D4)

A delay of up to 12 months between a property being acquired and the owner taking up residence does not prejudice the exemption; the property is still treated as if it were his main residence. The 12-month period can be extended by up to a further 12 months if it can be shown that there were good reasons for the owner not taking up residence, for example the need to carry out alterations or building work, or there was an unavoidable delay in the owner being able to dispose of his previous residence.

The last three years of ownership are treated as qualifying for the exemption, whether the owner lives in the property or not, provided the property has previously been his main residence.

16.1.3 The permitted area

The legislation also provides exemption for an area of gardens or grounds larger than 0.5 hectare if it can be shown that it was 'required for the reasonable enjoyment' of the property as a residence. If the taxpayer and the Inspector cannot agree on this, the Commissioners can determine the matter.

Relevant factors here include considerations such as the extent to which other similar properties have gardens or grounds larger than 0.5 hectare, the need for an area of land to provide either privacy or a buffer between the property and, for example, a motorway and the need to have room for other facilities and amenities appropriate to the property.

The last-mentioned factor is often the most difficult to argue with the Revenue, which relies on a judgment by Du Parcq J in a 1937 compulsory purchase case, the so-called *Newhill* case [1938] 2 All ER 163:

> 'Required' … does not mean merely that the occupiers of the house would like to have it, or that they would miss it if they lost it, or that anyone proposing to buy the house would think less of the house without it … 'Required' means … that without it there will be such a substantial deprivation of amenities or convenience that a real injury will be done to the property owner …

The Revenue's interpretation is not free from doubt, as the CGT legislation is worded differently from the compulsory purchase legislation, but *Longson v Baker* [2001] STC 6 has lent support to the Revenue. Mr Longson had used land for equestrian pursuits, but the High Court upheld the Commissioners' decision that, while it may have been convenient for him to be able to stable his horses and exercise them on land attached to his home, the facility was not required for the reasonable enjoyment of the property.

This is an area where it is essential to take professional advice.

16.1.4 What is 'the residence'?

There have been several cases concerning property where servants occupy a part of the premises.

In *Batey v Wakefield* [1981] STC 521 the property consisted of the main house and a caretaker's lodge. The caretaker/gardener and his wife (who was the owner's housekeeper) occupied the lodge rent free. The main house and the lodge were separated by the width of a tennis court. The Court of Appeal upheld the taxpayer's claim that his residence consisted of the main house and all related buildings that were part and parcel of the property and were occupied for the purposes of the owner's residence.

Yet in *Lewis v Rook* [1992] STC 171 the Court of Appeal decided against a taxpayer who claimed the exemption should cover a gardener's cottage located some 170 metres away, as it was not within the same curtilage as the taxpayer's house. Following that decision, the Revenue, which set out its views in *Tax Bulletin* August 1994, said that the exemption could not apply to a separate building at all, regardless of how close it is to the house occupied by the owner.

Specialist advice should be taken if substantial sums are involved.

16.2 POSSIBLE RESTRICTIONS ON EXEMPTION

16.2.1 Part of property used for business purposes
(TCGA 1992, s 224(1))

If part of the property has been used exclusively for the purposes of a trade, business, profession or vocation, the exemption does not cover the part of the gain attributable to that part. This restriction does not apply where the relevant rooms are used for part business/part personal reasons. So, if a journalist's living room doubles up as a workroom from which he carries on his business, there is no restriction under this provision.

16.2.2 Part of property let out
(TCGA 1992, s 223(4))

A similar restriction may apply where the owner has let out part of his home. Thus, if the owner had let approximately one-third of his home, the exemption would normally be confined to two-thirds of the gain on disposal. This rule may be overridden if the lettings are as residential accommodation: the gain on the part of the property let out in this way may still be exempt up to the lesser of:

(1) the exemption on the part of the property occupied by the owner; and
(2) £40,000.

A husband and wife who own a property jointly can each claim an exemption of up to £40,000 against their share of the gain.

16.2.3 Expenditure incurred with view to gain
(TCGA 1992, s 224(3))

The exemption is not available if a gain arises from the purchase of property made wholly or partly for the purpose of realising a gain.

Example – Expenditure with a view to gain

> *K*, a partner, lived in a flat owned by his firm. He was offered the opportunity to buy it for £75,000. He accepted because he knew he could fairly quickly find a buyer at £120,000. He sold it, and realised a gain of £45,000. The Revenue is likely to argue that the gain is a chargeable gain because of s 224(3). Similarly, a person who holds a leasehold interest and acquires the freehold because it will enable a better price to be obtained may suffer a restriction under s 224(3) if the Revenue can show that this was the only purpose of buying the freehold.

Some guidance on the circumstances in which the Revenue may seek to deny exemption on these grounds is contained in *Tax Bulletin* August 1994.

16.2.4 Sale of part of gardens

Special care is needed if it is decided to sell surplus land for development. In *Varty v Lynes* [1976] STC 508 the taxpayer had owned and occupied a house and the garden was less than one acre (the permitted area at that time). He sold the house and part of the garden in June 1971. Slightly less than 12 months later, he sold the rest of the garden to a builder and realised a substantial gain because he had secured planning permission in the meantime. He was assessed on the gain on the land sold to the builder. The High Court decided that the main residence exemption did not apply. Brightman J held that the exemption for the garden or grounds could apply only in relation to garden or grounds occupied as such by the owner at the date of sale. The Revenue subsequently stated that it will invoke this only where land is sold with development value. The following principles should be borne in mind:

(1) A sale of land out of a parcel of land greater than 0.5 hectare may be vulnerable even where the owner remains in occupation. The fact that the owner continues to live in the property suggests that the surplus land was not required for the reasonable enjoyment of the property.
(2) A sale of land with development value at the same time as the owner ceases to live in the property is not open to attack in the same way as in *Varty v Lynes*.
(3) A sale of land with development value after the owner has moved out is likely to result in a tax charge.

16.2.5 What happens where there are two homes?

An individual may live in two (or more) properties without necessarily owning both (or all) of them. The Revenue view is that a person has two residences if, for example, he owns a large house in Gloucestershire and rents a modest flat in Central London where he lives during the week.

If necessary, the Commissioners decide which of an individual's two or more residences is his main residence. The test is not necessarily where the individual lives most of the time, and it is often not clear in a particular case what view the Commissioners might take.

16.2.6 Taxpayer's right of election
(TCGA 1992, s 222(5))

Fortunately, the owner can settle the matter by formally electing one property to be treated as his main residence. The election may be varied from time to time, but only in relation to the last two years prior to the variation.

There is a time limit for a notice under s 222(5) of two years. The Revenue's view has been that the time limit refers to the point in time the individual starts to have a second residence. This interpretation was upheld by the High Court in *Griffin v Craig Harvey* [1994] STC 54.

There is one circumstance where the Revenue will accept an election outside the two-year time limit. ESC D21 provides:

> Where for any period an individual has more than one residence, but his interest in each of them, or in each of them except one, is such as to have no more than a negligible capital value on the open market (for example a weekly rented flat or accommodation provided by an employer) the two-year time limit will be extended where the individual was unaware that such a nomination could be made. In such cases the nomination may be made within a reasonable time of the individual becoming aware of the possibility of so doing, and it will be regarded as effective from the date on which the individual first had more than one residence.

16.3 LIVING IN JOB-RELATED ACCOMMODATION

16.3.1 Meaning of job-related accommodation

Job-related accommodation is defined as accommodation provided for an individual or his spouse by reason of his employment where:

(1) it is necessary for the proper performance of his duties that he should live there; or
(2) it is provided for the better performance of his duties and the employment is one where employers customarily provide accommodation; or
(3) the accommodation is provided as part of the special security arrangements for the employee's safety.

16.3.2 Right to nominate a property
(TCGA 1992, s 222(8))

Where an individual is required to live in job-related accommodation, a house owned by him and intended to be occupied as his residence in due course is treated as if it were his residence. Such a house may therefore qualify for exemption even if the owner had let it and never actually occupied it himself before disposing of it, provided he nominates it as his only or main residence.

16.3.3 Similar provisions for self-employed individuals

A self-employed individual who is required to live at or near his place of work (eg a publican) can nominate a property under s 222(8) for eventual use as his main residence. This also applies if his spouse is required to occupy such premises. Only periods after 5 April 1982 can qualify under this heading.

16.4 TREATMENT WHERE PROPERTY NOT OCCUPIED THROUGHOUT OWNERSHIP PERIOD

16.4.1 Proportion of gain may be exempt

The s 222 exemption is not necessarily an 'all or nothing' test. The legislation makes provision for a proportion of the capital gain to be exempt where the necessary conditions are satisfied for part of the period of ownership. The exempt proportion of the gain is normally:

$$\frac{\text{Period of qualifying use}}{\text{Total period of ownership}} \times \text{Indexed gain}$$

16.4.2 Periods prior to 31 March 1982 ignored

A period of non-qualifying use is ignored if it is prior to 31 March 1982.

Example – Incomplete period of occupation

A property was acquired in March 1975 and let as an investment until March 1984. Thereafter it is the owner's sole residence. It is sold in March 2004 for a gain of £340,000. The exempt proportion of the gain would be:

$$^{20}/_{22} \times £340{,}000 = £309{,}091$$

16.4.3 Last 36 months of ownership
(TCGA 1992, s 223(2))

Provided the property has at some time qualified as the owner's main residence, the last three years of ownership also qualify for exemption. This still applies if the property is let or another property is nominated as his main residence for all or part of that period. It also applies even where the period when the property was occupied as the individual's main residence was before 31 March 1982.

The period was 24 months for disposals prior to 19 March 1991.

16.4.4 Periods spent working abroad

(TCGA 1992, s 223(3)(b))

If, during a period when his property was used as his main residence, the owner has to work abroad, the property continues to be regarded as his main residence (and therefore exempt from CGT) if he was employed abroad under a contract of employment and all the employment duties were performed overseas. The condition requiring the property to be the owner's only or main residence after working abroad is treated as satisfied if he is unable to resume residence because the terms of his new employment require him to work elsewhere (ESC D4).

16.4.5 Periods spent working elsewhere in UK

A period of up to four years during which the owner's employment necessitated his living elsewhere in the UK is also a qualifying period. A period (or periods in total) that exceeds four years is covered to the extent of four years. Again, it is normally necessary that the period be followed by a period of occupation, but ESC D4 applies if the individual cannot resume occupation because his current employment prevents this.

16.4.6 Other qualifying periods

A further period of absence of up to three years can be treated as qualifying for exemption, provided the period is both preceded and succeeded by a period of actual occupation.

16.4.7 Summary

Table 16.1 may help in computing the position in a particular case. The exempt gain is (X) + (Y).

16.4.8 Dependent relatives

(TCGA 1992, s 226)

In addition to the main residence exemption, an individual may qualify for exemption in respect of a property occupied by a dependent relative as his main residence provided the property was so occupied before 6 April 1988. To qualify for this exemption, the property must have been occupied by the dependent relative rent free, and without any other consideration.

A widowed mother (or mother-in-law) is automatically regarded as a dependent relative. In other situations, the relative is regarded as dependent only if prevented by old age or infirmity from maintaining himself. The exemption is not available for a property acquired after 5 April 1988, even if the property is a replacement for another property previously occupied by a dependent relative.

In some cases, it may be appropriate to form a settlement with the trustees owning the property occupied by the dependent relative as the trustees may still qualify for exemption in respect of a property occupied by a beneficiary as his main residence (see 20.4.10).

Table 16.1 – Computation of exempt gain on main residence

Number of complete months since 31 March 1982 when the property was actually occupied as the owner's main residence. See 16.1.2	(A)
The lesser of 36 months or such part of the last 36 months which does not already fall within A (24 months for disposals prior to 19 March 1991). See 16.4.3	(B)
Months spent working abroad when the property was not occupied as the individual's main residence provided that the individual resumed residence after his overseas employment ceased or would have done so if he had not been required to take up employment elsewhere in the UK. Note: exclude any period which already falls to be included in B above. See 16.4.4	(C)
Number of months spent living elsewhere because the individual's employment required him to live in another part of the UK (subject to a maximum of 48 months). Again, exclude any period already included in B. Note, an entry is appropriate here only if the individual resumed occupation of the property at the end of the period. See 16.4.5	(D)
Any further period of absence which was both preceded and succeeded by the individual occupying the property as his main residence (subject to a maximum of 36 months). Again exclude any period already included in B. See 16.4.6	(E)
Apply the following fraction to the overall gain which arose on the disposal of the property: $\dfrac{A + B + C + D + E}{\text{Months of ownership since 31 March 1982}}$	(X)
A further exemption may also be due where the property has been let. The additional exemption is the lesser of X or £40,000. See 16.2.2	(Y)

17

CAPITAL GAINS TAX AND BUSINESS TRANSACTIONS

ROGER BLEASBY

This chapter focuses on the CGT aspects of various business transactions. It deals with the following matters:

(1) Loans to private businesses.
(2) Losses on unquoted shares.
(3) Relief for replacement of business assets.
(4) Roll-over relief for reinvestment in unquoted shares.
(5) Hold-over relief for gifts of business property.
(6) Partnerships and capital gains.
(7) Transfer of a business to a company.
(8) Retirement relief: general provisions.
(9) Retirement relief: unincorporated traders.
(10) Retirement relief: full-time directors or employees.

Taper relief on business assets is dealt with in Chap. 14.

17.1 LOANS TO PRIVATE BUSINESSES

A very common type of transaction is a loan to a sole trader or partnership (an 'unincorporated business') or to a private company. Almost as common are situations where a person gives a guarantee to a bank, etc that makes a loan to a business. This section deals with the CGT position if a loan becomes written off or a person is required to make a payment under a bank guarantee that he has given.

17.1.1 Loans to unincorporated businesses (TCGA 1992, s 253)

A CGT loss may be deemed to arise if the Revenue is satisfied that a loan has become irrecoverable. There are various conditions that need to be fulfilled, ie the borrower must:

(1) not be the lender's spouse;

(2) be resident in the UK;
(3) have used the loan wholly for the purposes of a trade carried on by him. The trade must not have consisted of (or included) money-lending.

When a claim is submitted, the Inspector must satisfy himself that any outstanding amount of the loan is irrecoverable and that the lender has not assigned or waived his right to recover the loan.

A claim can be made that has up to two years' retrospective effect provided the loan was irrecoverable at the end of the tax year or accounting period for which the claim is made (s 253(3A)).

The allowable loss is restricted to the amount of the loan that is irrecoverable; there is no indexation relief in these circumstances; this has always been the case, even where the disposal took place before 30 November 1993.

17.1.2 Loans to companies

(TCGA 1992, ss 253 and 254)

Similar provisions apply where a person has made a loan to a company that proves to be irrecoverable. The principal conditions that need to be satisfied are:

(1) the company must be UK-resident;
(2) it must be a trading company;
(3) the lender must not be a company that is a member of the same group of companies.

In all other respects, relief normally applies exactly as described in 17.1.1.

Loan notes and debentures

There is an additional complication that may apply to a loss on a loan that constitutes a 'debt on a security', which is a special type of loan. In broad terms, the loans is usually evidenced by a debenture deed and is transferable. A typical example is a loan stock.

If a loan falls into this category, it is necessary to ascertain whether it also falls into another subclass, ie a qualifying corporate bond (see 13.4.2(10)). If it is a QCB, relief can be due as set out in 17.1.1 provided the disposal took place before 6 April 1998. No loss relief is available where the disposal of a QCB takes place after 5 April 1998. However, losses on other debts on security continue to attract relief.

17.1.3 Payments under loan guarantees

(TCGA 1992, s 253(4))

Instead of lending money to a relative or friend or his private company, a person may have given a guarantee to a bank, etc. Similarly, a company director may have had to give personal guarantees in respect of bank loans to his company.

Where the borrower cannot repay the loan, the bank will call on the guarantor to pay the amount due. In these circumstances, the guarantor may be able to claim a CGT loss as if he had made a loan that was irrecoverable. The following conditions must be satisfied for relief to be claimed:

(1) payment has been made under a guarantee;
(2) the payment should arise from a formal calling in of the guarantee – a voluntary payment attracts no relief;
(3) the original loan met the requirements listed in 17.1.1;
(4) the amount paid under the guarantee cannot be recovered either from the borrower or from a co-guarantor.

17.2 LOSSES ON UNQUOTED SHARES

(TA 1988, s 574)

From time to time, an individual may invest in a private company, either as a working director/shareholder or perhaps as a 'passive' investor with a minority shareholding. Investments may also be made in companies that, while they are technically public companies as defined by the Companies Act, are not quoted companies.

17.2.1 Special relief for subscribers

A loss may arise on a disposal of shares in such a company. If the investor acquired existing shares by purchasing them, the loss is a normal CGT loss and the only way it can be relieved is as set out in 13.1.3. However, if he acquired his shares by subscribing for new shares, it may be possible to obtain income tax relief for the loss. Subject to certain conditions, the capital loss may be offset against his income for the year in which the loss is realised.

The following conditions must be satisfied:

(1) The loss must arise from one of the following:
    (a) a sale made at arm's length for full consideration (this rules out a sale to a connected person); or
    (b) a disposal that takes place when the company is wound up; or
    (c) a deemed disposal where the shares have become of negligible value.
(2) There are conditions that attach to the company itself. In particular:
    (a) the company must not have been a quoted company at the date the individual subscribed for his shares or at any time during the period that starts with the individual's acquisition and ends with 6 March 2001. If any class of shares in the company are quoted this rules out

relief under s 574 even though the loss may have arisen on another class of share that were not quoted;

(b) the company must be a trading company, or the holding company of a trading group, at the date of disposal or it must have ceased to have been a trading company not more than three years prior to the date of disposal and it must not have been an investment company since that date;

(c) the company's trade must not have consisted wholly or mainly of dealing in shares, securities, land, trades or commodity futures (further restrictions apply in relation to shares issued after 6 April 1998 so that the company must have met the conditions necessary to qualify for EIS relief: see 11.6);

(d) the company's trade must have been carried on on a commercial basis.

17.2.2 Relief also available for subscriber's spouse

The spouse of a person who subscribed for shares may also claim s 574 relief where he or she has acquired the shares in question through an *inter vivos* transfer from his or her spouse. Shares acquired on a spouse's death do *not* entitle the widow(er) to s 574 relief on a subsequent disposal.

17.2.3 Nature of relief

The loss is calculated according to normal CGT principles. If the loss is eligible for s 574 relief, the individual may elect within two years for it to be set against his taxable income for either the year of the loss or the preceding year. Either claim may be made independently of the other. Where he has losses that are available for s 574 relief and he is also entitled to relief for trading losses, he can choose which losses should be relieved in priority to the others.

Any part of the capital loss that cannot be relieved under s 574 can be carried forward for offset against capital gains in the normal way.

17.2.4 Shares acquired by exercising a share option

If you acquired your shares by exercising a share option, and you were taxed under Schedule E on your profit, your CGT acquisition cost may be much higher than you think (see 14.4.3). You may therefore have a CGT loss when you dispose of your shares. If the other conditions are satisfied, you can get income tax relief under s 574.

17.3 RELIEF FOR REPLACEMENT OF BUSINESS ASSETS
(TCGA 1992, ss 152-160)

'Roll-over' relief may be available where a person sells an asset used by him in a trade (or in certain circumstances, by his family company) and reinvests in replacement assets used for business purposes.

17.3.1 Nature of roll-over relief

A gain is said to be rolled over in that it is not charged to tax, but is deducted from the person's acquisition cost of the new assets. Note that the rolled-over gain is that which arises before taper relief.

Example – Roll-over relief

L sells a farm for £450,000. His capital gain is £200,000. He starts up a new business and invests £500,000 in a warehouse. By claiming roll-over relief, he avoids having to pay tax on the gain of £200,000. The acquisition cost of his warehouse is reduced as follows:

	£
Actual cost	500,000
Less: rolled-over gain	(200,000)
Deemed acquisition cost	300,000

The relief is really a form of deferment since a larger gain will arise on a subsequent disposal of the replacement asset.

17.3.2 Conditions that need to be satisfied

The asset disposed of must have been used in a business and must have fallen into one of the following categories:

(1) land and buildings;
(2) fixed plant and machinery;
(3) ships;
(4) goodwill (but not for companies that buy goodwill after 31 March 2002: see 26.6);
(5) milk and potato quotas;
(6) aircraft;
(7) hovercraft, satellites and spacecraft;
(8) Lloyd's syndicate rights ('capacity');
(9) ewe and suckler cow premium quotas and fish quota.

The replacement asset must also fall into one of these categories.

It is not possible to claim roll-over relief on the disposal of shares in a family company, nor is it possible to claim s 152 relief for expenditure on such shares on the basis that this is replacement expenditure.

The replacement asset must normally be acquired within a period starting one year before and ending three years after the date of the disposal of the original asset. The time limit can be extended (at the Revenue's discretion) if the acquisition of the replacement asset within three years was not possible because of circumstances outside the person's control.

Example – Full relief available only where all the sale proceeds are reinvested
(TCGA 1992, s 152(3)-(11))

> Using the same figures as in 17.3.1, *L* sells his farm for £450,000, making the same capital gain of £200,000. He starts up a new business but invests only £400,000 in the new warehouse. The part of the £450,000 disposal consideration for the farm that is not applied in acquiring the warehouse is £50,000. This is less than the gain that arose on the disposal of the farm and the balance of the gain may be rolled over. The warehouse's acquisition value is reduced by £150,000.

17.3.3 Old assets not used for business throughout ownership

If the old asset was not used for business throughout the period of ownership, s 152 applies as if a part of the asset used for the purposes of the trade was a separate asset to that which had not been wholly used for those purposes.

Example – Old assets

> In April 2003, *M* sells a warehouse for a gain, before taper relief has been calculated, of £50,000. It had originally been bought in April 1995 but had been used in his trade only since April 1997. The amount of gain that can be rolled over into the purchase of a new asset is calculated as follows:
>
> $$\text{Chargeable gain £50,000} \times \frac{\text{Period of trading use of old asset}}{\text{Period of ownership}}$$
>
> This equals £50,000 × $\frac{6}{8}$, ie £37,500. The balance of £12,500 (£50,000 – £37,500) is a chargeable gain before taper relief.

17.3.4 Treatment where replacement assets are wasting assets
(TCGA 1992, s 154)

The roll-over relief is modified where the replacement expenditure consists of the purchase of a wasting asset (ie with an expected useful life of less than 50 years) or an asset that will become a wasting asset within ten years. Plant and machinery is always considered to have a useful life of less than 50 years. Furthermore, the acquisition of a lease with less than 60 years to run also constitutes the acquisition of a wasting asset. Paradoxically, the goodwill of a business is not regarded as a wasting asset.

The capital gain in these circumstances is not deferred indefinitely, but becomes chargeable on the first of the following occasions:

(1) the disposal of the replacement asset; or
(2) the asset ceasing to be used in the business; or
(3) the expiry of ten years.

Examples – Roll-over relief on wasting assets

(1) *N* sells a factory and reinvests in a 59-year lease of a warehouse that he uses in his business. In Year 6 the warehouse is let as an investment property. The rolled-over gain becomes chargeable in Year 6.
(2) *O* also rolls over into a 59-year lease. He is still using the property after ten years, but because it has become a wasting asset within that period, the rolled-over gain becomes chargeable in Year 10.

17.3.5 Reinvestment in non-wasting assets

If the person acquires new non-wasting replacement assets during the ten years, the capital gain that was originally rolled over into the purchase of the wasting assets can be transferred to the new replacement assets. Assume in example (1) above that *N* had bought the goodwill of a business in Year 5. He could transfer his roll-over relief claim to the new asset. No gain would then become chargeable in Year 6 when he lets the warehouse.

17.3.6 Furnished holiday lettings

A property acquired for letting as furnished holiday accommodation (see 6.5) may qualify for roll-over relief; gains from the disposal of such properties may be rolled over.

17.3.7 Assets used by partnership
(SP D11)

Roll-over relief can be secured where the replacement assets are used by a partnership in which the owner is a partner.

17.3.8 Assets used by family company
(TCGA 1992, s 157)

Relief can be obtained where an individual disposes of a property, etc used by his 'personal trading company', but only if the replacement asset is acquired by him and is used by the same company. A company is an individual's personal trading company if he personally owns at least 5% of the voting shares.

He need not be a director of the company – indeed, he need not even be employed by it. Also, roll-over relief is not lost because he has charged the company rent (contrast the position for retirement relief: see 17.10.3).

17.3.9 Assets owned by employee or office-holder

An employee or office-holder may claim roll-over relief where he disposes of an asset used in the employment. This condition may apply to, for example, a sub-postmaster who has an 'office' for tax purposes, but who generally owns the sub-post office premises. For further details, see SP 5/86.

There are circumstances where these provisions can mean that a director of a family company who has sold an asset used by one company and bought new assets used by another family company is entitled to roll-over relief: this is a difficult area where professional advice is essential.

17.4 ROLL-OVER RELIEF FOR REINVESTMENT IN UNQUOTED SHARES

(TCGA 1992, s 164A)

Reinvestment relief made it possible for individuals and trustees to roll-over gains by reinvesting in ordinary shares in a qualifying unquoted trading company. The relief was abolished with effect from 6 April 1998, although similar relief can be available under the new EIS (see 11.6).

Reinvestment had to take place within a period beginning one year before and ending three years after the disposal that gave rise to the capital gain. Most trustees were eligible for reinvestment relief. The main exclusion was where some of the trust's beneficiaries were not individuals.

17.4.1 Qualifying companies

A company was a qualifying company only if it did not carry on a prohibited business (defined in a similar way to the EIS rules: see 11.6). The fact that a company's shares were dealt in on the AIM did not mean that it was a quoted company and such shares could qualify – although not all AIM companies carried on a qualifying trade.

Reinvestment relief was not available if the company was a subsidiary of another company. If the company had subsidiaries, it had to hold at least 75% of their share capital. It did not need to be a UK company, but if it was a foreign company it had to carry on its business wholly or mainly in the UK.

Relief was not available where an individual had disposed of shares in a company and reinvested in the same company or in a subsidiary of it the shares of which he had sold to realise his original capital gain.

17.4.2 Clawback of relief

The relief is clawed back where a company ceases to meet the qualifying conditions within three years of the reinvestment – unless the company becomes quoted, in which case its relevant period comes to an end. The mere fact that it becomes quoted does not cause the relief to be withdrawn.

Table 17.1 – Prohibited activities of a company for reinvestment relief

(1) dealing in land, in commodities or futures or in shares, securities or other financial instruments;
(2) dealing in goods otherwise than in the course of any ordinary trade of wholesale or retail distribution;
(3) banking, insurance, money-lending, debt factoring, hire-purchase financing or other financial activities;
(4) leasing (including letting ships on charter or other assets on hire) or receiving royalties or licence fees;
(5) providing legal or accountancy services;
(6) providing services or facilities for any trade carried on by another person (other than a parent company) which consists to any substantial extent of activities within any of (1)-(5) above and in which a controlling interest is held by a person who also has a controlling interest in the trade carried on by the company.

Note. Property development and farming were also prohibited activities up to 29 November 1994.

A clawback may also arise where the individual who has qualified for reinvestment relief ceases to be UK-resident within the three-year period.

The gain that has been covered by reinvestment relief is clawed back by being brought into charge as if it were a gain arising at the point in time when the company breached one of the conditions or, where the individual emigrates, immediately prior to his becoming non-UK resident.

17.5 HOLD-OVER RELIEF FOR GIFTS OF BUSINESS PROPERTY

(TCGA 1992, s 165)

17.5.1 Background and nature of hold-over relief

Under the legislation that applied up to 5 April 1989, a UK-resident individual could transfer any asset to another UK-resident person on a no gain/no loss basis by claiming hold-over relief.

The relief was abolished in 1989 for gifts of most types of assets, although the same type of relief can still be claimed on gifts of business property to a UK-resident person.

17.5.2 Definition of 'business property'

Business property is defined for these purposes as:

(1) an asset used by the transferor in a trade, profession or vocation;
(2) an asset used by the transferor's family company in a trade;
(3) an asset used for a trade by a subsidiary of the transferor's family company;
(4) unquoted shares in a trading company, or holding company of a trading group, which does not to any substantial extent have investment activities;
(5) agricultural land that qualifies for the IHT agricultural property relief.

Hold-over relief cannot be claimed in respect of a gift of shares or securities to a UK company where the gift took place after 8 November 1999. The relief can, however, be claimed on a gift to a company of an unincorporated business.

The rules concerning gifts of shares which qualify for hold-over relief changed with effect from 6 April 2003. Previously, a gift of shares in a trading company could qualify even if the company had investments which made up a substantial (ie 20% or more) part of its assets. The gain then had to be apportioned and the proportion found by applying the fraction

$$\frac{\text{Business chargeable assets}}{\text{Total chargeable assets}}$$

could be held-over. The position is now 'all or nothing'; if the company has substantial investment activities hold-over relief is not available at all.

17.5.3 Claiming the relief

You should obtain a copy of Helpsheet IR295, which incorporates an election that needs to be signed by the donor and donee (see opposite).

17.6 PARTNERSHIPS AND CAPITAL GAINS

How CGT affects partnership transactions can at times be complex. Partners should familiarise themselves with SP D12 and take regular professional advice. The following section describes some key aspects.

17.6.1 Partnership's acquisition value

Although individual partners' entitlement to profits may vary over the years, the partnership's acquisition value for the firm's chargeable assets is not affected unless there are cash payments from one partner to another to acquire a greater interest in the firm or unless assets are revalued as part of the arrangements for changes in profit-sharing.

HELP SHEET IR295

For the Capital Gains Pages

Claim for hold-over relief - Sections 165 and 260 TCGA 1992

	Transferor		**Transferee**
Name		Name	
Address	Postcode	Address	Postcode
Inland Revenue office		Inland Revenue office	
Tax reference		Tax reference	

Except in case of a gift in settlement, the claim must be made by both transferor and transferee. If the transferor or transferee has no Inland Revenue office or reference please explain why.

I/We hereby claim relief under Section 165/Section 260 TCGA 1992 in respect of the transfer of the asset specified below. The particulars given in this claim are correctly stated to the best of my/our information and belief.

Description of asset and date of disposal

√ one box

The gain held over is £ A calculation is attached ☐

We apply for deferment of valuations and have completed the second page of the claim form. ☐

We qualify for relief because:

√ one box

- the asset is used for the business of ☐
  Please insert name of person
- the asset consists of unlisted shares or securities of a trading company or holding company of a trading group ☐
- the asset is agricultural land ☐
- the asset consists of listed shares or securities of the transferor's personal company or, where trustees are the transferors, a company in which they had 25% of the voting rights ☐
- the disposal was a chargeable transfer, but not a Potentially Exempt Transfer, for Inheritance Tax purposes ☐
- Capital Taxes Office reference number
- the disposal was exempt from Inheritance Tax under IHTA Section ☐
  Please insert Section number

Signed Signed

Date / / Date / /

BS 12/2001net

17.6.2 Assets held by firm at 31 March 1982

The partnership may make a universal rebasing election for the values at 31 March 1982 to be used instead of cost (see 14.3.2). This is quite separate from the individual partners' position in relation to their personal assets when a disposal of an asset takes place. There may be partners who were not in the partnership at 31 March 1982, but this does not affect the computation of the gain.

17.6.3 Partnership gains divisible among partners

Where a partnership asset is sold at a capital gain (or loss), the gain is divided among the partners in accordance with their profit-sharing ratios. Each partner is personally assessable on his share of the gain.

The partner's actual CGT liability depends on his own situation, ie whether he has other gains for the year, has available losses, can claim roll-over relief or is entitled to retirement relief (see 17.8).

17.6.4 Revaluations and retirement and introduction of new partners

Problems may arise where a partnership has substantial assets that are chargeable assets for CGT purposes and worth more than their book value (ie the value at which they are shown in the firm's accounts). A revaluation to bring the assets' book value into line with their market value can produce a liability for individual partners if there is a reduction in their profit-sharing ratios. This commonly happens when existing partners retire or new partners are introduced.

Example – Retirement of partner

P is a partner in a five-partner firm and is entitled to 20% of the profits. He retires and his colleagues then share profits on the basis of 25% each. As part of the arrangements for his retirement, the book value of the firm's office block is increased from £150,000 to its current value of £750,000. The surplus is credited to each partner's account so that *P* is credited with £120,000.

P is treated as if he had realised a gain on the disposal of a one-fifth share of the building. This would be based on the £120,000. The remaining four partners are not treated as having made a disposal. Indeed, they each have made an acquisition of a 5% interest in the building for an outlay of £30,000.

Example – Introduction of new partner

Q and *R* are partners. Their premises are included in their firm's balance sheet at £200,000 (original cost), but are actually worth £500,000. *Q* and *R* agree to admit *S* as an equal partner in return for his paying new capital into the firm of £700,000. They revalue the premises before admitting *S* as a partner, and the surplus of £300,000 is credited to their accounts. In this case, *Q* and *R* are each regarded as having made a disposal of a one-sixth interest in the premises. This is because *S*'s new capital will go into the firm as a whole. After coming in, he effectively owns one-third of all the assets (and is responsible for one-third of the liabilities).

The former partners' ownership of the premises has been reduced from 50% to a one-third interest.

17.6.5 Retirement and introduction of partners with no revaluation of assets

There is no such problem where partners leave or come in and there is no revaluation of assets. In such a case, the remaining or incoming partners normally take over the outgoing partners' acquisition values for the firm's asset.

Example – Change of partners with no revaluation of assets

T and *U* are in partnership. They own premises that have a book value of £94,000 (equal to cost in 1980). *T* retires and is replaced by *V*. The premises are not revalued. Later the premises are sold for £244,000. *U* and *V* are assessed on their share of the gain.

The gain is computed by reference to the original cost (£94,000) or the premises' market value at 31 March 1982, not their value at the time that *V* became a partner. This does not apply where the partners are connected persons (eg because they are relatives), or where cash payments are made to acquire an interest in the firm. In either of these categories you should seek specialist advice.

17.7 TRANSFER OF A BUSINESS TO A COMPANY

(TCGA 1992, s 162)

Where a person transfers a business to a company (ie he 'incorporates the business'), there is a disposal of the assets that are transferred to the company. Not all the assets necessarily become chargeable assets for CGT purposes, but a gain may arise on assets such as land, buildings and goodwill. Fortunately, there is a relief that may cover such situations.

17.7.1 Nature of relief

The main relief applies only where a business is transferred to a company in return for an issue of shares to the former proprietors of the business. Where the necessary conditions are satisfied so that s 162 relief is available, the gains that would otherwise arise on the transfer of chargeable assets are rolled-over into the cost of the shares issued.

Example – Transfer of a business to a company

W transfers a business to B Ltd in return for shares worth £75,000. There are capital gains of £48,000 on the assets transferred to the company. If s 162 relief applies, *W* will not have any assessable capital gain, but her shares in B Ltd will be deemed to have an acquisition cost of £27,000 computed as follows:

	£
Market value	75,000
Less: rolled-over gain	(48,000)
	27,000

17.7.2 Conditions that must be satisfied

In order for s 162 relief to be available, all the business's assets other than cash must be transferred to the company. It is not acceptable to the Revenue for certain assets of the unincorporated business (eg trade debts) to be excluded, even though this might otherwise be advisable to save stamp duty.

Relief is available only in so far as shares are issued by the company instead of other forms of payment such as loan stock. The market value of the shares issued in return for the transfer of the business must be at least equal to the capital gains arising on the transfer of assets.

Example – Limitations of s 162 relief

X transfers a business with a net value of £400,000 to C Ltd, a new company specially formed for the purpose. Shares in C Ltd are issued to him, and these have a value of £400,000. However, closer examination reveals that the business's value is depressed by heavy bank borrowings. Furthermore, capital gains totalling £490,000 arise on chargeable assets transferred as part of the business.

Section 162 relief would be limited to £400,000. The balance of £90,000 would be taxable in the normal way.

17.7.3 Conditions that are not required

(1) Relief is not confined to a transfer of a business to a company by a sole trader; the same relief is available where a partnership transfers its business to a company.
(2) The shares that are issued need not be ordinary shares.
(3) Relief does not seem to be confined to a business that is classified as a trade that falls under Schedule D Case I or II. It is arguable that the relevant business might, for example, consist of letting a group of properties.
(4) There is no requirement that the company should be incorporated or

resident in the UK. It can be both of these things, but relief is not prejudiced just because a foreign company is involved.

17.7.4 Relief may be due on proportion of capital gains

Some relief will still be available if the business is transferred to the company in return for a mixture of shares and loan stock, or shares and cash. The formula to be used is:

$$\text{Chargeable gain} \times \frac{\text{Value of shares received}}{\text{Value of whole consideration received}}$$

17.7.5 Alternative incorporation relief

It may sometimes be possible to transfer a business to a company and avoid any CGT liability by relying on the hold-over provisions (see 17.5). Professional advice is essential when implementing such arrangements.

17.8 RETIREMENT RELIEF: GENERAL PROVISIONS

(TCGA 1992, ss 163-164)

This was a relief that may be available on a disposal before 6 April 2003 of a business, or an interest in a partnership, or on a disposal of assets used in a partnership, or on a sale of shares in a family company, the liquidation of such a company, or sales of assets used by such a company. The relief was available only if the individual was aged at least 50 or had to retire early because of ill health.

17.8.1 Nature of the relief

The maximum relief for disposals in 2002-03 was £50,000 and one half of gains falling within the band £50,001-£200,000. The relief was abolished with effect from 6 April 2003.

The maximum relief was based on all of the requirements being met for a ten-year period. The relief was tapered using the 'appropriate percentage', which started at 10% for one year and rose to 100% for the full ten years.

Example – Retirement relief

In May 2002 *Y*, who is 57 years old and fulfils all of the criteria, disposes of his business in which he has been a full-time working director for 15 years. He realises gains of £400,000. The relief is available on the first £200,000 only, as follows:

	£	£
Qualifying gain		200,000
Less: 100% relief on first £50,000		(50,000)
		150,000
50% relief on remaining £150,000	75,000	
Plus 100% first relief	50,000	
Total relief	125,000	
Taxable gain (£400,000 – £125,000)		275,000

The relief can be split between gains on disposals of two or more different businesses, but the aggregate relief will be restricted to the £50,000 and £200,000 limits. In some cases, the gains may arise in different tax years.

17.8.2 Interaction with taper relief

Taper relief (see 14.5) is calculated on gains after deducting retirement relief.

17.8.3 Retirement through ill health

The legislation provided that retirement relief should be available to an individual who was being required to dispose of his business because ill health made it impossible for him to carry on.

In practice, the Revenue required claimants to provide a medical certificate, signed by a qualified medical practitioner (whether or not the claimant's own GP). The Board will take advice from the Regional Medical Service of the Department of Health, and in some cases a further medical examination by the Regional Medical Officer can be required.

Retirement relief is not due to someone aged below 50 where he ceased work because of someone else's ill health, for example that of his spouse.

If you wish to claim retirement relief on these grounds, you should complete form CG85.

17.8.4 Conditions to be satisfied for ten years if full relief is to be available

The full relief was given only if the individual satisfied various requirements for a ten-year period. During that period he must have been in business as a sole trader or partner or have been a full-time officer (eg a director) or employee of a personal trading company (see 17.3.8).

Separate periods during which an individual satisfied one of these requirements can be aggregated in certain circumstances.

Example – Limited relief

In the example at 17.8.1, if *L* had owned the business for six years the relief, again based on total gains of £400,000 and qualifying gains of £200,000, would be as follows:

	£	£
Qualifying gain		200,000
Appropriate percentage of £50,000 = £30,000 × 100% relief due	30,000	
Appropriate percentage of £150,000 = £90,000 × 50% relief due	45,000	
Total relief due	£75,000	
Taxable gain (£400,000 – £75,000)		325,000

17.8.5 Specific conditions for unincorporated traders and full-time directors and employees

There are a number of very specific requirements for disposals by sole traders, partners and full-time directors and employees of personal trading companies. These are dealt with separately at 17.9 and 17.10 respectively.

17.8.6 Retirement relief for trustees

There are certain circumstances where the sale by trustees of family settlements of business property or shares could attract retirement relief. This is an area where professional advice should be taken.

17.9 RETIREMENT RELIEF: UNINCORPORATED TRADERS

The sale of a business may be broken down for tax purposes into the disposal of distinct assets (goodwill and buildings, plant and equipment, stock debtors and cash). The CGT position must be looked at separately in relation to each asset.

17.9.1 Retirement relief for sole traders

The legislation required that a capital gain should arise on the disposal of a business or a part of it. There have been several cases concerning farmers where an individual disposed of part of his land. In each case the courts held that retirement relief was not due since the asset disposed of was an asset used in the business rather than part of the business itself. A similar point would arise if a sole trader sold a warehouse or office block, but continued in business.

In practice, the Revenue resists relief for farmers unless the disposal concerns at least 50%+ of the total area being farmed. Problems sometimes arise even where this condition is satisfied.

17.9.2 Retirement relief for partners

A gain may attract retirement relief where it arises on a disposal that took place on the introduction of a new partner or on some other change in profit-sharing ratios combined with a revaluation of partnership assets (see 17.6.4). In some cases, a partner may own an asset used by his firm. Retirement relief is available to cover a gain arising from the disposal of such an asset provided the following conditions were satisfied:

(1) disposal must take place as part of the withdrawal of the individual from participation in the business carried on by the partnership;
(2) immediately before the disposal (or the cessation of the business), the asset must have been used for the partnership's business purposes;
(3) during the whole or part of the period in which the asset has been in the individual's ownership, it must have been used for the purposes of:
    (a) the business; or
    (b) another business carried on by the individual or by a partnership of which he was a member; or
    (c) another business carried on by the individual's family trading company (in this instance, he must have been a full-time working director at the time).

The amount of retirement relief on the disposal of an asset of this nature may be restricted where the partner had charged his firm a commercial rent for use of the property.

17.10 RETIREMENT RELIEF: FULL-TIME DIRECTORS OR EMPLOYEES

(TCGA 1992, ss 163-164, as amended by FA 1993, s 87)

This section focuses on the way the capital gain on the sale of shares in a personal trading company and assets owned privately by the shareholder may qualify for retirement relief.

17.10.1 Full-time working directors

It was necessary for the individual to work for the company on a full-time basis in a managerial or technical capacity.

There was no statutory definition of what 'full-time' means in this context. In practice, the Revenue accepted that a director whose normal working week was 30 hours (excluding meal breaks) qualified for relief. A person was required to devote more or less the whole of his time if that is what his job and service contract involved. Absence through illness did not prejudice entitlement to the relief.

In some cases, the individual worked full-time for a group of related companies. Relief was available where a person was required to devote more or less the whole of his time to the service of a commercial association of companies that carried on businesses and were of a nature that the business of a company and the associated companies taken together might be reasonably considered to make up a single composite undertaking.

This is clearly an area where professional advice may be required in the light of the circumstances of the particular case.

A director who has retired from full-time employment, but who continues to spend an average of at least ten hours pw in the conduct and management of the company's business, may qualify for relief. However, his entitlement was based on the period of full-time service that he had up to the date of his retirement.

It was also a condition for an individual to qualify for retirement relief that he had a shareholding in the company of at least 5%.

17.10.2 Possible restriction of retirement relief

Where a company had investments as well as business interests, the gain that could attract retirement relief was restricted to the proportion of the gain determined by the following fraction:

$$\frac{\text{Chargeable assets used for business purposes}}{\text{Total chargeable assets}}$$

Where a company had disposed of business assets within six months of a disposal of shares, the individual could elect for the restriction to be computed by reference to the position if the company had not sold the assets concerned.

17.10.3 Sale of premises, etc used by company

An individual who had been a full-time director or employee might have owned property or some other assets used by his personal trading company. Retirement relief could be claimed in respect of a disposal of such an asset provided the following conditions were satisfied:

(1) its disposal had to take place as part of the withdrawal of the individual concerned from participation in the business carried on by the company; and
(2) it had to be in use for the company's business purposes at the time of the disposal or it must have been so used at the time the company's business ceased; and
(3) it had to have been used in the whole or part of the period in which the individual had owned it for the purposes of:

(a) the business carried on by the company; or
(b) another business carried on by the individual or by a partnership of which he was a member; or
(c) another business carried on by a personal trading company.

The Revenue generally sought to restrict relief where the individual had charged rent (but see *Plumbly v Spencer* CA 1999 71 TC 399).

18

SOME WAYS OF REDUCING CAPITAL GAINS TAX

Where a capital gain arises, the transaction tends to be an exceptional or 'one-off' event. Instead of being spread evenly over the whole period of ownership, the capital growth on an investment that may have been held for many years falls entirely into the tax year in which the disposal takes place This can often mean that a large amount of tax is involved. There are a number of possible ways of mitigating tax and it is usually a good idea to take professional advice. The following should be borne in mind – but they are only suggestions rather than definitive advice:

(1) Make use of both spouses' annual exemptions.
(2) Realise gains to avoid wasting the annual exemption.
(3) Make sure you get relief for capital losses.
(4) Try to make gains taxable at your lower rates rather than 40%.
(5) Save tax by making gifts to relatives.
(6) Claim roll-over relief on furnished holiday accommodation.
(7) Selling the family company.

18.1 MAKE USE OF BOTH SPOUSES' ANNUAL EXEMPTIONS

18.1.1 Inter-spouse transfer can be a way of saving tax

All individuals are allowed to realise capital gains of £7,900 in 2003-04 before they become liable for CGT. This applies to husband and wife, but there are no provisions under which any unused amount may be transferred to a spouse.

Example – Inter-spouse transfers

If *A* has gains of £5,400 and his wife *B* has gains of £10,000, the position is as follows:

A	*B*	£
No CGT	Gains	10,000
liability	*Less:* exempt	(7,900)
Taxable		2,100

There is often a way of avoiding this type of mismatch. If *B* had transferred assets worth £2,100 to *A* and he then sold them, she could effectively transfer her gain to him. A transfer between spouses does not count as a disposal for tax purposes and *A* would take over *B*'s base cost. So, with a little forethought, the position could have been:

A	£	*B*	£
Gains	7,500	Gains	7,900
Exemption	(7,900)	Exemption	(7,900)
	Nil		Nil

18.2 REALISE GAINS TO AVOID WASTING THE ANNUAL EXEMPTION

Any unused annual exemption cannot be carried forward for use in a future tax year. Dealing costs may be a disincentive but, provided you expect to sell shares, etc at some time or other in the future, it can make sense to 'top up' any net gains to make full use of the £7,900 exemption.

The rules for matching sales and purchases within a 30-day period mean that 'bed and breakfast' transactions will not achieve this. However, you may be able to realise gains and then have your ISA buy the same shares (ie 'bed and ISA'). Alternatively, your spouse or family trust can buy the shares.

A small word of warning, though: do bear in mind the effect on taper relief. If you sell and your spouse buys, he or she will have to start from scratch in building up a qualifying period for taper relief purposes.

18.3 MAKE SURE YOU GET RELIEF FOR CAPITAL LOSSES

It may be possible to save tax in a different way by a transfer of an asset between spouses before it is sold to an outsider. Capital losses for previous years attach to each spouse separately and can be set only against that spouse's gain.

Example – Relief for capital losses

If *C*'s wife *D* has losses of £35,000 and *C* has an asset that has appreciated by £50,000, it will make sense for him to transfer it to *D* before it is sold. Instead of the position being like this:

	£
C's gains	50,000
Less: exemption	(7,900)
Taxable	42,100

the position will be:

D's gains	50,000
Less: capital losses	(35,000)
	15,000
Less: exemption	(7,900)
Taxable	7,100

Of course, the ideal position would be achieved by *C* transferring part of the asset to *D*, so that they eventually make a joint disposal, use *D*'s losses and take full advantage of both of their annual exemptions.

18.3.1 Negligible value claims

You may have made an investment in the past that has gone badly. Indeed, you may have written it off in your own mind but, if you have not sold it, the loss is normally only a paper loss that is not allowable for CGT purposes. There is an exception to this rule: you may be able to establish an allowable loss even though there has been no disposal. If the Revenue can be persuaded that the asset has become of 'negligible value' (ie virtually worthless), you can claim a loss (see 13.5.9). In practice, the Revenue issues lists of quoted shares that have been suspended and are recognised to be of negligible value, so you should ask your Inspector whether your defunct investments are on list. It may also be possible to establish losses on unquoted shares and other investments.

18.3.2 Interaction with taper relief

If you have gains that qualify for taper relief and capital losses, the losses are set against gains before taper relief. In some cases, it may be better to defer realising losses until a later year.

Thus, if *E* has gains of £100,000 on disposal of business assets in 2003-04 and these gains qualify for 75% taper relief, he may be advised not to realise losses of £30,000 until after 5 April 2004. His 2003-04 chargeable gains will then be £25,000 rather than £17,500, but the full £30,000 capital loss can then be available to cover future gains that may not attract taper relief at all.

Some married couples may approach matters differently by keeping all taper relief disposals in one name and putting all loss-making transactions through the other spouse who will then realise all their short-term gains.

18.3.3 Timing of disposals

Timing is very important in some cases. Suppose your position in 2003-04 is as follows:

	£
Losses brought forward	80,000
Gains on disposals of business assets qualifying for 75% taper relief as asset owned on 5 April 1998	100,000

The tax position is as follows:

	£
Gains	100,000
Less: losses	80,000
	20,000
Less: taper relief	15,000
Taxable gain	5,000

It will be rather sad if you then realised a gain of £90,000 that does not qualify for taper relief on 6 April 2004, making your combined taxable gains for the two years £95,000. If you had brought the disposal forward one day, the computation would be:

	£	£
Gains not qualifying for taper relief	90,000	
Less: loss brought forward	80,000	
		10,000
Gains qualifying for taper relief	100,000	
Taper relief	75,000	
		25,000
Total gains chargeable for 2003-04		35,000

18.3.4 Actively review holdings

In the US, under-performing stocks are sometimes referred to as 'dogs'. If you find yourself holding shares that have failed to live up to your expectations when you purchased them and, worse, made a loss, consider selling these shares to materialise a loss to offset against your capital gains. By taking positive action before the end of the tax year, you may be able to save 40% on your CGT bill and recoup in part the loss you suffered on a disappointing investment.

18.4 TRY TO MAKE GAINS TAXABLE AT YOUR LOWER RATES RATHER THAN 40%

The tax rate depends on the level of your income, rather than the amount of gain you make. If you have taxable income of more than £30,500 after deducting your personal allowances, etc, the gains are taxed at 40%. If you have little or no income, the first £30,500 of any capital gains normally attracts tax at a maximum rate of 20%. It can therefore make sense for you to transfer an asset to your spouse to sell and realise a gain if the gain will be taxed at a lower rate.

Example – Transfers to reduce the rate of CGT

If *F*'s wife has no income, he could transfer shares with a paper gain of £35,500 to her. If *F* sold them he would be taxed at 40%, but his wife's disposal will attract tax only as follows:

	£
Gain	35,500
Less: exemption	(7,900)
Taxable	27,600
First £1,960 at 10%	196
Tax at 20% on £25,640	5,128
Tax liability	£5,324

18.5 SAVE TAX BY MAKING GIFTS TO RELATIVES

If you are planning to sell unquoted shares it may be possible to save tax, but note that hold-over relief applies to the gain before taper relief (see 14.5).

Example – Sale of unquoted shares

G holds all the shares in a private trading company. He has reached broad agreement with a potential purchaser to sell his shares for £1,000 each, which will produce a gain of £600 per share. The resultant capital gain will attract tax at 40% because of the level of *G*'s other income and gains.

If *G* so wishes, he could transfer some shares to his son *H* to enable him to use his annual exemption, ie *G* would give *H* 14 shares in the company and claim hold-over relief. No capital gain need arise for *G* on his gift to *H* who would then dispose of the shares to the ultimate purchaser. *H*'s capital gain would then be as follows:

	£
Capital gain: 14 × £600 =	8,400
Less: annual exemption	(7,900)
Taxable	500

The overall effect is that *G*'s family saves tax of at least £3,160 (ie 40% of £7,900).

Gifts of listed shares and securities

It is sometimes possible to achieve a similar saving by transferring quoted securities even though hold-over relief is not normally available unless a donor owns at least 5% of the voting shares. But you have to plan some way ahead.

The key point is that it is possible to claim hold-over relief where you make a chargeable transfer for IHT purposes, normally on your putting assets into a discretionary trust (see 13.8 and 19.10). The first thing to do is to either create such a trust or add property to an existing family trust and make a hold-over election under TCGA 1992, s 260 so that you do not have to pay any CGT. If the trustees subsequently appoint property in favour of the trust beneficiaries (eg your children, grandchildren, etc), they can make a similar hold-over election to avoid any CGT charge on them. The overall effect will be that the trust beneficiaries will have taken the property that you put into trust at a value equal to your original acquisition cost plus indexation; if they do not have very much income or gains, a large part of the proceeds from their eventually selling the assets will have escaped CGT altogether.

You will need to take professional advice. Bear in mind that if transfers into a discretionary trust take your cumulative transfers over the nil rate band (at present £255,000), you may have to pay IHT at the rate of 20% on the excess. And do not try to do all this in rapid succession as the Revenue may well attack the transactions as a preordained scheme.

18.6 CLAIM ROLL-OVER RELIEF AND FURNISHED HOLIDAY ACCOMMODATION

Where a person has realised a capital gain on the disposal of a business and does not wish to embark on further trading activities, roll-over relief may still be available. A particular type of property investment qualifies in this way because where a property is acquired for letting as furnished holiday accommodation, the owner is deemed to have acquired an asset for a trade and roll-over relief may be available. Two points are of particular interest:

(1) The property need not be located at the seaside. A property in (eg) Central London could qualify provided it is let for at least part of the year on a short-term basis (see 6.5 and 17.3.6).

(2) Roll-over relief may be obtained provided the property is let as furnished holiday accommodation for a period. If the property is subsequently let on a longer-term basis or used for some other purpose (eg as a second home) the relief is not normally withdrawn. The one exception to this would be if the owner has acquired a leasehold interest on the property and the lease has less than 60 years to run at the time it is acquired. Taking such a property out of use as furnished holiday

accommodation would mean that the deferred gain would become chargeable (see 17.3.4).

18.7 SELLING THE FAMILY COMPANY

18.7.1 Make the most of taper relief

It is absolutely crucial that you qualify for the business rate of taper relief. Take advice if your trading company also has significant investments as this could prevent your qualifying for relief (see 14.6.5).

If your spouse owns shares in a quoted company for which you work, business taper relief may not be due unless he or she transfers the shares to you before sale (see 14.6.2).

Seek professional advice if you have substantial unrealised gains on shares that did not qualify as business assets until 6 April 2000 (see 14.6.4).

18.7.2 Pre-sale dividend

In cases where the vendors of a private company do not qualify for the business rate of taper relief, it can make sense for them to take a dividend that is taxable as income, before disposing of their shares. Clearly, the purchaser will pay less, but the difference in the tax treatment of dividends and capital gains may mean that the vendors are better off.

Example – Sale of a family company

K owns all the shares in X Ltd. He is planning to sell the shares for a total of £1.2m. The resulting capital gain would be £900,000 and *K* will qualify only for 5% taper relief. However, his accountant advises him that no additional tax would be payable by X Ltd if a dividend were taken of £900,000. Assume that the payment of the dividend is acceptable to the purchaser (provided the price for the shares is reduced to £300,000). If *K* receives a dividend he will be liable only for higher rate tax, ie:

	£
Dividend	900,000
Tax credit	100,000
	1,000,000
32.5% income tax	325,000
Less: tax credit	(100,000)
	225,000

Because the sale price is reduced to £300,000, *K* has no CGT liability. If he had not taken the dividend, his capital gain would have been £900,000 on which tax could be payable of £360,000 (40%). So by taking the dividend he has cut his tax bill by £135,000.

19

INHERITANCE TAX AND INDIVIDUALS

HILARY SHARPE

Inheritance tax (IHT) is a combined gift tax and death duty. It applies to gifts and deemed gifts made during a person's lifetime and to his estate on death. The first £255,000 of chargeable transfers (the 'nil rate band') is free of IHT. Cumulative transfers in excess of this that take place either at or within seven years of death are taxed at 40% (though the overall impact may be reduced on transfers that take place more than three years before death). On all other occasions when IHT is payable, the rate is 20%.

This chapter covers the following topics:

(1) Who is subject to IHT?
(2) When may a charge arise?
(3) Transfers of value.
(4) Certain gifts are not transfers of value.
(5) Exempt transfers.
(6) Potentially exempt transfers.
(7) Reservation of benefit.
(8) Business property.
(9) Agricultural property and woodlands.
(10) Computation of tax payable on lifetime transfers.
(11) Tax payable on death.
(12) Life assurance and pension policies.
(13) Heritage property.
(14) Planning: the first step.

19.1 WHO IS SUBJECT TO IHT?

A UK-domiciled individual is subject to IHT on all property owned by him, whether located in the UK or overseas. By contrast, a person of foreign domicile is subject to IHT only on property situated in the UK. There are various specific exceptions to this. For example, with effect from 16 October 2002, UK unit trusts and OEICs (open ended investment companies) held by non-UK domiciled individuals have been excluded from any UK IHT charge. Also, transfers of exempt gilts are excluded from any IHT charge if the transferor is not resident or ordinarily resident in the UK even though he may be domiciled in the UK.

See Chaps. 23 and 24 on domicile, residence, etc.

Section 267 of the Inheritance Tax Act (IHTA) 1984 contains a special rule that applies for IHT purposes whereby an individual may be deemed to be UK-domiciled for a tax year if he has been resident in the UK for 17 out of the 20 tax years that end with the current year. However, this is overruled by provisions contained in a few of the UK's double taxation agreements.

19.2 WHEN MAY A CHARGE ARISE?

IHT can apply in the following circumstances:

(1) On a gift made by an individual during his lifetime.
(2) On a lifetime transfer of value regarded as a 'chargeable transfer'.
(3) On an individual's death.

A person who has an interest in possession under a trust or settlement is normally regarded as if he were entitled to the capital. When the beneficiary dies, the trust property's full value is treated as part of his estate for IHT purposes (see 20.4.15).

Figure 19.1 indicates the circumstances under which a gift may be a chargeable transfer for IHT purposes.

19.3 TRANSFERS OF VALUE

19.3.1 Not all transfers are gifts

(IHTA 1984, s 3)

The legislation refers mainly to transfers rather than gifts. The reason for this is that all gifts are transfers of value, but not all transfers of value are gifts. For example, where a person deliberately sells an asset at less than market value he may not be making a gift, but he is certainly making a transfer of value. Similarly, deliberately omitting to exercise a right can be a transfer of value, but this is not a gift in the normal sense of the word. To give a third example, a transfer can even involve property not owned by the person since the IHT legislation deems a person to make a gift if his interest in possession under a trust comes to an end.

19.3.2 There must be gratuitous intent

(IHTA 1984, s 10)

IHT does not normally apply to a gift unless there is an element of 'bounty', ie there is a deliberate intention to make a gift. An unintentional loss of

Figure 19.1 – Is a gift a chargeable transfer?

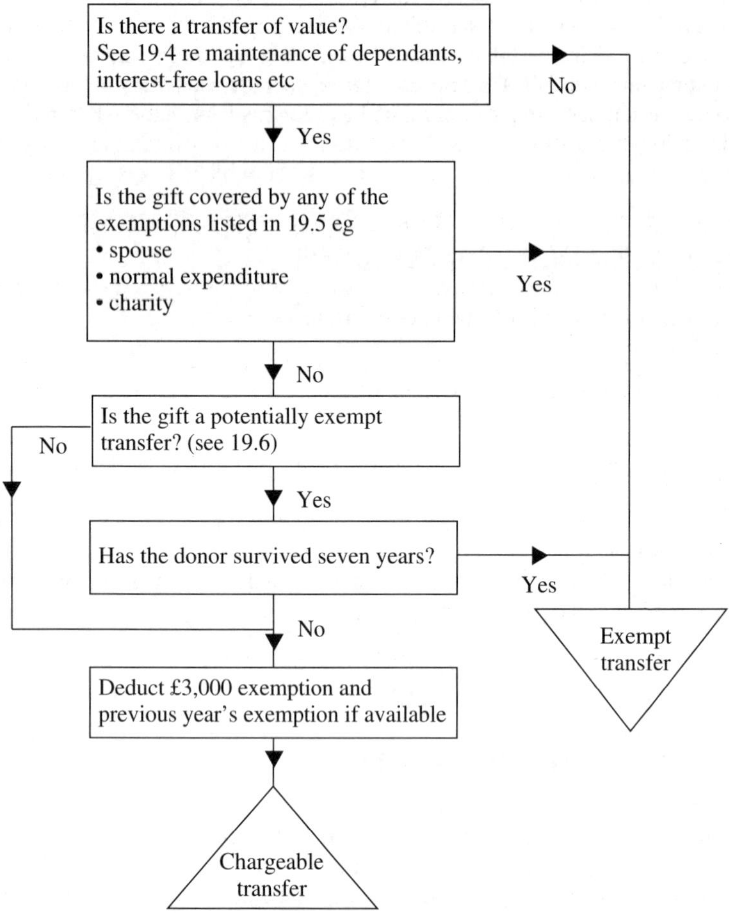

Is there a transfer of value?
See 19.4 re maintenance of dependants, interest-free loans etc
→ No: Exempt transfer
↓ Yes

Is the gift covered by any of the exemptions listed in 19.5 eg
• spouse
• normal expenditure
• charity
→ Yes: Exempt transfer
↓ No

Is the gift a potentially exempt transfer? (see 19.6)
→ No: Deduct £3,000 exemption
↓ Yes

Has the donor survived seven years?
→ Yes: Exempt transfer
↓ No

Deduct £3,000 exemption and previous year's exemption if available
↓

Chargeable transfer

value (eg a loss made on a bad business deal) is not subject to IHT because there was no intention to pass value to another person.

19.3.3 How a transfer is measured

(IHTA 1984, s 3)

The amount of any transfer of value is determined by the reduction in the donor's wealth. This is not necessarily the same as the increase in the recipient's wealth.

This can be shown by considering the situation where a person owns 51 out of 100 shares in a company. He has control because he has the majority of the shares. If he were to give two shares to his son, he would relinquish control of the company and his remaining 49 shares might be worth considerably less because of this. The two shares given to his son might not be worth very much in isolation, and the son may not have acquired a very valuable asset, but the father's estate would have gone down in value by the difference between the value of a 51% shareholding and that of a 49% shareholding.

19.4 CERTAIN GIFTS ARE NOT TRANSFERS OF VALUE

Certain gifts and other transactions are not regarded as transfers of value, so the issue of whether they are chargeable transfers simply does not arise. These include:

- Maintenance of dependants, family, etc;
- Waivers of dividends;
- Waivers of remuneration;
- Interest-free loans;
- Disclaimers of legacies;
- Deeds of variation;
- Transfers involving trusts where the settlor has retained powers of appointment.

19.4.1 Maintenance of dependants, family, etc

(IHTA 1984, s 11)

The legislation specifically provides that the following lifetime payments are not transfers of value:

(1) Payments for the maintenance of a spouse or former spouse.
(2) Payments for the maintenance, education or training of a child or stepchild under age 18.
(3) Payments made to maintain a child over age 18 who is in full-time education or training.
(4) Reasonable provision for the care or maintenance of a dependent relative, ie someone who is incapacitated by old age or infirmity from maintaining himself, or a widow or a separated or divorced mother or mother-in-law.

19.4.2 Waivers of dividends

(IHTA 1984, s 15)

A waiver of a dividend is not regarded as a transfer of value provided certain conditions are satisfied:

(1) The dividend must be waived by deed.

(2) The deed must not be executed more than 12 months before the right to the dividend has accrued.
(3) The deed waiving the dividend must be executed before any legal entitlement to the dividend arises.

The position is slightly different for interim and final dividends as the point in time at which entitlement may arise can be different.

Interim dividends

A shareholder has no enforceable right to payment prior to the date on which a board resolution has declared that a dividend shall be payable. However, the directors can declare an interim dividend that is payable immediately, and without having to first seek shareholders' approval. Therefore, a deed waiving a dividend should be executed in good time before any board resolution is passed.

Final dividends

A company might declare a dividend without stipulating any date for payment. In such circumstances, the declaration of the dividend creates an immediate debt and it is therefore too late to execute a waiver.

In other cases where a final dividend is declared as being payable at a later date, a shareholder may waive his entitlement provided he does so before the due date for payment.

In practice, a final dividend will require the shareholders' approval and an individual shareholder may therefore waive a dividend provided the deed is executed before the company's AGM.

19.4.3 Waivers of remuneration

(IHTA 1984, s 14)

There is a specific provision whereby a waiver of remuneration does not constitute a transfer of value. The terms of this exemption are based on the income tax treatment. In practice, the Revenue accepts that remuneration is not subject to income tax under Schedule E if it is waived and the Schedule E assessment has not become final and conclusive, and:

(1) the remuneration is formally waived (usually by deed); and
(2) the employer's assessable profits are adjusted accordingly.

19.4.4 Interest-free loans

(IHTA 1984, s 29)

The IHT legislation specifically provides that an interest-free loan is not to be treated as a transfer of value provided the loan is repayable on demand.

This exemption would not cover a situation where a loan was made for a specific period, with the lender having no legal right to call for repayment before that time. The grant of such a loan could be a transfer of value, with the Revenue assessing the transfer as the difference between the loan amount and its present market value if it were to be assigned.

19.4.5 Disclaimer of legacies

(IHTA 1984, s 142)

If a person becomes entitled to property under a will or an intestacy or under a trust (eg on a life tenant's death), he may disclaim his entitlement. Such a disclaimer is normally effective for IHT purposes and is not treated as a transfer of value provided that:

(1) no payment or other consideration is given for the disclaimer; and
(2) the person has not already accepted his entitlement, either expressly or by implication.

19.4.6 Deeds of variation

(IHTA 1984, s 142)

A deed of variation may be entered into where a person has died leaving property to a beneficiary, the effect being to redirect property. Where the necessary conditions are fulfilled, the revised disposition is treated as having taken place on the deceased person's death. Once again, a person who gives up an entitlement is not treated as making a transfer of value.

The following conditions need to be satisfied:

(1) The deed of variation must be executed within two years of a death.
(2) It must be in writing and must specifically refer to the provisions of the will, etc that are to be varied.
(3) It must be signed by the person who would otherwise have, and anyone else who might have, benefited.
(4) Only one deed of variation in respect of a particular piece of property can be effective for IHT purposes.
(5) No payment or other consideration may pass between beneficiaries to induce them to enter into the deed of variation (except that a variation is permitted that consists of an exchange of inheritances and a cash adjustment).
(6) For deeds executed before 1 August 2002, a formal election must be submitted to the Revenue within six months of execution.
(7) For deeds of variation executed on or after 1 August 2002 there is no need for a formal election provided that the deed refers to the relevant legislation. However, the deed must still be submitted to the Revenue within six months of being executed.

The Revenue's booklet IHT8, *Alterations to an inheritance following a death*, can be obtained by calling the CTO's orderline 08459 000 404.

19.4.7 Powers of appointment over settled property

Legislation was amended from 17 April 2002 to ensure that such rights and powers are not treated as being part of an individual's estate for IHT purposes. The relief applies retrospectively in relation to IHT charges that otherwise might have applied on death.

The change followed the decision in *IRC v Melville* CA [2001] STC 1297. This case concerned an individual who transferred property to a new discretionary settlement but had power to direct the trustees to return the property to him after three months. The Court of Appeal held that the chargeable transfer was only a modest amount as the settlor had retained a valuable right. Although this suited the taxpayer in *Melville*, it caused concern for settlors who had retained such powers, particularly individuals who had created settlements while domiciled abroad (see 24.15.2).

19.5 EXEMPT TRANSFERS

Even if a transfer takes place, it will not attract IHT if it is an exempt transfer. The full list of exempt transfers is as follows:

(1) Gifts to spouse.
(2) Normal expenditure out of income.
(3) £250 small gifts exemption.
(4) Annual £3,000 exemption.
(5) Exemption for marriage gifts.
(6) Gifts to charities.
(7) Gifts for national purposes.
(8) Gifts to political parties.
(9) Gifts to housing associations.
(10) Certain transfers to employee trusts.
(11) Compensation paid to POWs and holocaust victims.

19.5.1 Gifts to spouse

(IHTA 1984, s 18)

There is normally an unlimited exemption for transfers between husband and wife. For this purpose, a couple is regarded as husband and wife until a decree absolute has been obtained. The exemption covers outright gifts, legacies and a transfer of property to a trust under which the spouse has an interest in possession. (The transfer may be either a lifetime transfer or a transfer that takes place on death.)

The exemption is restricted where a UK-domiciled spouse makes transfers to a foreign domiciled spouse. In this situation, the exemption is limited to £55,000. However, the 'deemed domicile' rule (ie UK-resident for 17 out of 20 years: see 19.1) applies for all IHT legislation purposes except where expressly excluded. Consequently, a gift by a UK-domiciled individual to a spouse who has a foreign domicile, but who is treated as UK-domiciled for IHT purposes under the 17-year rule, qualifies for the unlimited exemption.

19.5.2 Normal expenditure out of income

(IHTA 1984, s 21)

A lifetime gift is exempt if it is shown that the gift was made as part of the donor's normal expenditure and comes out of income. The legislation requires that the gift should be normal, ie the donor had a habit of making such gifts. The legislation also requires that by taking one year with another, the pattern of such gifts must have left the donor with sufficient income to maintain his normal standard of living.

Gifts that take the form of payments under deed of covenant or the payment of premiums on life assurance policies written in trust frequently qualify as exempt because of this rule.

19.5.3 £250 small gifts exemption

(IHTA 1984, s 20)

Any number of individual gifts of up to £250 in any one tax year are exempt. If a person wanted to, he could make 100 separate gifts of £250 per time. However, where gifts to a particular individual exceed £250, the exemption does not apply.

19.5.4 Annual £3,000 exemption

(IHTA 1984, s 19)

This exemption is available to cover part of a larger gift. The exemption is £3,000 for each tax year. Furthermore, both husband and wife have separate annual exemptions.

If the full £3,000 is not used in a given year, the balance can be carried forward for one year only and is then allowable only if the exemption for the second year is fully utilised.

Example

Situation 1	£	£
Gifts made in Year 1		1,000
Balance of exemption carried to Year 2		2,000
Gifts made in Year 2		4,000
Annual exemption for Year 2	3,000	
Part of unused exemption for Year 1	1,000	(4,000)
Chargeable gifts		Nil

The balance of exemption from Year 1 of £1,000 may not be carried forward to Year 3.

Situation 2	£	£
Year 1 as in Situation 1 – unused exemption		2,000
Exemption for Year 2	3,000	
Gifts in Year 2	2,000	
Balance of Year 2 exemption to be carried forward to Year 3	1,000	

The balance of the Year 1 exemption of £2,000 may not be carried forward to Year 3.

19.5.5 Gifts in consideration of marriage

(IHTA 1984, s 22)

Gifts made to the bride or groom in consideration of their marriage are exempt up to the following amounts:

Gifts made by	*Maximum exemption*
Each parent	£5,000
Grandparents (or great grandparents)	£2,500
Bride or groom	£2,500
Any other person	£1,000

Parents may make gifts to either party to the marriage: their exemption is not restricted to gifts made to their own child but covers gifts made to both parties rather than £5,000 for each recipient. This means that for example in relation to the groom, each of the bride's parents may give up to £5,000. The gifts should be made so that they are conditional upon the marriage taking place.

19.5.6 Gifts to charities

(IHTA 1984, s 23)

Gifts to charities established in the UK are exempt regardless of the amount. A charity may be established or registered in the UK even though it carries out its work overseas, and the exemption covers gifts to such charities. Donations made to a foreign charity established abroad do not normally qualify.

19.5.7 Gifts for national purposes

(IHTA 1984, s 25)

Gifts to certain national bodies are totally exempt. These include colleges and universities, the National Trust, the National Gallery, the British

Museum and other galleries and museums run by local authorities or universities.

19.5.8 Gifts to political parties

(IHTA 1984, s 24)

Gifts to 'qualifying political parties' are exempt only if certain conditions are satisfied. A political party qualifies if it had at least two MPs returned at the last general election, or if it had at least one MP and more than 150,000 votes were cast for its candidates.

19.5.9 Gifts to housing associations

(IHTA 1984, s 24A)

Gifts of UK land to registered housing associations are exempt.

19.5.10 Certain transfers to employee trusts

(IHTA 1984, s 28)

Transfers by an individual to an employee trust of shares in a company can be exempt provided the following conditions are satisfied:

(1) The trust's beneficiaries include all or most of the persons employed by or holding office with the company.
(2) Within one year of the transfer:
    (a) the trustees must hold more than 50% of the company's ordinary share capital and have voting control on all questions that affect the company as a whole; and
    (b) the trustees' control is not fettered by some other provision or agreement between the shareholders.
(3) The trust deed must not permit any of the trust property to be applied at any time for the benefit of:
    (a) a participator in the company (ie a person who holds a 5% or greater interest);
    (b) any person who has been a participator at any time during the ten years prior to the transfer;
    (c) any person connected with a participator or former participator.

A further restriction may apply where a company makes a transfer to an employee trust.

19.5.11 *Ex-gratia* payments to POWs

There is an exemption for compensation and *ex-gratia* payments made to former prisoners of war by the Japanese Government. This has recently been extended to cover compensation received by prisoners of war from the German Government. Ask for a copy of ESC F20.

19.5.12 Holocaust compensation

Compensation paid to Holocaust victims or their families is exempt.

19.6 POTENTIALLY EXEMPT TRANSFERS

(IHTA 1984, s 3A)

19.6.1 Definition of 'potentially exempt transfer'

Irrevocable gifts made during an individual's lifetime may, provided certain conditions are satisfied, be potentially exempt transfers (PETs). These gifts become actually exempt only if the donor survives seven years. If he dies during that period, the PET becomes a chargeable transfer. The tax payable depends on the IHT rates in force at the date of death. The donee is liable to pay the tax.

The main conditions to be satisfied for a gift to be a PET are that the gift is made to:

(1) an individual; or
(2) a trust under which an individual has an interest in possession (see 20.4.18); or
(3) a trust for the disabled (see 20.7); or
(4) an accumulation and maintenance trust (see 20.6).

A gift that is subject to a reservation of benefit (see 19.7) cannot be a PET. Furthermore, a gift to a discretionary trust is a chargeable transfer.

19.6.2 Taper relief

(IHTA 1984, s 7)

Where an individual makes a PET or chargeable transfer and dies within the seven-year period, taper relief may reduce the amount of tax payable. The tax payable on the transfer that has become chargeable is reduced so that only a proportion is charged. The proportion is as follows:

Years between gift and death	*Percentage of full charge*
Three to four	80
Four to five	60
Five to six	40
Six to seven	20

Taper relief cannot reduce the tax on a lifetime chargeable transfer below the tax payable at the time the transfer was made.

If a gift falls within the nil rate band, the taper relief is of no real benefit and does not reduce the tax that arises on other property that passes on the donor's death.

19.7 RESERVATION OF BENEFIT
(FA 1986, s 102 and Sched 20)

19.7.1 Introduction

Property that has been given away may still be deemed to form part of a deceased person's estate unless:

(1) possession and enjoyment of the property was bona fide assumed by the donee; and
(2) the property was enjoyed virtually to the entire exclusion of the donor and of any benefit to him by contract or otherwise.

The reference to the property being enjoyed 'virtually to the entire exclusion' of the donor means that for all practical purposes this is an 'all or nothing' test. The Revenue's view is that the exception is intended to cover trivial benefits such as might arise where, for example, the donor of a picture enjoyed the chance to view it when making occasional visits to the donee's home.

The Act refers to a benefit reserved 'by contract or otherwise' and this is meant to refer to arrangements that are not legally binding but amount to an honourable understanding. This might arise where a person gifts away a house but remains in occupation. A reservation of benefit would arise even if there is no legal tenancy and the donee could, in law, require the donor to vacate the property at any time.

The rules on gifts of land and buildings were tightened up in FA 1999 to block the type of arrangements upheld by the House of Lords in *IRC v Ingram* [1999] STC 37. Here, the late Lady Ingram carved out a 20-year lease that entitled her to occupy the property rent free and then gave away the freehold. It was decided that this did not constitute a gift with reservation, but the law has been amended with effect from 9 March 1999 to block this loophole.

Starting date

The reservation of benefit rules apply to gifts made on or after 18 March 1986. Where a gift or transfer was made before that date, and the donor reserved a benefit, the gift is effective for IHT purposes and the capital does not form part of that person's estate.

19.7.2 Three specific exemptions

The FA 1986 specifically provided that occupation of property or use of chattels does not count as a benefit provided the donor pays a market rent. The legislation also provides that a benefit enjoyed by a donor occupying property can be ignored where the donor's financial circumstances have changed drastically for the worse after the gift has been made.

The FA 1999 introduced a further exemption whereby an individual who transfers an interest in a residence to another individual who resides there is not regarded as reserving a benefit provided that he continues to meet his share of all expenses and outgoings.

19.7.3 Position where reservation of benefit ceases

Where a person makes a gift and initially reserves a benefit, but then relinquishes that reservation, he is normally treated as making a PET at the time he gives up the reserved benefit. The amount of the PET is governed by the property's market value at that time.

Example – Giving up reservation of benefit

A gives property worth £150,000 in July 1992 but reserves a benefit. The benefit is relinquished in July 1997 when the property is worth £220,000. *A* dies in October 1999.

If no benefit had been reserved, the gift would have been completely exempt by August 1999 (ie seven years after the gift), but because a benefit was retained until July 1997 the seven-year period starts only from that date. The full £220,000 (ie the value at July 1997 when the reservation of benefit came to an end) would form part of *A*'s estate for IHT purposes.

19.7.4 Settlements and trusts

The position is less clear cut where a person has sought to reserve the possibility of a benefit, for example where he has created a settlement and is a potential beneficiary. It is the Revenue's opinion that a benefit is reserved where the settlor creates a discretionary trust and is a member of a class of potential beneficiaries. This would also apply where the settlor may be added to a class of potential beneficiaries.

In contrast to this, the Revenue has confirmed that no reservation of benefit arises where a person creates a settlement and is a contingent or default beneficiary. This might apply, for example, where property is put into trust for the settlor's children but the property would revert to the settlor in the event of the children dying or becoming bankrupt.

The legislation does not require that the donor's spouse should be excluded from benefit, and where a discretionary settlement is created it would be possible to include his spouse, any future spouse or widow(er) as a potential beneficiary. However, if property were to be distributed to the donor's spouse from the trust and that property were then to be applied for the benefit of the settlor, the Revenue might well take the view that, looked at as a whole, there had been a reservation of benefit.

The Revenue has confirmed that a settlor may be a trustee of a settlement created by him without this constituting a reservation of benefit. Also, where the settled property includes shares in a family company, the settlor/trustee may also be a director of the company and may be permitted

Figure 19.2 – Is there reservation of benefit?

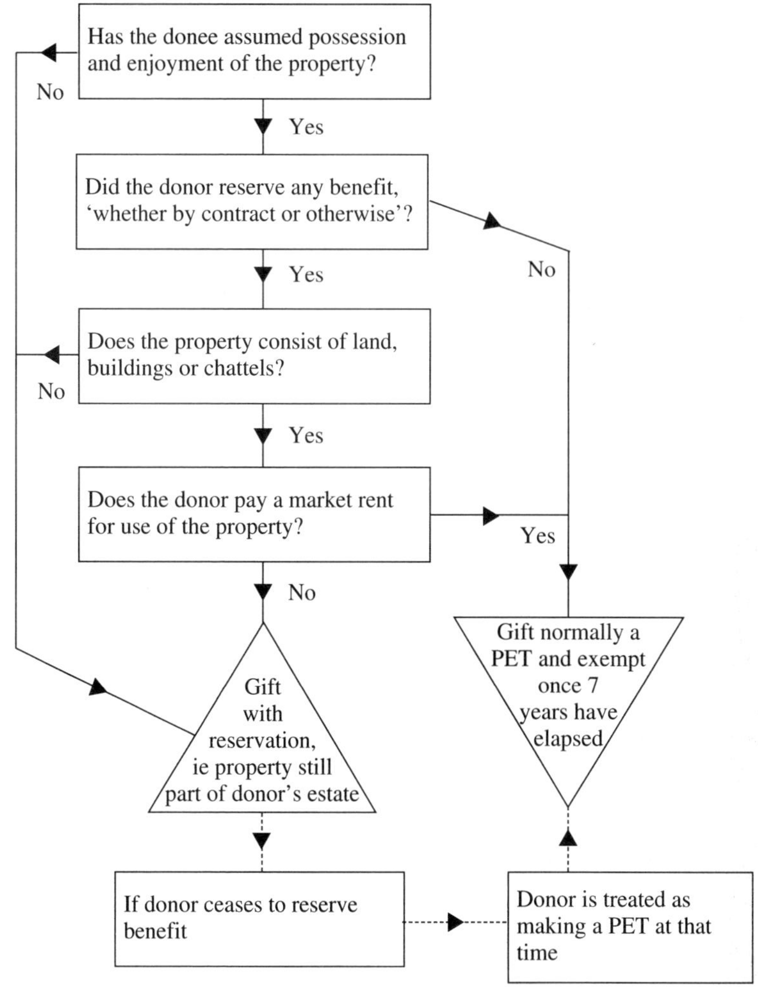

under the trust deed to retain his remuneration provided it is reasonable in relation to the services rendered.

19.7.5 Eversden case

The Court of Appeal held in *IRC v Eversden* [2003] STC 822 that the reservation of benefit rules did not apply where a woman transferred property into a trust under which her husband had an interest in possession even though that interest subsequently came to an end and the settlor was then able to benefit. The point was that the original transfer (gift into settlement) was covered by spouse exemption and the gifts with reservation (GWR) rules were therefore not applicable. The subsequent termination of the spouse's interest in possession was not caught by the GWR rules because it was a transfer of value and not a gift (the GWR legislation applies only to gifts).

Unfortunately, this loop was closed with effect from 20 June 2003.

19.8 BUSINESS PROPERTY

(IHTA 1984, ss 103-114)

19.8.1 Basic requirements

A special deduction is given against the value of business property where the following conditions are satisfied:

(1) The property must have been owned during the previous two years or have been inherited from a spouse and, when the spouse's period of ownership is taken into account, the combined period of ownership exceeds two years.
(2) Property must not be subject to a binding contract for sale.

(See also 19.11.10 on replacement property.)

19.8.2 Rates of business property relief

(IHTA 1984, s 103)

Unincorporated businesses

A sole proprietor's interest in his business qualifies for a 100% deduction, as does a partner's interest in his firm.

A 50% deduction is available for an asset owned by a partner but used by his firm.

Shares and debentures

Business relief is available on shares only where the company concerned is a trading company or the holding company of a trading group. The 100% relief is available on shares and debentures in an unquoted company. Where the company is a quoted company, 50% relief is due if (and only if) the person making the capital transfer had voting control before the transfer.

Shares dealt in on the AIM are treated as unquoted.

Prior to 6 April 1996, the 100% relief was available for a transfer of shares in an unquoted trading company only if the transferor had control of more than 25% of the voting rights before the transfer. A 50% deduction was given for smaller shareholdings in unquoted trading companies.

Where a controlling shareholder transfers an asset used by his trading company, or where such an asset passes on his death, 50% relief is available.

19.8.3 Businesses that do not qualify

Business relief is not normally available where the business carried on consists wholly or mainly of dealing in securities, stocks or shares, land or buildings or in holding or making investments.

Where a transfer involves shares, business relief may be restricted if the company owns investments. The legislation refers to such investments as 'excepted assets', which are defined as assets that are neither:

(1) used wholly or mainly for the purposes of the business, nor
(2) required for the future use of the business.

Where a company has subsidiaries, it is necessary to look at the group situation (ie shares in subsidiaries may have to be treated as excepted assets if the subsidiaries are investment companies).

19.9 AGRICULTURAL PROPERTY AND WOODLANDS

(IHTA 1984, ss 115-124B)

Agricultural relief is available on the agricultural value of farmland in the UK, Channel Islands or Isle of Man.

19.9.1 Land occupied by the transferor

A 100% deduction is available where the individual has occupied the farmland for the two years prior to the transfer date. Where a farm has been sold and another acquired, the replacement farm normally qualifies for agricultural property relief provided the owner has occupied the two farms for a combined period of at least two years in the last five years. Agricultural property relief is also available for land owned by an individual but occupied by a firm of which he is a partner or a company of which he is the controlling shareholder for the two years preceding the transfer date.

19.9.2 Relief for other land

A 100% deduction is also available on land not occupied by the owner provided he has (or had) the legal right to regain vacant possession within a period not exceeding 12 months. To qualify under this head, the individual must normally have owned the land for at least seven years.

19.9.3 Relief for tenanted farmland

A 50% deduction is available for farmland let on a tenancy granted before

1 September 1995 and where the owner cannot obtain vacant possession within 12 months. This would generally be the case where the land is let under an agricultural tenancy. Once again, the land must normally have been owned for seven years.

The 50% deduction is increased to 100% for land under a tenancy granted on or after 1 September 1995. This also includes a tenancy over property in Scotland acquired after that date by right of succession.

19.9.4 Woodlands

(IHTA 1984, ss 125-130)

The tax treatment of UK woodlands is largely beneficial as business relief is normally available after two years of ownership. In very unusual circumstances where business relief is not available, alternative relief may be due under s 125 after five years of ownership.

19.10 COMPUTATION OF TAX PAYABLE ON LIFETIME TRANSFERS

In practice, IHT is likely only to be paid during a person's lifetime for chargeable transfers made by him to a discretionary trust. The tax payable is calculated as follows:

Initial calculation

Chargeable transfers made during the preceding seven years		A
Add	Amount of chargeable transfer	B
		C
Deduct	Nil rate band	D
		E
	IHT thereon at 20%	X
Deduct	IHT on a notional transfer of A minus D as if it took place at the same time	Y
	IHT payable in respect of the chargeable transfer	Z

Position if the donor dies within three years

Chargeable transfers made during the previous seven years		A
Add	PETs caught by the seven-year rule	B
		C
Add	amount of chargeable transfer	D
		E
Deduct	Nil rate band	F
		G
	IHT thereon at 40%	H
Deduct	IHT at 40% on a notional transfer of C minus F	I
		J

The donee is liable to pay additional IHT of J minus the amount Z above already paid.

Position if the donor dies during years four to seven

The above will be liable for additional IHT computed as J above, but subject to the IHT on PETs caught by the seven-year rule being reduced by taper relief (see 19.6.2).

19.11 TAX PAYABLE ON DEATH

19.11.1 Normal basis of computation

The charge on death is normally computed as shown in the flowchart (see Figure 19.3). The IHT will be the tax on the figure in Box 6 minus the tax payable on a normal transfer equal to the amount in Box 4 as if the notional transfer took place immediately prior to the death. Some taper relief may be due on the PETs caught by the seven-year rule (see 19.6.2).

However, there are a number of special reliefs that may be available.

19.11.2 Death on active service

(IHTA 1984, s 154)

Ever since World War II the death duty legislation has contained an exemption for a person who dies from wounds suffered while on active service. The exemption applies to the estates of those killed in the Falklands conflict

Figure 19.3 – Charge on death computation

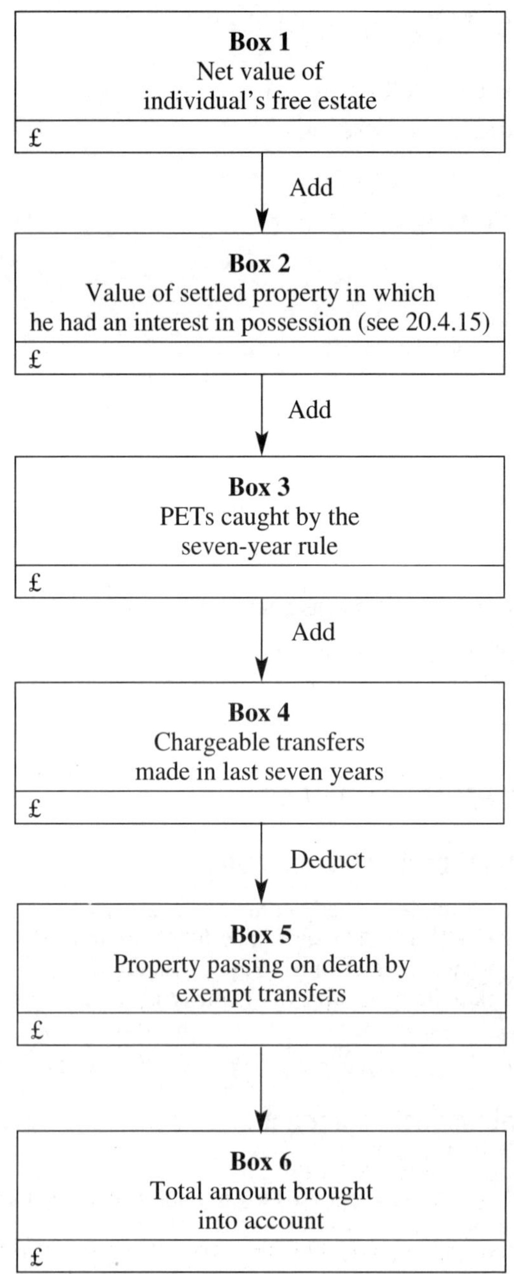

and the Gulf War, and of members of the RUC killed by terrorists in Northern Ireland.

The exemption may well apply more often than people think. Death does not have to be immediate, nor need the wound be the only cause of death. The High Court held in 1978 that the exemption was owed to the estate of the fourth Duke of Westminster because serious wounds that he had suffered in 1944 contributed to his death in 1967.

19.11.3 Sales of quoted securities at a loss

(IHTA 1984, ss 178-189, as extended by FA 1993, s 198)

Relief is given where quoted securities or unit trusts are sold at a loss within 12 months of death. Where shares are suspended, FA 1993, s 198 permits similar relief to be claimed by reference to the shares' value when they return from suspension. It is not possible to pick and choose: the relief is confined to the amount of any overall loss. Executors must, in effect, elect that the total proceeds of any sales should be substituted for the value at date of death.

Example – Sale of quoted securities at a loss

B died on 1 October 2001. His estate included a portfolio worth £70,000. The executors had to sell all of the securities in December 2001 and realised an overall loss of £25,000. The estate can be reduced by this amount so that, in effect, only £45,000 is taken into account.

The overall loss of £25,000 may have been made up of a gain of £5,000 and losses of £30,000. Relief is, however, limited to the net figure.

19.11.4 Relief restricted where executors purchase quoted securities

Furthermore, the relief is restricted where the executors repurchase quoted securities within two months of the last sale.

Example – Restriction of relief on quoted securities

B's executors sold the securities in December 2001. On 10 January 2002, they reinvested £10,000 in new securities. The £25,000 loss cannot be claimed in full, it has to be reduced by

$$\frac{10{,}000}{45{,}000} \times \text{£}25{,}000\text{, ie £}5{,}556$$

19.11.5 Sales of land at a loss

(IHTA 1984, ss 190-198, as amended by FA 1993, s 199)

Relief is due where land and buildings are sold at a loss within four years of death, provided the loss is at least £1,000 or 5% of probate value (whichever is less). The net proceeds are substituted for the value at the date of death and the IHT is recomputed. This relief applies only where the property is sold to an arm's length purchaser, and not to a connected person.

19.11.6 Debts that may be disallowed

(FA 1986, s 103)

There is a general rule that debts are not deductible where the deceased has made a capital transfer to the person who subsequently made a loan back to the deceased. This rule applies only to loans made after 18 March 1986, but there is no such time limit on the capital transfers. A debt may be disallowed because the deceased had made a capital transfer to the lender even though that capital transfer took place before 18 March 1986. It is also of no help that the loan was made on normal commercial terms and a market rate of interest was payable.

19.11.7 Legitim: special rules for Scotland

(IHTA 1984, s 147)

Scottish law provides that a person must leave a set part of his estate to his children: their entitlement is called 'legitim'. If a person makes a will that does not take account of this, the children can have it set aside. In practice children often decide to renounce their right to legitim, especially where a person's Will bequeaths all his property to his widow. The legislation provides that children who renounce their entitlement within two years of the death are not treated as making a chargeable transfer and the property is treated as passing to the widow in accordance with the will.

The deed renouncing the rights must satisfy the provisions as to variations: see 19.4.6.

Practical problems arise where minor children are involved. The IHT legislation provides that children under age 18 (at the date of death) may renounce their entitlement within two years of attaining age 18 without this constituting a chargeable transfer by them. The property is then treated (for IHT purposes) as passing to the widow in accordance with the will. As a child under age 18 does not have the legal capacity to renounce his entitlement, the executors have a difficult choice: they can either account for IHT on the basis that the child takes his entitlement or on the assumption that the child will renounce his rights when he reaches 18.

Position where executors assume legitim rights are taken

IHT will have to be paid to the extent that the property that passes to the children exceeds the nil rate band. When each child attains 18, he may elect to renounce his rights so that the widow benefits. The spouse exemption will then mean that no tax should have been paid. The Revenue will then repay the IHT paid and pay interest.

Position where executors assume that legitim will be renounced

No IHT will be paid in the first instance. However, if it turns out that one of the children decides not to renounce his entitlement, IHT on the death is recomputed and the tax payable attracts interest from the date it should have been paid.

19.11.8 Quick succession relief
(IHTA 1984, s 141)

Suppose a person has recently inherited property from someone else. If he were to die and the full rate of IHT applied, the same property would have been subject to IHT twice within a relatively short period of time.

Quick succession relief is intended to alleviate this. The relief works by giving credit for a proportion of the tax charged on the first occasion against the tax payable on the second death. The proportion is set out below:

Both deaths occur	*Proportion*
within one year	100%
within two years	80%
within three years	60%
within four years	40%
within five years	20%

Example – Quick succession relief

D inherited property worth £150,000 in June 2000. IHT was paid on that estate at an average rate of 25%, so the grossed-up amount was £200,000 (£150,000 × $^{100}/_{75}$) and the tax suffered was £50,000. *D* dies in August 2003. The maximum amount on which quick succession relief can be claimed is:

$$\frac{150{,}000}{200{,}000} \times \text{£50,000, ie £37,500}$$

This has to be reduced to 40% of £37,500 (ie £15,000) as three complete years have elapsed. The relief is not affected by the fact that property has been sold or given away before the second death takes place.

19.11.9 Treatment of gifts caught by seven-year rule
(IHTA 1984, s 113A)

Tax on a PET that becomes a chargeable transfer because of the transferor's death is payable by the recipient of the gift. Business relief is available on a PET that becomes a chargeable transfer only if the conditions in 19.8 are satisfied both at the time of the gift and at the time of death.

Examples – Business relief on PETs

(1) *E* owns all the shares in a family company. He gives his son *F* a 24% shareholding. Three years later, the company is sold and *F* receives cash for his shares. One year after that *E* dies.

Business relief will not normally be available as the necessary conditions are not satisfied by the donee at the time of *E*'s death. If *F* had reinvested the proceeds in another private company, business relief might have been available after all.

(2) The basic position is as in (1) (ie *E*'s gift to *F* of a 24% shareholding). This time, *F* retains his shares, but by the time *E* dies the shares are quoted. No relief is due as *F* does not control the company and his shares are quoted shares.

(3) The basic position is as in (1), but *F* retains the shares and they are still unquoted at the time of *E*'s death. The shares attract the 100% relief and this is not lost even if *F* disposes of the shares shortly after *E*'s death.

19.11.10 Replacement property

(IHTA 1984, s 107)

Where a donee has disposed of business property, but acquires replacement property, the PET may still attract business relief provided the replacement property is acquired within three years of the disposal. Prior to 30 November 1993, the replacement property had to be acquired within one year. Similar rules apply for agricultural property.

19.11.11 Acceptance of property in lieu of IHT

The Revenue has power to accept certain types of property in satisfaction of IHT liabilities. Such property includes pictures, prints, books, manuscripts, works of art, scientific objects and other items regarded as being of national, scientific, artistic and historic interest. The Revenue has to clear such arrangements with Heritage ministers and in practice only property regarded as of 'pre-eminent interest' is accepted.

Taxpayers who own such items that have been acknowledged as being first rate can enquire further about these arrangements by obtaining a copy of *Capital Taxation and The National Heritage* (price £5.20) from:

The Inland Revenue Reference Room
Room 8, New Wing
Somerset House
London WC2R 1LB

19.11.12 Double taxation agreements

The UK has only a handful of tax treaties that cover inheritance tax. There are treaties with France, India, Italy, Netherlands, Pakistan, Ireland, South Africa, Sweden, Switzerland and the USA.

Where no double taxation arrangement exists, unilateral relief will normally be available by way of a foreign tax credit against the UK IHT charge.

19.12 LIFE ASSURANCE AND PENSION POLICIES

19.12.1 Life assurance

Life assurance is one of the best ways of providing for the payment of IHT, but the tax treatment of policies needs to be watched carefully. The following is only a summary of a complex area.

19.12.2 Death of policyholder

A life assurance policy beneficially owned by the deceased is property subject to IHT in the same way as any other property owned by him.

19.12.3 Gifts of policies

Gifts of policies may generally be made in two ways:

(1) Writing the policy in trust or making a subsequent declaration of trust.
(2) Assignment of the policy.

In either case subsequent premiums may be paid:

(a) by the donor direct;
(b) by the beneficiary out of cash gifts from the donor;
(c) by the beneficiary out of his resources;
(d) by a combination of the above.

In general, if the gift is to an individual, an accumulation and maintenance trust, a trust for the disabled or a trust in which there is an interest in possession, it will constitute a PET and will only be taxable if the donor dies within seven years of making the gift. Gifts to other trusts such as discretionary trusts may attract lifetime IHT.

If any of the usual IHT exemptions applies (see 19.5), neither the gift of the policy nor any gifts of premiums that have been made will be taxable, for example:

(1) The gift of the premium or policy falls within the annual exemption – currently £3,000 (note that if the policy is a qualifying policy and premiums are payable net of life assurance relief, it is the net premium that constitutes the gift; if the premiums are paid gross, it is the gross premium that constitutes the gift).
(2) The premiums come within the donor's normal expenditure out of income exemption (note that this applies to payment of premiums, not to the gift of an existing policy).

(3) The gifts fall within the marriage settlement exemption.
(4) The gifts fall within the small gifts exemption – outright gifts of not more than £250 per donee (eg a premium on a policy written in trust for the absolute benefit of a child).
(5) Policies written by husband or wife in trust for the other.

If none of the exemptions applies, IHT may be payable in respect of the gift of the policy or the payment of subsequent premiums (unless they fall within the £255,000 nil rate band).

If IHT is payable, the chargeable transfers are the premiums paid by the donor; or, if a gift of an existing policy is made by assignment or declaration of trust, the chargeable transfer is generally the greater of the total gross premiums paid or the policy's market value (usually the surrender value).

If cash gifts have been made to enable the premiums to be paid by the beneficiary, the amount of the cash gifts will usually be PETs. The proceeds of the policy on death, maturity or surrender will not be subject to IHT in the hands of the recipient of the assignment or a beneficiary having an interest in possession in the trusts.

19.12.4 Life of another policies

On the death of the life assured the proceeds are totally free of IHT. Clearly they do not form part of the life assured's estate, as the policy is not owned by him. The surrender value will, however, be potentially chargeable in the policyholder's estate if he dies before the life assured.

If the policyholder is enabled to pay the premiums by virtue of cash gifts from the donor, the cash gifts will be taxable for the donor, unless the exemptions mentioned above apply, but the proceeds will be free of IHT in the policyholder's hands.

19.12.5 Use of policies

Life assurance policies can be used in two main ways in IHT planning:

(1) as a vehicle for making gifts to beneficiaries; and
(2) to create a fund for the eventual payment of the tax.

Thus they may help to both minimise the amount of tax payable and offer a means of paying any unavoidable liability whenever it arises.

19.12.6 IHT and pension plans

Although the legislation does not permit a policyholder to alienate his right to a retirement pension, it is possible to assign any death benefits provided under retirement annuity or personal pension plans, whether provided as a sum assured or as a return of the retirement fund. The IHT rules are broadly similar to those applicable to life policy assignments except that:

(1) discretionary trusts of these assignable benefits will not be subject to the usual IHT charging regime of ten-yearly and exit charges provided the benefits are distributed within two years of the individual's death;
(2) the right to a pension is not treated as giving rise to an interest in possession in the pension fund;
(3) the gift of a 'return of fund' death benefit will usually be regarded as having no value, provided the individual is in good health. Similarly, subsequent contributions to the pension will be treated as being attributable to the provision of the pension benefits and not the death benefit, provided the individual is in good health at the time the contribution is made.

Occupational schemes are usually written under discretionary trusts and also achieve the same IHT exemptions on payment of contributions and distribution of benefits.

19.13 HERITAGE PROPERTY

It is possible to claim exemption for transfers of qualifying heritage assets, for example chattels of museum quality, land of outstanding natural beauty or of historic or scientific interest, and buildings and amenity land deemed to be of outstanding historic or architectural interest. The exemption is currently conditional on the new owner undertaking to maintain and preserve the asset and to provide reasonable public access to it. It is no longer possible to restrict access by requiring a prior appointment with the asset's owner.

The rules for defining qualifying chattels have also been made more restrictive by FA 1998. There used to be no time limit for claiming heritage tax exemptions, but for tax charges arising after 16 March 1998 a claim for exemption normally has to be made within two years of the date of the relevant chargeable event. In addition, transfers made after 16 March 1998 no longer qualify for the special exemption previously available for gifts and bequests to certain non-profit making bodies.

19.14 PLANNING: THE FIRST STEP

Planning for IHT is something that many people would rather not think about. The first step should be to sit down with a piece of paper and work out the value of your estate: its something that your next of kin may already have done if you've ever argued! If the net value of your estate is close to the IHT threshold, then perhaps the time has come to talk with your financial or tax advisor to discuss ways in which you can ensure the people you would like to benefit from your estate are provided for. As part of this process you should review your existing will. If you do not have a will, this should be the starting point for any planning. If your affairs and estate are more complicated you may wish to consider the use of a trust during your lifetime. This can simplify matters on death by effectively accelerating or side stepping probate problems.

20

THE TAXATION OF TRUSTS

MARK FRANCIS

This chapter covers the taxation of trusts under the following headings:

(1) When are trustees liable to pay income tax?
(2) When are trustees liable for UK capital gains tax?
(3) Bare trusts.
(4) Fixed-interest trusts.
(5) Discretionary trusts.
(6) Accumulation and maintenance trusts.
(7) Trusts for the disabled.
(8) Protective trusts.
(9) Charitable trusts.
(10) Executors and personal representatives.

20.1 WHEN ARE TRUSTEES LIABLE TO PAY INCOME TAX? (FA 1989, s 110)

20.1.1 General rules

A liability to pay UK income tax arises for all trusts that have at least one UK-resident trustee (even though there may be a majority of non-resident trustees) unless the trust was created by a person of foreign domicile, in which case the UK trustee is liable only in respect of UK income.

In the main, trustees are liable for tax at 20% on income from savings, with other income being taxed at the basic rate, but trustees of discretionary and accumulation trusts are subject to additional tax so that in total they pay 34%.

A non-resident trust is subject to tax on UK income, for example interest taxed at source and dividends. Where the non-resident trust receives untaxed interest, there is in theory a tax liability, but in practice the trustees may escape tax because of ESC B13.

Trustees are not entitled to personal allowances.

Where the settlor or spouse can benefit, the trust income may be deemed to be that of the settlor for higher rate purposes (see 22.5) but any income received gross by the trustees still needs to be reported in the trust return.

20.1.2 Insurance bonds owned by trustees

Prior to 9 April 2003 legislation taxed individuals when they cashed in a non-qualifying insurance policy or 'bond'. It also imposed a charge on the individual taking a loan against the policy; the loan was treated as if it were an encashment. Where a trust was involved, the charge was normally computed as if the settlor had realised the policy.

Where the settlor died, a 34% tax charge arose on a policy being encashed but there were no existing provisions which taxed a loan. This lacuna was closed with effect from 9 April 2003.

20.1.3 Trusts and self-assessment

The same general rules apply to trustees as they do to individuals under self-assessment (SA). If a trust has UK chargeable income and gains, then the trustees have to file a self-assessment form by 31 January following the relevant tax year.

20.2 WHEN ARE TRUSTEES LIABLE FOR UK CAPITAL GAINS TAX?

(TCGA 1992, ss 2 and 69)

20.2.1 General rules

Trustees are subject to CGT only if the trust is resident in the UK. A trust is regarded as resident unless:

(1) the majority of the trustees are not UK-resident; and
(2) the ordinary administration of the trust is carried on outside the UK.

This rule is therefore slightly different from that used for income tax purposes.

There is an exception to the above general rule in the case of property settled by a person of foreign domicile who was neither resident nor ordinarily resident in the UK at the time the trust was created. Provided the UK trustees are professional trustees whose business consists of or includes the management of trusts, the facts that the majority of the trustees are UK-resident and the management of the trust is carried on within the UK do not make the trust UK-resident.

20.2.2 UK-resident trusts

In general, trustees are responsible for reporting gains and paying tax.

Where either the settlor or his spouse can receive benefit and the settlor is UK-resident, capital gains are generally taxed as if they were personal gains of the settlor (see 22.12). However, such gains still need to be reported in the trust tax return, but any tax payable is paid, initially, by the settlor who can recover it from the trustees. Where a trust is caught by this rule, any surplus capital losses are carried forward to cover future gains of the trustees and cannot be set against the settlor's personal capital gains.

Since 6 April 1998, it has not been possible for a settlor to set a personal capital loss against a capital gain attributed to him under the special rules for UK resident settlements in which he has an interest. With effect from 2003-04, the gain attributed to the settlor will be computed before taper relief and the settlor will set personal losses first against his personal gains and then against attributed gains. In this way, taper relief is effectively given by the settlor as opposed to the trustees in calculating the net gains taxable on the settlor. This new rule will not apply in certain cases where the settlor has been temporarily non-UK resident and returns to the UK.

A settlor may elect for the treatment that will apply from 2003-04 to also have effect for any of the tax years 2000-01, 2001-02 or 2002-03 with such an election being made by 31 January 2005 in each case. If the election results in the trustees having to reimburse the settlor a greater aggregate amount for those three years than would otherwise have been the case, the election must be made jointly by the settlor and the trustees.

20.2.3 Annual exemption

(TCGA 1992, Sched 1)

For a number of years the annual CGT exemption available to trustees has been half the individual exemption, for example for 2003-04, £3,950 (half of £7,900).

Where a settlor has created a number of settlements since 6 June 1978, the annual exemption is shared equally. The minimum annual exemption for each settlement is currently £790 (ie 1/10 of the annual individual exemption). An unused part of the exemption for one settlement cannot be utilised by another settlement.

Consequently, if a person created three trusts in 1975 and four in 1989, the 2003-04 exemption for the 1975 trusts would be £3,950 each, and the four trusts created after 6 June 1978 would each have an exemption of £987. If all seven trusts had been created after 6 June 1978, each would have an annual exemption of £790.

20.2.4 Taper relief

Trustees may qualify for the business rate of taper relief for business assets if they own shares in an unquoted trading company or have at least 5% of the voting rights in a quoted trading company. Certain fixed-interest trusts can also qualify where the trustees' shares are in a company that is the life tenant's qualifying company (see below).

The requirements were stricter until 5 April 2000 in that trustees were eligible for business taper only if they held 25% of the voting rights in a trading company (quoted or unquoted) or an eligible beneficiary worked full-time for the company and held 5% of the voting rights.

20.3 BARE TRUSTS

A bare trust is one where trustees hold property on behalf of someone who is absolutely entitled to that property, or would be absolutely entitled if he were not a minor. Income and capital gains received by trustees of a bare trust belong to the person who is absolutely entitled to the property concerned. The trustees normally have no liability to tax.

Prior to 6 April 1996, the trustees of some bare trusts accounted for income tax at basic rate on the income they paid over to the beneficiaries. These amounts became taxed income in the hands of the beneficiaries, who were required to give full details of that income in their tax returns, but were liable to pay further tax only if they were higher rate taxpayers. Conversely, they were entitled to a repayment of the tax paid by the trustees if they had no personal liability.

Under self-assessment, the Revenue no longer allows trustees to account for tax in such circumstances because there is no entitlement in law for trustees to deduct tax from income arising to bare trusts. Any income received gross by the trustees must be paid gross to the beneficiaries. The only exception to this rule is that UK-resident trustees may be required, under the non-resident landlords scheme, to deduct and account for tax on the rental income of beneficiaries whose usual place of abode is outside the UK (see 23.6).

Trustees of bare trusts are not required to complete SA tax returns, or to make any payments on account. Beneficiaries are still required to give details of all their income and gains from bare trusts in their own tax returns, and in addition are required to account to the Revenue for the full amount of any tax due.

See 22.5.4 on the position where a parent gives money to a bare trust for his minor child.

20.4 FIXED-INTEREST TRUSTS

A fixed-interest trust is one where a beneficiary is entitled to receive income as it arises, either during his lifetime or for a specific period. A simple type of fixed-interest trust would be where the beneficiary is entitled to receive all the income during his lifetime with the trust coming to an end on his death, perhaps with the capital then passing to his children. A beneficiary who is entitled to receive trust income in this way during his lifetime is called a ‘life tenant’.

There may also be a situation where a life tenant is entitled to receive a proportion of the trust income, say 50%, with the other 50% being held on different types of trust. Additionally, it is possible to have an entitlement to income (an 'interest in possession') for a specific period, so that a trust under which someone had a right to all of the income for a fixed period of ten years would be a fixed-interest trust until the end of that period.

20.4.1 Income tax

Where property is held on fixed-interest trusts, income tax is charged on the trustees at the basic rate except in so far as the income is dividend income (which is taxed at 10%) or 'income from savings' (which is taxed at the 'lower rate' of 20%). There is no deduction for personal allowances (only individuals are entitled to them), but if a trust owns investment properties on which an entitlement to capital allowances arises, such capital allowances may be set against the trustees' income in the same way as for individuals. Similarly, if the trustees carry on a trade, any losses may be relieved against other income. Subject to this, the trustees will either suffer basic rate/lower rate tax at source or be assessed to basic rate/lower rate tax on all income arising to them, with the assessments being made under the different Schedules.

20.4.2 Ascertaining the beneficiary's income

It will not generally be possible for the trustees to pay over to a beneficiary the full amount of the income left to him after tax. Inevitably, there will be some expenses (eg bank charges, interest, professional fees) that are properly charged to income, and there may also be the trustees' own fees. Such expenses may not be deducted in arriving at the trustees' taxable income, but they need to be taken into account in determining the amount of the beneficiary's income.

In broad terms, the proper procedure is to ascertain the trustees' taxable income for a year. The tax paid by the trustees for the year should then be deducted, and a further deduction made for expenses that are properly charged against income. The net amount must then be 'grossed up' and this is the amount the beneficiary will need to declare on his tax return.

Example – Tax treatment of income from a fixed-interest trust

The trustees of a fixed-interest trust have taxable deposit interest of £20,000 for 2002-03. They pay tax of £4,000 (20%). There are expenses of £1,700 that are properly chargeable against the income. The balance belongs to the life tenant, whose gross income will be ascertained as follows:

	£
Trustees' taxable income	20,000
Less: basic rate tax	(4,000)
	16,000

Less: expenses	(1,700)
	14,300
£14,300 grossed up lower rate (25%)	17,875

This income forms part of the life tenant's income for the year whether or not it is actually paid out to him. If the life tenant is subject to higher rate tax, he must pay the difference between the 40% rate and the rate paid by the trustees.

20.4.3 Income from savings

(FA 1993, s 79 and Sched 6)

It is necessary to distinguish income from savings. The lower Schedule F rate of tax means that income from savings should be separated into that from dividends and that from other sources. Dividend income is taxable at 10% as opposed to 20% on other savings income. Trustees' expenses are deemed to be set first against UK dividend income, so as to minimise the restriction of the tax deemed to be withheld from the trust income.

20.4.4 Tax returns

The returns usually completed for trusts are forms SA900 and additional pages as necessary. For fixed-interest trusts a tax deduction certificate (Form R185 (Non-discretionary)) should also be completed by the trustees or their professional advisers, showing the appropriate gross, tax and net figures in respect of the beneficiary's income. It is necessary to show the different types of income separately on the certificate.

20.4.5 Income mandated to a beneficiary

Trustees sometimes take the view that it is simpler to mandate dividends and other income to the beneficiary so that such income does not pass through the trustees' hands. This does not alter the fact that the trustees are still the legal owners of the assets that produce the income.

Although this income can be entered directly in the beneficiary's personal tax return, care should be taken to ensure that it is entered in the correct section for trust income so as to avoid any confusion with his personal income. Where this happens, the Revenue will assess the beneficiary rather than the trustees. If the trustees incur expenses, these may not be deducted as in 20.4.2; this applies even where the beneficiary reimburses the trustees for such expenses later on.

20.4.6 Beneficiary's exempt income

It is sometimes possible for UK-resident trustees to take advantage of a beneficiary's tax exemption to avoid paying tax that he would then have to claim back. For example, where a beneficiary is entitled to all the income of the trust and he is resident outside the UK, the trustees can agree with the Revenue that the income that arises outside the UK (and any other income that is exempt for a non-resident, for example, interest from exempt gilts: see 23.6.3) should not be taxed in the trustees' hands.

This treatment is not normally available where a non-resident beneficiary is entitled only to a proportion of the trustees' income.

20.4.7 Taxable income that is not income for trust purposes

Difficulties can arise where the trustees receive something that constitutes income for tax, but not for trust, purposes. For example, if trustees of a fixed-interest trust receive a lump sum premium that is taxable income for Schedule A purposes (see 6.3), this is not income that belongs to the life tenant. Similarly, a distribution such as may arise on a company buying back its own shares may be income for income tax purposes (see 7.9.7), but is capital for trust purposes. In both these situations, the trustees must pay tax on such deemed income, but the amounts must be excluded when calculating the life tenant's income for tax purposes.

Another situation where taxable, but not trust, income may arise is where trustees have acquired an enterprise zone building (or indeed any type of industrial building) and a balancing charge arises on a disposal. Such a charge is taxed at basic rate only. Because it is a capital receipt, it is not normally possible for the trustees to pay it to a life tenant and it therefore does not constitute part of his income for tax purposes.

There are certain situations where the legislation makes special provision. Where trustees dispose of a loan stock cum-interest, the trustees will generally be subject to assessment under the accrued income scheme (see 7.6) in respect of the interest that has arisen on the loan stock during their period of ownership. However, this is not income that the trustees will be able to pay out to a beneficiary since a life tenant will be entitled only to actual, not deemed, income. In this specific case, the legislation provides that trustees should be taxed at 34% on income assessed under Schedule D Case VI in respect of the accrued income scheme.

A similar rule applies where trustees realise gains on the disposal of shares in an offshore roll-up fund (see 8.2) and also income distributions from a purchase of own shares on or after 7 December 1996.

Enhanced scrip dividends can give rise to special problems, as the tax treatment depends on the way the dividend is treated for trust purposes (this may be affected by the way the trust deed is worded). You should obtain a copy of SP4/94.

20.4.8 Exempt receipts that are income for trust purposes

The converse may happen. For example, a trustee may receive income in the form of a repayment supplement that is exempt. This will still constitute income for trust law purposes and the life tenant will generally be entitled to receive the full amount, but it is not taxable income for him.

The treatment of dividends arising from demergers (see 7.8.7) also gave rise to concern, but a test case involving the ICI demerger has established that such receipts by trustees are generally capital rather than income from the point of view of trust law, so in this particular case the treatment for trust law and taxation will normally be the same. It is important to take professional advice where significant sums of money are involved as the Revenue distinguishes between different types of demergers (remind your accountant to refer to *Tax Bulletin* October 1994).

20.4.9 Capital gains tax

Trustees of fixed-interest trusts are subject to tax at 34% on any capital gains.

No further CGT (or income tax) liability will normally arise on the trustees distributing cash to a beneficiary after they have realised a capital gain by selling an asset.

20.4.10 Exemption for property occupied by a beneficiary (TCGA 1992, s 225)

There is an exemption for trustees in respect of a property owned by them, but occupied by a beneficiary as his main residence (provided he is entitled to do so under the terms of the trust deed). The beneficiary may not also claim exemption for a property owned by him. Where an individual has more than one residence, and it is desired to elect that a property owned by trustees be treated as his main residence, a joint notice must be given by the trustees and that individual.

20.4.11 Disposals of business assets

Where trustees of a fixed-interest trust dispose of an asset that has been used by an 'eligible beneficiary' for the purposes of a trade carried on by him, or by a firm in which he is a partner, the asset may be treated as a business asset for taper relief purposes (see 14.5). Similar provisions apply where trustees sell an asset used in a business carried on by an eligible beneficiary's qualifying company, or where they sell shares in the company itself.

An 'eligible beneficiary' is a beneficiary entitled to an interest in possession over the whole of the settled property or over a part of the settled property that included the asset concerned.

A company is the eligible beneficiary's qualifying company if he is employed by it.

Relief may be restricted where the eligible beneficiary has rights to only part of the income from the settled property. Professional advice should therefore be sought if the trust fund has more than one life tenant and one or more beneficiaries are not employed by the company.

If the trustees own shares in an unquoted trading company or hold 5% of the voting shares in a quoted company, they may qualify for taper relief as business assets even though the life tenant is not employed by the company.

20.4.12 Liability may also arise on deemed disposals

A capital gain may arise on a deemed disposal such as where the trustees distribute assets to a beneficiary, or where a beneficiary becomes absolutely entitled to capital under the terms of a trust. Hold-over relief is available only if the disposal involves business property (see 17.5).

20.4.13 Transfer of capital losses to a trust beneficiary

Until 15 June 1999, where capital was distributed to a beneficiary by the trustees exercising their discretionary powers, or when he became absolutely entitled to the capital on attaining a certain age, capital losses that were attributable to the property to which he became entitled passed across and were available to cover capital gains realised by him in that or a future year. Thus if the trustees had unrelieved capital losses of £100,000 and a beneficiary became entitled to one quarter of the trust capital, he would be treated as if he had personal CGT losses of £25,000.

Where a beneficiary becomes absolutely entitled on or after 16 June 1999, losses realised in the past by the trustees do not pass across. Furthermore, if a loss arises for the trustees on an asset passing across to the beneficiary, he may use this only against a capital gain that he may subsequently realise on a disposal of that asset.

20.4.14 Death of the life tenant

(TCGA 1992, s 73)

There is one type of deemed disposal that does not give rise to a CGT charge. Where an interest in possession ceases on a death, the assets are treated as having been disposed of and reacquired at their value at that date, but there is no chargeable gain for the trustees. This does not apply where the trustees hold assets that were subject to a hold-over claim by the settlor at the time he transferred the assets to the trustees.

20.4.15 Inheritance tax

(IHTA 1984, s 49)

Where a beneficiary has an interest in possession, he is treated for IHT purposes as if he owned the trust capital. On death, the value of the trust capital is brought into account as part of the individual's estate and IHT is charged accordingly. However, the trustees are responsible for paying the IHT on the proportion of the tax attributable to the trust property.

Example – IHT liability on a fixed-interest trust

A died on 1 December 2003 owning property in his personal capacity worth £205,000 (this is called his 'free estate') and he is also the life tenant of a trust that has a capital value of £350,000. The total IHT payable is:

	£
Free estate	205,000
Trust	350,000
	555,000
Less: nil rate band	(255,000)
	300,000
IHT thereon at 40%	120,000

IHT is payable as follows:

Executors $\frac{205,000}{550,000} \times 120,000 = £44,727$

Trustees $\frac{350,000}{550,000} \times 120,000 = £76,363$

20.4.16 Exempt pre-13 November 1974 will trusts

(IHTA 1984, Sched 6, para 2)

These are trusts created by the will of a person who died before 13 November 1974 and left property in trust on the following terms:

(1) his surviving spouse was entitled to an interest in possession;
(2) the surviving spouse was not entitled to demand that the capital should be paid out to her.

These trusts are exempt from the normal charge that arises when the surviving spouse's interest in possession comes to an end. The reason for this is that prior to 13 November 1974, estate duty was levied on an individual's death even if he left property in trust for his spouse. However, the estate duty legislation then provided an exemption on the death of the surviving spouse and this has been carried over to IHT.

Will trusts that came into being after 12 November 1974 are treated differently because of the exemption that applies for IHT purposes where property passes to a surviving spouse. Property held in a post-12 November 1974 will trust is subject to IHT on the life tenant's death.

20.4.17 No charge where life tenant becomes absolutely entitled to trust property

(IHTA 1984, s 53(2))

There are no IHT implications where a life tenant (or any other beneficiary entitled to an interest in possession) becomes absolutely entitled to the trust property. This is because the beneficiary was already regarded for IHT purposes as if he owned the capital concerned. All that has happened is that the beneficiary's interest has been enlarged and, while this may have CGT consequences, it does not give rise to an IHT charge.

20.4.18 Consequences of interest in possession terminating during a person's lifetime

(IHTA 1984, ss 3A, 23 and 52)

Where a beneficiary's interest in possession comes to an end during his lifetime and he does not personally become entitled to the trust property, he is treated as making a transfer of value. The transfer is normally either a PET (see 19.6) or a chargeable transfer, according to what happens as a result of the interest in possession coming to an end.

Potentially exempt transfer

If the effect of the beneficiary's interest coming to an end is that:

(1) another individual becomes entitled to an interest in possession, or
(2) another person becomes absolutely entitled to the trust property, or
(3) the trust becomes an accumulation and maintenance trust,

the person whose interest in possession has terminated is treated as having made a PET. In such instances, IHT is charged if (and only if) the person dies within the following seven years. If this should happen, the trustees are liable to pay the IHT unless the settled property passes to a beneficiary through his becoming absolutely entitled on the termination of the interest in possession. In such a situation the person who becomes absolutely entitled is liable to pay any such IHT.

Exempt transfer

Occasionally, the effect of a person's interest in possession coming to an end is that the spouse becomes entitled to an interest in possession. Where this happens, the person whose interest in possession has come to an end is treated as having made an exempt transfer. This treatment also applies if a trust becomes a charitable trust as a result of a beneficiary's interest in possession coming to an end.

Chargeable transfer

Where a person's interest in possession comes to an end, and the trust thereby becomes a discretionary trust, he is treated as having made a chargeable transfer. If his cumulative chargeable transfers bring him over the nil rate band, IHT is payable right away at the lifetime rate of 20%. If he should then die within three years, the rate increases to 40% (see 19.10).

20.4.19 How transfer of value is computed on lifetime transfer

The legislation contains an anomaly. Where an individual makes a gift in his personal capacity, the transfer of value is deemed to be the amount by which his estate is reduced in value (see 19.3.3). This rule does not apply where a person's interest in possession comes to an end as, in this case, the amount of the transfer of value is taken as the value of the property in which the interest in possession has terminated.

Example – Calculation of value of lifetime transfer

B owns 90% of a company in his personal capacity and is the life tenant of a trust that owns the remaining 10%. The value of a 100% shareholding in the company is worth £500,000. The value of a 90% shareholding is £450,000, but a 10% shareholding valued in isolation is worth only £20,000. If *B* had made a gift of 10% out of his personal shareholding, his transfer of value would be taken to be:

	£
Value of a 100% shareholding	500,000
Less: value of remaining 90% shareholding (taking his own shares and the trust together)	(450,000)
Reduction in value of his estate	50,000

However, if *B* surrenders his life interest in the trust so that his interest in possession comes to an end, the value transferred is taken as £20,000.

20.5 DISCRETIONARY TRUSTS

In contrast to a fixed-interest trust, a discretionary trust is one where the trustees can control the way the income is used. In most cases, they have power to accumulate income, in which case it may be retained by them either with a view to its being paid out in later years or as an addition to the trust capital.

In other cases, they have no legal right to accumulate income, but the trust is regarded as discretionary because no beneficiary has a fixed entitlement (ie the trustees must distribute the income, but they can choose how it is distributed and which particular beneficiary should receive it).

20.5.1 Rate applicable to trusts

(TA 1988, s 686)

Trustees of discretionary trusts are liable for tax at 34% on income that is not dividend income.

Where part of the trust income is subject to a fixed-interest trust and the balance is held on discretionary trust, the 34% rate is charged only on the income held on discretionary trusts.

In most cases, the trustees suffer lower or basic rate tax at source and then pay additional tax to bring the total up to 34%.

Notional income that is left out of account

Certain types of income are not taken into account for additional rate purposes, ie sums that are capital profits under trust law, for example:

(1) premiums treated as rent (see 6.3);
(2) profits on sale of certificates of deposit (see 8.1).

This income is subject to tax at only 22%.

Income taxed under the accrued income scheme arising from a purchase of own shares on or after 7 December 1996 is charged at 34%. This comes to the same thing, but such deemed income is not technically subject to the additional rate.

20.5.2 Computing the trustees' liability to the rate applicable to trusts

The trustees' liability for basic and lower rate taxes on income from savings is calculated in exactly the same way as for trustees of fixed-interest trusts. A separate computation is then required for the purposes of the 34% rate.

Expenses paid out of net income are 'grossed up' and the resulting amount is then deducted. Examples of such expenses are:

(1) Bank charges.
(2) Interest that does not qualify for tax relief.
(3) The costs of administering the trust.
(4) Charges made by professional trustees.
(5) Deficits on properties where the deficiency cannot be relieved against other Schedule A income.

Costs such as premiums on an insurance policy (excluding fire insurance), or property expenses such as the cost of maintenance or insurance of a property or charges made for collecting rents, cannot be included directly as a deduction in computing liability for additional rate tax.

Example – Calculating the additional tax on discretionary trusts

A discretionary trust receives income from savings of £15,000 in 2002-03. It has no other income. Expenses that are not allowable in computing income for basic rate tax purposes, but are properly chargeable to income, amount to £960. The trustees' liability for tax at the 34% rate is computed as follows:

	£
Income from savings	15,000
Less: expenses – grossed up: £960 × 100/80	(1,200)
	13,800
Tax at 14%	1,932

If the trustees had also received some other income subject to basic rate, this would normally be taxed at 12%, ie 34% less tax withheld at source. Administrative expenses are set off against income from savings first. Any balance is then grossed up at the rate of 100/78 and set against other income for the purposes of calculating the additional rate.

20.5.3 Additional rate on dividend income

Trustees of discretionary trusts are taxed at 25% on dividend income received after 5 April 1999. Dividends received from UK companies carry a 10% tax credit.

Example – Calculating the additional tax on dividend income

A discretionary trust receives cash dividend income of £80 in a tax year. The trustees' tax liability on that income is computed is follows:

	£
Cash dividend received	80.00
Tax credit (10/90)	8.89
Taxable income	88.89
Rate applicable to trusts (25%)	22.22
Less: tax credit	(8.89)
Tax payable	13.33

Furthermore, when the trustees distribute income to beneficiaries, they will be required to pay additional tax unless the distribution can be shown to have come out of a 'pool' that has suffered 34% tax. Thus in the case of a new trust with only dividend income, the trustees will be required to pay additional tax that brings the total tax paid by them up to 34%.

Example – Situation where dividend income distributed between beneficiaries

In the above example, the trustees had dividend income of £80.00 on which they paid tax of £13.33, leaving them with £66.67. If they distribute the whole of this income to the beneficiaries, the trustees will have to pay further tax. The calculation is complicated and is as follows:

	£
Maximum distribution	52.80
Tax thereon (£80 × 34%)	27.20
Gross income for beneficiary	80.00

This income is regarded as having suffered 34% tax. The trustees then pay tax of £13.87 over to the Revenue so that they have paid a total of £27.20, ie:

	£
Tax payable on the dividend	13.33
Tax payable on the distribution to bring payment up to tax of 34% of £80	13.87
	27.20

Trustees should obtain a copy of *Tax Bulletin* February 1999, which covers all this in detail.

20.5.4 Treatment prior to 1999-2000

A different treatment applied to dividends up to 1998-99. For details see 2001-02 *Tax Handbook* at 19.5.1 *et seq*.

20.5.5 Income distributions in excess of trustees' taxable income

(TA 1988, s 687)

There may be situations where trustees make distributions in excess of their taxable income. Such distributions also give rise to a liability for the trustees to account for tax at 34%. There are several situations in which such a liability can arise:

(1) A trust may have income on which income tax does not have to be paid. If such income is paid out to a beneficiary as an income distribution, the trustees must account for tax at 34%.
(2) Similarly, trustees may make payments of an income nature that are subject to tax as income in the hands of the beneficiary even though they come out of the trust capital. In practice, the Revenue would not normally assess such distributions unless they were made regularly.

If the income is fully distributed cach year and foreign securities are held, there will be an additional liability to tax when the foreign income is distributed to beneficiaries. The liability is equal to the credit allowed against basic rate tax for double taxation relief.

20.5.6 Tax returns

One tax return (form SA900) is now completed whether the trust is fixed-interest or discretionary. There are supplementary forms to be completed for various types of income, for capital gains, and where the trust is a non-resident or charitable trust.

The Revenue provides a tax calculation guide for trusts and estates, but as the calculation layout is of Byzantine complexity the form is generally not used.

Where payments are made to beneficiaries, a tax deduction certificate form R185 should be completed by the trustees or their professional advisers, showing the appropriate gross, tax and net figures.

20.5.7 The beneficiary's position

A beneficiary needs to include on his tax return the grossed up amount of any income distributed to him by the trustees during the tax year. Since the trustees are subject to the additional rate, the beneficiary's income is treated as net of 34% tax.

20.5.8 Accumulated income subsequently distributed as capital

A distribution of capital that represents income that has been accumulated is not normally taxable income for the beneficiary. Such a distribution is treated as a capital distribution, though this presupposes that the trustees have power to accumulate income. In cases where they have no such power, any distributions will remain as income.

20.5.9 Capital gains tax

(TCGA 1992, s 5)

All the capital gains of a discretionary trust are taxed at 34% except for the amount covered by the annual exemption.

As with a fixed-interest trust, no further CGT (or income tax) liability will normally arise on the trustees' distributing cash to a beneficiary after they have realised a capital gain by selling an asset.

20.5.10 Exemption for property occupied by beneficiary

(TCGA 1992, s 225)

The courts have held that trustees of a discretionary trust are entitled to this exemption where they permit a beneficiary to occupy a property as his main residence, even though the trust deed did not confer a right for him to require the trustees to provide such a property (but see SP8/79).

20.5.11 Businesss taper relief

Trustees of a discretionary settlement are entitled to business taper where they hold shares in an unquoted trading company or hold more than 5% of the voting shares in a quoted trading company.

20.5.12 Deemed disposals/hold-over relief

(TCGA 1992, s 71)

A capital gain may arise on a deemed disposal such as where the trustees distribute assets to a beneficiary, or where a beneficiary becomes absolutely entitled to capital under the terms of a trust. Hold-over relief is normally available under TCGA 1992, s 260 where a disposal of the property arises on a capital distribution to a UK-resident beneficiary (see 13.8 on s 260 relief).

20.5.13 Inheritance tax

(IHTA 1984, ss 64-65)

By definition, no beneficiary has an interest in possession in a discretionary trust and it follows that the trust capital is not treated as forming part of his estate. Therefore, no IHT charge arises on his death.

To make up for the absence of such a charge, the legislation imposes a lower charge every ten years (the 'periodic charge'). The theory is that a generation is approximately 30 years and the tax charged on three separate occasions by reason of the periodic charge will approximate to the tax payable on property passing down to the next generation.

There is also an 'exit charge' that applies where property leaves a discretionary trust. There are different rules for discretionary trusts created before and after 26 March 1974.

20.5.14 Trusts created after 26 March 1974

Periodic charge

(IHTA 1984, s 66)

The periodic charge arises on the tenth anniversary of the creation of the trust and on every subsequent tenth anniversary. The maximum rate is currently 6%, computed as follows:

Tax payable at lifetime rate (20%) × 30%.

The computation is actually more complex and involves the following process:

Amount of chargeable transfers made by settlor in the seven years prior to creation of the trust	A
Value of trust property at tenth anniversary	B
Add A and B	C
Deduct nil rate band	D
	E

The next step is to compute the IHT payable on E and on A – D. The tax payable by the trustees on the periodic charge is 30% of the difference.

Example – Periodic charge

C created a discretionary trust in June 1993. He had previously made chargeable transfers of £194,000. In June 2003 the trust is worth £160,000. The periodic charge is therefore computed as follows:

		£
Amount of previous chargeable transfers	(A)	194,000
Value of trust property in 2002	(B)	160,000
	(C)	354,000
Deduct nil rate band	(D)	255,000
	(E)	99,000
IHT on E		19,800
IHT at lifetime rates on A – D		Nil
		19,800

Periodic charge is 30% of £19,800, ie £5,940.

20.5.15 Trusts created prior to 26 March 1974

This type of trust is simpler in that there cannot have been any chargeable transfers made by the settlor prior to the creation of the trust. The computation is therefore:

Value of trust property at tenth anniversary	X
Deduct nil rate band	Y
	Z

IHT at lifetime rates on Z

Periodic charge is 30% of this amount.

20.5.16 Position where trustees have made capital distributions during preceding ten years

Where the trustees have made a capital distribution within the previous ten years or property has otherwise ceased to be held upon discretionary trusts (eg by reason of a beneficiary being entitled to an interest in possession), the capital distribution value must also be brought into account in arriving at the periodic charge. The computation is as follows:

Amount of chargeable transfers made by settlor in the seven years prior to creation of the trust and capital distributions since last periodic charge	A
Value of trust property at tenth anniversary	B
Add A and B	C
Deduct nil rate band	D
	E

The next step is to compute the IHT payable on E and on A – D. The tax payable by the trustees on the period charge is 30% of the difference.

20.5.17 Treatment of undistributed income

The Revenue accepts that undistributed income that has not been accumulated should be excluded in arriving at the value of the trust capital at the tenth anniversary. The reason for this is that such income remains income held for the benefit of beneficiaries and is not capital.

Where income has been formally accumulated, it must be brought into account for the purposes of the periodic charge. However, such accumulated income is treated as if it were additional capital added to the trust at the date the trustees resolved to accumulate it.

20.5.18 Exit charge (also known as 'proportionate charge')

The way in which the exit charge is computed varies according to whether capital leaves a discretionary trust within the first ten years or only after there has been a periodic charge.

Exit charge during first ten years

(IHTA 1984, s 68)

The position here is that a notional rate of charge should be computed which is the average rate of IHT that would have been payable had the settlor made a chargeable transfer at the time he created the trust equal to the trust property's value at that time.

Example – Exit charge during first ten years

D created a trust in February 1993 and the original trust property was worth £300,000. The entry charge would have been computed as follows:

	£
Value of trust property in February 1993	300,000
Less: nil rate band at that time	(128,000)
	172,000
£172,000 at 20% =	£34,400

$$\text{Effective rate} = \frac{34{,}400}{300{,}000} \times 100$$

The entry charge would therefore have been 11.47% and the tax payable if property leaves a discretionary trust within the first ten years is levied as a proportion of this rate. The exact proportion is determined by the number of complete periods of three months (or quarters) during which the trust has been in existence. Thus, if the exit charge occurred after the trust had existed for six years and seven months, the charge would be at the rate of:

$$\frac{26}{40} \times 30\% \text{ of } 11.47\%.$$

Exit charge after a periodic charge

(IHTA 1984, s 69)

The position here is that the charge applies only to the proportion of the property that leaves the discretionary trust, with the proportion being determined by the following formula:

$$\frac{\text{Number of complete quarters since the periodic charge}}{40}$$

A distribution during the first quarter following the ten-year charge is entirely free of IHT.

The tax rate charged is normally fixed by the effective rate charged on the previous periodic charge. However, the effective rate is calculated by using the scale of rates in force at the time the exit charge arises. Thus, the notional effective rate may be slightly lower than the effective rate of IHT that actually applied on the last periodic charge.

20.6 ACCUMULATION AND MAINTENANCE TRUSTS

(IHTA 1984, s 71)

An accumulation and maintenance trust is a special form of discretionary trust that has been set up for a stated class of beneficiaries. The following conditions must normally be satisfied:

(1) One or more beneficiaries will become entitled to an interest in possession in the trust property on attaining a specified age that must not exceed age 25.
(2) Until one of the beneficiaries becomes beneficially entitled, the trust income must be held on a discretionary basis with income being applied only for the maintenance, education or benefit of the beneficiaries or accumulated for their benefit.
(3) The trust must have a life of not more than 25 years or it must be a trust for the benefit of grandchildren of a common grandparent.

Where an accumulation and maintenance trust was in existence at 15 April 1976, the 25-year period runs from that date, ie to 14 April 2001, and not from the date the trust was created.

20.6.1 Taxation

The same rules apply, and the same returns and certificates need to be completed, for income tax and CGT as for discretionary trusts. There are, however, different rules for CGT hold-over relief and IHT.

20.6.2 Hold-over relief for trustees

(TCGA 1992, s 260)

Where trustees dispose of assets to a beneficiary, hold-over relief may be available if the property concerned is business property (see 17.5). As regards other assets, hold-over relief normally is available if the disposal takes place when a beneficiary becomes absolutely entitled to capital and income at the same date.

There is a problem area for trustees of accumulation and maintenance trusts in that many trusts provide that a beneficiary should become entitled to income when he reaches age 18, but capital vests only at age 25. If the beneficiary became entitled to the capital at age 18, there would be no problem but, because there is a gap in time between the accumulation period coming to an end and the beneficiary becoming absolutely entitled to the capital, it is not possible for trustees to claim hold-over relief (unless the trust property consists of business assets).

20.6.3 IHT privileges

An accumulation and maintenance trust is not subject to the periodic charge described above. Furthermore, there is no exit charge on a beneficiary becoming entitled to an interest in possession under the trust or becoming absolutely entitled to trust property.

20.7 TRUSTS FOR THE DISABLED

(TCGA 1992, Sched 1; IHTA 1984, ss 74 and 89)

A trust for a disabled person is a type of discretionary trust that enjoys certain tax privileges. The trustees are entitled to the full CGT exemption of £7,700 for individuals and there is no liability for the IHT periodic and exit charges.

The terms of the trust must be such that not less than half of the settled property and income must be applied for the benefit of a disabled person who is treated as if he had an interest in possession. A disabled person is one who, at the time the trust was created, was:

(1) incapable by reason of mental disorder within the meaning of the Mental Health Act 1983 of administering his property or managing his affairs; or
(2) in receipt of an attendance allowance under the Social Security Contributions and Benefits Act 1992, s 64; or
(3) in receipt of a disability living allowance under s 71 of the 1992 Act.

The two conditions that need to be satisfied are as follows:

(1) not less than half of the property within the trust should be applied for the benefit of the beneficiary concerned; and
(2) the person should be entitled to not less than 50% of the income arising from the property (this condition is regarded as satisfied where the trust provides that no income may be applied for the benefit of any other person).

Income is deemed to be applied for the benefit of a person where it is held by the trustees for that person on protective trusts.

20.8 PROTECTIVE TRUSTS

This is a term under the Trustee Act 1925, s 33. The protective trust is one under which a person (known as the principal beneficiary) is entitled to an interest in possession in the trust unless he forfeits his interest, for example, by assigning it or by becoming bankrupt. Protective trusts are normally worded so that if a principal beneficiary forfeits his interest, the trust property is held on discretionary trusts for a class of beneficiaries that includes the principal beneficiary.

20.8.1 IHT position where principal beneficiary dies

The periodic charge does not apply while property is held on protective trusts because the principal beneficiary has forfeited his interest. However, an IHT charge arises on his death. The charge varies according to whether he forfeited his interest before or after 12 April 1978.

Where forfeited before 12 April 1978, the tax charged on his eventual death is calculated at a fixed rate on the trust property's value according to the following formula:

	Cumulative total
0.25% for each of the first 40 quarters	10%
0.20% for each of the next 40 quarters	8%
0.15% for each of the next 40 quarters	6%
0.10% for each of the next 40 quarters	4%
0.05% for each of the next 40 quarters	2%
Maximum rate chargeable after 50 years	30%

The nil rate band is not available.

Where the interest is forfeited after 11 April 1978, the trustees are subject to a charge on the principal beneficiary's death as if he had an interest in possession at the date of his death.

20.9 CHARITABLE TRUSTS

Provided property is held for charitable purposes only, income and capital gains received by the trustees are normally exempt from tax.

Exemption from income tax

(TA 1988, s 505)

There is total exemption from income tax for all income other than trading profits. The exemption is dependent on income being applied for charitable purposes.

Exemption from CGT

(TCGA 1992, s 256)

There is also total exemption from CGT provided the charitable trust applies the capital gains for charitable purposes.

20.9.1 Application for charitable purposes

(TA 1988, s 505)

A charity's exemption from tax may be restricted where income is not applied for charitable purposes. In particular, where a charity has income and capital gains that exceed £10,000 in a tax year, exemption is restricted where the following two conditions are satisfied:

(1) The charity's relevant income and gains exceed the amount of its qualifying expenditure.
(2) The trust incurs or is treated as incurring non-qualifying expenditure.

'Qualifying expenditure' for these purposes means expenditure actually made during the year for charitable purposes and commitments for such expenditure entered into during the year.

Payments made to bodies outside the UK count as qualifying expenditure only to the extent that the charity can show that it has taken such steps that are reasonable in the circumstances to ensure the payments will be applied for charitable purposes. Expenditure for charitable purposes also includes reasonable administrative and fund-raising expenses.

Non-qualifying expenditure includes eg political activities, trading expenses and excessive administration costs. Furthermore, the legislation specifically mentions certain types of investments or loans that are to be regarded as not being qualifying expenditure. This is intended to catch investments in a company controlled by a connected person (eg the settlor) or loans to such a company. Indirect arrangements may also be caught such as where a charity makes loans or investments used as security for borrowings by a connected person.

Where a charitable trust makes a payment to another connected charitable trust, this does not count as application of the income for charitable purposes unless the trust that receives the payment actually applies it for charitable purposes.

20.9.2 IHT position

Property held on charitable trusts is exempt from the periodic and exit charges. If the property is held on temporary charitable trusts, a charge arises on those charitable trusts coming to an end with tax being charged according to the same formula in 20.8.1.

20.10 EXECUTORS AND PERSONAL REPRESENTATIVES

20.10.1 Meaning

When a person dies, his assets vest in his executors/personal representatives. If he does not leave a will, it is normally necessary for letters of administration to be obtained and the person who acts in this way is treated for tax purposes as if he were an executor. The term 'personal representative' covers both executors in the case of a will and administrators in the case of intestacy.

The fact that at least one personal representative is UK-resident would normally mean that the estate is subject to UK tax. There is an exception to this where the deceased was not resident, ordinarily resident or domiciled in the UK at the time of his death. In such a situation, provided at least one of the personal representatives is not UK-resident, the estate is not regarded as UK-resident.

Personal representatives of a deceased person are treated as a single body of persons so that there is no tax implication if an executor retires or dies. The estate is treated as a single entity for tax purposes.

20.10.2 Income tax

(TMA 1970, s 40)

The deceased's personal representatives are liable to pay tax on income received by the deceased up to the date of his death.

The tax is assessed in exactly the same way as if the individual were still alive, ie all the normal allowances and reliefs are due. The only difference is that the personal representatives are responsible for settling the tax (they are also entitled to any repayments).

Quite separately, personal representatives are also charged to tax on income received by them following the death. No personal allowances are given. During the administration period, the income is charged at 20% on gross income from savings, with other income, ie rent, being taxed at the basic rate; there is no higher rate liability for the personal representatives.

Although there are cases where income has to be apportioned pre- and post-death for legal purposes, for tax purposes any income received after a person's death is treated as income of the estate.

Where, under the terms of the will, a trust evolves, the executors become trustees upon the completion of the administration period. Depending on the type of trust, the trustees may become chargeable to additional rate income tax first on the balance of accumulated income at that date and secondly on receipt of subsequent income. There is no date fixed by law to determine the completion of the administration period, but it is generally agreed that it is the date on which the residue is ascertained.

20.10.3 Beneficiary's position

(TA 1988, ss 695-696)

A beneficiary of a will may receive an annuity. This income is taxable for the year in which it is payable unless, as a matter of fact, the annuity is paid out of capital in which case it is income for the year in which it is paid.

Beneficiaries of specific legacies are normally entitled from the date of death to the income that arises on the property they have inherited. Other beneficiaries will be entitled to the residue, either through a limited interest (eg a life tenant entitled to income arising from the residuary estate) or by an absolute entitlement.

During the administration period, sums paid to a beneficiary are normally treated as income for the year of payment.

Where income that has accrued to the date of death is treated as capital of the estate for IHT purposes and as residuary income, there is higher rate tax relief available to beneficiaries. Form 922 is used to calculate this relief.

20.10.4 Capital gains tax

(TCGA 1992, ss 3 and 62)

Personal representatives are subject to CGT at the rate of 34%. They are entitled to the full annual exemption due to an individual for the year of death and the following two tax years.

In computing capital gains, assets held by the deceased at the date of his death are deemed to be acquired by the personal representatives at their market value at that date (the probate value). The probate value may need to be adjusted where securities are sold at a loss within 12 months of the death and relief from IHT has been claimed (see 19.11.3). A similar rule applies where land is sold within four years of death at a loss and the sale proceeds are substituted for the probate value.

Assets transferred to beneficiaries, either during the course of or on the completion of the administration period of an estate, do not give rise to a chargeable gain since the beneficiary is regarded as having himself acquired the asset at the date of the person's death and at the probate value.

Certain expenses incurred by the personal representatives in establishing legal title to assets are allowed in computing gains on the sale of the assets (see SP8/94).

Personal representatives of an estate in the course of administration are not entitled to an annual exemption if they realise capital gains after two full tax years have elapsed since the date of death. However, if a will trust evolves upon completion of the administration period, the trustees will then become entitled to their own exemption.

Losses made by personal representatives during the administration period, and not utilised, are not available to be transferred to residuary beneficiaries with absolute interests or trustees of a trust established by the will that takes effect on the administration of the estate being completed.

20.10.5 Property owned by the estate, but used by beneficiary as main residence

The Revenue treats the beneficiary's main residence exemption (see 20.4.10) as applying where personal representatives dispose of a property that has been used by a beneficiary of the estate as his only or main residence both before and after the deceased's death and he is entitled to at least 75% of the proceeds when the estate has been administered (see ESC D5 and *Tax Bulletin* August 1994).

20.10.6 Deeds of variation

Where the terms of a will have been varied by a deed of variation (also known as a deed of family arrangement), there are important consequences so far as IHT is concerned (see 19.4.6). Basically, the revised way in which property passes to beneficiaries is read back into the will and effectively treated as something done by the testator so far as IHT is concerned. However, the House of Lords held in *Marshall v Kerr* [1994] STC 813 that where the variation creates a trust, the person(s) who relinquish their original entitlement under the will are treated as the settlor for CGT purposes.

The income tax treatment is also less favourable than the IHT treatment. Even where the deed specifically provides that all income is to be paid to a beneficiary named in the deed, this has no effect for income tax purposes for income that arose prior to the deed's execution. If payments have been made to the original beneficiary or beneficiaries named in the will, they remain liable for any higher rate tax on such income that arose at a time when they were entitled to it. Furthermore, a person who gives up an entitlement under a will by executing such a deed is treated as a settlor for income tax purposes.

21

DEDUCTING TAX AT SOURCE – AND PAYING IT OVER TO THE INLAND REVENUE

This chapter outlines the requirements imposed by law on employers, etc to act as unpaid tax collectors on the Treasury's behalf. If you are caught up in this, the administrative burden can be onerous and the penalties for non-compliance severe.

The chapter covers the following:

(1) Employers.
(2) Contractors.
(3) IR35.
(4) Non-resident landlord scheme.
(5) Payments to non-resident sportsmen and entertainers.
(6) Other payments to non-UK resident persons.

21.1 EMPLOYERS

An employer has an obligation to collect tax and operate the following schemes on the Revenue's behalf in respect of the following payments:

- PAYE/NICs;
- Working Families' Tax Credits (WFTC) and Disabled Persons' Tax Credit (DPTC) – now replaced by the Working Tax Credit;
- Student loans.

21.1.1 Payment of PAYE over to the Revenue

Employers are required to withhold tax under PAYE and NICs and pay them over to the Revenue on a monthly basis unless the PAYE and NICs do not normally exceed £1,500 pm, in which case it is possible to account for tax deductions on a quarterly basis. The £1,500 pm is inclusive of sums collected under the Student Loans Scheme and sums paid out under the WFTC and DPTC schemes. At the end of the year, the employer must give employees form P60 showing the tax withheld from their earnings.

21.1.2 Emoluments subject to PAYE

All payments of 'emoluments' by a UK-resident employer to directors and employees are subject to Pay As You Earn (PAYE). Emoluments are cash payments (salary, wages, bonus, etc) other than expense payments. The *Employer's Guide* lists the following payments as emoluments that are subject to PAYE:

- Salary;
- Wages;
- Fees;
- Overtime;
- Bonus;
- Commission;
- Pension;
- Honoraria;
- Pay during sickness or other absence from work;
- Holiday pay;
- Christmas boxes in cash;
- Employee's income tax borne by his employer;
- Payments for the cost of travelling between the employee's home and his normal place of employment;
- Payments for time spent in travelling;
- Cash payments for meals;
- Payments in lieu of benefits-in-kind;
- Certain lump sum payments made on retirement or removal from employment;
- Certain sums received from the trustees of approved profit-sharing schemes;
- Gratuities or service charges paid out by the employer.

As stated in the *Employer's Guide*, PAYE cannot be deducted from the following benefits even though they are regarded as taxable income for Schedule E purposes:

- Living accommodation provided rent free or at a reduced rent;
- Gifts in kind such as Christmas hampers;
- Luncheon vouchers in excess of 15p per day;
- Employee's liabilities borne by the employer (even though such payments are earnings for NICs purposes).

The scope of PAYE was extended by FA 1994, s 127 and further extended by successive Finance Acts. FA 1994 required employers to account for PAYE when they pay their staff in 'tradable assets' (eg gold bars, commodities, fine wine or diamonds) or with non-marketable assets where the employer has made arrangements for the employee to convert them into cash. FA 1998 replaced the concept of tradable assets with the yet more all-embracing term 'readily convertible assets'. This term includes (but is not limited to):

(1) money debts;
(2) property subject to a warehousing or fiscal warehousing regime;
(3) assets that give rise to cash without the employee taking any action; and
(4) assets for which trading arrangements come into existence in accordance with other arrangements or an understanding that is in place when the assets were provided to the employee.

PAYE may also have to be accounted for on gifts of shares in the employing company or profits realised on the exercise of non-approved share options (see 4.13).

National insurance contributions

The PAYE and NICs rules have largely been aligned from 6 April 2000 and it is now unusual for a payment or benefit to be taxable under Schedule E but not subject to NICs. See further Chap. 25.

21.1.3 Anti-avoidance of PAYE and NICs

In 1997 the Government decided that PAYE would apply to assignments of trade debts by employers to their employees. Legislation was included in FA 1998 to bring remuneration in the form of trade debts within the scope of PAYE from 2 July 1997. Employers need to ensure that they have accounted for PAYE on assignment of trade debts to employees that took place on or after that date.

Under these provisions, the term 'tradable assets' was replaced by 'readily convertible assets': these include items (1)-(4) in 21.1.2 above.

If an employee becomes liable under Schedule E on the exercise, assignment or release of an option for shares that are readily convertible assets, these provisions require the employer to operate PAYE. Similarly, PAYE will apply if the employee is rewarded by the enhancement of a readily convertible asset that he already owns. PAYE must be operated on a reasonable estimate of the income likely to be charged under Schedule E. Similar rules were also introduced for NICs.

21.1.4 Payment in shares

Background

Section 203F TA 1988 provides that employers must account for tax under PAYE whenever an employee is provided with assessable income in the form of readily convertible assets.

Shares in an employer or company which controls the employer are not caught by this legislation if they are acquired through the exercise of options granted before 27 November 1996 or if they are acquired under a Revenue-approved share scheme (see 25.1.4 for an exception to this where approved options are exercised after 8 April 2003 in circumstances which give rise to an income tax charge).

All other cases where employees acquire shares will be subject to the rules on readily convertible assets if either:

(1) they are capable of being sold or otherwise realised on a recognised investment exchange; or
(2) trading arrangements exist in respect of them.

Trading arrangements are defined … as being

arrangements for the purpose of enabling the person to whom the asset is provided to obtain an amount greater than, equal to or not substantially less than the expense incurred in the provision of the asset.

FA 2003 extends the definition

The FA 2003 has extended the scope of the legislation so that shares which are not ordinary share capital of the issuing company are deemed to be readily convertible assets with effect from the date of Royal Assent. Any shares issued by a company which is a subsidiary of another company are similarly treated with effect from that date unless the subsidiary is the employing company.

Revenue guidance

The Inland Revenue Personal Tax Division issued guidance on this in a question and answer format. The notes refer to 'tradable assets', this term had virtually the same meaning as 'readily convertible assets'.

Q1. Does the exercise of a share option amount to the provision of assessable income?

Yes. The legislation applies where an employee is provided with 'assessable income'. If the exercise of an option gives rise to a liability to tax under Schedule E then there is assessable income. If the shares acquired are tradable assets then that assessable income has been provided to the employee in the form of tradable assets and the employer is obliged to account for tax under PAYE. The legislation does not, however, apply to charges under [TA 1988, s 162] because this liability can only be calculated after the end of the relevant tax year.

Q2. Does *CIR v Herd* prevent the application of PAYE to share option gains?

No. *CIR v Herd* [1993] STC 436 considered the application of PAYE to payments of emoluments within [TA 1988, s 203(1)]. Where income is provided in the form of tradable assets there is no 'payment' of emoluments, actual payments of emoluments are specifically excluded from [TA 1988, s 203F by subs (4)(a)]. *CIR v Herd* does not prevent PAYE being applied to awards of tradable assets.

Q3. What code number should the employer use in operating PAYE?

The employer should use the code number that has been issued for the employee, even if this is code NT. Where the employer has to account for tax under PAYE in respect of an ex-employee he should account for tax at the basic rate …

Q4. What about awards made by third parties?

When an employee is provided with an assessable income in the form of tradable assets an obligation to account for tax falls on the employer even if the shares are provided by a third party such as a parent company. It is the employer's responsibility to put in place arrangements to ensure that he has the information necessary to comply with his statutory obligations.

Q5. On what figure should the employer operate PAYE?

Where the shares are tradable assets because they are capable of being sold or otherwise realised on a relevant investment exchange, then PAYE should be operated on the amount obtainable.

Where the shares are tradable assets because trading arrangements exist, PAYE should be operated on the amount obtained by the employee under those arrangements. There should therefore be no need for independent valuations for PAYE purposes.

Where assessable income is provided in the form of tradable assets the employer is treated as having made a payment of that income and should not operate PAYE on an amount which exceeds the amount of that assessable income, namely the amount chargeable to tax under Schedule E. The total amount in respect of which the employer should deduct tax … and, where appropriate, account for tax … should also therefore be limited to the amount chargeable to tax under Schedule E.

Q6. What happens where the employer cannot deduct the necessary tax because there is insufficient cash pay?

The employer remains responsible for accounting for the right amount of tax to the Collector within 14 days of the end of the income tax period. It is up to employers whether they make arrangements to recover this tax from the employees and if so how they go about this. If the employee does not make good to the employer the tax which could not be deducted within 30 days [extended to 90 days by FA 2003 in relation to share acquisitions after 8 April 2003] of the tradable assets being provided then the amount of the tax will be treated as a benefit in kind … This charge … is not reduced nor eliminated if the employee makes good after the time limit has expired.

Payments to surrender options

FA 1998 imposed an obligation for an employer to account for PAYE where employees received a cash sum in return for surrendering options over shares which are readily convertible assets.

21.1.5 Payments to agency workers

Where the services of an individual are provided to a trader through an agency, and the manner in which he performs his work is controlled and supervised as if he were an employee, TA 1988, s 134 requires the trader to operate PAYE.

There are situations where the Revenue regards payments to a 'one man' company as caught by this provision so that the person paying the money to the company should deduct PAYE as if he had made payments to the individual worker concerned. This is increasingly relevant as many employers use service contracts to reduce their overheads and maximise the benefits available to the worker. The Revenue, however, is likely to apply the same criteria to payments made in such circumstances as those they apply to the self-employed, as covered in detail in 5.2.2.

See 23.9 re payments to employment agencies operating in the Netherlands.

21.1.6 Failure to operate PAYE

An employer who fails to operate PAYE takes a substantial risk. The primary liability to account for the tax rests with the employer and the scope of PAYE does not extend simply to deducting tax from an employee's gross pay and remitting it to the Revenue. Instead, an employer must remember that PAYE can also apply to all forms of casual labour, which may or may not be paid through the payroll, and to individuals considered to be self-employed (see 5.2).

Another area frequently overlooked is expenses (see 4.4.1) that constitute part of an employee's emoluments and accordingly fall within the scope of PAYE. While genuine business expenses incurred wholly, exclusively and necessarily in the course of an employee's duties are allowed tax free, there remain several areas where employers are required to operate PAYE. These include the payment of all round sum allowances that have not been approved by the Inspector in the form of a dispensation, and the payment of unauthorised or unvouched expenses. Even the payment of travel expenses may not be permitted tax free in circumstances where the place visited is deemed to be his normal place of work. As an example, a site-based employee living in London and working on a site in Aberdeen will be taxed on all his expenses for travel between London and Aberdeen. This shows that special attention must be paid to such payments and the circumstances surrounding them.

While the Collector of Taxes will invariably seek to recover any unpaid tax from the employer in the first instance, the relevant Regulations (SI 1993/744) permit the Collector to direct that unpaid tax shall be recovered from the employee, but there is no legal requirement that he should give such a direction. The Regulations make it clear that he will make such a direction only if he is satisfied that the employer took reasonable care to comply with the PAYE regulations and the under-deduction of tax was an error made in good faith. Errors arising simply from confusion or ignorance of the rules are not considered to be a reasonable excuse: in such situations, the Collector will not only seek recovery of all duties underpaid but is likely to add interest and penalties as well.

SI 1993/744, reg 42 provides that the Collector may pursue the employee if he has received his remuneration knowing that the employer has wilfully failed to deduct PAYE tax, but the Revenue will normally pursue this course of action only after it has endeavoured to collect from the employer.

All lump sum payments generally should be treated with caution in times when termination payments are increasingly common. Basically, if there is any contractual obligation or expectation, on the part of the employee, to receive a sum then the Revenue is likely to take the view that the employer should have deducted tax.

21.1.7 Interest and penalties for late payment of PAYE

Over recent years, the Revenue has progressively tightened its policing of employers operating PAYE schemes. The current position is as follows:

(1) Interest is charged on any PAYE tax and employers' and employees' NICs not remitted to the Collector of Taxes by 14 days after the end of the tax year (ie by 19 April 2003 for 2002-03).
(2) Penalties may be imposed on employers who do not submit their end-of-year returns (Forms P14, P38S and P35) by 19 May following the end of the tax year. The maximum penalty is £100 pm per unit of 50 employees (rounded up, so that 51 employees count as two units).

These very substantial financial penalties mean that all employers must devote adequate resources to the preparation of PAYE returns.

Electronic Filing

In the 2002 Budget Speech, Gordon Brown announced the intention for all year-end returns to be filed electronically. The deadline for this has been set out as follows:

Number of employees in PAYE scheme	*First return to be filed electronically*	*Deadline*
250 or more	2004/05	19 May 2003
50–249	2005/06	19 May 2006
Fewer than 50	2009/10	19 May 2010

Table 21.1 Summary of year-end deadlines

Deadline		*Result of missed deadline*
19 April 2004	Due date for all remittances of PAYE, Class 1 NICs and subcontractor deductions for 2003-04 tax year	Automatic interest charge
19 May 2004	Due date for submission of forms P35 and CIS36 detailing deductions made under PAYE and under the subcontractors scheme	Automatic penalties
31 May 2004	Forms P60 to employees in employment as at 5 April 2004	Penalties
6 July 2004	Forms P11D and P9D to reach Revenue	Penalties of up to £300 per return
6 July 2004	Copies of P11D and P9D information to be given to employees, including any who have left the company since 5 April 2004	Penalties

21.1.8 Other returns required from employers

Forms P46 (car)

These forms report details of changes in company car allocations. They are due quarterly within 28 days of the end of the periods ending 5 July, 5 October, 5 January and 5 April. Reportable events are when an employee or director:

- receives a company car for the first time;
- changes company car;
- receives an additional company car;
- gives up a company car; or
- exceeds the £8,500 threshold (see below) having been below it previously.

Late returns may be liable to penalties of up to £300 per return, plus a further £60 per day while the failure continues.

Forms P11D and P9D

An employer must file forms P11D to report benefits and expenses for all employees earning £8,500+ pa. Directors are automatically included in this category unless they:

- are full-time working directors or directors of a not-for-profit organisation; and
- earn less than £8,500 pa; and
- do not control directly or indirectly more than 5% of the company's ordinary share capital; and
- do not have directorships in other businesses under the same control.

All benefits and expenses payments (including business expenses) must be reported, except those covered by dispensations. The amount is the cash equivalent (see 4.4-4.9 on taxation of benefits in general).

Except where special rules apply, the cash equivalent is normally the VAT-inclusive cost to the provider. Where the special rules apply, employers are responsible for calculating the cash equivalent and entering the appropriate amount on the P11D. The Revenue can supply the following P11D Working Sheets to assist you:

1 – Living accommodation and associated benefits
2 – Car and fuel benefits
3 – Vans available for private use
4 – Interest-free and low interest loans
5 – Relocation expenses.

If an arrangement has been made for someone else to provide benefits to the employees, the cash equivalents must be reported on P11D as though the employer itself provided the benefits. If the provider cannot or will not give details of the benefits to the employer, the employer must make a best estimate of the cash equivalent and notify the Revenue of this. Such arrangements are where an employer has guaranteed or facilitated provision of benefits or the benefits were part of a reciprocal arrangement with another employer.

P11D returns are due for submission to the Revenue by 6 July following the end of the tax year. Filing an incorrect return can result in a penalty of up to £3,000. Further, a penalty of £300 may be imposed for each form not submitted by 6 July, with a daily penalty of £60 per return if the forms are not submitted once the initial penalty has been imposed.

Details of taxable benefits must be supplied to employees by 6 July. Forms P9D may also be required for benefits provided to employees earning less than £8,500 pa.

The deadlines for submitting returns of Classes 1A and 1B NICs must also be borne in mind (see 25.1.7-25.1.8).

21.1.9 Working Families' and Disabled Persons' Tax Credits to 5 April 2003

As from 6 April 2000, employers acquired a new responsibility as dispensers of WFTC and DPTC. The amounts paid by employers by way of tax credits are set against their PAYE tax and NICs liabilities due to the Revenue each month or quarter. Where the employer has not collected enough PAYE and NICs to cover the tax credits payable for a particular period, application to the Revenue for additional funding may be made. At the end of the tax year, employers must provide employees with details of the credits paid to them. This information must also be shown on payslips and P60 forms.

21.1.10 Working Tax Credits from 6 April 2003

The working family and disabled persons' credits were replaced by a single Working Tax Credit (WTC) from 6 April 2003. The WTC is for working people regardless of whether they have a child. With the exception of any childcare element (which is paid direct to the main carer of the children in the family) Working Tax Credit is normally paid to employees through the payroll with their wages.

The Inland Revenue offers employers the following advice in respect of the payment of the WTC:

> When we want you to pay Working Tax Credit to an employee we will send you a Start Notice (form TC700). This document will be on watermarked paper with a blue and pink background print. If you receive a start notice which does not have these features please return it to the address shown at the top of the TC700.
>
> The TC700 will show
>
> - the employee's details;
> - the start date from which you are responsible for paying tax credit (this will be at least 42 days after the date we send you the TC700);
> - the daily rate of tax credit payable; and
> - a daily rate table showing the daily rate multiplied by 1-31 to help you work out how much to pay in each pay period.
>
> You are required by law to pay tax credits to the employee from the date shown on the TC700 unless:
>
> - the employee stops working for you before the start date on the TC700;
> - you do not expect to pay the employee for at least three consecutive pay periods starting with the pay period that includes the start date; or
> - you are not currently required to complete form P11 for any of your employees.
>
> In these circumstances you should tick the relevant box on the TC700 and return it to the Tax Credit Office.

You should fund tax credit by using the PAYE, payments NICs and/or Student Loan Deductions you are accountable for each pay period.

If you don't expect to make sufficient deductions to cover the amount of tax credit payable you can apply for funding from the Inland Revenue by completing a Tax Credit Funding Application, form TC711. This will be sent to you with the first Start Notice, form TC700. You can request extra copies of the form TC711 from the Employer's Orderline on 0845 7646646.

You will be sent a funding notification, form TC712, each month that will tell you how much funding you will be receiving for the following funding period. A standard funding period runs from the 6th of a month to the 5th of the following month. A form TC717 is sent with the first TC712, you can use this to tell us if any of the information given in your application for funding has changed. Return forms TC711 as soon as possible to your usual Accounts Office. You may send them by post or by fax using one of the following numbers

Accounts Office Cumbernauld	0845 602 3519
Accounts Office Shipley	0845 602 3517

To ensure that you receive funding in time, you should apply at **least nine working days** before you need it, provided that it can be paid by direct automated credit transfer into your Bank or Building Society account. If you have not applied this far in advance we will do our best to get the funding to you as soon as possible.

All payments will be made by direct automated credit transfer into your Bank or Building Society account so that they are available to be drawn from the 6th of each month to pay tax credit in the period 6th of the month to the 5th of the next month. The one exception to this is the initial payment, which covers the first two funding periods.

Working Tax Credit is not subject to PAYE tax or NICs.

You must pay tax credit at the same frequency and for the same period as you pay wages/earnings, for example, weekly, fortnightly or monthly. Tax credit is payable for every calendar day in a pay period, not just working days.

The first time you pay tax credit to an employee you must pay the daily rate for the start date itself and for each calendar day up to and including the last day of the pay period in which the start date falls. The TC700 table shows examples of how this works. On each subsequent pay day you must pay tax credit for each calendar day in the pay period.

Example of tax credit paid in arrears

Employer pays wages every Wednesday, 1 week in arrears for work done in previous week. Pay period Monday to Sunday.

Tax credit start date (on TC700) is Friday 14th. Daily rate is £5.50.

On Wednesday 19th (when paying wages for the period 10th–16th) employer pays 3 days' tax credit (£16.50) (for Friday 14th, Saturday 15th and Sunday 16th).

On each subsequent pay day employer pays 7 days' tax credit (£38.50) for the whole pay period.

Every time you pay tax credit to an employee you must

- pay the tax credit as an addition to the employee's net pay;
- show the amount of tax credit paid as a separate item on your employee's payslip;
- record the amount of tax credit paid on the form P11 in column 9 at the appropriate week/month.

If, exceptionally, you have not been required to prepare form P11 (or equivalent record) for the employee for PAYE and NICs purposes, you should prepare one to record the tax credit paid. There is no need, however, to record wages/salary on form P11 if you are preparing the form solely for tax credit purposes. Even if the pay in the period is not made up of earnings but for example SSP, SMP or a tax refund, you must still pay the tax credit for that pay period. In the case of a paid holiday where wages/salary are paid in advance tax credit should also be paid in advance. If we want you to amend the daily rate of tax credit that you pay we will send you an Amendment Notice, form TC701. We will always give you 42 days' notice before you have to start paying tax credit at the amended daily rate.

At the end of each month or quarter you will have to reflect, in the payment you make to your Accounts Office, the amount of tax credit you have paid to your employees.

A copy of the booklet is available at www.inlandrevenue.gov.uk/leaflets/credit.htm or you can get a copy from the Employer's Orderline on 08457 646 646.

You can stop paying tax credit only if

- we tell you to by sending you a stop notice (form TC702 giving you 42 days' notice);
- we agree with you a stop date with less than 42 days' notice (in which case an emergency stop notice, form TC703, will be issued to confirm this);
- you are not due to pay the employee any wages, SMP, SPP, SAP or SSP in a pay period, in which case you do not have to make up a pay packet simply to pay the tax credit;
- the employee leaves or dies.

The Inland Revenue offered additional advice in respect of tax credits and employers' obligations in the 64th edition of *Tax Bulletin*:

Overpayments of WTC by employers

Whereas WFTC and DPTC were awarded for six months at a time and remained payable for the full six months of the award, even if the recipient stopped working in that time, WTC is payable only while the claimant is actually in qualifying remunerative work. It is therefore possible that employers might, through no fault of their own, pay too much WTC to an employee, for example, if the employee leaves his job.

The following paragraphs explain what will happen if we find that an employer has paid too much tax credit to an employee in specific circumstances.

When an employee leaves

Under the old tax credits system, if an employee receiving WFTC or DPTC through the payroll left his job, the employer could choose whether to pay the tax credit up to the date of leaving or up to the end of the pay period in which the date of leaving fell. This choice was possible because the fixed tax credit award continued for six months even if the recipient stopped working.

However, if an employee receiving WTC stops working, his entitlement to WTC may cease, unless he starts another job within seven days. So the employer should not pay WTC beyond the employee's date of leaving.

An employer may inadvertently pay the employee beyond his last day of employment, for example, because the payroll department has not been made aware that the employee has left. If this happens, the employer or payroll department should, within seven days of finding out that the employee has left, call the Employer's Helpline on 08457 143 143 to report the latest day for which WTC has been paid to this employee. (Regulation 12(8) of The Working Tax Credit (Payment by Employers) Regulations 2002 covers this situation.) Provided he does this, the employer will not be held responsible for the overpaid tax credit, that is, WTC paid in respect of any day after the date of leaving.

When an employee dies

Similarly, an employer or payroll department may not know that an employee has died and may pay tax credit beyond the date of death. Within seven days of becoming aware that this has happened, he should call the Employer's Helpline on 08457 143 143 to report the latest day for which he has paid tax credit to this employee. (Regulation 12(7) of The Working Tax Credit (Payment by Employers) Regulations 2002 refers.) Provided he does this, the employer will not be held responsible for the overpaid tax credit, that is, WTC paid in respect of any day after the date of death.

When an employer does not receive an amendment or stop notice

Because tax credit awards respond to in-year changes in a claimant's household income or circumstances, we will sometimes need to ask an employer to amend the daily rate of WTC that he pays or to stop paying tax credit to an employee altogether. In these circumstances we will send the employer an amendment notice or a stop notice, giving him 42 days to amend the daily rate or such shorter period as may have been agreed between us and the employer in the case of a notice to stop paying WTC.

If an employer tells us that he has not received an amendment or stop notice that we have sent, and has continued to pay tax credit at the old daily rate, the employee may receive an overpayment of WTC. Provided we have no reason to doubt the employer's word, we will assume that the amendment or stop notice was lost in the post. We will deal with any overpayment arising in these circumstances by contacting the claimant rather than seeking to recover it from the employer.

21.1.11 Collection of student loans

Student loans are the main source of funding higher education. The Student Loans Company (SLC) is responsible for recovering the repayment of loans made up to August 1998; loans made after that date are recovered via deductions from salary.

The system is similar to that for WTC in that the employers will receive start and stop notifications from the Revenue. The employer is not responsible for identifying employees who are liable to make these repayments nor for answering questions from the employee on the loan. Such queries should be referred to the SLC. Only questions about operating the scheme should be referred to the Revenue.

The calculation of student loan repayments is very similar to that of NICs. There is an annual limit of £10,128 pa (£844 pm) below which no deductions are made. This limit is non-cumulative as with NICs so an employee who earns £800 in one month and £900 in the next will only be liable to deduction in the second month. The deduction made would be as follows:

£900 – £844	=	£56.00
Rate of deduction	=	9%
Student loan repaid	=	£5.04

The initial rate of repayment has been set at 9% and this will be applied to those earnings subject to secondary Class 1 NICs. For any employees not liable to NICs (eg employees working abroad in non-agreement countries) there will be no deductions due.

An employer should only begin to make deductions when a start notice (form SL1) is received from the Revenue. The notice gives at least six weeks' notice before deductions should commence. Deductions should begin on the first pay day after this date.

If a new employee hands over a P45 with a 'Y' in the SL box it means the previous employer had received a start notice. In this situation, deductions should be made as soon as possible. If the P45 is received some time after the employee has started work, no attempt should be made to deduct any arrears. The employer collects Student Loan repayments by making deductions from the borrower's pay using the Student Loan Deduction Tables. These tables are available from the Employer's Orderline, on 08457 646 646. Further information is available in the Revenue leaflet IR59, which is available online at inlandrevenue.gov.uk/pdfs/ir59.pdf.

21.2 CONTRACTORS

The Revenue has seen the way in which contractors pay subcontractors as an obvious area in which tax is being lost to the Treasury. Over the past few years, measures have been introduced to tighten rules and ensure that taxes are accounted for. Payments made by a contractor (see below) will now be made:

- Net after the deduction of PAYE;
- Net under the Construction Industry Scheme;
- Gross under the Construction Industry Scheme.

Construction industry

Construction workers supplied by employment agencies or other third parties were brought within the PAYE system by FA 1998. This aligned the tax and NICs treatment of such workers, who were in the past regarded as self-employed for tax purposes but as employees for NICs purposes.

Note that this change does not only apply to agencies. Companies acting as 'in-house' agencies within the construction industry that supply labour to others, and anyone else who supplies construction workers to others, fall within the legislation.

21.2.1 Payments to subcontractors in construction industry

Where a person carries on a business that includes construction work, the payments to a subcontractor in respect of 'construction operations' may be subject to a deduction of tax.

A contractor includes any person carrying on a business that includes construction industry operations even where these are not the main trading activity. If construction work is commissioned regularly on a person's own trading or investment properties, he is considered to be a contractor for the purposes of deducting tax if his expenditure exceeds £1m on average over a three-year period.

Construction operations

The Regulations define 'construction' as including the installation of heating, lighting or drainage, the internal cleaning of buildings in the course of their construction, alterations or repair work, internal or external painting, and the construction, alteration, repair or demolition of buildings.

Construction Industry Scheme

Tax must be deducted from payments to a subcontractor at the rate of 18% unless one of the exemptions applies. Subcontractors must hold one of the following:

- A registration card CIS4(P);
- A temporary registration card CIS4(T);

- Certificate CIS6;
- Certificate CIS5.

CIS4 and CIS6 must be presented in person. Certificate CIS5 is issued only to companies or partnerships that can show a turnover of at least £1m.

The certificates are issued by the Revenue and determine the basis on which the contractor makes a payment to a subcontractor or company.

Payments to registration cardholders

If the subcontractor holds a valid CIS4(P) or (T) and the contractor is satisfied with the card, the payment is made under the Construction Industry Scheme with a deduction of 18% on the net payment after taking into account deductions for materials, VAT and Construction Board Levies where appropriate. The contractor must supply the subcontractor with a CIS25 voucher within 14 days of the end of the tax month in which the payment is made.

Payments to certificate holders

If the contractor can answer 'Yes' to the three questions in advance of any payment then a payment is made gross and a voucher CIS6 supplied:

- Does the photo match the person?
- Is the certificate in date?
- Do you know the subcontractor?

The subcontractor must send the contractor a CIS24 gross payment voucher within 14 days of the end of the tax month.

The certificate CIS5 is for payments to a company and once again the contractor must be satisfied that the certificate and person presenting it are genuine. To qualify for a CIS5 certificate, a turnover threshold is applied. Prior to 21 March 2000 this was £5m; it is now £1m.

Regardless of the above, if the contractor-subcontractor relationship is one of employer-employee, then the contractor is under an obligation to deduct PAYE. Any payments falling outside of the scheme should be made under the usual PAYE rules.

For further details on the operation of the scheme, contact the Revenue or visit the CIS website www.inlandrevenue.gov.uk/cis.htm.

Electronic filing

Contractors can file the tax payment voucher CIS (E), Construction Gross Payment Voucher (CIS23) and the end-of-year details for those two vouchers electronically. For further details e-mail the Inland Revenue Business Support Team at pms.ir.sh@gtnet.gov.uk.

Payment of tax

The amounts of tax a contractor should have collected from payments made to subcontractors must be paid to the Revenue Accounts Office within 14 days of the end of the month to which the payment relates. Thus if the payment relates to the month 6 May 2003 to 5 June 2003, the payment must be made by 19 June 2003.

Future changes to the CIS

The Government announced on 9 April 2003 that the Construction Industry Scheme will be reformed in April 2005 in line with a consultation paper published in the 2002 Pre-Budget Report.

21.3 IR35

The revised version of the controversial rules and regulations on personal service companies came into effect as at 6 April 2000. These new rules use existing case law (see Chap. 5) to determine whether an individual performs services that would be taxed under Schedule E as employment income were it not for the fact that his services are provided through an intermediary such as a service company. Those caught by the new rules will pay approximately the same PAYE and NICs as an individual who is an employee of the end customer.

The Revenue has laid out a nine-point plan for determining the deemed Schedule E tax charge for a tax year:

- *Step 1* determines that the starting point for the calculation is the total amount received by the intermediary during the tax year from relevant engagements. This figure includes any benefits-in-kind provided to the intermediary in respect of those engagements. This total amount is then reduced by 5%, which is an allowance for the intermediary's running costs.
- *Step 2* adds in any payments or benefits-in-kind received by the worker or his family in respect of any relevant engagements from anyone other than the intermediary, which are not otherwise taxable under Schedule E, but which would have been so taxable had the worker been employed by the client.
- *Step 3* deducts any amounts spent by the intermediary that could have been claimed as expenses against income tax had the worker been the client's employee and met them himself.
- *Step 4* allows a deduction for any capital allowances that could have been claimed by the worker had he been the client's employee.

- *Step 5* deducts any contributions paid by the intermediary to an approved pension scheme for the worker's benefit.
- *Step 6* deducts any employer's NICs (Classes 1 and 1A) paid by the intermediary in respect of salary or benefits-in-kind provided to the worker during the year.
- *Step 7* deducts any amount of salary and benefits-in-kind provided by the intermediary to the worker during the year, which has already been subject to Schedule E tax and Classes 1 and 1A NICs (excluding any amounts that have already been deducted at Step 3).

  Note: if, after Step 7, the result is nil or a negative amount, there is no deemed Schedule E payment and no further tax or NICs are payable. If the result is positive, a deemed Schedule E payment must be calculated in accordance with Steps 8 and 9.
- *Step 8* allows for a deduction of the employer's NICs payable on the deemed payment. So Step 8 requires the calculation of the amount that, together with the employer's NICs due on it, equals the result of Step 7.
- *Step 9* states that the result after Step 8 is the amount of the deemed Schedule E payment.

Note that if the worker is within the Construction Industry Scheme (see above), it is the amount before deduction of tax under that scheme that must be brought in at Step 1 of the calculation.

Table 21.2 – Deemed Calculation: Inland Revenue Template

Step One	Enter in this box the amount of all payments and benefits received by your company or partnership in the year for contracts to which these rules apply.	1
	Enter in this box 5% of the amount in box 1.	2
Step Two	Enter in this box the amount of any payments and benefits received directly by you in the year for contracts to which the rules apply and which are not already taxable.	3
Step Three	Enter in this box the amount of any expenses met by your company or partnership in the year which you could have claimed personally if the worker had been an employee of the client and had paid for them yourself.	4
Step Four	Enter in this box the amount of any capital allowances for purchases made by your company or partnership which you could have claimed yourself if you had been employed by your client and had made the purchases yourself.	5

Step Five	Enter in this box the amount of any contributions to an approved pension scheme made by your company or partnership for your personal benefit.	6
Step Six	Enter in this box the amount of any employer's Class 1 and Class 1A NICs which your company or partnership paid in the year in respect of salary or non-cash benefits which it provided to you in the year.	7
Step Seven	Enter in this box the amount of any salary you received from your company or partnership in the year which is already taxable under Schedule E (this does not include anything for which a deduction has already been given at Step Three).	8
	Enter in this box any benefits in kind or expenses you received from your company or partnership in the year which are already taxable under Schedule E (this does not include anything for which a deduction has already been given at Step Three).	8a
	Add together the figures in boxes 1 and 3 and enter the total in this box.	9
	Add together the figures in boxes 2, 4, 5, 6, 7, 8 and 8a and enter the total in this box.	10
	Deduct the figures in box 10 from the figures in box 9 and enter the answer in this box. If the answer in box 11 is nil or a negative number there is no deemed payment. If the answer in box 11 is a positive number you will need to process this figure to get the deemed payment and the employer's Class 1 NICs on that deemed payment.	11
Step Eight	Multiply the figure in box 11 by 100 and enter the answer in this box.	12
	Divide the figure in box 12 by (100+11.9) and enter the answer in this box (case a), unless the figure in box 8 is less than the secondary Class 1 NICs earnings threshold, in which case complete the steps below (case b). The final figure in box 13 is the deemed payment.	13
	Case b: subtract the figure in box 8 from the Class 1 NICs earnings threshold and enter in this box.	13a
	Case b: subtract the figure in box 13a from the figure in box 11 and enter in this box.	13b
	Case b: multiply the figure in box 13b by 100 and enter the answer in this box.	13c

	Case b: divide the figure in box 13c by (100+11.8) (see footnote 1) and enter the answer in this box.	13d
	Case b: add the figure in box 13d to the figure in Box 13a and enter the answer in box 13.	
Step Nine	Deduct the figure in box 13 from the figure in box 11 and enter the amount you are left with in this box. This amount is the amount of employer's Class 1 NICs due on the deemed payment.	14
	Enter the figure from box 13 in this box. This amount is the deemed payment.	

1. The employer's contribution rate can vary. Contracted-out or contracted-in rates are different. The figure you add to 100 at this stage should be the contributions rate that is applicable to you. See Inland Revenue National Insurance tables CA38 and the Employer's Annual Pack for further details.

Example

Mr and Mrs A work through a service company in which they own all the shares. They each carry out some engagements during the year that fall within the new rules ('relevant engagements') and some that do not.

Assume the service company receives £20,000 in respect of relevant engagements for Mr A and £40,000 of those for Mrs A with a further £40,000 income from other business activities that do not fall within the new rules. Assume the service company also incurs the following expenses during the course of the year 2002-03:

Expense	*Mr A*	*Mrs A*	*Notes*
Salaries	£20,000	£20,000	Paid in year. PAYE and NICs deducted and accounted for under normal provisions.
Employer's NICs	£1,815	£1,815	Paid in year. NICs calculated on an annual earnings period, as for directors. Assumes that the employer's threshold (£4,615) has been set against these earnings, and 11.8% paid on remainder.
Employer's pension contributions	£4,000	£4,000	To an approved scheme.
Travel costs related to relevant engagements	£2,000	£500	All would be deductible under normal provisions relating to employees.

Other expenses: £10,000 business expenses, all allowable for corporation tax purposes.

Under the IR35 legislation, at the end of the tax year the service company must calculate the amount of PAYE and NICs due on Mr and Mrs A's earnings. If they have not paid enough PAYE and NICs during the year, these will be payable on a 'deemed payment' on the last day of the tax year.

Calculation of deemed payment		*Mr A*	*Mrs A*
Step 1:	Income from relevant contracts	20,000	40,000
Less:	Expenses (**Step 3**)	(2,000)	(500)
	Employer's NICs paid in year (**Step 6**)	(1,815)	(1,815)
	Pension contributions (**Step 5**)	(4,000)	(4,000)
	Flat rate 5% relevant income (**Step 1**)	(1,000)	(2,000)
		11,185	31,685
Deduct: Salary paid in year (**Step 7**)		(20,000)	(20,000)
Step 7		No deemed payment	11,685
Employer's NICs on deemed payment (**Step 8**)			(1,233,260)
Deemed payment (**Step 9**)			10,452

Company accounts		£	£
Turnover			100,000
Less:	Salaries	(40,000)	
	Employer's NICs	(3,630)	
	Pension contributions	(8,000)	
	Expenses	(12,500)	
			(64,130)
Accounting profit			35,870
Deemed payment		(10,452)	
Employer's NICs on deemed payment		(1,233)	
			(11,685)
Profits for corporation tax purposes			24,185

Summary

Mr A brought in £20,000 from relevant contracts during the course of the year. The service company paid the whole of that amount onto him in salary and deducted and accounted for full PAYE and NICs. No further action is required.

Mrs A brought in £40,000 from relevant contracts during the course of the year and the service company paid £20,000 onto her in salary and deducted and accounted for PAYE and NICs on that salary. This left £20,000 from her relevant contracts on which PAYE and NICs had not been deducted and accounted for during the course of the year. Under the new rules this £20,000, less the deductions allowed, is deemed to be paid to Mrs A as salary.

Example

Mr and Mrs B work as members of a partnership, of which they are the two partners. They carry out relevant engagements during the year. Of the partnership income 50% arises from such engagements and 50% from other sources. Profits are split equally, but for the relevant engagements the services are performed 60% by Mrs B and 40% by Mr B. Each is provided with a car, both of which are held as partnership assets. The private use proportion of the motoring expenses is 30%. Partnership accounts show the following results:

Year ended 5 April 2003	£	
Income	80,000	
Expenses	17,000*	
Profit	63,000	
Tax adjusted profit	65,000	(reflects adjustments for depreciation, private expenses etc)

* includes motoring expenses of £3,000

Calculation of deemed payment at 5 April 2003		*Mrs B*	*Mr B*
(**Step 1**)	Payments from relevant engagements:	24,000	16,000
Less:	5% allowance (**Step 1**)	(1,200)	(800)
	Schedule E expenses[1] (**Step 3**)	(630)	(420)
	Employer's NICs on deemed payment (**Step 8**):	(1,853)	(1,073)
Deemed payment (**Step 9**)		20,317	13,707

Recalculation of partnership taxable profit		£
Partnership profit:		65,000
Plus:	disallowed expenses: (7,500 – (2,000 + 1,050))[2]	4,450
		69,450
Less:	total deemed payments	(34,024)
Taxable profit		35,426

Recalculation of personal liability	*Mrs B*	*Mr B*
Partnership profit:	17,713	17,713
Deemed payment	20,317	13,707

[1] This amount is calculated from the business proportion of the motoring expenses that relate to the relevant engagements.

[2] This amount reflects the difference between the expenses incurred and allowable for taxation purposes in respect of the relevant engagements and the amounts allowed as part of the 5% allowance and Schedule E expenses.

Payment of tax

Tax and NICs under IR35 regulations in respect of deemed payments are due for payment by 19 April following the end of the tax year. In some situations, the Revenue believes that the P35 should be filed on the basis of estimates of the deemed payment and the tax and NICs due on it. See the advice published on www.inlandrevenue.gov.uk/ir35.

21.4 NON-RESIDENT LANDLORD SCHEME

If you rent a property from a non-resident landlord, you have an obligation to withhold basic rate tax and pay this over to the Revenue on a quarterly basis. There are two main exceptions to this rule, ie where

(1) the rent paid is less than £100 pw; or
(2) you have received confirmation from the Revenue that you may make the payment gross.

If you are in this situation you should contact:

The Inland Revenue Centre for Non-Residents
St John's House
Merton Road
Bootle
Merseyside L69 9BB.

The Revenue will forward you a form to complete within 30 days of the end of each quarter, explaining how the tax is calculated and how to make a payment to the Account's Office.

Example – Calculation of quarterly payment

Tax is calculated at the basic rate on the rent due in quarter less allowable expenses. Therefore, if the rent due in the quarter to 31 March 2003 is £3,000 but during the quarter you have paid £300 out of this sum to repair a broken window, then the calculation would be as follows:

	£
Rent	3,000
Less: Allowable expenses	(300)
	2,700
Tax at 22%	594

At the end of each tax year you must provide by no later than 5 July a return including details of the rent paid, allowable expenses and tax deducted. Within the same time frame you should also supply the landlord with a certificate of the tax deducted. The payments are dealt with by the Centre for Non-Residents (previously FICO) at the address above.

21.5 PAYMENTS TO NON-RESIDENT SPORTSMEN AND ENTERTAINERS

Basic rate tax must be withheld from most payments made to non-UK resident sportsmen and entertainers for work performed in the UK. In addition, where benefits-in-kind are provided to them, the cost must be 'grossed up' for tax at the basic rate and accounted for. A tax voucher must be provided for each payment and the person making the payments must account for tax on a quarterly basis.

21.5.1 Payments caught by this scheme

Payments or benefits subject to these regulations include:

(1) Prize money.
(2) Appearance or performance fees.
(3) Endorsement fees where the individual has appeared in the UK (whether or not his appearance is to promote the goods he is endorsing).
(4) Payments that finance any of the above (eg commercial sponsorship).

Certain payments specifically excluded from the scheme are those:

(1) subject to deduction of tax;
(2) subject to PAYE;
(3) solely for the use of copyright in words or music;
(4) made to the Performing Rights Society;
(5) made to UK residents and ancillary to a performance (including the cost of hiring a venue and payments for the services of UK-resident performers appearing with a non-resident);
(6) that are royalties on the sale of records and tapes; and
(7) amounting to less than £1,000 in a tax year. This *de minimis* limit applies to all payments made in a tax year in connection with the same event. Furthermore, payments made by the same or connected persons must be aggregated and the £1,000 exemption applies only if the total is less than £1,000.

21.5.2 Special arrangements

It is possible for a payer to secure the Revenue's agreement to a lower rate of withholding tax provided an application is made at least 30 days in advance. Such authorisation may be given on the basis that:

(1) the organiser can arrange that he is responsible for accounting for the tax; or
(2) the sponsor can apply for clearance on the grounds that the tax will be collected from someone else; or
(3) the payer can see authority to withhold tax at a lower rate, possibly to

reflect the fact that the non-resident will have certain allowable expenses or perhaps because only some members of a group are non-resident.

21.5.3 Indirect payments also caught

The regulations provide that the withholding system should apply to payments made to any person:

(1) who is under the control of the non-resident sportsman or entertainer;
(2) who is:
   (a) not resident in the UK; and
   (b) not liable to tax in a territory outside the UK where the rate of tax charged on profits exceeds 22%;
(3) in receipt of a connected payment or value transferred by a connected transfer;

who receives any connected payment or connected transfer where there is a contract or arrangement under which it is reasonable to suppose that the entertainer (or other person connected with him) is, will or may become entitled to receive amounts not substantially less than the amount paid.

21.6 OTHER PAYMENTS TO NON-UK RESIDENT PERSONS

21.6.1 Interest paid to non-resident lender

Tax at 20% must normally be deducted where the interest is chargeable under Schedule D Case III and the lender is not UK-resident. It may be possible for the lender to make a claim under a double taxation agreement; where such a claim has been made, the Revenue may authorise payment of interest without deduction of tax.

21.6.2 Patent royalties paid to non-residents

Patent royalties paid to a non-resident are normally subject to deduction of basic rate tax.

It will be possible from 1 October 2002 for a company to pay royalties without deducting tax if the recipient is a person resident in a country for which the relevant double tax treaty contains an exemption from UK tax. If it turns out that the exemption was not in fact due, the company paying the royalty will then have to account for the tax that should have been withheld.

21.6.3 Copyright royalties

Copyright royalties paid to a non-resident are also normally subject to deduction of tax. Where the payment is made via a commission agent, basic rate tax must be withheld for the net amount paid on to the non-resident. A statement made in the House of Commons in 1969 indicates that this obligation to withhold tax does not apply where copyright payments are made to professional authors who are resident abroad.

21.6.4 Purchase of British patent rights

There is an obligation for basic rate tax to be withheld where a person sells all or part of his patent rights and the vendor is not UK-resident. Once again, the provisions of a double taxation agreement may override this, but a person making payment for such rights must deduct tax unless he is authorised not to do so by the Inspector of Foreign Dividends.

22

ANTI-AVOIDANCE LEGISLATION

While the UK still does not have a GAAR (General Anti-avoidance Rule), there are numerous specific anti-avoidance provisions that must be borne in mind, especially when a tax planning exercise is being carried out. These provisions are generally intended to ensure that a person cannot reduce his tax liability by carrying out a given transaction in a roundabout way.

This chapter covers:

Income tax

(1) Interest income.
(2) Transactions in land.
(3) Transactions in securities.
(4) Transfer of assets overseas.
(5) Trust income taxed on the settlor.
(6) Transactions involving loans or credit.

Capital gains tax

(7) Bed and breakfast transactions.
(8) Disposals by a series of transactions.
(9) Transfers to a connected person.
(10) Qualifying corporate bonds.
(11) Value shifting.
(12) UK-resident settlements where settlor has retained interest.
(13) Offshore companies.
(14) Non-resident trusts.

INCOME TAX

22.1 INTEREST INCOME

22.1.1 Background

The Taxes Acts contain extensive legislation that is designed to prevent the conversion of taxable income into capital.

22.1.2 Sale of loan stock with right to purchase

(TA 1988, s 729)

At one time it was possible to enjoy the benefit of income in a capital form that was not subject to tax by selling loan stock or other interest-bearing securities and retaining a right to repurchase them. For example, a person holding £1m 3 1/2% War Loan could sell the stock to a charity for £400,000 cum-interest while retaining the right to repurchase the War Loan once it had gone ex-interest for, say, £385,000 – an overall profit of £15,000. He had to forgo the income of £17,500 but that was taxable and worth less than £15,000. The charity, meanwhile, got the income tax free.

There is now specific legislation designed to catch such arrangements. Where s 729 applies, the interest is treated as remaining taxable income of the person who sold the loan stock with a right to repurchase. Thus, using the above example, the interest payments actually received by the charity are now treated as income of the individual who had sold the War Loan stock with the right to repurchase it.

22.1.3 Sale of right to income

(TA 1988, s 730)

A variation on the above scheme worked for a number of years. It was common for individuals to sell to a charity or other exempt body the right to receive interest payments for a specified period of time, while retaining legal ownership of the securities themselves. This is now caught by s 730. If the loan stock is a UK security, the arising income is assessed on the vendor. If it is a foreign loan stock, the sale proceeds are assessable as if they were income.

22.1.4 Manufactured dividends

Manufactured payments arise during a stock loan or repo transaction. They involve the person who currently holds the securities paying over to the original owner an amount equal to dividends or interest received. Individuals could deduct such payments from their total income for tax purposes. FA 2002 introduced anti-avoidance provisions to counter perceived abuses. This is a specialised area and those affected will no doubt already be aware of the changes and should have taken professional advice.

22.2 TRANSACTIONS IN LAND

(TA 1988, s 776)

22.2.1 Introduction

Section 776 was intended to prevent tax avoidance by persons concerned with land or development of land. It may apply where a capital gain is realised and one of the following conditions applies:

(1) The gain arises from UK land (or some other asset deriving its value from land) and the land was acquired with the sole or main object of realising a gain.
(2) The gain arises from the disposal of UK land held as trading stock.
(3) The gain arises from a disposal of UK land that has been developed with the sole or main object of realising a gain on its disposal.

Where s 776 applies, all or part of the capital gain is charged as income under Schedule D Case VI.

The definition of land includes buildings, and also assets deriving their value from land (eg options). Consequently, s 776 could apply if a person received a lump sum for assigning the benefit of an option.

22.2.2 Exemption

There is an exemption for gains that arise on the disposal of an individual's principal private residence. This exemption continues to be available even where the CGT exemption is not due because the property was acquired with a view to realising a gain (see 16.2.3).

22.2.3 Sales of shares

Section 776 may apply where a person disposes of shares in a land-owning company. If a non-resident individual were to dispose of, say, a controlling shareholding in a company that itself owned a valuable UK property, he might be subject to tax under Schedule D Case VI on the whole of his capital gain.

There is a let-out in the case of a land-owning company that holds land as trading stock (ie a company that is a builder or developer or deals in land as a trade). No liability arises under s 776 on a sale of shares in such a company, provided the land held by the company is disposed of in the normal course of its trade and a full commercial profit from that land is received by the company.

Despite this let-out, s 776 may still be a problem on a sale of a land-owning company since the company may be an investment company (in which case it will not hold the land as trading stock).

22.2.4 Clearance procedure

It is possible for a person to apply for advance clearance from the Revenue that s 776 will not apply to a particular disposal. This clearance may be sought either for a sale of land or of shares in a land-owning company. The legislation requires the person to supply full written particulars to the Inspector who must then make his decision within 30 days. Once clearance is given, the Revenue cannot subsequently charge tax under s 776 unless the clearance application was invalid because it did not accurately set out all the facts.

22.3 TRANSACTIONS IN SECURITIES
(TA 1988, s 703)

22.3.1 Introduction

Legislation was originally introduced in 1960 to enable the Revenue to counteract tax advantages obtained by transactions in securities. The legislation is often applied by the Revenue to prevent tax savings being achieved because a right to income has been converted into a capital gain. An example of the type of transaction that might be caught in this way is where a person sells shares with a right to repurchase them for a lower amount after a dividend has been received by the purchaser (this is not caught by s 729, as mentioned at 22.1.2, because that legislation applies only to loan stock and other fixed interest securities). The legislation also applies to other more devious types of transactions where the tax advantage is less obvious at first sight.

22.3.2 Conditions to be satisfied before legislation can apply

For s 703 to apply, the following three conditions must be satisfied.

(1) there must be one or more transactions in securities; and
(2) a person must have obtained, or be in a position to obtain, a tax advantage; and
(3) one of the prescribed circumstances set out in s 704 must have occurred.

If s 703 does apply, an income tax assessment may be made under Schedule D Case VI to counteract the tax advantage.

22.3.3 The term 'transactions in securities'

This term is widely defined to include transactions of whatever description relating to securities. It includes in particular:

(1) the purchase, sale or exchange of securities;
(2) the issuing of new securities;
(3) alteration of rights attaching to securities.

'Securities' is, in turn, defined as including shares and loan stock.

22.3.4 Tax advantage

In general, a tax advantage is deemed to arise if there is any increased relief, or repayment of tax, arising from transactions in securities, or if the transactions result in a reduction in the amount of tax that would otherwise be assessed.

The courts have taken the view that a tax advantage may arise wherever the Revenue can show that an amount received in a non-taxable form could have been received in a way that would have given rise to an income tax liability. Going back to the example given in 22.3.1, the Revenue would say that a tax advantage arises when a person sells shares and has a right to buy back at a lower price after a dividend has been paid because he could simply have retained the shares and received the dividend.

22.3.5 Prescribed circumstances

Section 704 lists five circumstances, outlined in ss 704A-704E, and at least one of them must apply before the Revenue can invoke s 703. Sections 704B and 704E apply to special situations that are outside the scope of this book; the remaining three are as follows.

Section 704A

This requires:

(1) the receipt of an abnormal dividend;
(2) a dividend should be received by someone entitled to an exemption or relief.

One example of this would be where shares are sold to a charity, the company then pays a dividend and the charity is able to reclaim tax because it is exempt from income tax. Another less obvious example is where an abnormally large dividend is paid to an individual who is able to set losses against the dividend.

Section 704C

This applies where a person receives consideration without paying income tax on it as a result of a transaction whereby another person subsequently receives an abnormal amount by way of dividend. The consideration received must represent:

(1) the value of assets available for distribution by way of dividends; or
(2) future receipts of the company; or
(3) the value of trading stock of the company.

Section 704D

This subsection applies where a person receives consideration that is not subject to tax and represents:

(1) the value of assets available for distribution by way of dividends; or
(2) future receipts of the company; or
(3) the value of the trading stock of the company.

This is obviously similar to s 704C, but s 704D can apply even though there has been no abnormal dividend.

Section 704D can apply only to transactions involving specified companies, ie:

(a) companies that are under the control of not more than five persons; or
(b) transactions involving any other unquoted company.

22.3.6 Exemption for bona fide commercial transactions

If there is a transaction in securities and the prescribed circumstances apply, a taxpayer may still avoid assessment if he can show that transactions were carried out for bona fide commercial reasons or in the ordinary course of making or managing investments, and that none of them had as their main object the obtaining of a tax advantage.

22.3.7 Clearances

Section 707 provides a procedure whereby a person can give details of the proposed transactions to the Revenue and request clearance that the Board will not apply s 703.

Once a written application has been made under s 707, the Revenue has 30 days in which to request further particulars, which must then be provided within 30 days.

The Revenue must give a decision either within 30 days of receiving the original application or within 30 days of receiving the further particulars.

Where the Revenue has notified someone that it is satisfied that s 703 should not apply, it may not subsequently change its mind. Where information given in the application is incomplete or inaccurate, any clearance given by the Revenue may be void.

22.3.8 Situations where clearance should be sought

It is standard practice for vendors or their advisers to seek clearance under s 707 where a private company is being sold for a substantial amount. Quite apart from anything else, the vendor would otherwise be at the mercy of the purchaser who might extract an abnormal dividend and thus bring s 707 into consideration.

It is also advisable to seek clearance under s 707 where a company is liquidated, the reserves are extracted in a capital form and it is intended that the company's business should be carried on by a new company owned by the current shareholders.

22.4 TRANSFER OF ASSETS OVERSEAS

Legislation was originally introduced in 1936 to prevent tax savings for UK-resident and ordinarily resident individuals arising from their transferring assets overseas. The legislation refers to avoidance of income tax. Capital tax avoidance is not subject to counteraction by s 739 or 740, although separate anti-avoidance legislation also exists for CGT (see 22.13).

22.4.1 Where the individual or his or her spouse can benefit

Section 739 applies where a UK-resident has made a transfer of assets and either he or his spouse may benefit as a result of it. He is deemed to meet this test if he has 'power to enjoy' income that arises overseas. Power to enjoy income exists in the following circumstances:

(1) The income accrues for his benefit.
(2) The receipt of the income increases the value to him of any assets held by him or for his benefit.
(3) He may become entitled to enjoy the income at some future point in time.
(4) He is able in any way whatsoever, and whether directly or indirectly, to control the way the income is used.

Where s 739 applies, the transferor or spouse is assessed on the income as it arises, even if it is not actually paid out to them.

22.4.2 Exemption for bona fide transactions

Section 741 provides a clearance procedure. The individual must show to the Revenue's satisfaction that:

(1) the purpose of avoiding tax was not one of the purposes for which the transfer of assets was carried out; or
(2) the transfer of assets, and any associated operations, were bona fide commercial transactions and not designed for tax avoidance.

In *Carvill v IRC* SpC 233, the Special Commissioners held that the test was a subjective, and not an objective, one.

22.4.3 Transfer of assets by non-residents

The Revenue's view has always been that s 739 could apply to income arising from a transfer of assets made by an individual at a time when he was not UK-resident. The House of Lords found against the Revenue on this in *IRC v Willoughby* [1997] STC 995, but FA 1997 restored the position to what the Revenue always believed to be the case in relation to income arising on or after 26 November 1996.

22.4.4 Assessment of income caught by s 739

Income caught by s 739 normally is assessed under Schedule D Case VI. Where it is UK dividend income, or other income that has borne tax at source, relief is given for such tax and the assessment will be for higher rate tax purposes only.

22.4.5 Liability of non-transferors

(TA 1988, s 740)

A person may not be assessed under s 739 unless he or his spouse has made a transfer of assets. However, a UK-ordinarily resident individual may be assessed under s 740 if he receives a benefit from a transfer made by another person. This applies particularly to beneficiaries of non-resident settlements created by someone other than the individual and his spouse. It is also arguable that s 740 might apply to a person who had made a transfer of assets but was not 'caught' by s 739, perhaps because he was not resident at the time of the transfer.

In contrast to s 739, a liability may arise under s 740 only when the individual concerned receives a benefit. 'Benefit' is not specifically defined, although the legislation states it includes a payment of any kind. It is understood that the Revenue regards an interest-free loan or the provision of accommodation as constituting a benefit.

This is an area where professional advice is essential.

22.4.6 Matching income with benefits

The legislation provides for benefits to be matched with income received in either earlier or later years.

Example

An overseas trust receives income of £10,000 in 1994-95. In 1996-97 a capital payment of £100,000 is made to a UK-resident and ordinarily resident individual. In the year 2001-02, the trustees receive further income of £120,000. If s 740 applies, the individual will be taxed as follows:

	£
1996-97	10,000
2001-02	90,000

22.4.7 An interest-free loan may constitute a benefit

The High Court decided in January 2000 in *Billingham v Cooper* [2000] STC 122 that an interest-free loan that was repayable on demand gave rise to a benefit equal to interest at the 'official rate'.

22.4.8 Assessment under s 740

Where income is taxed under s 740, there is no credit for any UK tax suffered at source. This can give rise to double taxation. Thus, going back to the previous example, if the trustees' income represented interest from UK companies, the total tax suffered would really be as follows:

	£
Tax at source on interest: £100,000 × $\frac{20}{80}$ =	25,000
Tax charged on beneficiary under s 740 =	40,000
	65,000

22.4.9 Clearances

Once again, it is possible to obtain clearance from the Revenue that s 740 should not apply because the transfer of assets concerned was not carried out for tax avoidance purposes.

22.4.10 Foreign domiciliaries

Where the income arising to the non-resident trust or company is foreign source income, no liability can arise for a foreign domiciled individual except to the extent that he remits such income to the UK (see 24.10).

22.4.11 Reporting income taxable under s 739 or s 740

The relevant sections of your tax return are as follows:

Extract from tax return, page 2

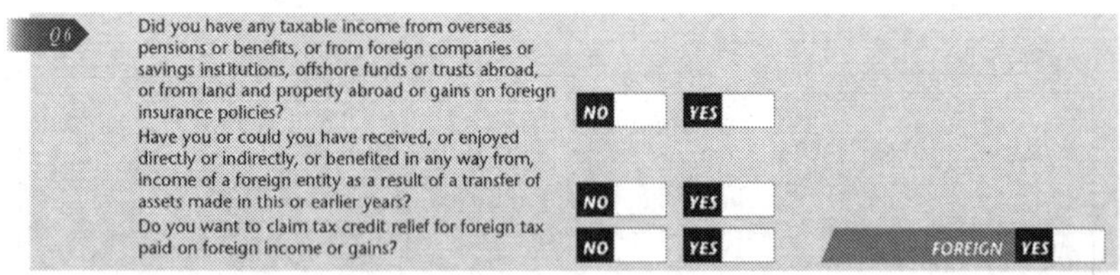

Q6 Did you have any taxable income from overseas pensions or benefits, or from foreign companies or savings institutions, offshore funds or trusts abroad, or from land and property abroad or gains on foreign insurance policies? NO YES

Have you or could you have received, or enjoyed directly or indirectly, or benefited in any way from, income of a foreign entity as a result of a transfer of assets made in this or earlier years? NO YES

Do you want to claim tax credit relief for foreign tax paid on foreign income or gains? NO YES

FOREIGN YES

If you tick either YES box, you are required to complete a Foreign Schedule.

Extract from foreign schedule, page F2

- Disposals of holdings in offshore funds, income from non-resident trusts and benefits received from overseas trusts, companies and other entities · *see Notes, page FN11.* 6.5 £

Tick box 6.5A if you are omitting income from boxes 6.4, 6.4A or 6.5 · *see Notes, pages FN11 and FN12.* 6.5A

Extracts from Revenue notes to the tax return

If you have transferred, or taken any part in the transfer of, assets as a result of which income has become payable to a trust, company or other entity situated abroad and,

- you are ordinarily resident in the UK and you or your husband or wife may at any time enjoy any of that income (in whatever form), or
- you or your husband or wife have received or are entitled to receive a capital sum connected in any way with the transfer,

enter that income in columns A to E on Page F2 and include it in the total amounts in boxes 6.3, 6.3A, 6.4 and 6.4A unless you are ticking box 6.5A …

Benefits received from overseas trusts, companies and other entities

boxes 6.5 and 6.5A If someone else has made the same sort of transfer of assets … the value of the payment or any other benefit you receive is treated as your income for tax purposes to the extent that the company, trust or other entity has 'unexpended income'. Unexpended income means income that has not already become that of another individual or that has not otherwise been spent by the company, trust or other entity. Income which arose before 10 March 1981 is not counted for this purpose …

… 'Benefits' include, for example, loans at less than a commercial rate of interest and the occupation or use of property at less than a commercial rental, the value of the benefit being the difference between the commercial rate of interest or rental and any amount actually paid to you.

A trust will be non-resident if all trustees are themselves resident outside the United Kingdom. A trust may also be non resident if at least one of its trustees is resident outside the United Kingdom – ask the trustees or your tax adviser if you are not sure whether the trust is treated as non-resident. 'Indirect' receipt must also be included, for example, if the capital or benefit came from a company controlled by the trustees or from a United Kingdom resident trust that has been, or has received funds from, an overseas trust.

If you received capital or benefit (other than income) from a trust which either is, or has been, non-resident, or which has received assets from a trust which either is or has been non-resident, enter that amount in box 6.5.

Enter in box 6.5 (unless you are ticking box 6.5A for the reason given below), the value of any payment or benefit received directly or indirectly to the extent that it is matched by unexpended income. If the payment or benefit is greater than the unexpended income, enter in box 6.5 the amount of the unexpended income. You may need to ask the overseas company, trust or other entity for this information. Include the value of any payment or benefit received in an earlier year if and to the extent that this was not taxed in earlier years. If the value of what you have received or benefited from exceeds the unexpended income that the overseas company trust or other entity has, you may be liable to Capital Gains Tax on the excess. You may need Help Sheet IR301: Calculation of the increase in tax charge on capital gains from non-resident, dual resident and immigrating trusts as well as the Capital Gains Pages; both are available from the Orderline. Otherwise that excess will need to be taken into account when completing your Tax Return next year. Also enter in the 'Additional Information' box on Page F3 the full name and address of the company or other entity receiving the income. Where the capital or other benefit has come from a resident trust in the circumstances described above, also give details of the circumstances including the full name of any other trust involved.

box 6.5A These provisions relating to transfers of assets do not apply if you can show that the purpose of the transfer and any associated operations was not to avoid tax. But if you are omitting income for this reason from columns A to E on Page F2 and boxes 6.4, 6.4A or 6.5 you must tick box 6.5A.

22.5 TRUST INCOME TAXED ON THE SETTLOR

22.5.1 Introduction

There are a number of separate provisions under which income on property that belongs to trustees may be taxed as if it were income that belonged to the settlor. FA 1995 recast these sections in relation to 1995-96 and subsequent years, but the overall effect of the new legislation (TA 1988, ss 660A-660J, inserted by FA 1995, Sched 17) is virtually identical.

22.5.2 Trust where settlor may benefit

(TA 1988, s 660A)

Legislation may catch income that arises to a trust under which the settlor or his spouse may benefit. The legislation provides that the settlor/spouse should be treated as capable of benefiting where they may benefit in any circumstances whatsoever except in one of the following exceptional cases:

(1) The bankruptcy of a person who is beneficially entitled under the settlement.
(2) The death under age 25 of a person who would be beneficially entitled to the trust property on attaining that age.
(3) In the case of a marriage settlement, the death of both parties to the marriage and of all or any of the children of the marriage.

The Revenue interprets this legislation rather literally. For example, if a person creates a trust for the benefit of his son, and the trust deed states that the property should revert to the settlor if the son dies before age 35, the Revenue takes the view that s 660A applies because the let-out applies only where property reverts on the death of someone before he attains age 25.

Sometimes the trust deed is silent on a matter. For example, a person creates a trust for the benefit of his three children and deed makes no reference to the capital coming back to the settlor. In such circumstances, the Revenue is apt to say that the property could revert to the settlor if all his children died and they left no children of their own. To avoid this kind of argument, it is normal for a trust to contain a clause that provides the capital shall in no circumstances whatsoever come back to the settlor but shall be held for the benefit of, say, a charity in the event that all the named beneficiaries die before the capital is distributed.

The Revenue does not take the view that a person has reserved the benefit simply because his spouse may benefit after his death as his widow. On the other hand, cases have actually arisen where the settlor and his wife were excluded but the Revenue said that s 660A should apply because the settlor's current marriage might come to an end and he might marry someone who could benefit. Once again, it is best to make sure that the trust deed excludes such an interpretation by expressly providing that any future spouse of the settlor should be excluded from all benefit.

Where a settlor's spouse can benefit, the settlor is assessed on the trust income. This means that the benefits of independent taxation cannot be secured by putting capital into trust for a spouse.

FA 2000 has introduced a concession. Where a settlor is not totally excluded but one of the beneficiaries under the trust is a charity, income arising after 5 April 2000 that is actually paid out to the charity will not be assessable on the settlor under s 660A.

22.5.3 Settlements where the property given is just a right to income

(TA 1988, s 660A)

The legislation contains a very wide definition of 'settlement'. It can even apply to an outright gift where the property given is 'wholly or substantially' a right to income. It can also apply where there is no gift at all but there are arrangements which amount to a settlement as might apply where an individual lets someone else subscribe for shares in a new company.

The Revenue arguments seem to have a 'seasonality'. In the early 1990s, Inspectors often tried to apply these provisions where a husband had admitted his wife into partnership. The argument was that this was uncommercial and the partnership's profits should be assessed on the husband who contributed most to the business (and invariably paid tax at a higher rate). But as the Revenue met dogged resistance from tax accountants these arguments largely ceased, but without the Revenue ever conceding that the principle was incorrect.

In 2003, these arguments resurfaced in the context of small companies. The Revenue argued that where the husband was the main contributor to the company's profits, s 660A allowed the Revenue to treat dividends paid to the wife as the husband's income.

It has to be said that there are no decided cases which underpin the Revenue arguments. The case of *Young v Pearce* [1996] STC 743 is often cited by Inspectors but the key feature of this case was that the wives had only non-voting shares and were totally dependent on their husbands voting them dividends. Similarly, another case often cited by the Revenue, *Butler v Wildin* [1989] STC 22, was decided on its special facts. Moreover, in that case some of the shares issued to minor children were held not to be caught by the settlement provisions.

At the time that this edition goes to Press, the position is that the Revenue has set out its views in the April 2003 edition of *Tax Bulletin*. Time will show whether the Courts will uphold the Revenue arguments.

Many professionals believe that there are ways of side stepping this type of Revenue attack. You should consult a tax specialist if you are setting up a new company.

Bear in mind s 660A if you are entering into a dividend waiver. Again, see the *Tax Bulletin* article for guidance on the Revenue's position.

22.5.4 Settlements on minor children

(TA 1988, s 660B)

Where a person gives capital to his minor children, the resulting income may be taxed as if it belonged to the parent. This treatment applies where the following three conditions are satisfied:

(1) The child is a minor.
(2) The child is unmarried.
(3) The income exceeds £100 per tax year for each child.

Similarly when a person makes a settlement under which his minor children may benefit, income distributed to the children before they are age 18 is treated as the settlor's income (subject to the £100 *de minimis* exemption). This applies even where he is separated or divorced and the children live with his former wife.

For s 660B purposes, 'child' includes an adopted child and illegitimate child. Again, the Revenue interprets this legislation strictly and it has been known to tax a grandparent who set up a trust for his daughter's (illegitimate) child whom he subsequently adopted and brought up as his own.

There are two circumstances where s 660B does not apply:

(1) Where the child has married.
(2) Where the settlor is not resident in the UK.

The legislation does not stop here. Any capital payments made to the children are also caught so far as the capital payments may be matched with accumulated income within the trust. This is less serious than in the past since trustees normally pay 34% tax on accumulated income (see 20.5.1), so even if the income is then deemed to be the settlor's income because a capital sum has been paid out to the child, the additional tax payable cannot exceed 6% (ie the difference between the 40% top rate and 34% paid by the trustees).

Until recently there was a gap in the legislation so that if a parent made an outright gift of capital to a minor child, with the capital being held by a bare trustee, and the trustee did not pay out the income or pay it into a bank account in the child's own name, the income was not caught by the anti-avoidance legislation and was treated as the child's own for all income tax purposes. The same treatment applied where a parent created a settlement under which a minor child had a life interest or other interest in possession. Provided the resulting income was not paid out to the child, or paid into a bank account in the child's own name, it was not assessed on the parent.

This loophole was closed in the March 1999 Budget, and so the above treatment applies only to parental gifts made before 9 March 1999.

Roll-up funds

A way that remains open for achieving a tax saving may be for a parent to give capital to a minor child, with the money being invested in a roll-up fund or some other investment that does not produce taxable income. If the roll-up fund is cashed in shortly after the child's 18th birthday, the income counts as the child's income, and not the parent's. This may be a good strategy where a child is unlikely to have much income in his own right, perhaps because he will be in full-time education during the year in which he attains age 18.

22.5.5 Capital payments to settlor

(TA 1988, s 677)

Section 677 may apply to enable the Revenue to charge tax on income received by the trustees of the settlement under which the settlor and spouse are both totally excluded from benefit. Thus it may apply where the trustees of the settlement have accumulated income and make a capital payment to the settlor. The capital payment is then treated as if it were income for the year in which the payment was made provided there is sufficient undistributed income.

If only part of the capital payment can be 'matched', the balance is matched with income for subsequent years, and amounts matched in this way are then taxable for those years.

Example – Matching of capital payments

In 1997-98 *A* received a capital payment of £18,000 from a trust set up by him in 1985. The trust has net undistributed income of £30,000. *A* will be assessed under s 677 as if he had received gross income that after tax at the rate applicable to trusts (34%) would have left £18,000, ie £27,272.

In 1998-99 *A* received a capital payment of £50,000. The trustees had undistributed income for that year of £20,000. The trustees made no further capital repayments but in 1999-00 and 2003-04 they had undistributed income of £10,000 and £8,000. The following amounts are taxable under s 677:

			£
1997-98	£18,000 grossed up	=	27,272
1998-99	£32,000[1] grossed up	=	48,484
1999-00	£10,000 grossed up	=	15,151
2003-04	£8,000 grossed up	=	12,121

[1]ie balance of the undistributed income available at the end of the year 1997-98.

22.5.6 Income may be matched with capital payments made in previous 12 years

Undistributed income can be identified with past capital payments for up to 12 years. The only way to get round this is for the whole of the capital sum to be repaid by the settlor, but even doing this does not affect the position for past years and the year in which the capital sum is repaid.

22.5.7 Loans may also be caught

A loan from the trustees to the settlor or spouse may be treated under s 677 as if it were a capital payment. Furthermore, the repayment of a loan made by the settlor to the trust can also be treated as a capital payment.

Example – Treatment of loans

In 1997-98 *B* made a £150,000 loan to a trust created by him. The trustees repaid the loan in full during 2000-01. At that time, the trustees had undistributed income of £45,000. *B* was taxed under s 677 on £45,000 grossed up at 34%, ie £68,181.

If the trustees had undistributed income of £30,000 for 2002-03 and £85,000 for 2003-04, the position would be that assessments could be made on £30,000 grossed up for 2002-03 and £75,000 grossed up for the year 2003-04.

22.5.8 Payments by companies connected with trustees

A liability could arise under s 677 if a company connected with the trustees makes a capital payment to the settlor. There have to be three conditions here:

(1) The trustees must have undistributed income.
(2) There must be 'associated payments' by the trustees to the company. An associated payment may include a capital payment (eg a subscription for shares) or the transfer of assets at an undervalue by the trustees to the company.
(3) The company must make a capital payment to the settlor, or make a loan to him or repay a loan made by the settlor to the company. This event must occur within five years of the associated payment having taken place.

22.6 TRANSACTIONS INVOLVING LOANS OR CREDIT

(TA 1988, s 786)

Specific legislation exists to prevent any tax avoidance that could otherwise arise if a person who was liable to pay non-allowable interest found a way of converting his liability to pay interest into some other payment that is tax deductible. Section 786 may apply where a transaction is effected with reference to money-lending. It can apply whether the transaction is between the lender and borrower or involves other persons connected with them.

(1) Section 786(3) states that if the transaction provides for payment of any annuity or other annual payment it shall be treated as interest for all purposes of the Taxes Act.
(2) Section 786(4) states that if the borrower agrees to sell or transfer to the lender any securities or other property carrying a right to income, the borrower may be chargeable under Schedule D Case VI on an amount equal to the income that arises from the property before he repays the loan.
(3) Section 786(5) refers to income being assigned, surrendered, waived or forgone and states that the person who has assigned, surrendered, etc may be charged to tax under Schedule D Case VI on the amount of income assigned, surrendered, etc.

In theory, s 786 could apply to interest-free loans. The Revenue has given some degree of comfort in that it has said that in the straightforward situation where one person lends money to another and then waives the interest, and there is no further transaction linked in any way to the arrangements, s 786 will not be invoked. There has been some concern in the past that s 786 could apply where, for example, a client deposited a large lump sum with his accountant on the basis that the accountant would not pay interest but would reduce his accountancy fees by the amount of interest that would have been paid at commercial rates on the client's deposit. It is possible to read s 786(5) as permitting the Revenue to make an assessment in this way even though the type of transactions described are somewhat different from those envisaged when the legislation was originally enacted.

CAPITAL GAINS TAX

22.7 BED AND BREAKFAST TRANSACTIONS

For disposals of shares by individuals or trustees on or after 17 March 1998, any shares of the same class and in the same company that are sold and then repurchased within a 30-day period will be matched so that the gain or loss that would otherwise have arisen by reference to shares already held will not be realised. This blocks a widely used way in which individuals have realised losses and then brought back the same shares on the following day.

It would appear that it is still possible to circumvent this rule by one spouse selling and the other purchasing the same securities. However, the Revenue may attack this as an artificial transaction entered into solely for tax avoidance, especially if the purchasing spouse subsequently transfers the shares to the original owner.

22.8 DISPOSALS BY A SERIES OF TRANSACTIONS

22.8.1 Basic principle behind the legislation (TCGA 1992, s 19)

There are certain assets that are worth more in total than the sum of their various parts. For example, a 55% shareholding in a private company will almost always be worth a great deal more than five times the value of an 11% shareholding since a 55% shareholder has control of the company. It follows from this that if there were not specific anti-avoidance legislation, a person could reduce his exposure to CGT on a gift to a relative, etc by transferring the asset in stages.

In fact, in certain circumstances, the Revenue may look at the value transferred by a series of transactions and assess that value by each separate transaction according to an appropriate part of the total value transferred.

22.8.2 Legislation may have wide application

The legislation can also apply in unexpected ways. Thus, if an individual with a 75% shareholding in an investment company decided to give 25% to each of his brother's three children and even arranged to make the gifts over a period of two (or more) years, the Revenue could still apply s 19 to catch the total value transferred.

22.8.3 Circumstances that cause s 19 to apply

The following circumstances may result in the Revenue applying s 19:

(1) A person disposes of assets to another person (or other persons) who falls within the definition of a connected person.
(2) There are 'linked transactions' that fall within a period of six years.
(3) The disposals have all taken place since 19 March 1985.
(4) The aggregate value transferred by the series of linked transactions is greater than the total of the values transferred by the individual transactions.

A transaction may be caught by s 19 even if it is a sale rather than a gift.

22.8.4 Section 19 can result in retrospective adjustments

If the Revenue invokes s 19, it may result in assessments for previous years being reopened. For example, *C* may have made a gift to her father in 1997-98 of a 10% shareholding in X Ltd and the shares' value may have been agreed with the Revenue as, say, £20,000. If *C* made a further gift to her brother in 2003-04 of a 70% shareholding, the position may have to be reopened. If the Revenue establishes that an 80% shareholding is worth £800,000 at the time of the gift to *C*'s brother, the effect of applying s 19 will be:

Deemed disposal proceeds on the 1997-98 gift	£100,000
Deemed disposal proceeds on the 2003-04 gift	£700,000

22.8.5 Hold-over relief may cover the position

In some circumstances, the donor may not have to pay extra tax because he and the donee have agreed that the hold-over provisions should apply (see 17.5). However, hold-over relief will not always be available since the asset will not always fall within the definition of business property or the donee may not be UK-resident.

Professional advice is clearly essential where a person is contemplating making a series of gifts to connected persons.

22.9 TRANSFERS TO A CONNECTED PERSON

Another potential pitfall arises from special rules that govern the way market value is to be determined when assessing a gain on a transaction between connected persons (whether the transaction is a gift or a sale).

22.9.1 Some restrictions may be taken into account (TCGA 1992, s 18)

A gift or sale to a connected person may involve an asset over which the acquirer already has certain rights. Thus, *D* may own the freehold of a building and his daughter, *E*, may have valuable rights as a tenant. Suppose the freehold is worth £230,000 with vacant possession, but is worth only £180,000 if *E*'s lease is taken into account. When *D* sells the freehold to *E*, will the market value be taken as £230,000 or £180,000?

The legislation states that the market value shall be taken to be the asset's market value less the lower of:

(1) the value of the interest held by the connected person who acquires the asset; or
(2) the amount by which the transferor's asset would increase in value if the connected person's rights did not exist.

Consequently, *D* would be deemed to make a disposal of an asset worth £180,000.

22.9.2 Some restrictions are ignored

(TCGA 1992, s 18(7))

Certain valuable rights may have to be left out of account. One example of this is an option. Suppose the facts set out in 22.9.1 had been slightly different so that *D* had vacant possession of a property worth £230,000, but his daughter had an option under which she could acquire it for £180,000. If *D* sells the property to *E* or if she exercises her option he will receive only £180,000, but he may be assessed as if he had received £230,000.

This is because the legislation requires options to be ignored or left out of account when computing an asset's market value. Similarly, legal rights that, if exercised, would effectively destroy or impair the asset also have to be ignored. Market value is determined as if such rights did not exist.

22.10 QUALIFYING CORPORATE BONDS

(FA 1997, s 88)

Anti-avoidance provisions took effect from 26 November 1996. They concern situations where an individual or groups of individuals dispose of their private company shares and take loan stock issued by the acquiring company as part of the sale consideration (referred to as 'rolling over' into loan stock since no capital gain normally arises until the loan stock is sold). Since 1984, legislation has made specific provision for the situation where a person receives QCBs in exchange for shares. The capital gain that would have arisen had he taken cash rather than QCBs is calculated but held over until such time as he disposes of the bonds. The legislation did not make express provision for the situation where the vendor receives loan notes that are not QCBs at the time of acquisition but become QCBs before a disposal takes place. As QCBs are normally an exempt asset for CGT purposes, the legislation seemed to allow a capital gain to escape a charge altogether, which gave rise to the term 'disappearing trick'.

The Revenue was sceptical that these arrangements succeeded in their objective. However, and without prejudice to litigation on past transactions, FA 1997 clarified the position.

The CGT legislation has been amended so that when a loan stock changes from a non-QCB into a QCB, the change is treated as a conversion of securities. This ensures that any gain that has been rolled over on an exchange of shares for loan stock is preserved and does not escape charge. The new rules apply to disposals after 25 November 1996, even where the loan stock was converted before the Budget.

22.11 VALUE SHIFTING
(TCGA 1992, s 29)

The legislation contains provisions that are intended to ensure that disguised gifts are assessed as a disposal at market value.

22.11.1 Type of transaction that may be caught

A controlling shareholder might exercise his control over a company to transfer value in an indirect way.

Example – Value shifting

F owns all the shares in Y Ltd. The company has 1,000 £1 ordinary shares in issue. Assume that the value of these shares is £300,000. If *F* allowed his son *G* to be issued with 2,000 £1 shares at par, he would not have made a disposal of his own shares. However, *G* would have acquired a valuable asset in that his 2,000 shares will probably be worth in excess of £200,000 compared with the £2,000 that he had paid to acquire them. Furthermore, *F*'s 1,000 shares will have gone down in value since he will have become a minority shareholder.

Where the Revenue can apply s 29, the person who has transferred value (in this example, *F*) is treated as if he had disposed of an asset.

22.11.2 Omission to exercise a right

There can be circumstances where s 29 is relevant because a person has failed to exercise a right. For example, if *H* and his grandson *J* were 50:50 shareholders in Z Ltd and the company announced a rights issue of three new shares for every one share already held and the amount payable for each share was £1 (par), s 29 would come into operation if *H* chose not to exercise his entitlement to the rights issue, as this omission would mean that after the rights issue the shares in Z Ltd would be owned as to:

H	20%
J	80%

Control would have thereby passed to *J*.

22.12 UK-RESIDENT SETTLEMENTS WHERE SETTLOR HAS RETAINED INTEREST

22.12.1 Introduction
(TCGA 1992, s 77)

Capital gains realised by trustees of a UK-resident settlement may be taxed as if they were the settlor's own gains if he is deemed to have retained an interest in the trust. The gains are simply added to his personal gains and he is responsible for paying the CGT. He can, however, reclaim the tax from the trustees.

This does not apply unless the settlor is UK-resident or ordinarily resident for the tax year concerned. These provisions can apply to a settlement created some years before the introduction of this legislation in 1988.

22.12.2 Circumstances where settlor is deemed to have retained an interest

A settlor is regarded as having retained an interest if there are any circumstances whatsoever under which the property within the settlement or income arising to the trustees may become payable to him or his spouse. Furthermore, he may be deemed to have retained an interest if he or his spouse enjoys a benefit derived directly or indirectly from the settled property.

There are some circumstances in which a settlor is not deemed to have retained a benefit even though he might receive a benefit. These exceptions relate to the possibility of the settlor or spouse benefiting in the event that a beneficiary becomes bankrupt or dies under age 25 or, in the case of a marriage settlement, the death of the married couple and their children.

22.12.3 Considerable care needed

There is no 'proportionality' here, so the retention of even a very small interest could result in the settlor being taxed on considerable gains that he did not (and perhaps never could) enjoy. There are two areas of special concern: loans by a settlor and remarriage.

Loans by a settlor

If the settlor lends money to the trustees there is a risk that he might be said to have an interest in the settled property. This situation should therefore be avoided.

Remarriage

The possibility of the settlor's current marriage coming to an end and his remarrying may be remote, but will be considered by the Revenue to bring s 77 into operation if such a future spouse is not specifically excluded from benefiting under the settlement.

22.12.4 Death of settlor

Once the settlor has died, s 77 ceases to apply. His widow cannot then be charged on the trustees' gains.

22.12.5 Relief for personal CGT losses

Until now, it has not been possible for a settlor to set his personal CGT losses against capital gains attributed to him under this legislation. This restriction will cease to apply from 2003-04 onwards. Furthermore, settlors may elect for this offset also to be available for any of the years 2000-01, 2001-02 and 2002-03. Such an election needs to be made by 31 January 2005.

22.13 OFFSHORE COMPANIES

(TCGA 1992, s 13)

A person who is resident and ordinarily resident in the UK (see 23.2) may be liable for a proportion of capital gains realised by a non-resident company in which he has a shareholding.

Example

> *K* owns all the shares in X Ltd, a company incorporated and resident in Bermuda. The company realises a capital gain by disposing of a US property that it owns. The legislation enables the Revenue to assess *K* as if he made the capital gain himself. However, certain conditions need to be satisfied before the Revenue can assess a capital gain in this way (see 22.13.1).

22.13.1 Conditions that need to be satisfied

First, the company must be controlled by five or fewer shareholders, or shareholder directors must between them own more than 50% of the company's shares.

Secondly, the individual must be resident (or ordinarily resident) and domiciled in the UK (see 24.1 and 24.14).

Thirdly, he and persons connected with him must between them have an interest in the company of at least 10%. Until 27 November 1995, the legislation could apply only if the individual was a shareholder who was entitled to at least 5% of the company's assets on a winding-up. From 27 November 1995 to 6 March 2001, the legislation applied if he had an interest of more than 5% in the company.

22.13.2 Certain gains not assessable under s 13

The legislation is really intended to catch gains on investment assets, etc held through an offshore company. There is therefore an exemption under s 13(5) for gains arising:

(1) on the disposal of foreign currency where the currency represents money in use for a trade carried on by the company outside the UK;

(2) from the disposal of 'tangible property' used for the purposes of a trade carried on by the company outside the UK;
(3) from disposals of assets used by a UK branch of the company.

22.13.3 Distribution test

(TCGA 1992, s 13(5)(d))

Where an offshore company has realised gains that are not exempt under 22.14.3, the individual may still escape assessment on gains realised before 28 November 1995 if he can show that the offshore company has distributed the gains within two years, either as a dividend or on the company being wound up. However, if he is UK-resident at the time he receives such a distribution, he will be assessed on it (either for income tax or, in the case of a liquidation, for CGT).

22.14 NON-RESIDENT TRUSTS

(TCGA 1992, s 86 and Sched 5)

22.14.1 Introduction

Trustees of a trust may be resident outside the UK and the administration of the trust may be carried out overseas. Provided both these conditions are satisfied, the trust is not resident and there will not normally be any liability for the trustees so far as UK CGT is concerned. There may be a liability for either the settlor (ie the person who set up the trust) or the beneficiaries (who may include the settlor).

22.14.2 Qualifying trusts

(TCGA 1992, s 86 and Sched 5)

The legislation refers to 'qualifying settlements'. In fact, they qualify for an adverse CGT treatment in that the trustees' gains are deemed to be the settlor's personal capital gains. The conditions under which the trust's capital gains will be treated in this way are as follows:

(1) The settlor must be UK-resident or ordinarily resident for the year concerned.
(2) He must not have died during the course of the year.
(3) The people who benefit from the trust include one of the following:
    (a) the settlor;
    (b) his spouse;
    (c) his children (and spouses);
    (d) a company connected with him;
    (e) for trusts created after 16 March 1998, his grandchildren.

22.14.3 Special treatment of pre-March 1991 trusts
(TCGA 1992, s 97(1))

Provided the trust did not become a qualifying settlement (see 22.14.5), there was no CGT liability for beneficiaries for years up to 1998-99 until such time as 'capital payments' are received.

UK-resident and domiciled beneficiaries may be assessed for CGT purposes on a proportion of the trustees' capital gains that can be 'matched' with capital payments received.

The receipt of a benefit may count as a deemed capital payment (the rules are virtually the same as under s 740: see 22.4).

Example – Pre-19 March 1991 offshore trusts

Trustees of an offshore trust make capital gains in 1989-90 of £200,000. In 1989-90 to 1991-92 the trustees distribute income, but their doing this does not have any CGT consequences. In 1997-98 they make a capital payment of £50,000 to *L*, who is UK-resident.

L would be assessed as if she had personally made capital gains of £50,000 for 1997-98. The tax actually payable will depend on whether she has made other capital gains, whether she has capital losses available for offset and her rate of tax.

22.14.4 Supplementary charge

A supplementary charge may be made of 10% of the tax for each complete year between 1 December following the year in which the trustees realised the gain and the time the trustees make the capital distribution. The supplementary charge cannot exceed 60%.

22.14.5 Pre-19 March 1991 trusts could become qualifying settlements

A pre-19 March 1991 offshore trust could become a qualifying settlement if:

(1) property is added after 18 March 1991;
(2) the trust is varied so that a person becomes a beneficiary who previously could not have been expected to benefit.

22.14.6 Finance Act 1998 changes

Protection for pre-March 1991 trusts removed

From 6 April 1999, the distinction between pre- and post-19 March 1991 trusts created by UK domiciliaries ceased to be relevant. If the settlor, his spouse or his children can benefit, the trustees' gains may be taxed as if they had been realised by the settlor.

The only circumstance where this does not apply is where the trust is a qualifying settlement only because the settlor's children are potential beneficiaries and the children are under age 18. Once the children attain age 18, this protection is lost.

Where a qualifying settlement has gains in the period 17 March 1998 to 5 April 1999, they may be taxed on the settlor as if he had realised them on 6 April 1999.

Settlements created by foreign domiciliaries

UK domiciliaries can be taxed on capital payments from trusts created by foreign domiciliaries. With effect from 17 March 1998, UK-resident and domiciled beneficiaries can be assessed where they receive capital payments from a non-resident trust created by a foreign domiciled settlor; this can apply only where payments made after 16 March 1998 can be matched with gains realised by the trustees after that date.

22.14.7 Finance Act 2002 changes

Until recently, it has not been possible for an individual who has been taxed on capital gains under s 86 to set off his personal CGT losses against these attributed gains. This restriction will cease to apply from 2003-04. Furthermore, an individual may elect for personal losses to be set against attributed gains for any of the tax years 2000-01, 2001-02 and 2002-03. Such an election needs to be made by 31 January 2005.

22.14.8 Sale of trust interest by beneficiary

A disposal of an interest in a non-resident trust has been a disposal of a chargeable asset for CGT purposes since 1981. On the other hand, a disposal of an interest in a UK resident trust has not normally been subject to CGT.

FA 1998 introduced a further rule so that if beneficiaries of UK-resident trusts dispose of their interest, and the trust has been non-resident in the past, the beneficiaries' disposal is subject to CGT.

22.14.9 Flip-flop arrangements

It was considered to be possible to avoid s 87 by arranging for a trust to borrow and to use the borrowed funds to make a gift to another settlement. The terms of the original trust were varied so that no UK person could benefit and any gains subsequently realised within that trust were not taxable under s 86. The settlement which received the transfer had no capital gains and could therefore make a capital appointment to UK beneficiaries without their being liable under s 87.

The legislators have made several attempts to block all such loopholes. The FA 2003 appears to have done so comprehensively but only time will tell as to whether the tax-avoidance industry can find some new way of getting round this legislation.

23

RESIDENCE STATUS

MIKE PRICE OF AMICORP

This chapter covers the following:

(1) Consequences of residence in the UK.
(2) Various criteria for determining residence status.
(3) Individuals who are resident but not ordinarily resident
(4) Basis on which individuals are regarded as ordinarily resident.
(5) Ceasing to be resident in the UK.
(6) UK income and capital gains received by non-residents.
(7) Non-resident investment companies.
(8) When tax should be withheld from payments to non-residents.
(9) Employment agencies operating in the Netherlands

23.1 CONSEQUENCES OF RESIDENCE IN THE UK

The basic principle of UK taxation is that an individual may be charged tax on his worldwide income if he is resident in the UK. If he is not, he is still liable for tax on income that arises in the UK, but not for tax on income that arises overseas.

There is an exception to this in that an individual who is UK-resident but not ordinarily resident and/or not domiciled there may have to pay tax only on UK income. The concept of domicile is different from residence (see 24.1).

The rest of this chapter proceeds on the basis that an individual has a UK domicile.

23.2 VARIOUS CRITERIA FOR DETERMINING RESIDENCE STATUS

23.2.1 Introduction

For UK taxation purposes, 'the UK' means England, Scotland, Wales and Northern Ireland. It does not include the Republic of Ireland, the Channel Islands and the Isle of Man. A person may be resident in more than one country so the fact that he is treated as resident in, for example, the USA or South Africa does not necessarily mean that he is not resident in the UK.

A person is resident or not resident for a tax year. A person may also be ordinarily resident if he is habitually resident in the UK as opposed to simply being resident for one year in isolation.

Somewhat surprisingly the word 'resident' is not defined in the Taxes Acts, but there is considerable case law and the position is summarised below.

23.2.2 Two basic tests

An individual will always be treated as UK-resident for a tax year if he is caught under either of the following tests:

(a) The six-month rule, ie he is present in the UK for 183 days or more during the tax year.
(b) The three-month average rule, ie he is present in the UK for an average of 91 days or more pa measured over a period of four tax years.

Days of arrival and departure are normally left out of account for these tests but this may change as a result of the consultative document issued by the Government in April 2003.

Mobile workers may be treated differently: see *Tax Bulletin* April 2001, which sets out the Revenue's view that individuals whose home and settled domestic life are in the UK may be regarded as remaining UK-resident despite frequent and regular trips abroad.

23.2.3 Existing UK residents

So far as a person who has been resident in the UK for a number of years is concerned, he is likely to continue to be regarded as UK-resident despite temporary periods of absence from the UK unless the following conditions are satisfied:

(a) he works full-time abroad, and the period spent overseas includes a complete tax year, or
(b) he has no accommodation in the UK and he lives abroad for at least one full tax year.

The treatment of UK residents who move overseas is covered at 23.5.

23.2.4 Foreign nationals coming to the UK

The residence status of individuals who come to the UK is now governed by the six- and three-month rules set out in 23.2.2. Individuals who regularly visit the UK, and are therefore caught by the three-month rule, are normally treated as ordinarily resident only from Year 4. However, an individual may be regarded as ordinarily resident from Year 1 if it is clear he intended to spend an average of three months pa in this country.

23.2.5 Double taxation agreements

The UK has entered into a large number of double taxation agreements (also known as double tax treaties) with other countries. Provisions of such an agreement may override UK tax law. Specifically, the agreement may provide exemption for certain income received by a person resident overseas even though the income arises in the UK. For example, most double taxation agreements provide that a resident of the foreign country concerned may claim exemption from UK tax in connection with interest income arising in the UK.

Most double taxation agreements also make provision for the situation that an individual may be resident in both the foreign country and the UK. They usually contain a clause along the following lines:

(1) If the individual has a permanent home in only one country, he is deemed to be resident there.
(2) If the position has not been resolved by (1), he is treated as resident where he has the centre of his personal and economic interests.
(3) If the above tests do not resolve the position, he is treated as resident in the country where he has an 'habitual abode'.
(4) If he has an habitual abode in both countries, he is deemed to be a resident of the country of which he is a national.
(5) If he is a national of both countries, or he is not a national of either country, the Revenue authorities of the UK and the foreign country may settle the matter by mutual agreement.

These provisions apply only for the purposes of determining residence under the agreement. They are deeming provisions and, under UK law, an individual might still be regarded as UK-resident even though he may be treated as resident in the foreign country for the purposes of the double taxation agreement. However, the terms of a double taxation agreement override UK tax law and, if an individual is deemed to be resident in a foreign country under the agreement, his liability to UK tax is then computed in accordance with other provisions of the agreement.

23.3 INDIVIDUALS WHO ARE RESIDENT BUT NOT ORDINARILY RESIDENT

An individual who is resident but not ordinarily resident in the UK has certain tax privileges.

23.3.1 Employment income

Earnings from duties performed outside the UK are taxable on the remittance basis. This applies even where the employment relates to a mixture of

UK and overseas duties. Furthermore, this treatment can apply even where the employer is UK resident (contrast foreign emoluments where the employer must be non-resident: see 24.2).

TA 1988, s 203D allows an employer to require a direction from the Revenue as to how much of a not ordinarily resident employee's remuneration should be subject to PAYE deductions.

Table 23.1 – Basis of assessment for earned income (Schedule E)

	Services performed			
	Wholly in UK	*Partly in UK*	*Partly abroad*	*Wholly abroad*
Non-resident	All	That part	None	None
Resident but not ordinarily resident	All	That part	Remittances	Remittances
Resident and ordinarily resident	All	All	All	All

23.3.2 Overseas investment income

This is taxable under the remittance basis.

23.3.3 April 2003 consultative document

The logic of retaining the remittance basis is questioned in a consultative document issued by the Government in April 2003 (see further on this in Chapter 24).

23.4 BASIS ON WHICH INDIVIDUALS ARE REGARDED AS ORDINARILY RESIDENT

23.4.1 Intention to make a permanent home in the UK

Where an individual arrives with the intention of staying in the UK for at least three years (apart from holidays and short business trips), he is regarded as ordinarily resident from the outset. If he arrives with no definite intention but stays in the UK he will be regarded as becoming ordinarily resident for the tax year in which the third anniversary of his arrival falls (unless he decides to stay in the UK on a longer term basis during the first three years in which case he will become ordinarily resident from the start of the tax year in which he makes such a decision).

Different rules apply to an individual who spends a significant part of his time overseas (see below).

23.4.2 Accommodation in the UK

Where an individual does not spend all his time in the UK but has UK accommodation available for his use, he is normally regarded as ordinarily resident as well as resident. He does not have to own the accommodation, it is sufficient if it is made available to him. Accommodation is regarded as available if it is kept in a permanent state of readiness for his occupation. Rented accommodation is ignored if the lease is for a period of less than 12 months (unfurnished) or for a period of less than two years (unfurnished).

23.4.3 Regular visitors

An individual who comes to the UK with the intention of spending at least 91 days in the UK for a period of four tax years is regarded as ordinarily resident from Year 1. An individual who comes without any such clear intention becomes ordinarily resident in Year 5 unless he forms a definite intention during the intervening years (in which case he becomes ordinarily resident from 6 April of the year in which he decides to reside in the UK for at least four tax years).

23.4.4 Visits for education

A person who comes to the UK for a period of study or education expected to last more than four years is regarded as resident and ordinarily resident from the date of his arrival. If the period is not expected to exceed four years, he may be treated as not ordinarily resident, but this depends on whether he:

(1) has accommodation available in the UK, or
(2) intends to remain in the UK when his education is complete, or
(3) proposes to visit the UK in future years for average periods of three months or more per tax year.

If, despite his originally intending not to do so, he remains in the UK for more than four years, he is treated in any event as ordinarily resident from the beginning of Year 5 of his stay. This applies to both a person who comes to the UK for his own education or a parent or guardian of a child who comes in connection with the child's education.

23.5 CEASING TO BE RESIDENT IN THE UK

23.5.1 Working abroad

Up to 1992-93 there was an important distinction between individuals who worked full-time abroad and others who lived overseas in that the legislation provided specifically that, where an individual worked full-time abroad, the fact that he had accommodation available for his use was not regarded as a relevant factor in determining his residence status. As from 6 April 1993, this distinction became less important as the legislation now provides that an individual shall not be regarded as resident just because he has available accommodation in the UK. Nevertheless, it is still easier to establish non-resident status if you are working overseas.

A key Revenue publication (IR20) states that if a person goes abroad for full-time service under a contract of employment and:

(1) all the duties of his employment are performed abroad or any duties he performs in the UK are incidental to his duties abroad; and
(2) his absence from the UK and the employment itself both extend over a period covering a complete tax year; and
(3) any interim visits to the UK during the period do not amount to:
  (a) six months or more in any one tax year; or
  (b) an average of three months or more per tax year,

he is normally regarded as not resident and not ordinarily resident in the UK on the day following the date of his departure until the day preceding the date of his return. On his return, he is regarded as a new permanent resident.

The treatment whereby a person is treated as not resident for part of a tax year is called the 'split year' concession. The latest edition of IR20 indicates that this concession will also apply to self-employed people who leave the UK to work full time in a trade, profession or vocation providing they are able to meet the conditions similar to those set out above.

23.5.2 Involuntary residence

(SP2/91)

The Revenue operates a concession that covers individuals who are forced to spend time in the UK because of exceptional circumstances outside their control, for example, someone who was working abroad in a Gulf state, but who had to return to the UK prematurely at the outbreak of the Gulf War, may be allowed some leeway when the Revenue applies the three-month average test. Similarly, where an individual spends days in the UK because of illness, these may be left out of account in certain circumstances.

These concessions do not apply where an individual returns to the UK because his employer has prematurely terminated his employment contract. Also, and more fundamentally, the Revenue's concession does not affect the rule that an individual is treated as UK-resident if he spends 183 days or more in the UK during a particular tax year.

23.5.3 Other individuals who live abroad

Different rules apply where a person does not work full-time abroad (eg where an individual moves to a foreign country on retirement), or where he works overseas but continues to perform duties in the UK that are not incidental to the work carried out abroad. A person who falls into this category continues to be treated as resident where he spends an average of three months pa in the UK over a four-year period.

23.5.4 Temporary non-residence

An individual who leaves the UK on or after 17 March 1998 and who

(1) has been tax resident in the UK for any part of at least four out of the seven tax years immediately preceding the year of departure; and
(2) becomes not resident and not ordinarily resident for a period of less than five tax years; and
(3) owns assets before he leaves the UK

remains liable to tax on any gains realised on those assets after departure from the UK. Gains made by him in the year of assessment in which he leaves the UK are chargeable for that year. Gains made after that year are chargeable in the year of assessment in which he resumes residence in the UK. Losses are allowable on the same basis as gains are chargeable. Gains of non-resident trusts and companies may also be taxed if they would have been taxable had the individual been resident (see 22.13).

Any gains made in the intervening years (ie between the tax years of departure and of return) on assets acquired by the taxpayer after becoming tax resident abroad are exempt from the charge. This exemption will not apply to assets held in a non-resident trust or closely controlled non-resident company. Special rules prevent gains on assets held before departure from escaping the charge, where gains are rolled over or otherwise deferred on the acquisition of assets during the period of absence.

Certain double taxation agreements may protect a temporary non-resident from the five-year rule. It is essential to take specialist advice if you decide to rely on this.

23.6 UK INCOME AND CAPITAL GAINS RECEIVED BY NON-RESIDENTS

A person who is not UK-resident for a tax year may still be subject to tax on UK source income, but is not liable to tax for income that arises abroad. The following types of income are deemed to arise within the UK and are therefore subject to tax even where the individual is not resident there:

(1) employment income that relates to duties performed in the UK;
(2) trading profits from a branch or permanent establishment in the UK;
(3) rents from UK properties;
(4) dividends from UK companies;
(5) interest paid by a person who is UK-resident;
(6) 'annual payments' made by a UK-resident person.

Since 1995-96, tax charged on investment income of a non-resident individual has normally been limited to the tax deducted at source. This does not apply to income from property in the UK or from trading in the UK through a broker or investment manager.

The provisions of a double tax agreement or extra statutory concession may also limit the tax charged on a non-resident individual.

23.6.1 Earned income

Where an individual is non-resident, profits from a trade carried on outside the UK are not subject to UK tax. Where such a person has a branch or permanent establishment in the UK, a liability to UK tax may arise from profits earned by that branch. Double taxation agreement provisions may govern what type of presence in the UK is deemed to constitute a branch or permanent establishment.

Earnings from an employment may attract UK tax where the duties are performed in the UK (see 23.6.5 on double taxation agreements).

Where an individual works full-time abroad under a contract of employment, the resulting income is not subject to UK tax even though the employer may be a UK company. However, a Crown employee or a member of the Armed Forces is regarded as performing the duties of his employment in the UK and he may therefore be subject to UK tax even though he performs all his duties overseas and is not resident in the UK.

Problems have arisen in recent years where an individual was granted a non-approved share option at a time when he was UK-resident and subject to tax under Schedule E Case I, with the option subsequently exercised after he ceased to be UK-resident. The Revenue's view is that a liability may arise in these circumstances even if he is no longer employed by the company concerned (but see *Tax Bulletin* October 2002 on the Revenue's views on treaty relief).

Pensions paid by UK residents are subject to tax unless the recipient can claim the benefit of a double taxation agreement (see 23.6.5).

23.6.2 Concession for bank and building society interest

In practice, certain income arising from a UK source is not subject to UK tax. In particular, bank deposit interest is not subject to deduction of UK tax at source provided the non-resident certifies he is not ordinarily resident in the UK (TA 1988, s 481(5)(k)). The Revenue will not assess such income unless the account is managed or controlled by a UK-resident agent. This also applies to interest or dividends paid gross by a building society, discount (eg on deep discount bonds), gains on deep gains securities, and interest on certificates of tax deposit.

23.6.3 Exempt gilts

Interest paid on all British Government securities is exempt from UK tax where the person who owns the security is not UK-resident (unless the interest forms part of the profits of a trade carried on in the UK). Different rules applied up to 5 April 1998 so that only some gilts were classified as FOTRA (free of tax to residents abroad); see *Tax Handbook 1998-99* at 21.4.3.

23.6.4 Income from property

Rental income received by an individual from a UK property is subject to UK tax even if he is not UK-resident. A tenant who pays rent exceeding £100 pw direct to a non-resident landlord should withhold basic rate tax at source unless the Revenue has authorised the tenant to pay the rent gross. Where rent is paid to a UK agent, the tenant should pay the rent without deduction, but the agent must then deduct tax from the net rental income.

The Revenue will authorise a tenant or agent to make no tax deductions if the landlord has registered for self-assessment and his tax affairs are up to date. See leaflet IR140, *Non-resident landlords, their agents and tenants.*

23.6.5 Double taxation agreements

Where an individual is not UK-resident but is resident in a foreign country that has a double taxation agreement, it may be possible for certain income that would normally suffer UK tax at source to be exempt from UK tax, or subject only to a lower rate.

Remuneration for work performed in the UK

Most double taxation agreements provide an exemption from UK tax for employment income, provided the following conditions are satisfied:

(1) the recipient of the remuneration is present in the UK for a period not exceeding 183 days in aggregate in the tax year concerned; and
(2) the remuneration is paid by, or on behalf of, an employer who is not UK-resident; and
(3) the remuneration is not borne by a permanent establishment or a fixed base that the employer has in the UK.

Pensions

Double taxation agreements generally provide for exemption from UK tax in respect of a pension paid by a UK company or pension scheme, although such a pension is normally subject to tax in the foreign country concerned.

Interest

In general, most double taxation agreements provide for a person resident in the foreign country concerned to be exempt from UK tax on interest. The company, etc that pays the interest can be given authorisation to pay it gross. In cases where tax has been withheld at source, the individual may be entitled to a repayment.

Dividends

A double taxation agreement usually includes a provision that the person who receives a dividend from the UK company is entitled to the benefit of a reduced tax credit and any balance should be repaid.

Royalties

Most double taxation agreements provide that where a royalty is received by a person resident in the foreign country concerned, the royalties shall be free from UK tax.

23.6.6 Allowances and reliefs

A British subject is entitled to full personal allowances for a tax year, even if he is not a UK resident.

Nationals of EU countries also became entitled to a full personal allowance from 1996-97 (in many cases such nationals may have been entitled to allowances for earlier years because of relevant double taxation agreement provisions). This change also applied to nationals of the following EEA countries: Iceland, Norway and Liechtenstein.

A non-resident person is not generally entitled to repayment supplement so it is normally important that tax should not be overpaid where this can be avoided. However, EU nationals may be entitled to supplement even though they are not UK-resident.

23.6.7 Capital gains

A non-UK resident is not normally subject to CGT except where capital gains arise from the disposal of assets used by a branch or permanent establishment of a business carried on by him in the UK (but see 23.5.4 on the taxation of gains realised by former UK residents who are non-resident for less than five complete tax years).

23.7 NON-RESIDENT INVESTMENT COMPANIES

A non-UK resident who has significant investment income arising within the UK may take certain steps to minimise his UK tax liability. In particular, where he cannot claim the benefit of a double taxation agreement, it may be advisable for UK assets such as real estate to be held through a non-UK resident company. This means that any tax liability is confined to basic rate tax and there is no question of any higher rate liability.

In such a case, it would still be sensible for some portfolio investments to be retained in his own name if he is a British subject or is otherwise entitled to claim a personal allowance. Sufficient personal income should arise to use such an allowance as this will be wasted if all income arises within an offshore company.

In some cases, a non-resident landlord should form an offshore company to acquire UK properties already owned and let by him. The offshore company may raise a qualifying loan to purchase the properties from the individual concerned and interest payable on the loan may then be offset against the non-resident company's rental income. This is a way in which an individual who already owns a property that is not subject to a mortgage may create a situation where interest is payable on a qualifying loan that is deductible in computing Schedule A income. However, see *Tax Bulletin* April 2000 on the possibility of the Revenue challenging a deduction for excessive interest under the transfer pricing legislation.

23.8 WHEN TAX SHOULD BE WITHHELD FROM PAYMENTS TO NON-RESIDENTS

23.8.1 Non-resident sportsmen and entertainers

A person paying a non-UK resident sportsman or entertainer for work carried out in the UK is liable to withhold tax at basic rate and pay this over to the Revenue (see 21.5), although it may be possible to agree an alternative withholding rate with the Inspector of Taxes at Special Compliance Office.

23.8.2 Rent payable to non-resident landlord

A person who pays rent to a non-resident landlord must withhold tax at the basic rate and account for this to the Revenue unless he has been authorised to pay gross (see 23.6.4). This obligation arises whether the payment is made within the UK or by payment out of a bank account held overseas.

Where a UK resident pays a premium to a non resident landlord, the same requirement to withhold tax arises.

Where a tenant has failed to withhold tax, he may be required to account for it to the Revenue. In such circumstances, he may withhold sums from subsequent payments of rent to cover the amounts paid over to the Revenue.

The obligation to withhold tax does not arise where the tenant pays rent to an agent in the UK. Also the Revenue would not normally pursue a tenant who had failed to deduct tax where he could not have known that the landlord was non-resident and nothing had happened to put him on notice.

For further details, see 21.4.

23.9 EMPLOYMENT AGENCIES OPERATING IN THE NETHERLANDS

IR Tax Bulletin 64 contained a special article about such agencies. It states:

> The Double Taxation Treaty with the Netherlands confirms their general taxing right at Article 15(1):
>
> > 'wages and other similar remuneration derived by a resident of one of the States in respect of an employment shall be taxable only in that State unless the employment is exercised in the other State. **If the employment is so exercised, such remuneration as is derived therefrom may be taxed in that other State.**'
>
> However, the second paragraph of this Article provides a let-out for short-term business visitors from the UK where their earnings will not end up being a deduction against Netherlands tax.
>
> UK residents who work in the Netherlands will be solely liable to tax in the UK provided *all* of the following criteria are satisfied:
>
> - they are not in the Netherlands for more than 183 days in total in the Dutch tax year, 1 January to 31 December;
> - their wages are not a deduction for a Netherlands employer; and
> - their wages are not borne by a permanent establishment or fixed base that a non-resident employer has in the Netherlands.
>
> Where an agency is supplying workers to a Dutch company the Netherlands Tax Authority may decide that these conditions are not fulfilled, though this depends on the precise facts of the case.
>
> **Agency obligations in the Netherlands**
>
> Employers that are treated as situated in the Netherlands are obliged to withhold a wage tax. This wage tax is calculated on a periodic base on the assumption that the employee works the whole year. If that assumption is not correct the income tax finally due can differ from the wage tax withheld, resulting in additional payments or money back for the taxpayer. The same thing can happen because of special deductions or expenses that are not taken into account when calculating the wage tax.
>
> In most cases it will be clear that the worker will be liable for wages tax in the Netherlands. The agency should deduct Dutch wages tax from remuneration from the start of the employment. However, if the UK Employment Agency fails to account for wages tax, the Dutch company will be liable for unpaid tax. In order to protect themselves against this liability, it is common practice for Dutch companies to withhold part of the payments to foreign Employment Agencies until arrangements have been made by the UK Agency to withhold tax on behalf of the employee.

To protect against the legal liability the client can pay part of the fee due to the Employment Agency into a G account. This is a blocked account of the Agency, which can only be used to pay wages tax and social security contributions to the Netherlands Tax Authority (NTA). The amount paid into a G account cannot be seen as an advance levy. Wages tax is not legally paid until the Agency uses the G account to pay taxes to the NTA. De-blocking will not happen automatically and can only take place on special request. A special form is needed to unblock a G account. This can be obtained from the Belastingdienst/Centrale administratie, sector betalingsverwerking (previously Centrale betalingsadministratie (Central Payment Administration)) WKA department. To unblock the account the employment agency will need to demonstrate that the money in the G account is no longer needed for the payment of the relevant tax due. Each payment to a G account relates to particular employees and periods. If, for example from a wage tax declaration, it appears that there is no, or less, tax due for those employees and that period, and that there are no other Dutch tax liabilities of the company, then the surplus can be released.

Agency obligations in the UK

Workers who remain resident in the UK will still be subject to the PAYE system. Paragraph 122 on page 70 of the Employer's Further Guide to PAYE and NICs (CWG2 2002) advises employers who are faced with making two lots of deductions from pay to contact their Inland Revenue Office. The Revenue may agree a procedure whereby PAYE can be operated net of credit relief; that is PAYE deductions will take account of overseas tax actually payable on, and deducted from, an employee's wage. This is set out in the Employment Procedures manual at Appendix 5.

It is important to note though that for this procedure even to be considered the tax must be deducted on a monthly or weekly basis in the Netherlands so that it can be matched with the PAYE deductions in the UK.

Credit in the UK for foreign tax paid

If Netherlands wages tax is correctly due and borne by the worker concerned he will be able to claim credit for this against UK tax due on the same earnings. If the worker pays no wages tax, his earnings have not borne any foreign tax and so when those earnings are taxed in the UK there is no credit due for foreign tax paid.

If the Agency pays Dutch wages tax on behalf of its workers from the G account without deducting it from them in turn, this cannot be relieved against its own UK corporation tax as it is not a tax on its profits.

24

THE INCOME AND CAPITAL GAINS OF FOREIGN DOMICILIARIES

MIKE WILKES

This chapter deals with the tax treatment of individuals resident but not domiciled in the UK. The following subjects are discussed:

(1) Meaning of 'domicile'.

Earned income

(2) Foreign emoluments.
(3) Travelling expenses.
(4) Subsistence allowances for employees seconded to the UK
(5) 'Corresponding payments'.
(6) Overseas pension funds.
(7) Self-employment.
(8) Partnerships controlled outside the UK.
(9) Pension benefits.

Investment income

(10) The remittance basis for investment income.
(11) What constitutes a remittance?
(12) Position if foreign domiciliary acquires UK domicile.
(13) Managing the remittance basis.

Capital gains tax

(14) Remittance basis for capital gains on foreign assets.
(15) Use of offshore companies and trusts.

Inheritance tax

(16) UK and foreign situs property.

24.1 MEANING OF 'DOMICILE'

Domicile is a fundamentally different concept from residence and ordinary residence. It is not the same as nationality, although an individual's nationality may be one relevant factor in determining his domicile. The basic concept is that a person is domiciled in the country he regards as his real home. The fact that he may be prevented from living in that country or may need to live elsewhere because of temporary reasons (eg business and/or employment) does not mean he is domiciled in the country in which he resides. Under English law, an individual normally acquires his father's domicile at birth and retains it unless his father changes his own domicile before the child attains age 16. The mother's domicile may apply instead where a child is illegitimate or the parents divorce. The domicile acquired in this way is called the individual's 'domicile of origin'.

An individual may change his domicile to a 'domicile of choice'. Normally this would happen by his leaving his country of origin and taking up permanent residence abroad with the intention of never returning to live in the country of origin on a permanent basis. His domicile of origin will revive if his intentions alter and he decides not to make his permanent home in the new country after all.

24.1.1 Married women

A woman married before 1 January 1974 generally acquired her husband's domicile (referred to as a 'domicile of dependency'), which continued after divorce or the husband's death, although she could discard her domicile of dependency and regain her domicile of origin. A domicile of dependency in the UK may be discarded by the woman establishing that she no longer intends to remain permanently in that country and by her ceasing to be resident there. The mere intention is not itself sufficient: an Australian woman who had acquired a domicile of dependency in England was held to be domiciled in the UK, despite her intention to return to Australia, because she had not ceased to be resident.

The law is somewhat different for couples married after 31 December 1973. The Domicile and Matrimonial Proceedings Act 1973 allows a woman to retain an independent domicile on her marriage.

There may be exceptions to this rule imposed by the taxation treaty with the other state. For example, the treaty with the USA treat wives as if they were married after 31 December 1973, regardless of the actual date of marriage.

24.1.2 Registration as an overseas elector

FA 1996, s 200 states that where an individual registers as an overseas elector to vote in UK elections, this is not to be taken into account in determining his domicile status for tax purposes.

24.1.3 A further review, discussion and consultation

Following the publication in 1992 of a report by the Law Commission on the law of domicile, the then Conservative Government announced it intended to introduce new legislation. A draft Domicile Bill contained the following provisions:

(1) A child will be domiciled in the country with which he is, for the time being, most closely connected.
(2) On becoming an adult, a person retains the domicile he had immediately before becoming an adult.
(3) An adult will acquire a domicile in another country if he is both present there and intends to settle there for an indefinite period.
(4) The burden of proof to demonstrate a change of domicile will not be so great as it is under the present rules.

However, on 26 May 1993, a reply given by the Prime Minister indicated that these proposals had been shelved

On 17 April 2002 Gordon Brown announced that a fresh review would be carried out with a view to possible changes to apply in the future for foreign domiciliaries who have become long-term UK residents. To date, this fresh review has resulted only in what amounts to yet another discussion paper that was released on Budget Day 2003.

The paper avoids some of the issues and certainly does not amount to the Government's roadmap on reform. It instead summarises the current UK domicile system and briefly looks at how other countries treat their long-term residents. However, it is widely seen as setting out the ground rules for debate.

The document contained Table 24.1 summarising the UK domicile and resident rules.

EARNED INCOME

24.2 FOREIGN EMOLUMENTS

24.2.1 Introduction

A foreign-domiciled individual who is employed by a UK-resident employer is basically treated no differently from a UK-domiciled individual in a similar position. The earnings from such an employment are taxed under Schedule E Case I or II according to whether he is ordinarily resident in the UK as well as resident there (for the taxation of such earnings, see Chap. 4).

Table 24.1 – Summary of rules

Box 2.1 A Summary of the Residence and Domicile Rules

UK Status			Income Tax on Employment	Income Tax on Savings Income	Capital Gains Tax	Inheritance Tax
Resident	**Ordinarily Resident**	**Domiciled**				
·	·	·	Worldwide (1)	Worldwide (2)	Worldwide	Worldwide
·	·	×	Worldwide (1) (3)	Worldwide (2) (4)	Worldwide (4)	UK
·	×	·	Worldwide (5)	Worldwide (2) (6)	Worldwide	Worldwide
·	×	×	Worldwide (5)	Worldwide (2) (4)	Worldwide (4)	UK
×	·	·	Duties performed in the UK	UK Source (7)	Worldwide	Worldwide
×	·	×	Duties performed in the UK	UK Source (7)	Worldwide (4)	UK
×	×	·	Duties performed in the UK	UK Source	None (8)	Worldwide

For Income Tax and Capital Gains Tax all sources are taxed on the full amount of the income or gain arising except:
(1) Foreign Earnings Deduction of 100 per cent may apply – this only applies to seafarers.
(2) Special rules apply for foreign pensions in certain circumstances.
(3) Where an individual is non-domiciled and works for a non-resident company, earnings from employment wholly outside the UK are taxed on the Remittance Basis.
(4) Foreign sources taxed on the Remittance Basis.
(5) Income from duties of employment performed overseas taxed on Remittance Basis.
(6) Commonwealth and Irish citizens taxed on the Remittance Basis for all foreign sources (except Irish sources).
(7) Taxable on UK source income and FOTRA's.
(8) Gains on the disposal of assets used or held etc. for the purposes of a trade carried on in the UK by a branch or agency are chargeable.

Where a person domiciled outside the UK is employed by a non-UK resident employer, the tax treatment is fundamentally different. Earnings from such an employment are called 'foreign emoluments'. Their tax treatment is as set out Table 24.2.

24.2.2 Employer's resident status need not be same as individual's domicile

It is not necessary that the employer should be resident in the same country as that in which the individual is domiciled (although this is often the case). An individual domiciled in eg Switzerland and employed by a company resident in the USA has foreign emoluments.

24.2.3 Earnings from Republic of Ireland-resident employer
(TA 1988, s 192)

There is one exception to the general rule that foreign emoluments arise from an employment by a person not domiciled in the UK from an office or

Table 24.2 – Tax treatment under Schedule E of earnings by foreign domiciled individual from non-UK resident employer ('foreign emoluments')

	Duties of employment performed wholly or partly in the UK		*Duties of employment performed wholly outside the UK*
	In the UK	*Outside the UK*	
Employee resident and ordinarily resident in the UK	Liable to UK tax (Case I)	Liable to UK tax (Case I)	Liable if remitted to the UK (Case III)
Resident but not ordinarily resident	Liable to UK tax (Case II)	Liable if remitted to the UK (Case III)	Liable if remitted to the UK (Case III)
Not resident	Liable to UK tax (Case II)	Not liable	Not liable

employment with a non-UK resident employer. Where the employer is resident in the Republic of Ireland, the earnings are not regarded as foreign emoluments.

24.2.4 Earnings of person not ordinarily resident in UK

Where an individual has foreign emoluments and is resident in the UK, but not ordinarily resident (see 23.2.1 for meaning of ordinary residence), it is necessary to divide the emoluments between those that relate to duties performed in the UK and those performed overseas. The remuneration referable to the UK duties is taxed on an arising basis under Schedule E Case II, but the remuneration for duties performed overseas is taxed on the remittance basis under Schedule E Case III.

24.2.5 Split contract needed for person resident and ordinarily resident in UK

A different rule applies where an individual is both resident and ordinarily resident in the UK. The earnings from an employment with a foreign employer are all subject to tax in the UK on an arising basis where all or any part of the duties are performed there. There are no provisions whereby remuneration can be split between earnings relating to work done in the UK and work performed overseas. However, if a foreign-domiciled individual has a contract of employment where all the duties are performed outside the UK, the earnings are taxed on the remittance basis under Schedule E Case III.

It may be possible to take full advantage of this treatment by an individual having two separate contracts of employment, one covering duties performed in the UK and the other covering duties performed overseas.

Where a foreign national is given a right to tax equalisation in his service contracts, the amount charged on the UK employment may be carefully scrutinised by the Revenue. This is an area where you should take advice from a specialist.

24.3 TRAVELLING EXPENSES

(TA 1988, s 195)

There are special provisions that apply for individuals of foreign domicile. Certain travel expenses paid or reimbursed by an employer are not assessable income where all the following conditions are satisfied:

(1) The expenses must be paid during the five-year period that begins from the date of arrival in the UK.
(2) The expenses must relate to a journey between the individual's usual place of abode and the place in the UK where he works.
(3) The expenses must relate to journeys made by the employee, unless he is in the UK for a continuous period of 60 days or more for the purposes of performing duties. In this event, the expenses of a visit by his spouse or minor child will also be allowable, although there is a limit of two visits by any such person in a tax year.

In order to secure this exemption it is also necessary that he must not have been resident in the UK in either of the two tax years that precede the year in which he took up his UK employment.

24.4 SUBSISTENCE ALLOWANCES FOR EMPLOYEES SECONDED TO THE UK

The Revenue accepts that an employer may bear certain costs where an employee is seconded to the UK for a period not exceeding 24 months. An article in *Tax Bulletin* December 2000 analyses what is meant by 'secondment' and outlines circumstances in which an employee of an overseas company may actually be coming to the UK to take up a new office or employment rather than be working there under a continuation of his existing employment contract.

The article also goes on to explain that if the employer provides, for example, a flat for the seconded employee to use instead of hotels, the expenditure is not regarded as a taxable benefit provided 'the total cost of the accommodation is appropriate to the business need and is reasonable and not excessive'. Examples are given of what might be regarded as not being reasonable.

24.5 'CORRESPONDING PAYMENTS'

(TA 1988, s 192(3))

Certain payments made by an individual out of foreign emoluments qualify for tax relief where they are made 'in circumstances corresponding to those in which the payments would have reduced his liability to income tax' had they been paid in the UK. The main type of payments that can be relieved under this heading are contributions to an overseas pension fund (see below). Before 2000-01, mortgage interest, alimony and maintenance could also be deducted from foreign emoluments.

24.6 OVERSEAS PENSION FUNDS

An overseas pension fund will not normally be an approved retirement benefit scheme for UK tax purposes. However, where the benefits provided by an overseas pension fund are broadly similar to those that arise from UK-approved retirement benefit schemes, the Revenue may regard the employer's contributions as not constituting remuneration for Schedule E purposes and any contributions made by the employee may be deducted as corresponding payments (see above). In some situations, the Revenue will accord this treatment only where the individual's rights under his overseas pension scheme are adapted or restricted. For example, a US national who has an individual retirement plan may be required to give notice to the US administrators so as to waive his ability to take a lump sum in circumstances where this would not be permitted under the rules that govern UK-approved retirement benefit schemes.

24.7 SELF-EMPLOYMENT

Where an individual is resident in the UK, any earnings from a business carried on as a sole trader are taxed under Schedule D Case I on the arising basis. This even applies in a situation where all the work is actually performed overseas. The basis for this interpretation by the courts is that a business is deemed to be carried on from where it is controlled and, in the case of a sole trader, control is located where the proprietor is resident.

A foreign-domiciled individual who carries on self-employment and who performs a substantial amount of work overseas should consider forming a company. In particular, if an overseas company were to be formed and the company employed him and supplied his services outside the UK to customers, the earnings from that employment would constitute foreign emoluments. Provided no work is performed in the UK under the employment contract, interposing an offshore company in this way would mean that he could take full advantage of the remittance basis for earnings taxable under Schedule E Case III.

24.8 PARTNERSHIPS CONTROLLED OUTSIDE THE UK

Where a UK-resident individual is a partner in a firm controlled outside the UK, his earnings from that firm are taxed as follows:

(1) *Profits from a UK branch:* under Schedule D Case I on the arising basis.
(2) *Overseas profits:* under Schedule D Case V under the remittance basis.

24.9 PENSION BENEFITS

24.9.1 Lump sums paid under overseas pension schemes (ESC A10)

Income tax is not charged on lump sum benefits received by an employee (or by his personal representatives or any dependant) from an overseas retirement benefit scheme or overseas provident fund where the employee's overseas service comprises:

(1) not less than 75% of his total service in the employment concerned; or
(2) the whole of the last ten years of his service in that employment (subject to the total service exceeding ten years); or
(3) not less than 50% of his total service in that employment, including any ten of the last 20 years, provided the total service exceeds 20 years.

If the employee's overseas service does not meet these requirements, relief from income tax is given by reducing the amount of the lump sum that would otherwise be chargeable by the same proportion as the overseas service bears to the employee's total service in that employment.

24.9.2 Pensions

An individual who receives a pension paid by a non-UK resident person is subject to tax under Schedule D Case V on the remittance basis. There is no such reduction as exists for UK-domiciled individuals taxed on only 90% of such pensions. If the whole pension is remitted, tax arises under Case V on the full amount.

INVESTMENT INCOME

24.10 THE REMITTANCE BASIS FOR INVESTMENT INCOME

24.10.1 Remittance basis

Chapter 8 covers the overseas investment income of an individual who is ordinarily resident and domiciled in the UK; such individuals are taxed under Schedule D Cases IV and V in respect of income as it arises. A completely different rule applies for individuals who are not ordinarily resident or not domiciled in the UK; their assessable income is fixed by reference to the amount of income remitted to the UK.

24.10.2 Exception for income arising within Republic of Ireland

(TA 1988, s 68)

Where a foreign-domiciled individual has income that arises within the Republic of Ireland, it is taxed as it arises and not on the remittance basis. It is taxed on the CY basis.

24.10.3 Change from PY to CY basis

See *Tax Handbook 1999-2000* at 22.9.3-22.9.5.

24.10.4 No assessment can be made if individual ceases to have source of income

A Schedule D Case IV or V assessment can only be made for a tax year if the individual had the source of income during that year. Care must be taken over what constitutes a source of income. Some advisors do not consider it prudent to rely on this principle by closing a bank account and opening a new deposit account with the same bank, although the Revenue appears to accept that this represents the cessation of one source and the creation of another. It is arguable that the source of income is represented by the debt due by that particular bank and so the individual continues to have the source of income in question.

24.10.5 Income from savings

Investment income assessed on the remittance basis cannot qualify for the 20% rate that applies to income from savings (see 7.1.5). If dividend income is remitted, a liability arises for basic rate rather than the normal 10%.

24.10.6 Relief for foreign tax

(TA 1988, s 793)

Where overseas income has borne foreign tax, credit may be claimed for this against the UK tax assessed on the same income.

24.11 WHAT CONSTITUTES A REMITTANCE?

24.11.1 General principles

A remittance arises where an individual brings money into the UK, either in cash or by transferring money to a UK bank account. No remittance occurs if money is spent abroad or if liabilities that fall due for payment overseas are settled directly from a foreign bank account.

24.11.2 Constructive remittances
(TA 1988, s 65)

The legislation deals with constructive remittances and states that a remittance is deemed to have occurred if an individual applies overseas income towards the satisfaction of:

(1) a debt (or interest thereon) for money lent to him in the UK;
(2) a debt for money lent to him abroad and brought to the UK;
(3) a loan incurred in order to satisfy such debts.

Case law also indicates that a constructive remittance is deemed to have occurred if an individual borrows from a UK bank but has his borrowings formally secured against money held in an overseas bank account.

The courts have held that a complex arrangement whereby money was transmitted between two South African companies, with the individual receiving a loan from one of them, constituted a constructive remittance of income. Since the courts are increasingly having regard for the overall consequences of a series of transactions, it would be unwise to rely on an artificial scheme that enabled an individual to enjoy sums in the UK that could be matched with overseas income.

24.11.3 Unauthorised remittances

In one case, a bank remitted untaxed overseas income by mistake. Because the bank acted contrary to its customer's instructions, it was held there was no liability under the remittance basis.

24.11.4 Gifts of unremitted income

The safest course of action is for a gift to take the form of a cheque to be drawn on a foreign bank account, with the recipient paying the sum into a foreign bank account. If matters are handled in this particular way, there can be no question of the gift constituting a remittance.

Where an individual makes a gift of foreign income, he is not affected by what happens subsequently. The money loses its income quality once it has been given away and the recipient can bring the money into the UK without any liability under the remittance basis. In principle, this rule ought also to apply to gifts between spouses, although one should expect the Revenue to carefully scrutinise such arrangements so as to ensure that there are no hidden arrangements that govern the way the recipient must use the money given.

24.12 POSITION IF FOREIGN DOMICILIARY ACQUIRES UK DOMICILE

Where an individual is assessable under the remittance basis, but then acquires a UK domicile of choice, the remittance basis ceases to apply for income tax purposes and his overseas income is taxable under the arising basis. No tax liability arises if he then remits money that would formerly have given rise to an income tax liability under the remittance basis. The Special Commissioners have held that this rule does not apply for CGT purposes and gains that are remitted after the time the individual acquired a UK domicile continue to attract a tax liability (see 24.14.5).

24.13 MANAGING THE REMITTANCE BASIS

24.13.1 Maintaining separate bank accounts

Where a foreign-domiciled individual has substantial overseas income, it is normal for arrangements to be put in place so that remittances to the UK may be identified, as far as possible, with capital. The way this is normally dealt with is by arranging for him to have three separate bank accounts, as follows:

(1) The first account is capital, ie the cash actually held by him at the time he took up residence in the UK. It is normal for further sums to be paid into this bank account where the cash relates to the sale proceeds of assets sold at a loss for CGT purposes or the proceeds arise from the sale of exempt assets. The bank should be instructed that any interest on this bank account should not be credited to the account, but paid to a separate income account (see below).
(2) The second account should contain the sale proceeds of assets that give rise to capital gains.
(3) The third account should be kept for income, including interest on the capital account and the capital gains account.

Clearly, in practice, an individual may minimise his liability under the remittance basis by taking remittances from the capital account in (1).

In some situations, it may be sensible to go one stage further and keep two income accounts with one account containing income that has not borne tax at source (eg overseas bank deposit interest) and the other containing income that has borne foreign tax. By organising matters in this way, remittances of income can come out of the account that contains income that has suffered foreign tax, and this will further minimise any UK tax liability.

There may be CGT savings from having different types of capital gains account (see 24.14.4).

24.13.2 Use overseas income accounts to fund expenditure outside UK

A foreign-domiciled individual should also organise matters so that all possible expenditure outside the UK is funded out of the income account and, where relevant, out of the income account that represents income that has not borne any foreign tax at source.

24.13.3 Closing bank account so source ceases to exist

Where an individual has a separate source of income (eg a bank deposit account) it may be possible to take full advantage of the rule that no assessment may be made for a tax year after the individual ceases to have the source of income concerned. He could achieve this by closing the bank deposit account, and transferring the cash to a new account (see 24.10.4). Remittances from that new account may then be made in the following tax year and no liability should arise under the remittance basis since such remittances will represent capital (even though the capital was built up out of income that arose while he possessed the particular source of overseas income concerned).

24.13.4 Trustees using unremitted income to buy investments from settlor

A further possibility whereby a foreign-domiciled individual may minimise the income he requires in the UK is for him to transfer unremitted income to foreign trustees who then use that income to make capital investments by buying property from the settlor.

Example – Trustee's use of unremitted income

> *A* has accumulated overseas income of £45,000 that will become taxable if it is remitted to the UK. If he transfers the £45,000 to an offshore trust and then sells his main residence to the trustees, he should not be chargeable to tax under Schedule D Case IV or V as if he had remitted the income, even though the £45,000 is brought into the UK after the sale of the property. If *A* remains in occupation as a beneficiary of the trust, this will not of itself constitute a remittance or a deemed remittance.

CAPITAL GAINS TAX

24.14 REMITTANCE BASIS FOR CAPITAL GAINS ON FOREIGN ASSETS

24.14.1 Introduction

(TCGA 1992, ss 12 and 275)

A person of foreign domicile may be subject to CGT if he is either resident or ordinarily resident in the UK. Gains on UK assets are charged in the same way as gains realised by UK-domiciled individuals. Gains realised on assets situated overseas are subject to UK CGT only if the proceeds are remitted to the UK.

The following rules determine whether an asset is deemed to be situated in the UK or abroad:

(1) Real estate and rights over such property are situated in the country where the real estate is located.
(2) Tangible movable property and rights over such property are situated in the country where the property is located.
(3) Debts are normally situated in the country where the creditor is resident.
(4) Stocks, shares and securities are generally situated in the country where the company maintains its principal register.
(5) Goodwill is treated as situated where the trade or business is carried on.
(6) Patents, trademarks and designs are situated in the country where they are registered.

24.14.2 Definition of 'remittance'

Capital gains are remitted if they are brought into the UK or enjoyed there. For example, payment of the disposal proceeds into a UK bank account counts as a remittance, as does a payment into a UK bank account from an overseas bank account containing such proceeds. Less obviously, the gains will be enjoyed in the UK if an individual has a large deposit account outside the UK and he formally secures a UK bank loan against this deposit account. However, if the money is spent outside the UK, it is not deemed to have been remitted. Payment of disposal proceeds into a bank account in the Channel Islands or Isle of Man does not constitute a remittance to the UK. An outright gift that takes place outside the UK will not normally be a remittance provided a cheque, etc is paid into an overseas bank account for the recipient.

24.14.3 Losses not allowable

(TCGA 1992, s 16(4))

Where a loss arises on an overseas asset, a person of foreign domicile cannot claim a capital loss. In some situations this could give rise to hardship.

Example – Losses not allowable

B has gains of £90,000 on UK assets and capital losses of £60,000 on foreign assets. Unfortunately, there is no relief for the £60,000 losses so he would be taxed on gains of £90,000.

24.14.4 How to take full advantage of remittance basis

In some cases it may be that there is no likelihood of the individual needing to bring the proceeds of a sale of foreign assets into the UK. In such a situation the payment of CGT is something that he may or may not choose to do since he can control the amount of his chargeable gains. Where it is going to be necessary to bring money into the UK at some stage in the future, it is advisable for him to keep separate bank accounts.

One account should receive the proceeds of assets that have been sold at a loss when measured for UK CGT purposes. This account may be used to fund remittances to the UK that are not going to give rise to a CGT liability. A second account should contain the sale proceeds of assets subject to foreign CGT. Remittances out of this account will give rise to a CGT assessment, but double tax relief will be due in respect of the foreign CGT that has been paid. Other sales of assets that have produced a gain should be kept in a third account, and should be remitted only as a last resort.

24.14.5 Position where foreign domiciliary acquires UK domicile

The law is not clear here. A Special Commissioners' decision indicates that a CGT liability may arise for a UK-domiciled individual if he remits sums that would have been subject to CGT had they been remitted before he acquired a UK domicile of choice. Special Commissioners' decisions do not constitute binding precedents, but caution is advisable here.

24.15 USE OF OFFSHORE COMPANIES AND TRUSTS

The formidable range of anti-avoidance provisions covered in Chap. 22 do not have the same impact where a foreign-domiciled individual is concerned.

24.15.1 Offshore companies

The anti-avoidance legislation contained in TCGA 1992, s 13 (see 22.13) does not apply to foreign-domiciled individuals and there are no other ways in which a person may be charged to tax on capital gains realised by an offshore company, even though the UK-resident individual may own all of its share capital. Consequently, gains on UK assets may be taken outside the ambit of CGT if a foreign-domiciled individual makes his investments indirectly by setting up an offshore company which then makes the relevant investments. Care needs to be taken to ensure that a company which is incorporated overseas is non-UK resident because central management and control are exercised there (see SP1/90).

It is also dangerous for the individual to occupy a property owned by an offshore company as the Revenue may seek to assess him under Schedule E as a 'shadow director'. The Revenue at one stage indicated that it might also raise assessments under transfer-pricing legislation introduced in FA 1998, but relented.

24.15.2 Offshore trusts

Offshore or non-resident trusts can be extremely tax-efficient where foreign-domiciled individuals are concerned. A settlement established by a foreign-domiciled individual after 18 March 1991 cannot be a 'qualifying settlement', which means there are no provisions for charging a settlor to tax on gains realised by the trustees of his non-resident settlement.

The provisions of TCGA 1992, s 86, which charge beneficiaries when they receive capital payments, had no application until 17 March 1998 where the settlor was not UK-domiciled and was not domiciled there at the time gains were realised. Even if these exemptions do not apply, s 86 still does not come into force if a beneficiary who receives a capital payment is not domiciled there. There are no other provisions that may allow the Revenue to tax a beneficiary on gains realised by offshore trustees and so the creation of an offshore trust may enable a foreign-domiciled individual to escape from any CGT charge, whether on foreign or UK assets.

Professional advice should be taken to avoid potential pitfalls arising from income tax and other legislation.

INHERITANCE TAX

24.16 UK AND FOREIGN SITUS PROPERTY

IHT may be charged on the death of an individual who is not deemed to be domiciled in the UK, but only to the extent that his estate consists of property situated there. No charge arises on foreign situs property as this is classified as 'excluded property'. Table 24.3 indicates which types of property are regarded as situated in the UK.

There is a special rule for IHT whereby an individual may be deemed to be domiciled in the UK if he has been resident for 17 of the 20 tax years ending with the current year.

Table 24.3 – Assets chargeable to IHT

	Not chargeable	*Chargeable*
Channel Island property	✔	
Isle of Man property	✔	
Other foreign property	✔	
UK property		✔
Bank deposits outside the UK	✔	
UK sterling bank deposits		✔
UK foreign currency deposits	chargeable only if the owner is resident in the UK	
Shares in UK companies		✔
UK unit trusts and OEICs	✔	
Registered shares in foreign companies	✔	
Bearer securities	depends where the bearer certificates are held	
Debts owed by a UK resident person		✔ (normally)
Debts owed by foreign resident person	✔	

25

NATIONAL INSURANCE CONTRIBUTIONS AND SOCIAL SECURITY BENEFITS

This chapter covers the following topics:

(1) Class 1 contributions.
(2) Class 2 contributions.
(3) Class 3 contributions.
(4) Class 4 contributions.
(5) Social security benefits.
(6) Tax credits.

Where rates are quoted, they are the 2003-04 figures with 2002-03 figures in brackets where different.

25.1 CLASS 1 CONTRIBUTIONS

25.1.1 Introduction

Employed individuals are liable for Class 1 NICs. Secondary contributions are paid by employers (see 25.1.7).

No contribution is payable unless the employee earns £89+ pw, although entitlement to benefits starts for earnings in excess of £75. If he earns £89+, contributions are calculated at 11% (10%) on the excess amount over £89 on earnings between £89 and £595 (£585) pw (eg on weekly earnings of £100, employee NICs due are £100 – £89 = £11, × 11% = £1.21p). In 2002-03 no employee contribution was payable on earnings in excess of £585 (the 'upper limit') but for 2003-04 an additional 1% charge is imposed on all earnings above £595 pw.

Women who married on or before 6 April 1977 and have chosen to pay a reduced rate are subject to pay NICs of only 3.85%. This right is lost if the woman is divorced, but is not lost if she is widowed.

Contributions are normally assessed by reference to weekly earnings, but if the employee is paid less frequently, contributions are calculated on the corresponding figures for a monthly basis or whatever other period is covered by the payment to him.

An individual's liability to NICs is not affected by a previous period of unemployment during the year. Each 'earnings period' is looked at in isolation and there is no principle that corresponds to the cumulative method used for income tax where a tax year is looked at as a whole. There is a slight exception to this for company directors (see 25.1.3), but this is basically an anti-avoidance provision.

On 1 April 1999 the Contributions Agency transferred from the Department of Social Security to the Revenue to become the Inland Revenue National Insurance Contributions Office (NICO). NICs, statutory sick pay (SSP) and statutory maternity pay (SMP) are now handled by the Revenue including responsibility for NICs policy and appeals.

During the 1999-2000 tax year, new arrangements were introduced so that most NICs, SSP and SMP appeals can be heard by an independent tribunal in the same way as tax appeals. Previously, the Secretary of State was asked formally to determine one of a range of 'questions' via the Office for the Determination of Contribution Questions (ODCQ) based in Newcastle. Note, however, that appeals on contracting-out pensions issues and WFTC will not be heard by tax tribunals.

25.1.2 Deferment

An individual who has more than one job and total earnings likely to exceed the upper limit may apply for deferment so that NICO may authorise certain employers not to withhold contributions from his remuneration (form CA 2700). The deferment application is made on form CF 379. Ideally this form should be submitted before the start of a tax year for which deferment is sought. In any event, deferment will not be granted for 2003-04 unless NICO had received the application by 14 February 2003. NICO is also reluctant to grant deferment for a year in which the individual will reach pensionable age. Where a deferment application is made, the individual cannot choose which earnings should be subject to deduction for NICs. In addition, NICO will always defer contributions at the non-contracted out rate if any of the employments is not contracted out.

The position is reviewed after the end of a tax year. It may be that the individual has not had the anticipated level of earnings from a particular employment and this may mean that the liability for the year has not been satisfied. In such a case, NICO will apply for payment of the balance and this falls due for payment within 28 days of NICO making such a demand.

There is an entitlement to a repayment of contributions withheld from the remuneration, where they exceed the maximum for the year, even if the individual has not applied for deferment.

25.1.3 Company directors

Remuneration paid to a company director is normally assessed for NICs as if it arose on a yearly basis. Therefore, a large lump sum payment of fees or a bonus could attract the maximum contributions for a year, rather than the maximum contributions for one week or one month.

Example – Assessment on lump sum payments

A weekly paid company director receives remuneration of £35,000 paid in a single sum. The liability for contributions is the liability for the year, ie

> 52 × 506 (£595 upper limit – £89 lower limit) × 11% ie £2,894.32
> + 1% on the excess ie £35,000 – (52 × £595) = 4,060 × 1%

It is not just the maximum for one week's earnings, ie 10% of £506.

Since 6 April 1999, a new administrative arrangement for the assessment and payment of NICs for directors came into effect (Social Security Act 1998). Regulation 6A of the Social Security (Contributions) Regulations 1979 still ensures that the earnings period is annual, but it is possible to make payments on account. When the last payment is made to the director in the tax year, the employer is required to reassess the NICs due on the total earnings for the tax year on an annual, or pro rata annual, earnings period, as appropriate. To qualify for these new arrangements the following three conditions must be satisfied:

(1) the director agrees to NICs being assessed this way;
(2) he normally receives his earnings in a regular pattern; and
(3) those payments normally exceed the lower earnings limit for the pay period.

Directors (and officers) may be held liable for the employer's contributions where it has failed to pay NICs on time and the failure appears to be attributable to fraud or neglect by the culpable officers.

25.1.4 Definition of earnings

'Earnings' for NICs purposes include all cash remuneration. Contributions are also payable on sick pay, holiday pay, etc. The NICs definition of 'earnings' is quite different from that used for income tax purposes. For example, NICs are assessed on an individual's pay before pension contributions and before any charitable donations made under a payroll deduction scheme. Profit-related pay was another type of earnings that was exempt for income tax purposes, but gave rise to a liability for NICs.

Where an employer settles an employee's pecuniary liability, the sum paid is treated as earnings for NICs purposes even though it is not pay for PAYE purposes. Previously, only certain types of benefits-in-kind that could easily be converted into cash were liable to NICs. For example, premium bonds and National Savings certificates are regarded as earnings for NICs purposes because they may be encashed by the holder surrendering them. With effect from 6 April 2000 the definition of earnings for NICs purposes was extended to cover all benefits-in-kind that are taxed as emoluments or deemed emoluments (see 25.1.8).

Non-cash vouchers are also treated as earnings with the following exceptions (see 4.4.7 and 4.4.8):

- Transport vouchers where the employee earns less than £8,500;
- Transport vouchers for the disabled;
- Transport vouchers for the armed forces;
- Vouchers exchangeable for the use of sports or recreational facilities;
- Vouchers associated with long service awards;
- Vouchers in respect of staff functions (less than £150 per person);
- Vouchers exchangeable for meals provided on employer's premises or at a staff canteen;
- First 15p per working day of luncheon vouchers (maximum £1.05 pw);
- Incentive awards up to £150 pa per donor;
- Childcare vouchers for children up to age 16.

NICs are also due on an employer's contribution to a FURBS established specifically for an individual director or employee.

Share options

No NICs arise on the grant or exercise of approved share options, unless the shares are readily convertible assets, the exercise takes place after 8 April 2003 and it gives rise to an income tax charge, for example where the option is exercised within three years of grant.

There is no NICs liability on the grant of an unapproved option, except where the option can be exercised more than ten years after the date of the grant.

The exercise of unapproved share options involving shares that are 'readily convertible assets' attracts NICs if the option was granted on or after 6 April 1999. The charge arises on the same amount as is chargeable to tax (see 4.13.2), ie it is based on the amount the shares would realise if sold on the day the option is exercised.

No NICs liability arises on the exercise of a non-approved option over shares that are not readily convertible assets at the time of exercise. This is because TA 1988, s 135 does not deem such a profit to be an emolument, it merely states that the profit shall be charged to tax under Schedule E.

An employer could make an election in respect of options granted between 6 April 1999 and 19 May 2000. This involved the employer paying 12.2% contributions based on the shares' value at 7 November 2000. If the election was made, the employer had no further liability as and when the option was exercised. The election to do this had to be made by 11 August 2001.

Dividends

NICs ought not to arise where a director receives a dividend, or interest on a loan made to the company, or rent for a property used by the company. Investment income of this nature is clearly not earnings but there may be borderline cases where a so-called dividend is really remuneration that has been given a misleading label. NICO may have a point if the dividend payment does not conform to company law requirements.

25.1.5 Problem areas

One major problem area concerns directors' drawings. NICO takes the view that where a director arranges for a personal liability to be settled by the employer and charged to his drawings account, the payment constitutes earnings for NICs purposes unless the drawings account is in credit.

Example – Directors' drawings

A has a drawings account with his company which is £60 in credit. The company pays a personal bill for *A* of £100 and debits his drawings account with £100, thus turning the credit balance into an overdrawn balance of £40.

NICO takes the view that £60 of the payment of the £100 bill is a repayment of a loan and attracts no NICs, but the balance of £40 is a payment of earnings and the grossed up amount is subject to NICs.

25.1.6 Loans from the employer

Curiously, NICO takes the view that if an individual arranges for a loan from his employer that is used to settle a personal liability, there is no NICs liability unless (and until) the employer writes off the loan. Considerable care should be taken when dealing with any documentation and the structure of such arrangements to minimise liability.

25.1.7 Employer's NICs

In addition to the 'primary' contributions paid by the employee, employers are required to pay 'secondary contributions'. There is no ceiling on the amount of an employee's earnings that attracts secondary contributions. No liability for secondary contributions can arise unless there is a liability for primary contributions, except when an employee with other employment has a deferment form CA 2700 or is a pensioner (Table C or S). An employee can agree to pay his employer's NICs on profits from the exercise of non-approved share options after 19 May 2000. The NICs borne by the employee are then deducted in arriving at his Schedule E income (see 4.13.2). The Revenue has published model agreements under which an employee can agree to pay his employer's NICs on his share option.

Employers are also liable for Class 1A NICs where the employee has benefits-in-kind (see 25.1.8). For company cars, the cash equivalent used for income tax purposes is treated as if it were additional earnings subject to secondary contributions. A further charge may arise if the employee is provided with fuel for private mileage, with the Class 1A charge again being based on the scale benefit used for income tax purposes.

Since 6 April 1998, Class 1A NICs on cars are due on unremunerated employees and directors (Social Security Act 1998, s 52). This section states that the person liable to pay Class 1A NICs in these circumstances is the person who would normally have been liable to pay secondary Class 1 NICs had the benefit of the car been earnings.

Unfortunately for employers, although SI 1998/2209 made this new provision operative only from 8 September 1998 to 5 April 1999, since Class 1A is an annual liability, if the car was available for the whole of the year, a Class 1A liability existed for the whole of 1998-99. The issue was clarified in the Employer's Budget update pack, despite the fact that in the *Employer's Bulletin* sent out by the Revenue in February 1999 the start date is given as 6 April 1999.

In November 1996, the Secretary of State for Social Security announced that NICs would be aligned with the Revenue's treatment of PAYE Settlement Agreements (PSAs). With effect from 6 April 1999, Class 1B NICs are payable on PSAs and are payable at the same time as the tax (19 October). Class 1B NICs are currently payable at 11.8% on the total value of:

(1) all items covered by the PSA that would give rise to a Class 1 or 1A liability, and
(2) the tax payable by the employer under the PSA.

25.1.8 Class 1A NICs

As mentioned above, Class 1A NICs already apply to company cars and fuel, but from 6 April 2000 they were extended to include most benefits-in-kind. The payment date of Class 1A NICs is 19 July after the end of the year of assessment. Payment of the increased charge therefore first arose on 19 July 2001.

The amount of the charge is normally equivalent to the highest rate of employer's secondary Class 1 NICs, which is currently 12.8% (from 6 April 2003). The Class 1A liability is an employer's charge only and is a tax-deductible expense. The charge is not payable by employees or directors.

Class 1A NICs are not charged if:

(1) NICs are already due (eg on expense payments);
(2) the expense payment or benefit-in-kind is covered by a P11D dispensation, extra-statutory concession or specific exemption;

(3) the expenses payment or benefit-in-kind is included in a PSA (where Class 1B NICs will be payable); or
(4) the benefit-in-kind is provided to an employee earning at a rate (inclusive of benefits) of less than £8,500 pa.

To reduce the reporting requirements, the Revenue has announced an exemption from income tax and NICs for the following:

(1) tools and equipment provided for work use where there may be a small amount of private use in the home, workplace or elsewhere;
(2) qualifying beneficial loans;
(3) general welfare counselling (but not private medical treatment or consultation); and
(4) refreshments provided by employers.

Class 1A NICs reports are merged with the existing forms P11D.

25.2 CLASS 2 CONTRIBUTIONS

25.2.1 Introduction

A self-employed individual is liable to Class 2 NICs of £2.00 pw unless his earnings are less than £4,095 (£4,025) pa and he has applied for a Certificate of Exemption. A penalty can be charged if he has not notified NICO within three months of taking up self-employment. See *Tax Bulletin* June 2001.

The Class 2 NICs for sharefishermen is £2.65 pw and for volunteer development workers is £3.35 pw.

25.2.2 Earnings from employment and self-employment

Where an individual has income from both employment and self-employment, both Classes 1 and 2 NICs are payable unless he applies for deferment. The maximum he may pay for any year is an amount equal to the maximum Class 1 primary contributions on 53 weeks' earnings; consequently, for 2002-2003 the maximum was £2,628.80 (no equivalent maximum figure exists for 2003-04 as a consequence of the introduction of the additional 1% charge). A repayment may be claimed if he has paid a mixture of Classes 1 and 2 NICs in excess of this amount.

25.2.3 Small earnings exemption

A person may avoid paying Class 2 NICs by applying in advance for the small earnings exemption. The amount of the limit for small earnings exemption for 2003-04 is £4,095.

Earnings for this purpose are measured by reference to actual earnings for the tax year. For example, if a trader makes up accounts to 30 September, the small earnings exemption is available only if his earnings for 2003-04 are less than £4,095 when computed as follows:

$\frac{6}{12}$ × profits for the year ended 30 September 2003
$\frac{6}{12}$ × profits for the year ended 30 September 2004

An individual may apply for repayment if Class 2 NICs have been overpaid. The repayment claim must normally be made between 6 April and 31 December following the end of the tax year and thus the deadline for making a repayment claim for 2002-03 will be 31 December 2003.

A false economy?

In general, choosing not to pay Class 2 NICs could prove a false economy as entitlement to benefits such as pensions and sick pay may be affected.

25.3 CLASS 3 CONTRIBUTIONS

These are a type of voluntary contribution. A person who is neither employed nor self-employed (or whose earnings fall below the exemption) may pay voluntary Class 3 NICs to secure the State retirement pension. The weekly rate is set at £6.85 for 2002-03.

Following an 'oversight' by the Revenue, the time limit for paying voluntary NICs for the tax years from 1996-97 to 2000-01, to make up for any gaps in a contributor's record, is extended. The limit for these years will now be 5 April 2008, the same as for 2001-02. The deadline for 1996-97 should have been 5 April 2003. However, notices informing people about their contributions were not sent out at the appropriate time. The Inland Revenue has promised to contact people who could have gaps in their records for the years from 1996-97 to 2001-02, to allow them to check their positions and make voluntary contributions if they wish to do so. Voluntary contributions must usually be paid within six years of the date they were due, however because of this Revenue error, for the years 1996-97 up to 2001-02 any late applicants will be allowed extra time to pay. This means that payments may be made up to the new deadline of 5 April 2008, payable at the original rate.

Class 3 weekly rates are:

1996/1997	£5.95
1997/1998	£6.05
1998/1999	£6.25
1999/2000	£6.45
2000/2001	£6.55
2001/2002	£6.75
2002/2003	£6.85
2003/2004	£6.95

25.4 CLASS 4 CONTRIBUTIONS

These are payable by self-employed individuals according to the level of their profits as determined for income tax purposes. At present, Class 4 NICs are levied at the rate of 8% (7%) of Schedule D profits between £4,615 and £30,940 (£30,420). Earnings in excess of the upper profits limit will attract Class 4 NICs at the rate of 1%.

Where an individual pays interest on a business loan or has suffered trading losses, such amounts may be set against his earnings for the purposes of assessing liability for Class 4 NICs. This situation applies even where the losses have been relieved for income tax purposes by way of offset against his other income.

25.5 SOCIAL SECURITY BENEFITS

(TA 1988, s 617)

The following benefits are taxed as earned income under Schedule E:

• Incapacity benefit • Income support paid to unemployed and strikers • Industrial death benefit (if paid as pension) • Invalid care allowance • Invalidity allowance when paid with retirement pension • Job release allowance • Jobseeker's allowance (contributions-based) • Old person's pension • Retirement pension l Statutory maternity pay • Statutory sick pay • Unemployment benefit • Widowed mother's allowance • Widow's pension.

(Note: The jobseeker's allowance was introduced from 7 October 1996. Payments are dependent on the NICs record and/or the income.)

The following benefits are not taxable:

• Attendance allowance • Child benefit • Child dependency additions paid with widow's allowance, widowed mother's allowance, retirement pension, invalid care allowance, unemployment benefit or supplementary benefits • Child's special allowance • Christmas bonus for pensioners • Disability living allowance • Disability working allowance • Employment rehabilitation allowance • Fares to school • Guardian's allowance • Home improvement, repair and insulation grants • Invalidity allowance when paid with invalidity pension • Invalidity pension • Job search allowances • Maternity allowance • Mobility allowance • One parent benefit • Severe disablement allowance • Sickness benefit • Employment training allowance • War orphan's pension • War widow's pension • Widow's payment • Youth training scheme allowance.

Means-tested benefits

• Educational maintenance allowance • Family credit • Hospital patients' travelling expenses • Housing benefit • Jobseeker's allowance (income-based) • Income support • Social fund payments • Student grants • Uniform and clothing grants.

(Note: The jobseeker's allowance was introduced from 7 October 1996. Payments are dependent on the NICs record and/or the income.)

War disablement benefits

Disablement pension, including: Age allowance • Allowance for lowered standard of occupation • Clothing allowance • Comforts allowance • Constant attendance allowance • Dependant allowance • Education allowance • Exceptionally severe disablement allowance • Invalidity allowance • Medical treatment allowance • Severe disablement occupational allowance • Unemployability allowance.

Industrial injury benefits

Disablement benefit, including: Constant attendance allowance • Exceptionally severe disablement allowance • Reduced earnings allowance • Retirement allowance • Unemployability supplement • Industrial death benefit child allowance.

Adoption allowances

(ESC A40)

Sums paid under schemes approved under the Children Act 1975, s 32 are exempt from income tax.

25.6 TAX CREDITS

25.6.1 Working Families' Tax Credit – to 5 April 2003

WFTC was in effect from October 1999 to 5 April 2003. The credits were paid through the individual's employer. The employer was informed by the Revenue how much the payments should be and when they should commence. The Revenue also notified the employers when the payments should cease. If an employer was not paying the credit, either because the credit has just started or the employment has ended, then payments were made directly from the Revenue. For further details on WFTC, see Chap. 10.

25.6.2 Disabled Person's Tax Credit – to 5 April 2003

This was also administered by employers. It was paid to people who had an illness or disability that put them at a disadvantage for getting a job. As with WFTC, claimants must be resident and entitled to work in the UK and must work at least 16 hours pw. In addition, they must be eligible for one of a number of qualifying benefits for disability, or have been receiving them up to 182 days prior to their application.

An award of the tax credit is effective for 26 weeks at a time, although when employers began to distribute the credits they were paid at the same intervals as pay (eg monthly or weekly).

The above credits were replaced by the working tax credit with effect from 6 April 2003. For further details see Chap. 10.

25.6.3 The role of employers

The new Working Tax Credit continues to be the responsibility of the employer. The amounts paid by employers by way of tax credits are set against the PAYE tax and NICs liabilities due to the Revenue each month or quarter as appropriate. Where the employer has not collected enough PAYE and NICs to cover the tax credits payable for a particular period, application to the Revenue for additional funding may be made. At the end of the tax year, employers are obliged to provide employees with details of the credits paid to them. This information must also be shown on payslips and P60 forms.

If the applicant is self-employed, he continues to receive his credits directly from the Revenue. It is not usually necessary for recipients to have to complete a tax return unless they are required to do so for some other reason. If an applicant does not agree with the Revenue's decision about qualification or the amount awarded, he can ask for the case to be reviewed. If he still disagrees, he can appeal to the Unified Appeals Tribunal.

Table 25.1 – Taxable social security benefits

	2002-03	*2003-04*
Retirement pension	£	£
Single	75.50	77.45
Adult dependant	45.20	46.35
*Incapacity benefit**		
Long-term benefit	70.95	72.15
increase for age higher	14.65	15.15
increase for age lower	7.35	7.60
Short-term benefit		
under pension age		
lower rate	53.50	54.40
higher rate	63.25	64.35
Short-term benefit		
over pension age		
lower rate	68.05	69.20
higher rate	70.95	72.15

Income support		
Single/lone parent		
– under 18	32.50	32.90
– 18 to 24	42.70	43.25
– 25 or over	53.95	54.65
Couple		
– both under 18	32.50	32.90
– one/both 18 or over	84.65	85.75
Statutory sick pay		
Earnings threshold	75.00	77.00
Standard rate	63.25	64.35
Statutory maternity pay		
Earnings threshold	75.00	77.00
Lower rate	75.00	100.00
*Jobseeker's allowance (contribution based)***		
Single people under 18	32.50	32.90
Single people 18-24	42.70	43.25
Single people 25 and over	53.95	54.65
Widow's payment		
Widowed mother's allowance	75.50	77.45
Widow's pension (standard)	75.50	77.45

* Incapacity benefit replaced invalidity benefit and sickness benefit from 6 April 1995. It is taxable (under Schedule E) except for short-term benefit payable at the lower rate.

** The jobseeker's allowance was introduced from 7 October 1996 and replaced unemployment benefit.

Table 25.2 – Non-taxable social security benefits

	2002-03	*2003-04*
Attendance allowance	£	£
Higher rate	56.25	57.20
Lower rate	37.65	38.20
Child benefit		
First or only child	15.75	16.05
Each subsequent child	10.55	10.75
Severe disablement allowance		
Basic rate	42.85	43.60
Age-related addition		
higher rate	14.90	15.15
middle rate	9.50	9.70
lower rate	4.75	4.85

Bereavement allowance		
Single lump sum	2,000.00	2,000.00
Christmas bonus		
Single annual payment	10.00	10.00

26

TAX AND COMPANIES

PETER HARRUP

This chapter looks at the taxation of companies under the following headings:

(1) Who pays corporation tax?
(2) Self-assessment.
(3) How 'profits' are defined.
(4) Accounting periods, rates and payment of tax.
(5) Loan relationships.
(6) Intangible assets
(7) Companies' capital gains.
(8) Dividends.
(9) Losses.
(10) Double taxation relief on foreign income.
(11) Groups of companies.
(12) Investment companies.
(13) Close companies.
(14) Corporate venturing.
(15) Research and Development (R&D) tax credits.
(16) Claims and elections.

26.1 WHO PAYS CORPORATION TAX?

(TA 1988, ss 11-12; FA 1988, s 66)

Corporation tax is levied on the chargeable profits of companies resident in the UK for tax purposes. A company is generally defined as meaning any body corporate or unincorporated association, but does not include a partnership, local authority or local authority association. The definition extends to authorised unit trusts, the detailed provisions for which are set out in TA 1988, s 468.

Corporation tax also extends to non-resident companies carrying on a trade in the UK through a branch or agency. Such companies are chargeable to tax on any income attributable to the branch or agency and on any capital gains arising on the disposal of assets used in the UK for the branch or agency's trade purposes. Any income of a non-resident company from sources within the UK that is not charged to corporation tax is liable to income tax.

A company that was incorporated in the UK is regarded as resident there regardless of where the directors exercise their management and control. Some of the double taxation conventions negotiated with other countries override this in practice and treat a dual resident company as if it were not UK-resident.

A company that was incorporated overseas may still be regarded as resident in the UK on the basis that its central management and control is exercised in the UK. Questions relating to a foreign incorporated company's residence status are usually determined by reference to the guidelines set out in SP1/90 dated 9 January 1990.

26.2 SELF-ASSESSMENT

(TA 1988, ss 8 and 10; FA 1989, s 102; FA 1990, ss 91-103 and Scheds 15-17)

Self-assessment applies to all companies with accounting periods ending on or after 1 July 1999. This is a similar system to that which was already in operation for individuals and trustees.

Where a 'large' company (as defined in 26.4.5) has taxable profits for such an accounting period, and it also had such profits in the preceding year, it must make four payments on account of its expected corporation tax liability for the year.

Self-assessment for companies brings with it extensive record-keeping obligations.

A copy of the relevant manual, *A Guide to Corporation Tax Self-assessment* (CTSA/BK2), can be obtained from the Revenue.

26.3 HOW 'PROFITS' ARE DEFINED

26.3.1 Computation of profits

(TA 1988, s 6)

The income and chargeable gains of a company, collectively termed 'chargeable profits', are chargeable to corporation tax. The computation of chargeable profits can be a very complex process bearing in mind the detailed tax legislation and extensive case-law. There are also myriad Revenue statements of practice, press releases and extra-statutory concessions that may need to be borne in mind when calculating chargeable profits on which corporation tax is payable.

The general principles of profit adjustment closely follow the rules for income tax, and the assessment of income under the various schedules is computed on an actual or arising basis.

26.3.2 Special computational rules for companies

Rental income

All income from UK rental activities is now treated as arising from one source and taxed along the same lines as trading profits taxable under Schedule D Case I. Any losses are relieved first against other income and gains of the same period, and any excess is available for carrying forward against all future income, or may be surrendered as group relief (subject to certain restrictions).

Forex transactions

Special rules apply for foreign exchange profits and losses; professional advice should be taken if the company has significant foreign assets or borrowings in foreign currency.

Loan relationships

Specific rules govern the treatment of loan relationships such as gilts and other fixed-interest investments in relation to accounting periods ending after 31 March 1996. Basically, any profits on disposal of such assets are taxed as income and any losses are allowed against the company's income. It is necessary to revalue gilts and fixed interest investments at the end of each accounting period. Any increase compared with the market value at the start of the period (or the date of acquisition where the gilt, etc was acquired during the course of the year) is taxable income; any reduction in value is an allowable loss. See 26.5.

Capital allowances

(CAA 1990, s 144)

Although depreciation is not regarded as an allowable expense for tax purposes, tax relief is given for expenditure on qualifying capital assets by means of capital allowances. The principles follow very closely those that apply to individuals (see 5.5) and therefore the main provisions are not covered in detail here. Capital allowances for a trade carried on by a company are regarded as trading expenses for the accounting period in which they arise. They are therefore taken into account in arriving at the chargeable profits or overall tax loss for the accounting period.

Capital allowances for non-trading activities are primarily deductible from the income arising from that source. Any surplus allowances may be carried forward against similar source income arising in later accounting periods or deducted from overall chargeable profits for the accounting period in which they arise.

Contributions to Employee Benefit Trusts

Contributions made on or after 27 November 2002 attract tax relief only if an employee receives sums within nine months of the company's year end on which PAYE and NIC are charged. If this condition is not satisfied, the company receives a deduction only for the accounting period in which sums are paid out.

Employee options

A company may secure a corporation tax deduction for accounting periods commencing after 31 December 2002 if an employee exercises an option over ordinary share capital. Where the company is a subsidiary, the shares must be shares in the parent company or the employee must be employed by the subsidiary.

The amount of the deduction is the amount which is taxed as employment income or which would be so taxed if the option were not an approved option.

Intangible assets

The tax treatment for expenditure on and gains from the sale of intangible assets was introduced by FA 2002. See 26.6.

Annual payments

(TA 1988, s 338)

Certain annual payments (termed 'charges on income') are deductible from a company's profits in arriving at the amount assessable to corporation tax. Examples of such annual payments are annuity and Gift Aid payments. The basic principle is that these charges on income are offset against the payer's total profits, not merely against a particular source of income with which the payment is connected.

A payment counts as a charge on income only if the following conditions are met:

(1) It has been made out of the company's profits brought into charge to corporation tax.
(2) It is made under a liability incurred for a 'valuable and sufficient consideration' (or the payment is a covenanted donation to charity).
(3) The payment must not be one charged to capital or one not ultimately borne by the company.
(4) It must not be in the nature of a dividend or distribution made by the company.

The basic rule is that payment must actually be made in the accounting period for it to count as a charge for that period. In certain restricted circumstances, some companies that are owned by charities are able to treat Gift Aid payments made within nine months of their year end as if they had been paid during the year.

Where the total profits for an accounting period are insufficient to absorb charges on income, excess charges in respect of payments made wholly and exclusively for the purposes of the company's trade may be carried forward and utilised against its future trading income. Non-trade charges may not be carried forward in this manner and no further relief is available.

26.4 ACCOUNTING PERIODS, RATES AND PAYMENT OF TAX

26.4.1 Accounting periods for tax purposes

(TA 1988, s 12)

Companies pay corporation tax by reference to their accounting periods and the chargeable profit included is assessed on an actual or accruals basis. Accounting periods may straddle two financial years (which for corporation tax purposes run from 1 April to 31 March and are named after the year in which it begins). If this is the case, the chargeable profits are apportioned on a time basis for the purposes of determining the rate of tax to apply to the overall profit.

An accounting period begins for corporation tax purposes when:

(1) the company comes within the charge to corporation tax either by becoming UK-resident or acquiring a source of income; or
(2) the company's previous accounting period ends without the company ceasing to be within the charge to corporation tax.

An accounting period runs on for a maximum of 12 months from its commencement. It will end earlier if the company's own accounting date falls within the 12 months and it will also end if the company:

(a) ceases to trade;
(b) begins or ceases to be UK-resident; or
(c) ceases to be within the charge to corporation tax altogether.

Where accounts are made up for a period of more than 12 months, the income is usually apportioned on a time basis to the relevant accounting period. Where a more appropriate basis of apportionment is available, the Inspector may apply that basis instead (see *Marshall Hus & Partners Ltd v Bolton* [1981] STC 18). In some instances, the accounts year end may vary slightly for commercial reasons (eg where accounts are made up to the last Friday of a specified month). Provided the variation is not more than four days from the 'mean' date it is normally acceptable to treat each period of account as if it were a 12-month accounting period ending on the mean date.

26.4.2 Corporation tax rate

(TA 1988, s 6)

The corporation tax rate is fixed for each financial year, which for these purposes starts on 1 April. The rate for the financial year 2002 (ie 1 April 2002 to 31 March 2003) is 30%. Profits include both income and capital gains.

26.4.3 Small companies rates and associated companies

(TA 1988, s 13)

A reduced corporation tax rate (known as the 'small companies rate') applies to a company's profits that do not exceed a minimum level. The rate for the financial years 2000 and 2001 was 20% and the profit level below which the small companies rate applied was £300,000. This rate and limit applied from 1994 until 2001. The rate was reduced to 19% for the financial year 2002 (ie 1 April 2002 to 31 March 2003).

Where profits exceed the maximum profit limit for small companies rate purposes, an element of marginal relief is given for profits between £300,000 and £1.5m. This relief operates on a tapered basis by charging the profits to the full corporation tax rate but gives an element of credit for the reduced corporation tax rate that would have been applicable to the initial tranche of profit.

The profit limits applicable to small companies relief are restricted, based on the existence of any 'associated' companies that the company has during the accounting period concerned. A company is an associated company of another if they are under common control or one has control of the other. 'Control' for this purpose is defined as the ability to exercise direct or indirect control over the company's affairs and in particular:

(1) the possession or entitlement to acquire more than 50% of the share capital or voting rights in the company;
(2) entitlement to receive the greater part of income distributed among the shareholders;
(3) entitlement to receive the greater part of the company's assets in the event of a winding-up.

For example, if a company has one associated company, the small companies profit limits are divided by two, ie one plus the number of associated companies. An associated company that has not carried on any trade or business at any time during the accounting period concerned is disregarded. Where a company's accounting period straddles more than one financial year and the marginal relief limits for each financial year differ, the 12-month period is treated as separate accounting periods for the purpose of calculating marginal relief.

26.4.4 Special rate for very small companies

A 10% rate was introduced with effect from 1 April 2000. This rate applied to taxable profits of up to £10,000, and companies with profits of between £10,000 and £50,000 were subject to an effective marginal rate of tax of 22.5%, so that the overall rate for a small company (a company with taxable profits of less than £300,000) did not exceed 20%. For example, a taxable profit of £25,000 would give rise to a corporation tax charge of £5,000 for 1999 (20%), but this would be only £4,375 for 2000 on the same level of profit.

The following table demonstrates how the starting rate worked for companies with profits between £5,000 and £50,000:

Total taxable profits £	*Years 2000 and 2001 corporation tax payable* £
5,000	500
10,000	1,000
15,000	2,125
20,000	3,250
25,000	4,375
30,000	5,500
35,000	6,625
40,000	7,750
45,000	8,875
50,000	10,000

The £10,000 and £50,000 limits were subject to reduction if they were associated companies.

The 2002 Budget changed the starting rate from 10% to nil and the effective marginal rate for profits between £10,000 and £50,000 to 23.75%. This means that tax is now payable as follows:

Total taxable profits £	*Corporation tax payable* £
10,000	Nil
15,000	1,187.50
20,000	2,375.00
25,000	3,562.50
30,000	4,750.00
35,000	5,937.50
40,000	7,125.00
45,000	8,312.50
50,000	9,500.00

26.4.5 Payment of tax

(TA 1988, s 10)

Corporation tax automatically becomes due and payable nine months and one day from the end of the accounting period. Since 1 July 1999 large companies must pay corporation tax by instalments. For these purposes, a 'large' company is one that has taxable profits of over £10m in the year, or profits of £1.5m divided by the number of associated companies, for the year and the preceding year. The instalment payments commence 14 days after the first six months of the year in question, and are due in four equal quarterly instalments. A company with a year end of 31 December will pay on 14 July, 14 October, 14 January and 14 April.

There are transitional rules where the company pays 60% of the liability due by instalments in Year 1 (ie the first accounting period ending on or after 1 July 1999), with the balance due nine months after the year end. This increases gradually from 60% to 72% in Year 2, 88% in Year 3, and 100% in Year 4.

Interest is charged on any unpaid tax due and is an allowable deduction. Interest is payable to the company on any overpayments; this interest is taxable.

26.5 LOAN RELATIONSHIPS

In broad terms, for all accounting periods ending after 31 March 1996 the tax treatment of profits and losses from loan relationships follows the accounting treatment. The new rules introduced in FA 1996 affect the tax treatment of items such as interest received and paid, premiums and discounts.

26.5.1 Scope of legislation

The legislation applies to all UK-resident companies and UK branches of overseas resident companies. The commencement date for the new regime is the start of a company's first accounting period ending after 31 March 1996 for interest, and 1 April 1996 for gains and losses on debt.

26.5.2 'Loan relationships'

(FA 1996, s 81)

The legislation refers to 'loan relationships' rather than loans, and these can arise where:

(1) a company is a debtor or creditor in respect of a money debt, and this debt arose as a result of a transaction for the lending of money; or
(2) an instrument is issued for the purpose of representing security for, or the rights of a creditor in respect of, a money debt.

Loan relationships therefore include bank loans, director's loans, gilts, inter-company accounts and debentures. Even where a money debt does not fall within the definition (eg trade creditors and debtors), the interest charged on such debts falls within the new regime.

26.5.3 Tax treatment

(FA 1996, s 84)

In general, the income and expenditure is taxed or allowed in the year it is credited or debited to the profit and loss account or, if appropriate, reserves. The company's accounting treatment must comply with an 'authorised accruals' accounting policy. Where a company accounts for debt using normal accounting practice (as set out in FRS4, *Capital Instruments*) this should satisfy the authorised accruals accounting policy.

Banks are also permitted to use an authorised market-to-market basis where a loan relationship is brought into account in each accounting period at the fair value.

26.5.4 Taxation of corporate debt

(FA 1996, ss 82-83)

The tax treatment of corporate debt depends on whether the item arose from the trade. Debits and credits arising in an accounting period from loan relationships entered into for the company's trade purposes are treated as forming part of its trading profits or losses, whereas any debits and credits arising from activities outside the company's trade are aggregated in coming to a profit or loss on non-trading loan relationships.

Where any expenditure or income arises partly from trading and partly from non-trading, it is split on a pro rata basis.

Taxation of non-trading profits and losses

(FA 1996, s 83)

Net profits from non-trading loan relationships are taxed under Schedule D Case III. If there are net losses, these can be relieved in a number of ways, ie by:

(1) offset against the company's profits chargeable to corporation tax for that accounting period; or
(2) surrender as group relief to other group companies; or
(3) carry back against the last three year's profits from non-trading loan relationships, setting off the loss against later years before earlier years; or
(4) carry forward against all profits, other than trading profits, of the next period; or
(5) carry forward against future profits from non-trading loan relationships.

Claims must be made within two years of the accounting period in which the loss arose for (1)-(3), and two years of the next period for (4). No claim is required for losses carried forward under (5).

26.5.5 Connected parties

(FA 1996, s 87)

Special rules apply when the other party to a loan relationship is a connected company. A company and another party are connected for these purposes if they are under the same control, or one controls the other, in that accounting period or in the two years before. A person controls a company by owning the greater part of the shares, voting rights, or other capital giving entitlement to more than one-half of the assets in a winding-up.

The same rules also apply if the other party, or its 'associate', is a 'participator' in the accounting period or was at any time in the two years before. In general participators are shareholders, and associates are relatives, partners or trustees of settlements where a relative or the participator is or was the settlor.

26.5.6 Late interest

(FA 1996, s 87)

If two parties are connected, then interest is only allowable on an accruals basis when paid to a connected party where the recipient is liable to UK corporation tax on the full amount of interest received, or the interest is paid within 12 months of the end of the accounting period. Therefore, if the recipient is an individual, trustee, non-resident company or exempt body such as a charity, the interest must be paid by the anniversary of the accounting period if a deduction is to be obtained.

26.5.7 Bad debts and waivers

(FA 1996, Sched 9)

No tax relief has been available for any bad debts on connected party loan relationships, and conversely no liability to tax arose when a debt is waived. FA 2002 modifies this from 1 October 2002 so that tax relief may be available for bad debts on connected party loan relationships where the debtor company is in liquidation. This aspect of the legislation is extremely technical and specialist advice should be taken where material sums are involved.

26.5.8 Annual charges

(TA 1988, ss 338-339)

Apart from interest, a company may make annual payments in respect of annuities, royalties, covenanted payments, etc that are available for offset as charges on income against the company's chargeable profits on a paid basis.

26.5.9 Income tax deduction at source

Until recently, companies were required to deduct and account to the Revenue for income tax on payments of annual interest and other charges on income, with the exception of annual interest paid to a UK bank. A return form CT61 had to be submitted on a quarterly basis, detailing payments made and computing the income tax payable to the Revenue. In arriving at the income tax liability due, any income tax suffered on income received under deduction of tax could be offset. Where the income tax suffered on income received exceeded the income tax payable on annual charges, the surplus could be carried forward to the next quarterly return. If at the end of the accounting period it had not proved possible to obtain credit against income tax payable, credit could be obtained against the corporation tax liability for the accounting period (and if there was no or insufficient corporation tax liability to offset any income tax credit, a repayment could be obtained from the Revenue).

These rules were substantially changed by FA 2001, with effect from 1 April 2001. There is no longer any requirement for a company paying interest, etc to deduct income tax provided the recipient is a UK-resident company.

A company is still required to deduct tax where the recipient is an individual or a non-resident company.

26.6 INTANGIBLE ASSETS

A new tax regime for intangible assets applies with effect from 1 April 2002 and is designed to achieve the following:

- Provide tax relief to companies for the cost of acquired intangibles;
- Give relief in line with the amortisation in the company's accounts;
- Treat related sales receipts as taxable income but allow for roll-over relief where the proceeds are reinvested in new intangibles;
- Provide transitional provisions that preserve the existing regime for intangibles held currently.

The legislation applies to intangible fixed assets as recognised under generally accepted accounting principles. It is specifically stated to apply to goodwill and intellectual property, which includes patents, trademarks, registered designs, copyright and design right; licensing and similar rights are also included.

Assets representing rights over real property, tangible moveable property, oil licences and financial assets are among the several categories of intangibles specifically excluded from the new regime.

26.6.1 Key concepts

The structure of the legislation is similar to that relating to corporate debt in that it identifies tax-effective accounting debits and credits in respect of expenditure incurred after 31 March 2002 on intangible fixed assets.

Debits that attract tax relief for expenditure and losses include all expenditure on an intangible fixed asset charged to the profit and loss account. This includes the amortisation of capitalised costs (or, at the taxpayer's option, 4% annually of that cost) and even abortive expenditure of realisation of an intangible fixed asset. A loss on the sale of such an asset (compared against its tax written-down value) also qualifies for relief.

Taxable credits include all receipts in respect of intangible fixed assets credited to the profit and loss account, gains over the tax written down value on disposal of the asset and the total proceeds of realisation of intangible fixed assets not carried on the balance sheet. Any 'negative' goodwill arising on the acquisition of a business that is recognised in the profit and loss account is also taxable.

26.6.2 How debits and credits are given effect

Debits and credits are brought into account for corporation tax purposes as follows:

(1) Assets held for the purposes of a trade – treated as a trading expense or receipt.
(2) Assets held for the purposes of a property business – treated as an expense or receipt of the business.
(3) Any other assets – the debits and credits are described as giving rise to non-trading losses and gains and aggregated. Credits are taxed while debits may be relieved against total profits, carried forward or surrendered as group relief.

26.6.3 Roll-over relief

Where the proceeds of the realisation of a chargeable intangible fixed asset are reinvested in whole or in part in the purchase of other intangible fixed assets, the legislation provides for a form of roll-over relief. Entitlement to relief is subject to certain conditions being met. The amount of the relief is calculated as follows:

(1) If the expenditure on new assets exceeds the proceeds of old assets, relief is the excess of proceeds over the cost of the old asset.
(2) If the expenditure on new assets is less than the proceeds of old assets, relief is the excess of expenditure over the cost of the old asset.

Roll-over relief in respect of goodwill held on 31 March 2002 will be available under the new regime. In all other respects, intangibles held on 31 March are excluded from these provisions.

26.7 COMPANIES' CAPITAL GAINS

26.7.1 Computation of gains

Capital gains made by companies are included in their chargeable profits and are subject to corporation tax. CGT therefore does not apply to companies, although chargeable gains and losses are computed in accordance with the detailed provisions of CGT. The main differences between CGT and corporation tax on chargeable gains for companies are, first, that provisions that clearly apply only to individuals (eg annual exemption) have no application as far as companies are concerned and, secondly, that computations of chargeable gains are prepared on an accounting period basis rather than by income tax years of assessment. Furthermore, taper relief does not apply to companies, but they remain entitled to indexation allowance on increases in the RPI after 31 March 1998. The total chargeable gains for an accounting period less a deduction for allowable losses are brought into charge to corporation tax in the same way as any other source of income.

Capital losses can only be offset against chargeable gains; they cannot be offset against trading or other income. However, it is possible for a company that realises a loss after 31 March 2000 to surrender its loss to another group company for it to offset against its chargeable gains.

26.7.2 Roll-over relief

(TCGA 1992, ss 152-158 and 175)

Roll-over relief is available where the proceeds on the disposal of a qualifying asset are reinvested in further qualifying assets. It operates as a deferral of the corporation tax liability arising on the chargeable gain if the proceeds are fully reinvested in qualifying assets within 12 months before and three years after the date of disposal.

Where the proceeds are only partly reinvested, a proportion of the gain is deferred or 'rolled over' and the balance (equivalent to the amount of proceeds not reinvested) is brought into charge. The element of gain deferred or rolled over is deducted from the new asset's base cost for capital gains purposes. This operates to increase the potential gain on the eventual sale of the new asset acquired, hence the term 'roll-over relief'.

Qualifying assets for this purpose are freehold and leasehold land and buildings, ships, aircraft and hovercraft, fixed plant and machinery, satellite space stations and spacecraft. Expenditure on an asset acquired from a group company (see 26.11) does not rank as qualifying expenditure for roll-over relief.

26.7.3 Disposals of substantial shareholdings

With effect from 1 April 2002, a gain accruing to a company on the disposal of a substantial shareholding in another company is not taxable provided certain conditions are met. The exemption also applies to a disposal of an asset that derives its value from a substantial shareholding, including put or call options in the shares, securities that carry rights to acquire or dispose of the shares and interests in such securities.

A 'substantial shareholding' is one where the investing company is beneficially entitled to not less than 10% of:

- the ordinary share capital; and
- the profits available for distribution to equity holders of the company; and
- the assets available for distribution to equity holders of the company on a winding-up.

In order to qualify for this relief, there are a number of tests that must have been met for different specified periods within the two years prior to the disposal:

(1) The 'investing company' must have been a trading company or a member of a trading group. For this purpose, a 'group' refers to a capital gains group but with a 51% ownership requirement. Non-trading activities must not be a substantial part of the vendor company/group's business, for this purpose a group company carrying on activities which contribute to the trade of another member of the group qualify. 'Substantial' is taken to be 20% or more.

(2) The company that has been invested in must have been a qualifying trading company. In practice this means that less than 20% of its assets consist of investments.

Note that this exemption can apply to disposals of shares in foreign trading companies.

In the same way that gains are exempt, losses are not normally be available for offset against other chargeable gains.

See the flow charts overleaf (Figure 26.1) on the key conditions which need to be satisfied. However, this relief has complex provisions and professional advice should be taken. See December 2002 *Tax Bulletin* for guidance.

26.8 DIVIDENDS

(TA 1988, ss 238-241)

26.8.1 Taxation of company distributions

Company distributions are defined as any dividends, and any other distribution out of the company's assets, paid by a company in respect of shares in

Figure 26.1 – Exemption for disposals of substantial shareholdings

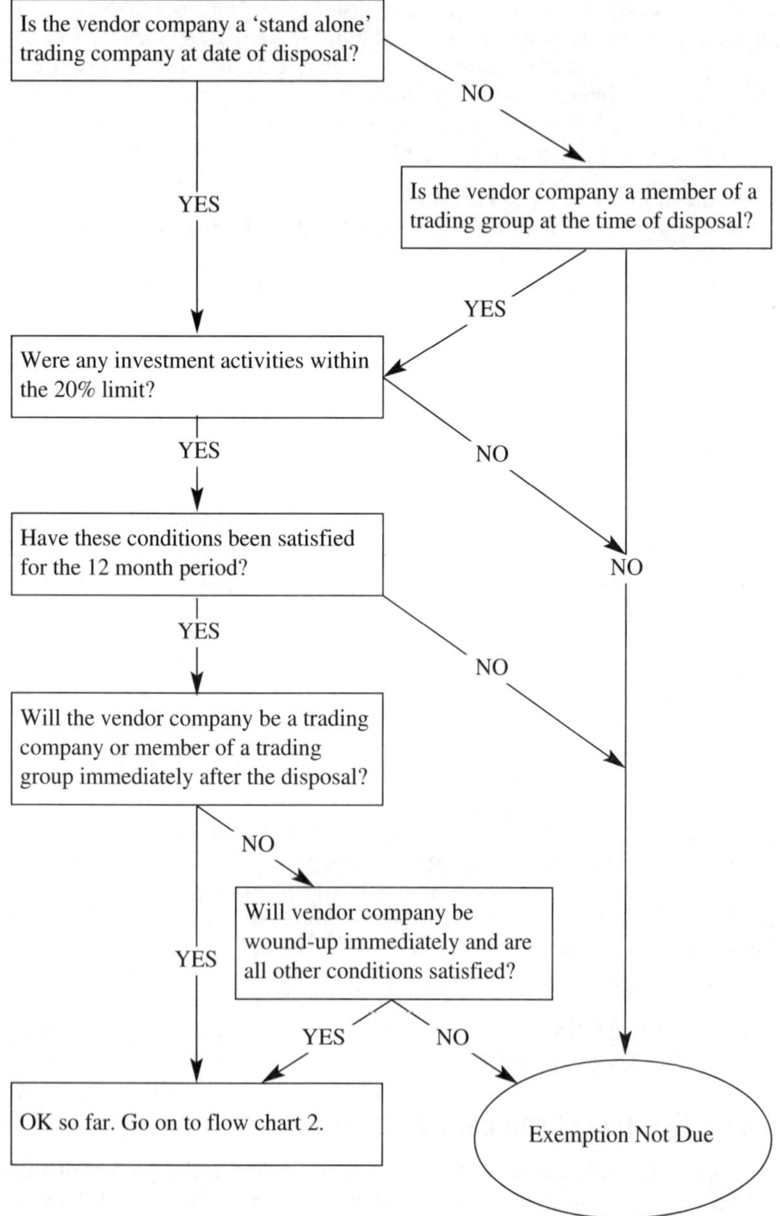

Conditions regarding the shares which are being sold

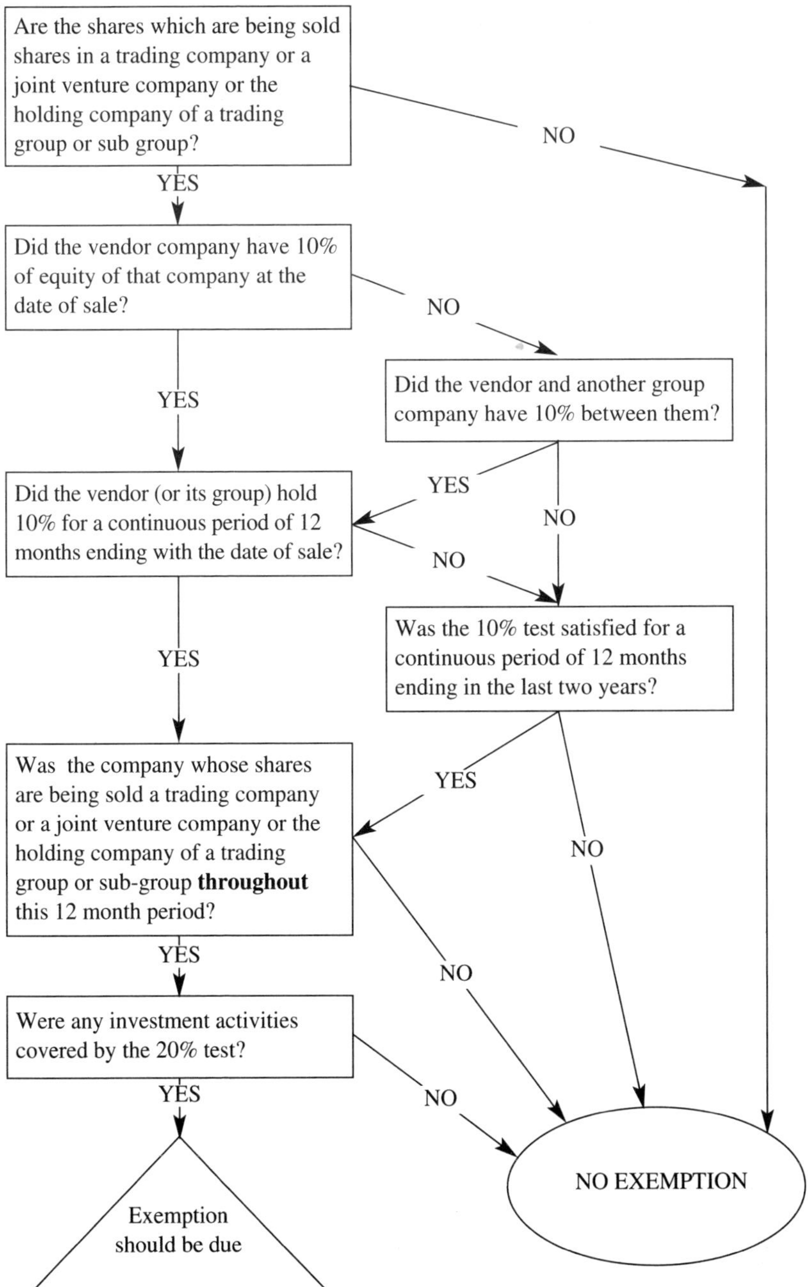

the company. The main exception to this is that any repayment of share capital is not regarded as a distribution of assets.

UK recipients of the distribution are entitled to a tax credit. This aggregate amount is described as a 'franked' payment and, as far as individuals are concerned, represents the gross equivalent of the dividend received. This amount is taxable income, but the shareholder may set the tax credit against his tax liability on the 'grossed-up' amount.

Dividends received by a company from another UK company are termed 'franked investment income'. This income is regarded as having already borne tax and does not form part of the chargeable profits of a company; it is therefore non-taxable.

26.8.2 Advance corporation tax (abolished from 6 April 1999)

(TA 1988, s 238)

Until 5 April 1999, a liability to account for ACT arose when a company made a qualifying distribution to its shareholders. The rate was $^{20}/_{80}$ of the dividend, ie 20% of the 'grossed up' amount. As its name suggests, ACT was treated as an advance payment of corporation tax and relief was obtained by deduction from the mainstream corporation tax liability payable on the profits for the accounting period in which the distribution had been made.

The collection of ACT on dividends and other distributions made by a company was undertaken on Revenue form CT61. The company was required to submit this return on a quarterly basis to the Revenue in respect of the ACT liability arising on dividends and other distributions made during the three-month period. ACT was then payable 14 days after the end of the quarterly period concerned.

ACT was abolished with effect from 6 April 1999.

26.8.3 Relief for payment of ACT

(TA 1988, s 239)

The maximum relief against mainstream corporation tax for ACT paid on distributions made in an accounting period was equivalent to the ACT that would have been due on a franked payment equal to the profits chargeable to corporation tax (ie 20% of the taxable profits). Where the ACT exceeded this maximum, relief could be obtained in the following ways:

(1) It could be carried back to accounting periods beginning in the six years preceding the accounting period in which the surplus ACT arose, taking later years before earlier years. A claim had to be lodged within two years of the end of the accounting period in which the surplus ACT arose.

(2) It could be carried forward and treated as ACT payable for the next accounting period. If it could not be utilised in the next accounting period, it was treated as surplus ACT in the following accounting period

and carried forward indefinitely until utilised (see below for accounting periods ending after 5 April 1999).

(3) It could be surrendered to a 51% subsidiary company resident in the UK. It was then treated as ACT paid by the subsidiary (see 26.11.3). A claim to surrender ACT had to be made within six years of the end of the accounting period in which the ACT was paid and required the consent of the subsidiary or subsidiaries concerned.

Even after the abolition of ACT on 6 April 1999, surplus ACT remains available for relief. However, the company will have to calculate the ACT that would have been due on any distributions after 5 April 1999. This fictitious ACT is referred to as 'shadow ACT'.

26.8.4 Shadow ACT

Shadow ACT is not actually payable to the Revenue, but merely serves as a method to calculate the extent to which surplus ACT can be offset against future corporation tax liabilities.

The Shadow ACT position has to be computed for each accounting period ending on or after 6 April 1999 as if ACT were still payable on dividends and the Shadow ACT were then set against mainstream corporation tax according to the rules covered in 26.8.2.

Shadow ACT is relieved in priority to surplus ACT brought forward from before 6 April 1999. Where there is spare capacity (ie where the Shadow ACT does not amount to the maximum that may be offset against mainstream corporation tax), surplus ACT brought forward from before 6 April 1999 will be set against the company's mainstream corporation tax.

Any unrelieved Shadow ACT will be carried forward and must be 'utilised' before actual unrelieved ACT. Surplus Shadow ACT also must be relieved in priority to any surplus ACT in any other group companies (parent or subsidiary).

Some companies may abandon the struggle and simply accept that they will never access unrelieved ACT. If they take this line they will not be required to carry out Shadow ACT calculations.

26.9 LOSSES

26.9.1 Losses arising in accounting period

(TA 1988, s 393)

When a company makes a tax loss in respect of its trading activities for an accounting period, it may claim that the loss arising may be offset against other profits including chargeable gains arising in that accounting period. A tax loss is computed in the same manner as taxable profits, but is restricted to losses arising from trading activities carried out on a commercial basis and with a view to realising profit.

26.9.2 Utilisation of loss relief

There are a number of ways in which a trading loss may be relieved for tax purposes apart from being offset against other profits arising in the accounting period. The loss can be carried forward to offset against trading profits from the same trade arising in succeeding accounting periods. Losses can be carried forward indefinitely in this manner for as long as the company carries on the trading activity that generated the loss. A loss may also be carried back.

Losses incurred after 1 July 1997 can be carried back and offset against profits in the 12 months immediately preceding the accounting period in which the loss was incurred. Losses before 2 July 1997 can be carried back three years. Where a loss is incurred in an accounting period straddling 1 July 1997, it is apportioned accordingly. Normally the apportionment is on a time basis.

The company must have been carrying on the relevant trade in the earlier periods. Partial relief claims are not allowed, and relief is obtained for later years before earlier years. Relief must be obtained for the loss against other profits of the accounting period before computing the balance of the loss available for carry-back.

26.9.3 Capital losses

Capital losses, like capital gains, are computed in accordance with CGT rules, although the net capital gains are subject to corporation tax as part of the overall chargeable profits for the accounting period. Capital losses may be offset against capital gains in computing net chargeable gains, and capital losses that cannot be relieved in this way may be carried forward and offset against gains arising in subsequent accounting periods without limit. The carry-forward of capital losses is not dependent on whether the company continues to carry on its trading activity, and may be offset against gains arising on trade and non-trade assets.

26.9.4 Surplus charges on income

(TA 1988, s 393(9))

Relief for charges on income is generally given as the last of all reliefs other than group relief (see 26.11). It is given against the total profits of the period in which the charges are paid. If profits are insufficient to absorb the charges, the amount of charges paid wholly and exclusively for the purposes of the company's trading activities may be carried forward to the next accounting period and treated as a trading loss to be offset against the company's future trading income. Non-trade charges on income may not be so carried forward and therefore relief will be lost.

26.9.5 Terminal losses

(TA 1988, ss 393A and 394)

A trading loss arising in the accounting period in which the trade ceases may be carried back and offset against profits of the three years ending immediately before the commencement of the final period of trading. Charges on income paid wholly and exclusively for trade purposes are treated as trading expenses for the purpose of computing the terminal loss available for carry-back.

26.9.6 Changes in company ownership

(TA 1988, s 768)

There are anti-avoidance provisions designed to ensure that trading losses carried forward can only be utilised against future trading income from the trading activity that generated the losses. Losses may not be carried forward if:

(1) within any period of three years there is a change in the ownership of the company preceded or followed by a major change in the nature or conduct of the trade carried on by the company; or
(2) there is a change in ownership of the company at any time after the scale of activities in a trade carried on by the company has become small or negligible, and before any considerable revival in the trade.

A 'change in ownership' means a change in more than 50% of the ownership of the ordinary share capital in the company. A 'major change in the nature or conduct of a trade' includes a major change in the type of property dealt in, or the services or facilities provided in, the trade or in customers, outlets or markets. The Revenue issued SP10/91 on some of the factors that are relevant in determining whether there has been a major change in the nature or conduct of a trade or business.
Similar provisions apply for surplus ACT and for excess management expenses brought forward by an investment company.

26.10 DOUBLE TAXATION RELIEF ON FOREIGN INCOME

(TA 1988, ss 788-806)

26.10.1 The main reliefs

A UK-resident company may claim a credit for foreign tax paid on income or capital gains arising from any overseas source. Credit is available against the corporation tax liability payable on the same income or gains. Relief may be due either under the provisions of a double taxation agreement between the UK and the overseas country concerned, or under the general rules for 'unilateral relief' as provided in TA 1988, s 790. Where credit is due under a double taxation agreement, the relevant agreement takes precedence over UK domestic legislation.

For most types of income and gains, the full amount is brought into charge for the purpose of computing the corporation tax liability on chargeable profits for the accounting period. Any overseas tax suffered is then offset by way of credit against the corporation tax liability. The amount of credit available is limited to the corporation tax liability on the source of income or gain that has suffered overseas tax. No relief is due for the excess foreign tax paid.

Further relief may be available for dividends received. In addition to relief for withholding or other taxes suffered on payment of the dividend, relief may also be available for the foreign tax suffered on the profits out of which the dividend has been paid. This is known as 'underlying tax', for which relief is given automatically if the UK-recipient company controls 10% or more of the voting share capital in the overseas company paying the dividend. The dividend taxable in the UK is grossed up at the rate of underlying tax applicable to the profits out of which the dividend has been paid. This, together with any withholding and other taxes suffered on payment of the dividend, can then be offset against the corporation tax liability arising on the grossed up equivalent of the dividend received (subject to the restriction that underlying tax relief cannot exceed the corporation tax liability on the same income).

Where double tax relief would be lost (eg where no corporation tax liability arises for the accounting period) it is possible to obtain relief for overseas tax paid by treating the tax as an expense in computing profits for Schedule D Case I purposes.

26.10.2 Anti-avoidance legislation

The Government has introduced complex anti-avoidance legislation aimed at the use of overseas 'mixer' companies, usually resident in the Netherlands. Until 31 March 2001, the use of a mixer company enabled UK groups to average the rate of tax on dividends from overseas subsidiaries. This meant that if, for example, the Netherlands company received a dividend of £100,000 from a German company that carried credit for 50% German tax and a dividend of £100,000 from another subsidiary that carried a 20% credit, and the Netherlands company then paid a £200,000 dividend to its UK parent company, the UK company was able to claim credit for underlying tax of £97,500, ie

	£
German dividend	100,000
Add underlying tax	100,000
	200,000

Other dividend	100,000
Add underlying tax	25,000
Total income	325,000

The corporation tax payable by the UK parent company of £97,500 (30% of £325,000) was covered by double tax relief.

If the UK company had received the dividends directly rather than via the Netherlands company, its double tax relief credit would have been limited to £85,000: the effect of FA 2000 changes is that this is the position from 1 April 2001 onwards even if the dividends come via an offshore mixer company.

26.10.3 Unremittable income

Where an overseas source of income is taxable on an arising basis but it is not possible to remit the income because of government actions in the overseas territory, it is possible to make a claim to defer the corporation tax liability until such time as sufficient funds are remitted to the UK to satisfy the liability. A claim under these circumstances may be made to the Revenue at any time within six years of the end of the accounting period in which the income arises.

26.11 GROUPS OF COMPANIES

26.11.1 Group relationships

(TA 1988, s 402)

There are special rules that apply to groups of companies. For corporation tax purposes, a group relationship exists between two companies if one company holds not less than 75% of the other's ordinary share capital, or if both companies are 75% subsidiaries of a third company. Before 1 April 2000, such companies had to be UK-resident 75% subsidiaries of a UK-resident parent company, but FA 2000 has now amended the rules to allow UK-resident subsidiaries of non-resident companies to constitute a group for UK tax purposes.

26.11.2 Use of losses

(TA 1988, ss 402-413)

Where one company in a group makes a tax loss for an accounting period, it may 'surrender' that loss to a member of the group for offset against that company's taxable profits. For this purpose, losses available for surrender include charges on income to the extent that they exceed profits chargeable to corporation tax. Where the accounting periods of the surrendering and claimant companies do not coincide, the amount of loss to be surrendered is restricted on a time basis reflecting the length of the accounting periods common to both companies.

For group relief purposes, the requirement for a 75% shareholding relationship is extended so that the company owning the shares must also be beneficially entitled to 75% or more of the profits available for distribution to equity shareholders, and of assets available for distribution in a winding-up.

26.11.3 ACT surrenders

(TA 1988, s 240)

Where a company has paid ACT on a dividend distribution to shareholders prior to 6 April 1999, it may surrender the ACT to a 51% UK-resident subsidiary. The 51% relationship refers to ordinary share capital and the shareholding relationship must subsist throughout the whole of the accounting period during which the dividend was paid. If a surrender of ACT is made, the subsidiary is treated as if it had itself paid both the dividend and the ACT. It may therefore offset the ACT against its own corporation tax liability for that accounting period, or carry it forward to subsequent accounting periods. It is not possible to carry back surrendered ACT, although for the purpose of determining the amount of surplus ACT to be carried forward or back, surrendered ACT is offset against the subsidiary's mainstream corporation tax liability before ACT paid by the subsidiary itself.

26.11.4 Transfers of assets between group companies

(TCGA 1992, ss 171-174)

Where a trading activity is transferred from one group company to another, relief is available under TA 1988, s 343 to ensure that the company transferring the trade does not suffer balancing charges on assets that have qualified for capital allowances. The successor company merely takes over the tax residue for capital allowances purposes relating to those assets. It is also possible to elect under CAA 1990, s 158 that properties may be transferred between group companies at tax written-down value for the purpose of industrial buildings allowances.

Section 343 can also apply where a trade is transferred to another company that is under common control, even though it is not a member of a group.

26.11.5 Capital gains

(TCGA 1992, ss 171 and 175)

For capital gains purposes, chargeable assets may be transferred from one group company to another without tax consequences. Such transfers are treated as if made at a no gain/no loss price and the recipient company will take over the assets' capital gains base cost from the transferor company.

For assets held on 31 March 1982, it is possible for the principal company of a group (normally the holding company) to make an election on behalf of all companies in the group that assets held on 31 March 1982 should be subject to the general rebasing rule for capital gains purposes (see 14.3). Such an election is required within two years of the end of the accounting period in which the first disposal occurs after 5 April 1988 of an asset held on 31 March 1982 by a group company.

For roll-over relief purposes, all the trades carried on by group companies are treated as a single trade and therefore it is possible to roll over a gain made on qualifying assets by one group member against qualifying expenditure incurred by another group member within the appropriate timescale. Roll-over relief is generally available only for trading companies within a group although, concessionally, relief is also available for a property-holding company where the properties are used for trading purposes by the other group members.

TCGA 1992 does not allow losses of one company in a group to be set off against gains of another group company. However, from 1 April 2000 two members of a group may jointly elect that an asset that has been disposed of outside the group by one of them may be treated as if it had been transferred between them immediately before that disposal. Previously the asset had to be actually transferred to the company with the losses.

26.12 INVESTMENT COMPANIES

(TA 1988, ss 75 and 130)

An investment company is any company the business of which consists wholly or mainly of making investments and the principal part of its income arises as a result of that activity. The expenses of managing a UK-resident investment company are deductible in computing its total profits for corporation tax purposes. Where management expenses exceed the company's chargeable income and gains for an accounting period, the surplus may be carried forward and treated as management expenses incurred in the next succeeding accounting period, and may continue to be carried forward until relieved. Surplus management expenses may also be surrendered as group relief from one group company to another. Expenses brought forward from previous periods are not available for surrender as group relief. Unrelieved management expenses of an accounting period may also be offset against surplus franked investment income by a claim under TA 1988, s 242(2), for the purposes of claiming repayment of the tax credit attaching to it.

26.13 CLOSE COMPANIES

(TA 1988, s 13A)

26.13.1 Definition

(TA 1988, ss 414-415)

Companies that are under the control of five or fewer persons, or under the control of their directors, are known as 'close companies'. There are special provisions designed to ensure that such individuals cannot take undue advantage of corporation tax legislation by virtue of their positions of influence over a company's affairs.

A person controls a company if, in fact, he is able to exercise control directly or indirectly over its affairs by owning the greater part of its share capital, voting capital, or other capital giving entitlement to more than half the assets on a winding-up. Shareholders and certain loan creditors in a close company are known as 'participators'.

26.13.2 Loans to participators

(TA 1988, s 419)

Where a close company makes a loan or advances any money to a participator, or an associate of a participator, there is a liability to account for an amount of tax equal to 25% of the loan.

This tax falls due nine months after the end of the company's accounting period in which the loan is made; no tax need be paid if the loan is repaid before the tax falls due. Where the loan is repaid after the tax falls due, the repayment of tax is not due until nine months after the accounting period in which the loan is actually repaid.

Regardless of when the loan was originally made, if it is wholly or partly written off or released, the borrower is treated as receiving, as part of his total income, an amount equal to the amount so written off, grossed up at the lower rate of income tax. While no basic or lower rate tax liability arises, there may be a further liability to higher rate tax.

26.13.3 Close investment-holding companies

(TA 1988, s 13A)

These are close companies carrying on specific investment-holding activities. For this purpose, investment-holding activities do not include carrying on a trade on a commercial basis, property holding, or holding shares in companies carrying on either of these activities.

A close investment-holding company does not qualify for the small companies corporation tax rate.

The Revenue has also been able to restrict repayment of tax credit to shareholders receiving dividends from a close investment-holding company where it appears arrangements have been made for the distribution of profits, the main purpose of which is to enable the individual shareholder to obtain the tax repayment. This is academic from 6 April 1999 now that such credits cannot be reclaimed by individuals.

26.14 CORPORATE VENTURING

Companies that subscribe for new ordinary shares in EIS-type companies (see 11.6) after 31 March 2000 may qualify for tax relief at 20% on the sum invested. This relief is dependent on the shares being retained for three years. The investment may also attract a capital gains deferral so that if the company invests £50,000 it may defer £50,000 of capital gains realised during the preceding three years or the following 12 months. These gains are then brought into charge as and when the company disposes of the shares or if the qualifying conditions are breached within a three-year period.

If all or part of the investment eventually has to be written off, the loss may be set against any of the company's profits for the year in which the loss is realised or the preceding accounting period.

The company in which the investment is made must meet basically the same tests as apply under the EIS (see 11.6), ie its gross assets must not exceed £15m before the investing company subscribes for its shares, nor exceed £16m after that subscription.

The investing company must not have more than 30% of the equity. Furthermore, at least 20% of its shares must be held by individuals.

26.15 RESEARCH AND DEVELOPMENT (R&D) TAX CREDITS

Small and medium-sized companies qualify for 150% relief on sums invested in R&D after 31 March 2000. If the company eventually pays the 30% corporation tax rate, this amounts to relief at an effective rate of 45%.

Furthermore, an SME can surrender its right to relief for a cash sum payable by the Treasury if it does not have sufficient profits to utilise the relief. A company paying corporation tax at the small companies rate can receive a cash sum equal to 24% of the amount invested subject to this not exceeding the amount paid over to the Revenue for PAYE and NICs during the year.

An SME is defined for these purposes as a company with less than 250 employees and turnover not exceeding £25m or a balance sheet total of not more than £17m.

The company must spend at least £10,000 (£25,000 up to 9 April 2003) on R&D to qualify for the increased rate of relief.

FA 2002 introduced credits for companies that are not SMEs. From 1 April 2002, such companies may obtain 125% relief for R&D expenditure.

26.16 CLAIMS AND ELECTIONS

Throughout the Taxes Acts there are various claims for relief from corporation tax that must be lodged with the Revenue and, in practice, are made to the Inspector dealing with the company's affairs. Unless otherwise specified by legislation, claims must be made within six years of the end of the accounting period to which they relate. The most common claims and elections are set out below, together with the time limit by which the claim or election must be made. The Inspector does not generally have discretion to accept claims made after the time limit has expired for a particular claim unless the legislation (or Revenue practice) allows otherwise.

In practice, most claims are normally made in the SA return form CT200.

Claim	*Time limit for submission*	*Reference*
Trading losses carried forward	6 years	TA 1988, s 393
Trading losses offset against other income of accounting period	2 years	TA 1988, s 393A
Trading losses carried back	2 years	TA 1988, s 393A
Terminal loss relief	2 years	TA 1988, s 393A
Disclaimer of capital allowances	2 years	CAA 1990, s 24
Group relief	2 years	TA 1988, s 412
Surrender of ACT	6 years	TA 1988, s 240
Carry back of ACT	2 years	TA 1988, s 239
Roll-over relief	6 years	TCGA 1992, s 152
CGT rebasing at 31 March 1982	2 years after the end of the accounting period in which the first relevant disposal is made after 31 March 1988	TCGA 1992, s 35

Error and mistake relief claims

Relief may be claimed within the normal six-year time limit against any over-assessment to corporation tax because of an error or mistake in, or an omission from, any return or statement. No relief is due where the information was not used to form the basis of an assessment, or where the assessment was made in accordance with practice generally prevailing at the time of issue. An error or mistake claim under TMA 1970, s 33 should be made to the Revenue.

27

SHOULD YOU OPERATE THROUGH A COMPANY?

There is no simple answer to this question. There are both advantages and disadvantages in carrying on business through a limited company rather than operating as an unincorporated business. Some of the considerations arise from commercial rather than tax aspects. Limited liability may be an important consideration, either for the business's proprietors or in order to attract finance from an outside investor. However, the apparent protection given by limited liability is often illusory since banks or other lending institutions normally require personal guarantees from directors for any bank loans made to the company. Furthermore, if limitation of liability is the main concern, you may find that having an LLP (Limited Liability Partnership) gives you the best of both worlds.

This chapter covers:

(1) Tax advantages of having a company.
(2) Possible disadvantages.
(3) Capital gains tax considerations.
(4) Limited liability partnerships.
(5) Transferring existing business to a company or an LLP.

27.1 TAX ADVANTAGES OF HAVING A COMPANY

27.1.1 Lower rate of tax on profits

Having a company means that a lower rate of tax will apply to retained profits. The small companies rate of 19% applies to profits up to £300,000 provided there are no associated companies. If there are associated companies, the threshold at which profits attract tax at either the normal 30% rate or the marginal small companies rate is reduced. If there are no associated companies, the small companies rate can produce a very substantial saving.

Example – Tax saving through incorporation

Unincorporated business	£
Profits	400,000
Tax and NICs (assuming single personal allowance)	158,329
Incorporated business	£
Profits before director's remuneration	400,000
Less: director's remuneration and NICs, say	(150,000)
	250,000
Corporation tax at 19%	47,500
Tax and NICs on director's remuneration	68,095
Total tax and NICs on profits of £400,000	115,595
Annual saving in tax through operating via a company	42,734

Some of this saving might have to be handed back as and when the retained profits are extracted from the company.

27.1.2 Other tax considerations

Timing difference

There is a useful timing difference where a business is carried on through a company in that remuneration can be deducted from the company's profits even though it is not paid (and is not taxable income of the individuals until it is paid). Provided the remuneration is actually paid within nine months of the company's year end, the company is normally entitled to a deduction in arriving at its profits.

Example – Timing of tax payments

If a company draws up accounts to 31 March 2003, it may secure a deduction for director's remuneration of £150,000 even though the remuneration is not paid until 31 December 2003, in which case PAYE does not have to be paid over until 14 January 2004. Contrast this with an unincorporated business where tax needs to be paid on account on 31 January 2003 and on 31 July 2003, with a balancing payment on the following 31 January.

Pension contributions

Another aspect that favours having a company is that it is generally possible for a company to fund pensions for directors at a greater rate than the legislation permits them to make personal pension contributions.

Payment of remuneration may prevent personal allowances going to waste

Where an unincorporated business operates at a loss, and the individuals have no other private income, the benefit of their personal allowances is lost forever. By trading through a company, it is possible to vote remuneration equal to their personal allowances and the remuneration voted in this way will increase the amount of the company's loss that can be carried forward and set against subsequent profits.

Certain reliefs are only available to companies

Companies can qualify for R&D tax credits (see 26.15) and get allowances for expenditure on intangibles (see 26.6). These reliefs are not available to unincorporated businesses.

Small company consideration – a case study

The introduction of the nil per cent corporation tax rate by FA 2002 introduces an interesting tax opportunity for the small sole trader. If in the tax year ended 5 April 2003 the trade has a net trading profit of £20,000 compare the situation for the individual where he operates either as a sole trader or as a company, drawing a salary of £3,900 and drawing the balance of profit as a dividend:

Income	*Sole trader*	*Corporation*
Trading profit	20,000	
Salary		3,900
Dividend		
less		
Corporation tax	Nil	1,187.50
Income tax	3,154.30	Nil
NIC Class 1	1,076.95	Nil
NIC Class 2	104.00	Nil
Net income	15,664.75	

27.2 POSSIBLE DISADVANTAGES

Possible disadvantages of operating through a company include the following:

27.2.1 Extra administration

There are more statutory requirements concerning book-keeping, filing annual accounts, disclosure, etc. An unincorporated business does not normally need to file annual accounts at all, whereas a company must file accounts with Companies House and make an annual return.

27.2.2 IR35 regulations

Some companies may fall foul of the regulations on personal service companies (see 21.3).

27.2.3 Admitting future partners

If profits are retained, this may make it increasingly difficult for individuals who come up through the business to become shareholder directors. For example, if a company has 100 £1 shares in issue and retains profits after tax of £15,000 pa for ten years, each share will be worth £1,500 more at the end of the ten years than at the start of the period. In order for an individual to acquire a 10% shareholding, he must find sufficient finance to purchase shares that reflect this. The problem does not arise in the case of a partnership, since the normal procedure is to allocate past profits to partners' capital accounts and then admit a new partner on the basis that he would share in future profits at a specified percentage.

27.2.4 Tax savings may only be a deferment

The traditional analysis has been that tax generally becomes payable by the shareholders on their share of retained profits, either when they sell their shares and realise a capital gain, or as and when they extract retained profits by taking a dividend. On this analysis, the tax saving on retained profits is often little more than a deferment of tax. However, there can be a true saving following the recent changes in the taxation of capital gains which mean that up to 75% of any gain can be received tax free because of taper relief. The traditional analysis is therefore no longer valid since shareholder directors are generally able to enjoy the full value of the shares on the sale or liquidation of the company.

27.2.5 Increased liability for NICs

A company must pay Class 1 NICs on all amounts paid as remuneration. There is no ceiling such as applies to the employees' own contributions. This can give rise to a substantially increased burden for a company as compared with an unincorporated business. Comparing an unincorporated business owned by four equal partners with a company that has four 25% shareholders (and it is assumed that in both cases the individuals will have income of £75,000 each), the national insurance bill for 2003-04 is as follows:

	Partnership		*Company*
	£		£
Class 2	416	Employees' Class 1 (not-contracted-out)	13,346
Class 4	10,186	Employer's Class 1	36,034
	10,602		49,380

While the benefits payable to employees are better than those received by the self-employed (a larger pension because of SERPS and entitlement to unemployment benefit), the higher NICs costs can be a very expensive way of financing such benefits.

27.2.6 Work in progress

In principle, a professional firm should not include partner time in arriving at the cost of work in progress. This means the figure brought into account should be lower because of this. However, if a business is carried on by a company, time put in by a director should be included when valuing work in progress.

27.2.7 Treatment of wives' earnings

If a wife is a partner in an unincorporated business, it is most rare for the Revenue to dispute the level of profits allocated to her. In this regard, unincorporated businesses are treated more favourably than companies where the Revenue regularly argues that a wife's remuneration is excessive and part of the remuneration should be disallowed in computing profits.

27.3 CAPITAL GAINS TAX CONSIDERATIONS

27.3.1 Potential double charge for capital gains

Where a valuable asset is held within a company, a tax liability may arise at two stages before the shareholders can enjoy the sale proceeds. For example, if a company acquired a property at a cost of £100,000, and five years later it is worth £550,000, there might be a gain for the company (after indexation) of £400,000. The company will pay tax on this capital gain either at the marginal small companies rate or at 30%. If a tax charge at 30% is assumed, the company will have net funds available after paying tax of £330,000, ie

	£
Profits for accounting purposes	450,000
Less: tax on gain (£400,000 at 30%)	120,000
	330,000

If the company is then wound up and the cash distributed to the shareholders, they are likely to have a personal CGT liability on the £330,000. The CGT payable by them could be as much as £132,000 (ie £330,000 at 40%). This latter figure assumes that other assets and retained profits within the company are such that there would have been capital gains for the shareholders in any event, even if the company had not held the property concerned.

However, the traditional analysis is open to question. If the company had paid a dividend to transmit the £330,000 cash to shareholders, their personal liability could not exceed £82,250. Furthermore, taper relief is likely to mean that CGT is paid at less than 40%. If the shares qualify as business assets, the CGT rate may well be only 10%, producing a tax bill of £33,000.

Consequently, while it is not generally good policy to have appreciating assets within a company, the extent of the extra tax payable is not as great as it was in the past. While some additional tax is likely to be payable if an appreciating asset is held within a company, this is not an argument in itself against a business operating through a company. Correctly analysed, the treatment of capital gains within a company is an argument in favour of shareholder directors holding such assets in their personal capacity rather than through a company.

Where shareholder directors own a property used by their trading company, roll-over relief (see 17.3) and business taper relief (see 14.5) should be available. If they need to take a loan to buy the property, they can secure relief on the interest by charging rent. Doing this will not prejudice roll-over and taper reliefs.

27.4 LIMITED LIABILITY PARTNERSHIPS

An alternative that should be borne in mind is to operate through an LLP (see 5.11). These are treated as companies for company law (and for VAT) purposes but are taxed as partnerships. Using an LLP means you can limit your personal liability towards customers, etc while keeping the Schedule D tax treatment that applies to partnerships.

27.5 TRANSFERRING EXISTING BUSINESS TO A COMPANY OR LLP

27.5.1 Transferring to a company

Some care is necessary when transferring a business to ensure that no CGT charge arises. Fortunately there is a special CGT relief intended to cover this (see 17.7). See also Chap. 29 *re* stamp duty. The VAT consequences should also be explored but in most cases the transfer of the business will be treated as a transfer of a going concern.

The timing of the transfer may be important. Bear in mind that if you were carrying on your unincorporated business in 1997-98, transferring it to a company may enable you to utilise your transitional relief (see 5.3.4). If your future Schedule E income is expected to be much lower than your current Schedule D tax, consider applying for a reduction in your payments on account (see 3.1.3).

If you have substantial qualifying loans used to put money into a partnership, you should take advice. But a Revenue concession will cover most situations (see 9.4.4).

27.5.2 Transferring to an LLP

Transferring an existing unincorporated business to an LLP does not normally involve a disposal for CGT purposes or a cessation for Schedule D. Remember to keep your VAT office advised.

28

OUTLINE OF VAT

TIM BUSS

Value added tax was introduced by FA 1972 and became operational on 1 April 1973 when it replaced purchase tax and selective employment tax. In concept, it is a simple tax, although various exclusions from a VAT charge and the European influence have resulted in a simple concept becoming one of the most complicated taxes of all time.

This chapter covers some of the detail of VAT under the following headings:

(1) Introduction.
(2) Legal authorities.
(3) Liability to VAT.
(4) Practical implications.
(5) Anti-avoidance measures.
(6) Special schemes.
(7) Control and enforcement procedures.
(8) Fraud.
(9) Appeals.

28.1 INTRODUCTION

The introduction of VAT was a precondition of the UK's acceptance into the then European Economic Community (EEC) which, as a result of the European Communities Act 1982, became the European Community (EC), now commonly referred to as the European Union (EU). Part of the EU philosophy is the harmonisation of taxing statutes, particularly those that affect cross-border trading activities. For example, customs duty is an EU tax, payable when goods enter the EU and charged at the same rate when or wherever the goods enter the Community.

Once customs duty is paid the goods can move freely between member states without payment of any further duty or being subject to customs' controls. The legislative authority for customs duty is to be found in EC Regulations, which, once agreed by the EC Commission, have immediate direct effect in each member state.

The harmonisation of VAT has been the subject of much discussion by the EC Commission, resulting in the introduction of transitional rules with effect from 1 January 1993 and commonly referred to as The Single Market Legislation. The rules implement a degree of harmonisation on the VAT accounting requirements of the movement of goods between member states. The Commission has proposed a staged work programme to introduce complete harmonisation for EC VAT, and has agreed the system will not take effect until two years after the European Council adopts the measures; the present transitional system will therefore remain for some time.

A number of EC directives are the ultimate legal authority for VAT, and they must be reflected in the national legislation of each member state. To that extent, directives have direct effect. For example, if the national law is not in accordance with a directive and thereby disadvantages the taxpayer, the taxpayer can argue his case, using the directive, in the national court, which must recognise the directive, and with the ultimate right of appeal to the European Court of Justice.

The UK administration of VAT was given to HM Customs & Excise (Customs), which introduced a completely new system of tax enforcement to the majority of businesses and the accounting profession. Customs, which is steeped in the history of duty enforcement, brought with it its practical approach to controlling the taxpayer. For the first time, many businesses and their professional advisers had to justify, face to face with the enforcement agencies (the VAT control officer), what had been declared in the VAT return and the amounts shown in the annual accounts.

In principle, for the majority of businesses VAT is *not* a tax on profits. It is a tax on the consumer that is collected in stages throughout the business chain and, eventually, by the businessperson supplying the consumer, whether that be an individual or a business that is not registered for VAT. If a business fails to charge and account for VAT correctly, it must account for both the VAT and any penalties from its own resources and thereby, by default, VAT becomes a charge on profits. Put simply, the businessperson is a tax collector.

For VAT purposes, the UK consists of England, Scotland, Wales, Northern Ireland and the Isle of Man; the Channel Islands are not included.

28.2 LEGAL AUTHORITIES

No single piece of legislation covers the administration and collection of VAT. The VAT legislation is described briefly below.

28.2.1 The VAT Act 1994 (VATA 1994)

This consolidation Act brought together the VATA 1983 and subsequent Finance Acts amending the original legislation. It deals with the administration of the tax and provides for certain aspects to be dealt with by delegated legislation.

28.2.2 VAT (General) Regulations 1995

This consolidates 60 sets of existing regulations and amendments introduced since 1972. It deals with a wide range of administrative procedures that must be complied with, for example the detail to be shown on tax invoices, the method of recovering VAT when a VAT-registered person is not entitled to a full recovery of VAT paid to its suppliers, and special VAT accounting procedures for particular transactions.

28.2.3 Treasury orders

Certain Treasury orders describe among other things what is or is not chargeable to VAT, and give certain organisations legal authority to recover VAT that would otherwise not be recoverable. Treasury orders are published in the *London Gazette*.

28.2.4 Customs notices and leaflets

Generally, VAT public notices are not part of the law, although certain notices are published pursuant to VATA 1994 and the VAT Regulations 1995 and, thereby, become part of the law. As such they have the same status as Acts of Parliament and are legally binding on the taxpayer. For example, Notice 700 (General Guide) is principally Customs' interpretation of the law, but the section dealing with the maintenance of accounting records is part of the law, as is the Public Notice on the special VAT Retail Schemes (Notice 727).

Customs' leaflets are not strictly part of the law, but certain leaflets explaining the Commissioners' requirements for particular types of transactions are, in practical terms, legally binding. This applies to relatively few of the leaflets, the vast majority being simply the Commissioners' interpretation of the law.

28.2.5 EC directives

All VAT law has its roots in the EC Sixth VAT Directive, which has direct effect in the UK and other EU countries through their respective national laws. A number of other EC directives deal with specific aspects such as that which, on 1 January 1993, introduced VAT harmonisation in the Single Market and others that provide the right to recover VAT incurred in other countries.

28.3 LIABILITY TO VAT

Basically, VAT is chargeable on the supply of any goods and services (for a consideration) in the UK when supplied 'in the course or furtherance of any business'. Supplies made outside the UK are outside the scope of UK VAT. There are complex rules for determining the place of supply, which differ depending on whether the supply is one of goods or services: professional advice should be taken if you are unsure about the place of supply of a transaction.

28.3.1 Business

(VATA 1994, s 94)

'Business' is not defined, but has been widely interpreted to cover all organisations that carry on an activity in a business-like way. This has resulted in a number of organisations that do not consider themselves to be carrying on a business (eg clubs and associations, charities) having to conform with the VAT legislation and, where appropriate, register and account for VAT on their business income. If it can be demonstrated that the activity is purely and simply a hobby, there is no requirement to charge VAT on any resulting income. An employee's services to an employer in return for a salary meets the definition of a supply of services, but the law specifically provides that they are not in the course or furtherance of a business and so are outside the scope of VAT.

Charities

There is no automatic relief from VAT for supplies either to or made by charities. A charity carrying on a business activity must register and account for VAT on its business income the same as any commercial organisation.

Certain supplies to charities are zero rated (see 28.3.2), but these are mainly in the health and welfare area, and new commercial property used wholly for charitable non-business activities, known as 'qualifying buildings'. If a qualifying building is to be used for non-business and business use, the purchase price is apportioned between the standard and zero-rated elements.

Zero rating was extended in FA 2000 to include supplies of advertising when made to charities and all costs incurred in producing the advertising material when supplied with advertising. In addition certain goods used in connection with collecting monetary donations became zero rated by concession from 1 April 2000.

A more generous regime for fundraising by charities was introduced by FA 2000. This allows charities, in certain circumstances, to treat fundraising income as exempt from VAT.

Clubs and associations

(VATA 1994, s 94(2)(a))

Many local clubs and associations, including those formed by local residents, consider they are not carrying on a business, but this is not correct. The law specifically provides that the admission to premises for a consideration and the provision of benefits to members in return for a subscription or other payment is a business activity.

Certain trade and professional organisations consider they either are not in business or qualify for exemption as professional associations, and consequently have no requirement to register for VAT. Yet because they generally provide other benefits that are not within the exemption to their members and, possibly, non-members, they may be liable to register.

Admission to premises

(VATA 1994, s 94(2)(b))

Admitting persons to any premises in return for a payment is a business activity. Anyone carrying on such an activity must register and account for VAT if the income exceeds the registration threshold. To avoid the risk of penalties all clubs, associations and similar organisations should review their activities to ensure they meet their VAT obligations at the correct time.

Under FA 2001, several national museums and galleries granting free admissions are treated in the same way as local authorities and similar organisations covered by VATA 1994, s 34. Thus, these museums and galleries can recover VAT on related costs. The museums and galleries eligible to recover VAT on costs are chosen by the Treasury. Normally free admission is a non-business activity and museums and galleries granting free admission cannot recover VAT on costs.

28.3.2 Supplies

The application of VAT differs depending on whether there is a supply of goods or of services.

A supply of goods is where legal title to the goods is, or is to be, transferred to another person. This includes, for example, the transfer of title in land by means of a freehold sale or a lease exceeding 21 years.

Anything that is not a supply of goods and supplied for a consideration is a supply of services and, therefore, subject to VAT. A charge to VAT arises only where consideration is present, so a free supply of services is outside the scope of VAT. Care is required, because what may appear to be free is not necessarily so in real terms and a hidden VAT liability could arise.

With effect from 1 January 1996, processing work carried out on goods is treated as a supply of services. Prior to that date, processing work was treated as a supply of goods in the UK. The change follows the adoption by all member states of the EC Second Simplification Directive.

It has been agreed that zero rating will still apply to processing services carried out on goods that are themselves zero-rated.

Zero-rated supplies

Zero-rated supplies are exports of goods to places outside the EU (VATA 1994, s 30) and those listed in VATA 1994, Sched 8. There are 16 groups in Sched 8:

(1) Food for human consumption.
(2) Sewerage services and water (but not bottled water).
(3) Books and newspapers, etc.
(4) Talking books and wireless sets for the blind.
(5) Construction and sales of new dwellings.
(6) Approved alteration of listed residential buildings and listed buildings used by charities for non-business purposes.
(7) International services (note that qualifying services were greatly reduced on 1 January 1993).
(8) Transport.
(9) Caravans and houseboats.
(10) Gold.
(11) Bank notes.
(12) Drugs, medicines, aids for the handicapped, etc.
(13) Imports, exports, etc.
(14) Tax-free shops.
(15) Charities (certain supplies to or by charities).
(16) Clothing and footwear (children's and protective).

The VAT liability of supplies can fall into three main headings.

Taxable

These are supplies subject to VAT at either the zero (see above) or the standard (currently 17.5%) rate. Fuel and power supplies are taxable at 5% when supplied for domestic use or for use by a charity otherwise than in the course or furtherance of a business.

FA 2001 introduced a 5% rate on the services of converting certain residential accommodation. Prior to the change on 11 May 2001 the services were subject to VAT at the standard rate. This is to encourage developers to reclaim existing brown field sites.

Exempt

These are supplies that are exempt from VAT by statute, ie those listed in VATA 1994, Sched 9 (see 28.4.5). Exemption and zero-rating must not be confused because the overall effect on a business is totally different. As discussed below, zero-rating gives entitlement to recover VAT on underlying costs whereas exemption does not.

'Outside the scope'

Certain supplies or business activities are outside the scope of VAT. This includes an employee's services to an employer but can also include, on the face of it, an organisation's normal trading activities. For example, the supply of goods situated outside the UK, although part of the UK business activities, is outside the scope of UK VAT. Similarly, with effect from 1 January 1993, certain services either physically performed or to be received outside the UK are deemed to have been supplied outside the UK and so are outside the scope of UK VAT.

Generally, 'outside the scope' activities of an organisation do not permit the recovery of VAT on related costs. The exception to this general principle is where a VAT-registered person supplies goods or services outside the UK that would be subject to VAT if supplied in the UK.

28.3.3 Imports

VAT is normally charged on the importation of goods into the UK from outside the EC. Payment is due at the time of importation, but can be deferred provided approval is obtained. The VAT payable can be recovered as input tax, subject to the normal rules. Security is required for VAT and duty payable in the form of a bank guarantee. With effect from 1 December 2003, the duty deferment scheme will be relaxed. Approved importers will no longer have to provide security for the full amount of VAT and duty deferred.

28.3.4 European Community

The terms 'acquisitions' and 'supplies' replaced 'imports' and 'exports' respectively for transactions with other member states. It is not necessary to make an import declaration on an acquisition of goods from a supplier in another EC country.

Subject to certain conditions (eg showing the customer's VAT number on each invoice), supplies to a customer registered for VAT in another EC country can be zero-rated. VAT is chargeable if the conditions cannot be met on supplies to non-registered customers.

28.3.5 Commercial property

The sale of the freehold of a new commercial property (ie a property less than three years old) is subject to standard rate VAT. The grant of the freehold of old commercial property or the grant of a leasehold interest is exempt from VAT, but the landlord has the right to elect to waive the exemption and charge VAT on the sale or on rental payments, commonly known as 'the option to tax'. The major advantage of making an election is that a landlord can recover VAT on costs relating to an elected property.

The tenant can recover VAT charged on rent provided he is using the property for taxable purposes.

The election is not available for certain supplies where, at the time the interest was granted, there is an intention or expectation that the land will become 'exempt land'. In broad terms, exempt land is land or buildings used wholly or mainly for non-VATable purposes. See further 28.5.6.

28.4 PRACTICAL IMPLICATIONS

The administration of VAT is by a system of VAT registration, the submission of regular VAT returns and control verification visits (known as 'assurance visits') by Customs.

28.4.1 VAT registration

Registration is required where a business or any other organisation makes taxable supplies over a predetermined limit. The limits, which are based on gross turnover, are increased each year, generally in line with inflation.

It is the person who is registered, not the business activity. Once registered, all business activities must be reflected in the VAT accounting records; for example a solicitor VAT-registered as a sole proprietor must also include his farming or writing income in his VAT accounts.

Currently registration is required when one of the following two conditions is satisfied:

(1) When, at the end of any month, the gross taxable turnover during the previous 12 months, on a rolling basis, exceeds £56,000 (£55,000 prior to 10 April 2003). Such a liability must be notified within 30 days and registration is effective from the first of the month following the month in which a liability to notify arose.

    For example, where taxable turnover in the 12 months to 31 May 2003 is, say, £57,000, notification must be made within 30 days and registration is effective from 1 July.

    There is no VAT liability on income received prior to the effective date of registration.

(2) As soon as there are reasonable grounds to believe the value of taxable supplies to be made during the following 30 days will exceed £56,000. Notification has to be made immediately.

Only taxable turnover (ie goods or services liable to VAT at either the zero or standard rate) is taken into consideration when determining a liability to register for VAT. Income that is exempt or outside the scope of VAT is ignored.

Voluntary registration

There is an entitlement to voluntarily register for VAT where the taxable turnover of the business is below the VAT registration limits. This could be an advantage to an expanding or small business as VAT on costs is recoverable and, providing the VAT charge on supplies does not reduce demand for the product, will increase profitability. Businesses based in the UK that do not make any supplies in the UK but make what would be taxable supplies overseas are entitled to register and can thereby recover VAT on UK costs.

VAT groups

Incorporated companies under common control may register as a single unit – a VAT group. All supplies between the companies in the VAT group are disregarded for VAT purposes; ie no VAT or other consequence arises. One company is nominated as the representative member and is responsible for submitting the VAT returns and accounting for VAT on all supplies to or received from persons outside the group. There is a joint and several liability on all companies within a VAT group for any VAT due to Customs.

28.4.2 VAT returns (VAT 100)

Once a business is registered, VAT returns must be submitted on a regular basis. Each VAT-registered person is allocated a three-monthly VAT accounting period, but it is possible to request a particular VAT period (eg to coincide with the business's financial year). It is also possible to request monthly returns if the business regularly recovers VAT from Customs.

Returns must be submitted with full payment by the end of the month following the end of the VAT accounting period. Failure to submit returns and make full payment by the due date is subject to a default surcharge (see 28.7.2).

The VAT chargeable on supplies made during the period (known as 'output tax') must be declared on the VAT return provided automatically each period by Customs. Output tax is due on all tax invoices issued during the period, irrespective of whether they have been paid. Special schemes are available to ease this particular requirement for certain classes of business, as explained in 28.6. In addition, VAT is also due on all monies received for supplies made during the period and for which a tax invoice has not been issued, for example scrap sales, vending machine income, emptying 'phone boxes, staff canteen sales, and certain deductions from salaries for supplies to staff.

For businesses that do not issue tax invoices (eg retailers), VAT is due on the gross taxable income received during the VAT period.

With effect from 1 January 1993, VAT on the value of goods that have been both supplied by other EU VAT-registered persons and received from another EU country must be declared as output tax in Box 2 of the return.

Payments on account

Businesses that normally pay more than £2m annually to Customs must make monthly payments on account with a balancing payment when the three-monthly VAT return is submitted; payments must be by electronic means. Monthly payments on account are 1/24 (before 1 June 1996, 1/12) of the annual VAT liability. Businesses have the option of paying their actual monthly VAT liability instead of the set amount. Unfortunately payments on account are subject to the default surcharge (see 28.7.2) and the seven-day period of grace given to taxpayers who pay their VAT liability by electronic means does not extend to businesses that have to pay on account.

28.4.3 VAT recovery

VAT-registered businesses may offset any VAT paid to suppliers (known as 'input tax') against the output tax declared, subject to the following conditions:

(1) Goods/services have been supplied to and have been, or will be, used by the business to make taxable supplies.
(2) Documentary evidence of the supply received, ie a tax invoice to the business by the supplier, is obtained and retained. If there is no tax invoice or other documentary evidence, the VAT officer will refuse claims for input tax.

However, Customs has discretion and may accept alternative evidence of VAT paid.

Supplies of zero-rated goods or services are taxable supplies with an entitlement to recover VAT on related costs, whereas there is no such entitlement in respect of exempt supplies.

VAT is recoverable on the purchase of a motorcar used wholly for business purposes. Customs interpret 'wholly for business purposes' strictly, and in practice most businesses cannot recover the VAT.

SI No 3222 was amended with effect from 1 March 2000 to allow for the sale of items on which input tax deduction had previously been blocked to be treated as VAT exempt. This follows an ECJ decision against the Italian Government in favour of an appeal made by a taxpayer.

VAT is not recoverable on business entertainment expenses. In addition, VAT on goods or services received by the VAT-registered person and used for either a non-business activity, transactions outside the scope of VAT or private use is not recoverable as input tax. Many people believe that merely because a VAT-registered person pays an invoice, there is an automatic entitlement to recover the VAT shown on it. This belief is not correct and recovery of VAT that is not input tax may give rise to penalties.

The recovery of VAT by businesses that make both taxable and exempt supplies is described in 28.4.5.

Bad debt relief

A claim for bad debt relief may be made for any debt that is more than six months old, whether or not the debtor has gone into formal bankruptcy, liquidation or winding-up. Prior to 1 April 1989 there had to be a formal insolvency before VAT bad debt relief was available. When a claim for such relief relates to a supply made after 26 November 1996, the debtor must repay Customs the VAT previously reclaimed as input tax. The claimant had to notify VAT-registered debtors of his claim within seven days of making it. However, from 1 January 2003 such notification will not be required. Businesses that have not paid for supplies within six months of the due date for payment will have to repay the input tax to Customs.

Once a debt is six months old and providing the VAT has previously been accounted for to Customs, the debt may be written off by being entered in a Refund for Bad Debt Account (ie not written off in the accounting sense, as for corporation tax). The VAT is recovered by including the sum in Box 4 (input tax recovery). Any payment received after the claim has been made is VAT inclusive and the VAT element must be repaid to Customs. VAT bad debt relief is not available for businesses that use either a retail or the cash accounting scheme; such relief is built into the scheme.

28.4.4 Three-year cap

On 18 July 1996, the Treasury announced that claims for refund of overpaid VAT would be limited to a period of three years. Following a consultation process, the measures were introduced in the 1996 Budget. One welcome change from the original announcement is that Customs' power to issue assessments for underdeclared VAT is also limited to the three-year period. However, the 20-year limit remains in cases of fraud. It should be noted that there is currently a legal challenge to the legality of the three-year cap following a decision from the European Court of Justice in the case of *Marks & Spencer*.

28.4.5 Partial exemption

A business that makes both exempt and taxable supplies is known as 'partly exempt' and is generally unable to recover all VAT paid to its suppliers. However, if the VAT on costs relating, directly and indirectly, to the exempt activities (known as 'exempt input tax') is below prescribed limits (known as '*de minimis* limits'), all the VAT is recoverable in full. The current limits are that the exempt input tax must not exceed £625 pm on average and 50% of the total input tax incurred. This means that a business can incur approximately £42,800 pa of costs that relate to its exempt activities without having to restrict its recovery of input tax provided the 50% qualification is not breached. Once the exempt input tax limit is exceeded in any VAT year (the VAT year ends March, April or May depending on the business's VAT return period), all the relevant VAT is irrecoverable, ie the £625 pm is not an automatic entitlement.

There are other minor limits that apply in particular circumstances. The rules are complex and it is advisable to obtain professional advice. Full details may be found in the VAT Regulations 1995 (SI No 2518), regs 99-109 and Customs VAT Notice 706.

VAT-exempt goods and services are listed in VATA 1994, Sched 9. The main headings are:

(1) Land (with a number of exceptions, and see 28.3.2).
(2) Insurance.
(3) Postal services.
(4) Betting, gaming and lotteries.
(5) Finance.
(6) Education (when provided by eligible bodies, which include youth clubs).
(7) Health and welfare.
(8) Burial and cremation.
(9) Trade unions and professional bodies.
(10) Sports competitions, sport and physical education.
(11) Works of art, etc (in limited circumstances).
(12) Fundraising events by charities and other qualifying bodies.
(13) Cultural services.
(14) Supplies of goods where input tax cannot be recovered.
(15) Investment gold.

As the headings are a general description and the rules for exemption can be complex, it is advisable to take professional advice before exempting a particular transaction.

28.5 ANTI-AVOIDANCE MEASURES

A number of anti-avoidance measures are available to Customs. These include the following.

28.5.1 Business splitting

Where a business activity has been divided among a number of legal entities (eg a series of partnerships with a partner common to all) and the reason for splitting the business is to avoid accounting for VAT, Customs may issue a direction informing all the businesses that they are registered as a single unit (see 28.4.1) and that VAT must be accounted for on all taxable income. The direction can only be from a current or future date.

Customs is not obliged to prove the division was for VAT avoidance; it can treat connected businesses as one entity for VAT purposes, whether or not there is genuine commercial reason for the division.

28.5.2 Sales to connected parties

Where a VAT-registered business supplies goods or services at below market value to a connected party that is not entitled to a full recovery of input tax, Customs may direct at any time, during the three years following the supply, that VAT is accounted for on the open market value.

28.5.3 Self supplies, etc

In certain circumstances, an output VAT charge will arise on normal business activities that are not supplies made to third parties, ie a VAT charge arises on business expenditure (usually referred to as 'self supplies'). The value of such supplies is taken into consideration when determining a liability to register for VAT; the more important ones are described below. The reasons behind such a liability are both anti-avoidance and to reduce possible trade distortion.

Stationery

Until 1 June 2002, if an exempt, or partially exempt, business prints its own stationery there is an output VAT liability on the total printing cost (including all overheads). If the in-house printing costs of an otherwise exempt business exceed the VAT registration threshold there is a liability to register and account for VAT on such costs. This measure was abolished on 1 June 2002.

Reverse charges

Certain professional and intellectual services purchased from overseas persons give rise to an output tax liability on the recipient. The services are deemed to be both supplied and received by the UK organisation, ie there is an output tax liability and the VAT may also be recovered under the normal rules (restricted if partially exempt). The services include royalty and/or licence payments; financial, insurance advertising, legal, accountancy and consultancy services; and the hire of staff or equipment.

28.5.4 Transfer of a business

Where the assets of a business are transferred to another person who intends to use them to carry on the same kind of business as the vendor, the transaction is not subject to a VAT charge. However, where a partly exempt VAT group (ie a VAT group that is not entitled to a full recovery of input tax) acquires assets in these circumstances, there is a deemed taxable supply by the VAT group and output tax must be accounted for on its VAT return. The corresponding input tax is restricted by whatever method has been agreed with the local VAT office.

28.5.5 Group registration

Customs can direct, in exceptional circumstances, that VAT be charged on intragroup supplies, which are normally disregarded for VAT purposes. In addition, it can treat an associated company as part of a VAT group retrospectively from a particular date or remove a VAT group member from that group with effect from a particular date.

These powers are used only where to group structure will result in a loss to the Revenue; they are designed to have an effect only in cases involving VAT avoidance. Customs consulted with professional bodies and issued a statement of practice in May 1996. The statement of practice gives examples of proposed structures where the powers will be used.

Customs is also able to remove companies that are no longer eligible and companies presenting a revenue risk from a VAT group.

Overseas companies, which subject to certain conditions had been eligible to be included in VAT groups, no longer qualify unless they have a branch or substantial establishment in the UK.

28.5.6 Election to tax commercial property

The election, or option, to tax the grant of freehold or leasehold interests in commercial property is not available in certain circumstances if the purchaser or tenant does not use the property wholly or mainly for taxable purposes. The Customs' view is that 'wholly or mainly' means more than 80%, although this has not been tested at a VAT Tribunal. This does not apply to leases granted prior to 26 November 1996. This subject is beyond the scope of this book; those entering into property transactions should seek professional advice.

Landlords and vendors of commercial property must enquire about a tenant's or purchaser's legal relationship with the vendor, the financing arrangements and likely use of the property as, if the election is disapplied, this may affect the landlord's or vendor's right to recover VAT on related costs. Indemnity clauses may therefore need to be inserted into leases and agreements.

28.6 SPECIAL SCHEMES

A number of special schemes are either designed to simplify accounting for VAT or reduce the VAT liability.

28.6.1 Flat-rate scheme

A flat-rate scheme for VAT-registered businesses with a turnover not exceeding £100,000 was introduced on 25 April 2002. The turnover threshold was increased on 8 April 2003 to £150,000. A business that elects for the flat-rate scheme will simply account for VAT at a flat rate on turnover rather than on every single transaction. The flat rate percentage applied depends on the trade sector of the business concerned, and is calculated to include relief for input tax. Customs has published full details of the scheme in VAT Notice 733.

28.6.2 Retail schemes

These are special schemes used by retailers, ie businesses that sell, hire or repair goods direct to the general public rather than to other VAT-registered businesses and are in trade classification Groups 24 (Retail Division) and 28 (Miscellaneous Services). Generally it is those who deal direct with the public on a cash basis and who do not normally issue tax invoices.

It was announced in the 1996 Budget that future use of retail schemes would be restricted. Taxpayers are only allowed to use a retail scheme when normal VAT accounting is not possible. Since then the measures have been implemented on an individual basis as part of Customs' normal VAT assurance visit programme.

As retailers normally account for VAT on receipt of payment, retail schemes provide automatic bad debt relief, although with effect from 1 March 1997 retailers must account for VAT on all credit sales at the time of sale.

28.6.3 Second-hand schemes

A number of special second-hand schemes allowed VAT to be charged on the profit, if any, as opposed to the full selling price. Schemes were available for:

(1) Cars.
(2) Motorcycles.
(3) Caravans/motor caravans.
(4) Works of art, antiques and collectors' items.
(5) Boats and outboard motors.
(6) Electronic organs.
(7) Aircraft.
(8) Firearms.
(9) Horses and ponies.
(10) Second-hand goods, works of art, antiques, and collectors' items except precious metals and gemstones.

Special stock recording and records are required.

It has been recognised that dealers in low-value, high-volume goods have difficulty maintaining the detailed records required, so a simplified VAT accounting method, 'Global Accounting', was introduced. Under the system 'eligible businesses' can account for VAT on the difference between total purchases and sales in each tax period rather than on individual items.

28.6.4 Cash accounting

The general principle is that VAT must be accounted for on all tax invoices issued, whether or not the customer/client has paid for the supply. Businesses that cannot use a retail scheme and with a turnover of less than £600,000 pa, excluding VAT, may use the cash accounting scheme, provided certain conditions are satisfied. The conditions are laid down in regulations as described in C&E Notice 731, which in this respect has the force of law. Output VAT is not due until payment has been received but, similarly, input tax on purchases/expenses cannot be recovered until the supplier has been paid and a receipt obtained.

28.6.5 Annual accounting

To avoid having to submit returns quarterly, businesses registered for at least 12 months and with an annual turnover not exceeding £600,000, excluding VAT, may be authorised, in writing, by Customs to use the annual accounting scheme. Nine payments, based on the previous year's VAT liability, are made by direct debit and a final, balancing payment is made with the VAT return at the end of the second month following the allocated VAT year.

Businesses with a turnover below £100,000 pa can make quarterly interim payments of 20% of the previous year's net VAT liability. Where the net tax liability is below £2,000, businesses can choose whether to make interim payments. With effect from 25 April 2002 businesses with a turnover below £100,000 can opt to make nine interim payments with the balance payable with the annual return. The 12-month qualifying period has been removed for such businesses.

28.6.6 Tour operators' margin scheme

This scheme must be used by any VAT-registered business that supplies packaged travel/accommodation services. As the name implies, VAT is accountable on the margin, if any, on the taxable element of the package. Special record keeping and an annual calculation are required.

28.6.7 Agricultural flat-rate scheme

This is a special scheme under which farmers and other agricultural businesses need not register and submit VAT returns in order to recover VAT on overhead expenses, etc. Instead, the farmer charges VAT at a nominal 4% on all his supplies that he retains (in lieu of input tax) The recipient is entitled to recover the charge as input tax under the normal rules. The scheme requires authorisation by Customs and is not applicable to all farmers: farmers who would benefit by more than £3,000 compared to being VAT registered are not entitled to join the scheme.

28.7 CONTROL AND ENFORCEMENT PROCEDURES

28.7.1 VAT visits

Customs officers regularly visit VAT-registered businesses to verify the returns submitted. Their powers are extensive and include the right to see any documents, accounts, etc relating to the business activities, and to inspect (but not search) the business premises. The frequency of visits depends on a number of factors such as business size, types of business activity and compliance history. Visits can range from half a day every few years for smaller business to several weeks a year for multinationals.

Where errors are discovered, the visiting officer will raise an assessment for any VAT previously underdeclared and, where appropriate, impose penalty and interest charges (see 28.7.2). It is therefore advisable to have all assessments independently reviewed. Customs collects over £1,000m by way of additional assessments from approximately 450,000 visits each year, but most visits do not result in assessments being issued. If the accounting records have been well kept and independently reviewed regularly, no problem should arise at the visit.

28.7.2 Penalties

Customs may impose, automatically and arbitrarily, a number of penalty provisions for a failure to comply with the many complex VAT regulations. These were introduced with the view to improving compliance and reducing the amount of VAT outstanding at any one time.

Late registration

(VATA 1994, s 67(1))

Failure to notify and register at the correct time (see 28.4.1) results in Customs imposing a financial penalty. With effect from 1 January 1995, the penalty is a percentage of between 5% and 15% (depending on the length of the delay) of the net tax due between the date notification was required and the actual date of notification.

Late returns
(FA 1994, s 59)

With effect from 1 October 1993, if one payment is submitted late in any 12-month period, Customs notifies the VAT-registered person that payments submitted late during the following 12 months will be subject to a default surcharge. Prior to that date, the business would be notified if two returns or payments were submitted late in any 12 months.

If a payment is submitted late during the 12-month surcharge period, a 2% penalty is imposed and the surcharge period extended for a further 12 months. The surcharge rises for each successive late payment to 5% and by increments of 5% to a maximum of 15%. If payments have been submitted by the due dates for 12 months, the business is removed from the default surcharge regime and the cycle starts again.

The surcharge is waived if it is assessable at the lower rate and below a minimum amount of £200.

Misdeclaration penalty
(FA 1994, s 63)

If a VAT officer discovers an underdeclaration that exceeds specified limits, he will assess a misdeclaration penalty of 15% of the additional VAT assessed. The penalty, which is based on each individual period (ie it is not accumulative), is imposed where the additional VAT assessed exceeds the lesser of:

(1) £1m; and
(2) 30% of the gross amount of tax due for the appropriate return period.

Interest
(VATA 1994, s 74)

An interest charge is imposed on assessments for additional tax issued by VAT visiting officers. The interest rate is the prescribed rate as enacted by Treasury order and is not deductible for income or corporation tax. Customs has stated that interest may not be imposed where there is no overall loss of revenue, for example where a supplier has failed to charge VAT to a customer who would have been entitled to recover the VAT charge. Customs has indicated that each case will be decided on its merits, but that officers have been made aware of the need to consider whether there has been a loss of revenue.

Other penalties

There are a number of other penalty provisions such as failure to maintain or produce records, unauthorised issue of a tax invoice (by non-registered persons), persistent incorrect returns, etc. There are, in fact, over 60 regulatory offences that could give rise to a penalty.

28.8 FRAUD

There are two forms of fraud in VAT law: civil and criminal.

28.8.1 Civil

(FA 1994, s 60)

If, after an investigation, Customs is satisfied there has been an element of dishonesty, it may seek to impose a civil fraud penalty of 100% of the tax involved. If there has been full co-operation by the taxpayer, Customs, or (on appeal) a VAT tribunal, may reduce the penalty by whatever percentage is considered reasonable.

In a civil fraud investigation, Customs has only to prove on a balance of probabilities that a fraud had been committed in order to impose a penalty.

Customs' civil evasion procedures are currently being challenged as a result of the UK enacting the European Convention on Human Rights with effect from October 2000. As a result of this challenge, Customs may be required to alter the way civil evasion cases are investigated and dealt with.

28.8.2 Criminal

(VATA 1994, s 72)

The more serious cases are dealt with under the criminal law with penalties of up to three times the VAT involved, or imprisonment, or both. In these cases Customs must use the criminal rules of evidence, etc and prove beyond reasonable doubt that a fraud has been committed deliberately.

28.9 APPEALS

28.9.1 VAT tribunals

There is a right of appeal to an independent VAT tribunal on a number of matters, including:

(1) Assessments considered to be incorrect or not issued to the Commissioners' best judgement.
(2) Liability rulings by Customs in respect of a specified supply.
(3) Penalties, other than the interest charged for errors, if there is a reasonable excuse for the error. The law does not define 'reasonable excuse' but does state that the insufficiency of funds or the reliance on another is *not* a reasonable excuse.
(4) The amount of the reduction, if any, of a penalty for a civil fraud where the taxpayer considers he has provided full co-operation with the investigating officers.

The details of appeal procedures are outside the scope of this book.

However, the procedure for lodging an appeal to a VAT tribunal (which must be made within 30 days of the notification of appealable decision) is straightforward. It is prudent to obtain professional advice before appealing and it is advisable to be represented at the tribunal hearing, which in many ways resembles a court hearing, although less formal.

A VAT tribunal decision may be appealed to a higher court on a point of law and, in limited circumstances, an appeal may be referred to the ECJ for a ruling.

28.9.2 Departmental reviews

Many disputes are settled by negotiations with Customs by formally requesting a departmental review of the disputed ruling/assessment within the 30-day time limit. This allows discussions to continue without the loss of the right to appeal to an independent VAT tribunal. The departmental review may become compulsory. Taxpayers will not be able to lodge an appeal to a VAT tribunal until a departmental review has been completed. The Commissioners, if requested, usually review an assessment after the 30-day limit has expired and, where appropriate, reduce the amount assessed. In certain circumstances it is also possible to make an application to a VAT tribunal to hear a case that is out of time.

29

STAMP DUTY, STAMP DUTY RESERVE TAX AND STAMP DUTY LAND TAX

DAVID GUBBAY OF DECHERT

It is believed that stamp duty originated in Holland in 1624 as a result of a competition to discover a new form of tax. It appeared in England in 1694 and was originally only intended as a temporary measure.

Throughout its history stamp duty has been imposed in a variety of ways, but is now a tax on certain written instruments that have legal effect. The tax is governed primarily by the Stamp Duties Management Act 1891 and the Stamp Act 1891. These Acts have been amended and supplemented on numerous occasions and some significant changes have been made to stamp duty in the last decade or so.

The tax is administered by the Inland Revenue. The department within the Revenue responsible for stamp duty is known as the Stamp Office. Documents are often submitted by post, but an over-the-counter service is available in a number of cities (Belfast, Birmingham, Bristol, Edinburgh, London and Manchester).

The tax is an extremely important revenue raiser for the Government. In recent years it has raised between 2% and 3% of the total UK tax take and more than the combined total for CGT and IHT. It is also extremely cheap to collect in view of its essentially voluntary nature.

However from 1 December 2003, stamp duty will, broadly, cease to apply to all transactions relating to UK property, and a new tax, to be called stamp duty land tax will apply. Three regimes will then apply: stamp duty in respect of shares and marketable securities and transactions in partnership interests; stamp duty reserve tax, which applies to agreements to transfer shares and marketable securities; and stamp duty land tax which will apply to land transactions. This chapter looks at those three regimes.

(1) General principles.
(2) Documents liable to duty.
(3) Mitigating duty.
(4) Stamp duty reserve tax (SDTR).
(5) Stamp duty land tax (SDLT).

29.1 GENERAL PRINCIPLES

29.1.1 A stamp on instruments

It is of vital importance to understand that stamp duty is a tax on instruments and not a tax on persons or transactions. The duty is evidenced by physically embossing a stamp on the instrument itself. The word 'instrument' has a wide meaning and includes 'every written document upon every sort of material'. Therefore, if a transaction can be effected orally or by a person's actions (eg delivery) there will generally be no charge to stamp duty (as there is nothing upon which a stamp may be fixed).

Stamp duty is only payable on certain instruments, the most significant being 'conveyances or transfers on sale' and leases. (More detail on the types of instrument are set out 29.2.) Therefore, the first step in deciding whether a document should be stamped is to check whether it falls within one of these categories. It is also important to note that the description given to the document on its cover may not always accurately reflect its true nature for stamp duty purposes.

29.1.2 The rate of duty

The rate at which stamp duty is charged is either fixed or 'ad valorem' (literally, 'accordingly to value'). The usual fixed duty is £5 and as a general rule is levied on certain types of instrument where no consideration is provided and/or no change in beneficial ownership is involved. Ad valorem duty is payable upon the consideration set out in the instrument and will be a specified percentage of that consideration.

Conveyance or transfer on sale

Shares and securities

Stamp duty is charged on sales of shares and other marketable securities at 0.5%, rounded up to the next £5. Thus if the consideration for the sale of shares is £8,800, the duty is £45.

Other property

For all other property (principally land and debts up to 1 December 2003) the rates are as follows:

Consideration	*Rate*
Up to £60,000	Nil
£60,001–£250,000	1%
£250,001–£500,000	3%
£500,001 +	4%

Duty is rounded up to the next £5. As the rates are tiered, duty is payable on the entire purchase price at the rate indicated. Thus, if the consideration for the purchase of land is £600,000 plus VAT, the duty is £28,200. Where reduced rates of duty apply the document should contain a certificate of value so that higher duty is not charged. Note that transfers on sale of certain types of property, for example goodwill, patents and other intellectual property and some corporate loan capital are exempt from duty.

From 1 December 2003 stamp duty will be abolished on debts and the benefit of contracts, and stamp duty land tax will apply to transactions in UK property in place of stamp duty.

Leases of real property

Where a premium is charged on the grant of a lease, duty is charged at the rates set out above as for transfers on sale. In addition, if rent is payable under the lease, lease duty is also chargeable on the basis set out below:

Average yearly rent	*Lease duty*
Term less than seven years or indefinite:	
Rent £5,000 or less	Nil
Rent more than £5,000	1%
Term more than seven years but not more than 35 years	2%
Term more than 35 years but not more than 100 years	12%
Term more than 100 years	24%

Note that if a dwelling is let furnished for less than a year and the rent exceeds £5,000, fixed duty of £5 is payable.

Exemption for land in disadvantaged areas

Transfers and lease of non-residential property in certain 'disadvantaged areas' specified in a Treasury list are totally exempt from stamp duty. For residential property this only applies if the value does not exceed £150,000.

29.1.3 Chargeable consideration

Only certain forms of consideration attract stamp duty:

(1) Cash.
(2) The release or assumption of a liability (eg a mortgage on a property).
(3) The issue or transfer of any stock or marketable security.

Thus if one block of shares is exchanged for another, duty is payable on both transfers. The exception to the above is where land is involved: here the restriction on what constitutes consideration does not apply and any property given as consideration for the sale or lease of land will be chargeable consideration. So if two plots of land are exchanged, stamp duty is potentially payable on both transfers (although it is normally possible to structure matters so that duty is only payable on the transfer of the more expensive plot).

29.1.4 Calculating the duty payable

The amount upon which stamp duty is payable is generally the actual consideration for the transaction. Stamp duty is (with the exception of certain transactions in land) stamped upon the consideration payable, and not upon open market value.

Sales and rentals of some commercial property may be subject to VAT. In such cases, stamp duty is charged on the VAT-inclusive sale price, premium and/or rent. Moreover, in certain circumstances the landlord may have the right to add VAT to the rent at a later date, in which case the VAT-inclusive figure must be taken.

Problems can arise where the consideration paid is determined by a formula. If the elements of the formula are determinable as at the date of the instrument but remain to be collated (eg details of the net assets of a company being sold in completion accounts), the Stamp Office will wait for the result of the formula and stamp on the result. If the consideration is unascertainable at the date of the instrument, for example part of the price on the sale of a company is linked to future profits or earnings, the 'contingency principle' operates to determine the consideration. If there is a maximum consideration, the stamp duty will be assessed on that figure. If there is no maximum, but there is a minimum, stamp duty is payable on the minimum. If there is no maximum or minimum, but there is a 'base' figure subject to adjustment, stamp duty is assessed on the 'base' figure. If no figure can be found under these rules, no ad valorem duty is payable. There is an exception to this where the instrument relates to a conveyance of land or the grant of a lease over land. In such cases the stampable consideration will generally be deemed to be the market value of the interest conveyed or leased.

In addition, under changes introduced by FA 2000, where land or buildings are concerned, if the vendor and purchaser are connected (eg companies in the same group) the conveyance or lease may, in certain cases such as a gift or where the consideration is not arm's length, be stampable on the property's market value.

29.1.5 Why stamp an instrument?

Stamp duty is not enforceable directly. Subject to very limited exceptions, there is no obligation to stamp any instrument, and no audit or investigation powers for the Stamp Office to determine if documents have been stamped. Failure to stamp does not of itself reduce the document's legal effect; however, in certain circumstances documents that have not been stamped are treated unfavourably.

It is an offence for an unstamped instrument to be entered into any register located in the UK (eg the Land Registry or a shareholder's register). Thus in practice it is essential to stamp transfers of UK land and UK shares in order to obtain legal title to these assets.

In addition, unstamped documents may not be produced in court as evidence, except in criminal proceedings. Also the Revenue might refuse to recognise the effect of a document unless it has been stamped (eg when claiming capital allowances on assets purchased).

29.1.6 Jurisdiction

Generally, all instruments

(a) executed in the UK,
(b) relating to property situated in the UK, or
(c) relating to any matter or thing done or to be done in any part of the UK

are within the scope of stamp duty. Instruments transferring only assets situated outside the UK (eg non-UK land or shares of an overseas company the register of which is kept outside the UK) are not normally stamped, even if the instrument is executed within the UK. This is because there is nothing in the legislation that would prevent the transfer being recorded in a non-UK located register.

29.1.7 Timing and penalties

If it is to be stamped, an instrument should be stamped as soon after execution as possible. Instruments may be stamped within 30 days of execution without any penalty or interest being incurred. Thereafter stamp duty is payable together with a penalty and interest. The penalty is a price paid for late stamping; it does not indicate any culpability. Stamping more than one year after execution can give rise to a penalty equal to the amount of the duty. Stamping within a year of execution gives rise to a maximum penalty of £300. If stamp duty is paid later than 30 days from execution interest is charged at market rates on the amount of the duty.

While there is no express provision in the Stamp Act, it is generally the purchaser or transferee who takes responsibility for stamping an instrument. This is because it is the transferee who is liable for a penalty in the event that the instrument is stamped late. However, especially in land transactions, the purchaser may seek to negotiate a sharing of the stamp duty cost.

It has been possible to delay the payment of stamp duty in all cases (sometimes indefinitely) without risk of penalty by executing a document offshore. The document could be retained offshore until required in the UK. Payment of the duty was postponed until the document was brought onshore and there were no penalties for late stamping providing the document was stamped within 30 days of its arrival in the UK. However, interest on the unpaid duty will run from the date of execution even if this was offshore. However, FA 2002 has extended the penalty provisions for documents relating to UK land and this change means that a penalty may now arise if such a document is not stamped within 30 days of its being executed even if executed offshore.

29.1.8 Adjudication

It is possible that the instrument will need to be 'adjudicated upon'. This is the process whereby the instrument is sent to the Stamp Office to formally determine the amount of duty (if any) chargeable. Adjudication may be voluntary or compulsory. You may submit a document for adjudication voluntarily if you want to be certain that the right amount of duty has been paid. Compulsory adjudication is required where for example exemption from stamp duty is claimed on transactions between associated companies.

If adjudication is required then the instrument, together with any other necessary documentation (eg the contract or a statutory declaration), needs to be sent to the Stamp Office adjudication section. If the instrument does not require adjudication then generally the document can be taken for stamping 'over the counter' at various Stamp Offices.

29.2 COMMON DOCUMENTS ON WHICH STAMP DUTY IS PAYABLE

29.2.1 Conveyance or transfer on sale

The head of charge most often encountered is that of 'conveyance or transfer on sale'. Instruments typically within this head are stock transfer forms for shares and securities (where the rate is 0.5%), transfers of land, and business asset sales involving the assignments of book debts (where the rate can be as high as 4%).

It is essential to every 'sale' that there should be a purchaser, a vendor, property sold and consideration. Beneficial interest in property must therefore move from one person to another.

Note that certain types of property are exempt from duty. Most common examples are patents and other forms of intellectual property and certain types of company loan capital. The FA 2002 took transfers of goodwill outside the scope of stamp duty with effect from 23 April 2002. Debts, the benefit of contracts and UK land will be removed from the scope of stamp duty from 1 December 2003.

29.2.2 Grant of a lease of real property

Where a lease is granted (as opposed to transferred or assigned, which amounts to a conveyance on sale), ad valorem duty is payable on the rent and any premium. The premium is subject to ad valorem duty at the same rate as a conveyance on sale. Stamp duty is also payable on the average annual rent for the property. The amount of ad valorem duty payable on the rent depends on the length of the lease and the amount of the rent.

Agreements for the grant of a lease of real property are subject to stamp duty as if they were leases. An agreement for lease can, however, be left unstamped until 30 days after the lease is executed without incurring a penalty for late stamping. This means that the agreement can be stamped at the same time as the lease itself. If the terms of the agreement conform to those of the lease, the stamp duty payable on the lease is reduced by the amount payable on the agreement, usually to nil. There should generally be no need for the agreement to be stamped until the lease is executed.

29.2.3 Conveyances not on sale

Instruments falling under this head are stampable with the fixed duty of £5. This head includes transactions where no consideration is paid and conveyances by way of security. Certain instruments are exempt from even the £5 fixed duty. A common example of this is gifts and transfers to nominees.

29.2.4 Agreements for sale

Certain agreements for the sale of assets (as opposed to actual conveyances) are subject to stamp duty as if they were conveyances. The most important of these are agreements for the sale of:

(a) equitable interests in any property;
(b) any property other than (*inter alia*) land, non-UK property, goods, wares or merchandise, marketable securities and ships.

Thus agreements for the sale of debts are *prima facie* liable to stamp duty. The agreements are stampable as if they were actual conveyances. If a conveyance follows the agreement, this will not be stampable in addition unless the consideration exceeds that set out in the agreement.

This is of particular relevance on the sale of a company's business assets. The consideration payable on the sale is apportioned in the business acquisition agreement among the various assets. Stamp duty is only payable on the consideration attaching to the assets in respect of which stamp duty is payable on an agreement for their sale, in particular debts, and not on, for example, loose plant and machinery and stock.

29.3 MITIGATING STAMP DUTY

Various common methods mitigating stamp duty are set out below. In certain cases, especially involving land, specialist advice should be sought as in some cases additional planning can be undertaken to reduce the duty.

29.3.1 Leaving document unstamped

In view of the voluntary nature of stamp duty, the simplest way to avoid paying duty is to leave the document unstamped. If the document is required to be stamped at a later date, interest and penalties will be payable. Since leaving a document unstamped merely defers payment of the duty (although possibly indefinitely), it is preferable to try to ensure at the outset that a statutory exemption or relief applies, or to structure the transaction so that the charge is avoided or reduced. However, where the purchaser wants title to the property to be registered (eg land or shares) he will need to pay the duty in most cases.

29.3.2 Execution abroad

The benefits of executing documents relating to UK land overseas have been eliminated by FA 2002. This provides that penalties may now be levied if such a document is not stamped within 30 days of its execution. However for other documents, for example, for the sale of book debts penalties are still charged only if the document is not stamped within 30 days of its being brought into the UK.

29.3.3 Goods passing by delivery

Title to certain property (eg goods and stock) can pass by delivery, so provided a document of transfer is not executed, stamp duty can be avoided or the rate of duty reduced. A mere agreement for the transfer of goods does not attract duty. This is important in the case of business sales where duty can be reduced by apportioning consideration to, say, stock and loose plant and machinery. This principle can also be applied on the sale of land by apportioning part of the consideration to loose items such as carpets, curtains and appliances. Provided the apportionment of consideration in these cases is reasonable, this cannot be attacked by the Stamp Office.

29.3.4 Oral contracts

As stamp duty is only chargeable on documents, stamp duty may be avoided in certain cases by contracting verbally or by conduct. For example, if a business sale is effected by means of a detailed letter of offer from the vendor to the purchaser and the offer is accepted by the conduct of the purchaser, for example by causing the consideration to be paid to the vendor, then since there is no written 'agreement for sale' there is no duty payable. This is particularly useful where valuable book debts are being transferred. However, duty cannot be avoided to the extent that the oral agreement will be followed by vesting documents that the purchaser will have to stamp (eg for land). This method raises evidential issues and care needs to be taken not to create a memorandum the purposes of which are to record the unwritten contract, since it could constitute a stampable document.

29.3.5 Land: resting on contract

Stamp duty is payable on a conveyance of freehold land but not generally on the contract to convey, even though the contract is sufficient to transfer ownership to the purchaser. Therefore, if vendor and purchaser sign and exchange contracts, but never 'complete' by conveyance, generally no duty is payable and the purchaser can protect his position by registering a caution or notice against the title. The drawback is that, without a stamped conveyance, the purchase cannot be registered at the Land Registry, and this means that this is not normally a practical proposition where the purchaser is raising a mortgage. Furthermore, FA 2002 means that it is no longer possible to avoid stamp duty by resting on contract where the purchase price exceeds £10m as the contract itself will be stampable.

29.3.6 Use of an unlimited company

Stamp duty is payable where a sole trader's or partnership business is incorporated, because the trader or the partnership is treated as having sold the business in exchange for shares in the new company. Where the successor company is a limited company, the company must produce to the Registrar of Companies a properly stamped copy of the contract by which the business was sold to the company. It is therefore necessary to pay stamp duty on the consideration attributable to the debts and certain other assets.

No stamped contract is required where a business is transferred to an unlimited company. It is thus possible to transfer a business to an unlimited company by means of an unstamped contract (which could be signed and kept offshore) and then to re-register that company as a limited company.

29.3.7 Associated company relief

Sales of assets between companies in the same group give rise to stamp duty in the same way as sales between unconnected parties. However, associated company relief is available on intra-group transactions if

(1) one company is the beneficial owner of not less than 75% of the issued ordinary share capital of the other; or
(2) the issued ordinary share capital of both of them is beneficially owned as to not less than 75% by a third company.

In addition, various economic tests (similar to those for corporation tax group relief) requiring an entitlement to 75% of dividends and to assets on a winding-up must be satisfied.

Non-UK companies can satisfy these tests provided they have a share capital. In order to obtain relief the effect of the instrument must be to transfer the beneficial interest in the property. Relief is granted if the necessary conditions exist at the date of execution of the document and is not subject to forfeiture if conditions later change.

Relief will not be available if certain 'offensive' arrangements were present at the time of the transaction. In practice it may be difficult to show these did not apply, in particular if it is proposed to sell the transferee company or the assets transferred to a non-group person.

Furthermore recent changes relating to intra-group transfers of UK land provide that relief is clawed back and stamp duty plus interest payable if the transferee company ceases to be an associated company within three years of the intra-group transfer, even if there were no arrangements for this to happen at the time of the transfer.

29.3.8 Reconstructions and acquisitions

Various statutory 'reconstruction' reliefs are available. In each case the acquiring company must be a UK company and the transaction must be effected for a bona fide commercial purpose and not form part of an arrangement entered into for the purpose of avoiding tax.

A full exemption applies where the whole or part of a company's undertaking (assets or share capital of a subsidiary) is transferred to a company (the acquiring company) in pursuance of a scheme of reconstruction and where the consideration shares are issued to all shareholders of the company.

The consideration must consist of the issue of non-redeemable shares in the acquiring company to the shareholders of the target company and may include nothing other than the assumption or discharge by the acquiring company of the liabilities of the target company.

29.3.9 New holding company exemption

If a UK company acquires the entire issued share capital of another company for a consideration consisting entirely of the issue of shares in the acquiring company, this will not, in certain circumstances, be liable to stamp duty.

29.4 STAMP DUTY RESERVE TAX (SDRT)

Unlike stamp duty, SDRT is a compulsory tax payable when there is an unconditional agreement to transfer chargeable securities for consideration in money or money's worth.

Chargeable securities include UK stocks, shares, loan capital and interests in or options over such securities. Securities in a foreign company kept on a UK register are also included. Any written or oral agreement to transfer these securities gives rise to a charge to SDRT of 0.5% of the consideration (the same rate as stamp duty on share transfers). SDRT thus applies to the UK's paperless system of dealing in UK listed stocks and shares called CREST. But the 0.5% charge is cancelled if a written instrument pursuant to the agreement to transfer the securities is executed and stamped. For instance, if *A* agrees to sell shares to *B*, a charge to SDRT arises, but is cancelled or refunded if (within six years of the date of the agreement) a stock transfer form is executed and stamped.

Sometimes the stamp duty on a sale of shares can be less than the SDRT on the underlying agreement, for example because there is a stamp duty relief that has no SDRT equivalent or because whereas stamp duty is charged only on certain specified forms of consideration (eg cash and shares) SDRT is charged on the amount of consideration given in money or money's worth. In these cases the agreement should be completed by an instrument, such as a stock transfer form or declaration of trust, because the stamped instrument (perhaps attracting an exemption or a small charge) will cancel the (possibly large) charge to SDRT.

29.5 STAMP DUTY LAND TAX (SDLT)

29.5.1 Introduction to SDLT

The Finance Act 2003 will completely replace stamp duty in respect of UK property transactions, with a new tax, stamp duty land tax (SDLT). This is in part to block avoidance techniques which have become common place in respect of large property transactions and in part in preparation for e-conveyancing. Instead of being a voluntary tax on documents SDLT becomes a compulsory tax on all UK property transactions and is chargeable whether or not there is a document, wherever it is executed and wherever the parties are located or resident.

The changes are expected to come into force on 1 December 2003. Note that the Government is consulting further on certain aspects of the new regime and changes may be made in some areas.

29.5.2 Application of SDLT

SDLT will be charged upon the acquisition of any 'chargeable interest' in UK land. Chargeable interest is widely defined and includes not merely freehold and leasehold interests but easements, restrictive covenants and powers over land. The grant of options and pre-emption rights are also caught as are the surrender or release of rights such as the cancellation of restrictive covenants and the surrender of leases as well as the variation of leases.

SDLT must be paid within 30 days of the 'effective date' of the transaction. The effective date will usually be completion, when the transfer is delivered or the lease granted and payment made. However, if a contract is 'substantially performed', which is widely defined as providing a substantial amount of consideration (expected to be around 90% of the purchase price) or entering into 'possession', then SDLT must be paid within 30 days of this date.

29.5.3 SDLT rates

On a sale of a freehold or an existing leasehold interest or where a premium is paid on the grant of a new lease or consideration is paid in respect of any other chargeable interest (apart from lease duty, see 29.5.4 below) the same rates of duty as currently apply to stamp duty will apply to SDLT. Thus where the consideration exceeds £500,000 a rate of 4% will apply. However, for non-residential property no SDLT will be payable if the consideration does not exceed £150,000. (For residential property the exempt amount is still £60,000.)

29.5.4 SDLT on rent

Instead of SDLT being payable on the average annual rent as is currently the case with stamp duty, SDLT will be charged on the net present value of the lease – the total rent payable over the whole term of the lease, discounted by a statutory rate. The formula to calculate net present value is complex although the Revenue have promised an online facility to facilitate calculations.

The SDLT on the rent will be 1% of the net present value. However, for non-residential property there will be a nil rate band where the net present value of the rent does not exceed £150,000 (eg a lease at £20,000 for five years will pay no stamp duty as against £200 now). Although short leases at modest rents may pay less SDLT than they would stamp duty, for many leases of commercial property the new charge will be 4-8 times more than the current lease duty charge (eg a lease for 15 years at £50,000 pa will pay SDLT of £5,758 as compared to stamp duty of £1,000).

Provided the first rent review of the lease is after the end of the second year of the term, then rent post-review is assumed to be the same as the rent in the year preceding the review. If there is a rent review before the end of the second year of the term, then the rent post-review is treated as uncertain and the provisions at 29.5.5 below in respect of unascertainable consideration apply.

29.5.5 Consideration

SDLT is chargeable on the total consideration provided (monetary and non-monetary). This will include the value of services or works provided by the purchaser to the vendor (unless certain exemptions apply) and includes VAT unless the landlord has not elected at the time of the transaction. It includes deferred consideration without any discount for the period of deferral (although in some cases a postponement may be available). Land exchanges will now give rise to an SDLT on both transfers.

Where the consideration is contingent SDLT is payable on the basis that the amount will become payable (or the sums will continue to be payable). Where the consideration is uncertain or unascertained, it is valued at the best current estimate. If the contingency occurs or the uncertainty is resolved, the purchaser/lessee must notify the Inland Revenue if more SDLT would be payable and can claim a refund if SDLT has been overpaid.

29.5.6 Exemptions from SDLT

A number of exemptions which apply to stamp duty have been replicated in the SDLT regime. Thus the exemptions for charities, intra-group transfers, reconstructions and new holding companies are included in the new regime. In addition disadvantaged areas relief (described in paragraph 29.1.2) will apply to SDLT as well. In addition a number of new reliefs will be introduced. These include relief from a double charge to SDLT which could otherwise apply in the context of Islamic financing arrangements and a relief which applies where an employee is required by his employer to relocate.

29.5.7 Compliance obligations

SDLT is a compulsory tax and there are wide ranging requirements relating to filing of SDLT land transaction returns, payment, provision of information and record keeping. Under the new regime it is the purchaser or lessee which is responsible for notifying the Inland Revenue within 30 days of the effective date of a transaction taking place and of paying the SDLT at the same time. The Inland Revenue have substantial powers, similar to those available in respect of income and corporation tax, to enquire into returns, to require the production of documents, to issue assessments for non or underpayment of SDLT and to charge property in the event of non or underpayment of SDLT. Interest and penalties will be charged in the event of late payment of SDLT, and the amount of the penalty can equal the amount of SDLT payable.

29.5.8 Commencement and transitional provision

The SDLT regime will apply to transactions entered into on or after 1 December 2003. There is an exception where the transaction is pursuant to an agreement or contract entered into before the Finance Bill 2003 gets Royal Assent (provided the agreement is not varied or assigned after that date) in which event stamp duty and not SDLT will apply to the lease or transfer whenever it is completed. Additionally, if agreements for lease or contract are exchanged after Royal Assent but complete before 1 December 2003, the current stamp duty regime will also apply.

30

SOME SPECIAL TYPES OF TAXPAYER

This chapter gathers together special tax provisions and Revenue practices that are relevant only to specific occupations. The chapter covers:

(1) Authors.
(2) Barristers.
(3) Doctors.
(4) Dentists.
(5) Farmers.
(6) Lloyd's underwriters ('Names').
(7) Ministers of religion.
(8) Members of Parliament.
(9) Independent financial advisers and insurance agents.
(10) Business economic notes.
(11) US citizens working in the UK.
(12) Australians living in the UK.

30.1 AUTHORS

30.1.1 Averaging profits

FA 2001 introduced provisions that enable authors' profits to be averaged. With effect from 2001-02, authors are allowed to average the profits of two consecutive tax years provided the profits of the lower year are less than 75% of those for the higher year. The averaged amount is then taken as the taxable figure for each year.

30.2 BARRISTERS

Detailed notes on the requirements following FA 1998 for barristers to produce accounts on an earnings basis are available from the General Council of the Bar, 3 Bedford Row, London WC1R 4TB. Bear in mind that barristers' accounts may be produced on the cash basis for the first seven years. (See also 5.4.14.)

Readers might also refer to a Bar Council publication, *Taxation and Retirement Benefits Handbook*, available at www.barcouncil.org.uk.

Among other things, this handbook gives detailed guidance on the amounts to be included in respect of disputed fees and offers the following practical advice for self-assessment:

> **Practical considerations**
>
> If you wish to complete your own returns and want the Inland Revenue to calculate the tax liability you should ensure that you obtain all the necessary information as soon after 5 April as possible. If an accountant will be completing the return on your behalf you should still ensure the information is provided as soon as possible: it is obvious that they will not be helped by receiving information at the eleventh hour.

30.3 DOCTORS

30.3.1 Locum and fixed practice expenses insurance

The Revenue formerly resisted claims for such premiums, but this policy changed on 30 April 1996. The premium should now be treated as an expense in the doctor's accounts. If any claim is made under the policy, the amounts paid out by the insurer are treated as taxable receipts. See *Tax Bulletin* August 1996.

30.3.2 Pension contributions

Doctors engaged as general practitioners (GPs) are actually independent contractors to the NHS but, rather uniquely, GPs are entitled to a pension under the NHS pension scheme as if they were employees. The NHS withholds 6% of GPs' NHS salary as a contribution towards these pension benefits and this is normally treated as an allowable deduction from a GP's earnings.

The strict position is that such contributions are allowed only by virtue of ESC A9. The GP can therefore insist on the legal basis whereby no relief is due in respect of his NHS pension contributions and he can then make contributions under a personal pension policy.

Where a GP renounces relief for his NHS contribution, he can do so in relation only to one particular tax year, ie he does not have to take an irrevocable decision in relation to later years.

As an alternative to making personal pension contributions, a GP can continue to claim relief for his NHS pension contributions and make additional voluntary contributions. These may take the form of the purchase of pension rights for past years (ie added years) or he may make FSAVC payments of up to 6% of his NHS earnings.

30.3.3 Capital gains tax

Many GPs have a surgery that is either attached to or part of their main residence. Where the property is sold, that part of any capital gain that relates to the surgery is not normally covered by the principal private residence exemption. However, it should be possible for the GP to claim roll-over relief (see 17.4) where he purchases another property to be used as a surgery. Also, if the GP is aged 50+ and retiring, the gain relating to the surgery should qualify for retirement relief.

The position is more complex where a GP is aged 50+ and a partner in a practice. If he disposes of his interest in the surgery when he retires, or he takes a material reduction in his share of the profits of the practice, he should qualify for retirement relief provided he has not charged a market rent to the practice.

Note that the notional rent reimbursed by the health authority to the practice as a whole is not rent for these purposes, as it is merely a 'grant' to cover part of the doctor's expenses.

If a capital gain arises on a qualifying business asset for taper relief purposes (see 14.5-14.6), the GP will benefit from the taper relief available for gains on business assets (see 14.5).

30.4 DENTISTS

Relief is due in respect of insurance premiums paid to secure locum cover (see 30.3.1). Self-employed dentists are given tax relief for their contributions to the NHS superannuation scheme contributions by ESC A9, in the same way as doctors (see 30.3.1); they too can renounce relief for these.

30.5 FARMERS

There are a number of tax provisions that are specific to farmers.

30.5.1 All farming a single trade

(TA 1998, s 53)

The legislation specifically provides that all farming activities carried on by an individual within the UK are treated as a single trade. However, where an individual is a sole trader but also a partner in a farming partnership, the two activities are regarded as separate and distinct trades for tax purposes.

30.5.2 What counts as farming income?

There have been cases where the Revenue has argued that profits arising from farm shops form a separate venture and are not part of the farming activity. This depends on the facts and, in particular, on the extent to which the produce sold in the shop is bought in rather than produce of the farm itself.

Where farmers engage in ancillary activities (eg providing B&B accommodation or self-catering facilities for holidaymakers), the Revenue normally regards the resulting profits as forming part of a separate business unless they are relatively modest, in which case they may be included in the profits of the farming business for administrative convenience.

30.5.3 Farmhouse

It was normal practice for many years to claim that one-third of the farmhouse expenses were an allowable expense in computing the farm's Schedule D Case I profits. The Revenue has since moved away from this practice and has emphasised that regard should be had to the actual usage of the farmhouse (see *Tax Bulletin* February 1993).

30.5.4 Valuation of stock

If you are dealing with the accounts of a farming business, the Revenue's booklet BEN 19 is required reading. It is one of a series produced for Revenue staff on 'Business and Economic Notes' to give Inspectors some background on the commercial practice of different industries.

30.5.5 Herd basis

The effect of a herd basis election is that the herd is treated as a fixed asset. The original cost of the herd and any additions are excluded in arriving at the farm's profit for tax purposes. If the whole herd (or a substantial part of it) is disposed of, the proceeds are not treated as a trading receipt. There is a free Revenue booklet IR9, *The Tax Treatment of Livestock – The Herd Basis*. Advice should be sought from an accountant about the mechanics of the herd basis.

30.5.6 Treatment of set-aside payments

Where farmers receive payments under the Government's set-aside scheme, the way such payments are taxed depends on the use to which the land is put. If the farmer allows the land to become fallow, income received under the set-aside scheme is normally treated as farming income. In contrast, where the land that has been set aside is used for non-agricultural purposes, income received under the set-aside scheme is not regarded as farming income, but rather as Schedule A rental income.

30.5.7 Averaging

(TA 1988, s 96)

It is possible for a farmer to make a claim under which his profits of two consecutive years of assessment are averaged. This election cannot be made where the profits of the lower year exceed three-quarters of the other year's profits.

Where the profits of one year are no more than 70% of the other year's profits, the results of the two years are simply averaged. Where the profits of the lower year are between 71% and 75% of the other year, averaging is done as follows:

Take three times the difference between the two years' profits	A
Deduct 75% of the profits for the higher year	B
	C

Take the resulting figure (C) away from the taxable profits for the higher year and add it to the profits for the lower year

30.5.8 Farming losses

Restrictions under TA 1988, s 397 may apply to losses suffered by farmers. The legislation may prevent a farming loss being set against the individual's other income where he has suffered losses for each of the preceding five tax years. This period is extended to 11 years for thoroughbred horse breeders. The only way of avoiding this restriction is to show that no reasonably competent farmer would have expected to have made a profit during the period in question.

The Revenue has published an ESC on s 397. The concession enables a farmer to claim such relief for 2000-01 provided he has not made losses for more than six consecutive years and there was at least one other year of profit in the preceding three tax years. For 2001-02 he may claim relief provided he has not made losses for more than seven consecutive years. See *Tax Bulletin* December 2000.

30.5.9 Capital gains tax

The availability of retirement relief where a partner sells part of his farmland is a difficult and contentious matter. At one time the Revenue's yardstick was that retirement relief would be available if the farmer disposed of more than half of his land, but the position is not now clear cut even here. It is very much an area where a farmer should seek specialist advice. However, with the phasing out of this relief this point becomes less important as the land will normally qualify as a business asset for taper relief purposes.

30.5.10 Foot and mouth

Both the Revenue and Customs & Excise stated that they will take a very sympathetic view with businesses affected by the foot and mouth outbreak. The text of the Revenue's statement on foot and mouth, issued on 10 April 2001, is reproduced below and should be cited by taxpayers where necessary:

> The Inland Revenue have tonight reminded all their offices that interest on tax debts can be waived in cases of extreme hardship. To help streamline decisions on businesses facing extreme hardship as a result of the foot and mouth outbreak, the Revenue has authorised its offices to exercise this discretion themselves. A Revenue spokeswoman said, 'We always do our best to help businesses in trouble through no fault of their own. We recognise the acute problems faced by many businesses as a result of foot and mouth, and it is timely to remind our offices of this discretion. Short-circuiting our usual processes will enable our offices to take decisions quickly, and businesses to know where they stand. We issue penalties automatically when people don't send in their returns on time. But, nobody who is suffering severe personal or financial stress because of the effect of the foot and mouth outbreak on their business will have to pay these penalties provided they send in their returns as soon as they are able.'

The key point is to keep both the Revenue and Customs informed of the difficulties you are experiencing with any filing or payments deadlines to ensure a sympathetic handling of your affairs. A number of specific concessions are set out in a special issue of *Tax Bulletin* May 2001.

30.6 LLOYD'S UNDERWRITERS ('NAMES')

It is beyond the remit of this book to cover the taxation of Underwriters' in any depth, although the following sections act as a general guide.

30.6.1 General principles

An individual who is a Name at Lloyd's is deemed to carry on a trade the profits of which are charged to tax under Schedule D Case I. All underwriting profits (including syndicate and other Lloyd's investment income and syndicate capital appreciation) are now treated as earned income. The Contributions Agency originally took the view that any profits arising to individuals who had previously been regarded as non-working Names were not liable to Class 2 or 4 NICs, but has since revised this view. Thus, Class 2 NICs are payable by all Names with effect from 5 January 1997, and Class 4 NICs from 1997-98, unless they are already paying maximum NICs on other sources of earned income.

There is a time delay in that Lloyd's syndicates make up their accounts only after a period of two years has elapsed. The basis of assessment of individual Names changed for the 1994 and subsequent accounts. The profits will be assessed for the year of assessment in which the results are declared and not for the year in which they arose. Thus, 1999 profits are assessed for 2002-03.

30.6.2 Allowable deductions

A deduction may be claimed for the following personal expenses borne by the Name strictly on a calendar year cash basis:

(1) Premiums for insurance policies (known as 'Personal Stop Loss' policies) paid to minimise a Name's exposure to underwriting losses. The premiums are allowable as a deduction for the calendar year in which they are paid. Any recovery from the insurance company will in turn be treated as additional underwriting income for the year of the loss to which the recovery relates.
(2) The annual cost of maintaining a letter of credit or bank guarantee.
(3) Interest on a loan raised to finance an underwriting loss and on money borrowed to fund the Lloyd's deposit and personal reserves (and Lloyd's expenses).
(4) Personal accountancy fees. The Revenue takes the view that only fees relating to the agreement of income tax assessments or to the earning or calculation of profits for the Name are allowable (and, therefore, those relating to the computation of transfers to the special reserve fund or the submission of loss claims are not). The deduction is on a cash basis.
(5) Premiums paid to an estate protection plan (an insurance arrangement intended to facilitate the winding-up of a Name's estate following death).
(6) Subscriptions to the Association of Lloyd's Members and certain expenses of attending meetings.
(7) Purchase of Lloyd's 'blue book' (annual listing of syndicate members), Chatset tables (Lloyd's league tables) and certain other publications.
(8) Subscriptions to Names' Action Groups (eg Lime Street Action Group).
(9) Central Fund payments, Members Agency fees and commissions and personal run off contract premiums.
(10) Payment for EXEAT policies.

30.6.3 The special reserve fund

(FA 1993, Sched 20)

The purpose of the special reserve fund is to enable Names to set aside some of their Lloyd's income, free of tax, as a reserve against future liabilities. Subject to the rules set out below, the amount transferred (if any) is entirely at the Name's discretion.

Transfers to the special reserve fund

The fund operates as follows:

(1) Transfers into and withdrawals from the fund are made gross rather than net of tax at basic rate.
(2) Payments into the fund are deducted as a trading expense and withdrawals are taxed as trading receipts.
(3) A transfer into the fund is permitted of up to 50% of the profits for an underwriting year provided the fund's value at the end of the year does not exceed 50% of the Name's overall premium limit.
(4) Transfers are voluntary and must be made by the earlier of:
    (a) the date in which the balance of the Name's profit is paid to him; or
    (b) 31 October of the year of distribution.
(5) Income and gains on the investments in the fund are exempt from income tax and CGT.
(6) If an underwriting loss is sustained, a withdrawal must be made from the fund of the lower of the loss and the amount of the fund.
(7) If a cash call is made, a withdrawal must be made of the lower of the cash call and the amount of the fund and, if the cash call is greater than the ultimate loss, the excess must be transferred back.
(8) The fund is valued each year at 31 December and if the fund's value exceeds 50% of the premium limit for that year, the excess must be withdrawn.
(9) When a Name ceases to underwrite, the fund's balance is repaid to him or his estate. This repayment may take the form of money or money's worth. Where assets are transferred, the Name (or his personal representatives) acquires the assets at market value for CGT purposes.
(10) The fund managers can claim repayment of tax suffered by deduction and payment of tax credit, because it is a gross fund. However, it is not possible to reclaim tax credits on dividends after 5 April 1999.
(11) Although funds accumulate tax free in the fund, there is a potential tax liability on withdrawal and this is on the fund's full value.
(12) If a withdrawal is made when a Name ceases to underwrite, the payment is treated as a trading receipt received immediately after the end of the year preceding the one in which his Lloyd's deposit is repaid to him, ie normally a receipt of their final year of underwriting.

30.6.4 Payment of tax

The 1999 Account was declared in the summer of 2002 and will form the basis of assessment for the tax year ended 5 April 2003. Names or their agents will receive form CTA1 and CTA2 to help them complete the relevant pages of the SA form. In recent years the Lloyd's Members' Service Unit has even included numbers on these forms that correspond with the boxes on the SA form.

30.6.5 Treatment of underwriting losses for UK taxation purposes

(TA 1988, ss 380-381, 385; FA 1994, Sched 1(2))

Underwriting losses for an underwriting year arise where a Name's total syndicate net claims and expenses (including reinsurance costs and personal allowable expenses) exceed his total syndicate income from premiums, investments, capital gains and personal Lloyd's income (including stop loss recoveries). A formal claim for the relief of such losses must be made by the Name to the Inspector of Taxes not later than 31 January following the end of the tax year after the year of the loss and would normally be incorporated in the SA tax return. Thus a loss arising from the 1999 underwriting account (ie a loss for the tax year 2002-03) must be claimed by 31 January 2004.

Order of set-off

Such losses are now set off against the claimant Name's income in the following order:

(1) Other income of the same, or the previous, year of assessment, for example the 1999 account, can be set against other income for 2002-03 or 2001-02.
(2) Any balance of loss can only be carried forward under TA 1988, s 385 against future underwriting income and investment income from the Lloyd's deposit, special reserve fund and personal reserves (but not personal capital gains). Consequently, if beneficial, a Name can choose to carry forward all losses against future Lloyd's income.
(3) Underwriting losses can be set off against a Name's capital gains in certain circumstances.

Names have the option, in any of their first four years of underwriting, to carry back any loss under TA 1988, s 381(1) against any income of the three years immediately preceding that in which the loss arose (see 5.9.5).

Terminal loss relief under TA 1988, s 388 can be claimed in the year that a Name ceases underwriting. Normally this is the year in which the final syndicate account closes. Run-off syndicates can therefore delay such a claim, which has led to the use of EXEAT policies to close an account.

The Inland Revenue recently announced that it would allow provisional relief in respect of the 2000 year of account in the PAYE codings for the tax year ending 5 April 2004. Names or their accountants wishing to claim relief in this fashion can find a calculation sheet at www.lloydstaxation.com under market bulletins.

30.6.6 Capital gains tax

A Name may have several sources of capital gains as a result of his participation in Lloyd's, and it is necessary to distinguish between each type in order to determine the correct tax treatment. Capital gains or losses that arise within each of the syndicates in which a Name participates are not subject to CGT, but are charged or allowed as Lloyd's syndicate income or expenses. They form part of a Name's Lloyd's trading income for the year of account in which the disposal takes place.

Capital gains or losses that arise within the new Lloyd's special reserve fund are free of all taxes while in the fund, but are effectively taxed on withdrawal as trading income.

By contrast, capital gains or losses that arise from the disposals of assets held in a Name's Lloyd's deposit or personal reserves (other than the special reserve fund) are treated as personal gains or losses for the tax year in which the disposal takes place. They are therefore added to any other personal gains or losses arising during the same fiscal year.

Similarly, the sale or transfer of syndicate capacity is treated as a personal disposal and any gain or loss arising must be included with other capital gains or losses for the tax year in which the disposal takes place. Some Names write insurance through Members' Agent Pooling Arrangements (MAPAs), which allows them to buy into a preselected portfolio of syndicates, rather than participate directly in a much smaller number of syndicates. This enables them to spread the risk of their underwriting activities. FA 1999 gave Revenue practice a statutory basis in treating a MAPA as a single asset for CGT purposes. Effectively a CGT liability will only arise when there is a distribution from the MAPA manager of surplus funds (normally at the time of the annual auctions) or if the MAPA Name withdraws from the MAPA.

FA 1999 extended the classes of assets that qualify for roll-over relief to include syndicate capacity whether held directly or through a MAPA.

Capacity is treated as a business asset for taper relief purposes; additional investment in an existing syndicate or MAPA is treated as enhancement expenditure (ie the taper will run from the date of the original purchase, not the date of the additional expenditure).

30.6.7 Inheritance tax

The value of a Name's underwriting interests at Lloyd's is potentially chargeable to IHT when transferred on death. The valuation of these interests is normally based on the insolvency statement for the underwriting account ending with the calendar year preceding that in which the death occurs, and includes the value of investments held as funds at Lloyd's, underwriting profits or losses for open and running off accounts, and undistributed profits or losses for closed accounts.

Normally, underwriting interests qualify for business property relief (currently 100%), but the CTO investigates all claims for relief, and may seek to reduce the relief where it believes a Name's combined reserves are excessive in relation to the amount and nature of the underwriting activities.

30.6.8 Other issues

Names should be aware that special rules apply on the cessation or death of a Name who was underwriting prior to the 1972 Account. Details can be obtained on this subject along with any other taxation points from the Lloyd's Taxation Department at the number given below.

FA 2000 also changed the rules in respect of non-UK tax credits and their availability to non-resident Names. These, in general terms, will be available to be claimed as a credit with effect from 6 April 1999 (in the past they had only been allowed as a deduction to those Names). The Revenue also announced that its treatment of EU/EEA Names had been incorrect and these Names were invited to make claims for earlier years for non-UK tax credits in respect of their Lloyd's UK income, which had only been allowed as a deduction.

Lloyd's no longer accepts new Names underwriting with an unlimited liability and discussions are underway to allow underwriting losses to be carried forward when converting from unlimited personal liability to limited liability status. It is intended that any such measures introduced be included in the 2004 Finance Act.

30.6.9 Useful numbers

Lloyd's Members' Service Unit: 020 7327 5311
Lloyd's Taxation Department: 020 7327 6046

30.7 MINISTERS OF RELIGION

30.7.1 No tax on rent-free accommodation

A clergyman is not normally liable for tax in respect of his occupation of a vicarage or other living accommodation provided by the church, charity or ecclesiastical body for carrying out his duties (TA 1998, s 332).

ESC A61 also provides exemption for payment or reimbursement of heating, lighting, cleaning and gardening expenses. This does not apply if the clergyman is a P11D employee because his earnings exceed £8,500 pa (see 4.4.1).

Where the minister's earnings exceed £8,500, any tax charge on such 'service benefits' in respect of his vicarage or manse is limited to 10% of the net emoluments (after deducting expenses). All this is covered in Helpsheet 124.

If the clergyman pays his wife wages for cleaning the part of the house used for official duties, this may be treated as a tax deductible expense for him.

30.7.2 Allowable expenses

The following expenses commonly incurred by clergy are allowable deductions under TA 1988, s 198:

- Stationery, postage and use of telephone for clerical duties;
- Secretarial costs (including wages paid to the clergyman's wife for providing such assistance provided this is separate and distinct from work she performs as an active member of the church);
- Travelling in the course of his duties (including the 12p per mile for 'business use' of a bicycle);
- Cost of repair or replacement of robes;
- Communion expenses;
- Cost of providing a locum;
- Reasonable entertainment on official functions.

White v Higgingbottom [1983] STC 143 decided that a clergyman was not entitled to allowances for an OHP and screen that he paid for personally.

30.7.3 Capital gains tax

Where a clergyman buys a property, he can often nominate it as his main residence for CGT purposes on the grounds that his work requires him to live elsewhere (see 16.3.1).

For further background information, contact the Churches Main Committee, Fielden House, Little College Street, London SW1P 3JZ for a circular, *The Taxation of Ministers of Religion*.

30.8 MEMBERS OF PARLIAMENT

As one would expect there are special rules that apply to MPs, Members of the Scottish Parliament and Members of the Welsh Assembly. MPs are dealt with by a central Inland Revenue office in Cardiff. They complete a supplementary form SA101 (MP), which is available on the Revenue's website, together with help notes. The Revenue also publishes a leaflet, *MPs, Ministers and Tax*.

Additional costs allowance

MPs receive a tax-free additional costs allowance that covers the additional costs of living away from home while engaged in Parliamentary duties either in London or in their constituency (TA 1988, s 200). This means an MP can effectively receive tax relief on interest on a mortgage to buy a second home in London, as the allowance is calculated to allow for the payment of either rent or mortgage interest in the case of a property owned by him.

Travel

MPs are issued with rail/air warrants. No taxable benefit arises where these are used to travel from Westminster to a home in the constituency. Where the MP's home is not in the constituency, the extent to which a benefit is taxable is as follows:

- Where his home is not more than 20 miles from the constituency, no amount is taxable
- Where the home is within 20 miles of Westminster, no amount is taxable
- In other cases, the cost of the rail/air warrant is taxable.

Where a warrant is used for travel to/from the constituency via home, only the excess cost over a direct journey from Westminster to the constituency is taxed. This treatment depends on the MP staying at home for only one night unless the journey spans a weekend.

The position of car allowances is complex because the cash mileage reimbursement that the MP receives from the Fees Office includes the cost of travel between his home and Westminster, or between home and constituency. All this ranks for tax purposes as private travel. In strictness, the car mileage allowance paid by the Fees Office (54.4p per mile for the first 20,000 miles) is assessable as an emolument and an expenses claim should be made. However, for practical purposes the allowance is generally not taxed.

Incidental travel costs in London, for example taxi fares between London rail and air terminals and Westminster, and in visiting ministers on parliamentary business, are allowable expenses.

Where an MP uses a bicycle for Parliamentary business, the Fees Office pays an allowance of only 7p per mile. The MP can claim tax relief for the difference between this and the authorised mileage rate (see 4.4.9) of 12p per mile.

Office costs allowance (OCA)

MPs receive an allowance for office, secretarial and research expenses, currently around £50,000 pa. This is taxable, but a deduction is made for the actual costs of any secretarial and clerical assistance, general office expenses and research assistance undertaken in the proper performance of the MP's parliamentary duties. Such expenses include the normal costs of office accommodation such as rent, heat and light, including the use of part of the home as an office and the costs of repairs and renewals of office equipment. Telephone, stationery and postage costs, if not provided free, are also allowable. An MP's secretary is paid direct by the Fees Office rather than the MP receiving the salary as part of a claim for office expenses; PAYE is operated by the Fees Office.

Incidental expenses

An MP can claim a deduction for the following:

- Costs of hiring a room to meet constituents;
- Costs of expenses incurred in participation in delegations organised by all-party Parliamentary organisations such as the Parliamentary Group for European Unity;
- Payments to a local agent or party organisation for assistance in constituency work;
- Extra cost of meals taken while travelling on parliamentary business.

Pensions and retirement lump sums

Parliamentary pensions accrue at the rate of $^1/_{50}$ final remuneration for every year of service. MPs can buy extra years pension by making regular contributions or by paying a lump sum within 12 months of election to the House of Commons.

Ministers are able to pay contributions into a personal pension scheme if their ministerial salary is not pensionable under the Parliamentary Pension Scheme. Terminal grants to a person ceasing to be an MP are regarded as tax free up to £30,000.

30.9 INDEPENDENT FINANCIAL ADVISERS (IFAs) AND INSURANCE AGENTS

IFAs and insurance agents will either be employed or self-employed. As such there are no special rules outside of those already outlined in Chaps 4 and 5, and it is outside the scope of this book to examine why certain individuals in the insurance business are treated as self-employed while others in apparently similar positions are employed. The following areas have received comment from the Revenue in regard to this anomaly.

30.9.1 Commissions

The time at which commission is brought into account depends on the terms of the contract. If the agent has carried out the majority of his work when the policy is sold, the full amount of the initial commission receivable should be charged in the tax period in which the policy is sold. In such circumstances a specific provision will be allowed to take into account the contingent liability to repay the commission, should the policy lapse. *IRC v Gardner Mountain* 29 TC 69 and *D'Ambrumeni and Owen v Southern Railway of Peru* 36 TC 602 give some guidance, but specialist advice should be taken.

30.9.2 Agent's book

Agents may have a financial interest in their business, known as a 'book'. The book is a single asset for tax purposes and will give rise to a CGT charge on a material disposal. The Revenue has issued its guidance and views on how such a disposal may be treated; these can be found in the Inspector's manuals at the Revenue website.

30.10 BUSINESS ECONOMIC NOTES

Even if there is no special legislation that governs the way in which your particular occupation is taxed, you may well find it interesting to see the background information the Revenue provides to its staff.

The Revenue publishes a series of Business Economic Notes that are primarily intended to aid Inspectors in the examination of accounts. The notes, listed in Table 30.1, are available for purchase from the Inland Revenue, Room 28 New Wing, Somerset House, Strand, London, WC2R 1LB.

Table 30.1 – Business Economic Notes

	Subject	*Date of issue*
1	Travel Agents	February 1987
2	Road Haulage	February 1987
3	Lodging Industry	February 1987
4	Hairdressers	February 1987
5	Waste Materials Reclamation and Disposal	March 1987
6	Funeral Directors	May 1987
7	Dentists	July 1987
8	Florists	September 1987
9	Licensed Victuallers	May 1988
10	Jewellery Trade	1989
11	Electrical Retailers	1989
12	Antique and Fine Art Dealers	March 1990
13	Fish and Chip Shops	October 1990
14	The Pet Industry	October 1990
15	Veterinary Surgeons	October 1990
16	Catering – General	October 1990
17	Catering – Restaurants	October 1990
18	Catering – Fast Foods, Cafes and Snack Bars	October 1990
19	Farming – Stock Valuation for Income Tax Purposes	April 1993
20	Insurance Brokers & Agents	August 1994
21	Residential Rest & Nursing Homes	November 1994
22	Dispensing Chemists	May 1995

23	Driving Instructors	June 1997
24	Independent Fishmongers	June 1997
25	Taxicabs and Private Hire Vehicles	July 1997
26	Confectioners, Tobacconists and Newsagents	November 1997

For further details, go to www.inlandrevenue.gov.uk/bens/.

30.11 US CITIZENS WORKING IN THE UK

30.11.1 US taxation

A US citizen or green card holder is liable to US taxation on a worldwide basis regardless of where this income is paid, earned or received. Reliefs are available in respect of foreign earned income and housing credits. This section deals in brief with these allowances and some of the filing requirements that apply to a US citizen living and working in the UK.

The examples quoted are in respect of the 2002 US calendar year, but the general principles hold true for the current year, 2003.

30.11.2 Filing requirements

The filing date for the US Federal return for the calendar year to 31 December 2002 was 15 April 2003. There is an automatic extension to the date to file, though not to pay taxes, for a US individual working outside the US who fulfils either the foreign residence or physical residence test (see 30.11.4).

Table 30.2 shows the requirements for each filing status for the last three years. If your income was below the income limit for your filing status, you are not required to file a US federal income tax return for that year.

Filing status

When filing a US tax return the taxpayer must first determine his filing status which will decide the appropriate standard deduction and tax rates to apply, the five choices are:

- Single;
- Head of Household;
- Married Filing Jointly;
- Married Filing Separately;
- Qualifying Widow(er) with Dependent Child.

Filing extensions

If a US individual cannot file the return by the normal due date, he can file for an extension using the IRS Form 4868. This form should be filed by the due date of the return together with a 'good faith' estimate of the tax due.

Table 30.2 – Requirements for each filing status

IF your filing status is:	**AND** at the end of the year you were:	**THEN** file a return if your gross income for **2000** was at least:	**THEN** file a return if your gross income for **2001** was at least:	**THEN** file a return if your gross income for **2002** was at least:
Single	Under 65	$7,200	$7,450	$7,700
	65 or Older	$8,300	$8,550	$8,850
Head of Household	Under 65	$9,250	$9,550	$9,900
	65 or Older	$10,350	$10,650	$11,050
Married Filing Jointly	Under 65 (Both Spouses)	$12,950	$13,400	$13,850
	65 or Older (One Spouse)	$13,800	$14,300	$14,750
	65 or Older (Both Spouses)	$14,650	$15,200	$15,650
Married Filing Separately	Any Age	$2,800	$2,900	$3,000
Qualifying Widow(er) with Dependent Child	Under 65	$10,150	$10,500	$10,850
	65 or Older	$11,250	$11,600	$11,750

Notes: Table 30.2 refers to 'gross income', which means *all* income received in the form of money, goods, property and services that is not exempt from tax. *This includes any income from sources outside the US, even if you may exclude part or all of it.* Foreign currencies must be converted to US dollars. Do not include social security benefits unless you are married filing a separate return and you lived with your spouse at any time in 2002.

The filing date is automatically extended by two-months for US individuals living and working outside the US or Puerto Rico on the date the return is due, ie for 2002 the normal filing date for those qualifying will be 16 June 2003. Individuals relying upon this auto extension do not need to file the extension but should reference that it applies when filing the Form 1040. For an additional two-month extension to this filing date, Form 4868 should have been filed by 16 June 2003 together with an estimated payment of the tax due. Alternatively, if there are good grounds for assuming that no tax would be due on foreign earned income, a longer extension could be applied for using Form 2688.

30.11.3 Foreign earnings exclusion

A US citizen or green card holder living outside the US may elect to exclude up to $80,000, for the 2002 US tax year, of foreign earned income and certain housing allowances (see 30.11.5). The exclusion can only be claimed if the tax home is outside the US and the individual meets either the foreign residence or physical presence test. If only part of the qualifying period falls within the tax year, the amount of exclusion available is scaled down proportionally.

30.11.4 The foreign residence and physical presence test

The bona fide foreign residence test applies to US citizens only and requires that a US citizen is physically present in any one or a number of foreign countries for a period that includes a complete US tax year. The physical presence test extends to resident aliens as well as US citizens and to qualify the individual must be physically present in any one or a number of foreign countries for 330 days during any consecutive 12-month period.

Example

A was resident in the UK from 20 February 1999 until 30 June 2001. On 1 July 2001 she returned to the US. Since her period of foreign residency included all of 2000, thereby satisfying the foreign residence test, she may claim a pro rated exclusion for 2001. As *A* was abroad for 181 of the 365 days in 2001, she can exclude earnings of up to $38,679, or $^{181}/_{365}$ of the $78,000 maximum exclusion. If she earned more than $38,679 from January to June 2001, the exclusion is limited to $38,679.

30.11.5 Housing costs

A US citizen can elect to exclude from his US taxable income the excess of reasonable un-reimbursed housing expenses. The housing exclusion is claimed on Form 2555 and is limited to the excess of foreign earned income over the housing exclusion.

30.11.6 Foreign tax credit

A US citizen can elect to claim tax paid on his non-US earnings as a credit as opposed to a deduction. The credit is limited to the ratio of foreign source taxable income to worldwide taxable income multiplied by the US tax. The foreign tax credit available will also be scaled down if he uses the foreign earned income exclusion.

Excess credits may be carried back two years and carried forward five years.

30.11.7 Coming to work in UK

A US individual coming to work in the UK should review his residence position as discussed in Chap. 23. If he is on secondment to the UK for less than two years, all reasonable subsistence accommodation expenses can be paid tax free. Split contracts for non-UK duties are a way of mitigating UK, but not US, tax. There are also NICs and other exemptions from UK tax included in the US/UK Double Taxation Treaty and the reciprocal social security agreement.

Tax rates

Individuals are charged according to their filing status (see 30.11.2) at the rates for 2002 shown in Table 30.3.

Capital gains are taxed depending upon the nature of the gain and the holding period of the asset, with assets held for less than a year (short-term), taxed at higher rates than long-term gains (assets held for more than a year). The rates applicable to net gains in a year will be 8%, 10%, 20%, 25% or 28% but will not exceed the marginal income tax rate for the year.

Alternative Minimum Tax (AMT)

To counteract the tax savings that legislative changes have created over the years the US Congress enacted the Alternative Minimum Tax (AMT). In brief the AMT ensures that where a taxpayer takes legitimate advantage of the tax relief available to him in the tax code, the IRS clawback part of this by use of the AMT calculation. Overseas, taxpayers who offset their US income tax with a substantial foreign tax credit often become liable for AMT, and the resulting calculations can be extremely complex. AMT is computed using IRS Form 6251. In effect, individuals with incomes that are offset by large deductions have those deductions and exemptions either reduced or eliminated. The remaining income is taxed at 28%.

If an individual has foreign tax credits equal to or greater than 90% of the AMT figure, the credit is reduced to 90% of the AMT. This makes all of the income over the limit effectively taxed at a rate of approximately 2.8%. This commonly applies to US taxpayers who have income in excess and are claiming the foreign earnings exclusion.

Table 30.3

Schedule X—Use if your filing status is **Single**

If the amount on Form 1040, line 41, is: *Over*—	*But not over*—	Enter on Form 1040, line 42	*of the amount over*—
$0	$6,000	-------- 10%	$0
6,000	27,950	$600.00 + 15%	6,000
27,950	67,700	3,892.50 + 27%	27,950
67,700	141,250	14,625.00 + 30%	67,700
141,250	307,050	36,690.00 + 35%	141,250
307,050	---------	94,720.00 + 38.6%	307,050

Schedule Y-1—Use if your filing status is **Married filing jointly** or **Qualifying widow(er)**

If the amount on Form 1040, line 41, is: *Over*—	*But not over*—	Enter on Form 1040, line 42	*of the amount over*—
$0	$12,000	-------- 10%	$0
12,000	46,700	$1,200.00 + 15%	12,000
46,700	112,850	6,405.00 + 27%	46,700
112,850	171,950	24,265.50 + 30%	112,850
171,950	307,050	41,995.50 + 35%	171,950
307,050	--------	89,280.50 + 38.6%	307,050

Schedule Y-2—Use if your filing status is **Married filing separately**

If the amount on Form 1040, line 41, is: *Over*—	*But not over*—	Enter on Form 1040, line 42	*of the amount over*—
$0	$6,000	-------- 10%	$0
6,000	23,350	$600.00 + 15%	6,000
23,350	56,425	3,202.50 + 27%	23,350
56,425	85,975	12,132.75 + 30%	56,425
85,975	153,525	20,997.75 + 35%	85,975
153,525	--------	44,640.25 + 38.6%	153,525

Schedule Z—Use if your filing status is **Head of household**

If the amount on Form 1040, line 41, is: *Over*—	*But not over*—	Enter on Form 1040, line 42	*of the amount over*—
$0	$10,000	-------- 10%	$0
10,000	37,450	$1,000.00 + 15%	10,000
37,450	96,700	5,117.50 + 27%	37,450
96,700	156,600	21,115.00 + 30%	96,700
156,600	307,050	39,085.00 + 35%	156,600
307,050	--------	91,742.50 + 38.6%	307,050

30.11.8 Forms and publications

The following forms and guidance notes can be found on the IRS web pages www.irs.gov or via the US Embassy website for London.

Form 1040	–	US Individual Return and supporting schedules
Form 1116	–	Foreign Tax Credit
Form 2350	–	Automatic filing extension for individuals resident outside of US on 15 April
Form 2555	–	Foreign Earned Income
Form 4868	–	Application for Automatic Extension of Time to File US Individual Income Tax Return
Form 5471	–	Information Return of US Persons With Respect To Certain Foreign Corporations
Form W7	–	Application for IRS Individual Taxpayer Identification Number by non-US individuals
W8-Ben	–	Certificate of foreign status of beneficial owner for United States Tax Withholding.
Publn 54	–	Tax Guide for US Citizens and Resident Aliens Abroad

30.11.9 Double taxation agreement

The new UK/US double taxation treaty was ratified on 21 March 2003. The new treaty takes effect as follows:

UK & US withholding taxes	Payments made on or after 1 May 2003
Other US taxes	1 January 2004
UK Corporation Tax	1 April 2003
UK Income and Capital Gains Tax	6 April 2003

To coincide with the introduction of the new treaty the Inland Revenue released a special *Tax Bulletin* which can be found at inlandrevenue.gov.uk/bulletins/tbse6.pdf.

30.11.10 Useful contact details

Internal Revenue Service

The IRS in the UK can be contacted in the UK at:

United States Embassy/IRS
24/31 Grosvenor Square
London W1A 1AE
Tel: (44) 207 408 8077 (9 am to 12 noon Monday to Friday)
Fax: (44) 207 495 4224
Web page: www.irs.ustreas.gov

National Association of Enrolled Agents (EAs)

The IRS licenses and regulates tax preparers who have either passed exams or have experience with the IRS as Enrolled Agents (EAs). You can get details of EAs practising in your area from:

The National Association of Enrolled Agents
200 Orchard Ridge Drive, Suite 302
Gaithersburg, MD 20878
Tel: 001 301-212-9608
Fax: 001 301-990-1611
E-mail: info@naeahq.org
Web page: www.naea.org

30.12 AUSTRALIANS LIVING IN THE UK

Dan Foster, DMS

30.12.1 Australian taxation

Australian tax residents are taxable on their worldwide income on an arising basis, regardless of where it is earned, paid, held or remitted. Australian tax residency is distinct from citizenship, nationality, passport or visa status. It is possible to be a tax resident of both Australia and the UK (or elsewhere) and subject to tax in more than one country. Where this applies, certain exemptions and credits are generally available under local legislation and the DTA, where appropriate. Australians working in the UK who have ceased being Australian tax residents are only taxable in Australia on Australian-source income.

The Australian tax year runs from 1 July to 30 June. Returns are due 31 October. Australian personal tax is administered on a comprehensive self-assessment tax return basis. The marginal tax rates for Australian residents are as follows (non-resident rates are at 30 December 2005):

\$0–\$6,000	Nil
\$6,001–\$20,000	17%
\$20,001–\$50,000	30%
\$50,001–\$60,000	42%
\$60,001+	47%

Plus Medicare Levy of 1.5%, and surcharge of 1% on high earners without private medical insurance. The earliest due date for payment is 21 November.

30.12.2 Australian tax residency

Australian tax residency is a matter of fact, not choice. A resident is defined in subsection 6(1) of ITAA 1936 as:

(1) a person whose domicile is Australia, unless their permanent place of abode is outside Australia; or,
(2) a person present in Australia for more than 182 days of a tax year (whether continuous or not), unless their usual place of abode is outside Australia or they do not intend to take up residence in Australia; or,
(3) a person who is an eligible employee under the Superannuation Act 1976 (eg an Australian commonwealth civil servant).

The Australian Tax Office has summarised its views on residency in IT 2650.

The crucial test for Australian domiciles is therefore whether they have established a permanent home outside Australia. The two most important facts to consider are:

(1) The intended and actual length of the individual's stay in the UK. More than two years abroad is indicative of Australian non-residence, but not conclusive; and,
(2) Any intention either to return to Australia at some definite point in time or to travel to another country.

Intention to return is indicative of continued residence in Australia. All relevant evidence will be considered to determine the person's intention, including any remaining ties with Australia.

It is worth noting that Australians working in the UK on two-year working-holiday visas will usually remain Australian tax residents during their time abroad, and will therefore be taxable in Australia on their worldwide income.

30.12.3 Taxation of Australian residents working in the UK

UK employment income

UK salary income will be exempt from Australian tax provided that the UK engagement was for continuous service in excess of 91 days, and the earnings were subject to PAYE at source (ITAA 1936, s 23AG). This exempt foreign employment income will still have to be included on the supplementary pages of the Australian tax return. Although the income will not be subject to further tax, it will affect the rate of tax applied to any taxable income. The tax payable will be calculated as follows:

$$\frac{\text{Notional gross tax}}{\text{Notional gross income}} \times \text{Other taxable income}$$

where:

Notional gross tax = tax calculated at marginal rates on all income as if the foreign employment income were taxable
Notional gross income = Total income, including exempt foreign income
Other taxable income = Income subject to tax in Australia (eg any Australian income or foreign investment income).

Other UK income

Income that does not qualify for the foreign employment exemption will generally be taxed as foreign income at marginal rates. Foreign tax credits may be allowed for UK tax paid, for example tax paid on assessment in the UK or by way of withholding tax.

Examples

1. *A* is an Australian tax resident and self-employed person working in the UK in receipt of gross income, and pays UK income tax on assessment. The UK self-employment income is assessable in Australia, and a credit is given for the UK tax paid, but not the Class 4 NIC.
2. *B* is an Australian tax resident working in the UK as director/shareholder of a limited company and is in receipt of dividend income. He pays higher rate tax on that amount of the dividends over his £35,115 threshold. The UK dividends are taxable in Australia, and *B* receives a foreign tax credit in the Australian tax return for the UK higher rate tax paid on them. Credit is given for the notional 10% tax credit on the UK dividends.
3. *C* is an Australian tax resident living temporarily in the UK but not-domiciled in the UK and earns interest from an offshore investment. As the interest is not remitted to the UK it suffers no UK tax. However, the interest is taxable in Australia and no tax credit is available.
4. *D* is an Australian resident living in the UK and earns interest on a cash ISA. The interest is taxable in Australia and there is no tax credit.
5. *E* is an Australian resident living in the UK and earns interest on a UK deposit account, from which 20% tax is withheld. No higher rate tax is paid on the interest. The interest is taxable in Australia and a credit allowed for the tax withheld.

The ATO has published a guide on *How to claim a foreign tax credit*. The Inland Revenue also publish form FD2, an application for relief at source and claim for repayment of tax in respect of pensions, annuities, interest and royalties paid to Australian residents.

30.12.4 Ceasing to be an Australian tax resident

Australians leaving Australia permanently before the end of a tax year may request an early assessment for that year on Form NAT 3404, which can be submitted with the Return. If a person was resident at any time during a tax year then he should answer 'Yes' to the question 'Are you an Australian tax resident?' on the first page of the return, whether it is submitted early or after the end of the tax year.

Australians who cease being a resident during a tax-year are only entitled to a part-year tax-free threshold. The date that the person became non-resident, and the number of months that the tax-free threshold is claimed, should be declared in the appropriate section on the return. A person who is non-resident for a whole tax year is not entitled to any tax-free threshold and will pay tax on the first dollar of taxable income.

Non-residents do not pay the Medicare levy, and can claim an exemption from the levy for the number of days they were not resident.

Non-residents cannot claim certain tax offsets (formerly called rebates) or tax credits only available to residents, including the dependant spouse tax offset. Any offsets will be reduced according to the number of days of non-residence.

30.12.5 Non-resident returns and tax rates

Non-residents should notify their Australian financial institutions of their non-resident status, as well as of their foreign address. Non-resident withholding tax of 10% will then be deducted from bank interest. This is a final tax and the interest does not then need to be included on an Australian tax return.

Non-resident withholding tax of 15% will also be deducted from unfranked dividends (that is, dividends on which the paying company has not applied company tax credits). No tax will be deducted from fully franked dividends. Neither type of dividend should be declared on the tax return of a non-resident.

If a non-resident's only income is interest or dividends subject to withholding tax (or franked dividends), then no tax return is necessary. A final return can be submitted upon leaving Australia. However, if a non-resident earns Australian rental income or other Australian-source income then a return must be submitted. Unlike the UK, no tax is normally withheld from rents paid to non-residents.

Non-resident tax rates are as follows:

$0–$20,000	29%
$20,001–$50,000	30%
$50,001–$60,000	42%
$60,001+	47%

30.12.6 Capital Gains Tax (CGT)

Australian residents are subject to Australian CGT on their worldwide assets. Non-residents are subject to CGT on their Australian assets only. In general, when an asset is held for over 12 months, only half the gain is subject to CGT. Careful planning is required in this area, particularly if any properties are making tax losses.

Main residence exemption

An Australian resident may elect for their sole principal residence (SPR) to remain exempt from CGT for six years if it is rented out in their absence, or indefinitely if it is not let.

Deemed disposal and acquisition

Non-Australian assets are deemed to have been disposed of at market value on the day a person becomes non-resident. A taxpayer can elect for this rule not to apply. Non-Australian assets are deemed to have been acquired at market value on the day the owner becomes a tax resident of Australia.

30.12.7 Miscellaneous rules

'Negative gearing'

Australian property losses can be set off against income from other Australian sources. This is known as 'negative gearing', since typically interest on loan repayments is higher than rental income. These losses can generally be carried forward indefinitely. The losses cannot be used against UK income. Australian residents must first use their rental losses against exempt income, including exempt foreign employment income earned while they are abroad.

Using Australian losses

Residents can also elect to use carried-forward Australian losses (eg business losses) against taxable foreign income.

Foreign Investment Fund (FIF) rules and UK pensions

The FIF rules are Australian anti-avoidance legislation that attempt to tax income accruing in offshore trusts to the benefit of Australian residents as if it were paid to that person. A side effect of the rules is to tax gains within foreign pension funds. UK personal pensions are subject to the rules, however company funds are generally not. Australians returning to the UK should therefore consider transferring any UK pension to a complying Australian superannuation fund. If this is done within six months of becoming an Australian resident then no tax is due on the roll over.

Professional financial analysis and tax planning is recommend in these cases.

Living away from home allowance (LAFHA)

Australia levies a Fringe Benefits Tax (FBT) on employers who provide taxable benefits to employees. A LAFHA may be exempt from FBT, and can therefore provide a form of tax-free remuneration to relocated employees, including expatriates. However, the ATO will look critically at a LAFHA paid solely to avoid tax, and any such arrangement should be approached with caution. This does not affect any eligible tax-free relocation allowance, up to £8,000 pa, paid by a UK employer to an Australian worker moving to the UK.

UK personal allowance

As Commonwealth citizens, Australians are entitled to the UK personal allowance even when not resident in the UK.

31

CHARITIES AND NOT FOR PROFIT ORGANISATIONS

NIALL O'GARA

Most of this book is concerned with paying tax. However, many organisations enjoy exemptions, and their main involvement with the Revenue is in reclaiming tax.

We look at the following

(1) Charities.
(2) Community amateur sports clubs.
(3) Mutual associations.
(4) Holiday clubs and thrift funds.
(5) Investment clubs.

31.1 CHARITIES

Charities are dealt with by:

Inland Revenue (Charities)
St John's House
Merton Road
Bootle
Merseyside L69 9BB
Tel: 0151 472 6036/6037.

In Scotland, the address is:

Inland Revenue (Charities)
Meldrum House
15 Drumsheugh Gardens
Edinburgh EH3 7UL
Tel: 0131 551 8127.

Review of charity taxation

A thorough review of the tax regime for charities gave rise to important changes in FA 2000. We cover:

(1) exemption from income tax and CGT;
(2) tax credits on dividends;
(3) trading profits;
(4) Gift Aid scheme and record-keeping requirements; and
(5) payroll giving schemes.

31.1.1 Exemption from income tax and CGT

Charities are exempt from income tax on all income other than trading income (see 31.1.4), provided the income is applied for charitable purposes. Similarly, charities are exempt from CGT.

The exemption can be restricted in a year in which the charity accumulates income of more than £10,000 that is not reasonably required for application for charitable purposes in the foreseeable future or if it incurs non-qualifying expenditure. In practice, the rule on non-qualifying expenditure is most likely to arise where a private charity makes loans to a company connected with the settlor, especially if the loans are not on proper commercial terms. Professional advice should be obtained in such circumstances. (See further 22.9.1.)

The CGT exemption does not cover capital gains realised by personal representatives where the charity is a residuary legatee. In such cases, it may be more tax efficient for the executors to vest the assets in the charity before they are sold to a third party.

31.1.2 Tax credits on dividends

Although tax credits on UK dividends are not normally reclaimable, it is possible for a charity to make a claim for transitional relief. The claim must be made within two years of the year in question. The charity will then be entitled to relief as follows:

Dividends received in 2001-02	13%
Dividends received in 2002-03	8%
Dividends received in 2003-04	4%

31.1.3 Life policies held by charitable trusts

Provisions which take effect from 9 April 2003 ensure that trustees of charitable trusts do not have to pay any tax on most UK policies and no more than basic rate tax on gains from foreign policies.

31.1.4 Trading profits

Trading income is exempt only if the trade is exercised in the course of carrying out a primary purpose of the charity or if the work is carried out mainly by its beneficiaries. This includes the sale of donated goods. A major problem area in the past has been the tax treatment of profits from other types of trading.

Small fundraising events

ESC C4 has applied for many years and exempted profits from most fundraising activities. The concession used to state:

> Bazaars, jumble sales, gymkhanas, carnivals, firework displays and similar activities arranged by voluntary organisations or charities for the purpose of raising funds for charity may fall within the definition of 'trade' in ICTA 1988, s 832, with the result that any profits will be liable to corporation tax. Tax is not, however, charged on such profits provided all the following conditions are satisfied:
>
> (1) The organisation or charity is not regularly carrying on these trading activities;
> (2) The trading is not in competition with other traders;
> (3) The activities are supported substantially because the public are aware that any profits will be devoted to charity; and
> (4) The profits are transferred to charities or otherwise applied for charitable purposes.
>
> Profits from lotteries are exempt provided the profits are applied solely for charitable purposes and the lottery is promoted and conducted in accordance with the Lotteries and Amusements Act 1976.

However, it was argued that the terms of the concession were too restrictive and, as from 1 April 2000, a wider exemption applies for trading profits from fundraising events provided:

(1) the public are aware that the purpose of the event is to raise funds for charity; and
(2) the event does not last for more than four days; and
(3) the charity holds no more than 15 events of a similar type in the same location each year. Small-scale events with gross takings of up to £1,000 each do not count towards this total provided they are no more frequent than weekly.

Exemption for charity's trading profits

There is also a specific tax exemption for the profits of certain small trading and other fundraising activities carried on by a charity that are not otherwise already exempt from tax. This came into effect from 1 April 2000. It means that, for tax purposes, a charity no longer has to set up a trading company to carry on these activities.

The Charity Commission has confirmed that if a charity is governed by one of the Commission's model governing documents – which contain prohibitions on 'any substantial permanent trading activity' – it may lawfully carry on the activities falling within the new tax exemption without having to set up a trading company. If the charity has some other governing document, it should check that it permits it to carry on a fundraising trade before doing so.

The new exemption will apply to the profits of all trading activities, and most other incidental fundraising activities, that are not already exempt from tax, provided:

(1) the total turnover from all of the activities does not exceed the annual turnover limit, or
(2) if the total turnover exceeds the annual turnover limit, the charity had a reasonable expectation that it would not do so, and
(3) the profits are used solely for the purposes of the charity.

The annual turnover limit is:

(1) £5,000, or
(2) if the turnover is greater than £5,000, 25% of the charity's 'incoming resources', subject to an overall limit of £50,000.

For this purpose, 'incoming resources' has a very wide meaning. It means the total receipts of the charity for the year from all sources (grants, donations, investment income, etc).

Example

A charity sells Christmas cards to raise funds and the sales in the year total £4,000. Assuming this is the only taxable fundraising activity, any profits will be exempt from tax because the turnover does not exceed £5,000.

However, suppose the sales in the year total £40,000 instead of £4,000. Any profits will still be exempt from tax provided the charity's incoming resources are at least £160,000, because the turnover does not exceed either:
(1) 25% of the incoming resources (£160,000 × 25% = £40,000), or
(2) the overall limit of £50,000.

Even if, in the example above, the charity's incoming resources are below £160,000, so that the turnover exceeds the annual turnover limit, the profits will still be exempt from tax if it had a reasonable expectation at the start of the year that the turnover would not exceed the limit. Thus, suppose the sales in the year total £60,000. This exceeds the overall annual turnover limit of £50,000. Any profits will still be exempt from tax if there was a reasonable expectation at the start of the year that the turnover would not exceed the limit.

The reasonable expectation test

If the total turnover of the taxable fundraising activities for any tax year exceeds the annual turnover limit, any profits will still be exempt from tax if it can be shown that, at the start of the tax year, it was reasonable to expect that the turnover would not exceed the limit. This might be because:

(1) the turnover was expected to be lower, or
(2) the charity's incoming resources proved to be lower than expected.

The Revenue will consider any evidence the charity may have to satisfy this test. For example, if a charity has carried on an activity for a number of years, it might be able to show that the turnover increased unexpectedly compared with earlier years. If it started carrying on the fundraising activity in the year, it might be able to show that the turnover was higher than forecast when it was decided to start the activity. Alternatively, it might be able to show that its incoming resources were lower than forecast, perhaps because a grant it was expecting to receive was not paid in the year. Evidence might include minutes of meetings at which these matters were discussed, copies of cash flow forecasts and business plans, and copies of previous years' accounts.

Trading profits not covered by the exemption

If trading profits are not likely to be covered by the above exemption, consideration should be given to the establishment of a company that would carry on the trading activities and then pay away the profits to the charity by a Gift Aid donation. Professional advice should be taken on this.

Charities and membership subscriptions

In order to recover VAT on its expenditure (inputs), a charity must first split its activities between business and non-business activities. Input VAT can never be recovered on non-business activities. The charity must consider at what rate VAT is charged on its business activities (standard, reduced or zero) or whether they are exempt from VAT. Input VAT cannot be recovered on expenditure that relates wholly to exempt activities. Where expenditure relates to both exempt and non-exempt business activities, it will be partially recoverable.

Customs & Excise has given examples of types of activities that are always business activities (eg admission to premises for a charge) and activities that are always non-business (eg donations, legacies or other voluntary contributions from the public). However, most activities can be either business or non-business, depending on the exact circumstances, and some may even be partly business and partly non-business.

Frequently, a membership subscription entitles the charity supporter to free magazines and newsletters or free advice. In the past, charities have been able to allocate the subscription between the various benefits and charge VAT accordingly. However, at recent tribunal cases, it was decided that the membership subscription is for the provision of one service and not for a number of individual services. In such cases the whole of the subscription is liable to standard rate VAT. This has led to unexpected VAT liabilities.

Customs has proposed an extra statutory concession, allowing charities to continue to treat their subscriptions as a mixture of supplies, unless this is done for tax avoidance purposes. This may lead to a more restrictive regime for VAT recoveries. If the main benefit is zero rated, it may also be possible to reclaim VAT for the past three years.

Any special accounting scheme must, of course, be agreed with Customs in advance.

Inland Revenue leaflet

The Revenue and Customs have issued a leaflet jointly (CWL 4), *Fund-raising events: Exemption for charities and other qualifying bodies.*

31.1.5 Other changes following the review of charities

From 1 April 2000 companies – including those owned by a charity and unincorporated associations, such as clubs and societies – no longer:

(1) deduct tax from their Gift Aid donations; or
(2) have to give charities a Gift Aid declaration.

This applies to all Gift Aid donations by a company made on or after 1 April 2000, including covenanted payments (even if under a deed of covenant executed before that date). For example, suppose a deed of covenant executed on 1 April 1999 provides for a company to make covenanted payments of 'such an amount as after deduction of tax equals £1,000'. While the basic rate is 22%, the company is required to make gross payments of £1,282 (£1,282 – tax at 22% = £1,000). From 1 April 2000, the company simply pays this gross amount and claims tax relief for it when calculating its profits for corporation tax.

Therefore, a charity should not reclaim tax on donations received from a company on or after 1 April 2000. If a company incorrectly deducts tax from its donation, the charity should inform the company of the correct position and ask it to pay over the sum it has incorrectly deducted.

Individuals still have to deduct tax from their Gift Aid donations and provide a Gift Aid declaration. The guidance below regarding tax reclaims and Gift Aid declarations applies only to donations by individuals.

31.1.6 Simpler paperwork: Gift Aid declarations

From 6 April 2000, Gift Aid certificates have been replaced by new, simpler and more flexible Gift Aid declarations. Before a charity can reclaim tax on a donation by an individual, it must have received a Gift Aid declaration from the donor containing certain information and confirming that the donation is to be treated as a Gift Aid donation. Companies no longer have to give a Gift Aid declaration in respect of their donations.

Donors can give a declaration:

(1) in advance of, at the time of or at any time after their donation (subject to the normal time limit within which a charity can reclaim tax – normally around six years);
(2) to cover a single donation or any number of donations;
(3) in writing (eg by post, by fax or electronically through the Internet) or orally (eg over the 'phone).

The amount of information required on a Gift Aid declaration has been kept to the minimum consistent with proper administration of the tax relief and the need for the charity to be able to show an audit trail. A charity can design its own Gift Aid declaration, but must ensure that it satisfies all the requirements set out below and any other legal requirements under the Data Protection Act, the Charities Act, etc. The Revenue's approval is not needed for an own-design declaration, but Inland Revenue (Charities) (IR(C)) will be happy to approve it if required.

What a Gift Aid declaration must contain

All Gift Aid declarations must contain:

- The donor's name;
- The donor's address;
- The charity's name;
- A description of the donations to which the declaration relates;
- A declaration that the donations are to be treated as Gift Aid donations;

and, except in the case of a declaration given orally:

- A note explaining the requirement that the donor must pay an amount of income tax or CGT equal to the tax deducted from his donations;
- The date of the declaration.

There is no requirement for a declaration to contain the donor's signature.

In the case of a written declaration, the charity may pre-print the information (eg the charity's name) on the declaration form. In the case of an oral declaration, the information may be recited to the donor for him to confirm it, rather than asking the donor to recite the information.

Written records of oral declarations

If a charity receives an oral declaration it must send the donor a written record of the declaration showing:

(1) all the details provided by the donor in his oral declaration;
(2) a note explaining the requirement that the donor must pay an amount of income tax or CGT equal to the tax deducted from his donations;

(3) a note explaining the donor's entitlement to cancel the declaration retrospectively;
(4) the date on which the donor gave the declaration; and
(5) the date on which the written record was sent to the donor.

An oral declaration will not be effective unless and until the donor is sent the written record. This means that a charity cannot reclaim tax in respect of a donation covered by an oral declaration until it has sent the written record. Once it has sent the written record, it can reclaim tax in respect of any donations covered by the declaration, even if it received them before sending the written record.

Cancellation of declarations

Donors are entitled to cancel their declaration at any time. They may do so by notifying the charity in any form of communication. The charity should keep a record of the cancellation, including the date of the donor's notification. Cancellation has effect only in relation to donations received by the charity on or after:

(1) the date on which the donor notifies the cancellation, or
(2) such later date as the donor may specify.

The charity must not reclaim tax in respect of such donations. Any donations received up to the date of the donor's notification still qualify as Gift Aid donations.

If a donor who has given an oral declaration cancels it within 30 days of being sent the written record, the cancellation will have retrospective effect, so that it will be as if the declaration had never been made. The charity does not have to wait for the 30-day period to expire before reclaiming tax in respect of donations received. But if it reclaims tax and the donor subsequently cancels his declaration within the 30-day period, it must pay the tax back to the Revenue. It may be possible for the charity to pay the tax back by deducting it from its next tax reclaim and it should contact IR(C) on this.

31.1.7 Gift Aid donations by partnerships

In England, Wales and Northern Ireland a partnership does not have legal personality, so a donation by a partnership is treated as made by the underlying partners. One partner may make a Gift Aid declaration on behalf of all the partners, provided he has the power to do so under the terms of the partnership agreement, in which case it will be sufficient for the declaration to show the name and address of the partnership. Otherwise, it will be necessary for each partner to make his own Gift Aid declaration, in which case he may do so on the same declaration form, provided it lists all the partners' names and addresses.

In Scotland a partnership has legal personality, so in all cases one of the partners may make a Gift Aid declaration on behalf of the partnership, showing the name and address of the partnership.

In order to claim higher rate relief, the partners should enter their share of the donation on their own SA returns. How the donation is apportioned between the partners is a matter for them, but normally will be in accordance with their share of the partnership profits.

31.1.8 Deeds of covenant: transitional arrangements

From 6 April 2000 there is no longer any separate tax relief for payments made under a deed of covenant; all tax relief for such payments is now given under the Gift Aid scheme. As a transitional measure, the charity does not have to get a Gift Aid declaration in respect of payments under a deed of covenant already in existence before 6 April 2000. The deed of covenant will stand in place of the Gift Aid declaration. Any donations made outside the terms of, or after expiry of, the deed must be covered by a Gift Aid declaration.

Payments made under a deed of covenant executed on or after 6 April 2000 must be covered by a Gift Aid declaration.

31.1.9 New simpler forms for claiming repayments

A new, simpler claim form and schedules have been produced to enable charities to reclaim tax on Gift Aid donations (including covenanted payments that fall within the Gift Aid scheme) by individuals received on or after 6 April 2000. IR(C) issues them automatically when it receives a tax reclaim. Alternatively, charities can obtain them from the Forms Orderline 0151 472 6293.

A charity no longer has to complete separate schedules for Gift Aid donations and covenanted payments – in future there will only be one type of schedule for all donations. It will have to enter the following details on the new schedule for each donor:

- The donor's name;
- The date of the donation or, where the claim covers more than one donation by the donor, the date of the last donation;
- The total amount of donations by the donor on which the charity is claiming in the schedule.

The charity will have to complete a separate schedule for each tax year, or part tax year, included in the claim. It will no longer be necessary, however, to calculate the tax relating to each donation separately. The charity can simply calculate the total tax reclaimed for all the donations shown on each schedule.

31.1.10 Keeping records

A charity must keep sufficient records to show that its tax reclaims are accurate. In other words, it must keep records that enable it to show:

(1) an audit trail linking each donation to an identifiable donor who has given a valid Gift Aid declaration; and
(2) that all the other conditions for the tax relief are satisfied.

If a charity does not keep adequate records it may be required to pay back to the Revenue tax it has reclaimed, with interest. It may also be liable to a penalty.

The form of records that must be kept is not prescribed in the legislation and has not changed significantly as a result of the new Gift Aid measures. In practice, it will depend on the size of the charity, the number of donors and the kind of systems used.

In the event that IR(C) audits a tax reclaim, the auditor will usually ask to see in respect of a donation:

- Any written Gift Aid declaration;
- In the case of an oral Gift Aid declaration, a copy of the written record sent to the donor;
- Any correspondence to or from the donor that relates to the donation, including:
  - any notification of a change of name or change of address;
  - any notification of the cancellation of the Gift Aid declaration;
- The charity's bank statements;
- Its paying-in book stubs showing details of cheques and cash banked;
- Statements received from credit card companies showing details of credit card donations;
- A cash book recording the receipt of cash donations;
- If the charity uses envelopes to collect cash donations, a sample of the envelopes and a record of the sums enclosed;
- Any other records kept relating to the donation.

A charity does not have to keep records on paper. They may be held on the hard drive of a computer, floppy disc or CD ROM, or stored on microfiche.

Revenue COP5, *Inspection of Charities' Records*, explains how IR(C) carries out its audit inspections. In particular, it explains a charity's rights, and promises that it will be treated fairly and courteously. It also promises that IR(C) will provide help where appropriate. A copy of COP5 will be issued to the charity before any audit inspection.

How long must records be kept?

If the charity is a charitable trust, it must keep records until the later of:

(1) the 31 January next but one after the end of the tax year to which the tax

reclaim relates (eg if it makes a tax reclaim for the tax year 2002-03, until 31 January 2005);

(2) one year after it makes its tax reclaim, rounded to the end of the next quarter (eg in the case of a tax reclaim on 25 May 2003, until 30 June 2004); or

(3) when IR(C) completes any audit it has commenced.

If the charity is a company, it must keep records until six years after the end of the accounting period to which the tax reclaim relates.

These are the minimum periods for which a charity must keep records. In the event that IR(C) audits a tax reclaim and the auditor identifies errors, he may reopen tax reclaims for earlier years. Therefore, it may be in the charity's interests to keep records for longer than the minimum period.

Using envelopes to collect cash donations

A charity may choose to collect cash donations in envelopes (eg church stewardship envelopes) so that it can show an audit trail linking the donation to the donor. For one-off donations, it may choose to pre-print the Gift Aid declaration on the envelope for completion by the donor. If the donor is a regular supporter, the charity may already hold his Gift Aid declaration, in which case the envelope need simply contain either:

- The donor's name, or
- Some other unique identifier, such as a reference number that can be cross-referenced to a donor register.

Where a reference number is used, this should be unique to the donor. In practice, where envelopes containing the same unique identifier are used by the donor and his spouse and minor children, a charity can assume that all the donations are from the donor.

When the envelope is opened and the contents are counted, an official of the charity should record the sum that it contained:

- on the envelope, and
- in a donor record.

A charity should retain all envelopes on which a Gift Aid declaration is printed for the periods set out above, together with a sample of other envelopes (normally for one month of the year) and the donor record.

31.1.11 Donations from joint bank accounts, etc

If a charity receives a donation drawn on a joint bank account, and it has not been given a Gift Aid declaration by all of the account-holders, it will need to determine whether the donation is from a donor who has given a Gift Aid declaration. It is normally safe to assume that the donation is from the account-holder who signs the cheque, debit card slip or direct debit/standing order mandate. In the case of a donation received over the 'phone or through the Internet, a charity can normally assume that the donation is from the account-holder who authorises the transaction.

Similarly, if a charity receives a credit card donation drawn on an account in respect of which there is more than one authorised signatory, it can normally assume that the donation is from the authorised signatory who signs the credit card slip. In the case of a donation received over the 'phone or through the Internet, it can normally assume that the donation is from the person who authorises the transaction.

If there is any doubt whether the donation is from the person who signs the cheque, etc or authorises the transaction, the charity should ask him to confirm whether the donation is from him.

31.1.12 Gifts of shares and land

The reliefs due where an individual gives shares or land to a charity are covered at 9.9-9.10.

31.1.13 Gift Aid donations of tax rebates

From April 2004, self-assessment taxpayers will be able to donate their tax repayments to charities. If a charity wishes to participate in this scheme it must register with IR Charities, S-A Donate by 30 September 2003. See Inland Revenue press release of 24 June 2003.

31.1.14 Payroll giving schemes
(TA 1988, s 202)

Under a payroll giving scheme an employee asks his employer to deduct an amount from his wage or salary and pay that amount over to a charity (usually a clearing house such as the Charities Aid Foundation). PAYE is then operated by the employer as if the employee's wage or salary had been the amount remaining after the charitable donation, which has the effect of granting tax relief at the highest rate paid.

An employer is not obliged to offer a payroll giving scheme and, if a scheme is offered, employees may decide individually whether they wish to participate. Usually each employee will specify particular charities to the clearing house, but in some cases the money is paid into a fund administered by a workplace committee. Such funds can cause difficulties, especially where the fund's name suggests that it was established by the generosity of the employer, rather than the employees themselves.

The maximum donation under payroll giving arrangements used to be £1,200 per annum. This ceiling was abolished with effect from 6 April 2000. In addition the Government gave a 10% supplement on all donations made under the scheme between 6 April 2000 and 5 April 2003. The 10%

supplement was distributed to charities by payroll giving agencies along with payroll giving donations.

31.2 COMMUNITY AMATEUR SPORTS CLUBS

FA 2002 introduced similar reliefs to those enjoyed by charities.

Following the consultation period promised in the 2001 Budget, a new package of tax reforms has been introduced to support community amateur sports clubs (CASCs). These measures are designed for those clubs that do not wish to, or cannot, apply for charitable status with the Charity Commission.

To benefit from the new rules, CASCs must be open to the whole community and organised on an amateur basis, and their main purpose must be to provide facilities for, and promote participation in, an eligible sport. It is understood that an eligible sport will be defined as one of those currently recognised by the National Sports Council.

The main features of the new tax reforms are exemption from:

- Tax on interest income;
- Tax on rental income up to £10,000;
- Tax on trading income up to £15,000;
- CGT.

In addition, when giving to CASCs, donors will be able to take advantage of the following:

- Gift Aid for individual donors;
- Relief from IHT;
- Business tax relief on the gifts of trading stock;
- Relief from CGT for gifts of assets from both individuals and businesses.

These new measures are designed to provide a boost for community sport activities.

31.3 MUTUAL ASSOCIATIONS

Mutual trading arises where a company or association (eg a club) trades with its members. Profits from such trading are exempt from tax under TA 1988, s 491; thus, if a member receives a dividend paid out of profits from mutual trading, he is not liable for tax on it.

Problems are apt to arise if there is a mixture of mutual trading (exempt) and trading with non-members (which is taxable), for example, a golf club that also receives green fees from non-members and makes bar profits from them. The Revenue's views are set out in *Tax Bulletin* December 1997. You

Table 31.1 – Comparison of charitable status with community amateur sports clubs

	Charitable status	*Community amateur sports clubs*
Direct taxes	Primary purpose trading income exempt from tax	Gross income from fund raising and trading exempt from tax where turnover is less than £15,000 (all such income is taxable if the threshold is exceeded)
	All rental income exempt	Gross income from property exempt from tax where less than £10,000 (all such income is taxable if the threshold is exceeded)
	80 per cent mandatory relief from uniform business rates	Under separate legislation to take place in 2004 mandatory rates relief at 50% for clubs with a rateable value of less than £3,000 reducing to no relief for rateable values more than £8,000
Incentives to give	Gift Aid on individual and company donations	Gift Aid on individual and donations only
	Payroll giving	No payroll giving
	Income tax relief on gift of shares	No income tax relief on gift of shares
	Inheritance tax relief on gifts	Inheritance tax relief on gifts
	Gift of assets on no-gain no-loss basis for capital gains	Gift of assets on no-gain no-loss basis for capital gains
Fundraising	Business: relief on gifts or trading stock	Business: relief on gifts or trading stock
	Grants available from other charities, eg community foundations and other bodies supporting charities	Will not attract charitable sources of funding
Regulation	Charity Commission regulation and audit	Inland Revenue regulation and audit
	Public recognition of and trust in 'charity' and 'Gift Aid' concepts	Public awareness of community amateur sports clubs 'brand' to be developed
	Charity Commission definition based on health benefits of physical recreation	Inland Revenue definition based on the value of sport as a factor in community cohesion
	Sports must be capable of improving physical health and fitness	Likely to adopt Sports Council's list of adopted sports
	Significant social activity to be kept separate from charitable activities	Social membership permitted

By kind permission of David Betram

should consult an accountant if you are responsible for running a mutual company or association and the level of turnover is starting to become substantial.

If a company or association receives investment income, it will be subject to corporation tax in the normal way.

CGT roll-over relief

(ESC D15)

Roll-over relief may be due to an unincorporated association, the activities of which are not wholly or mainly carried on for profit, if it replaces an asset (eg a hockey club that sells its ground and uses the proceeds to purchase fresh headquarters). Where an asset is owned by a company of which 90% of its shares are held by such an unincorporated association or its members, roll-over relief may be due provided the other conditions are satisfied.

31.4 HOLIDAY CLUBS AND THRIFT FUNDS

In strictness, a holiday club might be regarded as an unincorporated association. However, where the club is formed on an annual basis, income earned on deposits, etc is simply apportioned among the members (for further particulars, see ESC C3).

31.5 INVESTMENT CLUBS

Capital gains and allowable losses are apportioned among the members and should be included in their tax returns. Provided all the following conditions are satisfied, the secretary can apply for the gains and losses to be agreed by the tax district in which he lives (Form 185-1 must be used when applying for this treatment):

- There are no more than 20 members;
- The average amount invested is not more than £5,000;
- The annual subscription does not exceed £1,000;
- Total annual gains are not more than £5,000.

The Revenue will then accept each member's share of the gains without further enquiry.

32

TAX TABLES

Table 32.1 – Rates of income tax

	Rate	*Taxable Income £*	*Cumulative Tax £*
2003-04			
Lower rate	10%	0-1,960	196
Basic rate	22%	1,961-30,500	6,474
Higher rate on dividends	32.5%	(see Note)	
Higher rate	40%	over 30,500	
2002-03			
Lower rate	10%	0-1,920	192
Basic rate	22%	1,921-29,900	6,347.60
Higher rate on dividends	32.5%	(see Note)	
Higher rate	40%	over 29,900	
2001-02			
Lower rate	10%	0-1,880	188
Basic rate	22%	1,881-29,400	6,242.40
Higher rate on dividends	32.5%	(see Note)	
Higher rate	40%	over 29,400	
2000-01			
Lower rate	10%	0-1,520	152
Basic rate	22%	1,521-28,400	6,065.60
Higher rate on dividends	32.5%	(see Note)	
Higher rate	40%	over 28,400	
1999-2000			
Lower rate	10%	0-1,500	150
Basic rate	23%	1,501-28,000	6,245
Higher rate on dividends	32.5%	excess	
Higher rate	40%	excess	
1998-99			
Lower rate	20%	0-4,300	860
Basic rate	23%	4,301-27,100	6,104
Higher rate	40%	over 27,100	
1997-98			
Lower rate	20%	0-4,100	820
Basic rate	23%	4,101-26,100	5,880
Higher rate	40%	over 26,100	

Note: Rates of tax applicable to dividends are 10% for income below the basic rate and 32.5% for income above it.

Table 32.2 – Personal allowances and reliefs (see Chap. 10)

Allowances (£s)	*1997-98*	*1998-99*	*1999-2000*	*2000-01*	*2001-02*	*2002-03*	*2003-04*
Single person:							
– under 65	4,045	4,195	4,335	4,385	4,535	4,615	4,615
– 65 plus	5,220	5,410	5,720	5,790	5,990	6,100	6,610
– 75 plus	5,400	5,600	5,980	6,050	6,260	6,370	6,720
Married couple's allowance:							
– under 65	1,830*	1,900*	1,970*	–[1]	–	–	–
– either spouse 65 plus[2]	3,185*	3,305*	5,125*	5,185	5,365	5,465	5,565
– either spouse 75 plus	3,225*	3,345*	5,195	5,255	5,435	5,535	5,635
Age allowances – reduced by:							
– £1 in £2 for income over	15,600	16,200	16,800	17,000	17,600	17,900	18,300
Additional personal allowance	1,830*	1,900*	1,970*	–[1]	–	–	–
Widow's bereavement allowance	1,830*	1,900*	1,970*	2,000	–[1]	–	–
Blind person's allowance	1,280	1,330	1,380	1,400	1,450	1,480	1,510
Children's tax credit[3]	–	–	–	–	5,200	5,290	–

*Allowance where relief was restricted to 15% for 1997-99 to 1998-99 and to 10% for 1999-2000 and 2000-01.

[1] The married couple's allowance for couples where neither partner has reached age 65 before 6 April 2000 and the associated reliefs (additional personal allowance, widow's bereavement allowance and relief for maintenance payments) were withdrawn from April 2000.

[2] Age 65 before 6 April 2000.

[3] The rate of relief for the continuing married couples allowance and maintenance relief for people born before 6 April 1935, and for the children's tax, is 10%.

Children's Tax Credit abolished and replaced by Tax Credits.

Table 32.3 – 'Official rate' of interest for beneficial loans (see 4.7)

	Average rate (%)
2003-04	5.00
2002-03	5.00 *
2001-02	6.25 *
2000-01	6.25 *
1999-00	6.25 *
1998-99	7.16
1997-98	7.08

The rate on 6 April 1998 was 7.25% and on 6 April 1999 was 6.25%.

* Now fixed in advance.

Table 32.4 – Personal pension schemes and stakeholder pensions – maximum contributions by individuals 1997-98 to 2003-04

Age at the beginning of the tax year	*Percentage of net relevant earnings*
up to 35	17.5
36–45	20
46–50	25
51–55	30
56–60	35
61 or more	40

Note – there is a 'cap' on relevant earnings as follows:

	£
2003-04	99,000
2002-03	97,200
2001-02	95,400
2000-01	91,800
1999-00	90,600
1998-99	87,600
1997-98	84,000

Table 32.5 – Retirement annuity premiums

From 1996–97

Age at beginning of tax year	*Percentage of net relevant earnings*
Up to 50	17.5
51–55	20.0
56–60	22.5
61 or more	27.5

Table 32.6 – Rates of capital gains tax

Annual exemptions	*1997-98*	*1998-99*	*1999-00*	*2000-01*	*2001-02*	*2002-03*	*2003-04*
Individuals	6,500	6,800	7,100	7,200	7,500	7,700	7,900
Trusts	3,250	3,400	3,550	3,600	3,750	3,850	3,950
Rates of tax							
Individuals							
Gains are effectively taxed as top slice of taxable income:							
Gain less than lower rate limit	20%	20%	20%	20%	20%	10%	10%
Gain less than basic rate limit	24%	23%	23%	20%	20%	20%	20%
Gain greater than basic rate limit	40%	40%	40%	40%	40%	40%	40%
Trusts							
Discretionary (including accumulation and maintenance)	34%	34%	34%	34%	34%	34%	34%
Interest in possession	24%	23%	34%	34%	34%	34%	34%
Where the settlor (or settlor's spouse) has retained an interest	Chargeable on settlor at his personal rate (see Individuals, above)						

Table 32.7 – Taper relief

Non-business assets

*Number of complete years after 5 April 1998 for which asset held**	*Percentage of gain chargeable*
0	100
1	100
2	100
3	95
4	90
5	85
6	80
7	75
8	70
9	65
10 or more	60

*Assets acquired before 17 March 1998 qualify for an addition of one year to the period for which they are treated as held after 5 April 1998. This addition will be the same for all assets, whenever they were actually acquired. So, for example, an asset purchased on 1 January 1998 and disposed of on 1 July 2000 is treated for the purposes of the taper as if it had been held for three years (two complete years after 5 April 1998 plus one additional year).

Business assets

(1) For disposals on or after 6 April 2000, a four-year taper for business assets applies for holding periods from 6 April 1998. The gains charged to tax are reduced as set out in the table:

Period asset held (years)	*Percentage of gain chargeable (%)*	*Equivalent rate for higher rate CGT payer (%)*
0-1	100	40
1-2	87.5	35
2-3	75	30
3-4	50	20

The additional year for assets held at 17 March 1998 has been consolidated into the new four-year taper so that it is not added for disposals on or after 6 April 2000.

(2) For disposals after 6 April 2002, the table is:

Period asset held (years)	*Percentage of gain chargeable (%)*	*Equivalent rate for higher rate CGT payer (%)*
0	100	40
1	50	20
2	25	10

Table 32.8 – Capital gains tax indexation allowance (see 14.5)

RETAIL PRICE INDEX FIGURES

	1982	*1983*	*1984*	*1985*	*1986*	*1987*
Jan		325.9	342.6	359.8	379.7	394.5/100.0
Feb		327.3	344.0	362.9	381.1	100.4
Mar	313.4	327.9	345.1	366.1	381.6	100.6
Apr	319.7	332.5	349.7	373.9	385.3	101.8
May	322.0	333.9	351.0	375.6	386.0	101.9
June	322.9	334.7	351.9	376.4	385.8	101.9
July	320.0	336.5	351.5	375.5	384.7	101.8
Aug	323.1	338.0	354.8	376.7	385.9	102.1
Sep	322.9	339.5	355.5	376.5	387.8	102.4
Oct	324.5	340.7	357.7	377.1	388.4	102.9
Nov	326.1	341.9	358.8	378.4	391.7	103.4
Dec	325.5	342.8	358.5	378.9	393.0	103.3
	1988	*1989*	*1990*	*1991*	*1992*	*1993*
Jan	103.3	111.0	119.5	130.2	135.6	137.9
Feb	103.7	111.8	120.2	130.9	136.3	138.8
Mar	104.1	112.3	121.4	131.4	136.7	139.3
Apr	105.8	114.3	125.1	133.1	138.8	140.6
May	106.2	115.0	126.2	133.5	139.3	141.1
June	106.6	115.4	126.7	134.1	139.3	141.0
July	106.7	115.5	126.8	133.8	138.8	140.7
Aug	107.9	115.8	128.1	134.1	138.9	141.3
Sep	108.4	116.6	129.3	134.6	139.4	141.9
Oct	109.5	117.5	130.3	135.1	139.9	141.8
Nov	110.0	118.5	130.0	135.6	139.7	141.6
Dec	110.3	118.8	129.9	135.7	139.2	141.9
	1994	*1995*	*1996*	*1997*	*1998*	*1999*
Jan	141.3	146.0	150.2	154.4	159.5	163.4
Feb	142.1	146.9	150.9	155.0	160.3	163.7
Mar	142.5	147.5	151.5	155.4	160.8	164.1
Apr	144.2	149.0	152.6	156.3	162.6	165.2
May	144.7	149.6	152.9	156.9	163.5	165.6
June	144.7	149.8	153.0	157.5	163.4	165.6
July	144.0	149.1	152.4	157.5	163.0	165.1
Aug	144.7	149.9	153.1	158.5	163.7	165.5
Sep	145.0	150.6	153.8	159.3	164.4	166.2
Oct	145.2	149.8	153.8	159.5	164.5	166.5
Nov	145.3	149.8	153.9	159.6	164.4	166.7
Dec	146.0	150.7	154.4	160.0	164.4	167.3

Table 32.8 – *cont.*

RETAIL PRICE INDEX FIGURES

	2000	*2001*	*2002*	*2003*
Jan	166.6	171.1	173.3	178.4
Feb	167.5	172.0	173.8	179.3
Mar	168.4	172.2	174.5	179.9
Apr	170.1	173.1	175.7	181.2
May	170.7	174.2	176.2	
June	171.1	174.4	176.2	
July	170.5	173.3	175.9	
Aug	170.5	174.0	176.4	
Sep	171.7	174.6	177.6	
Oct	171.6	174.3	177.9	
Nov	172.1	173.6	178.2	
Dec	172.2	173.4	178.5	

Table 32.9 – Rates of interest on overdue tax/repayment supplement

Rates from 6 August 1997:	
For overdue income and capital gains tax	9.5%
For overpaid income and capital gains tax	4.75%
Rates from 6 January 1999:	
For overdue income and capital gains tax	8.5%
For overpaid income and capital gains tax	4.0%
Rates from 6 March 1999:	
For overdue income and capital gains tax	7.5%
For overpaid income and capital gains tax	3.0%
Rates from 6 February 2000:	
For overdue income and capital gains tax	8.5%
For overpaid income and capital gains tax	4.0%
Rates from 6 May 2001:	
For overdue income and capital gains tax	7.5%
For overpaid income and capital gains tax	3.5%
Rates from 6 November 2001:	
For overdue income and capital gains tax	6.5%
For overpaid income and capital gains tax	2.5%

Note that different rates apply for late payment/repayment of inheritance tax. The current rate is 3%.

Table 32.10 – Rates of corporation tax

Financial year commencing 1 April	*1997 & 1998*	*1999*	*2000 & 2001*	*2002 & 2003*
Full rate (see 26.4.2)	31%	30%	30%	30%
Small companies rate (see 26.4.3)	21%	20%	20%	19%
Starting rate (see 26.4.4)			10%	–
Small companies rate – profit limit	£300k	£300k	£300k	£300k
Small companies Marginal relief Profit limit	£1.5m	£1.5m	£1.5m	£1.5m

Table 32.11 – Rates of inheritance tax

TRANSFERS ON DEATH				*GROSS*	*LIFETIME TRANSFERS*			*GROSS*
Cumulative chargeable transfers net	*Rate on gross % age*	*Rate on net fraction £*	*Cumulative tax £*	*Cumulative chargeable transfers £*	*Rate on gross % age*	*Rate on net fraction*	*Cumulative tax £*	*Cumulative chargeable transfers £*
from 6 April 1997								
0-215,000	nil	nil	nil	0-215,000	nil	nil	nil	0-215,000
over 215,000	40	2/3	–	over 215,000	20	1/4	–	over 215,000
from 6 April 1998								
0-223,000	nil	–	nil	0-223,000	nil	nil	nil	0-223,000
over 223,000	40	–	–	over 223,000	20	1/4	–	over 223,000
from 6 April 1999								
0-231,000	nil	–	nil	0-231,000	nil	nil	nil	0-231,000
over 231,000	40	–	–	over 231,000	20	1/4	–	over 231,000
from 6 April 2000								
0-234,000	nil	–	nil	0-234,000	nil	nil	nil	0-234,000
over 234,000	40	–	–	over 234,000	20	1/4	–	over 234,000
from 6 April 2001								
0-242,000	nil	–	nil	0-242,000	nil	nil	nil	0-242,000
over 242,000	40	–	–	over 242,000	20	1/4	–	over 242,000
from 6 April 2002								
0-250,000	nil	–	nil	0-250,000	nil	nil	nil	0-250,000
over 250,000	40	–	–	over 250,000	20	–	–	over 250,000
from 6 April 2003								
0-255,000	nil							
over 255,000	40							

INDEX